WHO
WAS REALLY WHO
IN FICTION

Who Was Really Who in Fiction

Alan Bold and Robert Giddings

Longman Group UK Limited,
Longman House, Burnt Mill, Harlow,
Essex CM20 2JE, England
and Associated Companies throughout the world.

First published 1987

Bold, Alan
Who was really who in fiction.
1. English fiction – History and criticism
2. Characters and characteristics in literature
I. Title II. Giddings, Robert
823'.00927 PR830.C47

ISBN 0-582-89251-1

Set in Linotron 202 8/9pt Plantin

Printed and bound in Great Britain by
Mackays of Chatham Ltd, Chatham, Kent

INTRODUCTION

Lord Byron, who features in this book as an authentic original, wrote memorably of the relationship between reality and romance in the fourteenth Canto of *Don Juan* (1819-24):

> 'Tis strange, but true, for truth is always strange,
> Stranger than fiction. If it could be told,
> How much would novels gain by the exchange!
> How differently the world would men behold!

Truth may occasionally be stranger than fiction but fiction is arguably stronger than truth. The writer perceives everyday reality through a highly personal vision and rearranges life as literature, actuality as art. We hope to show that even the strangest fiction has a solid factual foundation.

Anyone enjoying the exploits of the anarchic schoolgirls in the films *The Belles of St Trinian's* (1954) and *Blue Murder at St Trinian's* (1957) could be forgiven for thinking the whole comic spectacle beyond the bounds of belief. Yet there was a real St Trinian's school; actually St Trinnean's which opened in Edinburgh in 1922 and closed in 1946. It was after visiting a family with daughters at St Trinnean's that Ronald Searle created his cartoons about an institution more criminal than educational. Alastair Sim's headmistress Mildred Umbrage, in the aforementioned films (inspired by Searle's cartoons), is an outrageously eccentric character but then so was Catherine Fraser Lee, the headmistress of the real St Trinnean's. One year, for example, C.F. Lee had her girls eat their meals the wrong way round, starting with pudding and ending with soup. That fact is as strange as the fiction.

Moving from the deliberately ridiculous to the sublime it cannot, we feel, fail to fascinate the reader to realize that Franz Kafka's *The Trial* (1925) was prompted by the author's own experience of being interrogated in a hotel room in Berlin (as can be seen in the entry on Fräulein Bürstner on p56). Similarly, it enhances our appreciation of such literary immortals as Alice (p4), Dracula (p101), Gunga Din (p142), Dr Jekyll (pp165-6) and Trilby (pp325-6) when we are introduced to their prototypes.

Researching this book we made the assumption that the more substantial the character the more likely he or she was to have a factual foundation, so we went in search of the extraordinary originals behind Doyle's Sherlock Holmes (p156), Simenon's Maigret (pp197-8), Christie's Miss Marple (p204) and Le Carré's Smiley (p301). Sometimes we found the solution to our search in books, sometimes living authors answered our queries. John Le Carré gladly admitted that his George Smiley was based on the Rev Vivian Hubert Howard Green, Senior Tutor at Lincoln College when David Cornwell (Le Carré by his real name) was an Oxford undergraduate.

Not all creators of fiction are as frank as John Le Carré. Lillian Hellman has consistently refused to confirm rumours that her character Julia – in *Pentimento* (1973), then the 1973 film *Julia* – is based on Muriel Gardiner (1902-85), an American who went to Vienna in the 1930s and, using the codename Mary, saved people and papers from Nazi persecution until the outbreak of World War Two. Gardiner wrote to Hellmann, in 1973, pointing out the similarities between her life and the career of the fictional Julia. Hellmann never replied to Gardiner but was quoted as saying that her Julia had 'nothing to do with her – my word of honour'.

Some authors are understandably reluctant to own up to using models. Creative pride encourages novelists to project themselves as the only begetters: characters drawn from life demonstrate descriptive skill whereas (some authors suppose) characters conjured out of the thin air of the literary atmosphere provide irrefutable evidence of originality. Kingsley Amis's Lucky Jim (p95) used, initially at least, the character of the poet Philip Larkin. Amis now feels that Larkin's 'resemblances to Dixon are totally superficial or so general as not to be interesting'. We disagree and feel that literary sleuthing has a value in indicating how a work of art is built up from the raw material of life. Proust, D.H. Lawrence and Jack Kerouac – to cite three obvious examples – are writers who excel at appropriating the experiences of their friends and enemies.

In an interview of 1961, Muriel Spark observed that 'even if a particular character has struck my imagination, one person I've met, I never reproduce the character in the book. It's always my experience of hundreds of characters, and also a kind of memory that I can't explain, almost as if I remember the past before I was born.' Clearly Mrs Spark takes this view seriously for when we were on the track of the original Jean Brodie, and had identified a teacher who habitually took her holidays in Italy and impressed select groups of girls, Mrs Spark insisted 'there was no real Jean Brodie'. Later, though, in a letter of 1983 she recalled: 'There was a Christina Kay who died during the '40s, greatly esteemed, but not like Miss Brodie in character.'

It is, of course, difficult to determine how much of the model remains when the act of creation is accomplished; the real people inform the fiction which takes on a real life of its own. We are convinced that the identification of originals in no way detracts from any writer's artistic integrity and that the genesis of a literary character is as much a matter of impressive observation as an immaculately aesthetic conception. We accept that an imaginative novel does not simply comprise a series of verbal portraits drawn from life but suggest that it is enriched by being rooted in reality. This claim does not impose limitations on literature for originals are open to a variety of interpretations. The real Nancy Cunard, after all, became Iris March (pp202-3) in Michael Arlen's *The Green Hat* (1924), Lucy Tantamount (p317) in Aldous Huxley's *Point Counter Point* (1928) and Baby Bucktrout (p52) in Wyndham Lewis's *The Roaring Queen* (posthumously published in 1973): one propotype, three different ficitonal personalities.

'We all like to pretend we don't use real people, but one does actually,' said E.M. Forster who, for example, modelled Philip Herriton (p152), in *Where Angels Fear to Tread* (1905), on the musicologist Edward J. Dent. There can be problems in this practice which is why books and films come complete with a disclaimer rejecting any connexion between fiction and fact. When Somerset Maugham's *Cakes and Ale* was about to be published in 1930 Hugh Walpole, Chairman of the Book Society's Selection Committee, was aghast when he recognized himself as the literary careerist hero, Alroy Kear (p171). Realizing instantly that Kear was a vicious portrait of himself, he attempted to stop publication of the book and wrote a letter of protest to the author. 'I certainly never intended Alroy Kear to be a portrait of you', was Maugham's calculated reply.

A.J. Cronin's *Hatter's Castle* (1931), set in Levenford (that is, Dumbarton), tells a grim tale of family life dominated by a domestic tyrant – James Brodie, the hatter. Cronin's maternal grandfather, Archibald Montgomerie, owned a hatter's shop at 145 High Street, Dumbarton, and was seen as the original of the appalling Brodie. The publication of the book completely destroyed Cronin's relationship with his mother's family. It can, then, be a traumatic experience for an original to undergo a literary transformation. Peter Llewelyn Davies, one of the originals for J.M. Barrie's Darling family, hated people to remind him that he was the 'real' Peter Pan (pp245-6). 'If,' he complained, 'that perennially juvenile lad, if that boy so fatally committed to an arrestation of his development, had only been dubbed George, or Jack, or Michael, or Nicholas, what miseries would have been spared me.' He thought Barrie's play a 'terrible masterpiece' and in 1960 the 'real' Peter Pan took his own life.

Wyndham Lewis's novel *The Apes of God* (1930) scandalized literary London by the force of its satire. Edith Sitwell appeared as the 'old harpy' Lady Harriet (p292) while brother Osbert became Lord Osmund Finnian Shaw (p292), 'the licking, eating, sniffing, fat-muzzled machine'. Osbert did not accept the insult passively. At the Sitwell family home, Renishaw Hall, he found an old postcard showing two anonymous actors clad in the same sinister cloaks and hats that Lewis himself favoured. Osbert had the picture duplicated and mailed, from various parts of Europe, to Lewis who was, presumably, suitably irritated by the abusive captions on the cards.

Another victim of Lewis's was the Scottish poet Edwin Muir, cruelly caricatured as Keith of Ravelstone (p172) in *The Apes of God*: 'He is, as you see, a very earnest, rather melancholy freckled little being – whose dossier is that, come into civilization from amid the gillies and haggises of Goy or Arran, living in poverty, he fell in with that massive, elderly scottish lady next to him – that is his wife. She opened her jaws and swallowed him comfortably. There he was once more inside a woman, as it were – tucked up in her old tummy.' Muir's response to that description is not on record but the poet's son, Gavin, told us that his parents 'disliked that man Lewis'. Another Scottish poet – Hugh MacDiarmid – was delighted to be recreated as Hugh Skene (p297) in Eric Linklater's comic novel *Magnus Merriman* (1934). Enjoying the portrait of the multilingual Scots-writing Scottish Nationalist Communist, MacDiarmid exclaimed 'That's me to a T'. It all depends, obviously, on the tone of the finished product.

We can, then, enthusiastically enjoy the use writers make of the material that comes their way. When a gifted painter does a portrait of an individual the result lifts the sitter on to another sphere, one created by the artistic act of perception. Writers, too, remodel individuals by fitting them into a dramatic, poetic or narrative framework. André Gide said 'the work of art is a part of nature seen through a temperament' and in the following pages we focus on the temperamental authors as well as the natural originals. Like its predecessor, *True Characters: Real People in Fiction* (1984), this book has been an enjoyable one to write and research, representing a combination of scholarship and literary sleuthing. It is designed as both a work of reference and an entertaining experience. Unmasked, the originals have an appeal of their own.

Alan Bold
Robert Giddings

ACHILLES

William Shakespeare. *Troilus and Cressida* (1602)

Robert Devereux, Second Earl of Essex (1566-1601)

Further reading: A.L. Rowse: *William Shakespeare – A Biography* (1963)

In Shakespeare's play, Achilles is a Greek general who is portrayed as torn by two conflicting loyalties. On the one hand he is in love with Polyxena, the sister of Hector, the Trojan hero. On the other hand he is Greek commander, continually reminded of his duty by Ulysses. Achilles is blamed for the sluggish progress of the Greek war effort; instead of giving the lead expected of him, he lies in his tent all day in the convivial company of his friend Patroclus and the foul-mouthed Thersites (see THERSITES). Priam's son Hector sends a challenge to any Greek 'that holds his honour higher than his ease'. Ulysses realizes this is aimed at Achilles, but encourages his colleagues to send the 'dull brainless' Ajax (see AJAX) as this will provoke Achilles. When they meet in combat, Hector realizes that Ajax is related to the Trojan royal family and the fight is discontinued. When his friend Patroclus is killed in battle by Hector, Achilles is spurred to action. He slays Hector and drags his body around behind his horse.

This is Shakespeare's portrait of the Earl of Essex. The situation presented in this play is far closer to contemporary political and military affairs than it is to Homer's *Iliad*. Towards the end of 1600 Essex and his followers – the Earl of Southampton and the notoriously malcontented Henry Cuffe, were railing and plotting against the Queen's privy councillors. George Chapman, on whose translation of Homer Shakespeare based *Troilus and Cressida,* dedicated his work to the Earl of Essex, as 'most true Achilles, whom by sacred prophecy Homer did but prefigure in his admired object'. A.L. Rowse in *William Shakespeare – A Biography* (1963) suggests that Shakespeare is reflecting the 'shattering events of the past two or three years'. The Trojan war, like the long war with Spain, is drawing to an end and the similarities between Achilles and Essex are very strong: 'sulking in his tent, withdrawing from court and duty when he did not get his own way, had been Essex's regular method of bringing pressure on the Queen'. Essex had a habit, like Shakespeare's Achilles, of making 'things small as nothings' seem of overriding importance: 'Possessed he is with greatness/And speaks not to himself but with a pride/That quarrels at self-breath; imagined worth/-Holds in his blood such swollen and hot discourse.' Essex was a brilliant public figure and gathered other luminaries to him (see PATROCLUS). He had powerful enemies at court and was executed after attempting to raise a rebellion in London. He was the closest friend of Shakespeare's patron the Earl of Southampton.

SWEET FANNY ADAMS

Naval slang term for tinned mutton (circa 1889-1900)

Fanny Adams (1859-67)

Fanny Adams is a naval term for tinned meat, which was first introduced into the navy in the late 1860s. The phrase is still used today but means 'nothing' = sweet F.A., Sweet Fanny Adams. An eight-year-old girl and her younger sister Elizabeth were out playing in the fields near their home in Tanhouse Lane, Alton, Hampshire, on 24 August 1867. They met another friend, Minnie Warner, who was also eight years old. They were on their way to Flood Meadows, which was a favourite spot for children to play in, near the River Wey and the surrounding hop-gardens. Children could paddle and picnic safely here in the shallows. The three children had not gone very far on their way when they were accosted by Frederick Baker. He was a clerk of twenty-nine years of age with a firm of solicitors in Alton. He offered Fanny a halfpenny to accompany him to The Hollow, a road leading to the village of Shalden. He gave Minnie three halfpence to take Elizabeth safely back home. The two children watched as Frederick Baker carried Fanny bodily into the field and towards The Hollow. They then went back home. Fanny Adams was never seen alive again. When they got home a neighbour was suspicious about the account of Frederick Baker and Fanny and the payment of the money, and she went in search of the man and the missing child. This was a Mrs Gardiner, who soon met Baker on the footbridge over the Wey. 'What have you done with the child?' she asked. 'Nothing,' he calmly replied, and although he admitted paying the children money, he was cool and collected in his answers. Mr and Mrs Adams were very distressed when Fanny did not come back and eventually Baker was arrested. A thorough search of the fields revealed the dismembered body of Fanny. Several knives were found on Baker and his diary detailed the event: 'Killed a young girl. It was fine and hot.' Baker's family had a record of mental instability and the press had a field-day, one paper proclaiming: 'No tiger of the jungle, no jackal . . . could so fearfully have mutilated the victim . . .' Frederick Baker was found guilty and hanged before a crowd of some five thousand at Winchester on Christmas Eve 1867. It was the opinion of sailors in the Royal Navy that chopped tinned meat resembled the remains of the poor victim, sweet little Fanny Adams.

AJAX

William Shakespeare, *Troilus and Cressida* (1602)

Ben Jonson (1572-1637)

Further reading: Marchette Chute: *Ben Jonson of Westminster* (1953)

In Homer Ajax is king of Salamis and, apart from Achilles, the most heroic of the Greek commanders. In Shakespeare's play he is given vastly different treatment, and – as several scholars have argued – this must be to some purpose. In *Troilus and Cressida* he is muscular but slow witted and surly, far from brilliant. Thersites says to him: 'Thy horse will sooner con an oration than thou learn a prayer without a book.' (See THERSITES). When the challenge arrives at the Greek camp from Hector to fight any Greek 'that holds his honour higher than his ease' – although it is clearly directed at the sulking Achilles – Ulysses urges his fellow commanders to pass over Achilles and to send Ajax, knowing that this will infuriate Achilles, and may spur him to some action (see ACHILLES). Ajax and Hector meet in combat but the battle is given over after just a few passes, as Hector realizes that Ajax is related to Troy's royal family.

In the so-called 'War of the Theatres' – the feud between Ben Jonson on the one hand, and Dekker and Marston on the other, Jonson was satirized by Dekker. In this character of Ajax Shakespeare is giving us Dekker's version of the personality of Jonson. This is alluded to in the *Parnassus Plays* 1598-1602, where Will Kempe says:'Why here's our fellow Shakespeare puts them all down, I and Ben Jonson too. O that Ben Jonson is a pestilent fellow . . . but our fellow Shakespeare hath given him a purge that made him bewray his credit.' Jonson was born in Westminster and taught by William Camden; he was briefly at university at Cambridge and then served in the army in Flanders. He returned to England in 1592 and was involved in acting and play-writing. He killed a fellow actor in a brawl but escaped death by benefit of clergy. He had a quarrelsome temperament and was addicted to conviviality and riotous living; John Aubrey records in his *Brief Lives* that he 'was wont to wear a coat like a coach-man's, with slits under the arm pits. He would many times exceed in drink; canarie was his beloved liquor: he would then tumble home to bed; and when he had thoroughly perspired, then to his study.' His most celebrated comedies are *The Alchemist* and *Volpone*. Shakespeare's view of him as slow-witted, derivative and ponderous was well known: an anonymous jest-book of 1769 repeats the story of Shakespeare's seeing him in a 'necessary-house' (privy) with 'a book in his hand', at which Shakespeare says: 'I am sorry to see your memory is so bad, that you can't shit without a book.'

Another identification of Ajax is made by Harold Hillibrand and T.W. Baldwin in their edition of *Troilus* of 1953. They suggest he is Sir Walter Raleigh, who was chagrined at being replaced by Essex as England's leading courtier and nobleman.

ALBERTINE

Marcel Proust, *Remem-*

At Balbec (Cabourg, on the Normandy coast) the narrator of Proust's novel is attracted by the dark-haired Albertine Simonet, a member of a 'little band' of girls. On a second visit to Balbec, Marcel takes Albertine on trips by motor-car to Norman churches and spends nights with her on the Balbec beach. When Albertine, however, reveals her Lesbian nature to Marcel, he is shattered by jealousy and decides to keep her in seclusion at his home in Paris where she is installed in a bedroom twenty paces from his own. Eventually Albertine escapes from this domestic captivity and Marcel hears the news that she has died after being thrown against a tree by a horse. A subsequent telegram indicating that Albertine is alive does not revive Marcel's love for this voluptuous girl.

Initially Albertine was modelled on female originals. In August 1892 Proust stayed at Trouville, on the Normandy coast, and there became enchanted by Marie Finaly, daughter of a wealthy Jewish banker and sister of Proust's friend Horace Finaly. Proust and Marie enjoyed spending time together and he always recalled this period with affection. Later she married an Italian nobleman, gave birth to three children, and died in the influenza epidemic of 1918. In 1909, at Cabourg, Proust met a young girl whom he thought of marrying; not even her name is known. The Albertine of the Parisian captivity is modelled on the character's most important original, who was a man and (with Marie de Benardaky, the original of GILBERTE SWANN) one of the two great loves of Proust's life.

In 1906 Proust went to Cabourg to visit the ancient churches of Normandy and travelled in a taxi driven by Alfred Agostinelli who had been born in Monaco of an Italian father. Proust enjoyed his driver's company and was sympathetic when, in January 1913, Agostinelli turned up at Proust's home, 102 Boulevard Haussman, Paris, asking for a job. Proust employed Agostinelli as his secretary and set him to work typing *Swann's Way* (published, at Proust's expense, in November 1913). Moreover, Proust took in Agostinelli's mistress Anna (believing she was his wife) though he found it difficult to put up with her. Like Albertine in the novel, Agostinelli felt he was Proust's captive and in December 1913 he fled from Paris. The following March he enrolled at a flying school near Antibes under the significant pseudonym of Marcel Swann, and on 30 May 1914 crashed his monoplane at sea during his second solo flight. His body was washed up near Cannes on 7 June and Proust sent a 400-franc wreath to the funeral in Nice.

brance of Things Past (1913-27)

Alfred Agostinelli (1888-1914)

Further reading: George D. Painter, *Marcel Proust* (1959, 1965)

THE ABBESS ALEXANDRA

Muriel Spark, *The Abbess of Crewe* (1974)

Richard Milhous Nixon (1913–) **37th President of the USA**

Further reading: Alan Bold (ed.), *Muriel Spark: An Odd Capacity for Vision* (1984)

Muriel Spark's satire *The Abbess of Crewe* sets in an English abbey the scandal that eventually forced Richard Nixon to resign as President of the United States in 1974. Although Nixon's massive majority over George McGovern in 1972 was a foregone conclusion, the Committee to Re-elect the President (Creep) indulged in 'dirty tricks' including the burglary of the Democratic Party Headquarters in the Watergate complex in Washington D.C. Nixon denied any prior knowledge of the break-in, but his staff were implicated. Subsequently the presidential tapes revealed the President as a ruthless and often foul-mouthed operator. The Nixonian figure in Spark's novel is Alexandra, who rises from sub-prioress to abbess in an election campaign she personally orchestrates. She puts electronic surveillance on her rival, Sister Felicity, who (like McGovern) 'wants everyone to be liberated by her vision and to acknowledge it'. Aided by the trouble-shooting, globe-trotting Sister Gertrude (representing Nixon's Secretary of State Henry Kissinger) and abetted by Sisters Mildred and Warburga (for John Ehrlichman and Bob Haldeman, Nixon's closest advisers), Alexandra encourages a plan to discredit Felicity. Two Jesuit novices break into the Abbey to steal love-letters from Felicity's work-box; the trial run is discovered when Felicity notices her thimble is missing. When the scandal breaks Alexandra claims to be above everything because of the prestige of her position: 'I know nothing about anything. I am occupied with the administration of the Abbey, our music, our rites and traditions, and our electronics project for contacts with our mission fields.' When she is compelled to release her tapes she makes sure (as did Nixon) that the most scandalous parts are deleted. With her 'white-skinned English skull' Alexandra is self-destructive – gifted yet ultimately idiotic in her abuse of personal power.

ALICE
Lewis Carroll, *Alice's Adventures in Wonderland* (1865), *Through the Looking Glass* (1872)

Alice Liddell (1852-1934)

Further reading: M.L. Green, *Lewis Carroll* (1960), Martin Gardner, *The Annotated Alice* (1962) Stuart Dodgson Collingwood, *Life and Letters of Lewis Carroll* (1898), Colin Gordon, *Beyond the Looking Glass* (1982)

On Friday 4 July 1862, a 'golden afternoon', the Revd Charles Dodgson and his friend the Revd Robinson Duckworth took three young sisters – Lorina, Alice and Edith – on a three-mile rowing trip from Folly Bridge, near Oxford, up the Thames to Godstow. Dodgson amused the children by telling them stories and Alice later remembered that 'Nearly all of *Alice's Adventures Underground* was told on that blazing summer afternoon with the heat haze shimmering over the meadows where the party landed to shelter for a while in the shadow cast by the haycocks near Godstow.' Afterwards Alice implored Dodgson to 'write out Alice's adventures for me'; he obliged and spent almost the whole night writing out what he could recall of the tale. At the end of 1864 Alice received, as a 'Christmas present to a Dear Child in memory of a Summer's day', a handwritten copy of *Alice's Adventures Underground* complete with Dodgson's own illustrations.

Dodgson was a lecturer in mathematics at Christ Church, Oxford, and the Dean of the college was Henry George Liddell, a lexicographer. Fascinated by photography, Dodgson especially delighted in taking pictures of the Dean's daughter, Alice Liddell. She was a precocious child and, as fitted the daughter of a lexicographer, was enchanted by words – an interest Dodgson encouraged. Naturally she was greatly flattered by Dodgson's gift and, when the manuscript was shown around Oxford, pressure was put on the author to have his book published with professional illustrations. On 4 July 1865, the third anniversary of Wonderland Day, Alice was given the first copy of *Alice's Adventures in Wonderland*, as the story was retitled, at Dean Liddell's suggestion. Dodgson was a painfully shy man and used the pseudonym Lewis Carroll to protect his privacy.

SQUIRE ALLWORTHY
Henry Fielding, *The History of Tom Jones* (1749)

Ralph Allen (1694-1764)

Further reading: R.E.M. Peach, *The Life and Times of Ralph Allen* (1895)

Squire Allworthy is a noble character who more or less adopts Tom Jones, a foundling, not realizing that Tom is the son of his own sister. Allworthy is goodness and generosity personified: '[he] might well be called the favourite of both nature and fortune; both of these seem to have contended which should bless and enrich him most. In this contention, nature may seem to some to have come off victorious, as she bestowed on him many gifts, while fortune had only one gift in her power; but in pouring forth this, she was so very profuse, that others may think perhaps this single endowment to have been more than equivalent to all the various blessings which he enjoyed from nature. From the former of these he derived an agreeable person, a sound constitution, a solid understanding, and a benevolent heart; by the latter, he was decreed to the inheritance of one of the largest estates in the country.' He lives in the county of Somerset, and his generous hospitality is well known: 'Neither Mr Allworthy's house, nor his heart, was shut against any part of mankind, but they were both more particularly open to men of merit. To say the truth, this was the only house in the kingdom where you were sure to gain a dinner by deserving it. Above all others, men of genius and learning shared the principal place in his favour.'

This is a portrait of Fielding's friend, Ralph Allen, known as the 'Man of Bath'. His philanthropy was a byword. He was employed in the post office in Bath and earned the patronage of General Wade by his discovery of a Jacobite plot; he raised and equipped a troop of volunteers in 1745. He became Deputy Postmaster at Bath and evolved a system of cross posts for England and Wales which earned him a vast fortune. He built the magnificent mansion at Prior Park and there entertained celebrities including Pope and the Earl of Chatham. Fielding was of course a frequent visitor.

KASPAR ALMAYER

Joseph Conrad, *Almayer's Folly* (1895)

William Charles Olmeijer (died 1900)

Further reading: J.D. Gordon, *Joseph Conrad – The Making of a Novelist* (1940)

Kaspar Almayer is a failed trader on a river station in Borneo, but he suffers from illusions of a grand future for himself. He is convinced that it is to be his destiny to find treasure inland. To demonstrate his belief in himself and his golden future he constructs a new house for himself which is described by visiting Dutch naval officers as 'Almayer's Folly'. Almayer is married to a native woman who is bad-tempered and inefficient. Their daughter, Nina, is the apple of her father's eye and he builds all his hopes on her. She falls in love with a rajah's son, Dain Maroola, who is carrying some illicit gunpowder on his brig when it explodes and several Dutch sailors are killed. Consequently Dain becomes a fugitive from justice, and Nina flees to Bali with him, thus forsaking her besotted father who swears that he will never forgive her. In an attempt to destroy all memories of her, Almayer burns down his house and retires to live in his Folly. He takes to opium, and one morning is discovered dead, with a serene expression on his face which suggests to those who gaze on him that at last he had been 'permitted to forget before he died'.

Conrad based this tragic character on a trader he knew at Berouw river while he was serving on board the *Vidar* at Borneo. This was a steamship owned by an Arab, sailing under a Dutch flag. It was based at Singapore and voyaged through the Malay Archipelago, through the Carimata Strait to Banjermassim, then to Pulo Laut, Dongala, Coti Berouw and Bulangan, trading in cane, gutta percha and rubber. Here Conrad met many European or half-caste traders, many of them married to native women. William Charles Olmeijer was a Eurasian, married to a native, with eleven children. He traded in rattan, rubber and gutta percha, and made and lost a fortune. His good relations with the Dyaks, head-hunters from the interior, made him distrusted by the authorities. In fact he constructed a large house for himself which was locally known as The Folly.

JULIA ALMOND

F. Tennyson Jesse, *A Pin to See the Peepshow* (1934)

Edith Thompson (1893-1923)

A manageress/book-keeper for a London firm of wholesale milliners, Edith Thompson found her home life – in Ilford, Essex – far from lively with her husband Percy, four years her senior and a shipping clerk. In 1921 the Thompsons went to the Isle of Wight for a summer holiday with Avis Graydon, Edith's sister, and Frederick Bywaters, a twenty-year-old laundry steward with the P & O line. After the holiday Bywaters became a lodger in Edith's Ilford home, fell out with Percy Thompson, and sailed with his ship to the Far East. Edith kept in touch with Bywaters, sending him love letters together with newspaper cuttings relating to recent cases of murder by poison. She further informed Bywaters that she had tried to murder her husband and that she had had to abort Bywater's child. On 4 October 1922, a month after Bywaters docked in England, Percy Thompson was stabbed to death while walking home from Ilford Station. At a trial notorious for its moralistic posturing, Edith Thompson and Frederick Bywaters were condemned to death for this murder; Mr Justice Shearman called the affair 'a squalid and rather indecent case of lust and adultery'. Edith Thompson and Frederick Bywaters were hanged on 9 January 1923.

As readers realized, when her novel first appeared, F. Tennyson Jesse recreated the circumstances of the Thompson/Bywaters case in *A Pin to See the Peepshow.* The novel begins with Julia Almond as a romantic schoolgirl with a crush on her schoolmistress and ends with her agonizing over her imminent execution. While still at school, Julia looks into a peep-show belonging to a younger pupil, Leonard Carr, and sees 'a mad world, compact of insane proportions, but lit by a strange glamour'. Julia's whole life is a quest for romance and glamour for she 'knew she was something wonderful'. After marrying Herbert Starling, a gent's outfitter, Julia cannot accept life as 'just an ordinary respectable wife and wage-earner'. Then she meets Leonard Carr again and is delighted that the schoolboy who once showed her a peepshow (on payment of a pin) is now a handsome young man working as a fitter-mechanic on an aircraft-carrier. Julia and Leonard become lovers and are tried for murder when Herbert Starling dies after being assaulted by Leonard. The novel closes with a passionate plea against capital punishment.

CAPTAIN VON ALOESAM

Carl Zuckmayer, *The Captain of Köpenick* (1931)

Wilhelm Voight (1850-1922)

Further reading: E.T. Rosenthal, *Introducao à obra de Carl Zuckmayer* (1967). A.J. Jacobius, *Das Schauspiel Carl Zuckmayers* (1956)

A penniless shoemaker becomes obsessed against Prussian militarism and respect for authority. Feeling that he has been badly treated by society – he lives in continual poverty and has been in and out of jail; his criminal record stands in the way of being able to obtain a passport and try his fortunes abroad – he decides to take revenge on the system. He gets hold of a Prussian army officer's uniform and impersonates the authority he so deeply despises. He finds that he is given instant and unquestioning respect wherever he goes, and that his orders are unfailingly obeyed. He arrests the mayor of Köpenick (a suburb of Berlin) and steals the funds kept in the town hall (he really wants a passport, but has to be content with money). He finally gives himself up, and the authorities to whom he has surrendered find it difficult to believe that such an unlikely-looking person could have successfully passed himself off as an officer.

The real imposter of Köpenick was Wilhelm Voight. He was a cobbler who had spent nearly thirty years of his life in prison. He bought an officer's uniform in a second-hand shop. When questioned about the purchase, he explained that he needed it as he held this rank in the reserves. He tried out the disguise casually at first, and found that it worked like magic wherever he went. He then pulled off his great *coup*; he went to the barracks and rounded up ten soldiers whom he took by rail to the small suburban town of Köpenick. He went straight to the town hall and ordered the burgomeister to be arrested. Official doubts were allayed by his visiting the local police headquarters, where he assured the chief inspector that he was merely obeying orders. The burgomeister asked why he had been arrested, and Voight explained that he had been specially sent from Berlin to investigate certain irregularities. He took over the funds in the town hall – more than four thousand marks – and signed for them. He arrested the town council and sent them back to Berlin under armed guard. He returned to Berlin and left the train dressed as a civilian, ready to merge back into ordinary life. A reward was offered for the impostor, and he was arrested, in possession of much of the money he had acquired, trying to obtain a passport. Voight was given a sentence of four years imprisonment but was pardoned after serving two years, and given a pension by the Kaiser. He went to the USA where he earned a good living performing a cabaret act based on his exploits. He died in Luxembourg.

ALVAN

George Meredith, *The Tragic Comedians* (1880)

Ferdinand Lassalle (1825-64)

Further reading: George Meredith, *The Tragic Comedians*, edited by C.K. Shorter (1891)

The Tragic Comedians deals with the dramatic love affair between Clothilde and Alvan. She is the daughter of a noble family who disapprove of him. They hope to marry, but Alvan insists that they should not defy her family. On his advice, she returns to her family in the hope of gaining their approval of their marriage. But she is coerced into marrying a suitor from her own class of whom they approve – Marko. Alvan is deeply distressed and writes an insulting letter to Clothilde's father. Alvan and Marko fight a duel and Alvan is killed.

This is based on the real life tragedy of Helene von Dönniges and her love affair with Ferdinand Lassalle, the German socialist. Marko is based on Count Racowitza of Wallachia. Lassalle was the son of a Jewish banker, and was a disciple of Hegel. He met Heine in Paris. He defended the Countess Sophie Hatzfeld in litigation against her husband, a case which lasted eight years, and took part in the revolution of 1848. He founded the German Working Men's Association, which was pledged to universal suffrage and agitated in the Rhineland and Berlin. In 1864 he met Helene von Dönniges. In spite of considerable opposition from her family, they resolved to marry. Her parents exerted tremendous influence upon her and in the end she gave up Ferdinand Lassalle and intended to marry Count Racowitza. Lassalle responded to this news with a challenging letter both to Helene's father and to the Count. Count Racowitza and Lassalle fought their duel in Geneva, and Lassalle was mortally wounded, dying two days later. He was an idealist socialist who predicted the ultimate democracy of labour, the triumph of social democracy. He was greatly helped by Karl Marx, some of whose ideas he adopted and modified. Helene von Dönniges married Racowitza, the man who had killed her lover. She committed suicide in 1911.

FATHER AMAURY

Charles-Augustin Sainte-Beuve, *Volupté* (1834)

Charles-Augustin Sainte-Beuve (1804-69)

Further reading:
Vicomte d'Haussonville, *Charles-Augustin Sainte-Beuve, sa vie et ses oeuvres* (1875)

While on a voyage to the United States a priest, Father Amaury, writes the story of his life up to the point where he took orders, in the hope that it may prove spiritually supportive to a friend of his. The background is the royalist intrigues during the Consulate, in which Georges Cadoudal and Charles Pichegru conspire against Napoleon; but the real core of the novel is the inner biography of the man who becomes a priest. His soul is torn by the conflict between his spirituality and powerful physicality, which inclines even to sensuality. The spiritual side of his personality eventually triumphs over carnality, and believing he is immune from further temptations, he takes holy order and becomes a priest, strengthened by his religious faith. At the end of the novel he has to administer the last rites to Madame de Couaën, the wife of his friend and patron. For years he had been deeply in love with her, but she was a relentlessly virtuous woman, loving wife and fond mother.

This story is the history of the inner conflicts and torments experienced by the French writer and critic, Sainte-Beuve. He was the son of a commissioner of taxes, originally intended for the medical profession. One of his teachers, Paul-Francois Dubois, founded a journal, *Le Globe*, a literary and political paper, to which Sainte-Beuve contributed. He had now found his vocation. In 1827 he published a rhapsodic review of Victor Hugo's *Odes et Ballades*, and this led to the two writers meeting; it also led to Sainte-Beuve's meeting Victor Hugo's wife, Adèle Foucher. Victor Hugo had married when he was twenty-two and had been wholly sexually inexperienced. On their wedding night they coupled nine times. Adèle eventually found his sexual prowess exhausting, and after five pregnancies in eight years, she declared a sexual moratorium. Hugo then embarked on one of the most notoriously active and systematic sex-lives ever recorded. Nevertheless, when Sainte-Beuve fell in love with Adèle it led to a rupture in the friendship of the two men in 1834. It was at this time that Sainte-Beuve composed *Volupté*. It is generally believed that Sainte-Beuve's affair with Adèle was never consummated but it nearly led to Hugo and Saint-Beuve fighting a duel. The publication of *The Hunchback of Notre Dame* had established Hugo's genius, and women were finding him irresistible. Sainte-Beuve sublimated his passion in writing *Volupté* together with a huge critical output.

BLANCHE AMORY

William Makepeace Thackeray, *Pendennis* (1850)

Theresa Reviss and Cecilia Gore

Further reading:
Ann Monsarrat, *An Uneasy Victorian – Thackeray the Man* (1980)

Arthur Pendennis is a naive young man who has to learn about the world the hard way (see ARTHUR PENDENNIS). His naiveté leads him initially into an emotional entanglement with Emily Costigan, whose father is in favour of the match as he believes Arthur to be heir to a considerable fortune. Arthur is saved from this predicament by the intervention of his worldly uncle, Major Pendennis. He next falls prey to the wiles of Blanche Amory, daughter of Lady Clavering by her first husband. Blanche is: 'a muse – Miss Amory is a mystery – Miss Amory is a *femme incomprise*' by reputation. She paints, writes poems, composes music and rides like Diana. At her first appearance at the village church, always with an eye to the right effect, Blanche appeared meek in dove colour, 'like a vestal virgin'; she was fair, 'and like a sylph. She had fair hair, with green reflections in it. But she had dark eyebrows. She had long black eyelashes, which veiled beautiful brown eyes. She had such a slim waist, that it was a wonder to behold; and such slim little feet, that you would have thought the grass would hardly bend under them. Her lips were of the colour of faint rosebuds, and her voice warbled limpidly over a set of the sweetest little pearly teeth ever seen. She showed them very often, for they were very pretty. She was always smiling, and a smile not only showed her teeth wonderfully, but likewise exhibited two lovely little pink dimples, that nestled in either cheek.' She bespatters her conversation archly with French words and phrases, and writes poems in French and English which she keeps in a dear little book, which she calls 'Mes Larmes! isn't it a pretty name?' she asks, 'who was pleased with everything that she did.' This calculating young charmer almost ensnares Arthur Pendennis, but he is saved at the last minute (see HARRY FOKER).

Blanche is based on Theresa Reviss, who was in her teens when Thackeray first met her. Theresa was the bastard daugther of Thackeray's friend Arthur Buller, and was a monstrous child, precocious, arch, calculating and sophisticated to a degree far beyond her years (see also BECKY SHARP). In the summer of 1850, Thackeray visited Jane Brookfield in Southampton. During the return journey by rail to London he met the young beauty Cecilia Gore, daughter of the novelist Catherine Gore (1799-1861). Cecilia claimed she was Blanche Amory. Thackeray told Jane Brookfield: 'And I think she is Blanche Amory. Amiable (at times) amusing, clever and depraved.' Their talk helped him in the composition of the romance between Pendennis and Blanche, which finally purges Pen of his folly.

ESKER SCOTT ANDERSON

John Ehrlichman, *The Company* (1976) and TV series *Washington Behind Closed Doors* written by David W. Rintels and Eric Bercovici (Paramount 1977)

Lyndon Baines Johnson (1908-1973) Thirty-seventh President of the USA

Further reading: Doris Kearns, *Lyndon Johnson and the American Dream* (1976)

Esker Scott Anderson was 'nearly sixty' when he ran as Vice President with William Curry (see WILLIAM ARTHUR CURRY), and he seemed a logical choice: 'Curry was liberal, his running mate more conservative. Curry was rich, Anderson came from humble beginnings. Curry's wife was young and glamorous. Mrs Martha Anderson epitomized the all-American homemaker. . .Curry was devastating on television and in the great halls before friendly crowds. Esker Anderson was the master flesh-presser. . .in his element at the country fair, the fund-raising cocktail party and the small-town rally.' Within minutes of William Curry's death Anderson was sworn in as President. In his view he was qualified for this position after a lifetime of public service; he was elected Senator for the State of Oregon four times and was monumentally self-confident and seemingly unbeatable. He had a huge staff and the prettiest secretaries and was a raconteur of off-colour stories and a systematic amorist, though his wife affected to be oblivious of his reputation. Anderson retires from the Presidency, on the face of it because of illness, and goes on nationwide television to announce that he will neither seek nor accept the Democratic nomination for another term. He is ill, but the real reason for his retirement is that he has been forced out by his failure to win the war in Indo-China.

President L.B. Johnson was sworn into office immediately after the assassination of John Kennedy in November 1963. He made it his duty to get Congress to pass many of the measures which his predecessor had worked to get through – including the Civil Rights Act of 1964. He had a brilliant political career. He was born at Stonewall, Texas and entered politics in 1932. Between 1937 and 1949 he served in the House of Representatives and moved to the Senate in 1949. He was a renowned wheeler-dealer, and master of compromise and careful negotiation. Johnson was elected Democratic whip in 1951 and party leader in 1953. John F. Kennedy chose him for his Vice Presidential nomination, recognizing his skills as a political manipulator and also realizing that his influence would be very useful in winning the Southern states and getting his policies through the Senate. Johnson's Presidency was marked by liberal reforms at home – including a major education bill, a new tax plan and new economic initiatives. His victory over Barry Goldwater in the

Presidential elections of 1964 was a landslide. This gave him in one session of Congress major domestic reforms on immigration, housing, voting rights and education. His foreign policy was flawed by the escalation of the Vietnam war with no victory in sight. As oppositon to the war mounted and he sensed the strength of the challenge from Senator Eugene McCarthy, he announced in 1968 that he would not seek re-election.

DR ANGELUS

James Bridie, *Dr Angelus* (1947)

Dr E. W. Pritchard (1825–65)

James Bridie's drama *Dr Angelus*, set in the Glasgow of 1920, presents a protagonist who is convinced that his own greatness justifies any action against those he regards as his intellectual and spiritual inferiors. Dr Cyril Angelus (whose name suggests the fallen angel rather than a conventional melodramatic villain) poisons his mother-in-law and his wife, but feels smugly self-righteous about these crimes since they enable him to continue to exercise his ego and indulge his appetites. Before he is arrested at the end of the play he produces his credo: 'I regard religion, philosophy and science not as ends in themselves but as means to an end. This realisation of oneself is the aim and object of existence...Suppose [such a man as myself] to be subjected to the incessant attempts of two ignorant and narrow-minded women to mould him to their miserable conception of what a right-thinking domestic animal ought to be. . . What is he to do? . . . He must make circumstances, like Napoleon. He must break the bonds of oppression. He must be ruthless. He must hew Agag in pieces before the Lord. It is the only thing he can do consistent with his self-respect.'

Bridie took the material for his play from the trial of Edward William Pritchard, a Glasgow doctor found guilty of the murder of his mother-in-law and his wife in 1865. As Bridie discovered when he studied the trial, Dr Pritchard was regarded as a pillar of the local community and held court at home in Sauchiehall Street as a man of the strongest religious principles. Yet he was willing to murder to preserve his position and his reputation; it is likely that, some time before his trial, he had caused the death of a young girl by setting fire to the house she worked in as his maid and mistress. When he was arrested for the murder of his wife and mother-in-law he was involved with another servant-girl, Mary McLeod.

Further reading:
Alan Bold, *Modern Scottish Literature* (1983), Alan Bold and Robert Giddings, *The Book of Rotters* (1985), Winnifred Bannister, *James Bridie and his Theatre* (1955)

ANN

Mary Wollstonecraft, *Mary, A Fiction* (1788)

Fanny Blood (1757–85)

Mary Wollstonecraft's *Mary, A Fiction* is an account of the heroine's capacity for love and friendship. In the course of the story, Mary marries one man and forms a close relationship with another – Henry, an invalid. The love of her life, however, is for a young woman called Ann, a few years older than Mary and a victim of consumption: 'She [Mary] loved Ann better than any one in the world – to snatch her from the very jaws of destruction – she would have encountered a lion. To have this friend constantly with her; to make her mind easy with respect to her family, would it not be superlative bliss?. . .Her friendship for Ann occupiedher heart, and resembled a passion.' Distressed by Ann's economic and medical circumstances, Mary decides to accompany Ann to 'a more salubrious climate' and the two women go to Lisbon. There Ann dies of consumption and Mary is left to her sorrow: 'she wished to avoid a parade of grief – her sorrows were her own, and appeared to her not to admit of increase of softening. . .all was impenetrable gloom.'

In 1774, when her father moved back to the outskirts of London, Mary Wollstonecraft was befriended by the Clares, a clergyman and his wife who had earlier encouraged a girl called Frances (Fanny) Blood. Mary went to see the Blood family in south London and fell in love with Fanny, the original of Ann. In 1784 Mary encouraged her own sister Eliza to leave her husband and the two women set up a school with Fanny at Newington Green. The following year Fanny married the businessman Hugh Skeys in Lisbon. As Claire Tomalin writes, in *Mary*

Further reading:
Claire Tomalin, *Mary Wollstonecraft* (1974), Lillian Faderman, *Scotch Verdict* (1985)

Wollstonecraft (1974): 'Advanced tuberculosis did not prevent (Fanny) from becoming pregnant immediately, and it was not comfortable to be dying and breeding at the same time under the sun of Portugal. . .Mary decided to go out to Lisbon.' Fanny's baby was born in November 1785, but within days Fanny and the child died. Claire Tomalin comments: 'Mary's passionate love for Fanny, which had long since settled into a lesser, protective emotion, now flared up again; she could be restored to her position as ideal romantic friend and mourned with bitter sincerity.'

CARLEON ANTHONY

Joseph Conrad, *Chance* (1914)

Coventry Patmore (1823–96)

Further reading: J.C. Reid, *The Mind and Art of Coventry Patmore* (1957)

The leading theme which holds together the complexities of the narrative in Conrad's first successful major novel, *Chance*, is the collision between the ideals of the Christian civilization to which our culture pays lip service, and the realities of the cruelty, materialism, moral bankruptcy and confusions of the modern world. The plot shows the working out of two leading strands of narrative, involving love and marriage, and the ethics of finance. Flora de Barral is the daughter of a speculator who fails in business. She is brought up by a governess who taunts her about her father's failures and then leaves when the business finally fails. She resolves to kill herself, but is saved by the friendship of Mr and Mrs Fyne. Captain Roderick Anthony, Mrs Fyne's brother, persuades her to elope. When Flora's father comes out of prison he regards his daughter's marriage as a desertion of him in his hour of need and he tries to poison Roderick. He drinks the poison himself and dies, and his attempted crime is detected by Powell, the second mate of Roderick Anthony's ship, the *Ferndale*. Years pass and the *Ferndale* is sunk in an accident. Flora and Powell survive the collision, but Captain Anthony goes down with the ship. Conrad uses the figure of Roderick Anthony's father, Carleon Anthony, to stand for the ideals which *Chance* suggests are no longer relevant in the twentieth century. He is a poet and a tyrant, but his published work puts forward the Christian-humanist ideal: 'The late Carleon Anthony sang in his time of the domestic and social amenities of our age with a most felicitous versification, his object being, in his own words, "to glorify the result of six thousand years' evolution towards the refinement of thought, manners and feelings". Why he fixed the term of six thousand years I don't know.' This is a direct echo of the last lines of the first canto of Coventry Patmore's most famous work, *The Angel in the House*: 'The fair sum of six thousand years'/Traditions of civility'. *Chance* tells us that Carleon's verse 'expresses the supremely refined delicacy of tenderness' and 'the most highly civilized, chivalrous love'. Patmore was a friend of Tennyson, Ruskin and the Pre-Raphaelites. His work celebrating romantic love and loyalty, *The Angel in the House*, was designed to be the apotheosis of married life and love. He became a Roman Catholic in 1864 and wrote religious and meditative verse.

DR PESSIMIST ANTICANT

Anthony Trollope, *The Warden* (1855)

Thomas Carlyle (1795-1881)

Further reading: Julian Symons, *Thomas Carlyle: The Life and Ideas of a Prophet* (1952)

The matters debated during the public outcry about the warden of Hiram's Hospital and the sinecure he was supposed to enjoy (see MR POPULAR SENTIMENT) are taken up and treated to analysis by a fashionable pamphleteer, Pessimist Anticant. This is a satirical portrait of Thomas Carlyle: 'Dr Pessimist Anticant was a Scotchman, who had passed a great portion of his early days in Germany . . . and had learned to look with German subtlety into the root of things, and to examine for himself their intrinsic worth and worthlessness. . . . Returning from Germany, he had astonished the reading public by the vigour of his thoughts, put forth in the quaintest language. He cannot write English, said the critics. No matter, said the public; we can read what he does write, and that without yawning. And so Dr Pessimist Anticant became popular. Popularity spoilt him for all further real use. . .While. . . he confined his objurations to the occasional follies of mankind. . . we were glad to be told our faults and to look forward to the coming millennium, when all men, having sufficiently studied the works of Dr Anticant, would become truthful and energetic. But the doctor mistook the signs of the times . . . instituted himself censor of things in general, and began the great task of reprobating everything and everybody, without further promise of any millennium at all. This was not so well. . .'

The philosopher, historian and pamphleteer, Thomas Carlyle, was greatly influenced by German literature and used a Germanic syntax, as well as Scottish pulpit rhetoric and a somewhat biblical tone. One of his earliest essays was 'Signs of the Times' (1829) and Trollope is accurately characterizing his ranting and denunciatory tendencies.

MR APPOLINAX

T.S. Eliot, 'Mr Appolinax'. *Prufrock and other Observations* (1917)

Bertrand Russell (1872-1970)

Further reading: A.J. Ayer, *Russell* (1972)

In 1914 Bertrand Russell was teaching symbolic logic to a dozen postgraduate students at Harvard University, Cambridge, Mass. An outstanding member of his class was T.S. Eliot, subsequently the author of *The Waste Land* (1922), but then seriously contemplating a career as an academic philosopher. Writing to Ottoline Morrell, Russell said that on 27 March 1914 he was visited by two of his students: 'One, named Eliot, is very well-dressed & polished, with manners of the finest Etonian type'. In London, a year later, Eliot introduced his first wife Vivien to Russell, who let them stay with him at his flat at Russell Chambers, Bury Street. During this period, Vivien flirted with Russell, to the dismay of Eliot, who felt this experience affected his wife's stability. Russell admired Eliot's intellect and was sufficiently fond of him to give him $3,000 in engineering debentures (a debt the poet repaid in 1927 after Vivien inherited her father's shares in a trust fund).

When Eliot's collection *Prufrock and Other Observations* appeared in 1917 it contained a portrait of Russell in the poem 'Mr Appolinax' which, as Russell acknowledged in his *Autobiography* (1967-9), described a typical session over tea in the symbolic logic class. Eliot wrote: 'When Mr Appolinax visited the United States/His laughter tinkled among the teacups...He laughed like an irresponsible foetus./His laughter was submarine and profound./Like the old man of the sea's...I heard the beat of centaur's hoofs over the hard turf/As his dry and passionate talk devoured the afternoon.'

Russell was one of the greatest English philosophers and an immensely influential figure throughout the twentieth century. In collaboration with A.N. Whitehead he wrote the classic *Principia Mathematica* (1910-13) and during six months' imprisonment for pacifism during the First World War he wrote *An Introduction to Mathematical Philosophy* (1919). Though he married four times, he offended contemporaries with his radical criticisms of the institution of marriage. He received the Nobel Prize for Literature in 1950–Eliot, in a letter of 10 June 1949, described him as 'one of the few living authors who can write English prose' – and his later years were devoted to the cause of unilateral nuclear disarmament. Though he succeeded to the title of Third Earl Russell in 1931 he preferred to stand by his reputation as a writer.

SANDY ARBUTHNOTT

John Buchan, *Greenmantle* (1916), *In the Courts of the Morning* (1929), *The Island of Sheep* (1936)

Aubrey Herbert (1880-1923)

In *Greenmantle*, John Buchan's 'shocker', it is Sandy Arbuthnott who solves the problem that Sir Walter Bullivant of the Foreign Office sets RICHARD HANNAY, now a Major who has been through the Battle of Loos with his Lennox Highlanders. Bullivant's son Harry has died out East, leaving a message containing three words: *'Kasredin, cancer, v.I'*. When Hannay meets up with Sandy in Constantinople, he is told by his friend that *Kasredin* is a Turkish play about the coming of an Islamic prophet called Greenmantle whose female ally is Hilda von Einem, hence the *v.I. Cancer* means exactly what it says, for Greenmantle is dying of the disease. To resolve a difficult situation, Sandy himself becomes Greenmantle to save the East from German exploitation. Sir Walter Bullivant's description of Sandy Arbuthnott is a fair summary of the pre-war career of Buchan's Oxford friend Aubrey Herbert, the son of Lord Carnarvon: 'I know the fellow. . .tallish, with a lean, high-boned

Further reading: Janet Adam Smith, *John Buchan* (1965), Margaret FitzHerbert, *The Man Who Was Greenmantle* (1983)

face and a pair of brown eyes like a pretty girl's. I know his record too...He rode through Yemen, which no white man ever did before. The Arabs let him pass, for they thought him stark mad and argued that the hand of Allah was heavy enough on him without their efforts. He's blood brother to every kind of Albanian bandit. Also, he used to take a hand in Turkish politics, and got a huge reputation.' On learning of Sandy's assumption of the role of Greemantle, Hannay observes: 'Sandy was a man of genius – as much as anybody I ever struck – but he had the defects of such high-strung, fanciful souls. He would take more than mortal risks, and you couldn't scare him by any ordinary terror.'

The extraordinary career of Aubrey Herbert is told in Margaret FitzHerbert's *The Man Who Was Greenmantle* (1983). In 1914, when almost blind, Herbert tricked his way into the Irish Guards and fought in France until he was wounded. Later he was at Gallipoli, as a go-between with the Turks. With T.E. Lawrence he went on a secret mission to Mesopotamia, again because of his knowledge of the Turks. As an MP he championed the cause of small nations, and when he died John Buchan described him as 'the most delightful and brilliant survivor from the days of chivalry'.

ARCADIA

Sir Philip Sidney, *Arcadia* (1590)

Arcadia

The pastoral tradition begins with the poems of Theocritus (*c.* 310-250 BC),whose shepherds move in the Sicilian landscape of the poet's youth in Syracuse. It was Virgil, in his *Eclogues* (37 BC), who first idealized Arcadia as the perfect place for lovestruck shepherds. In fact, Arcadia was a mountainous part of the Peloponnesian peninsula in southern Greece, where the real life of the shepherds was harsh rather than idyllic. However, Arcadia was sufficiently far removed from Virgil's world to have an exotic appeal. In Eclogue vii. 4, Virgil refers to Corydon and Thyrsis as 'Arcadians both' (*Arcades ambo*). Virgil's lead was enthusiastically taken up in Italy, and Jacopo Sannazaro's *Arcadia* (1504) celebrates the pastoral Arcadia in a series of verse dialogues linked by a prose narrative.

Sir Philip Sidney's *Arcadia* was written as an entertainment to amuse his sister, Mary, Countess of Pembroke. In this prose romance – punctuated by pastoral eclogues – two princes, Musidorus and his cousin Pyrocles, have various adventures before they are married to Pamela and Philoclea, the daughters of Basilius, king of Arcadia. Sidney's descriptive powers emphasized the other-wordly beauty of the pastoral scene. Here is his description of the River Ladon: 'The banks of either river seemed arms of the loving earth that fain would embrace, and the river a wanton nymph which still would slip from it; either side of the bank being fringed with beautiful trees, which resisted the sun's darts from overmuch piercing the natural coldness of the river. There was among the rest a goodly cypress, who, boughing her fair head over the water, it seemed she looked into it, and dressed her green locks by that running river.' In one of the poems from *Arcadia*, Strephon, a lovestruck shepherd, addresses 'Ye goatherd gods, that love the grassy mountains,/ Ye nymphs which haunt the springs in pleasant valleys,/Ye satyrs joyed with free and quiet forests'.

Pastoral is one of the most persistent modes in English literature, and modern examples include Maurice Hewlett's *The Song of the Plow* (1916), a celebration of the indigenous English peasantry as personified by the hero Hodge, who champions the cause of the Angles. Meanwhile, Arcadia continues as one of the seven names of Peloponnese. It has an area of more than 2,000 square miles and a population estimated in 1961 at around 135,000.

MARIE ARNOUX

Gustave Flaubert, *Sentimental Education* (1869)

Sentimental Education is a novel which deals with the personal development and relationships of a group of characters in France between 1840 and the 1860s – the period of the July monarchy, the Second Republic and the Second Empire. The political background deals with the rising opposition to Louis Philippe, who abdicated in 1848, with the moderate republican government which followed it and the complex events which resulted in the *coup d'état* of Louis Napoleon in 1852.

The novel explores the parallels between the personal ambitions and personal failures of the various characters, and the similar failures and frustrations of hope to be found in the larger political and social context. The main character, Frédéric Moreau, is eighteen years old when the book begins. He is coming back by boat from Paris to his home at Nogent on the Seine. On the boat he meets and falls in love with Marie Arnoux, who is married to an art dealer and owner of a pottery business. Frédéric is immediately enchanted with the older woman: 'She was sitting in the middle of the bench, all alone; or at least he could not see anybody else in the dazzling light which her eyes cast upon him.' He had never seen anything like her before, 'her splendid dark skin, her ravishing figure . . . her delicate, translucent fingers'. He is befriended by the Arnouxs and naturally Marie becomes aware of his infatuation, but he is incapable of making any advances to her. He also has a friend from his childhood, Deslauriers, and there is some suggestion of homosexual attraction between them. Frédéric inherits money and tries to realize himself socially but his life remains empty at the centre. Arnoux fails in business and eventually it seems likely that Marie will give herself to Frédéric, but the illness of her child prevents her from keeping the arrangement. He believes she has betrayed him and embarks on an affair which results in the birth of a child who dies. Much later Marie visits him and offers herself, but he now cannot accept her affection. He is shocked that her hair is now grey. He is afraid of being disgusted later. She cuts him a lock of hair and leaves him.

When he was fourteen Flaubert had seen the 26-year-old wife of a music publisher at Trouville, Elisa Schlesinger, feeding her baby. He fell in love with her and she may have become his mistress for a time. They kept in touch. Her husband's business failed and he fled to Germany. The child was not his but the child of a lieutenant from whom Schlesinger had bought Elisa.

Elisa Schlesinger (1810–88)

Further reading:
Francis Steegmuller (ed.), *The Letters of Gustave Flaubert* (1954)

SIR ARTEGALL

Edmund Spenser, *The Faerie Queene* (1589, 1596)

Arthur Grey, Fourteenth Baron Grey de Wilton (1536-93)

Further reading:
Edmund Spenser, *View of the Present State of Ireland* edited by E. Greenlaw, C.G. Osgood and F.M. Padelford (1949) and R. Bagwell, *Ireland Under the Tudors* (1890)

Sir Artegall is the hero of Book V of *The Faerie Queene*: 'The Champion of true Justice'. He was taught the principles of justice by Astraea, the daughter of Zeus and Themis, who lived among men during the Golden Age: 'Whiles through the world she walked in this sort,/Upon a day she found this gentle childe/Amongst his peres playing his childish sport;/-Whom seeing fit, and with no crime defilde,/She did allure with giftes and speaches milde/To wend with her. So thense him farre she brought/Into a cave from companie exilde,/In which she noursled him till yeares he raught/And all the discipline of justice there him taught.' She taught him to weigh up right and wrong, and to measure out equity according to the line of conscience. In the seclusion of the forest there were no humans on whom he could practice his jurisprudence, so: 'She cause him to make experience/Upon wyld beasts, which she in woods did find/With wrongfull powre oppressing others of their kind.' The image of his magnificent visage is revealed to Britomart by means of a magic mirror and she falls in love with him. Her quest for him ends in their being united. He undertakes the task of rescuing Irena from the tyrant, Grantorto (see GRANTORTO). With the aid of Prince Arthur he then slays the evil Souldan. This is an allegorical portrait of Arthur Grey, the Fourteenth Baron Grey de Wilton, who was Lord Deputy of Ireland and had Edmund Spenser as his secretary. Irena represents Ireland, and the tyrant who threatens her stands for Philip II of Spain. Arthur Grey was the son of one of Henry VIII's commanders in France and Scotland and fought with his father on several campaigns. He fought at the battle of St Quentin and at Guines, and during the assault on Leith. He was appointed Lord Deputy of Ireland in July 1580. At first he suffered defeat at Wicklow, but soon quelled the rebels. In November he was responsible for the massacre of 600 Spaniards and Italians at Smerwick. He frequently requested the Queen to recall him to England, and returned in August 1582. He was one of the commissioners at the trial in 1572 of the Duke of Norfolk, who had been involved in Ridolfi's plot and had intrigued on behalf of Mary Queen of Scots (see DUESSA). Grey was also a commissioner at the trial of Mary Queen of Scots in 1586. He was active in preparations against the Spanish invasion of 1588.

GEORGE ARTHUR

Thomas Hughes, *Tom Brown's Schooldays* (1857)

Arthur Penrhyn Stanley (1815-81) or **Henry Walrond**

Further reading: G.G. Bradley, *Recollections of Arthur Penrhyn Stanley* (1883) and Sydney Self, *Chapters From the History of Rugby School* (1910)

As he moved on up through the school, Tom Brown had hoped to share a study with his close friend, East (see HARRY EAST) but on returning from the holidays Brown is put out to learn that he must share with a new boy: 'a slight pale boy, with large blue eyes and light fair hair, who seemed ready to shrink through the floor'. Tom recognizes that he is the kind of sensitive, delicate boy whose early days at public school would be a misery to him if he was not protected and advised. He takes him under his wing in a manly and gentlemanly way, even though it means sacrificing all the fun he had anticipated with East – having a bottled-beer cellar under his window, making night-lines and slings, plotting expeditions, talking about fishing, reading the novels of Captain Marryat and sorting birds' eggs – and his resolve is strengthened when the matron tells him that his father has died and that he has no brothers: 'And his mama. . .almost broke her heart at leaving him. . .' Dr Arnold believes that some Rugby air and cricket will do George Arthur a power of good, but the matter has to be handled with great tact. Tom advises Arthur never to talk about home or his mother and sisters, as he will get bullied. He saves Arthur from verbal and physical abuse on his first night in the dormitory, when his kneeling and saying his prayers is the cause of general scorn and jeering, and this scene preys on Tom's mind and makes him ashamed of his own neglect of his religious duties. Arthur's simple piety sets him an example he cannot ignore. Tom Brown also begins to say his prayers, and although he too is mocked at first: 'this soon passed off, and one by one all the other boys but three or four followed the lead. . .' The news spreads to the other rooms, and the example becomes generally followed: 'Before either Tom Brown or Arthur left the School-house, there was no room in which it had not become the regular custom.' Even East (see HARRY EAST) gets confirmed.

For many years George Arthur was supposedly a portrait of the young Dean Stanley, educated at Rugby and Balliol, who wrote a biography of Dr Arnold in 1844. Stanley was canon of Canterbury in 1851, travelled widely in the Middle East and was made Dean of Westminster in 1864, a post he held until he died. He published numerous theological, historical and academic works. Some doubt has been expressed as to whether Dean Stanley is, in fact, Arthur. He gained an Exhibition in 1834, and left Rugby that year, within a year of Hughes' arrival. Hughes would have known little about Stanley's days at Rugby, where he had been since 1828, except by repute. Hughes himself claimed that Arthur was based on the character of his school-fellow Henry Walrond, a religious and lovable boy.

KING ARTHUR

Welsh romance, *Kilhwch and Olwen* (tenth century), Geoffrey of Monmouth, *Historia Regum Britanniae* (circa 1150), Wace of Jersey, *Geste des Bretons* (circa 1154), Layamon, *Brut* (twelfth century), Chretien de Troyes, *Perceval, le Conte du Graal* (circa 1180), Sir

Many tales and elaborations have accumulated around the figure of King Arthur to form the Matter of Britain, and each storyteller over the years added various embellishments. In outline, the version that is handed on to us now is that Arthur is the son of Uther Pendragon and Igraine, the wife of Gorlois of Cornwall. Uther wins her favours with the aid of Merlin the magician (see MERLYN). He is brought up and instructed by Merlin and becomes King of Britain, demonstrating his true qualities by pulling the sword Excalibur out of the stone. He gathers round himself a fraternity of worthy knights and engages in various chivalrous feats. The problem of precedence among the brotherhood is solved by the famous Round Table. Among the famous quests is the search for the Holy Grail.

Arthur marries Guinevere, and the fellowship of the Round Table is finally destroyed by the love between Guinevere and Sir Lancelot. While campaigning on the continent Arthur learns that his kingdom is in danger of being seized by his evil nephew, Mordred. Arthur returns, but is mortally wounded. He is carried in a boat to the island of Avalon, where his wounds are to be healed. In Malory's version his parting words are: 'Comfort thyself. . .for I must into the vale of Avalon to help me of my grievous wound. And if thou hear nevermore of me, pray for my soul.' On his tomb in a chapel is engraved in Latin: 'Here lies Arthur, the Once and Future King'. Malory reports that many say he is not dead, but has been taken by the will of Jesus to another place, and shall come again.

These fabulous stories are magnificently rewrought by Tennyson and told with epic learning, wit and vigour by T.H. White in modern times. There is some historic evidence for the existence of a chieftain, Arthur or Artorius, who led armies to defend Britons from the invasions of Scots, Picts and continental barbarians after the Roman legions had left the country defenceless. He is associated with Cornwall and the South-West. Nennius credits him with twelve great victories, and records his death at the battle of Camlan. Arthur came to symbolize the collective effort to preserve the legacy of Roman civilization against pagan invaders.

Thomas Malory, *Le Morte D'Arthur* (1470), Alfred Tennyson, *Idylls of the King* (1842-85), T.H. White, *The Once and Future King* (1958) etc.

Arthur (died 537)

Further reading:
Geoffrey Ashe, *All About King Arthur* (1969)

PRINCE ARTHUR

Edmund Spenser, *The Faerie Queene* (1589, 1596)

Robert Dudley, Earl of Leicester (1532-88)

Further reading:
Robert Naunton, *Fragmenta Regalia* (1630) and Elizabeth Jenkins, *Elizabeth and Leicester* (1961)

Prince Arthur, who represents the knightly virtue of Magnificence, is introduced in Book I of *The Faerie Queen*. He assists the other knights in their adventures, and always brings their encounters with evil-doers to a successful conclusion. He slays the monster Gerioneo, who represents Philip II (see GRANTORTO), saves Belge (the Netherlands) from his powers, and aids Sir Artegall (see SIR ARTEGALL) in his destruction of the Souldan (another portrait of Philip II) who attacks with his horrendous chariot (which stands for the Armada). Arthur is granted a vision of Gloriana in a dream (see UNA) and goes to seek her: 'Gloriane, great Queene of glory bright'. He is described as 'a goodly knight' in magnificent armour and accoutrements: 'His glitterand armour shined far away,/Like glauncing light of Phoebus brightest ray;/From top to toe no place appeared bare,/ That deadly dint of steele endanger may./ Athwart his brest a bauldrick brave he ware,/That shind, like twinkling stars, with stones most pretious rare.' In the middle of his baldric there is a precious stone, shaped like a lady's head, which dazzles all who behold it. His sword is encased in an ivory sheath, the hilt burnished with gold and priceless jewels. His helmet is gold, with lofty plumes, and his shield was cut from one huge precious diamond. No sword could pierce it.

This is a flattering portrait of Robert Dudley, the Earl of Leicester, at the time of the first publication of Spenser's epic Queen Elizabeth's favourite. It was rumoured that caused the death of his wife, Amy Robsart, to further his cause with the Queen. These tales were encouraged by the publication of *Leicester's Commonwealth* in 1584. He tried to win Spanish support for his marriage in 1561 by promising to acknowledge papal supremacy. In 1573 he secretly married Lady Sheffield; It was rumoured that he had poisoned her husband. Leicester entertained Elizabeth lavisly at Kenilworth in 1575, though the proposed match was opposed by Cecil and the nobility. His military and political careers were not brilliant, but he was a glamorous personality and possessed magnificent armour for tilting. Robert Naunton wrote of him: 'He was a very goodly person, and singular well featured, and all his youth well favoured, and of a sweet aspect, but high-foreheaded, which. . .was of no discommendation; but towards his latter end. . .he grew high-coloured and red-faced. . .He was sent Governour by the Queen to the United States of *Holland*; where we read not of his wonders; for they say that he had more of *Mercury* than of *Mars*. . .' It was suggested he died from poison that he had prepared for others.

ASCHENBACH

Thomas Mann, *Death in Venice* (1912)

Gustav Mahler (1860-1911)

Further reading: Richard and Clara Winston, *The Letters of Thomas Mann* (1970), Erich Heller, *The Ironic German* (1958), David Holbrook, *Gustav Mahler and the Courage to Be* (1982)

Thomas Mann's story *Death in Venice* depicts the dying days of Gustav Aschenbach, a world-famous writer who has sacrificed his life on the altar of stylistic purity. Alone with his aesthetic ideals he comes to Venice to renew his creative energy. When Aschenbach beholds a beautiful long-haired boy of about fourteen he is captivated. He even has his own appearance retouched cosmetically in order to appear younger before the boy. While the vision of beauty appears before him Aschenbach is gradually aware of the progress of disease through the city and dies watching 'the pale and lovely Summoner' in the water.

In appearance Aschenbach has the features of Gustav Mahler: 'The nose-piece of his rimless gold spectacles cut into the base of his thick, aristocratically hooked nose.' When the artist Wolfgang Born sent him lithographs based on *Death in Venice* Mann replied: 'The conception of my story, which occurred in the early summer of 1911, was influenced by news of the death of Gustav Mahler, whose acquaintance I had been privileged to make in Munich and whose intense personality left the strongest impression upon me. I was on the island of Brioni at the time of his passing... Later, these shocks fused with the impressions and ideas from which the novella sprang. So that when I conceived my hero who succumbs to lascivious dissolution, I not only gave him the great musician's Christian name, but also in describing his appearance conferred Mahler's mask upon him. I felt quite sure that given so loose and hidden a connection there could be no question of recognition by readers.'

Mahler's exquisitely orchestrated music dwells on death with some justification: in 1907, for example, his elder daughter died at the age of four and he was told he had an incurable heart disease. He died in a Vienna sanatorium on 18 May 1911.

LADY BRETT ASHLEY

Ernest Hemingway, *The Sun Also Rises* (1926)

Duff Smurthwaite (1896–1938)

Further reading: Carlos Baker, *Ernest Hemingway – A Life Story* (1969)

The Sun Also Rises is a novel which concerns the 'lost generation' of expatriate Americans living in Europe after the First World War. The earth is seen as permanent and self-renewing, whereas man is a creature enduring between the twin polarities of birth and assured death. The key to the book is the text from Ecclesiastes: 'One generation passeth away, and another generation cometh; but the earth abideth forever... The sun also ariseth, and the sun goeth down, and hasteth to the place whence he arose.' War and death (symbolized by the bullfight) are present constantly in the background of the novel, which deals with a group of footloose and – on the face of it – fairly dissipated characters, trying to piece their lives together again somehow. They seem to be representative figures of modern man, starting the process of living all over again, attempting to rise from the ashes of the past. Jake Barnes, Bill Gorton and Pedro Romero represent various facets of Hemingway's concept of the heroic. The war has made Jake sexually impotent. Bill despairs of making any sense out of life. Pedro is able to come to terms with the idea of death within the ritual of the bullfight. Lady Brett has been marred by the war as she has lost the man she loved. There is something in her of the pagan deity, she is almost associated with Circe, who turned men into swine. In other respects she is like Helen of Troy. She is aware of the destruction she brings to others, and rejects Romero because she knows ultimately she would bring him destruction and ruin. 'She was damn good looking,' Hemingway writes, 'she wore a slipover jersey sweater and a tweed skirt, and her hair was brushed back like a boy's... She was built with curves like the hull of a racing yacht.' Carlos Baker, in *Hemingway*, describes Duff Smurthwaite as: 'Tall dark slant-eyed Englishwoman of thirty with a storied past and a notable capacity for drink and a string of admirers.' She was married to Sir Roger Twysden in 1917, and separated in 1926. Evelyn Waugh met her and considered her a monster. In Hemingway's novel, however, she emerges with more nobility , beneath the socialite exterior.

LUCY ASHTON

Sir Walter Scott, *The Bride of Lammermoor* (1819)

Janet Dalrymple

Further reading:
Coleman O. Parsons, 'The Dalrymple Legend in the Bride of Lammermoor' in *Review of English Studies* Vol. XIX (1943)

Scott's novel *The Bride of Lammermoor* and Donizetti's Scott-inspired opera *Lucia di Lammermoor* (1835) have familiarized the public with the story of the tragic Lucy Ashton who attempts to murder her husband, Bucklaw, and then dies insane. Anticipating criticism of the melodramatic nature of his book Scott wrote, 'those who are read in the private family history of Scotland during the period in which the scene is laid, will readily discover, through the disguise of borrowed names and added incidents, the leading particulars of AN OWER TRUE TALE.'

Janet Dalrymple was the eldest daughter of James Dalrymple, Lord of Session, and Margaret Ross of Balniel. She promised to marry her sweetheart Archibald, Third Lord Rutherford, but Lady Dalrymple disapproved of the match since Archibald had a title but no wealth to his name. It was Lady Dalrymple's wish that Janet should marry David Dunbar, son and heir of Sir David Dunbar of Baldoon. In order to persuade Janet to break her promise to Archibald, Lady Dalrymple cited the Bible's authority that a woman can break a vow 'if her father disallow her in the day that he heareth . . . and the Lord shall forgive her, because her father disallowed her' (Numbers 30:5). Although in despair, Janet duly married David Dunbar on 12 August 1669 at the Kirk of Glenluce, two miles from her home at Carscreugh. She then went to her husband's home at Baldoon, near Wigtown, and was dead within a month of her marriage.

Local gossip elaborated on the facts and Scott drew on this when composing *The Bride of Lammermoor* in which Janet becomes Lucy Ashton and Lady Dalrymple becomes the evil-minded Lady Ashton who is described, at the close of the book, without 'the slightest symptom either of repentance or remorse'.

RAFE ASHTON

H.D., *Bid Me To Live* (1960)

Richard Aldington
(1892-1962)

Hilda Doolittle, whose name was abbreviated to H.D. in 1912 by Ezra Pound (to whom she had been briefly engaged), married the English writer Richard Aldington in 1913. Two years later – the year of their joint poetic production *Images, Old and New* (1915) – H.D. and Aldington suffered a setback when she miscarried their child. Two years after this – when H.D. was living at 44 Mecklenburgh Square, Bloomsbury, London – Aldington spent his periods of leave from France not in the arms of his wife but in the embrace of Dorothy Yorke who lived in an attic in the same house.

This situation is recreated in *Bid Me to Live* which was drafted in 1927 and revised in 1933 under the influence of Sigmund Freud, who felt that H.D. should clarify her own past by writing about it. The autobiographical heroine Julia Ashton recalls '1915 and her death, or rather the death of her child. Three weeks in that ghastly nursing-home and then coming back to the same Rafe. Herself different. How could she blithely face what he called love, with that prospect looming ahead and the matron, in her harsh voice, laying a curse on whatever might then have been, "You know you must not have another baby until after the war is over." Meaning in her language, you must keep away from your husband, keep him away from you. When he was all she had, was country, family, friends. Well – that anyway.' Rafe (Richard Aldington) is having an affair with Bella Carter (Dorothy Yorke). As Rafe tells Julia: 'I love you, I desire *l'autre*.' Rafe is now something of a stranger to Julia; 'A great, over-sexed officer on leave. . .His body was harder, he was as they say well set-up, his head was bronze on the less bronze shoulders, he was perfectly proportioned, a little heavy but a late-Roman, rather than Greek image, that walked about a room, himself with no clothes on.' Julia eventually leaves London and goes to Cornwall with the composer VANE (Cecil Gray).

H.D. had a child (Perdita, born 1919) by Cecil Gray, and Aldington lived with Dorothy Yorke until 1928, when he left her for Brigit Patmore (the minor character Morgan le Fay in *Bid Me to Live*). Aldington became well-known on the publication of his novel *Death of a Hero*

(1929), an account of his marriage to H.D. (Elizabeth Paston in the Aldington novel) and affair with Dorothty Yorke (Fanny). A close friend of D.H. Lawrence, Aldington compiled *The Spirit of Place* (1935), an anthology of Lawrence's prose. He was divorced from H.D. in 1937 and in 1940 published his autobiography *Life for Life's Sake*. His account of D.H. Lawrence, *Portrait of a Genius, But...*, appeared in 1950.

ASTARTE

Lord Byron, *Manfred* (1816-17)

Augusta Leigh (1783-1851)

Further reading: Leslie A. Marchand, *Byron – A Portrait* (1970)

Manfred, published in 1817, is a dramatic poem, which portrays Manfred, a kind of Faustian outcast, who is living in exile as a result of some serious crime, tortured by remorse. He conjures various universal spirits, but they cannot grant him the one solace he seeks – oblivion. He tries to throw himself from a high peak in the Alps, and after other harrowing adventures is granted a vision of his beloved, Astarte. He had exhausted the entire scope of sensational experience, including an incestuous relationship with Astarte, who is his own sister. In her guilt she has taken her own life. Her spirit now tells him that the next day he is to die, and does not answer his appeals: 'Hear me, hear me – /Astarte! my beloved! Speak to me:/I have so much endured – so much endure – /Look on me! the grave hath not changed thee more/Than I am changed for thee. Thou lovedst me/Too much, as I loved thee: we were not made/To torture thus each other, though it were/The deadliest sin to love as we have loved./Say that thou loath'st me not – that I do bear/This punishment for both.' His time comes and demons appear to take him away on the morrow. Manfred denies their power over him, and they disappear. Manfred dies. Goethe characterized this key poem of the romantic period as possessing 'the gloomy heat of an unbounded and exuberant despair'.

It is another portrayal of Byron's illicit passion for his half-sister, Augusta. His publisher, Murray, hesitated to publish *Manfred* as he was concerned that the public would perceive the obvious identification with Byron as Manfred and Astarte as Augusta Leigh. Murray's fears were correct. When the poem was reviewed in the London *Day and New Times* the writer commented on the autobiographical significance of *Manfred*. Is Manfred's guilt expiated? The end of the poem is ambiguous. The Abbot who attempted to offer him comfort ends the poem with the lines 'He's gone – his soul hath ta'en its earthless flight – / Whither? I dread to think – but he is gone.' (See also ZULEIKA.)

J.L. ATKINS

John Davenport and Dylan Thomas, *The Death of the King's Canary* (1976)

T.S. Eliot (1885-1965)

Written in 1940 by John Davenport and Dylan Thomas, *The Death of the King's Canary* contains a series of satirical portraits of the principal artisitic figures of the 1930s. At the beginning of the novel the Prime Minister is considering a list of candidates for the vacant post of Poet Laureate (that is, the King's Canary) and comes across the name of John Lowell Atkins. We learn that Atkins is Boston born; Harvard, Heidelberg and Cambridge educated; and a naturalized British citizen (since 1917). Turning to Atkin's *Collected Poems*, Prime Minister Crewe reads a composition called 'West Abelard' whose third section starts: 'Even the end is similar. It ends/and there's an end./ A whispering under the door, a weeping/in violet darkness when the last wheels are still.' After Hilary Byrd is appointed Poet Laureate, Atkins is one of the guests at a 'Laureate-warming Party' at Dymmock Hall, Suffolk. Davenport and Thomas describe Atkins alighting from the train at Dymmock railway station: 'J.L. Atkins placed his luggage in a row; many hat-boxes, excellent, capacious cases, a typewriter and a cat-basket. He called the porter in a polite, level voice that admitted no nonsense or argument. He was plainly, but perfectly dressed.' At the head of his table at the banquet, Atkins is wary of fellow-guests who ask him questions about himself: 'He had long since laid Boston, and did not like the ghost to be raised.'

As is obvious from the parody of 'East Coker' (1940) – which opens with the phrase 'In my beginning is my end' – Atkins is a caricature of T.S. Eliot, whose collection *Prufock and Other Observations* appeared in 1917 and who became a British citizen in 1927. Eliot was born in St Louis, Missouri, but looked on Boston as the Eliot family seat. He was educated at the universities of Harvard, Oxford and Marburg (in Germany) before settling in England where he worked as a teacher, bank clerk, and publisher. After the publication of *The Waste Land* (1922), Eliot was admired as a great modernist, but he gradually adopted traditional values and proclaimed his conservative tastes. Atkin's 'cat-basket' is a reference to Eliot's great love of cats, celebrated in *Old Possum's Book of Practical Cats* (1939).

ATOSSA

Alexander Pope, *On the Characters of Women* (1735)

Sarah, Duchess of Marlborough (1660–1744)

Further reading: L. Kronenberger; *Sarah, Duchess of Marlborough* (1958)

Atossa is portrayed in Pope's poem as a bad-tempered and unforgiving creature, with mercurial changes of mood. The main positive characteristic which comes through is Atossa's incredible energy: 'With herself, or others, from her birth/Finds all her life one warfare upon earth:/Shines in exposing knaves, and painting fools,/Yet is whate'er she hates and ridicules.' She is as bold as a man, but as spiteful as a feline: 'Offend her, and she knows not to forgive;/Oblige her, and she'll hate you while you live.' She is married and in a position of power and influence, and spends her time and energies supporting her lord and helping her friends and quarrelling with her immediate family.

Pope takes the name from Atossa, the wife of Darius and mother of Xerxes, the Persian king who attempted in the 5th century BC to conquer the Greeks – without success – and is a leading figure in Aeschylus's tragedy, *The Persians*.

Atossa is generally taken to be Sarah, Duchess of Marlborough, whom Pope knew well. It has been claimed that Pope was paid £1,000 to suppress the character of Atossa, and indeed it is the case that Atossa and two other characters (see CHLOE) were not printed until the edition of 1751, ten years after Pope's death. Sarah Churchill was certainly a strong-willed and tempestuous character, although she and Pope were quite good friends. She married John Churchill in 1678 and became Lady Churchill four years later. She served as lady-in-waiting to Princess Anne and dominated her mind. She helped Anne receive a large parliamentary allowance and after Anne's accession in 1702 wielded considerable power to her husband's advantage, though ousted eventually by Abigail Masham (a relative) and lived abroad after 1713. When she sent in her accounts as keeper of the privy purse in 1711, she deducted £2,000 a year since 1702 as her pension.

ATTICUS

Alexander Pope, *Epistle to Dr Arbuthnot* (1735)

Joseph Addison (1672–1719)

Further reading: P. Smithers, *The Life of Joseph Addison* (1954)

In the *Epistle to Dr Arbuthnot* there is a portrait of a critic, named 'Atticus', who wants to attack writers but has not the courage to be straight about it, but he eggs others on to attack. Other critics, Pope says, such as Dennis and Gildon, can be dealt with in an open manner, but Atticus is too crafty, his method is to: 'Damn with faint praise, assent with civil leer,/And without sneering, teach the rest to sneer,/Alike reserved to blame or to commend,/A tim'rous foe and a suspicious friend:/Fearing e'en fools; by flatterers besieged,/And so obliging that he ne'er obliged;/willing to wound, and yet afraid to strike.'

This is a portrait of Addison, whom Pope disliked for the manner in which he received Pope's translation of Homer. Addison preferred Thomas Tickell's version, which Pope believed Tickell only did at the instigation of Addison. John Gay relayed to Pope remarks made about him and his translation, which further inflamed Pope's feelings. Gay told him: 'I am informed that at Button's (coffee house) your character is made very free with as to morals, etc., and Mr Addison says that your translation and Tickell's are both very well done, but that the latter has more of Homer.'

Addison was educated at Charterhouse and Oxford and was a distinguished classical scholar. He had quite a career in the diplomatic service and achieved fame as poet and essayist, but in 1711, when the Whigs fell from office and he too was out of office, he turned to the stage. His *Cato* was produced with great success in 1713. He was a major contributor to the *Spectator* and the *Tatler*. When the Whigs returned to office, he was appointed chief secretary for Ireland and undertook political journalism. He was buried in Westminster Abbey. His place in literary history is assured by his contribution to the establishment of periodic journalism, and his creation of the immortal squire, Sir Roger de Coverley.

AYESHA

H. Rider Haggard, *She* (1886), *Ayesha, or the Return of She* (1905), *She and Allan* (1921)

A rag doll

Further reading:
D.S. Higgins, *Rider Haggard: The Great Storyteller* (1981), M.N. Cohen, *Rider Hagard: His Life and Works* (1960)

H. Rider Haggard's celebrated romance *She* portrays a female figure who is exquisitely evil. When the narrator, Ludwig Horace Holly, asks to see Ayesha's face he is astonished: 'I have heard of the beauty of celestial beings, now I saw it; only this beauty, with all its awful loveliness and purity, was *evil*.' Ayesha, the white queen who rules over the Amahagger people of Kŏr, has been alive for two thousand years waiting for the rebirth of Killikrates, the Egyptian priest she killed for rejecting her offer of immortality. Holly is guardian of Killikrates's descendant, Leo Vincey, who watches as she steps into 'the flame of Life' and is consumed by it.

Haggard was a morbid child who was brought up by various nurses at the family home in Bradenham Hall, Norfolk. As the author's daughter, Lilias Rider Haggard, wrote in *The Cloak That I Left* (1951) one of the nurses terrified him by keeping, in a cupboard near his bed, 'a disreputable rag doll of particularly hideous aspect, with boot-button eyes, hair of black wool and a sinister leer upon its painted face'. When the nurse left the room she would assert her authority by opening the cupboard door and telling the child to behave since he was being watched by 'She-who-must-be-obeyed'. The figure haunted Haggard's imagination and lurks beneath the skin-deep beauty of Ayesha who, in the transformation scene in *She*, becomes hideous as she increasingly assumes the features of the figure of Haggard's childhood: 'smaller and smaller she grew; her skin changed colour, and in place of the perfect whiteness of its lustre it turned dirty brown and yellow, like an old piece of withered parchment... Smaller she grew, and smaller yet, till she was no larger than a baboon.'

B

BABES IN THE WOOD

Anon, *The Children in the Wood* (ballad on traditional subject, earliest version dates from 1595: reprinted in Percy's *Reliques of Ancient English Poetry*, 1765)

Male and female children of the family of Wayland Hall, Norfolk

The traditional British pantomime story tells how two children, a boy and a girl, are murdered by their wicked uncle, who stands to benefit from their father's will. He hires two murderers, one of whom does not have the heart to go through with the crime. In a quarrel he is killed by his partner. The children are left in the wood where they die during the night. Birds cover them with leaves. The wicked uncle does not profit from the deed. His farm is burned down. His own sons die. His cattle perish. He becomes a highwayman and dies in prison after confessing to his crime.

The ballad version, entitled *The Norfolk Gentleman*, was published in Norwich in 1595, and was the subject of a stage play, *Two Lamentable Tragedies; the one of the murder of Maister Beech, a chandler of Thames Street; the other of a young child murdered in a wood by two ruffians, with the consent of his uncle*, by Robert Yarrington. It dates from 1601. Yarrington's version sets the story in Padua, and there is but one child murdered by a stab wound.

The original incidents are supposed to have happened in the vicinity of Wayling Wood (or Wayland Wood) between Watton and Kimberley, in Norfolk. There is the stump of the oak tree where, it is claimed, the children's bodies were discovered. The master of Wayland Hall had a son and daughter: 'The one a fine and pretty boy,/ Not passing three years old;/The other a girl more young than he,/And fram'd in beauty's mold.' When he died, he left them in the care of his wife's brother. According to his will the children were to inherit his money. But if the children were to die, it was to pass to the uncle. A year after the father's death, the wicked uncle plans their murder: 'He bargain'd with two ruffians strong,/Which were of furious mood,/That they should take these children young,/And slay them in a wood.' Thomas Percy claims the ballad to be later than the play of 1601, yet it is clearly earlier, and based on a real murder case.

Further reading:
Thomas Percy, *Reliques of Ancient English Poetry* (1765), *Bishop Percy's Folio Manuscript*, edited by J.W. Hales and F.J. Furnivall (1867-8)

YVONNE BACON

John Davenport and Dylan Thomas, *The Death of the King's Canary* (1976)

Nina Hamnett (1889-1956)

In the 1930s the alcoholic centre of literary London was the Fitzroy Tavern, on the corner of Charlotte Street and Windmill Street. There painters such as Augustus John and Nina Hamnett mixed with writers like Dylan Thomas. In *The Life of Dylan Thomas* (1965), Constantine FitzGibbon says 'Nina [Hamnett] was queen of the Fitzroy. To enter ...and not to buy Nina a drink – if one had the price of two – was in those days and in that world a solecism that amounted to a social enigma. The payment was an anecdote or two from an apparently inexhaustible (but alas only apparently, for repetition quite soon set in) fund concerning the artistic and literary great. A tall bony, angular woman with a voice like a stage duchess and a laugh like a man, Nina had been a painter of very considerable talents.' Like her friend Augustus John, Nina came from Tenby, Wales. She once lived with the sculptor Gaudier-Brzeska, whose torso of her (in the Tate Gallery) prompted her to call her autobiography *Laughing Torso* (1933). She had also known Gertrude Stein, Ernest Hemingway, Picasso, Modigliani from her days in Paris. On 7 January 1933 the *South Wales Evening Post* carried an article by Dylan Thomas in which he mentioned Nina as 'author of the banned book *Laughing Torso*': a week later the newspaper apologized for mistakenly suggesting the book was banned, and Thomas was no longer asked to write for the paper.

In *The Death of the King's Canary*, which Thomas wrote with John Davenport in 1940, Nina appears as Yvonne Bacon (a childish reference to the 'ham' in her surname). She is one of the guests at a 'Laureate-warming Party' held by the newly appointed Poet Laureate,

Hilary Byrd, at Dymmock Hall, Suffolk. 'Yvonne Bacon was in heaven', we hear, because two cultural celebrities have agreed to sit for her. When she sees HERCULES JONES (Augustus John) talking seductively to a lovely blonde woman, she is annoyed; '"Dirty old man", said Yvonne Bacon. She had known Jones for thirty years, but he had not spoken to her for twenty.' With her 'raddled face' and affectations, Yvonne is faintly ridiculous (like the other guests). She is seen in strange situations: 'Round a corner at the far end of the corridor two women, one in underclothes, the other Yvonne Bacon, scampered, squealing.' When one of the guests throws her to the ground she reacts with a 'titter of anticipation' but accepts the inevitable anticlimax: 'Yvonne lay still. She had, anyway, never expected it to happen.'

MRS MARTHA BETHUNE BALIOL

Sir Walter Scott, *The Chronicles of the Canongate-The Highland Widow* (1827), *The Two Drovers* (1827) and *The Fair Maid of Perth* (1828)

Anne Murray Keith (died 1818)

Further reading: Edgar Johnson, *Sir Walter Scott-The Great Unknown* (1970)

The Chronicles of the Canongate is the collective title for three of Sir Walter Scott's later novels, all of them of a somewhat sombre and tragic hue. The situation of these tales is the fiction that they are written by a Mr Chrystal Croftangry, who composes them by drawing on the memories and recollections of his old friend, Mrs Martha Bethune Baliol, who lives in the Canongate, Edinburgh. Chrystal is a self-portrait of Scott, and the old lady, Mrs Bethune Baliol, is based on Mrs Anne Murray Keith, whom he got to know when he was a young man in Edinburgh society. It was in the late 1780s that Walter Scott was introduced to Lady Balcarres and her cousin, Mrs Anne Murray Keith, both of advanced years, who shared a flat in George Square. Both ladies enjoyed company, cards and gossip, and young Scott found them fascinating acquaintances. Lady Balcarres was a devotee of the drama, but Mrs Murray Keith was well versed in belles lettres and steeped in the oral tradition of Scottish history, legend, culture and manners – a living sourcebook of ancient Scottish days. Walter Scott was frequently in their company, either escorting Lady Balcarres to her box at the theatre, or soaking up Scotland's history and heritage from the stories told him by Mrs Murray Keith. She recognized them even when they had been reworked by the novelist's romantic imagination. Her comment has been preserved: 'D'ye think I dinna ken my ain groats among ither folks' kail'. Scott describes her lodgings in Canongate with the old-fashioned furniture, lacquer cabinets, old books, family portraits, valuable chinaware, and 'the spontoon which her elder brother wore when he was leading on a company of the Black Watch at Fontenoy'. Scott describes her: 'She had ordinary features and an ordinary form. She said herself that she was never remarkable for personal charms; a modest admission, which was readily confirmed by certain old ladies, her contemporaries, who, whatever might have been the youthful advantages which they more than hinted had been formerly their own share, were now in personal appearance, as well as in everything else, far inferior to my accomplished friend. Mrs Martha's features had been of a kind which might be said to wear well: their irregularity was now of little consequence, animated as they were by the vivacity of her conversation; her teeth were excellent, and her eyes, though inclining to grey, were lively, laughing and undimmed by time.' She was one of a large family from Craig in Kincardineshire and she was related to ambassadors and diplomats. When she died Scott wrote that much of the best kind of tradition had died with her.

BARABAS

Christopher Marlowe, *The Jew of Malta* (1592)

David Passi (died 1589)

Further reading: A.L. Rowse, *Christopher*

In Marlowe's drama, *The Jew of Malta*, the Grand Seignior of Turkey demands that the Jews of Malta should pay him tribute. Barabas is one of the wealthiest Jews on the island: 'Who hateth me but for my happiness?/ Or who is honoured now but for his wealth?/Rather had I, a Jew, be hated thus,/Than pitied in a Christian poverty.' He suffers the indignity of having his riches impounded and his mansion turned into a nunnery, as he attempted to resist the edict and pay the tribute. He hides a store of riches under the floor and gets his daughter, Abigail, to pretend

Christian conversion to gain access. She regains the gold and returns it to Barabas. He is aided in his machinations by the Christian-hating Arabian slave, Ithamore. They arrange the death of Abigail's lover, among others, and Abigail flees to become a genuine convert to Christianity. Barabas's revenge is to murder the whole convent with a gift of poisoned rice. Before she dies, Abigail betrays her father. Malta is now beseiged by the Turks. Barabas betrays the fortress to the invaders and his reward is to be made governor. His next plot is to destroy the Turkish garrison by means of a collapsible floor, beneath which is a boiling cauldron. He perishes when he is hurled through the floor himself.

Marlowe–His Life and Work (1964)

Marlowe's sources are various, including Lonicerus's chronicles and Contarini's history of the Turkish war in the Mediterranean. The latter involved an account of the extraordinary career of Joseph Nassi (or Miques). He was a Jew and a sworn enemy of the Venetians. He gave himself to the service of the Turks. His reward was to be made governor of the island of Naxos – which was Christian. This exactly parallels the story of *The Jew of Malta*. During the time Marlowe composed his drama the adventures of one David Passi, an ambitious Jewish merchant, were well known in the circle in which Marlowe moved, the Walsingham intelligence network. Walsingham was chief of the secret service in London from 1569, ambassador to France 1570-73 and Secretary of State 1573-90. Walsingham's system of espionage and bribery resulted in the convictions of William Parry in 1585 and Anthony Babington and Mary Queen of Scots in 1586. Passi was rewarded for his services to the Turks by being given the very highest offices at Constantinople. Marlowe based the political and military background on the Turkish siege of Malta in July 1551. François de Belleforest, a writer used by marlowe and other dramatists as a source of material, refers to the career of David Passi.

BARCHESTER, BARSETSHIRE

Anthony Trollope, *The Warden* (1855), *Barchester Towers* (1857), *Doctor Thorne* (1858), *Framley Parsonage* (1861), *The Small House at Allington* (1864), *The Last Chronicle of Barset* (1867)

Salisbury and the county of Somerset

In the Barsetshire novels Trollope created the perfect haven for the English imagination, a Victorian community where time stood still; an ideal small town community, supported by its agriculture, hardly touched by the railways and the thoughts which shake mankind; where the centres of civilization are small cathedral towns with ivy-covered church buildings and official dwellings; where the only sounds are church bells, horse traffic and cawing rooks. Endless summer days dapple the quiet streets and the darker side of human nature only shows itself in the intrigue over missing postal orders or rivalry in the matter of church preferments. The cathedral town that Trollope describes as Barchester he admitted was Winchester, not Wells in Somerset; but much of the details of the county were based on his experiences of Somerset in the West Country. He worked for the Post Office for two years in Gloucestershire and Somerset in the early 1850s and absorbed the local colour. He wrote in his autobiography: 'I spent two of the happiest years of my life at the task. I began in Devonshire; and visited I think, I may say, every nook in that county, in Cornwall, Somersetshire, the greater part of Dorsetshire, the Channel Islands, part of Oxfordshire, Wiltshire, Gloucestershire, Worcestershire, Herefordshire, Monmouthshire, and the six southern Welsh counties. In this way I had an opportunity of seeing a considerable portion of Great Britain, with a minuteness which few have enjoyed . . . I went almost everywhere on horseback . . . The object was to create a postal network which would catch all the recipients of letters . . .' He visited Salisbury and: 'whilst wandering there one midsummer evening round the purlieus of the cathedral I conceived the story of *The Warden*, from whence came that series of novels of which Barchester, with its bishops, deans, and archdeacons, was the central site . . .' He wrote *The Warden* while at Tenbury in Worcester, but with the impression of Salisbury, Wiltshire, strongly in his mind: 'I had stood for an hour on the little bridge in Salisbury, and had made out to my own satisfaction the spot on which Hiram's hospital should stand.' He admitted the location of Barchester and Barsetshire to the historian Edward Augustus Freeman while visiting him at his home in Somerset in October 1882.

AMOS BARTON

George Eliot, *Scenes of Clerical Life* (1858)

Revd John Gwyther (died 1873)

Further reading: Robert C. Rathburn and Martin Steinman Jr. (eds), *From Jane Austen to Joseph Conrad* (1967)

George Eliot's earliest writings deal with life and incident which she observed around her in her early days in Nuneaton. The three tales which make up *Scenes of Clerical Life* originally appeared in *Blackwood's Magazine*. 'The Sad Fortunes of the Rev Amos Barton' tells the story of a perfectly ordinary clergyman, who is the curate of Shepperton. He has neither deep learning, nor sophistication nor the human touch. He is devoid of humour and is not at all popular with his parishioners. But even so, this man – who in so many respects might be perceived as a mediocrity – does in fact earn in some measure the respect of his flock, through suffering and misfortune with which mankind can identify. He was married to a beautiful young woman, Milly Barton, who dies from hard work and the stress and strain of her life as the wife of a poor parish priest. In deep regret, the Revd Amos Barton moves to the north of England.

His character and the major incidents of the story were based on the Revd John Gwyther, who was the curate of the parish of Chilvers Coton, where Mary Ann Evans (George Eliot) went to church. She was seventeen when Mrs Gwyther died, and, like the Revd Amos Barton, John Gwyther left his parish and went to the north of England. He went to a parish in Sheffield and moved later to Fewston, in Yorkshire. In January 1857 the first part of *Amos Barton* appeared in *Blackwood's* and the Revd Gwyther's eldest daughter, Emma, exclaimed 'Who in the world could have written this? Is it you, papa?' Emma appears as Patty in the story. Gwyther wrote to congratulate the unknown author 'now the pain I felt at the first publication is past off. . .yet I fully forgive for old acquaintance sake'.

MISS HETTY BATES

Jane Austen, *Emma* (1816)

Miss Molly Milles

Further reading: R.A. Austen-Leigh, *Jane Austen – Her Life and Letters* (1913), C. Hill, *Jane Austen – Her Home and Her Friends* (1902)

Jane Austen's *Emma* contains one of her finest comic creations in the person of the tiresomely nice Miss Bates who lives with her mother Mrs Bates at Highbury. The self-indulgent altruism of Miss Bates provides Jane Austen with an amusing quality to contrast with the selfish magnanimity of her heroine Emma Woodhouse. 'Mrs Bates,' writes Austen, 'the widow of a former vicar of Highbury, was a very old lady, almost past everything but tea and qaudrille. She lived with her single daughter in a very small way, and was considered with all the regard and respect which a harmless old lady, under such untoward circumstances, can excite. Her daughter enjoyed a most uncommon degree of popularity for a woman neither young, handsome, rich, nor married. . .Her youth had passed without distinction and her middle life was devoted to the care of a failing mother, and the endeavour to make a small income go as far as possible. And yet she was a happy woman, and a woman whom no one named without good-will.'

When Jane Austen visited her brother Edward, at Godersham Park, Kent, in 1813 she had dinner with a Mrs and Miss Milles and agreed to call on them at Canterbury: 'I like the mother. . .because she is cheerful and grateful for what she is at the age of ninety and upwards [whereas] Miss Milles was queer as usual, and provided us with plenty to laugh at. She undertook in *three words* to give us the history of Mrs Scudamore's reconciliation, and then talked on about it for half-an-hour, using such odd expressions and so foolishly minute, that I could hardly keep my countenance.' In recreating Mrs and Molly Milles as Mrs and Hetty Bates, Jane Austen made good use of Molly's garrulous nature, for her dramatic monologues are among the finest moments of *Emma*.

NORMAN BATES

Film *Psycho*, written by Joseph Stefano, based on the novel by Robert Bloch;

Marion Crane (Janet Leigh) works in an office in Phoenix, Arizona. She cannot marry her lover, Sam, as he is hard up. She steals $40,000 from her employer in the hope that the couple can start a new life in California. She leaves town, but a sudden storm compels her to put up for the night at a lonely motel, where the owner, Norman Bates (Anthony Perkins), seemingly lives with his cranky old mother in a gothic house behind the motel. As Marion is taking a shower she is stabbed to death, apparently by Norman's mother. Norman then goes to great lengths to clear up all the evidence of his insane mother's crime, and disposes of Marion's body, sinking it in her car in a swamp. Marion's sister, with the help of an insurance investigator, attempt to solve the mystery of Marion's disappearance, believing it is connected with the theft of the $40,000. The detective is murdered in the Bates's house. Sam and Marion's sister Lila learn that Mrs Bates has been dead for some years. They go to the Bates's house and discover the rotting body of old Mrs Bates in the cellar. Norman, his personality totally overtaken by that of his mother, tries to murder Lila, but she is saved by Sam. It was Norman-as-Mother, dressed in her clothes, who committed the crimes. The film is full of clues suggestive of the Norman/Mother duality: 'My mother – what is the phrase – isn't quite herself today' he tells Marion when she first arrives at the Bates's Motel. He also tells her that a boy's best friend is his mother. Norman's hobby is taxidermy, and the motel is decorated with stuffed birds. He preserves his mother's body with chemicals. 'My mother's harmless,' he tells Marion, 'She's as harmless as one of these stuffed birds.'

This terrible story is based on the case history of Edward Gein, a psychopathic murderer. He was born in Wisconsin and doted on his mother, who was a religious fanatic. To the small community of Plainfield he seemed a quiet, solitary man; but inwardly he was a raging lunatic who longed to be a woman. He was obsessed with anatomy and sex-change surgery. He practised on bodies he exhumed from the local cemetery, secretly indoors in his farm, wearing the skin of dead women over his own person. He murdered two women, experimented on the bodies of several, and habitually wore women's clothes in secret. One of his victims was the mother of a deputy sheriff. Gein was tried in 1957 and committed to the local asylum. Psychiatrists testified at his trial that after his mother died he had wanted to turn into a woman and his house was full of the grisly evidence of his endeavours.

directed by Alfred Hitchcock (1960)

Edward Gein (1906-84)

Further reading:
Donald Spoto, *The Art of Alfred Hitchcock* (1977), John Russell Taylor, *Hitch – The Life and Work of Alfred Hitchcock* (1978)

BAZAROV

Ivan Turgenev, *Fathers and Sons* (1862)

V.G. Belinsky (1811-48)

Further reading:
David Magarshak, *Turgenev* (1954), N. Brodsky, *V.G. Belinsky*

Turgenev dedicated *Fathers and Sons* to the memory of V.G. Belinsky and gave his hero, Bazarov, characteristics in common with the great Russian critic. Bazarov is the son of a poor army doctor, as was Belinsky; moreover Bazarov's argumentative intensity is derived from Belinsky, a man Turgenev regarded with admiration and awe. Turgenev lived near Belinsky in St Petersburg, in 1843, and the aspiring novelist became part of the critic's literary circle. Though he could not accept all Belinsky's arguments Turgenev watched closely as his friend moved from a reactionary artistic and political position to an urgent advocacy of literary naturalism and socialism. A member of Belinsky's circle recorded the radical impact of Belinsky on Turgenev: 'Belinsky was the first of us to notice (his affections) and sometimes laughed at them mercilessly. . .Turgenev very much respected Belinsky and submitted to his moral authority without question...He was even a little afraid of him.' Belinsky died of consumption at the age of thirty-seven, and Turgenev speculated on how he might have developed, given his volatile temperament.

Bazarov, who also dies prematurely and pointlessly, is a nihilist, one of the 'sons' who treats with contempt the romanticism of the older generation of 'fathers'. His mission in life is the destruction of antiquated attitudes and he is sweeping in his statements on human nature: 'It is enough to have one single human specimen in order to judge all the others. People are like trees in a forest: no botanist would dream of studying each individual birch-tree.' When the novel first appeared young Russians misinterpreted the character of Bazarov, with his intolerance and love of wine and women, as an attack on the radicals N.A. Dobrolyubov and N.G. Chernyshevsky who wrote *What is to be done?* (1863) as a rejoinder to Turgenev's novel. Turgenev, however, thought of Bazarov as 'my favourite offspring' and meant the character to be sympathetic.

BAZHAKULOFF

Norman Douglas, *South Wind* (1917)

Rasputin (1871-1916)

Further reading: Nancy Cunard, *Grand Man* (1954), I. Greenless, *Norman Douglas* (1957), M.V. Rodzianko, *The Reign of Rasputin* (1927)

Norman Douglas's novel *South Wind* hangs a whole sensuous attitude to life on a slim narrative peg. Thomas Heard, Bishop of Bampopo in Africa, breaks his journey to England by stopping off on the island of Nepenthe where he encounters the strangest creatures. Among these is the self-styled Messiah Bazhakuloff, the ex-monk from Russia, who limits his disciples to the Sacred Number 63 and calls them Little White Cows. The Russian colony on the island is resented especially after violence breaks out over one of the Messiah's Revelations: he decides that the flesh and blood of warm-blooded beasts is Abomination to Little White Cows, a decision that enables him to continue to enjoy fish. Bazhakuloff is presented as a preposterous figure: 'The voluptuous surroundings of Nepenthe, the abundant food, adoration of disciples, alcoholic and carnal debaucheries, had impaired his tough Moujik frame and blunted his wit, worked havoc with that energy and peasant craftiness which once ruled an Emperor's court. His body was obese. His mind in a state of advanced putrefaction. Even his personal cleanliness left something to be desired. Sitting there, puffy and pasty, in a darkened room, he looked more than ever like some obscene vegetable that has grown up in the shade.'

Douglas intended Bazhakuloff as a caricature of Rasputin, the Russian prophet whose scandalous personal behaviour and influence over the Tsarina led to his assassination. Rasputin managed successfully to exploit the sectarianism that was so rampant in the Russia of his time and he managed, at first, to convey a sense of holiness that was above suspicion. He took over the mind of the Tsarina because she believed completely in his power to treat her son's haemophilia. Like Bazhakuloff in Douglas's novel, Rasputin 'fought and wormed his way into the favour of the Court. A good deal of his worldly success may well have been due, as his enemies assert, to an incredible mixture of cringing, astuteness and impudence.'

BEATRICE

Dante, *The New Life* (1292), *The Divine Comedy* (1307-21)

Beatrice Portinari (1266-90)

The love of Dante for Beatrice – as expressed in *The New Life (La Vita Nuova)* and *The Divine Comedy* (originally entitled *Commedia*, the epithet being added by admirers of the masterpiece) – is one of the glories of world literature. Though Dante's vision of Beatrice is an artistic triumph, the object of his attraction was a real woman, Beatrice Portinari, who married the Florentine banker Simone de' Bardi and died at the age of twenty-four – less than six months after the death of her father Folco Portinari.

In 1274, when he was nine and she eight, Dante first saw Beatrice at her father's house in Florence. 'Her dress, on that day,' says Dante in *The New Life* (as translated by Dante Gabriel Rossetti), 'was of a most noble colour, a subdued and goodly crimson, girdled and adorned in such sort as best suited with her very tender age. . .I say that, from that time forward, Love quite governed my soul'. On May Day, 1283 (exactly nine years after his first glimpse of Beatrice), Dante saw her, dressed entirely in white, walking along a Florentine street between two older women. This time he heard her speak, for she turned to him and greeted him: 'because it was the first time that any words from her reached mine ears, I came into such sweetness that I parted thence as once intoxicated'. In a dream that night, Beatrice appeared to him 'covered only with a blood-coloured cloth' in the arms of Love: 'From that night forth, the natural functions of my body began to be vexed and impeded, for I was given up wholly to thinking of this most gracious creature'. Rather than reveal his passion, Dante turned his attentions elsewhere so that Beatrice 'denied me her most sweet salutation, in the which alone was my blessedness'. After Beatrice's death, on 8 June 1290, Dante says 'the whole city came to be as it were widowed and despoiled of all dignity'. Dante wrote a poem containing the lines 'Beatrice is gone up into high heaven,/The kingdom where the angels are at peace'. In 1291 Dante married Gemma Donati, a wife chosen by his father, and at the end of *The New Life* announced his ambition to commemorate Beatrice: 'I shall yet write concerning her what hath not before been written of any woman'. This great plan resulted in *The Divine Comedy*, in which Beatrice appears as a symbol of Heavenly Wisdom, sent to guide the poet through Paradise. In Canto XXXI of *Paradiso*, St Bernard points out Beatrice in her appointed place – beside Rachel, in the third circle.

JOHN BEAVER

Evelyn Waugh, *A Handful of Dust* (1934)

Sir John Heygate, the Fourth Baronet (1903-76)

Further reading: Malcolm Bradbury, *Evelyn Waugh* (1964), *Evelyn Waugh Diaries*, edited by Michael Davie (1976), and *Evelyn Waugh Letters* edited by Mark Amory (1980)

John Beaver is the rather colourless villain, in *A Handful of Dust*, who breaks up the marriage of Tony and Brenda Last. He does not seem to be a strong character or a likeable personality, and was used by various society hostesses to make up their numbers: 'Most of Beaver's invitations came to him at the last moment; occasionally even later, when he had already begun to eat a solitary meal from a tray.' He is aimless. 'He was twenty-five years old. From leaving Oxford until the beginning of the slump he had worked in an advertising agency. Since then no one had been able to find anything for him to do. So he got up late and sat near his telephone most of the day, hoping to be rung up. Lady Brenda Last, beautiful, with a 'very fair, underwater look', has become rather bored after six years of married life to Tony Last, proud owner of Hetton Abbey, a Victorian gothic mansion in the country. When Tony invites Beaver to stay for the weekend, it leads to an affair between Brenda and Beaver which leads to ironic tragedy. Tony goes on an expedition to Brazil, led by a charlatan, Dr Messinger, from which he never returns. He had been deeply shocked by Brenda's adultery: 'He had got into habit of loving and trusting Brenda.'

The novel was written soon after Waugh's marriage to Evelyn Gardner had ended in divorce after her adultery with John Heygate. They had married in June 1928. He had suggested they marry 'and see how it goes'. It had not gone very well. She was unwell during a Mediterranean cruise in 1929, and when they returned to England he left her in London while he went to the country to complete his second novel, *Vile Bodies*. She had an affair with John Heygate, at that time a news editor at the BBC. In July 1929 she told her husband what had happened, and, after a reconciliation had failed, they were granted a decree nisi in January 1930. John Heygate was the son of a master at Eton, and was educated at Eton and Balliol College, Oxford. He worked for the BBC 1926-29, but was compelled to resign by Sir John Reith, the Director General, after he had been named co-respondent in the divorce proceedings. He married Evelyn Waugh in 1930, but the marriage was annulled in 1936. He realized that he was John Beaver, and wrote to Michael Davie, editor of Waugh's diaries: 'One realizes one was the rather feeble villain in *A Handful of Dust*. But much later Evelyn Waugh used to ask Tony Powell (Anthony Powell, the novelist) about me in a friendly manner.' The theme of the betrayed husband recurs in several of Waugh's novels.

SIXTUS BECKMESSER

Wagner, *The Mastersingers of Nuremberg* (1868)

Eduard Hanslick (1825-1904)

Further reading: Ernest Newman, *Wagner Nights* (1954)

In Wagner's comic masterpiece, *The Mastersingers*, the young knight, Walther von Stolzing, hopes to gain admittance to the Mastersingers Guild in order to compete in the coming singing festival. The prize is to be the hand in marriage of Eva, the beautiful daughter of Veit Pogner. The town clerk, Beckmesser, wants Eva for himself, and is bitterly jealous of Walther, whom – he suspects – Eva loves in any case. When Walther has to sing before the Guild before he can be considered, his song has to be assessed by the Marker. On this occasion the Marker is Beckmesser. He takes advantage of his position to mark Walther's trial song down. He finds fault with everyting – obscurity, bad rhyming, poor imagery, lack of balance – the whole thing is simply far, far too outlandish and outrageous for Beckmesser's taste and judgement. Some of the mastersingers who hear it find things to admire in it, others say they could not understand a word of it. Hans Sachs, the elder statesman of the Guild, suspects that Beckmesser is motivated by personal spite. Eva and Walther both turn to Sachs for advice and consolation. Sachs explains that tradition and rules are there as an aid to inspiration, not as a means to destroy it. In the meantime, Beckmesser is trying to write a song with which to win the competition – and Eva. Walther is inspired to compose a superb prize-song which Beckmesser attempts to purloin. Beckmesser has insufficient time properly to master it and on the day of the festival sings it, makes a fool of himself, and is laughed off the stage. Walther sings the prize-song, wins universal approbation and is united with Eva.

In the character of Beckmesser, Wagner portrays his arch-enemy Eduard Hanslick, the Viennese conservative music critic, who opposed the modernist tendency in his day, especially as represented by Liszt and Wagner. He found much to admire in Wagner's early operas – especially *Tannhäuser* – but bitterly opposed the 'music of the future' which Wagner pioneered in *Tristan* and *Der Ring des Nibelungen*. Beckmesser was originally called Hans Lick in Wagner's opera. Hanslick complained of the restless accompaniments and excessive modulations, long-winded and declamatory style, submarine and subterranean legends, melodic poverty and cacophany: 'we sit there, helpless and bored, amid these endless dialogues,m thirsting equally to articulate speech and intelligible melody'.

BELINDA

Alexander Pope, *The Rape of the Lock* (1712)

Arabella Fermor
(1689-1738)

Further reading: Bonamy Dobree, *Alexander Pope* (1951), Peter Quennell, *Alexander Pope – The Education of Genius* (1968), Maynard Mack, *Alexander Pope – A Life* (1985)

Alexander Pope's mock-heroic *The Rape of the Lock* (enlarged 1713) was written at the request of his friend, John Caryll, who wanted a poetic peace-offering to settle the differences between two of England's most prominent Catholic families. Caryll's ward, Lord Petre, had snipped a side-curl from the hair of the celebrated beauty Arabella Fermor; as a result the Fermors seethed with indignation at the audacity of Lord Petre and his apparently unrepentant family. Pope was called in, he said, because Caryll liked both families and wanted the poet to 'laugh them together again', which he did by inflating a trivial incident into an epic event. He also produced a glowing verbal portrait of Arabella in the person of Belinda: 'Her lively looks a sprightly mind disclose,/Quick as her eyes, and as unfixed as those:/Favours to none, to all she smiles extends;/ Oft she rejects, but never once offends./Bright as the sun, her eyes the gazers strike,/And, like the sun, they shine on all alike./Yet graceful ease, and sweetness void of pride,/Might hide her faults, if belles had faults to hide:/If to her share some female errors fall,/Look on her face, and you'll forget them all.' Although Arabella was flattered when she read a prepublication copy of the poem she had second thoughts when Belinda materialized in print and became public property.

On 8 November 1712 Pope told Caryll that 'the celebrated Lady herself is offended, and, which is stranger, not at herself but me'. However the two Catholic families were reconciled and Arabella learned to live with her celebrity and to enjoy it. When Arabella married Francis Perkins in 1715 she was pleased to receive the congratulations of the poet who had immortalized her. Subsequently she basked in being Belinda; when Mrs Hesther Thrale toured Europe in 1775 she met Arabella's niece, an abbess in a Parisian convent, who 'remembered that Mr Pope's praise made her aunt very troublesome and conceited'.

VISCOUNTESS DOWAGER BELLAIR

Benjamin Disraeli, *Henrietta Temple – A Love Story* (1837)

Henrietta Temple is a novel of love, intrigue and entanglement, and if the reader's concern for the fortunes of Ferdinand Armine and Henrietta may wane, he is bound to be impressed by the person of Lady Bellair: 'the prettiest, liveliest, smallest, best-dressed, and, stranger than all, oldest little lady in the world. Lady Bellair was of child-like stature, and quite erect, though ninety years of age; the tasteful simplicity of her

Mary Monckton, Countess of Cork and Orrery (1746-1840)

Further reading: Edwin Pugh, *The Charles Dickens Originals* (1912)

costume, her little plain white silk bonnet, her grey silk dress, her apron, her grey mittens, and her Cinderella shoes, all admirably contrasted with the vast and flaunting splendour of her companion ... ' (who is dressed in the 'extreme of gorgeous fashion'). Lady Bellair is the last remaining link between the eighteenth and nineteenth centuries. She was born to a noble family, and distinguished herself both for her beauty and her wit: 'she had reigned for a quarter of a century the favourite subject of Sir Joshua; had flirted with Lord Carlisle, and chatted with Dr Johnson. But the most remarkable quality of her ladyship's destiny was her preservation. Time, that had rolled on nearly a century since her birth, had spared alike her physical and mental powers. She was almost as active in body and quite as lively in mind, as when seventy years before she had skipped in Marylebone Gardens . . . The heroes and heroines of her youth, her middle life, even of her old age, had vanished; brilliant orators, profound statesmen, inspired bards, ripe scholars, illustrious warriors; beauties whose dazzling charms had turned the world mad; choice spirits . . . all had disappeared. She had witnessed revolutions in every country in the world; she remembered Brighton a fishing town, and Manchester a village . . . She had stimulated the early ambition of Charles Fox, and had sympathized with the last aspirations of George Canning; she had been the confidant of the loves alike of Byron and Alfieri; she had worn mourning for General Wolfe, and given a festival to the Duke of Wellington.' She loves Henrietta, who is her prime and permanent favourite, and attempts to guide her in the complexities of life. She is a great matchmaker.

This is a brilliant portrait of the Countess of Cork and Orrery, a celebrated blue-stocking and socialite, who knew everybody, outlived nearly everybody, and spanned the centuries. In her childhood Dr Johnson said to her: 'Dearest, you're a dunce'. She was also the original of Mrs Leo Hunter in *Pickwick*. (See MRS LEO HUNTER.)

CYRANO DE BERGERAC

Edmond Rostand, *Cyrano de Bergerac* (1897)

Savinien Cyrano de Bergerac (1620–55)

Further reading: L.R. Lefevre, *Cyrano de Bergerac* (1927)

Cyrano de Bergerac is the hero of Rostand's romantic play. He is a dashing and brave young officer, with a reputation for wit, panache and daring. Unfortunately, he has a monstrously large nose, which stands in the way of his romantically fulfilling the true potential of his soul. He loves the beautiful Roxane but knows that his facial disfigurement will always prevent her loving him. From the deep generosity of his heart, he enables another to woo and to win her, in the course of which romance he actually pens the love-letters. The wit and romance of Cyrano's character comes through in some of the sharp exchanges of Rostand's dialogue, even in translation: 'Twirling my wit as it were my moustache,/The while I pass among the crowd, I make/Bold truths ring out like spurs'; 'Tis my soul/That I thus hold erect as if with stays,/And decked with daring deed instead of ribbons'; 'Your name hangs in my heart like a bell's tongue'; 'To offend is my pleasure; I love to be hated'; 'A kiss, when all is said, what is it?/ ... a rosy dot/Placed on the "i" in loving; 'tis a secret/Told to the mouth instead of to the ear'.

Savinien Cyrano de Bergerac is the original of this hero. He was a French dramatist and romance-writer, born in Paris, and studied at the College de Beauvais, in company with Henri Lebret, who was later his biographer. Cyrano joined the guards and earned a reputation for dare and dashing, fighting some thousand duels and writing tragedies in the classical mode and several romances. His unique mixture of science and romance was later imitated by Voltaire, Swift and Poe. He was seriously injured by falling timber at the house of his patron, the Duke of Arpajon in 1654. He was persecuted as a free thinker and sought refuge with friends. He died in Paris.

FRIEDRICH BERGMANN

Christopher Isherwood's *Prater Violet*, set in the period October 1933 – March 1934, involves the author in scripting a film based on a banal musical comedy called 'Prater Violet' (about a girl who sells violets in the

Christopher Isherwood, *Prater Violet* (1946)

Berthold Viertel (1885-1953)

Further reading: Brian Finney, *Christopher Isherwood* (1979)

Vienna Prater). The film is to be directed by Friedrich Bergmann, an Austrian Jew who has abandoned his career in Germany to work in London for Imperial Bulldog Pictures. Isherwood (who appears under his own name in the novel) is immediately impressed by Bergmann: 'His head was magnificent, and massive as sculptured granite. The head of a Roman emperor, with dark old Asiatic eyes . . . He sparkled with epigrams, he beamed, he really amazed himself . . . Bergmann didn't really need a collaborator at all. But he needed stimulation and sympathy: he needed someone he could talk German to. He needed an audience.' Always aware of the European situation, Bergmann has an apocalyptic vision of a world war complete with the massacre of the Jews, the execution of intellectuals, the burning of books, the rise of a Hitler Religion. Throughout the novel the artistic problems Bergmann and Isherwood have, through their connection with an inconsequential film, are contrasted with political dramas such as the trial of Dimitrov (following the Reichstag Fire) and the suppression by Chancellor Dollfuss of the Austrian uprising. Bergmann feels that 'to make such a picture at such a moment is definitely heartless. It is a crime. It definitely aids Dollfuss . . . It covers up the dirty syphilitic sore with rose leaves, with the petals of this hypocritical reactionary violet.' Nevertheless Bergmann finishes the film and, because of its success, takes up an offer of work in Hollywood.

As Isherwood acknowledges in *Christopher and his Kind* (1976), Bergmann is based on Berthold Viertel. In October 1933 Isherwood was asked to write the dialogue for *Little Friend* (1934), a film Gaumont-British had hired Viertel to direct. A Viennese-born Jew, whose first love was poetry (especially his own), Viertel had moved to Hollywood in 1928, and when he arrived in London to work on three Gaumont-British films he found Isherwood to be 'a dialogue writer of unusual finesse and tenderness'. Isherwood, however, felt awed in the presence of this powerful personality, whose eloquence astonished him and whose energy exhausted him. When Isherwood settled in California in 1939, Viertel helped him to find work in Hollywood. In 1946, while plotting the Shirley Temple film *Adventure in Baltimore* (1949), Isherwood moved into an apartment in the Viertels' house in Santa Monica Canyon where Salka Viertel, the director's wife, ran a salon.

BERGOTTE

Marcel Proust, *Remembrance of Things Past* (1913-27)

Anatole France (1844-1924)

Further reading: George D. Painter, *Marcel Proust* (1959, 1965)

Staying at his aunt's house at Combray (actually Illiers, near Chartres, where Proust's father was born) young Marcel enjoys reading in the garden. Thus he discovers the work of the writer Bergotte, whose style seduces him (in the translation by C.K. Scott Moncrieff): 'One of these passages of Bergotte, the third or fourth which I had detached from the rest, filled me with a joy to which the meagre joy I had tasted in the first passage bore no comparison, a joy which I felt myself to have experienced in some innermost chamber of my soul, deep, undivided, vast, from which all obstruction and partitions seemed to have been swept away. For what had happened was that, while I recognised in this passage the same taste for uncommon phrases, the same bursts of music, the same idealist philosophy which had been present in the earlier passages . . . I now no longer had the impression of being confronted by a particular passage in one of Bergotte's works . . . but rather of the "ideal passage" of Bergotte, common to every one of his books, and to which all the earlier, similar passages, now becoming merged in it, had added a kind of density and volume, by which my own understanding seemed to be enlarged'. To his delight, Marcel discovers that Charles Swann, a friend of the family, knows Bergotte, and that ODETTE, Swann's wife, has built a salon around Bergotte's celebrity. Bergotte's death provides Proust's novel with one of its great visionary moments.

Marcel Proust met Anatole France (Jacques-Anatole Thibault) in the summer of 1889 at the salon of Mme Arman de Caillavet at 12 Avenue Hoche, Paris. France divorced his wife in 1893 (and we learn that

Bergotte behaved cruelly to his wife); 'Henceforth', says George D. Painter, 'France ate and spent his days at Mme Arman's. They made love every morning at his bachelor home, and then walked to Avenue Hoche for lunch.' France wrote an introduction to Proust's *Les Plaisirs et les Jours* (1896), and greatly impressed the younger man. According to Painter 'France was the only living novelist [Proust] met and enthusiastically admired in early youth, and in gratitude he built the character of Bergotte, an apotheosis of France, around him'.

In his lifetime Anatole France was regarded as one of the great French novelists, though his reputation has suffered since. After the publication of *The Crime of Sylvestre Bonnard* (1881), his first novel, he wrote many works, including *Monsieur Bergeret in Paris* (1901), whose eponymous hero suggested to Proust the name Bergotte. France was awarded the Nobel Prize for literature in 1921.

JOHN BIDLAKE

Aldous Huxley, *Point Counter Point* (1928)

Augustus John (1878-1961)

Further reading: Sybille Bedford, *Aldous Huxley* (1973, 1974), Michael Holroyd, *Augustus John* (1974, 1975)

John Bidlake, in Aldous Huxley's *Point Counter Point*, is a painter, a man of passion devoted to the art of life. In one of Huxley's flashbacks, Bidlake is seen at the age of forty-seven 'at the height of his powers and reputation as a painter; handsome, huge, exuberant, careless; a great laugher, a great worker, a great eater, drinker, and taker of virginities'. Bidlake's paintings are founded on the physical, as he explains: 'Painting's a branch of sensuality. Nobody can paint a nude who hasn't learnt the human body by heart with his hands and his lips and his own body. I take my art seriously. I'm unremitting in my preliminary studies'. Bidlake has a pivotal position in the novel. Married three times, he is the father of Elinor (who marries Philip Quarles, the novelist) and Walter (whose longing for LUCY TANTAMOUNT is the opening theme of *Point Counter Point*). Even when old and ill, Bidlake manages to paint, and sees the landscape in terms of 'curves and bulges and round recessions, like a body.'

Bidlake's profession and passionate nature were derived from the painter Augustus John, whose nudes show an obvious relish for the female form. John was one of the great characters of the 1920s, the source of endless gossip because of his appetite for sex and alcohol. His conversational powers and romantic manner endeared him to several leading writers; D.H. Lawrence, for example, portrayed him as the bad-mannered artist Struthers in *Aaron's Rod* (1922). John seemed to embody all the attributes of the Bohemian artist, and he was uncomfortable when, in 1928, the year Huxley's novel was published, he was made a Royal Academician. Ten years later, however, he resigned when the Royal Academy rejected Wyndham Lewis's portrait of T.S. Eliot. When he accepted re-election two years after this, he became – according to Lewis – 'the most distinguished Royal Academician . . . of a sleeping-partner order'.

BIG BROTHER

George Orwell, *Nineteen Eighty-four* (1949)

Joseph Stalin (1879-1953)

Further reading: Isaac Deutscher, *Stalin* (1949)

George Orwell's devastating critiquc of totalitarianism, *Nineteen Eighty-Four*, is dominated by the ubiquitous figure of Big Brother who permeates the story as a presence. As Winston Smith begins another day in 1984 he is immediately aware of Big Brother as he sees a coloured poster: 'It depicted simply an enormous face, more than a metre wide: the face of a man of about forty-five, with a heavy black moustache and ruggedly handsome features. . . . It was one of those pictures which are so contrived that the eyes follow you about when you move. BIG BROTHER IS WATCHING YOU, the caption beneath it ran.' After Smith's love affair with Julia, which amounts to an act of rebellion against the state, he is brainwashed back into the fold of total conformity and as the book ends he 'gazed up at the enormous face. Forty years it had taken him to learn what kind of smile was hidden beneath the dark moustache... He loved Big Brother.'

Orwell's state of Oceania is structured, politically, on the Soviet model and Big Brother is obviously made in the image of Stalin whose kindly avuncular appearance contrasted with his dictatorial habits. When Orwell wrote *Nineteen Eighty-Four* in 1948 (hence the title) Stalin was an apparently indestructible figure whose authority in the Soviet Union was absolute. Orwell had already portrayed Stalin as the boar Napoleon in *Animal Farm* (1945) where the dictator triumphs over his old adversary Trotsky, personified as the pig Snowball. The Stalin-Trotsky struggle is recreated in *Nineteen Eighty-Four* when the party propaganda suggests that the icon of Big Brother is threatened by the Trotsky-like face of Emmanuel Goldstein, the Enemy of the People – 'a lean Jewish face, with a great fuzzy aureole of white hair and a small goatee beard'.

BIG BROTHER

George Orwell, *Nineteen Eighty-Four* (1949)

Brendan Bracken
(1901-58)

Further reading: Charles Edward Lysaught, *Brendan Bracken* (1979), W.J. West (ed.), *Orwell: The War Broadcasts* (1958)

On 18 August 1941 George Orwell was accepted as an Empire Talks Assistant in the Indian Section of the BBC's Eastern Service. From then until November 1943, when he left the BBC, Orwell was responsible for initiating programmes, delivering talks and dealing with distinguished speakers. By the time he resigned from his post, Orwell said he felt like 'an orange that's been trodden on by a very dirty boot'. According to W.J. West's *Orwell: The War Broadcasts* (1985), this period had an important impact on the making of the author's *Nineteen Eighty-Four.*

The BBC's Eastern Service, housed in a building at Oxford Circus, contained a canteen which Orwell reproduces in *Nineteen Eighty-Four.* While at the BBC, Orwell wrote the first episode of a 'Story by Five Authors' (the five being himself, L.A.G. Strong, Inez Holden, Martin Armstrong and E.M. Forster) which has details that reappear in *Nineteen Eighty-Four.* Most telling of all circumstances was the atmosphere of censorship that prevailed. Orwell saw censors' stamps on scripts, and eventually broadcast under the scrutiny of a switch censor, who sat by the microphone and cut off the speaker if he departed from the officially approved script. The really menacing authority in all this was not the BBC itself, but the Ministry of Information, which regarded the BBC as an instrument of propaganda, not a cultural service. By 1941, when Brendan Bracken replaced Duff Cooper as Minister of Information, this government department had direct control over the output of the BBC. The Irish-born Bracken, Winston Churchill's closest friend, was the man to reckon with.

Known by his initials 'B.B.' in the corridors of the Ministry of Information at Senate House, in Malet Street, this formidable figure must have seemed to Orwell a symbol of great power in a country involved in a world war. Bracken was a member of the War Cabinet Committee on Basic English, C.K. Ogden's scheme to simplify English to a vocabulary of 850 words. Though Orwell was interested in the possibilities of Basic as an international means of communication, he was also suspicious enough of bureaucrats to realize they could abuse a limited linguistic system. Orwell thus satirized Basic as 'Newspeak', and the Ministry of Information as the 'Ministry of Truth'. Brendan Bracken – 'B.B.' – was, thus, an important part of the creation of Big Brother.

BIGGLES

W.E. Johns, *The Camels are Coming* (1932) and ninety-seven subsequent Biggles books

C.G. Wigglesworth
(1893-1961)

Captain James Bigglesworth – the First World War flying ace known to tens of thousands of readers as Biggles – made his first appearance in April 1932 in the pages of *Popular Flying*, an aviation magazine edited by W.E. Johns. Introducing *The Camels are Coming*, the first Biggles collection, Johns described his creation as 'a fictitious character, yet he could have been found in any RFC mess during those great days of 1917 and 1918 when air combat had become the order of the day and air duelling was a fine art'. As the hero of the Royal Flying Corps, Biggles is a dashing figure possessed, however, of some sensitivity: 'His deep-set hazel eyes were never still and held a glint of yellow fire that somehow seemed out of place in a pale face upon which the strain of war, and sight of sudden death, had already graven little lines. His hands, small and delicate as a girl's, fidgeted continually with the tunic fastening at his throat. He had killed a man not six hours before. He had killed six men during the past month – or was it a year? – he had forgotten. Time had become curiously telescoped lately. What did it matter anyway? He knew he had to die some time and had long ago ceased to worry about it'.

Johns himself flew with the RFC and was able to observe the air aces closely. One of these men was Air Commodore C.G. Wigglesworth who served with the Royal Naval Air Service and the Royal Air Force during the First World War. As Johns admitted in 1949, when hinting that the original Biggles had a similar name to his hero, he first thought of 'a shadowy figure created by my admiration for the courage and resource displayed by some of the men with whom it was my good fortune to spend several years of my life'. From Wigglesworth, Johns took the name and the nature of his flying ace and fleshed out this ideal with a projection of himself.

Further reading:
Peter Berresford Ellis and Piers Williams, *By Jove, Biggles! The Life of Captain W.E. Johns* (1981)

JAMES BLACKBURN

James Clavell, *Shogun* (1975)

William Adams (died 1620)

Shogun is an adventure story, set in sixteenth-century Japan. The hero, Captain James Blackburn, is an Elizabethan privateer who gets shipwrecked on the mainland of Japan with some of his crew. Several of them are very cruelly treated when they are captured by a warlord and his men. One of them is boiled alive over a slow fire. Captain Blackburn survives, however, and himself becomes a Shogun – a warlord, assimilating himself completely into the society which has taken him prisoner. He studies and masters the code of the Samurai caste, and becomes an exemplar of the way of Bushido; more polished, more honourable, more proficient and more pugnacious than the native-born Japanese Samurai. He fully realizes his manhood in the society of his brutal adoption, and he never returns to England.

This unlikely tale is very closely based on the career of William Adams. He was born in Gillingham, Kent, and served in the British navy and later as master and pilot to a company of Barbary merchants. In 1598 he sailed as pilot major with a fleet of five ships from Rotterdam, attempting to break into the Dutch trade with India. The fleet was driven to the coast of Guinea, where they attacked the island of Annabon, and then sailed for the Straits of Magellan. By spring 1599 the ships had been scattered, and only two vessels, the *Charity* (with Adams on board) and the *Hope* reached the coast of Chile. Here they met hostile Indians, and, fearing further trouble with the Spanish, they resolved to cross the Pacific. The *Hope* was lost, but in April 1600 the *Charity* anchored off the coast of the island of Kyushu. He was summoned to Osaka and interrogated by Iyeyasu, who was the guardian of the young son of Taiko Suma, the ruler, who had just died. Adam's knowledge of astronomy, navigation, mathematics and other practical subjects impressed his captors, and he was presented with an estate near Yokosuko. He was refused permission to return home, but worked to establish a factory for the East India Company, for which he obtained permission from the Shogun. He undertook several voyages to Siam, Cochin-China, and married a Japanese woman who bore him a family. Adams was given permission to return to England, but died before he could do so. His logs are preserved at the Bodleian Library, Oxford.

Further reading:
C.W. Hilary, *England's Earliest intercourse With Japan* (1905)

ANTHONY BLANCHE

Evelyn Waugh, *Brideshead Revisited* (1945)

Sir Harold Acton (born 1904)

The arrogant aestheticism of Oxford in the 1920s is observed with great accuracy in Evelyn Waugh's *Brideshead Revisited*. As the narrator Charles Ryder recalls his own days at Oxford, from the perspective of the Second World War, he thinks of Sebastian Flyte with his immature 'eccentricities of behaviour' and of the outrageously affected Anthony Blanche: 'He was tall, slim, rather swarthy, with large saucy eyes... This, I did not need telling, was Anthony Blanche, the "aesthete" *par excellence,* a byword of iniquity from Cherwell Edge to Somerville.' Blanche is an enthusiast for the modernist poetry of the 1920s and declaims T.S. Eliot's *The Waste Land* through a megaphone. Later he comes to an exhibition of Ryder's pictures and lectures him on art:

Further reading: Christopher Sykes, *Evelyn Waugh* (1975), Christopher Hollis, *Oxford in the Twenties* (1976)

'Charm is the great English blight . . . It kills love; it kills art; I greatly fear, my dear Charles, it has killed *you*.'

Blanche was modelled, somewhat maliciously, on Waugh's Oxford contemporary Harold Acton who combined an outlandish appearance with a determination to remake Oxford in his own aesthetic image. Some of the details of Blanche are borrowed from Acton's rival Oxford aesthete Brian Howard (1905-58), previously caricatured as Ambrose Silk in Waugh's *Put Out More Flags* (1942). Blanche's way of punctuating his speech with 'my dear' was taken from Howard as was the character's partly Jewish origin. Howard, however, was a pathetic figure in real life whose promise petered out in self-pity. Blanche, like Acton, is an intellectually alert individual who has a considerable impact on the Oxford of the 1920s. Ryder regards him with awe: 'At times we all seemed children beside him – at most times, but not always, for there was a bluster and zest in Anthony which the rest of us had shed . . . his vices flourished less in the pursuit of pleasure than in the wish to shock . . . He was cruel, too, in the wanton, insect-maiming manner of the very young, and fearless like a little boy.'

DOCTOR BLIMBER

Charles Dickens, *Dombey and Son* (1848)

Doctor Everard

Further reading: Edwin Pugh, *The Charles Dickens Originals* (1912)

Mr Dombey is very anxious that his young son Paul should do well, and should be pushed to the limit to be a son worthy of his father. In a letter Dickens wrote to his biographer, John Forster, before he started *Dombey and Son* he says that he intends to show the father: 'with that one idea of the Son taking firmer and firmer possession of him, and swelling and bloating his pride to a prodigious extent. As the boy begins to grow up, I shall show him quite impatient for his getting on, and urging his masters to set him great tasks, and the like..' The master to whom he sends him is Dr Blimber, the proprietor of a boys' boarding school at Brighton: 'The Doctor was a portly gentleman in a suit of black . . . He had a bald head, highly polished; a deep voice; and a chin so very double, that it was a wonder how he ever managed to shave into the creases. He had likewise a little pair of eyes that were always half shut up, and a mouth that was always half expanded into a grin, as if he had, that moment, posed a boy, and were waiting to convict him from his own mouth. The Doctor's was a mighty fine house, fronting the sea. Not a joyful style of house within, but quite the contrary. Sad-coloured curtains, whose proportions were spare and lean, hid themselves despondently behind the windows. The tables and chairs were put away in rows, like figures in a sum . . .' Doctor Blimber's academy is like a forcing-house in which boys are artificially cultivated to bloom before their time: 'All the boys blew before their time. Mental green-peas were produced at Christmas, and intellectual asparagus all the year round . . . Every description of Greek and Latin vegetable was got off the driest twigs of boys, under the frostiest circumstances. Nature was of no consequence at all. No matter what a young gentleman was intended to bear, Doctor Blimber made him bear to pattern, somehow or other.' When Doctor Blimber promises to make a man of young Paul, the boy replies: 'I had rather be a child' (see PAUL DOMBEY).

This is a portrayal of Doctor Everard, a worthy pedagogue of Brighton, whose famous school was locally known as the 'House of Lords' because so many members of the upper classes were educated there. The illustration by Hablot Browne of 'Doctor Blimber's Young Gentlemen as they appeared when enjoying themselves' shows the boys out walking with Doctor Blimber.

LEOPOLD BLOOM

James Joyce, *Ulysses* (1922)

Alfred Hunter/Ettore Schmitz

Leopold Bloom, the hero of James Joyce's *Ulysses*, is at once a convincing naturalistic figure and a mythical embodiment of various archetypes – Homer's Odysseus, the Wandering Jew, the eternal Everyman. In the Ithica section of the book Joyce concentrates on Bloom as the Wandering Jew: 'Ever would he wander, selfcompelled, to the extreme limit of his cometary orbit, beyond the fixed stars and variable suns and telescopic planets, astronomical waifs and strays, to the extreme boundary of space, passing from land to land, among peoples, amid events.' Ithica, in the novel, is Eccles Street, where, in 1904, Joyce was knocked down in a scuffle with the escort of a lady he had accosted. Joyce (Dedalus in the novel) was brushed down by Alfred Hunter, a Dublin Jew who came to his assistance; subsequently Joyce learned that Hunter was painfully aware of his wife's infidelity.

When Joyce left Ireland he settled, after some wandering, in Trieste where he earned a living as an English tutor. Among his pupils was Ettore Schmitz (1861-1928) who disclosed that he had once published two novels under the pseudonym Italo Svevo. Joyce read the novels, pronounced Schmitz a neglected writer and encouraged his gifted pupil to complete *Confessions of Zeno* (1923), now recognized as a comic classic. Schmitz was a lapsed Jew as well as a businessman (whose factories manufactured anti-corrosive paint) and he provided Joyce with details of his former religion. Joyce admired Schmitz and greatly appreciated his sense of humour. As he wrote *Ulysses* he used memories of Alfred Hunter and observations of Schmitz in his creation of Leopold Bloom who 'ate with relish the inner organs of beasts and fowls. He liked thick giblet soup, nutty gizzards, a stuffed roast heart, liver slices fried with crust-crumbs, fried hencod's roes.'

Further reading: Richard Ellmann, *James Joyce* (1959, 1982)

MOLLY BLOOM

James Joyce, *Ulysses* (1922)

Nora Barnacle (1885-1951)

According to the Homeric pattern of James Joyce's *Ulysses* the heroine, Molly Bloom, is Penelope. At the end of the book she lies in bed, dwells on life and love and thinks 'a woman wants to be embraced twenty times a day almost to make her look young no matter by who so long as to be in love or loved by somebody if the fellow you want isnt there'. Molly's affirmative monologue is regarded as one of the greatest of all literary insights into feminine psychology, a subject Joyce pursued energetically with Nora Barnacle – the woman he left Ireland with in 1904 and married, in London, in 1931.

Joyce met Nora on 10 June 1904 in Dublin and was immediately attracted to her. She worked as a servant in a hotel, and had no interest in, or knowledge of, literature. However, her interest in sex was strong and when she made a sexual advance to Joyce on 16 June 1904 the day became momentous to him and was subsequently commemorated as Bloomsday, the time of the action of Joyce's masterpiece. Nora's background was harsh: her father, a baker, drank what money he made; her mother was unable to look after her. Nora was brought up by her grandmother, sent to a convent, then employed as a portress by nuns in Galway City. Joyce was fascinated by Nora and encouraged her to write sexually frank letters to him. The unpunctuated style and erotic subject of these letters contributed to the making of Molly Bloom in Nora's image. Nora's erotic letters have been lost but a note she wrote to Joyce's brother Stanislaus shows the headlong style that would characterize Molly Bloom: 'I hope you are very well I am sure you would be glad to see Georgie now he is well able to run about he is able to say a lot he has a good appetite and he has eight teeth and also sings when we ask him where is Stannie he beats his chest and says non c'e piu'.

Further reading: Richard Ellmann, *James Joyce* (1959, 1982), Stan Gebler Davies, *James Joyce* (1982)

COTTON BLOSSOM

Edna Ferber, *Show Boat* (1926), Jerome Kern and Oscar Hammerstein, *Show Boat* (1927)

'Golden Rod' show-boat, St Louis, Missouri

The story of Captain Andy Hawks and his show-boat troupe, the amorous intrigues and plot complexities involving Gaylord Ravenal, Magnolia Hawks, Joe and Julie, captured public imagination and crystallized for all time the ethos of Mississippi steam-boat chic originated by Mark Twain. One source of the book's fascination is the masterly transferring of the pathos and comedy of show-business life to a glittering, romantic and golden setting aboard a floating palace of pleasure at the turn of the century. It is a well fabricated piece of genuine Americana. The boat commanded by Cap'n Andy was built for him in the St Louis shipyards. It is pushed by the steam-boat *Mollie Able* and he takes his company on tour as far as New Orleans: 'beginning with Bayou Teche . . . they would

Further reading:
Alfred Simon, *Songs of the American Theatre* (1973), Oscar Hammerstein, *The Jerome Kern Song Book* (1970)

proceed grandly upstream, calliope screaming, flags flying, band tooting, to play every little town and landing and plantation from New Orleans to Baton Rouge to Vicksburg; to Memphis, to Cairo, to St Louis, and up to Minnesota itself . . . following the crops as they ripened – the corn belt, the cotton belt, the sugar cane; north when the wheat yellowed, following the sun, the ripening of the peas, the tomatoes, the crabs, the peaches, the apples; and as the farmer garnered his golden crops so would shrewd Captain Andy Hawks gather his harvest of gold.' *Show Boat* was made into a very successful musical, in which Paul Robeson made *'Ol' Man River'* very much his own, and was filmed several times.

In *Life on the River* (1971) Norbury L. Wayman wrote: 'Family ownership and operation became a hallmark of successful showboats . . . creating the right atmosphere of quality to appeal to the rural families. The arrival of the showboat was much like that of a circus, its shrill calliope playing while a band paraded on the town's main street. It practically closed down the town to all but the performance. Vaudeville and melodrama were popularly programmed on showboats. Among plays presented were *Uncle Tom's Cabin, East Lynne, The Drunkard* and *Ten Nights in a Bar Room.'* After 1900 the trend was for boats of some 200 feet in length. W.R. Markle's *Golden Rod*, built in 1909, was electrically air-cooled and accommodated 1,400 persons. It was sold to R.W. Emerson in 1914, and from 1922 was run by Captain Bill Menke. Monte Blue, Red Skelton, Kathy Nolan and many others starred in *Golden Rod* productions. She took Major Bowes' 'Amateur Hour' up the Ohio River in 1936. The *Golden Rod* was renovated and re-opened at moorings on the levée at St Louis in 1965, and is one of the city's attractions. She was designated a national historic landmark in 1968, and still provides one of the best nights out in St Louis – dinner in the boat's restaurant followed by authentic burlesque melodrama and vaudeville. The film versions of *Show Boat* portray her as a self-propelled paddle-boat, this is inauthentic. She was a barge moved by an auxiliary steam-boat.

BISHOP BLOUGRAM

Robert Browning, *Bishop Blougram's Apology* (1855)

Nicholas Patrick Stephen Wiseman
(1802-65)

Further reading:
J.F. Reynolds, *Three Cardinals* (1958)

A journalist and a bishop agree to have dinner together, to take wine afterwards, and to see the dawn come up, while fundamental beliefs are discussed. The bishop senses that the journalist despises him for accepting the position of a beneficed priest even though his beliefs do not extend to all the doctrines of the Church of Rome. It is a classic analysis of the position of the 'worldly' priest: 'The common problem . . . Is not to fancy what were fair in life/Provided it could be – but, finding first/What may be, then find how to make it fair/Up to our means'. Blougram is not placed in a sympathetic light, and Browning's irony has a fine cutting edge.

The figure of Blougram was based on Cardinal Wiseman. He was an English Cardinal, born in Seville of Anglo-Irish parents, educated at Durham and in Rome. For twelve years he was rector of the English college in Rome, and was a brilliant scholar in his own right, who became curator of the Arabic manuscripts in the Vatican and professor of oriental languages at Rome. He came to England in the mid 1830s and preached the doctrines of the Roman Catholic faith and in 1840, now a consecrated bishop, made Oscott College, near Birmingham, the centre of English Catholicism. In 1850 he was appointed Cardinal Archbishop of Westminster, vehemently supporting Pius IX's policy of restoring the faith in England. He greatly influenced the Oxford Movement and earned a wide reputation as lecturer on social, aesthetic and literary topics. As he grew older his religious views hardened into a less liberal mould, he opposed Christian unity and forbade Catholic parents to send their sons to Oxford or Cambridge, though earlier he had managed to combine high principles in matters of faith with liberal views in ecclesiastical matters.

BLOUNDELL BLOUNDELL

William Makepeace Thackeray, *Pendennis* (1850)

Henry Matthew

Further reading:
Ann Monsarrat, *An Uneasy Victorian–Thackeray the Man* (1980)

While Arthur Pendennis is at Oxbridge University his Mephistophelean guide, philosopher and friend is the notorious bounder, Bloundell Bloundell. He has been at Camford University, but left in suspicious circumstances, after a dubious career in the cavalry. Arthur's uncle, Major Pendennis, tries to warn him, in the face of Arthur's assertions that Bloundell is the most popular man in the University, elected to the best clubs and descended from one of the best old families in Suffolk. 'A man may have a good coat-of-arms, and be a tiger,' the Major says. 'That man is a tiger . . . a low man. I will lay a wager that he left his regiment . . . in bad odour. There is the unmistakable look of slang and bad habits about this Mr Bloundell. He frequents low gambling-houses and billiard halls . . . he haunts third-rate clubs. Did you remark the quantity of rings and jewellery he wore? That person has Scamp written on his countenance, if any man ever had.' Bloundell leads young Pendennis astray with his 'flashy grace, and rakish airs of fashion'. He teaches Arthur the delights of gambling, cards and dicing. He tells his mother and uncle during the Easter vacation that he is going to stay at Oxbridge, to study, but in fact goes to town with Bloundell: 'They put up at a hotel in Covent Garden . . . and took the pleasures of the town very freely . . . Bloundell still belonged to a military club, whither he took Pen to dine . . . and here Pen was introduced to a number of gallant young fellows with spurs and mustachios, with whom he drank pale-ale of mornings and beat the town of a night. Here he saw a deal of life, indeed: nor in his career about the theatres and singing-houses which these roaring young blades frequented, was he very likely to meet his guardian.' Arthur is soon heavily in debt at University and in London. As a result of the influence of Bloundell over him, he is prevented from taking his degree. In Arthur's words: 'I have lost everything . . . my honour's gone; I'm ruined irretrievably; I can't go back to Oxbridge'.

This is a portrait of Henry Matthew, son of the rector of the village of Kilve, who had been Thackeray's companion in ruin and dissipation at Cambridge 1829-30. Matthew was four years older than Thackeray and was elected President of the Union. He was sent down from Oxford, eventually took his degree at Sidney Sussex College, Cambridge. He was a renowned rake and gambler, but Thackeray thought the world of him. Thackeray met him again late in his life and found him tall, imposing, but seedy, in a brown frock coat, at a rouge-et-noir table at Spa in Belgium. Bloundell is also the model for the gambler and swindler Deuceace.

BLUEBEARD

Charles Perrault, *Histoires et Contes du Temps Passé* (1697)

Gilles de Rais, Marshall of France (1404-40)

Further reading:
F. Winwar, *The Saint and the Devil* (1948)

This collection of tales was published in an English translation by Robert Samber in 1729. They were popular French tales from various sources, and included Little Red Riding Hood, the Sleeping Beauty, Puss in Boots, Cinderella, Hop o' my Thumb and the grisly tale of Bluebeard. This narrative is placed in an oriental setting and concerns a powerful potentate with a blue beard. He has an evil reputation as he has married several times but his wives have disappeared. He asks for the hand of the fair Fatima, the younger of two handsome daughters of a local lady of quality. Fatima agrees to the match but then Bluebeard says he has to go away on business and leaves Fatima in charge of his castle. As he gives her the keys he warns her not to use one particular key which he says opens a particular chamber. Of course she is overwhelmed by curiosity and as soon as he has gone opens the door and finds the bodies of all Bluebeard's previous wives. She is so shocked that she drops the forbidden key which is thus stained with blood. This leads to her discovery by Bluebeard, but her life is saved by her sister Anne and her brothers and Bluebeard is killed.

Although the story has many similarities with widespread folkloric tales of forbidden chambers containing dreadful secrets, there are some disturbing parallels with the life story of Gilles de Rais who was executed for abnormal sexual crimes in Brittany in October 1440, after a

15th-century *cause célèbre*, second only to the trial of Joan of Arc, with whom he is associated. A wealthy baron and landowner, patron of the arts and brilliant soldier, in 1420 he married Katherine of Thouars, a great heiress in Brittany, La Vendée and Poitou. He fought against the British and was an avid supporter of Joan of Arc at Orleans, Jargeau and Patay. Financial difficulties caused him to begin selling some properties, though his family protested. He hoped to regain his wealth by alchemy and necromancy, at the same time protecting his soul by charity and ritualistic devotion to the Church. Rumours began to circulate of his torturing and killing boys, procured for him by servants, reputed to number over 150. He was tried for heresy and murder and, terrified by excommunication, he confessed and was hanged.

MR BOBBE

Richard Aldington, *Death of a Hero* (1929)

D.H. Lawrence (1885-1930)

Further reading: Richard Aldington, *Life for Life's Sake* (1941)

Before he goes to fight (and die) in the First World War, George Winterbourne – the 'hero' of Richard Aldington's *Death of a Hero* – is a painter who writes articles to support himself. In the course of his precarious career he visits the London studio of Mr Shobbe (modelled on Ford Madox Ford), whose guests include Mr Upjohn (Ezra Pound), Mr Tubbe (T.S. Eliot) and Mr Bobbe. Bobbe is clearly a verbal portrait of Aldington's friend D.H. Lawrence; 'Mr Bobbe was a sandy-haired, narrow-chested little man with spiteful blue eyes and a malevolent class-hatred. He exercised his malevolence with comparative impunity by trading upon his working-class origin and his indigestion, of which he had been dying for twenty years. Nobody of decent breeding could hit Mr Bobbe as he deserved, because his looks were a perpetual reminder of his disease, and his behaviour and habits gave continual evidence of his origin . . . His vanity and class-consciousness made him yearn for affairs with upper-class women, although he was obviously a homosexual type. Admirable energy, a swift and sometimes remarkable intuition into character, a good memory and excellent faculty of imitation, a sharp tongue and brutal frankness, gave him power . . . George admired his feverish energy and talents, pitied him for his ill-health and agonised sense of class inferiority, disliked his malevolence and ignored his theories.'

Though Aldington was close to Lawrence over a long period, he was highly critical of him in his *Portrait of a Genius, But . . .* (1950). Lawrence liked Aldington, sympathized with him when his wife – the poet H.D. – had an affair with Cecil Gray, but disapproved when Aldington dropped Dorothy Yorke (who features as Fanny in *Death of a Hero*) for Brigit Patmore, with whom he lived on the Riviera in the late 1920s and early 1930s. Lawrence's illness was tuberculosis but, like Mr Bobbe, he enjoyed the company of upper-class women (such as Lady Cynthia Asquith). The homosexual reference is relevant too; Compton Mackenzie – in the fifth octave of *My Life and Times* (1966) – cites Lawrence as saying 'the nearest I've ever come to perfect love was with a young coal-miner when I was about sixteen.' Harry T. Moore, in *The Priest of Love* (1974), quotes Frieda Lawrence as saying that her husband 'did not disbelieve in homosexuality'.

NICODEMUS BOFFIN

Charles Dickens, *Our Mutual Friend* (1865)

Henry Dodd

Further reading: Edwin Pugh, *The Charles Dickens Originals* (1912)

Noddy Boffin started his career as confidential servant and foreman to Old Harmon, the wealthy dust-contractor. When the death of John Harmon, Old Harmon's son, is announced, Boffin comes into the Harmon fortune – some £100,000 – which earns him the sobriquet of the 'Golden Dustman.' Nicodemus and his wife, Henrietta, adopt Bella Wilfer, whom Old Harmon wished to be his son's wife. John Harmon comes back in disguise as Rokesmith, and is employed by Nicodemus as a secretary. They soon recognize him as Old Harmon's son, and help him to win the love of Bella. Silas Wegg had attempted to blackmail Boffin by producing a later will than the one which benefited Boffin, but Harmon's son exposes the scheme. He is: 'A broad, round-shouldered, one-sided old fellow in mourning ... dressed in a pea overcoat, and carrying a large stick. He wore thick shoes, and thick leather gaiters, and thick gloves like a hedger's. Both as to his dress and to himself, he was of an overlapping rhinoceros build, with folds in his cheeks, and his forehead, and his eyelids, and his lips, and his ears; but with bright, eager, childishly-enquiring grey eyes, under his ragged eyebrows, and broad-brimmed hat. A very odd-looking old fellow altogether.'

This is Henry Dodd, the well-known Hoxton dust-contractor. Edwin Pugh quotes an account of him by a Mr Braye, of Kensington, who knew Dodd well: 'This gentleman, who is still slightly connected with the dust business, I will call Boffin junior; he was well acquainted with the great novelist, made a fortune in the family business, devotes his time, and, I should think, a considerable sum of money, to the study of natural history (his place is a sort of zoological and botanical garden combined); and he is conversant with Darwin and the great men of science, as he is with the best means of making money out of dust-bin refuse. So, such is the force of habit, that he has set aside a corner of his park for the neighbour townsfolk to shoot their dust. He says he likes the smell; it reminds him of old times. The story told by Dickens is substantially correct. Mr Boffin had one daughter; she was sought in marriage by a gentleman of aristocratic connections. On the wedding morning the Golden Dustman, instead of coming down with a big cheque, to the dismay of the gentleman, said the only present he could make the bride would be one of his dust heaps. The bridegroom accepted, as he thought, a bad bargain; but he sold it to the brickmakers for £10,000. Mr Boffin lived in a corner house not far from Cavendish Square ...'

JAMES BOND

Ian Fleming, *Casino Royale* (1953), *Live and Let Die* (1954), *Moonraker* (1955), *Diamonds Are Forever* (1956), *From Russia with Love* (1957), *Doctor No* (1958), *Goldfinger* (1959), *For Your Eyes Only* (1960), *Thunderball* (1961), *The Spy Who Loved Me* (1962), *On Her Majesty's Secret Service* (1963), *You Only Live Twice* (1964), *The Man With the Golden Gun* (1965), *Octopussy and the Living Daylights* (1966)

Dusko Popov

When Ian Fleming wrote his first novel, *Casino Royale*, in 1952 he wanted to find 'the simplest, dullest, plainest-sounding name' for his hero and so turned to one of his favourite books – James Bond's guidebook *Birds of the West Indies*. Written rapidly at Fleming's Jamaican home of Goldeneye, the first Bond book was – so the author insisted – produced to 'take my mind off the shock of getting married at the age of forty-three'. But if the Bond saga began as a fond farewell to bachelor life it was not all fantasy. Bond is, superficially, Fleming writ large: both smoke heavily, drink discriminately, gamble cleverly and dress elegantly.

During the Second World War Fleming worked as personal assistant to the Director of Naval Intelligence and was able to observe several agents closely. Of these the most formidable was Dusko Popov, the Yugoslavian whose work as a British agent involved infiltrating the Nazi Secret Service. He was greatly valued by Britain's XX Committee which, as the name implies, double-crossed the enemy by feeding it misleading information through its own agents. Like Bond, Popov combined a taste for expensive living with a deadly efficiency. Some of Popov's audacious adventures are described in his book *Spy/Counterspy* (1974) where there are interludes with beautiful women, ferocious bouts of fighting and displays of coolness in the face of great danger. Popov writes: 'I'm told that Ian Fleming said he based his character James Bond to some degree on me and my experiences. As for me, I rather doubt that a Bond in the flesh would have survived more than forty-eight hours as an espionage agent. Fleming and I did rub shoulders in Lisbon, and a few weeks before I took the clipper for the States he did follow me about.' On one occasion Fleming watched Popov in action in the Casino which is where the whole Bond saga begins. Having argued in his *The Life of Ian Fleming* (1966) that Bond was a fantastic projection of Fleming's own personality, John Pearson subsequently gave Bond the benefit of the doubt and disguised as fact the fiction that Bond was a real man, the son of a Highland Scot.

Further reading:
John Pearson, *James Bond: The Authorised Biography of 007* (1973)

JULIANA BORDEREAU

Henry James, *The Aspern Papers* (1888)

Claire Clairmont (1798-1879)

Further reading: Leon Edel, *The Life of Henry James* (4 vols., 1953–72), Richard Holmes, *Shelley–The Pursuit* (1975)

The narrator of Henry James's *The Aspern Papers* is drawn to Venice on a shady literary mission. On learning that Juliana Bordereau, inspirational mistress of lyric poet Jeffrey Aspern, is living in the city he determines to relieve her of the priceless Aspern papers. When he first sees the legendary Juliana he is astonished by her age: 'The divine Juliana as a grinning skull – the vison hung there until it passed . . . She would die next week, she would die tomorrow – then I could seize her papers.' The narrator rents a room in the 'big, imposing house' so he can ingratiate himself with Juliana and her niece Miss Tita, 'a ridiculous, pathetic, provincial old woman'. When Juliana dies, Miss Tita offers the papers if the narrator will marry her; when he turns her down she burns them.

Such a fictional scenario was suggested to Henry James by the way Claire Clairmont was pestered in Florence by the Shelley-fanatic Captain Edward Augustus Silsbee when she was eighty-one and a recluse living at 43 Via Romana, Florence, with her niece Paula. After Claire Clairmont died, Silsbee approached Paula about the Shelley papers; she agreed to give them to him if he married her but it was too high a price for Silsbee to pay. Claire Clairmont was the stepsister of Mary Godwin. In 1814 Mary eloped with Shelley, and Claire came along too. Later Claire offered herself to Byron who took advantage of the offer. As a result, on 12 January 1817 Claire gave birth to a daughter Allegra. Hurtfully, Byron took the child from Claire and eventually put Allegra in a convent near Ravenna (where she died, of typhus, at the age of five). Byron liked to claim that Allegra was Shelley's child. There are persistent rumours that the baby, Elena, adopted by Shelley in 1818 was his child by Claire.

ISABELLE BORGE

F. Scott Fitzgerald, *This Side of Paradise* (1920)

Ginevra King

Further reading: Andrew Turnbull, *Scott Fitzgerald* (1962), Matthew J. Bruccoli, *Some Sort of Epic Grandeur: The Life of F. Scott Fitzgerald* (1981)

Both books of Fitzgerald's first novel contain a love story: in 'Book One: The Romantic Egotist' Amory Blaine courts Isabelle Borge without success; in 'Book Two: The Education of a Personage' he courts Rosalind Connage, a character partly suggested by the author's wife Zelda. Isabelle Borge is initially impressed by the autobiographical hero of Fitzgerald's book. At the age of eighteen, Amory, a student at Princeton, is 'exceptionally, but not conventionally, handsome'. Isabelle is a 'Speed', a flighty young woman of sixteen: 'She had that curious mixture of the social and the artistic temperaments found often in two classes, society women and actresses. Her education or, rather, her sophistication, had been absorbed from the boys who dangled on her favour; her tact was instinctive, and her capacity for love-affairs was limited only by the number of the susceptible within telephone distance. Flirt smiled from her large black-brown eyes and shone through her intense physical magnetism.'

Fitzgerald met Ginevra King, the model for Isabelle, in 1914, on his return from Princeton to St Paul, Minnesota. At that time she was known as a rich belle from Lake Forest, Illinois; she was sixteen and a student at Westover, a girls' school in Connecticut. When Fitzgerald went back to Princeton he wrote to Ginevra almost every day. In February 1915 he visited her at Westover, and in June she came to the Princeton prom, chaperoned by her mother. Fitzgerald took her to dinner at the Ritz, in New York, and eventually accepted that he was not financially in Ginevra's class.

In March 1916 Ginevra was dismissed from Westover and this disturbed Fitzgerald who felt it revealed a flaw in her character. Years later, when writing a letter of advice to his daughter Scottie (on 5 July 1937), he connected Ginevra's educational misfortune with Zelda's mental problems: 'The girls who were what we called "Speeds" (in our stone-age slang) at sixteen were reduced to anything they could get at the marrying time ... ["Speeds"] fool their parents but not their contemporaries. It was in the cards that Ginevra King should get fired from Westover – also that your mother should wear out young.'

As well as basing the character of Isabelle on Ginevra, Fitzgerald used her as the basis for his heroine Josephine Perry, a Chicago debutante who appears in five stories: 'First Blood', 'A Nice Quiet Place', 'A Woman with a Past', 'A Snobbish Story', and 'Emotional Bankruptcy'.

BOULE DE SUIF

Guy de Maupassant, *Boule de Suif* (1880)

Adrienne Legay

Further reading:
Michael G. Lerner, *Maupassant* (1975)

Set during the Franco–Prussian War, Maupassant's story 'Boule de Suif' contrasts the self-seeking hypocrisy of the French bourgeoisie with the self-sacrifice of a plump prostitute. Worried at the loss of trade due to the Prussian occupation of Rouen, some prominent local citizens decide to go to Le Havre, still in the hands of the French army. The coach party for Le Havre comprises merchants, nuns, members of old French families as well as Cornudet and Boule de Suif. Cornudet is a radical and sensualist and his friend Boule de Suif – 'Suet Dumpling' – is a well-known Rouen prostitute: 'Short, completely round, fat as a pig, with puffy fingers constricted at the joints like strings of tiny sausages, taut shiny skin, and huge breasts swelling underneath her dress, her freshness was so attractive that she nonetheless remained desirable and much sought after. Her face was like a ruddy apple, or a peony bud about to burst into flower; and out of it looked two splendid black eyes shaded and deepened by thick lashes.' Maupassant adds (in the translation by Roger Colet) 'She was also said to possess many other inestimable qualities.' On the first stage of the journey the respectable travellers avoid Boule de Suif until they are so overcome by hunger they accept offerings from her big basket of food and wine. When the coach reaches Tôtes, the travellers are at the mercy of a Prussian officer who refuses to let them continue unless Boule de Suif sleeps with him. She refuses. However, looking after their own interests, the respectable travellers persuade Boule de Suif to comply with the enemy's wishes so they can all go on to Le Havre. As the story ends Boule de Suif is in tears and again being ignored by her travelling companions, with the exception of Cornudet, who whistles the 'Marseillaise' as a tribute.

Maupassant based the tale on an incident told him by his uncle Charles Cordhomme, who is Cornudet in 'Boule de Suif'. Adrienne Legay, a Rouen prostitute well known to Uncle Charles, decided to go to Le Havre to bring food and messages to her boyfriend there. On the way her coach was detained while a Prussian officer demanded she sleep with him. She did, despite her detestation of the Prussians. Maupassant used the incident to criticize Rouen hypocrisy and told Flaubert: 'I will from now on be obliged to carry some pistols in my pocket when I walk in Rouen!'

HENRY BOUNCER

Cuthbert Bede, *The Adventures of Mr Verdant Green* (1853–7), *Little Mr Bouncer and His Friend, Verdant Green* (1878)

John George Wood (1827–89)

In Cuthbert Bede's novel *The Adventures of Mr Verdant Green* (first published in three parts) the hero, an innocent at large at Oxford, is constantly astonished at the uninhibited ways of his fellow undergraduates. Among these is Henry Bouncer, a small volatile fellow, whose outrageously ostentatious behaviour is in marked contrast to Verdant Green's diffidence. When the two first meet on the Oxford coach 'little Mr Bouncer made some most unearthly noises on a post-horn as tall as himself, which he had brought for the delectation of himself and his friends, and the alarm of every village they passed through.' Part of Verdant Green's education at Brazenface (Brasenose) College, Oxford, includes a series of encounters with Henry Bouncer. Though Bouncer's widowed mother wishes him to read for the bar, he spends much of his time pursuing convivial pleasures. On a visit to Woodstock, 'Mr Bouncer . . . led the way to an inn, where the bar was presided over by a young lady, "on whom", he said, "he was desperately sweet", and with whom he conversed in the most affable and brotherly manner . . . So [Verdant Green and friends] left this young lady drawing bitter beer for Mr Bouncer and otherwise attending to her adorer's wants.'

Cuthbert Bede was the pseudonym of Edward Bradley (1827–89), a clergyman who studied not at Oxford but Durham (patron saints: St *Cuthbert* and the Venerable *Bede*). After graduating BA in 1848, he spent about a year at Oxford where he became friendly with John George Wood, the model for Bouncer. Wood and Bradley had much in common; both were surgeon's sons, both were clergymen, both wrote books, and both were born in the same year (just as they were to die in the same year). Wood wrote many popular works of natural history and also produced *The Boy's Own Treasury of Sports and Pastimes* (1866). Having been a Merton postmaster while at Oxford, Wood became a parson devoted to choral services. In his introduction to the 1982 Oxford reprint of Bede's novel, Anthony Powell says that Wood 'may well have been small and noisy . . . but one doubts whether even as an undergraduate he ever behaved quite like Bouncer, ceaselessly blowing a post-horn, two rampageous terriers always at his heels, almost illiterate, and cribbing in his exams to avoid being "plucked".' Bede was obviously amused by the character and made him the hero of the sequel to *Verdant Green – Little Mr Bouncer*.

EMMA BOVARY

Gustave Flaubert, *Madame Bovary* (1857)

Louise Colet (1808-76) and **Delphine Delamare** (died 1848)

Further reading: Enid Starkie, *Flaubert the Master – A Critical and Biographical Study 1856–80* (1971)

Madame Bovary is set in Normandy, near Rouen. Emma is a convent-educated young woman whose mind is stuffed with notions of romantic love uncritically absorbed from shallow literature. She marries a youthful medical practitioner, Charles Bovary, but finds him boorish and her life unfulfilled. In desperate attempts to find romance she has affairs with a local landowner and a lawyer's clerk and runs up considerable debts. Her creditors threaten to expose her to her husband and she kills herself by taking arsenic. The power of the novel lies in Flaubert's ability to exploit creative tension between the shoddy activities and motivations of the characters and the brilliant beauty and precision of its style.

There are several significant contradictions at the basis of Flaubert's novel. One is his assertion that his art was impersonal: 'I have put nothing of my own feelings or life [in that book]'; and a further comment that 'I had no model for Madame Bovary. She is purely an invention.' This seems to be countered by his claim that 'Madame Bovary is myself.' But there is incontrovertible evidence that Flaubert was drawing on real-life characters and experiences when composing *Madame Bovary*. One source is the poetess Louise Colet, with whom Flaubert had a love affair. She was thirteen years older than he was, and separated from her husband. She was a romantic poetess who had twice won the poetry prize of the Académie Française. Their relationship lasted ten years. Flaubert found her shallow, possessive and affected and was distressed by her poor taste. She gave him a cigar case which had the same motto as that on the signet ring Emma gives her lover Rodolphe: 'Amor nel cor.'

Another, more influential, source was the story which Louis Bouilhet, the poet and friend of Flaubert, told the young writer about Delphine Delamare. She was a seventeen-year-old girl, daughter of one of the patients of Eugène Delamare near Rouen. They were married in 1839. Like Emma she was filled with romantic delusions and soon tired of her bourgeois existence and sought relief in numerous affairs. Debts mounted and rumours spread. She committed suicide with arsenic in March 1848. Emma thought at the end, 'no longer of her need for money, only of martyred love and her humiliation'.

SALLY BOWLES

Christopher Isherwood, *Sally Bowles* (1937), *Goodbye to Berlin* (1939)

Jean Ross (1912–73)

In 1930 Christopher Isherwood found lodgings at 17 Nollendorfstrasse, Berlin, where he was befriended by his landlady Fräulein Meta Thurau. Since she called him Herr Issyvoo the author retained the name for the observer of the episodes collected in *Goodbye to Berlin* in which Fräulein Thurau becomes Fräulein Schroeder. Among Isherwood's fellow lodgers was Jean Ross. As the daughter of a cotton merchant she was accustomed to comfort but by then earned her living singing in a seedy bar. By 1936 Isherwood had conceived a story 'about an English girl who sings in a Berlin cabaret'; *Sally Bowles* was first published in 1937 and then incorporated in *Goodbye to Berlin*. Sally herself is an innocent who remains unaltered by experience; even her abortion leaves her unchanged. For all her love affairs she remains vulnerable: 'Her face was long and thin, powdered dead white. . . "Hiloo," she cooed, pursing her brilliant cherry lips as though she were going to kiss the mouthpiece. "Ist dass Du, mein Liebling?".'

By the time Sally Bowles materialized in print Jean Ross was a committed left-winger married to the English writer Claud Cockburn and did not identify with Isherwood's creation though she remained friendly with the author. Sally Bowles subsequently appeared in John van Druter's Isherwood-inspired play *I am a Camera* (1951) which in turn inspired the stage musical *Cabaret* (1961) – filmed by Bob Fosse in 1971 with Liza Minelli as Sally. Isherwood recalled Jean Ross with affection in *Christopher and his Kind* (1977): 'Jean was more essentially British than Sally; she grumbled like a true Englishwoman, with her grin-and-bear-it grin. And she was tougher. She never struck Christopher as being sentimental or the least bit sorry for herself. Like Sally, she boasted continually about her lovers.'

Further reading:
Brian Finney, *Christopher Isherwood* (1979)

LAWRENCE BOYTHORNE

Charles Dickens, *Bleak House* (1853)

Walter Savage Landor
(1775–1864)

Boythorne is an old friend of John Jarndyce, with whom he had been at school. He lived near Sir Leicester Dedlock, with whom he was in endless conflict over various rights of way. Beneath all his ferocity he was as tender as a lamb: 'There was a sterling quality in his laugh, and in his vigorous healthy voice, and in the roundness and fulness with which he uttered every word he spoke, and in the very fury of his superlatives, which seemed to go off like blank cannons . . . He was not only a very handsome old gentleman . . . with a massive grey head, a fine composure of face when silent, a figure that might have become corpulent but for his being so continually in earnest that he gave it no rest, and a chin that might have subsided into a double chin but for the vehement emphasis in which it was constantly required to assist; but he was such a true gentleman in his manner, so chivalrously polite, his face was lighted by a smile of so much sweetness and tenderness and it seemed so plain that he had nothing to hide, but showed himself exactly as he was.' This is an affectionate portrait of Dicken's friend Landor, in which – as Dickens's biographer John Forster says – 'ludicrous traits were employed . . . to enrich without impairing an attractive person in the tale'.

Dickens named his second son Walter Savage in honour of his old friend Landor. It was while on a visit to Landor's house in Bath in 1840 that Dickens conceived the idea that was eventually to be developed into the novel *The Old Curiosity Shop*. The quarrels with Lord Dedlock are a reflection of his frequent disagreements with neighbours and tenantry at Llanthony Abbey, ten miles north of Abergavenny, after six years of constant battle and litigation to foist his 'improvements' on the area (which included planting thousands of cedar trees from Lebanon and importing a particular breed of sheep, merino, with soft wool) he left for France and Italy in 1813. He was a lifelong friend of Robert Southey. Landor wrote numerous works, poetry, historical plays, essays and periodic journalism; his epic poem *Gebir* 1798 contains the famous lines on a shell: 'Apply/Its polisht lips to your attentive ear;/And it remembers its august abode,/And murmurs as the ocean murmurs there'. His most its august abode,/And murmurs as the ocean murmurs there'. His most famous work was *Imaginary Conversations* (1824–29). He was hearty, irascible, bluff but big-hearted. He quarrelled with his wife in 1835 and later transferred his English estates to his son, thus becoming entirely dependent on his family. He described Dickens as: 'Truly extra-ordinary...a good as well as a delightful man'. He told Forster: 'Dickens has drawn from me more tears and more smiles than are remaining to me for all the rest of the world, real or ideal.'

Further reading:
John Forster, *Landor – A Biography* (1869)

LON BRACTON

J.B. Priestley, *London End* (1968)

Tony Hancock (1924-68)

Further reading: Freddie Hancock and David Nathan, *Hancock* (1969)

J.B. Priestley's novel *London End* features a neurotically self-destructive comedian, Lon Bracton, who achieves enormous popularity on television, yet can never come to terms with his own talent. Bracton's complex personality is scrutinized by his American agent, who admits that while Lon is at times a conscientious comedian he is also 'nutty as a fruit-cake. It's not the sauce, the hard stuff, though he can lap it up . . . It's Lon himself. He's several people. He goes to the can a good sweet guy and comes back a lousy bastard. You help yourself to a drink, turn around, and it isn't the same fella. He'll keep you up and you'll be falling about laughing, and the very next day he'll tell you he can't work. For weeks on end he can be more dippy-batty than half the people put away in mental homes. Yet when he's really working and it's all coming through, I tell you, this is a great comic – the best we've got.' As Freddie Hancock (the comedian's second wife) and David Nathan observe, in *Hancock* (1969), Lon Bracton is a shrewd portrait of Tony Hancock. 'Hancock was alive at the time,' Priestley said, 'so the physical description is different. All the rest is Hancock.'

Anthony John (not Anthony Aloysius St John, the forenames he affected in his act) Hancock was born in Birmingham and at the age of three moved to Bournemouth where his father – a semi-professional entertainer – had acquired a laundry. During the Second World War, he developed his skills and in 1951 met Ray Galton and Alan Simpson who scripted his best work, *Hancock's Half Hour,* which ran on radio (1954–7) and television (1956–61), and the film *The Rebel* (1961). Using Hancock's own mannerisms, Galton and Simpson created a loveable character perpetually at the mercy of his own pretensions. To the fifteen million people who regularly watched him on television, Hancock was a classic clown. In private he went through agonies of self-doubt which he attempted to drown in alcohol.

In 1961 Hancock sacked his scriptwriters Galton and Simpson, and the problems this decision caused were exacerbated by his personal crises: both his marriages ended in divorce, and his drinking led to a loss of comic timing as well as periods of hospitalization. Well aware that he could no longer meet his own artistic expectations, Hancock took his own life, while in Australia, by overdosing himself on amylo-barbitone tablets and vodka. A suicide note said: 'Things seemed to go wrong too many times.'

THE BARON OF BRADWARDINE

Sir Walter Scott, *Waverley* (1814)

Alexander Forbes, fourth and last Baron Forbes of Pitsligo (1678-1762) **Alexander Stewart of Invernahyle** (died 1795)

Further reading: Edgar Johnson, *Sir Walter Scott–The Great Unknown* (1970)

The Baron of Bradwardine is the father of Rose, who becomes the wife of Edward Waverley, the hero of Scott's novel. Bradwardine is described by Scott as tall and thin, with an athletic figure: 'old indeed, and grey-haired, but with every muscle rendered tough as whipcord by constant exercise. He was dressed carelessly, and more like a Frenchman than an Englishman of the period, while, from his hard features and perpendicular rigidity of stature, he bore some resemblance to a Swiss officer of the Guards who had resided some time in Paris, and had caught the *costume*, but not the ease or manners of its inhabitants.' He has been seasoned in foreign campaigns, accused of high treason after his part in the rebellion of 1715, he lived in semi-retirement, consorting only with his own fraternity, a leader among the discontented Jacobites: 'He was of a very ancient family . . . embarrassed of fortune: a scholar . . rather a reader than a grammarian . . . Latin he could speak with as great facility as his own good Scots.' This is a composite portrait of two leading Scots gentlemen. There are several close parallels with Lord Pitsligo, whose lands were formerly owned by the Comyn family, which probably gave Scott his Cosmo Comyn in *Waverley*. Like Bradwardine, Pitsligo had two bears as supporters on his shield. Pitsligo was born on 24 May 1678. His mother was a daughter of the Earl of Mar, Jacobite leader in 1715. He inherited title and estates while a boy. He served on the continent, where in Paris he became deeply influenced by the Quietists. As an MP he was opposed to the Union with England, the Act of Union bringing an end to his public political career. He gave his services to Mar in 1715 and was conspicuous at Sheriffmuir. He left the country after the failure of the rising, returned years later and again served the cause in the rising of 1745 when he was 67. He attainted after Cullodon and remained in hiding for years, the search for him gradually subsiding. He spent his last years at the house of his son, the Master of Forbes. He published several works of theology and philosophy – *Essays Moral and Philosophical* (1734), and *Thoughts Concerning Man's Condition* published a year after his death. He survived powerfully in oral tradition, the grand Old Man of the Jacobite cause, which is the main source of Scott's brilliant portrait. Scott also drew on Alexander Stewart, whom he knew personally and who taught him so much about Highland life, customs, scenery and Jacobite lore. Stewart had served in 1715 and gave distinguished service to Bonnie Prince Charlie at Prestonpans in 1745. He was wounded at Cullodon and pardoned under the Act of Indemnity. Scott met him in 1787.

BRAGGADOCHIO

Edmund Spenser, *The Faerie Queene* (1589, 1596)

François, Duke of Alencon, Duke of Anjou (1554–84)

Further reading:
M.P. Parker, *The Allegory of the Faerie Queene* (1961)

Braggadochio, the Elizabethan Englishman's stereotype portrait of the bragging continental knight, appears in Books II, III and V of Spenser's *The Faerie Queene*. He vaunts himself like a peacock with painted plumes, and constantly crows his own valour. He is forever smiting his courser, rattling his spear, waving his sword and bruiting forth his past glorious deeds and claims to future greatness. He is a coward at heart, and his actions seldom match his words. At one moment he says to a challenger: 'Sith then . . .needes thou wilt/Thy daies abridge through proofe of puissance,/Turn we our stees; that both in equall tilt/May meete againe, and each take happy chaunce.' But once he has turned his steed, he takes the chance to gallop off to safety. He is finally exposed and humiliated in Book V, when Sir Guyon said that it would be a dishonour to avenge one's wrath on such a wretched creature as Braggadochio: 'It's punishment enough that all his shame doe see.' The braggart has his beard shaved off and is totally discredited as a knight, his sword broken in two and his armour confiscated.

This unflattering caricature is a picture of the Duke of Alencon, who was well known in England when *The Faerie Queene* was first printed, as he had recently visited London for several months while negotiating a marriage contract with Queen Elizabeth. The proposed marriage was deeply unpopular in the country; the Privy Council failed to deliver the support which the Queen had expected, and Puritan opposition, led by John Stubbs, was very loudly voiced against it. In January 1571 negotiations had opened for a marriage between Elizabeth and Henri, Duke of Anjou. They were abandoned and a year later the Alencon marriage and treaty with France was negotiated (Francois was Henri's younger brother). The mutual defence treaty was signed at Blois and the marriage looked likely, but when the Duke came to Greenwich in October 1581 he was so unpopular that the marriage negotiations were given over and he left for Flushing in February 1582. He gained considerable territory and several titles in the various French Wars of Religion. He was declared Defender of Liberties by the States General in the Netherlands, and led an army of 2,000 cavalry and 10,000 infantry against the Spanish. By August 1581 he had reached Cambrai, causing the Duke of Parma to retreat. Hoping to conquer a principality for himself he sacked Antwerp; his brutalities here and at La Charité, Brussels, in 1577 became notorious. He died at Château-Thierry in June 1584.

GUDRUN BRANGWEN

D.H. Lawrence, *Women in Love* (1920)

D.H. Lawrence's friends John Middleton Murry and Katherine Mansfield (who lived together for several years before they were able to marry in 1918) helped create the literary climate of modernism in England. They had a close and typically tense relationship with Lawrence who often enchanted them and frequently enraged them with his self-centred sexual aesthetic. Although they did not at first realize it both of them

Katherine Mansfield
(1888-1923)

Further reading: Harry T. Moore, *The Priest of Love* (1974), A. Alpers, *Katherine Mansfield – A Biography* (1953), Jeffrey Meyers, *Katherine Mansfield* (1978)

featured in Lawrence's *Women in Love*: Murry was physically enlarged as Gerald Crich; Katherine became Gudrun Brangwen whose artistic gifts are visual rather than verbal. Gerald and Gudrun share a fierce physical passion whereas a more metaphysical love seems possible between Gerald and Rupert Birkin who (representing Lawrence himself) wants 'eternal union with a man too: another kind of love'. What Gerald sees in Gudrun is an independent quality he finds irresistible: 'Gerald watched Gudrun closely. . . . There was a body of cold power in her. . . . He saw her a dangerous, hostile spirit, that could stand undiminished and unabated. It was so finished, and of such perfect gesture, moreover. . . . The bond was established between them, in [her] look, in her tone. In her tone, she made the understanding clear – they were of the same kind, he and she, a sort of diabolic freemasonry subsisted between them. Henceforward, she knew, she had her power over him. Wherever they met, they would be secretly associated. And he would be helpless in the association with her. Her soul exulted.'

Katherine Mansfield was one of the most formidable intellectuals active in England. She came from New Zealand and made an early reputation as an incisive critic, then as Murry's assistant editor on *Rhythm*, a quarterly committed to revitalizing art. Mansfield's own short stories established her as one of the most subtle writers of the century. Two years after the publication of Lawrence's novel she went to G.I. Gurdjief's Institute for the Harmonious Development of Man at Fontainebleau, hoping to restore her spiritual as well as physical health, but died there of tuberculosis.

URSULA BRANGWEN

D.H. Lawrence, *The Rainbow* (1915), *Women in Love* (1920)

Louisa (Louie) Burrows

Further reading: Harry T. Moore, *The Priest of Love* (1974)

Between 1903–5 D.H. Lawrence attended the Pupil–Teacher Centre at Ilkeston, a municipal borough three miles from his native Eastwood, Nottinghamshire. Outside Ilkeston, at the village of Cossall, lived Louisa (Louie) Burrows, an attractive girl two and a half years younger than Lawrence. Her father Alfred Burrows (Will Brangwen in *The Rainbow*) ran a carving class at Cossall and Lawrence was somewhat reluctantly accepted as a visitor to the Burrows' home. With Louie, Lawrence liked to visit Marsh Farm (which he made a Brangwen stronghold in *The Rainbow*) just north of Cossall. He kept up a correspondence with her – published as *Lawrence in Love* (1968), edited by James T. Boulton – and wrote such poems as 'Snap-Dragon' and 'Kisses in the Train', expressing his feelings for her. In 1910 Lawrence, then teaching at Croydon, spent alternate weekends with his mother, then fatally ill. Some weeks before his mother's death (in December 1910) he became engaged to Louie, and in a letter of 5 December 1910 told A.W. Mcleod: 'She is a glorious girl; about as tall as I, straight and strong as a caryatid. . .and swarthy and ruddy as a pomegranate, and bright and vital as a pitcher of wine. I'm jolly glad I asked her. What made me do it, I cannot tell. Twas an inspiration. But I can't tell mother.' On 4 February 1912 Lawrence wrote to Louie saying that his illness (tuberculosis) made marriage inadvisable for him so she should break off the engagement. When he next wrote to her, on 19 November 1912, he was living in Italy with Frieda, his future wife. 'I want to say,' Lawrence told Louie, 'that it grieves me that I was such a rotter to you. You always treated me really well. . .the wrong was all on my side. I think of you with respect and gratitude, for you were good to me.' After Lawrence's death in 1930 his body lay at the Vence cemetery, in the south of France, for five years where Louie twice visited the grave. In 1940 she married Frederick Heath.

Although Frieda's personality played a part in the creation of Ursula Brangwen, the character was originally made in the image of Louie. In *The Rainbow*, Ursula loses her lover; in the sequel, *Women in Love*, she marries Rupert Birkin (a self-portrait of Lawrence). Ursula appears, in *The Rainbow*, as a passionate woman. 'She was always a woman, and what she could not get because she was a human being. . .she would get because she was a female, other than the man. In her femaleness she felt a secret riches, a reserve, she had always the price of freedom.'

ALAN BRECK

Robert Louis Stevenson, *Kidnapped* (1886), *Catriona* (1893)

Alan Breck Stewart (died 1789)

Robert Louis Stevenson's *Kidnapped* (which opens in the summer of 1751) is narrated by David Balfour, a schoolmaster's son who is cheated out of his inheritance by his uncle Ebenezer Balfour of Shaws, and kidnapped on a trading brig, the *Covenant*, bound for America. On the tenth day at sea the *Covenant* runs down a boat in the fog and takes on board the sole survivor, a Jacobite who has continued to fight for the cause since the defeat of the clans at Culloden in 1746. David Balfour's first impression of Alan Breck Stewart, the Jacobite, is favourable: 'He was smallish in stature, but well set and as nimble as a goat; his face was of a good open expression, but sunburnt very dark, and heavily freckled and pitted with the smallpox; his eyes were unusually light and had a kind of dancing madness in them, that was both engaging and alarming. . . Altogether I thought of him, at the first sight, that here was a man I would rather call my friend than my enemy.'

When the captain of the *Covenant* plots to kill Alan for his 'belt full of golden guineas', David warns the Jacobite and helps him fight the crew and subdue the captain. David learns that Alan is an Appin Stewart whose chief's lands have been forfeited and whose clan, captained by Ardshiel, has been 'harried and wasted' by the Campbells – especially the 'Red Fox', red-headed Colin Campbell of Glenure. After the *Covenant* sinks on the coast of Mull, David witnesses the murder of the Red Fox in the Wood of Lettermore 'in Alan's country of Appin'. David accepts Alan's assurance that he is innocent of the murder and the two friends go on the run in a series of adventures culminating in David's recovery of his inheritance and Alan's flight into exile. In *Catriona*, a sequel to *Kidnapped*, David unsuccessfully attempts to secure the release of Alan's foster-brother James Stewart of the Glens, who is held on a charge of murdering the Red Fox.

Alan Breck (meaning spotted or pock-marked) Stewart was an historical character who was in the vicinity when Colin Campbell of Glenure, the 'Red Fox', was murdered while on his way to evict tenants of Jacobite chiefs. Both Alan, and his foster-brother James Stewart of the Glens, were indicted for the murder, but whereas Alan escaped to France, James was hanged, above Ballachulish Ferry, on 8 November 1752 (Stevenson having put the murder a year earlier than its actual occurrence on 14 May 1752). It is generally agreed that both Alan and James were innocent, and that the murderer was Donald Stewart, (nephew of Alexander Stewart of Ballachulish) who had James buried at Keil.

GARETH BRENDAN

Harold Robbins, *Dreams Die First* (1977)

Hugh Hefner (born 1926)

Further reading: John Sutherland, *Bestsellers* (1981)

Dreams Die First deals with the attempts made by Gareth Brendan, who is young and power hungry, to create a sexually liberated magazine which will deal openly and honestly with sex. He puts *Macho* on the market, which stimulates some, but shocks and disturbs others, with its outspoken views and publisher's daring. Gareth soon learns that the success he undoubtedly achieves with *Macho* is not to be bought without cost, and he finds threats and obstructions from several directions, notably from the underworld, the law and other rivals attempting to break into the same market. The action of the novel is a series of confrontations, as gradually Gareth's ambition to liberalize sex in the modern world, through his power as a publisher, becomes sacrificed for other goals – a glamorous world of hedonism in which money and sex become almost synonymous. He has accidentally created a monster that he can no longer control. His dreams are turned into the roughage of his ambition and success.

Brendan is based on the career of the American publisher and gaming promoter, Hugh Marston Hefner. He was born in Chicago on 9 April 1926, and educated at the University of Illinois. He was editor and publisher of *Playboy* magazine from 1953, and president of the Hugh Marston Hefner Publishing Company, now called *Playboy* Enterprises, from 1953. *Playboy* certainly opened up a new kind of market for entrepreneurial publishing enterprises, who cashed in on the territory Hugh Hefner was the first to explore. As John Sutherland wrote in *Offensive Literature – Decensorship in Britain 1960-1982* (1982): 'Hugh Hefner's magazine (which started obscurely in 1953) was a miscellany which exploited post-1959 freedoms. It used new and visually imaginative pictorial techniques (the famous centrefolds, for instance). Hefner, like the sex shops, was in the absolution business. According to the *Playboy* philosophy, promiscuous hedonistic sex was normal.' *Playboy* also projected an intensely consumerist lifestyle: the real pin-ups sometimes seemed the Lamborghini cars or Sony hi-fis. Hefner took no 'inadequacy ads' (dealing with baldness, acne, impotence). The way of life valued by *Playboy* was unblemished, physically and morally. 'The initial liberating, and in some ways courageous, quality of the *Playboy* enterprise was soon dissipated in a vast capitalistic empire which diversified into clubs, films, books and the leisure industries.'

ALFRED BRICKNELL

D.H. Lawrence, *Aaron's Rod* (1922)

Alfred Brentnall (1834-1924)

Further reading: Harry T. Moore, *The Priest of Love* (1974)

As a child in Eastwood, D.H. Lawrence was often sent to collect his collier father's wages at the offices of Barber, Walker and Company on the Mansfield Road. The cashier for the firm was Alfred Woolston Brentnall, whose father had been cashier before him. When young, sensitive Bert Lawrence presented himself for his father's pay, Brentnall – who had been a heavy drinker – would taunt the boy by asking, 'Ho, lad wheer's your Pa – too drunk to come and collect the pay hissen?' Lawrence found this an excruciatingly embarrassing experience and recreated Brentnall first as Mr Braithwaite, the torment of Paul Morel's young life, in *Sons and Lovers* (1913): 'Mr Braithwaite was large, somewhat of the stern patriarch in appearance, having a rather thin white beard.' Braithwaite is 'the great cashier' and 'an important shareholder in the firm'.

In *Aaron's Rod* Lawrence improves on Brentnall's actual social status by making him Alfred Bricknell, a partner in a colliery firm. At the beginning of the novel Bricknell, a widower who lives in Shottle House, is at home, for it is Christmas Eve, and two of his children have come to be with him. Lawrence explains that Bricknell has the luxury of an enormous coal fire, since in his house 'there was no coal-rationing'. Bricknell is 'a large man, wearing a loose grey suit, and sprawling in the large grey arm-chair. The soft lamp-light fell on his clean, bald Michelangelo head, across which a few pure hairs glittered. His chin was sunk on his breast, so that his sparse but strong-haired white beard, in which every strand stood distinct, like spun glass, lithe and elastic, curved now upwards and inwards, in a curious curve returning upon him.' Though Bricknell seems to be meditating, Lawrence explains that he is asleep after a heavy meal. In the context of the mining town, he represents privilege. While the young people are celebrating Christmas, Bricknell is 'perfectly sober' (as Brentnall was in his later years). When they decide to stay up, he leaves the room and Lawrence notes that only Josephine, engaged to Bricknell's son Jim, had 'any feeling for him'.

SUE BRIDEHEAD

Thomas Hardy, *Jude the Obscure* (1895)

Tryphena Sparks (1851-90)

Introducing the first edition of *Jude the Obscure* Thomas Hardy wrote 'The scheme was jotted down in 1890, from notes made in 1887 and onwards, some of the circumstances being suggested by the death of a woman in the former year.' The woman was Tryphena Sparks, the model for Jude's 'darling little fool' Sue Bridehead. Jude, the stonemason who longs for learning, is enchanted by Sue as he sits watching her 'pretty shoulders' aware that 'his interest in her had shown itself to be unmistakably of a sexual kind'. Jude and Sue are 'simpletons' (Hardy's first title for the novel) whose attempt to put love before marriage ends in catastrophe and Sue's 'mental volte-face' back to convention. Hardy's fiction is an imaginative reconstruction of what might have happened had he pursued Tryphena in his youth.

In 1867 Hardy was working part-time in a Dorchester architect's office and about this time began to see his cousin Tryphena, a student-teacher at Puddletown School. On 16 January 1868 Tryphena was rebuked for 'neglect of duty' and probably dismissed; she went to Stockwell Training College, London, and was eventually appointed headmistress at Plymouth Public Free School in 1871, by which time Hardy had taken up with Emma Gifford. Hardy married Emma in 1874; three years later Tryphena married Charles Gale and had four children. When she died at the age of thirty-eight Hardy wrote a poem, 'Thoughts of Phena', in which she is described as his 'lost prize'.

In *Jude the Obscure* the Hardy-Tryphena relationship is transformed into a great tragedy but the origins of the story are still apparent: Jude and Sue are cousins as were Hardy and Tryphena; Jude uses books to better himself, as did Hardy; Sue trains as a schoolmistress, as did Tryphena. *Jude the Obscure* caused a sensation and Hardy said that 'the experience completely [cured] me of further interest in novel-writing'.

Further reading:
Robert Gittings, *Young Thomas Hardy* (1975), *The Older Hardy* (1980), F.E. Hardy, *The Early Life of Thomas Hardy 1840-1891* (1928), Anne Smith, *The Novels of Thomas Hardy* (1981)

REVD MR BROCKLEHURST

Charlotte Brontë, *Jane Eyre* (1847)

Revd Carus Wilson

Jane Eyre is orphaned as a baby and looked after by her aunt, the cold-hearted Mrs Reed of Gateshead Hall. For ten years Jane is treated like a servant, while Mrs Reed's own children are totally spoilt. As a punishment on one occasion, Jane is put into the room in which the late Mr Reed had died. Jane is a very sensitive girl, and she faints and becomes ill. When she is better she is sent to Lowood School, run by the Revd Brocklehurst, who seems to Jane like a 'black pillar', with the 'grim face at the top'. His regime is a tyrannical one, and the accommodation austere in the extreme, but in some ways it seems to Jane a relief after Gateshead Hall. Jane at one stage is punished by making her stand in isolation outside in the elements which makes her ill.

Brocklehurst is a portrait of the Revd Carus Wilson, who ran a school at Cowan Bridge, on the coach-road between Leeds and Kendal, where the daughters of the clergy could be educated for £14 a year plus extras. Charlotte Brontë was a pupil here, under the puritanical Revd Wilson. Wilson regarded himself as a philanthropist, but the conditions in the school seem to have been prison-like. He wrote little magazine stories for children, which are full of death-bed scenes. In one of them a child aged less than four is asked whether he would choose life or death, and answers: 'Death for me. I am fonder of death.' The desirability of continual prayer is stressed and in one story a child who screamed and cried is struck down by God and sent to hell. Children were punished, he claimed, in order to save their souls.

Cowan Bridge was cold all the time, and come rain or shine the pupils regularly had to walk to Revd Wilson's church at Tunstall. The food was uneatable. Two of Charlotte's sisters contracted tuberculosis there. Mrs Gaskell recorded of Wilson that 'his love of authority' led to much 'unnecessary and irritating meddling with little matters'.

Further reading:
Winifred Gèrin, *Charlotte Brontë* (1967) William Clarke, *The Brontes Were Here – Reflection on the Family's Life and Travels* (1977)

LEWIS BROGAN

Simone de Beauvoir, *The Mandarins* (1954)

Nelson Algren (1909-81)

After the liberation of France in 1945, Simone de Beauvoir visited the USA and was encouraged to go to Chicago to meet Nelson Algren. She was greatly impressed by the novelist who lived (as she said in her autobiography) 'in a hovel, without a bathroom or refrigerator, alongside an alley full of steaming trash cans and flapping newspapers'. Algren and de Beauvoir were deeply attracted to one another and when she returned to Chicago she lived with him for six weeks. Algren asked her to move in with him permanently but she was drawn back to France and her deep friendship with Jean-Paul Sartre. For several years Algren and de Beauvoir met regularly for holidays but he realized she could never be separated from Sartre for long and decided to end the affair.

This relationship was recreated by de Beauvoir as the romantic aspect of the otherwise rigorously intellectual *The Mandarins* which is

Further reading:
H.E.F. Donaghue, *Conversations With Nelson Algren* (1964)

dedicated to Nelson Algren. On a visit to the USA, Anne – wife of prominent French thinker Robert Dubreuilh – goes to meet the writer Lewis Brogan. She is overwhelmed by his personality: 'He was twenty when the great depression struck and for several years he lived the life of a hobo, crossing America hidden in freight cars, in turn peddlar, dishwasher, waiter, masseur, ditch digger, bricklayer, salesman, and, when necessary, burglar. In some forgotten roadside lunchroom in Arizona where he earned a living washing glasses, he had written a short story which a leftist magazine accepted for publication ... Through his stories, you got the feeling that he claimed no rights on life and that nevertheless he had always had a passionate desire to live. I liked that mixture of modesty and eagerness.' Like the author, Anne loves the American novelist but finally chooses to return to her life with 'the mandarins'.

FATHER BROWN

G.K. Chesterton, *The Innocence of Father Brown* (1911), *The Wisdom of Father Brown* (1914), *The Incredulity of Father Brown* (1926), *The Secret of Father Brown* (1927), *The Scandal of Father Brown* (1935)

Father John O'Connor (1870-1952)

Further reading: John O'Connor, *Father Brown on Chesterton* (1937), W. Ward, *Gilbert Keith Chesterton* (1944)

On his first appearance, in the 1910 story 'The Blue Cross', G.K. Chesterton's divine detective Father Brown is conspicuous by his singular appearance: 'he had a face as round and dull as a Norfolk dumpling; he had eyes as empty as the North Sea; he had several brown-paper parcels which he was quite incapable of collecting ... He had a large shabby umbrella, which constantly fell on the floor.' Father Brown goes on to outwit Flambeau, the 'colossus of crime'; and to astonish Valentin, 'the greatest detective alive'. When asked for the secret of his success he says 'a man who does next to nothing but hear men's real sins is not likely to be wholly unaware of human evil'.

Father Brown was (apart from the moon face) closely modelled on Father John O'Connor. An Irishman, he was curate at St Anne's, at Keighley in Yorkshire, when he wrote a fan letter to Chesterton in 1903. The following year Chesterton met Father O'Connor and the two became firm friends. O'Connor (like Father Brown) wore a flat black hat, frequently carried brown-paper parcels and sported a 'large shabby umbrella'. One evening he revealed to Chesterton how much he knew about human sin and suffering, whereupon Chesterton conceived the idea of 'constructing a comedy in which a priest should appear to know nothing and in fact know more about crime than the criminals'. The priest had a great influence on the author's life and when, on 30 July 1922, Chesterton was received into the Roman Catholic Church he made his confession to Father O'Connor. In 'The Sins of Prince Saradine' Chesterton describes Father Brown as 'an oddly sympathetic man... He had that knack of friendly silence which is so essential to gossip.' Father O'Connor's gift was recognized and he was made a Privy Chamberlain to Pope Pius XI and a Monsignor.

TOM BROWN

Thomas Hughes, *Tom Brown's Schooldays* (1857), *Tom Brown at Oxford* (1861)

Thomas Hughes (1822-96)

Further reading: Sydney Selfe, *Chapters From the History of Rugby School* (1910)

Tom Brown's Schooldays, probably the most celebrated account of Victorian public school life, was significant in constructing the public school ideal – with its emphasis on muscular Christianity, manliness, playing-the-game, discipline and outdoor games. It is an overtly romantic portrait of Rugby at the height of Dr Thomas Arnold's headmastership which lasted 1828-42. Tom Brown's father, a Berkshire squire, says to him as he leaves for Rugby: 'Remember you are going, at your own request, to be chucked into this great school, like a young bear with all your troubles before you... You'll see a great many cruel blackguard things done, and hear a deal of foul bad talk. But never fear. You tell the truth, keep a brave and kind heart, and never listen to or say anything you wouldn't have your mother or sister hear, and you'll never feel ashamed to come home, or we to see you.' Tom Brown is soon immersed in the world of fagging, flogging, bullying, cross-country running, cricket, rugby football; singing, tossing and roasting; fights in the playground, close personal friendships (see HARRY EAST, GEORGE ARTHUR) and the personal care and interest of the great Dr Arnold, who 'found time in those busy years to watch over the career, even of him,

Tom Brown, and his particular friends, and no doubt of fifty other boys at the same time'. The sequel follows the hero's career through Oxford. In its *Preface* the author denied that Tom Brown was a portrait of himself, but the parallels are very close.

Hughes was educated at Rugby and Oxford, where he gained his BA at Oriel College in 1845, where he was also a friend of Matthew Arnold, son of the great headmaster (see LUKE). Hughes was a follower of Frederick Denison Maurice, the Christian socialist. By profession a lawyer – entered Lincoln's Inn 1845, barrister, Inner Temple 1848, QC 1869 – Hughes was also active in various charities, and as a politician, sitting as Liberal MP for several constituencies. He was a county court judge 1882-96. *Tom Brown's Schooldays*, published anonymously, was an immense success. Hughes also published several biographies, including those of David Livingstone and of Alfred the Great. Tom Brown and Thomas Hughes were both born in the Vale of the White Horse, and they both entered Rugby in 1833, were placed in the third form and were members of School House. They were both rather slow academically, but sound in athletics, and outstanding at cricket. Major events in the novel parallel those which occurred during Hughes' days at Rugby – the famous football match was that played when Queen Adelaide visited the school in 1839; the great fight behind the old Chapel and the famous cricket match (part II Chapter VII) is based on the Rugby/MCC match of June 1841.

INSPECTOR BUCKET

Charles Dickens, *Bleak House* (1852)

Inspector Charles F. Field

Inspector Bucket is the detective officer used by Tulkinghorn and Lord Dedlock. It is Bucket's skill which finally unravels the mysteries which form the structure of the central plot of *Bleak House*, the murder of Tulkinghorn, and the discovery of Lady Dedlock. He finds out that the killer of Tulkinghorn was Hortense (see HORTENSE) the French maid and not George Rouncewell or Lady Dedlock. He seems to have the power to come and go without normal locomotion. Mr Snagsby suddenly sees: 'a person with a hat and stick in his hand, who was not there when he himself came in, and has not since entered by the door or by either of the windows . . . this person stands there, with his attentive face, and his hat and stick . . . and his hands behind him, a composed and quiet listener. He is a stoutly built, steady-looking, sharp-eyed man in black, of about the middle-age.'

This is Inspector Field. He was an Inspector in the Greenwich Division of Metropolitan Police in 1833 and later promoted to the Detective Force. Dickens's friend, the journalist George Augustus Sala, wrote that: 'There was something . . . of Dickens's Inspector Bucket about Inspector Field; and I venture to think that he was a much acuter and astuter detective in *Bleak House* than he was in real life.' Dickens wrote several times about Field. In one article in *Household Words* he is described as 'a middle-aged man of a portly presence, with a large, moist, knowing eye, a husky voice, and a habit of emphasizing his conversation by the aid of a corpulent forefinger'. Elsewhere he says he is 'of a burly figure', 'sagacious, vigilant . . . polite and soothing'. He had that capacity for being everywhere at once, knowing everyone and every place. Dickens wrote that Field's eye 'is the roving eye that searches every corner of the cellar as he talks ... Every thief cowers before him, like a schoolboy before his schoolmaster.' Field conducted Dickens through some of the worst London slums.

Further reading:
Philip Collins, *Dickens and Crime* (1962), Charles Dickens, *Reprinted Pieces* ('The Detective Police', 'Three Detective Anecdotes' and 'On Duty with Inspector Field')

BABY BUCKTROUT

Wyndham Lewis, *The Roaring Queen* (1973)

In Wyndham Lewis's satirical novel *The Roaring Queen*, various cultural figures assemble at Beverley Chase, the Oxfordshire home of Mrs Wellesley-Crook. The Honourable Baby Bucktrout, Mrs Wellesley-Crook's niece, is a rebellious young lady who indulges her passion for sexual slumming at every opportunity. When she first appears she is pursuing (in a chapter that makes satirical allusions to D.H. Lawrence's *Lady Chatterley's Lover*) a young handyman employed by Mrs

Nancy Cunard
(1896-1965)

Further reading:
Anne Chisholm, *Nancy Cunard* (1979)

Wellesley-Crook. Baby 'was clothed only in white tennis-shorts and a polo-singlet of the same Sienna sun-tan complexion as her skin, while she sucked in her lean cheeks without thinking, to enhance the attractive hatchet-lines of her close Eton crop. She was a pocket-amazon, for she stood no more than five feet high in her sandalled feet and was of an airy build.' Although a Miss Corse has been detailed to keep Baby under control, she insists on her right to act on impulse, which leads her to some peculiar situations. Despite her hearty heterosexual appetite, she is engaged to Donald Butterboy, the roaring queen of the title. She tells her mother, Lady Saltpeter, 'I hate effeminate boys who write books or do Gossip. It is only with workmen or with servants that you are sure of finding *the Goods*, and I don't mind saying so! . . . I want the Goods – you understand? I must have *The Goods*!'

The Roaring Queen was suppressed in 1936, and, when it eventually appeared, an introduction by Walter Allen identified Baby Bucktrout as Nancy Cunard. Apparently Cunard read the book, took no exception to the satirical portrait of herself, and offered to publish it with her Hours Press, Paris, though Lewis declined as there was no advance available. Nancy Cunard knew Lewis well, despite their political differences, and sat for him for a portrait. She was, as Walter Allen points out, friendly with the literary homosexual Brian Howard, a possible original of Butterboy, the roaring queen. Known as a minor poet, and notorious for her major break with her mother Lady Emerald Cunard, Nancy Cunard was devoted to radical reform all her life. She was, in the words of Walter Allen, 'one of the great rebellious figures of the twenties and thirties, a beautiful woman notorious for her flouting of the conventions and her passionate support of left-wing causes, a bohemian when the word still had a meaning'.

BILLY BUDD

Herman Melville, *Billy Budd Foretopman* (1924)

Philip Spencer
(1823-42)

Further reading:
Charles R. Anderson, *The Genesis of 'Billy Budd'* in *American Literature* (November 1940)

Billy Budd is a young foretopman, serving on board the *Indomitable* in 1797. He was a foundling, forcibly impressed for service. He is a very attractive and likable young man: 'He was young; and despite his all but fully developed frame, in aspect looked even younger than he really was. This was owing to a lingering adolescent expression in the as yet smooth face, all but feminine in purity of natural complexion . . . Cast in a mould peculiar to the finest physical examples of those Englishmen in whom the Saxon strain would seem not at all to partake of any Norman or other admixture, he showed in face that humane look of reposeful good nature which the Greek sculpture in some instances gave to his heroic strong man, Hercules . . . ' There is a quality of mystery about Billy. He does not know who he is. He was a foundling left on a doorstep in Bristol. He is very popular with the crew, and particularly liked by the captain, the Honourable Edward Fairfax Vere. But Billy is victimized by the evil master-at-arms, Claggart, who finally unjustly accuses him, before Captain Vere, of conspiring in a mutiny. Billy is struck speechless with rage and strikes out at Claggart, whom he kills with the blow. Vere is now torn between his love for Billy and his need to maintain social order on board the *Indomitable*. He has to administer justice within the context of the articles of war, and Billy is hanged at the yardarm. He goes to his execution crying: 'God bless Captain Vere'.

The story is based on the mutiny on board the American brig *Somers* in December 1842. The *Somers*, under Captain Alexander Slidell McKenzie, arrived at New York after an eight-day voyage from St Thomas, following a cruise on the African coast. Soon after the *Somers* left St Thomas a mutiny was suspected, led by Philip Spencer, son of John C. Spencer, Secretary of War. The plan was to murder the captain and another officer, take over the brig and ply the American coast, robbing other shipping. The master-at-arms learned of the conspiracy and told the captain, who confined the crew under hatches, held a court martial and hanged Spencer and two of his confederates at the yardarm. At the court of enquiry held immediately afterwards Captain McKenzie claimed he had acted under the articles of war in reference to mutiny. Acting Midshipman Philip Spencer was the youngest of three sons of the Secretary of War, and grandson of the Chief Justice of New York State. A college classmate remembered him as: 'a sprightly, delicate lad who was quite a favourite with many of his schoolmates, though his queer stories and sharp tricks made him unpopular with others . . . '

NATTY BUMPPO

James Fenimore Cooper, *The Pioneers* (1823), *The Last of the Mohicans* (1826), *The Prairie* (1827), *The Pathfinder* (1840), *The Deerslayer* (1841)

Daniel Boone (1734-1820)

Further reading:
J. Bakeless, *Master of the Wilderness – Daniel Boone* (1939)

James Fenimore Cooper's hero Natty Bumppo, a 'man of the forest', declares himself in *The Pioneers* as an archetypal loner: 'I have lived in the woods for forty long years, and have spent five at a time without seeing the light of a clearing bigger than a wind-row in the trees.' Natty, known as Hawk-eye in *The Last of the Mohicans*, and Leatherstocking elsewhere, has an appropriately odd appearence: 'His moccasins were ornamented after the gay fashion of the natives, while the only part of his underdress which appeared below the hunting frock was a pair of buckskin leggings that laced at the sides, and which were gartered above the knees with the sinews of a deer.'

As a fiercely independent individual who pushes back frontiers and impresses his rugged personality on the American soil, Natty was modelled on 'the venerable patriarch' Daniel Boone – as Cooper acknowledged in *The Prairie*, the third Leatherstocking tale. Boone, born near Reading, Pennsylvania, fought in the French and Indian War. In 1767 and, more spectacularly, in 1769, he explored Kentucky to which he returned in 1775 as an agent for the Transylvania Company. Boone led a group of settlers to Kentucky and erected a fort at what was to become Boonesborough. Captured by the Shawnees at the Lower Blue Licks in 1778 he escaped in time to warn Boonesborough of an imminent Indian attack which was thereby resisted in a long siege. The following year he brought more settlers to Kentucky and, when Kentucky was made a county of Virginia, Boone was made a lieutenant-colonel in the militia, was chosen for the legislature, and was (in 1782) appointed sheriff and county lieutenant. However his claims on land in Kentucky were invalidated as he had not registered them properly, so he left the county in 1788 going first to Point Pleasant and then to Missouri where he lived on land given to him by Congress.

BILLY BUNTER

Frank Richards, *Magnet* (issue numbers 1-1683)

Lewis Ross Higgins (1885-1919)

Further reading:
E.S. Turner, *Boys Will Be Boys* (1948)

On 15 February 1908 the halfpenny paper *Magnet* made its first appearance with a hero, Harry Wharton, and a school, Greyfriars in Kent. Wharton goes to Study No 1 along with Billy Bunter, 'a somewhat stout junior with a broad face and a large pair of spectacles'. Bunter's weekly adventures continued until 1940 when the paper closed down with *Magnet* issue number 1683. After the war Bunter appeared in books and (in 1952) on BBC television. He was an unforgettable character with his Fat Owl face, his faith in the imminent appearance of a postal order (on the strength of which he borrowed), his addiction to 'tuck', and his stock phrases 'Yarooh!', 'Oh, crumbs' and 'Oh, crikey'.

Frank Richards, the astonishingly prolific author who created Bunter, acknowledged his original: 'His extensive circumference came from an editorial gentleman who . . . seemed to overflow the editorial chair and almost the editorial office.' This was Lewis Ross Higgins who edited the comic paper *Chuckles* from 1914 until his death. He was a Welshman who, on account of his great girth, was sometimes mistaken for G.K. Chesterton; in addition to his work as editor, cartoonist and illustrator he wrote art criticism for *Punch*.

Two other sources were tapped to complete the picture of Bunter. The large spectacles came from Richards's sister Una who was 'wont to peer . . . somewhat like an Owl in boyhood days'. The celebrated postal order was 'a reincarnation of a cheque which a certain person constantly expected but which did not often materialise', the certain person being Richards's brother Alex whose literary submissions frequently resulted in rejection slips rather than the hoped-for cheques.

BUNTHORNE

Opera, *Patience* (1881, libretto by W. S. Gilbert, music by A. S. Sullivan)

Oscar Wilde (1854-1900)

Further reading: Mark Nicholls, *The Importance of Being Oscar* (1981)

Bunthorne, the leading character in Gilbert and Sullivan's comic operetta which attacks the aesthetic movement, is given a splendid character which portrays an aesthetic young thing who 'walked down Piccadilly with a poppy or a lily in his medieval hand'.

This is a picture of Oscar Wilde, who was then leading quite a flamboyant life and was often seen in Piccadilly in what was perceived as fancy dress. The craze for an almost feminine sartorial elegance, offset with flowers and a touch of medievalism, was under vehement attack from such philistine quarters as *Punch*. *Patience* struck a chord in the British middle-class soul: 'Then a sentimental passion/of a vegetable fashion/must excite your languid spleen,/An attachment à la Plato/for a bashful young potato,/or not-too-French French bean!/Though the philistines may jostle,/you will rank as an apostle/in the high aesthetic band,/If you walk down Piccadilly/with a poppy or a lily/in your medieval hand./And everyone will say,/As you walk your flowery way,/"If he's content with a vegetable love/which would certainly not suit me,/Why, what a most particularly pure/young man this pure young man must be!"'

Wilde had an answer for it, of course. Anybody could have walked down Piccadilly like that, he claimed, but: 'The difficult thing to achieve was to make people believe that I had done it.' His lecture tour of the United States coincided with the staging of *Patience* in America. He lectured on the 'Principles of Aestheticism'. Tour and opera were mutually successful. Wilde had been a brilliant student at Oxford, and easily achieved fame as essayist, attender at 'first-nights', conversationalist and dandy. Wilde was the leader of the art-for-art's sake movement and a poseur with the intention of outraging the bourgeoisie; he triumphed in America and Paris. *The Picture of Dorian Gray* (1891) struck a slightly more sinister note, foreshadowing characteristically flamboyant decadence. He produced brilliant comedies in the 1890s and then his trial in 1895, following his association with Lord Alfred Douglas, brought to an end one of the most spectacular literary careers. He died in Paris.

SIR BURBON

Edmund Spenser, *The Faerie Queene* (1589, 1596)

Henry IV, King of France (Henry of Navarre) (1553-1610)

Further reading: Hesketh Pearson, *Henry of Navarre* (1953)

In Book V of Spenser's epic, Prince Arthur (see PRINCE ARTHUR) goes to Belgae (the Netherlands), as the people have called for aid in their struggles against the tyrant, Gerioneo (see GRANTORTO), and puts an end to the rule of the tyrant. Arthur and Artegall (see SIR ARTEGALL) should have been aided in their attempts against tyranny by their ally, Sir Burbon, but he has been forced to yield to mob pressure. Arthur and Artegall strive against idolatry wherever they find it, and go to the aid of Irena (Ireland) only to find that her defender, Sir Burbon, has thrown down his shield in submission and disgrace. He has done this in order to retain power: 'O sacred hunger of ambitious mindes,/And impotent desire of men to raine!/Whom neither dread of God, that devils bindes,/Nor laws of men, that common-weales containe,/Nor bands of nature, that wild beastes restraine, /Can keepe from outrage and from doing wrong,/Where they may hope a kingdome to obtaine . . . '

This is a portrait of Henry of Navarre, the third son of Antoine de Bourbon and Jeanne d'Albret, heiress of Henry, King of Navarre. His mother was a devout Calvinist and he was reared in the same faith. During the third Huguenot war Henry of Navarre was the leader of the Protestant party. After the Peace of St Germain he married Margaret of Valois, sister of Charles IX, a week after the massacre of St Bartholomew. Henry's life was spared when he professed himself a Roman Catholic. Spenser calls upon Sir Burbon's behaviour to demonstrate the lengths of apostasy that men will go to in order to obtain worldly power: 'Witnesse may Burbon be; whom all the bands/Which may a Knight assure had surely bound,/Untill the love of Lordship and of lands/Made him become most faithless and unsound . . . ' For three years Henry was a prisoner at the French court but he escaped in 1576 and renounced his previous conversion to Catholicism. When the Duke of Anjou died in

1584, this made Henry heir presumptive to the throne; the succession was opened to him by the murder of Henry III in 1589. His claim was unpopular because his Protestantism was not acceptable to most of the population of France, but in 1593 he again reverted to Catholicism, making peace with Spain in 1598. By the Edict of Nantes he granted liberty of conscience to Protestants. He married Mary de Medici. He was assassinated by a Jesuit fanatic immediately prior to his embarking on a war with Germany. He was well built, broad-shouldered and had sparkling, attractive eyes, a large nose and short beard. His personality was amiable, impetuous, generous and humorous.

DENIS BURLAP

Aldous Huxley, *Point Counter Point* (1928)

John Middleton Murry (1889-1957)

Further reading:
John Middleton Murry, *Between Two Worlds* (1935).
Sybille Bedford, *Aldous Huxley* (1973, 1974)

Aldous Huxley's *Point Counter Point* ends ironically with Denis Burlap, editor and half-owner of the London *Literary World*, splashing about in the bath with his mistress Beatrice: 'Of such,' runs the final sentence of the novel, 'is the Kingdom of Heaven.' Burlap is introduced in the novel as 'a man of middle height with stoop and a rather slouching gait. His hair was dark, thick and curly, with a natural tonsure as big as a medal showing pink on the crown of his head.' Self-consciously, Burlap acts the part of the man of sorrows, forever grieving over his late wife, Susan, who died in the influenza epidemic. The self-styled 'Christ-like' Burlap, who constantly uses the language of the New Testament, recalls the nature of his relationship with his wife; 'his love was at once babyish and maternal; his passion was a kind of passive snuggling. Frail, squeamish, less than fully alive and therefore less than adult, permanently underaged, she [Susan] adored him as a superior and almost holy lover. Burlap in return adored . . . his own adorable husbandliness.' Burlaps's self-indulgent piety wins him the adoration of Beatrice (hence the childish bath at the end of the novel) and the scorn of the writer MARK RAMPION (modelled on D.H. Lawrence). 'A pure little Jesus pervert' is Rampion's description of Burlap.

Burlap is a caricature of John Middleton Murry, who was editor of the *Athenaeum* when Huxley joined the magazine in 1919. Born in London, Murry was educated at Oxford before beginning his journalist career with the *Westminster Gazette* and the *Nation*. He worked in the War Office (eventually as Chief Censor) in the First World War, and married Katherine Mansfield in 1918. After her death in 1923 he commemorated her life and art in *Letters of Katherine Mansfield* (1928), *The Life of Katherine Mansfield* (1933), *Katherine Mansfield and other Literary Portraits* (1949). He knew D.H. Lawrence well and criticized him in *Son of Woman* (1931), which Huxley described as 'a curious essay in destructive hagiography'. For his part, Lawrence portrayed Murry as Gerald Crich in *Women in Love* (1920).

STANLEY BURNELL

Katherine Mansfield, *Collected Stories* (1945)

Sir Harold Beauchamp

Further reading:
V. O'Sullivan and M. Scott, *Collected Letters of Katherine Mansfield* (Vol. 1, 1984)

Several of Katherine Mansfield's stories are drawn from her experiences as a member of a prosperous New Zealand family. She was the third daughter of Harold and Annie Beauchamp who had two further children so that Kezia, as Katherine appears in the stories, was the child in the middle. In 1893, when Katherine was five, the family moved from Wellington to Karori and this shift from a town to a country house is the subject of Mansfield's most distinctive story, *Prelude*, so called because it was conceived as the prelude to a projected novel entitled *Karori*. *Prelude* presents Kezia's father, Stanley Burnell, as a strong physical presence 'so delighted with his firm, obedient body that he hit himself on the chest and gave a loud "Ah"'. In *At the Bay* Stanley is still endearingly energetic – 'a figure in a broad-striped bathing-suit [who] flung down the paddock, cleared the stile, rushed through the tussock grass into the hollow' – but in *The Little Girl* the father-figure is a domestic tyrant.

Harold Beauchamp, Katherine Mansfield's father and the Stanley Burnell of the stories, was a successful businessman who became, in 1907, Chairman of the Bank of New Zealand. The following year he agreed to pay his daughter an allowance (initially of £100 a year) to enable her to live in England and pursue her literary ambitions. He provided her with an income for the rest of her life though he frequently disapproved of the company she kept and thought her husband John Middleton Murry was 'a perfect rotter'. For his services to the Dominion of New Zealand, Harold Beauchamp was knighted in 1923, the year his daughter died. Shortly after her death he bequeathed a large sum of money towards the encouragement of the arts in New Zealand, a demonstration of the sensitivity his wife noted in *At the Bay*.

FRAULEIN BURSTNER

Franz Kafka, *The Trial* (1925)

Felice Bauer (1887-1960)

Franz Kafka's posthumously published novel *The Trial* (which was edited by the author's friend Max Brod) immediately puts the central character in a nightmarish situation. The opening sentence (in the 1935 translation by Edwin and Willa Muir) states: 'Someone must have been telling lies about Joseph K., for without having done anything wrong he was arrested one fine morning.' Though no specific charge is brought against him, K. is haunted by guilt and at the end of the book is done to death in a stone quarry – 'Like a dog'. Before he dies he has a glimpse of Fräulein Bürstner, a typist who rents a room near his. When he sees her he realizes 'the futility of resistance' and hopes he will 'not forget the lesson she had brought into his mind'.

Fräulein Bürstner is an enigmatic figure in a mysterious novel. After his first early morning visit from the Interrogation Commission, K. waits for her: 'As she locked the front door she shivered and drew her silk shawl round her slim shoulders.' K. is increasingly drawn to her: 'He was gazing at her hair, evenly parted, looped low, firmly restrained reddish hair.' When she opens the door and slips into the entrance hall, K. reacts impulsively: '"I'm just coming," K. said, rushed out, seized her, and kissed her first on the lips, then all over the face, like some thirsty animal lapping greedily at a spring of long-sought fresh water. Finally he kissed her on the neck, right on the throat, and kept his lips there for a long time.'

Kafka's manuscript invariably refers to Fräulein Bürstner as F.B., also the initials of Felice Bauer, the girl he twice promised to marry. Felice, from Berlin, first met Kafka in 1912, and on 12 April 1914 they were engaged, though the commitment made Kafka feel 'like a criminal'. As a result of his procrastination Kafka found that, on the morning of 12 July 1914 his Berlin hotel room – as Ernest Pawel puts it in *The Nightmare of Reason* (1984) – was 'transformed into a courtroom, and himself the defendant in the dock'. After a trial of several hours, during which Kafka refused to defend himself, the engagement was formally dissolved to the satisfaction of the furious Felice. Shortly after that experience Kafka began to write *The Trial*. Felice Bauer, who trained as a stenographer-typist, was to endure another broken engagement to Kafka, who dreaded marriage as a threat to his artistic inviolability. She preserved most of the five hundred letters Kafka wrote to her, and they were subsequently published as *Letters to Felice* (1974).

MADAM BUTTERFLY

Opera, *Madam Butterfly* (1900, music by Giacomo Puccini, libretto by Giacosa and Illica)

Japanese wife of Thomas Blake Glover

Further reading: K.G. Millward, *L'Oeuvre de*

Lieutenant Pinkerton of the US navy goes through the formalities of marrying the young Japanese, Cio-Cio-San ('Madam Butterfly'). She has renounced her religion to marry him as she is really in love with him. She is convinced that he will return to her, not realizing that he embarked on the 'marriage' without sincerity, intending eventually to marry an American girl. Three years pass. The American Consul, Sharpless comes to tell Butterfly that Pinkerton is returning, and that he is now married to an American. Butterfly is so thrilled at hearing of his return that Sharpless has not the heart to tell her he is married. When Butterfly learns the truth she stabs herself just as Pinkerton enters, calling her name. The house is empty except for Butterfly's child by Pinkerton.

Puccini's tear-jerker was based on David Belasco's one-act melodrama (1900). This was a one-act version of a story he had read in an

American magazine by J. L. Long. Long had borrowed the story from a romance by an officer in the French navy, Pierre Loti (real name L. M. Julien Viaud, 1850–1923). Loti's story was called *Madame Chrysanthème* (1887). It may have been in part autobiographical; at one time he had proposed it be subtitled *Le Mariage de Loti*. He spent a great deal of his professional life in the East and was at Nagasaki when Japan was first opened up to the trade with the West. He doubtless heard the story of the successful trader and gunrunner, Glover, who was based in Nagasaki after 1859 (six years after Perry and the American fleet came to Tokyo Bay) and who married a Japanese girl. Sharpless was probably based on Townsend Harris, American Consul at Shimoda, who arrived in 1856. In Nagasaki the house where Glover lived is now called Butterfly House, and features Cio-Cio-San's Garden – bamboo fences, ponds, bridges, cherry trees and all. Harris's journals survive and record that he knew Glover well. Harris died in Japan in 1886, a year after Loti's story appeared.

Pierre Loti et l'esprit fin de siecle (1955)

JOHNNIE BYRNE

Jimmy Boyle and Tom McGrath, *The Hard Man* (1977)

Jimmy Boyle (born 1944)

The Hard Man, by Jimmy Boyle and Tom McGrath, is a play about the criminal life and imprisonment of Johnnie Byrne, a tough character from the Gorbals of Glasgow. Serving a life-sentence for a murder he claims he did not commit, Byrne addresses the audience directly from prison and relives his life in a series of flashbacks that show his brutal methods as a moneylender and leader of a Glasgow gang. Offering his own version of his past, Byrne projects himself as a man conditioned by a vicious urban environment: 'in the world that I come from, violence is its own reason. Violence is an art form practised in and for itself. And you soon get to know your audience and what it is impresses them. You cut a man's face and somebody asks you, "How many stitches?" "Twenty" you say, and they look at you – "Twenty? Only twenty? Christ, you hardly marked him." The next time you cut a face you make a bit more certain it will be news.' As Byrne sees it, prison exists to destroy men like himself. It is, thus, an oppressive institution made in the image of a violent society. Byrne, in the play, sees himself as a victim. When *The Hard Man* was first performed, in Edinburgh on 19 May 1977, Jimmy Boyle – co-author and original of Byrne – was serving a sentence of life-imprisonment for murder.

Born in the Glasgow Gorbals, Boyle drifted into crime and was, in 1967, sentenced to life-imprisonment. Categorized as Scotland's most dangerous criminal, Boyle began to see the possibility of changing his life when he was placed in the Special Unit of Barlinnie Prison in 1973. There he was able to practise a new art form, sculpture, with distinction. Encouraged by such as Tom McGrath, then director of Glasgow's Third Eye arts complex, Boyle substituted a creative urge for his former destructive rage. In his book *The Pain of Confinement* (1984) Boyle says he recognized that the Special Unit 'could be a golden opportunity to create a new model for the penal system and would be an important springboard for radical changes throughout'. In 1977 Boyle was visited in prison by Sarah Trevelyan, the woman he married in 1980. By the time of his release in 1982 he was a celebrity, known for his sculpture and his startling rehabilitation. On coming out of prison Boyle involved himself in social work, helping teenagers to overcome the problem of drug addiction. Since then Boyle has spoken out persuasively for the human rights of prisoners, arguing that reform comes through responsibility.

Further reading:
Alan Bold, *Modern Scottish Literature* (1983)

C

CALAMITY JANE
Edward L. Wheeler, *Deadwood Dick on Deck, or Calamity Jane the Heroine of Whoop Up* (1884)

Martha Jane Burke (née **Canary**) (1852-1903)

Further reading: Peter Neward, *The Illustrated History of the Old West* (1982)

The term 'Calamity Jane' is nowadays used for a person who always has a dismal tale to tell, or dire forbodings to unburden. It can also mean a person who seems to carry trouble with them wherever they go. The term was put in circulation in the 1880s as the result of a series of popular dime-novels which featured the adventures of Calamity Jane. However, the heroine was not a miserable person, nor one dogged by misfortune. Quite the contrary. She was called 'Calamity' Jane because she was such a dead shot with both revolver and rifle that she could guarantee to bring calamity to anyone who had the misfortune to provoke her. This noted markswoman was born in Princeton, Missouri. When she was eight years old she was taken by her parents to Virginia City, Montana. Her mother and father separated when the child was still quite young, and in order to survive the tough life she adopted the costume of the male, wore trousers and carried six-shooters. She became a well known frontier character, rode for the pony-express companies and was a celebrated scout. She moved to South Dakota after the peace agreement signed with the Sioux Indians had led to the state's gaining territorial status in 1861, and the gold rush made it a vast attraction to settlers and prospectors. She moved from one boom town to another and finally settled in the Black Hills, where she died in 1903. Many legends grew up about her, some less flattering than others – it was rumoured she had been a prostitute in Hays City, Kansas, and that she had been the lover of Wild Bill Hickock. It has also been claimed that she was a scout for General George Armstrong Custer and General Miles. She has been portrayed in several films, notably played by Jean Arthur in *The Plainsman* (1936), by Jane Russell in *The Paleface* (1948), by Yvonne de Carlo in *Calamity Jane and Sam Bass* (1949) and Doris Day in *Calamity Jane* (1953).

ROY CALVERT
C.P. Snow, *Strangers and Brothers* (1940), *The Light and the Dark* (1947), *Time of Hope* (1949), *The Masters* (1951)

Charles Allberry (1912-43)

Further reading: Philip Snow, *Stranger and Brother* (1982), John Halperin, *C.P. Snow – An Oral Biography* (1983)

Roy Calvert, the tormented hero of C. P. Snow's novel *The Light and the Dark,* is an academic who lives his life at a ferocious pace. Lewis Eliot comes to Cambridge as a fellow in 1933 and has rooms near Calvert, so he is able to study the young man who is poised to achieve an international reputation as an orientalist. Eliot notices, however, that Calvert's nature threatens any long-term achievement: 'He was born with this melancholy; it was a curse of fate, like a hereditary disease. It shadowed all his life.' Eliot also admits that 'my friendship with him became the deepest of my life'. Calvert's linguistic work brings him to Berlin where he is briefly impressed by Nazism; when the war comes he becomes a bomber pilot and is reported missing after going on one of his regular raids.

Calvert's character is closely modelled on Charles Allberry who was the youngest fellow at Christ's College when Snow worked at Cambridge in the 1930s. Allberry was athletically accomplished as well as intellectually dazzling and was considered to be one of Cambridge's brightest men; at the age of twenty-seven he was already considered to be among the finest orientalists in Europe. As Germany became more menacing Allberry affected an indifference to it all, in deference to the German professor in Berlin who was his collaborator; when war was declared, though, he volunteered as a bomber pilot. On 3 April 1943 he left for a raid on Essen and was later reported missing. In a letter to his brother, C.P. Snow wrote: 'His loss is harder to bear than that of any other of my friends would be. I learned from him more of the adventures and solitariness of the spirit than from anyone else; in some ways he was the most gifted & the most remarkable of all of us, and the most unhappy.'

TONY CAMONTE
Film, *Scarface* (1932,

Scarface traces the rise and fall of a gangster, and resembles a Chicago gangland version of the story of the Borgias, including the very strong suggestion of incest between Tony Camonte and his sister. The script contained at least fifteen killings, including a brief reference to something akin to the St Valentine's Day massacre, the shooting of a character called Big Louie Costillo in a telephone booth and the attempted slaying of one Johnny Lovo. Tony has a taste for high culture and Italian opera. He goes to a performance of *Rain*. 'I like to see shows like that,' he says, 'Serious.' Halfway through he is called out to see the killing of a mobster rival. Afterwards he asks what happened in the play. A fellow gunman who stayed for the show says: 'She climbed back in the hay with the Army.' Tony Camonte retorts: 'That's-a fine, she's-a smarta girl.' There is something engagingly child-like about Camonte. When he picks up his first tommy gun he says: 'I'm going to write my name all over this town in big letters. Outta my way, I'm spittin'.' He is deeply jealously protective of his sister and resents to an unnatural degree any association with males on her part. He is finally tracked down and killed by the police after he has shot and killed a fellow gangster who had seduced his sister.

This is clearly the life story of Al Capone. Both gangsters had facial scars and the narrative of the film has several key parallel moments – the killing of Big Louie is the killing of Big Jim Colosimo and Johnny Lovo is really Johnny Torrio. Capone was called 'Scarface Al' in the tabloids of the day. Although all spoken references to the city of Chicago were removed from the soundtrack, the parallels were obvious, and to a well-established extent *Scarface* was made with Capone's cooperation. Capone worked originally for Colosimo, and when he was killed, for Johnny Torrio. Torrio, who himself was nearly killed, retired as Capone became Mr Big, controlling Chicago's vice, gambling and bootlegging on a syndicate basis, with the law rendered powerless by bribery. He was finally imprisoned for tax offences and died in 1947.

directed by Howard Hawks, written by Ben Hecht, based on the novel by Armitage Triall, starring Paul Muni)

Al Capone (1899-1947)

Further reading:
Carlos Clarens, *Crime Movies* (1980), Hank Messick and Burt Goldblatt, *The Mobs and the Mafia* (1972), Jay Robert Nash, *Bloodletters and Badmen* (1973), Kenneth Allsop, *The Bootleggers* (1968)

REVD JOSIAH CARGILL

Sir Walter Scott, *St Ronan's Well* (1823)

Dr Alexander Duncan (1708-95)

Further reading:
John Gibson Lockhart, *The Life of Sir Walter Scott* (1838)

The Revd Cargill is the scholarly, absent-minded and solitary minister of St Ronan's Well, the Scottish spa (see MEG DODS). He was of humble origins and had been trained and educated for the ministry only at the cost of considerable family sacrifice. While he was private tutor to the beautiful Honourable Miss Augusta Bidmore, her marriage to another cuts him to the quick and he throws himself into his studies by way of compensation. He was a 'a thin spare man, beyond the middle age, of a dark complexion, but with eyes which, though now obscured and vacant, had been once bright, soft and expressive, and whose features seemed interesting . . . he had forgot neatness, but not cleanliness. His hair might have appeared much more disorderly had it not been thinned by time . . . black stockings, ungartered, marked his professional dress, and his feet were thrust into the old slipshod shoes which served him instead of slippers.' He was invariably to be found at the manse immersed in some folio volume and piles of books. When he moved in society he was wont to neglect his dress and other formalities, which tendency was increased by his truly astonishing absent-mindedness, frequently mistaking the person he was talking to, enquiring of an old maid for her husband, or a childless wife about her young people, of distressed widowers for their spouses at whose very funerals he had himself officiated in recent weeks. He was immensely familiar with strangers whom he had never seen before, and estranged to those who had known him for years: 'The worthy man perpetually confounded sex, age, and calling; and when a blind beggar extended his hand for charity, he has been known to return the civility by taking off his hat, making a low bow, and hoping his worship was well.' This splendid character was based on Dr Alexander Duncan, who was minister at Smailholm when Walter Scott was a boy. He was educated at Marischal College and ordained at Traquair in 1738. He had been Chaplain to the second Lord Marchmont, had seen Alexander Pope and knew many of the survivors of the Augustan age. He came to Smailholm in 1743. He was a considerable scholar; among his publications are *A Preservative Against the Principles of Infidelity, The Devout Communicant's Assistant, The Evidence of the Resurrection of Jesus as Recorded in the New Testament, History of the Revolution of 1688* and an unpublished account of the Jacobite rebellion of 1745. He was made a Doctor of Divinity in 1773. His wife died when she was quite young and Dr Duncan was a sorrowful widower for nearly half a century. In his autobiography Scott talks of Duncan as 'a most excellent and benevolent man, a gentleman in every feeling'.

SISTER CARRIE

Theodore Dreiser, *Sister Carrie* (1900, unexpurgated edn 1981)

Emma Wilhelmina Dreiser

Further reading: Helen Dreiser, *My Life with Dreiser* (1951), W.A. Swanberg, *Dreiser* (1965), Richard Lehan, *Theodore Dreiser – His World and His Novels* (1969)

Theodore Dreiser's *Sister Carrie* shows the inexorable rise of the heroine at the expense of the men in her life, particularly Hurstwood who steals for her. Dreiser based the story on his sister Em's adventures with, first, a Chicago architect, and then L. A. Hopkins, a saloon-manager. Dreiser described Emma Wilhelmina, his sister, as a 'showy, erotic' woman, 'one of the most attractive of all the girls in our family'. She had none of her brother's literary interests and, as such, she is introduced with critical caution as Caroline in the novel: 'Caroline, or "Sister Carrie" as she had been half affectionately termed by the family, was possessed of a mind rudimentary in its power of observation and analysis. Self-interest with her was high, but not strong. It was nevertheless her guiding characteristic. Warm with the fancies of youth, pretty with the insipid prettiness of the formative period, possessed of a figure which tended towards eventual shapeliness and an eye alight with certain native intelligence, she was a fair example of the middle American class – two generations removed from the emigrant. Books were beyond her interest – knowledge a sealed book.'

When Em met L. A. Hopkins in Chicago they became lovers and were found in bed by a detective acting on behalf of Hopkins's wife. In 1886 Hopkins took some three thousand dollars from the safe of the saloon he managed and eloped with Em to Montreal. Eventually they came to New York where fact parted from fiction. Hopkins set up in style on the proceeds of his corrupt connections with local government; however, when Dreiser joined Em and Hopkins in 1894 as a boarder, the couple were far from happy. Hopkins was given to bouts of violence and once suggested to Em that they rent out their rooms for prostitution. Dreiser observed all this and then advised his sister to leave Hopkins, which she did.

KIT CARRUTHERS

Film *Badlands* (1973) written and directed by Terrence Malick

Charles Starkweather (1940-59)

Further reading: Jonathan Green, *The Directory of Infamy* (1980)

Badlands was one of the cult movies of the 1970s, in which Martin Sheen turned in a splendidly moody portrayal of an aimless teenage multiple killer. Kit Carruthers is a young garbage collector in a small western town. His life is totally humdrum and devoid of hope or glamour. He meets and falls in love with a young schoolgirl daughter of a middle-class family, and they begin a torrid love affair. Her stepfather strongly disapproves of the relationship and in a row with them he is shot dead by Kit. To throw the police off the scent, Kit fakes a suicide pact and burns the house down. The fugitives try to live rough in the woods but are pursued by bounty hunters. Kit shoots four of them and they are then on the run again. Kit models his style on his hero, James Dean, turning his life into a psychopathic real-life fantasy. He shoots a pal of his, to whom he had turned for help, as well as two young friends of his who accidentally visit during the murder. Other killings follow as the authorities close in. They trek across the land hoping to cross the borders, but are captured. He is arrested by two policemen after troops and national guard have turned out to find them. When making the arrest one of the officers says to Kit: 'Well, I'll kiss your arse if you don't look like James Dean.' Holly gets long term probation and Kit is sent to the electric chair.

Although the film is described as 'fiction', this is clearly the story of Charles Starkweather, who was born in Lincoln, Nebraska. He worshipped James Dean and modelled his personality on his hero, believing that he resembled him. He was fascinated by guns. With his girl friend, Caril Ann Fugate, he left a trail of wanton killings across the plains states. He killed a petrol station attendant and robbing his till, drove to town, shot Caril's parents and killed their daughter, two-year-old Betty Jean. They kept people away by claiming there was a flu scare in the house, then made a dash for it in Charlie's car. He next killed a wealthy farmer, August Meyer, and a young couple. The head of the Capital Steel Works in Lincoln, his wife and servant were next, followed by a shoe salesman in Douglas, Wyoming. Starkweather's car failed to start and a passing oil agent, Joseph Sprinkle, stopped to help, recognized Starkweather, and held his rifle until the police arrived. Starkweather was electrocuted on 24 June 1959. His comment on his life: 'If we'd have been let alone we wouldn't hurt nobody.'

KIT CARSON

Joaquin Miller, *Kit Carson's Ride* (1871); numerous dime novels and comic book stories; film, *Kit Carson*, starring Jon Hall (1939)

Christopher Carson (1809-68)

Kit Carson is one of the legendary figures of the Old West, a resourceful trapper, guide and scout – the idealized figure of the frontiersman. He came to personify the masculine virtues of the West – honesty, integrity, immense personal prowess, tempered with the kind of basic human decency that Gary Cooper projected so well in various cowboy roles. Christopher Carson was born in Madison County, Kentucky, but raised on the Missouri frontier. He was apprenticed to a saddler and was a teamster in the Southwest. By 1826 he was a guide, hunter and trapper, and accompanied John Charles Fremont on his expeditions to explore and map the regions between the Mississippi and Missouri rivers, and to Oregon and California 1845–6, which aroused the interest which led to the opening up and development of the West. Carson took part in the Mexican War and was Indian agent at Taos, New Mexico in 1854. Here he performed valuable service and was a restraining influence on the belligerent Apache Indians, aided by his knowledge of Indian culture and languages. In the American Civil War he served in the Federal army in the Southwest. He was breveted a brigadier of volunteers in 1865 for 'important services in New Mexico, Arizona and the Indian Territory'. At the end of the war he was again an Indian agent, at Fort Lyon, Colorado, where he died on 22 May 1868. Stories about him began to appear in popular literature many years before his death. He truly had become a living legend. The *Arkansas Gazette and Democrat* in June 1851 described him: 'He was not dressed in the outlandish habiliments with which fancy, since the time of Boone, instinctively invests the hunter and the trapper, but in general American costume . . . Carson is rather under the medium height, but his frame exceedingly well-knit . . . His hair, a light auburn, and worn long, falls back from a forehead high, broad and indicating more than a common intelligence . . . (and) such an eye! gray, searching, piercing, as if with every glance he would reach the well springs of thought, and read your very silent imaginings.'

Further reading:
Blanche C. Grant (editor), *Kit Carson's Story of his Own Life* (1926)

EDWARD CASAUBON

George Eliot, *Middlemarch* (1872)

Dr Robert Henry Brabant

Dorothea Brooke, the heroine of George Eliot's *Middlemarch*, has an exaggerated idea of duty and feels that the 'really delightful marriage must be that where your husband was a sort of father, and could teach you even Hebrew, if you wished it'. Her marital philosophy is put to a severe test when she marries the Revd Edward Casaubon, a man thirty years her senior. Casaubon is soon revealed as a tiresome pedant whose abiding interest is his projected (but never completed) work of religious scholarship: 'Mr Casaubon, too, was the centre of his own world [for] he was liable to think that others were providentially made for him, and especially to consider them in the light of their fitness for the author of a *Key to all Mythologies*.' Only after his death can Dorothea resume her own life.

In 1843 May Ann Evans (George Eliot) was a bridesmaid at the wedding of her friends Charles Hennell and Elizabeth Rebecca Brabant – who had been nicknamed Rufa in some verses by Coleridge, once her

Further reading:
David Williams, *Mr George Eliot* (1983), Anne Smith, *George Eliot Centenary essays and An Unpublished Fragment* (1980), J.W. Cross, *George Eliot's Life as*

Related in Her Letters and Journals (1885)

father's patient. Dr Robert Henry Brabant considered himself to be a great scholar, despite his lack of actual scholarship, and claimed to be writing a definitive work dealing with the supernatural aspects of Christianity. After Rufa's wedding Dr Brabant took Mary Ann home with him to Devizes where she was to assist him in his literary labours. He called her Deutera, his second daughter, and she wrote to her friend Cara Bray, to say 'I am in a little heaven here, Dr Brabant being its archangel. . . . We read and walk and talk together, and I am never weary of his company.' However the arrangement was not to the liking of Dr Brabant's blind wife and her sister Susan Hughes pressurized Mary Ann into returning to Coventry after only two weeks. Mary Ann was mortified and never forgave the pedant who promised so much yet constantly failed to deliver.

LADY CASTLEWOOD

William Makepeace Thackeray, *The History of Henry Esmond* (1852)

Jane Octavia Brookfield (1821-95)

Further reading: Gordon Ray, *Thackeray* (1955, 1958), Charles and Frances Brookfield, *Mrs Brookfield and her Circle* (1905)

When young Harry Esmond, the hero of Thackeray's *The History of Henry Esmond*, first sees Rachel, Lady Castlewood – the woman he is eventually to marry – he is enchanted. As Thackeray writes 'The instinct which led Henry Esmond to admire and love the gracious person, the fair apparition of whose beauty and kindness had so moved him when he first beheld her, became soon a devoted affection and passion of gratitude, which entirely filled his young heart. . . . There seemed, as the boy thought, in every look or gesture of this fair creature, an angelical softness and bright pity – in motion or repose she seemed gracious alike; the tone of her voice, though she uttered words ever so trivial, gave him a pleasure that amounted almost to anguish.'

Thackeray himself conceived such a passion for Jane Brookfield, wife of his friend William Henry Brookfield, an eccentric and theologically daring preacher. Brookfield's lofty indifference to his wife's sensitivity offended Thackeray who offered Jane his devotion – as he demonstrated by portraying her first as Amelia in *Vanity Fair* (1848) then as Lady Castlewood. Thackeray called on Jane frequently, to the consternation of Brookfield, and believed she was in love with him. Then in 1849 he was shocked to learn that Jane was pregnant – by her husband. Jane had encouraged Thackeray to assume that her marriage was a loveless ordeal so he was consumed by jealousy at the thought of Brookfield's intimacy with his wife. In 1851 Thackeray told Brookfield what he thought of him and his treatment of his wife; the result was an angry scene leading to a break between the Brookfields and the celebrated author. Thackeray admitted 'I have loved his wife too much, to be able to bear to see her belong even to her husband any more – that's the truth.'

LORD CASTLEWOOD

William Makepeace Thackeray, *The History of Henry Esmond* (1852)

William Henry Brookfield (1810-74)

Further reading: Margaret Forster, *William Makepeace Thackeray – Memoirs of a Victorian Gentleman* (1978), Charles and Frances Brookfield, *Mrs Brookfield and Her Circle* (1905), Gordon N. Ray, *Life of William Makepeace Thackeray* (1955-58)

Young Henry Esmond serves as a page in the household of Lord Castlewood and develops a profound admiration for Lady Castlewood. Tragically it is Henry who introduces small-pox into the household, a disease which Lady Castlewood contracts. As a result of her illness her beauty is considerably marred and she loses much of her husband's esteem. The disintegrating relationship is observed in close focus: 'The persons whom he loved best in he world, and to whom he owed most, were living unhappily together. The gentlest and kindest of women was suffering ill-usage and shedding tears in secret: the man who made her wretched by neglect, if not by violence, was Harry's benefactor and patron. In houses where, in place of that sacred, inmost flame of love, there is discord at the centre, the whole household becomes hypocritical, and each lies to his neighbour.' He notices sadness in her eyes and plaintive vibrations in her voice. When Lord Castlewood was in his cups he warned Harry against all women: 'as cheats, jades, jilts. . .' Henry perceives that it was the husband's realization of his wife's superiority that was at the root of the problem: 'and that *he*, and not she, ought to be the subordinate of the twain . . . After the illumination, when the love lamp is put out . . . and by the common daylight we look at the picture, what a daub it looks! what a clumsy effigy! How many men and wives come to this knowledge . . . if it be painful to a woman to find herself mated for life to a boor . . . it is worse still for the man himself perhaps, whenever in his dim comprehension the idea dawns that his slave . . . is, in truth, his superior.'

Thackeray is here describing the relationship between William Henry Brookfield, a close friend of the novelist's since undergraduate days at Cambridge, and his beautiful wife, Jane. Thackeray fell deeply in love with Mrs Brookfield and had to endure the pain, not only of loving one was was married to another, but of seeing her abused by her husband. Earlier in their marriage the Revd Brookfield seemed proud to be married to an attractive woman adored and admired by all. Later he seemed to turn against her, and to treat her sarcastically, mimicking her in front of other people. The couple were incompatible. He was a reserved and meticulous person, but she was a warm and outward-going character. He had wit, but little humour. He did not get the church preferments he had expected, grew petulant, and became tyrannical at home. *Henry Esmond* enabled Thackeray imaginatively to act out his desire – Harry, the narrator, marries Lady Castlewood after her husband's death. The semi-incestuous relationship of the marriage shocked Victorian readers (see AMELIA SEDLEY).

ANNE CATHERICK, THE WOMAN IN WHITE

Wilkie Collins, *The Woman in White* (1860)

The case of the Marquise de Douhault (1787)

The opening of *The Woman in White* is supposed to be based on Wilkie Collins's own experiences. Out walking one evening he heard a young woman scream. Then he saw a female figure, dressed in flowing white, running from a large house. He ran to her aid and discovered from her own account that she had been held a prisoner there under hypnotism for several years. She became Collins's mistress and he used her story as the basis of his classic thriller, which opens in the dead of night as a stranger, walking alone down a moonlit road, is touched suddenly on the shoulder by 'a solitary woman, dressed from head to foot in white'. Thus is the life of Walter Hartright, a drawing master, changed for ever. The young woman appears to be demented and to have escaped from an asylum. Her name is Anne Catherick. She bears a strong resemblance to Laura Fairlie, daughter of Hartright's employer. Hartright falls in love with Laura, and leaves the country in despair when she marries Sir Perceval Glyde, of Blackwater Park. Glyde is really after the Fairlie family fortunes, and has planned to get Laura to sign a document in which she surrenders her wealth to him, and then to get her confined to the asylum as Anne Catherick, who has died in the meantime. When Anne dies she is to be buried as Lady Glyde and the wicked Sir Perceval will thus gain her wealth. Glyde's plot is revealed by the hero, and it is even discovered that the villain has no right to the title as he was born out of wedlock. He dies in a fire at the church where he is attempting to forge evidence by tampering with the parish register.

Wilkie Collins used as the outline for this plot the real-life case of the Marquise de Douhault. She came to Paris in 1787 to take the necessary legal steps to regain from her brother, a shifty and dishonest type, properties which were hers by right, as they had been left to her by her father. Her brother had her kidnapped, and kept her drugged and confined for years, until she managed to smuggle out a letter to friends which eventually effected her release and the exposure of her brother's villainy.

Further reading: W.C. Philips, *Dickens, Reade and Collins – Sensational Novelists* (1919)

THE COUNTESS CATHLEEN

W.B. Yeats, *The Countess Cathleen* (1892)

Maud Gonne (1866-1953)

W. B. Yeats's verse play *The Countess Cathleen* is set in the distant past of Ireland during a terrible famine. When two demons, disguised as merchants, tempt the peasants to sell their souls for food, the Countess Cathleen sacrifices her goods to protect her tenants. Eventually, she sells her own soul as a supreme sacrifice for the peasants: 'The people starve, therefore the people go/Thronging to you. I hear a cry come from

Further reading: Joseph Hone, *W.B. Yeats* (1943)

them/And it is in my ears by night and day,/And I would have five hundred thousand crowns/That I may feed them till the dearth go by.' She adds that all souls bought by the demons must be set free. As Joseph Hone points out in his biography of Yeats, the central character combined a figure from folklore with a contemporary heroine: 'Stories of how Maud Gonne had appeared as a sort of miracle-worker among the poor in Donegal associated themselves in the poet's thought with the legend, and made the play a symbolical song of his pity. Maud Gonne had given of her substance to the evicted tenants; exhausted by the effort, she had been told by her French doctor that she was threatened with serious illness, and must spend a winter among the pine trees at St Raphael.'

Shortly after the publication of his *The Wanderings of Oisin* (1889), Yeats was visited in London by Maud Gonne, who told the poet she had wept over passages in his poem. The daughter of an English Colonel who died of cholera in Dublin, Maud was both an actress and an Irish revolutionary. When Yeats dined with her, after their first meeting, she told him of her ambition to act in a play in Dublin. Yeats replied that, while researching his *Fairy and Folk Tales of the Irish Peasantry* (1888), he had come across the story of the Countess Cathleen, which would provide a good part for Maud. Visiting Ireland in 1891, Yeats heard that Maud was in Dublin and called on her. Later that same year he was back in Dublin and made the first of several proposals of marriage to her. She declined the offer but said she valued his friendship. Yeats read her the text of *The Countess Cathleen* and told her he saw Cathleen, in selling her soul, as a symbol of all souls who lose their peace by pursuing a political cause. Though Maud did not act in the play the published text is dedicated to her. In 1903 Maud married John MacBride, who was executed in 1916 for his part in the Easter Rising.

BENITO CERENO

Herman Melville, *Benito Cereno* (1856)

Don Bonito Cereno, of the Spanish ship 'Tryal', (1805)

Further reading: Harold H. Scudder, *Melville's 'Benito Cereno' and Captain Delano's Voyages*, in P.M.L.A., volume XLIII (June 1928)

In 1799 Captain Amasa Delano, of Duxbury, Massachusetts, is on board *the Bachelor's Delight*, a large sealer and general trader, at anchor at Santa Maria, on the coast of Chile. He sights the *San Dominick*, which shows no colours. Investigation proves the vessel to be a Spanish merchantman of the first class, carrying negro slaves from one colonial port to another. The ship is mysterious, and the Spanish captain: 'a gentleman, reserved looking, and rather a young man . . . dressed with singular richness, but bearing plain traces of recent sleepless cares and disquietudes . . .' He stands leaning against the main-mast and as Captain Delano boards the *San Dominick* he casts 'a dreary, spiritless look' upon his crew, and 'an unhappy glance towards his visitor'. Nevertheless, Don Benito Cereno seems to be in command of the ship. The reality turns out to be the opposite. He is a prisoner of the slaves. The slave mutiny has been led by Babo, a Senegalese who pretends to be Cereno's valet. The conspiracy is unmasked and Babo is brought to justice. Benito Cereno himself dies only months after these terrible events.

This is a true story which Melville found in Amasa Delano's *A Narrative of Voyages and Travels in the Northern and Southern Hemispheres; Comprising Three Voyages Round the World*, published in Boston 1817. Melville changes the names of the ships – Delano's ship is changed from the *Perseverance* to the *Bachelor's Delight*, and Beneto Cereno's from the *Tryal* to the *San Dominick*. He invents Cereno's death in the monastery. The Spanish captain's name is changed from Bonito to Benito. Melville changes the simple but terrible story of the slave mutiny he read in Amasa Delano's narrative into a dreadful allegory of the blackness of human behaviour and the inhumanity of social tyranny. At the end of the story Delano asks Melville's protagonist to realize that the past is past: 'Why moralise upon it? Forget it. See, yon bright sun has forgotten it all, and the blue sea, and the blue sky; these have turned over new leaves.' And Benito Cereno answers: 'Because they have no memory . . . because they are not human.'

PROFESSOR CHALLENGER

Sir Arthur Conan Doyle, *The Lost World* (1912), *The Poison Belt* (1913), *The Land of Mist* (1920), 'The Disintegration Machine', 'When the World Screamed' (two late stories)

Professor William Rutherford (1839-99)

Further reading: Owen Dudley Edwards, *The Quest for Sherlock Holmes* (1982)

The Lost World, first and most famous of the Professor Challenger stories, is narrated by Ed Malone, a journalist with the London *Daily Gazette*. Anxious to embark on a great adventure, Malone seeks out the notoriously irascible zoologist, Professor George Edward Challenger, to discover the facts behind 'some cock-and-bull story from South America . . . rank nonsense about some queer animals he had discovered'. Under the pretence of being deeply disturbed by Challenger's controversial attitude to Darwinism, Malone goes to see the Professor at his West Kensington home. Malone is astonished by Professor Challenger's appearance: 'It was his size which took one's breath away – his size and his imposing presence. His head was enormous, the largest I have ever seen upon a human being . . . He had the face and beard which I associate with an Assyrian bull . . . The hair was peculiar, plastered down in front in a long, curving wisp over his massive forehead. The eyes were blue-grey under great black tufts, very clear, very critical, and very masterful. A huge spread of shoulders and a chest like a barrel were the other parts of him which appeared above the table, save for two enormous hands covered with long black hair.' After being physically attacked by Challenger, Malone is allowed to join him on an Amazonian expedition which reveals the lost world of prehistoric monsters and primitive apemen.

As Doyle revealed, in *Memories and Adventures* (1924), he based the character of Professor Challenger on Professor William Rutherford of Edinburgh University, where Doyle studied medicine in 1876, and where the fictional Challenger was educated. Doyle vividly recalled 'Professor Rutherford with his Assyrian beard, his prodigious voice, his enormous chest and his singular manner. He fascinated and awed us . . . He would sometimes start his lecture before he reached the classroom, so that we would hear a booming voice saying: "There are valves in the veins", or some other information, when the desk was still empty. He was, I fear, a rather ruthless vivisector.' Rutherford had a single-minded dedication to his own method of teaching and resigned two London chairs of physiology before returning to Edinburgh in 1873. He also suffered from bouts of mental instability and no doubt this contributed to the demented determination of Professor Challenger.

ALLEN CHALMERS

Christopher Isherwood, *All the Conspirators* (1928), *Lions and Shadows* (1938)

Edward Upward (born 1903)

Further reading: Brian Finney, *Christopher Isherwood* (1979)

In *Christopher and his Kind* (1976) Christopher Isherwood describes Edward Upward as his 'closest heterosexual male friend' and his 'literary mentor', in honour of an association that began at an English public school. Isherwood, then fourteen, was sent to Repton School, near Derby, in 1919. When he entered the sixth form, the following year, he met Upward, who was a history-student with a hatred of public school life. In 1921 Isherwood and Upward, by then great friends, travelled to Cambridge together to take the scholarship examinations in which they both did well. While Isherwood remained for another year at school, Upward went to Cambridge to read history, and wrote letters to Isherwood denouncing university life and developing his artistic vision of rebellion. Reunited at Cambridge, Isherwood and Upward concocted the fantasy world of Mortmere, an imaginary village on the edge of the Atlantic ocean. Both wrote stories about Mortmere which so continued to fascinate Upward that in 1928 he wrote 'The Railway Accident', the only Mortmere story to materialize in print (in 1949). In the 1930s Upward worked as a schoolmaster and contributed Marxist analyses of English society to leftist periodicals. His Kafkaesque novel *Journey to the Border* (1938) was followed by a period of silence, but when Upward's trilogy *The Spiral Ascent* (1962–77) appeared, Isherwood welcomed it as a masterpiece. Isherwood dedicated his first published novel, *All the Conspirators*, to Upward; in an introduction to the 1957 edition he called Upward 'the judge before whom all my work must stand trial' and extended the dedication to include 'Edward's wife Hilda, his daughter Kathy and his son Christopher'.

As Allen Chalmers, Upward appears in both *All the Conspirators* and the autobiographical novel *Lions and Shadows*. The former features Philip Lindsay, a delicate creature dominated by his mother. Chalmers's role in the novel is to explain to Philip that his ill-health is a state of mind that can be remedied if he will only escape from his mother's clutches (though at the end of the novel Philip catches rheumatic fever). *Lions and Shadows*, a slightly fictionalized autobiography, gives an impression of Upward as Isherwood first encountered him at Repton: 'He was a natural anarchist, a born romantic revolutionary . . . Above all things, Chalmers loathed the school to which he invariably referred as "Hell". His natural hatred of established authority impressed me greatly and I felt that it was a weakness in myself not to share it; to be guilty, indeed, of having sometimes kissed the rod.'

CHARLIE

John Le Carré, *The Little Drummer Girl* (1983)

Charlotte Cornwell

John Le Carré's *The Little Drummer Girl* opens explosively with the impact of a Palestinian terrorist bomb-attack on Jews in Germany. As a counter-terrorist move Israeli intelligence decides to infiltrate a Palestinian group by using a double agent. The girl they choose for this work, Charlie, is an actress who naturally sees herself as a heroine in search of a strong, dramatic political role: 'Her name was actually Charmain but she was known to everyone as "Charlie", and often as "Charlie the Red" in deference to the colour of her hair and to her somewhat crazy radical stances, which were her way of caring for the world and coming to grips with its injustices. . . . Charlie was not the prettiest of the girls, by any means, though her sexuality shone through, as did her incurable goodwill, which was never quite concealed by her posturing.' Recruited by the Israelis she proves to be an effective double agent though at the end of the book she has cause to dwell on the implications of her roleplaying.

Le Carré based the character on his sister Charlotte Cornwell, the Shakespearean actress, who acknowledges that 'politically there are great similarities. When I was younger I was lured towards several extreme left-wing groups of people. I was desperate to find a place where I could hang [my beliefs and ideals] on a hook somewhere.' Le Carré recalls seeing his sister, when touring with the Royal Shakespeare Company, performing at the Camborne sports centre: 'It was pouring with rain, the most unbelievable noise on the roof. Charlotte was really having to belt it out and I thought she was very good but she was over the top, I mean she was booming in order to defeat the rain. It was actually the moment when I thought, yes, I'll have Charlotte for my character, at least as the raw material.'

COMUS

John Milton, *Comus, A Masque, presented at Ludlow Castle, 1634, before the Earl of Bridgewater, Lord President of Wales*

Mervyn Touchet, Lord Audley, Second Earl of Castlehaven (1592-1631)

Further reading: William Cobbett, *State Trials* (1809-12) Volume 3 pp. 401-26, *The Arraignment and Conviction of Mervyn Touchet* (1642)

Mervyn Touchet, the Second Earl of Castlehaven, was executed for abominable crimes in 1631, after being exposed by his eldest son, James Touchet (1617–84), who became Third Earl of Castlehaven. James was the son of Mervyn Touchet by his first wife, Elizabeth, daughter and heiress of Benedict Barnham, who was an alderman of London. Mervyn was a man of passionate and profligate habits. He married a second time, taking as his bride Lady Anne, daughter of Ferdinando Stanley, Fifth Earl of Derby, and widow of Grey Brydges, Fifth Baron Chandos. When James Touchet was thirteen he was married to Elizabeth Brydges, the daughter of his father's second wife, Anne, by her first husband, Grey Brydges. When this young girl had been barely twelve years old, she was forced by Mervyn Touchet into having criminal intercourse with her mother's paramour, one Skipwith. James Touchet was neglected by his father and disgusted with the scenes of depravity, debauchery and bestiality which he was compelled to witness; eventually, as state papers of the day put it: 'he appealed for protection from the Earl, his natural father, to the father of his country, the King's Majesty' and was instrumental in the initiation of proceedings which brought his father to justice. The Touchet family were kin of the Bridgewaters, for whom

Comus was written. Lady Alice Bridgewater played the Lady in the original production. She was the cousin of the young woman who had been so horribly abused at the hands of her stepfather, Mervyn Touchet, who was tried and executed on 14 May 1631. The Castlehaven scandal was very widely discussed at the time, especially as the exposure of the Earl by his son was such a feature of the case. Thus Lady Alice, daughter of the Earl of Bridgewater, is the original of the Lady in Milton's *Comus*: 'Let us fly this cursed place,/Lest the Sorcerer us entice/ With some other new device' would strike home with fearful relevance to those who knew about the dreadful Castlehaven scandal.

BARON DE CHARLUS

Marcel Proust, *Remembrance of Things Past* (1913-27)

Count Robert de Montesquiou (1855-1921)

Further reading:
George D. Painter, *Marcel Proust* (1959, 1965)

Baron Palamède Charlus, brother of the Duc de Guermantes, is one of the main characters in Proust's novel. At first Charlus, a great friend of CHARLES SWANN, is rumoured to be a lady's man, but the narrator discovers that he is in fact homosexual (in the C.K. Scott Moncrieff/ Terence Kilmartin translation): 'I now understood [why] M. de Charlus looked like a woman: he was one! He belonged to that race of beings . . . whose ideal is manly precisely because their temperament is feminine.' Later at Doncières (actually Orleans) station, the narrator sees Charlus, a nocturnal creature of society, by daylight: 'as he waddled along with his swaying paunch and almost symbolic behind, the cruel light of day decomposed, into paint on his lips, into face-powder fixed by cold cream on the tip of his nose, into mascara on his dyed moustache whose ebony hue contrasted with his grizzled hair, everything that in artificial light would have seemed the healthy complexion of a man who was still young.' Though he is an intelligent man capable of kindness (as when he adopts the niece of his friend Jupien) Charlus is besotted by the cynical violinist Morel for whose sake he descends to the level of Mme Verdurin's 'little clan'. After being rejected by Morel, Charlus declines morally and physically. During the First World War the narrator visits the male brothel run by Jupien and finds the Baron de Charlus acting out a sadomasochistic fantasy in which he is the 'Man in Chains' being flogged by a soldier.

As a young man anxious to infiltrate the aristocratic world of the Faubourg Saint-Germain, in Paris, Proust cultivated the members of the French nobility. In 1893, at the salon of Madeleine Lemaire, Proust met Count Robert de Montesquiou. 'In some ways', says George D. Painter, who identifies Montesquiou as the chief original of Charlus, 'this pseudo-poet and monster of vanity was the most extraordinary person [Proust] ever met.' A member of one of France's oldest noble families, Montesquiou (who was slim, unlike Charlus) had a country seat in the Hautes-Pyrénées and a bizarrely-decorated house in the Rue Franklin at Passy. He was a gifted raconteur, able to drop many impressive names in conversation; a technically adroit if banal versifier; and (says Painter) 'By far the most remarkable and original person in the empty milieu of the Faubourg Saint-Germain.' For years Proust flattered his influential friend, pandering to Montesquiou's arrogance by praising his writing. Though he had once slept with Sarah Bernhardt, Count Robert's main interest was in the attractive young men he employed as secretaries. When Montesquiou read Proust's novel he said 'Now people will call me Montesproust'.

CHARLES AND EDWIN CHEERYBLE

Charles Dickens, *Nicholas Nickleby* (1839)

William Grant (died 1842) **and Daniel Grant** (died 1855)

The Cheeryble brothers are self-made merchants of considerable wealth and generosity, exemplars of charity and benevolence, who are worthy and free-handed supporters of the Nicklebys, Madeline Bray and their nephew, Frank. They are quite unbelievable. The first Nicholas meets is Charles: 'A sturdy old fellow in a broad-skirted blue coat, made pretty large, to fit easily, and with no particular waist; his bulky legs clothed in drab breeches and high gaiters, and his head protected by a low-crowned broad-brimmed white hat, such as a wealthy grazier might wear. He wore his coat buttoned; and his dimpled double-chin rested in the folds of a white handkerchief – not one of your stiff-starched apoplectic cravats, but a good, easy, old fashioned white neckcloth that a man might go to bed in and be none the worse for . . . ' Edwin is his twin brother: 'Something stouter than his brother; this, and a slight additional shade of clumsiness in his gait and stature, formed the only perceptible difference between them.'

These are portraits of two remarkable brothers, William and Daniel Grant, who were merchants of Ramsbottom and Manchester. Dickens met them personally while he and John Forster were guests of Gilbert Winter at Stocks House, Cheetham Hill Road, Manchester in 1838. The qualities of charity and humanity which Dickens ascribes to the Cheerybles were exactly true of the Grant brothers. They were Scots from Elchies, formerly graziers in Scotland, who had failed as shopkeepers, but went on to become linen drapers and woollen dealers in Manchester. A marble tablet at St Andrews Presbyterian church, Ramsbottom, praises William Grant's 'vigour of understanding, his spotless integrity of character and his true benevolence of heart . . . If you are in poverty, grieve for the loss of so good a friend; if born to wealth and influence, think of the importance of such a trust, and earn in like manner by a life of charitable exertion the respect and love of all who know you, and the prayers and blessings of the poor.' Percy Fitzgerald wrote in *The Life of Charles Dickens as Revealed in his Writings* (1905): 'The novelist's father always held them out to him as a pattern to imitate. They were well known for their philanthropic character. A Liverpool merchant, who came to ask assistance at a crisis, was given £10,000 without any security.' The Grant brothers were identified as the originals of the Cheerybles by Frederick Kitton in his *The Dickens Country* (1905). It was estimated that William Grant gave away £600,000 in his lifetime.

COUNTESS OF CHELL

Arnold Bennett, *The Card* (1911)

Duchess of Sutherland (1851-1913)

Further reading: Margaret Drabble, *Arnold Bennett – A Biography* (1974)

One of Denry Machin's funniest exploits is to get himself invited, while still a humble solicitor's clerk, to the ball given by the Countess of Chell (see DENRY MACHIN). The Countess is known locally as 'Interfering Iris' for very good reasons; she is a local do-gooder and busybody.

Bennett based her on a local Hanley celebrity, the Duchess of Sutherland, known as 'Meddlesome Millie'. She took a great interest in affairs of the day, and was forever opening bazaars, church fetes, bring-and-buy sales and fund-raising functions for good causes. She spoke at school prize-givings, lectured on Benjamin Constant and infant mortality, lead poisoning in the pottery trade (a matter of considerable local interest in the pottery towns!) and expressed her concern at the widespread incidence of phthisis in the area and advocated the teaching of Gaelic. She had a finger in every pie and was involved in every fad and passing fashion.

Bennett was later to suffer the considerable personal embarrassment, perhaps well-deserved, of meeting the Duchess of Sutherland at a dinner in London. The identification of the Countess of Chell with the Duchess of Sutherland was well-established and the Lady herself was aware of it. She later returned to France and Arnold Bennett wrote to her there, saying he was: 'admiring, apologetic, and unrepentant'. She was a well-known eccentric and Frank Harris records an anecdote about her complaining in public that Queen Victoria's English syntax had been ruined by the German influence of her husband, and this unfortunate awkwardness rendered royal messages 'not being so pure as they used to be'. Arthur Balfour, to whom the complaint was made, bravely answered: 'I had nothing to do with it. . . . It doesn't matter much.' He was Prime Minister at the time.

LORD CHILTERN

Anthony Trollope, *Phineas Finn* (1869)

When Phineas goes to London and leaves Mary Flood Jones, he is soon deeply attracted by Lady Laura Standish, who is a very beautiful young woman who takes to him also. She has a brother, younger than her, Lord

Thomas Pitt, Second Baron Camelford (1775-1804)

Chiltern. These two are 'related to almost everybody who was anybody among the high Whigs'. When Phineas first notices him he sees: 'something in the countenance of the man which struck him almost with dread, something approaching ferocity'. Laura is very attached to her brother, saying that: 'he is not half so bad as people say he is. In many ways he is very good – very good. And he is very clever. . . . I think he loves me.' But Lord Chiltern is a violent character and drinks a great deal. He brings disgrace upon his family: 'He had fallen through his violence into some terrible misfortune at Paris, had been brought before a public judge, and his name and his infamy had been made notorious in every newspaper' in Paris and London. Chiltern grows very jealous of Finn's association with Violet Effingham, whom he had wooed without success, and he challenges Finn to a duel. It is fought in Belgium. Chiltern is killed. A radical newspaper publishes an account of the incident, attacking the principals, and commenting: 'There were old stories afloat . . . of what in a former century had been done by Lord Mohuns and Mr Bests; but now, in 186–', etc. Trollope's reference is clearly to Lord Camelford, and there are several important clues. The first is the reference to Mr Best. Camelford was shot and killed by Best in a duel of honour, fought over the reputation of one Fanny Loveden, in 1804. The second clue is the reference to Lord Mohun. Mohun was killed in a duel in 1712, and he was the last owner of Bocconnoc, which was later bought by Thomas Pitt, Lord Camelford's illustrious ancestor. Thomas Pitt, second Baron Camelford, had a notorious reputation for violence and eccentric behaviour. While in the navy he challenged his commander to a duel, and shot and killed a fellow officer in a dispute over seniority. Anthony Trollope may have got the story of Camelford from his sister, Anne Pitt, Lady Grenville, who died in 1864.

CHLOE

Alexander Pope, *On the Characters of Women* (1735)

Henrietta, Countess of Suffolk (1681-1767)

The story of Daphnis and Chloe is one of the most beloved of all pastoral romances. It is an ancient Greek tale of love. Two infants are discovered by Lamon and Dryas, who are shepherds of Mitylene. They are brought up to tend sheep and goats, and Daphnis and Chloe are constant and loyal companions whose virtue and affection serve as a model for all. It is eventually discovered that they are really the children of wealthy parents, and they are destined to live happily ever after.

Pope's treatment of this charming theme is somewhat mocking, as Chloe is presented as a shallow and cold young woman, who can neither really give nor receive love, as she totally lacks heart: 'She, while her lover pants upon her breast,/Can mark the figure on an Indian chest;/And when she sees her friend in deep despair,/Observes how much a chintz exceeds mohair. . . . Safe is your secret still in Chloe's ear;/But none of Chloc's shall you ever hear.'

This is Henrietta Howard, Countess of Suffolk, who was the mistress of George II. She was the daughter of Sir Henry Hobart, and married Charles Howard, who became the Ninth Earl of Suffolk, and they lived at Hanover. When George I came to England, she became woman-of-the-bedchamber to the Princess of Wales, and consequently came into contact with George II. Her house in Marble Hill, Twickenham, was the meeting place of the most distinguished company of the day, including Pope, Arbuthnot and Swift. She was a celebrated beauty and was admired by Charles, Third Earl of Peterborough (1658-1735) a patron of letters and science, general, diplomat and admiral. As mistress of George II she was much courted because of the power it was believed she wielded. She became Countess in 1731 and retired from court in 1734. In 1735 she married the Hon George Berkeley. This character, and that of Philomède (Henrietta, Duchess of Marlborough) were suppressed until later editions of the *Moral Essays*.

Further reading:
Horace Walpole, *Memoirs of the Reign of George II*, edited by Lord Holland (1846)

ANNA CHRISTIE

Eugene O'Neill's *Anna Christie* arranges, in an affirmative manner, the bits and pieces in the life of a so-called fallen woman. Anna, 'tall, blonde,

Eugene O'Neill, *Anna Christie* (1921)

Marie

Further reading: Arthur and Barbara Gelb, *O'Neill* (1962)
B. Clark, *Eugene O'Neill – The Man and His Plays* (1947)

fully-developed [and] handsome after a large, Viking-daughter fashion' turns up in New York in search of her father, Christopher Christopherson, captain of a coal barge. When he last saw Anna, fifteen years before, she was a child in Sweden and he is pleased she has been raised on a Minnesotan farm away from 'dat ole davil sea'. As the heroine explains, to Marthy Owen but not to her father, she has had an unfortunately eventful life. Seduced at the age of sixteen she ran away from the farm to find work as a nursemaid; subsequently she became a prostitute and, after a raid on the brothel, received a prison sentence. After she finds her father she renews her life on his barge and ends the play in the arms of Mat Burke, an Irish stoker.

The story is a dramatic version of the life of Marie, mistress of O'Neill's closest drinking-friend Terry Carlin (the original of Larry Slade in *The Iceman Cometh*). Marie was a nursemaid before she took to prostitution and was in despair when rescued and restored by Terry. After living with him she left to find herself in the hills of California and a letter she wrote provided O'Neill with the basis for Anna's sense of euphoria. 'I am intoxicated by all this beauty,' wrote Marie to Terry, 'and love the very air and earth . . . I feel newborn and free. The air is scented with balsam and bay, and a pure crystal stream flows through this valley between two hills covered with giant redwood trees . . . At night I sleep as I have never slept – a deep dreamless slumber. I awake to a cold plunge in the stream. Oh, it just suits me!. . . Everything in the past is dead. . . I have become happy, healthy, and free, free without hardness. . . I will now lave myself with the pure crystal waters and make myself clean again, and then look on the sun once more.'

CHRISTOPHER ROBIN

A. A. Milne, *When We Were Very Young* (1924), *Winnie the Pooh* (1926), *Now We Are Six* (1927), *The House at Pooh Corner* (1928)

Christopher Milne (born 1920)

Further reading: Christopher Milne, *The Enchanted Places* (1974)

The name Christopher Robin is immortalized in the poems A.A. Milne assembled in *When We Were Very Young* and its sequel *Now We Are Six*, and in the two books of prose that celebrate Christopher's adventures with 'a Bear of Very Little Brain' – *Winnie the Pooh* and *The House at Pooh Corner*. In 'Buckingham Palace' there is spectacle for 'They're changing guard at Buckingham Palace – /Christopher Robin went down with Alice', and in 'Vespers' there is pathos in 'Hush! Hush! Whisper who dares!/Christopher Robin is saying his prayers.'

Christopher Robin is Milne's son Christopher Robin Milne (1920-). In 1925 A.A. Milne bought Cotchford Farm, Sussex, which provided the setting for the Pooh books. Pooh was Christopher's teddy bear; Christopher would invent adventures for Pooh and his father would develop them as stories. The illustrator E.H. Shepard studied the teddy bear before making his first Pooh drawings. Shepard's drawings of Christopher Robin are an accurate portrayal of Christopher Milne as a boy, and in his autobiography *The Enchanted Places* (1974) Christopher explained his appearance: 'I suspect that, with my golden tresses, I reminded my mother of the girl she had always wanted to have. And I would have reminded my father of the boy with long, flaxen hair he once had been.' Later in life Christopher Milne resented the little-boy image associated with him and felt that 'Christopher Robin was . . . a sore place that looked as if it would never heal up.' Occasionally he thought his father 'had filched from me my good name and had left me with nothing but the empty fame of being his son'. However, he learned to live with the problem and in 1951 opened a bookshop in Dartmouth where he is still approached by visitors wishing to shake hands with the original Christopher Robin who still 'fills me with acute embarrassment'.

CHRYSOGANUS

John Marston, *Histriomastix* (1599)

Ben Jonson (1572-1637)

The title of this play, *Histriomastix*, means the scourging of the actors, and among the leading figures satirized in this production, in the person of Chrysoganus, is Ben Jonson. This public manifestation of ill-feeling between various playwrights and actors marks the beginnings of what came to be known as the 'War of the Theatres' or *Poetomachia*. It seems to last between the years 1599 and 1602, and particularly to concern Ben

Jonson, John Marston, Thomas Dekker and William Shakespeare (see HORACE, CRISPINUS, DEMETRIUS and VIRGIL). It may well have been a conflict between popular public theatres and the private theatres, which catered for a more sophisticated audience; but the strong feelings of personal animosity which come through in the satiric portraits of the various writers and actors must point to some serious rivalry. Jonson was not amused at Marston's portrait of himself in *Histriomastix* as a boring, boastful, pedantic windbag, and he parodied Marston in his plays *Every Man Out of his Humour* (1599) and *Cynthia's Revels* (1600). Here Jonson himself appears in the person of Asper, and answers the attacks of two young men about town – Hedon and Anaides – who are clearly John Marston and Thomas Dekker. These had accused Jonson of being: 'a bookworm, a candle-waster' who had devoted long years of study merely to accumulate no more learning 'than a schoolboy'. Dekker and Marston recognized themselves and began to co-operate on an answer, a play called *Satiromastix*, in which Jonson would be guyed once again (see HORACE), but Ben Jonson somehow heard rumours of their endeavours and struck first with yet another comic attack of their theatrical affectations – *Poetaster* – which was performed in 1601. During the height of the War of the Theatres Jonson figured in other satiric attacks – he appears as Brabant Senior in the anonymous comedy *Jack Drum's Entertainment* (1600). At one time the feeling between them was very strong. William Drummond (1585-1649) who knew Jonson quite well, recorded that: 'He had many quarrels with Marston, beat him, and took his pistol from him, wrote his *Poetaster* on him; the beginning of them were, that Marston represented him on the stage' (*Conversations With Drummond* (1711). Marston's portrait of Jonson, which he further developed in *Antonio and Mellida* (1600), seems in essence to have been just; most who knew Jonson personally agreed that he was a bragger, given to passionate friendships and enmity, and overzealous in scholarship.

Further reading:
Marchette Chute, *Ben Jonson of Westminster* (1978), A.F. Caputi, *John Marston Satirist* (1961)

BLESSED JEREMY CIBBER
Richard Aldington, *Stepping Heavenward* (1931)

T.S. Eliot (1888–1965)

Richard Aldington's satire *Stepping Heavenward* tells the story of the Blessed Jeremy Cibber, who is born and raised in the USA, comes and conquers the mind of England, and is beatified shortly after his death. Cibber discovers his destiny when he arrives in England: 'Jeremy knew that he had found his spiritual home. Here, in the ancient matrix of his race, he felt that the genius within him would be recognised, would be effective in a way impossible in a cruder and more turbulent land; and here the rewards offered to a noble life were worth winning.' Cibber later writes 'the first page and a half of his (unfinished) essay, "A Plea for Royalism in Western Europe," an exceedingly able paraphrase of [Charles] Maurras.' He also tries to cope with the 'acute personal problem of Miss Adèle Paleologue'. Cibber's unhappy marriage to Adèle, his meeting with the Pope, his decision to retire to a Roman monastery – all these events add to the reader's understanding of Cibber as a man devoted to his own piety. Although the Pope feels, on Cibber's death, that he cannot make a full saint of an American, he is pleased to pronounce the Beatification of Jeremy Cibber.

As Peter Ackroyd says, 'the publication of *Stepping Heavenward* hurt Eliot deeply ' since he recognized that the Blessed Jeremy Cibber was a satirical version of himself. Eliot's marriage to Vivien Haigh-Wood, in 1915, was a torment to him because of her mental problems. Nevertheless Eliot established himself as an outstanding poet and critic: *The Waste Land* (1922) was the key poetic text of modernism and the *Criterion*, edited by Eliot with assistance from Aldington, appealed to the elitist assumptions of many British intellectuals. Born in St Louis and associated with Boston, Massachusetts, Eliot identified himself with what he took to be quintessentially English qualities. On 29 June 1927 he was baptized and received into the Church of England and, in November of that year, became a British citizen. In 1928, in his volume of essays *For*

Further reading:
Peter Ackroyd, *T.S. Eliot* (1984)

Lancelot Andrewes, he declared himself a 'classicist in literature, royalist in politics, and anglo-catholic in religion'. Aldington admired Eliot but in *Life for Life's Sake* (1941) said he felt Eliot spent much time and energy during the First World War years 'laying the foundations of his future influence by cultivating the right people'.

EL CID

The Poem of the Cid (1140), Francois Du Pèrier, *La Hayne et l'Amour d'Arnoul et de Clairemonde* (1600), Guillen de Castro, *Los Mocedades del Cid* (1614), Pierre Cornielle, *Le Cid* (1636), film, *El Cid* written by Frederic M. Frank and Philip Yordan. Directed by Anthony Mann, starring Charlton Heston (1961)

Diaz de Bivar (died 1099)

Further reading: H. Butler Clarke, *The Cid Campeador* (1897)

The *Poema del Cid*, the national epic of Spain, presents the ideal Castilian warrior – shrewd, but generous; honourable, brave, ruthless, and not above a little cheating and swindling. He is pious, sentimental, and, in victory, magnanimous; yet, at the same time, boastful and scornful of weakness in others. The poem narrates the hero's gradual ascent from banishment and disgrace (the result of the intrigues of Count Garcia Ordonez) to wealth and position through conquest. He avenges all the wrongs done to him and his family. Among the most outstanding exploits described is his taking of the city of Valencia and making himself 'king' of the city, where his daughters are married to the young princes of the King of Lèon and Castille. El Cid exposes the princes' cowardice and in revenge they inflict dreadful treachery upon the two young ladies. El Cid demands that the king have them tried and punished. The king yields and the hero's family honour is restored when his daughters are married to the rulers of Navarre and Aragon: 'Great is the rejoicing in noble Valencia at the honour achieved by those of the Campeador. Ruy Diaz, their lord, grasps his beard and says, "I thank God, the King of Heaven, that my daughters are now avenged... I can give their hands in marriage, without shame!". . . and Dona Elvira and Dona Sol are wed again. Great as their first wedding feast had been, but this was far greater. See how his honour increases, he who was born in a happy hour, for the Kings of Spain are now among his kinsmen. My Cid, lord of Valencia, passed from this life on the Day of Pentecost . . .'

As the Canon in *Don Quixote* says: 'There is no doubt there was such a man as the Cid, but much doubt whether he did what is attributed to him.' Rodrigo Diaz, called de Bivar after his birthplace, was born of a noble family, about 1040. The Arabs named him El Seid, the lord. He served in the war between Castille and Navarre, and earned the name Campeador (Champion) by slaying the enemy king's champion in single combat. His greatest exploit was the capture of Valencia in 1065, the richest prize recovered from the Moors. He died after being defeated at Cuenca in July 1099.

LADY CIRCUMFERENCE

Evelyn Waugh, *Decline and Fall* (1928)

Jessie Graham (died 1928)

Further reading: *Evelyn Waugh Diaries* edited by Michael Davie (1976), *Evelyn Waugh Letters* edited by Mark Amory (1980)

As their son is a pupil at Llanabba Castle, Lord and Lady Circumference are distinguished guests at the school's sportsday. She is described as: 'A stout elderly woman dressed in a tweed coat and skirt and jaunty Tyrolean hat.' She advances on Dr Fagan, the headmaster, and harangues him in a deep voice: 'How are you? Sorry if we're late. Circumference ran over a fool of a boy. I've just been chaffing your daughter about her frock. Wish I was young enough to wear that kind of thing. Older I get the more I like colour. We're both pretty long in the tooth, eh?' When told her son is doing quite well she retorts: 'Nonsense! The boy's a dunderhead. If he wasn't he wouldn't be here. He wants beatin' and hittin' and knockin' about generally, and then he'll be no good.' Her attention suddenly turns to the school grounds: 'The grass is shockin' bad on the terrace, Doctor; you ought to sand it down and re-sow it . . .'

This formidable lady is based on Jessie Graham, the mother of Waugh's close friend Alastair Graham. She was, according to Waugh: 'high-tempered, possessive, jolly and erratic.' She was the daughter of a Scot, Andrew Low, who emigrated to the USA and made a cotton fortune in Georgia. Her brother William inherited £750,000, and was a friend of Rosa Lewis of the Cavendish Hotel. William was Alastair Graham's uncle, and it was through him that Waugh was introduced to the Cavendish set (see LOTTIE CRUMP). Waugh was a frequent guest at

Barford House, the Grahams' home near Warwick, and in fact he wrote much of *Decline and Fall* while staying there. His diaries are full of accounts of Mrs Graham's wayward behaviour and changing moods. In 1927 he noted a scene which might come from the pages of *Decline and Fall:* 'As usual Barford is in a ferment of reorganization – a lodge being torn down, and pond dug, two gardeners threatening to cut each other's throats and being placated by the construction of an earth-closet . . . the cook ruptured, a housemaid in bed with an ulcer, Mrs G. full of port roaring about directing everything.' She was very put out when her son went to Africa: 'Mrs Graham stands like some baffled archangel beating in the void her voluminous wings while anger fills the room up of her absent son' (Waugh's diary, 9 November 1924). On 25 August 1926 he recorded a car trip with the Grahams: 'Mrs G. was in a furious rage all the time . . . and was intolerably rude not only to Alastair who provoked her but to me who did not . . . It ended with my resolving heartily never to visit her again.' But he did and recorded further characteristically tense scenes.

CLARENCE, EARL OF EMSWORTH

P.G. Wodehouse, *Summer Lightning* (1929), *Blandings Castle* (1935), *A Pelican at Blandings* (1969), etc

Spencer Compton Cavendish, Marquess of Hartington and Eighth Duke of Devonshire (1833–1908)

Lord Emsworth, leading character in the Blandings Castle stories of P.G. Wodehouse, and proud owner of the Empress of Blandings – the greatest prize pig in English fiction, has many interesting parallels with the Eighth Duke of Devonshire.

He was the eldest son of the Seventh Duke of Devonshire and was awarded his MA at Cambridge in 1854. Three years later he was elected Liberal MP for North Lancashire. He travelled to the United States, where he met President Lincoln and held various government positions including Under Secretary at the War Office, Postmaster General, Chief Secretary for Ireland, Secretary of State for India, and with Joseph Chamberlain he founded the Liberal-Unionist party. He served under Gladstone, Lord Russell and Lord Salisbury and three times rejected the premiership himself. He was, in turn, MP for North Lancashire, the Radnor boroughs, North-East Lancashire and Rossdale. When Victoria congratulated him on his appointment as Minister for War he replied that there would not be much for him to do, and the Queen noted in her diary on 6 May 1885 that he was 'rather amusing about Britain's friendlessness'. He presided over the Cabinet when the decision was made to send Gordon to Khartoum. Chamberlain called him 'Rip Van Winkle'. He was a keen sportsman, generous landlord and public-spirited benefactor. He entertained King Edward VII frequently, though on one occasion he invited him to dinner and then forgot and went out to dine at the Turf Club. The King arrived at Devonshire House to find his host absent. Devonshire was also known to walk past his Cabinet colleagues so absent-mindedly that he did not seem to recognize them. When made Grand Commander of the Victorian Order he complained that the award would 'only complicate his dressing'. He was late for Edward VII's coronation. He genuinely preferred baggy old clothes and casuals to formal attire, notoriously neglected his guests and avoided 'bores'. Once when a fellow peer was going on in the Chamber about 'the greatest moment in his life', Devonshire opined: 'My greatest moment was when my pig won first prize at Skipton Fair.' Was this a reference to the Empress of Blandings?

Further reading:
Benny Green, *P.G. Wodehouse – A Literary Biography* (1979)

DARIUS CLAYHANGER

Arnold Bennett, *Clayhanger* (1910)

Enoch Bennett (1843–1902)

Clayhanger, the first novel in a trilogy completed by *Hilda Lessways* (1911) and *These Twain* (1915), contains a father-and-son conflict as Edwin Clayhanger, on leaving school at sixteen in 1872, tells his father Darius he does not want to enter the family printing business in Bursley (actually Burslem, one of the Five Towns of Arnold Bennett's childhood). Despite Edwin's wish to become an architect, Darius pressurizes him into the family business, and so the son lives in the shadow cast by his formidable father, a self-made man who worked at the age of seven in the potbanks, was rescued from the poorhouse by a

Further reading: Margaret Drabble, *Arnold Bennett* (1974)

Sunday School teacher, and rose to become Bursley's leading printer. Eventually Darius goes into a physical decline that ends with his death: 'It seemed intolerably tragic that the enfeebled wreck should have had to bear so much, and yet intolerably tragic also that death should have relieved him. But Edwin's distress was shot through and enlightened by his solemn satisfaction at the fact that destiny had alloted to him, Edwin, an experience of such profound and overwhelming grandeur. His father was, and lo! he was not. That was all, but it was ineffable.'

Bennett based the character of Darius Clayhanger on his father, Enoch Bennett, who left school at the age of twelve to become a potter. After two years working at the potbanks, Enoch Bennett went back to school as an apprentice pupil teacher, then returned to the potbanks and became a master potter with a partnership in the Eagle Pottery. When the business failed he set up as a pawnbroker and draper in a house in Hope Street, Burslem, where Bennett was born on 27 May 1867. Until 1870, when he inherited some money on the death of his father John, Enoch Bennett lived in considerable poverty. With his legacy he trained as a solicitor and qualified in 1876. Enoch Bennett was determined that his eldest son, Arnold, should also pursue a legal career, and took him into his office in Hanley. It required considerable strength of character for Bennett to break away from his father's influence and move to London where he abandoned the law for literature. As Margaret Drabble says, Enoch 'refused to consider that Arnold was not suited for a career in law, just as Darius Clayhanger refused to consider Edwin's desire to be an architect'. Enoch Bennett eventually died a slow lingering death, from cerebral arterio-sclerosis, in Arnold's home at Trinity Hall Farm, Hockliffe, Bedfordshire: the patriarch was eventually dependent on his successful literary son.

CAPTAIN CLEVELAND

Sir Walter Scott, *The Pirate* (1821)

John Gow (died 1725)

After the publication of his first novel *Waverley* (1814), Walter Scott went on a cruise with the Northern Lighthouse Commissioners, in the company of their Surveyor-Viceroy Robert Stevenson, grandfather of Robert Louis Stevenson. On 17 August 1814, Scott visited Stromness, in Orkney, and recorded the details of a visit to an 'old hag [who] subsists by selling winds . . . She told us she remembered *Gow the pirate*, who was born near the House of Clestrom and afterwards commenced buccanier.' Gow was born in Caithness and raised in Stromness, where his father was a respectable merchant. As Gow was an intelligent, personable youth, Captain Oliver Ferneau of the galley *Caroline* made him his second mate. On 5 November 1724, while the *Caroline* was sailing from Santa Cruz to Genoa, Gow – who had been entrusted with the ship's firearms – led a mutiny and murdered Captain Ferneau. He then renamed the galley *Revenge* and embarked on a career of piracy. Returning to Stromness, Gow visited the home of a Stromness merchant and fell in love with his daughter Katherine. In traditional Orkney style, Gow and Katherine made a love-pact at the Stone of Odin, five miles from Stromness. Shortly after this, Gow was captured and taken to London where he was hanged twice at Execution Dock, as the rope snapped after four minutes at the first attempt. As Scott recorded, in his *Journal*, Katherine went to London to shake hands with the corpse in order to dissolve her engagement to the pirate, since they had first pledged their faith by shaking hands at the Stone of Odin.

From the details supplied to him orally by the 'old hag' (Bessy Millie, who appears as Norna in the novel), Scott shaped his romantic version of *The Pirate*. In Scott's tale Gow is Captain Clement Cleveland: 'He was rather above the middle size, and formed handsomely as well as strongly [having] the frank and open manners of a sailor.' His vitality impresses Minna Troil and when (unlike Gow) Cleveland is spared the death sentence and dies 'leading the way in a gallant and honourable enterprise' Minna rejoices that 'the death of Cleveland had been in the bed of honour'. Indeed Scott's pirate is eventually transformed by 'new-born virtue'. Scott was not alone in finding the story fascinating: Daniel Defoe wrote an account of Gow's trial and execution and George Mackay Brown included two stories about Gow ('Perilous Seas' and 'The Pirate's Ghost') in his collection *The Sun's Net* (1976).

COCK-ROBIN

Nursery rhyme, *Who Killed Cock Robin?* (circa 1744)

Sir Robert Walpole (1676-1745)

Further reading: Iona and Peter Opie, *The Oxford Dictionary of Nursery Rhymes* (1977), J.H. Plumb, *Life of Sir Robert Walpole* (1956–61)

'Who killed Cock Robin?/I, said the Sparrow,/With my bow and arrow, I killed Cock Robin./Who saw him die?/I, said the Fly,/With my little eye,/I saw him die./Who caught his blood?/ I, said the Fish,/With my little dish,/I caught his blood. . .' This is one of the most celebrated and widely known of British nursery rhymes. It ends: 'Who'll toll the bell?/I, said the Bull,/Because I can pull,/I'll toll the bell./All the birds of the air/Fell a-sighing and a-sobbing,/ When they heard the bell toll/For poor Cock Robin.' These verses are similar in style and construction to several widely known European rhymes, and may go back as far Old Norse rhymes about the death of Baldur. The story of the rhyme is shown in the stained glass window at Buckland Rectory, Gloucester (fifteenth century) and is similar to Skelton's *Phyllyp Sparowe* (circa 1508). But the sudden popularity of the verses in the early 1740s points to the clear association with Sir Robert Walpole, leader of the Whig party and prime minister in all but name, until his dramatic fall from office in 1742. He was known as Robin, and was much satirized at the time. He is referred to as 'Bob Booty' and 'Robin of Bagshot' in *The Beggar's Opera* (1727), and appears as the protagonist in Fielding's *Jonathan Wild* (see JONATHAN WILD). He was born at Houghton in Norfolk (see TIMON'S VILLA) and entered parliament in 1701, holding several government offices before being brought to power by the financial crisis of the South Sea Bubble in 1720, and by the fact that his major rivals were discredited by Jacobite intrigue. He maintained tight control over the Commons by bribery, and dominated the political establishment by the astute awarding of public offices and sinecures. Swift wrote of him: 'Achieving of nothing – still promising wonders – /By dint of experience improving in blunders./Oppressing true merit, exalting the base,/And selling his country to purchase his place,/A jobber of stocks by retailing false news – /A prater at court in the style of the stews:/Of virtue and worth by profession a giber,/Of juries and senates the bully and briber.' In spite of such opposition he maintained himself in office until the crisis with Spain in 1739, and was finally driven to resign in 1742. George II wept. A special committee was set up to investigate alleged misdemeanours during his administration, but corruption was never proved. The rhyme celebrates his spectacular fall from office (see ORGILIO).

HARRY CONINGSBY

Benjamin Disraeli, *Coningsby* (1844)

George Augustus Frederick Percy Sydney Smythe, Seventh Viscount Strangford and Second Baron Penshurst (1818–57)

Further reading: B.R. Jerman, *The Young Disraeli* (1961)

Harry Coningsby is the young hero whose life story holds together the various threads of interest in *Coningsby* – Disraeli's belief in the social duties and responsibilities of the aristocracy, the need to return to the chivalrous values of the past, the empty nature of Peelite Conservatism and the evils of the factory system. Harry stands for the ideals of the young generation. The name 'Coningsby' was probably suggested to Disraeli by his reading of Sir Philip Sidney. Sidney was a central influence in Disraeli's thinking. Sir Thomas Coningsby was a companion of Sidney's.

Harry Coningsby's countenance is described as: 'radiant with health and the lustre of innocence. . . . The expression of his deep blue eyes was serious . . . the face was one that would never have passed unobserved. His short upper lip indicated a good breed; and his chestnut curls clustered over his open brow.' We follow his career through Eton and Cambridge, his marriage with Edith, daughter of Oswald Millbank, a rich manufacturer, the disinheritance by his aristocratic grandfather, Lord Monmouth (see LORD MONMOUTH), and a career in the law. He is finally elected an MP at Darlford, Millbank's constituency. We are told the exact date of Coningsby's birth, 1818, the year Lord Strangford was born. There is also the important link with the Sidneys of Penshurst.

Strangford went to Eton and St John's College, Cambridge, and wrote promising verse. He was an MA *jure natalium* in 1840, and MP for Canterbury and a leading member of Disraeli's Young England party. He supported Peel in the Corn Law issue and broke with Disraeli, who remained a protectionist, but this was after *Coningsby* was published. His wife said of him: 'He loved to recall the grandeur of the ancient nobility . . . to sing the days of chivalry . . . and together with his friend, Lord John Manners, he dreamed of a powerful aristocracy and an almsgiving church.' Young England personified.

CONRAD

Lord Byron, *The Corsair* (1814)

Jean Lafitte (1780–1826)

Further reading: C. Gayarré, *Pierre and Jean Lafitte*, in *Magazine of American History* Volume X (1883), G. Cusacks, *Lafitte – The Pirate and the Patriot* in *Louisiana Historical Quarterly* Volume II (1919)

Conrad is the pirate chief hero of Byron's poem. In a note to the 1815 edition the poet admitted that he had in mind Jean Lafitte, the French privateer, whose notorious exploits against the British and Spanish would have been daily reading in contemporary newspapers. There are strong parallels between Lafitte's devil-may-care character and the Byronic hero – 'there was a laughing Devil in his sneer' – as well as similarities in the pirate colony of Barataria run by Lafitte, and Conrad's pirate community on the Aegean island described by Byron.

Conrad has only one virtue – chivalry – but many vices. He learns that Seyd, the Turkish Pasha, is preparing to attack his Aegean community, and resolves to strike the first blow. Disguised as a Dervish, and having bidden farewell to his beloved Medora, he gains access to Seyd by claiming that he himself has recently escaped the pirates. His plot misfires as Conrad's men prematurely fire on the Pasha's ships. Conrad is wounded and captured but helped by Gulnare, the Pasha's leading slave-girl, who stabs Seyd in his sleep. The two then escape although Conrad is repulsed by Gulnare's violent act. He returns to his pirate island to find that Medora had died of grief, believing him slain. Conrad's adventures are continued in the sequel (see LARA).

Lafitte's early career is obscure until his exploits around New Orleans made him famous during the war of 1812. He and his privateers lived in a pirate colony on the Baratarian Gulf, off the coast of Louisiana. They earned their living by preying on Spanish and other vessels and trading in New Orleans. Efforts to destroy them failed, including one mounted by the US Navy commanded by Commodore Patterson. The Baratarian Gulf was strategically important in giving access to New Orleans and in 1814 the British offered Laffite £30,000 and a commission in the Royal Navy to cooperate against the US. Lafitte handed over these papers to the US authorities in exchange for a general pardon. His offer of help against the British was accepted by Andrew Jackson and the privateers played a significant part in the defeat of the British. Their pardon was proclaimed by President Madison He continued to operate from a base in Texas until the US government was pursuaded to act against him. He then left with his best ship the *Pride*.

HUNT CONROY

Thomas Wolfe, *You Can't Go Home Again* (1940)

F. Scott Fitzgerald (1896–1940)

Further reading: Matthew J. Brucolli, *Some Sort of Epic Grandeur: The Life of F. Scott Fitzgerald* (1981)

Towards the end of Thomas Wolfe's novel *You Can't go Home Again*, the autobiographical hero George Webber writes a long letter to his friend and editor Foxhall Edwards (based on the celebrated Scribner's editor Maxwell Perkins) and disassociates himself from one of Edward's writers: 'You have a friend, Fox, named Hunt Conroy. You introduced me to him. He is only a few years my senior, but he is very fixed in his assertion of what he calls "The Lost Generation" – a generation of which, as you know, he has been quite vociferously a member, and in which he has tried enthusiastically to include me. Hunt and I used to argue about it. . . If Hunt *wants* to belong to "The Lost Generation" – and it really is astonishing with what fond eagerness some people hug the ghost of desolation to their breast – that's *his* affair. But he can't have me.'

A decade before the publication of Wolfe's first novel *Look Homeward, Angel* (1929) by Scribner's, Maxwell Perkins had persuaded Scribner's to accept F. Scott Fitzgerald's first novel *This Side of Paradise*

(1920). Though Fitzgerald was a fastidious man with an exquisite prose style and Wolfe was (as he told Fitzgerald in a letter of 26 July 1937) a 'putter-inner' rather than a 'taker-outer', Perkins felt his two authors had a bond in common. 'In some occult way', Perkins wrote to Fitzgerald, 'the appearance of [Wolfe's] manuscript here, and of himself, recalled to me your apparition eight or nine years ago. It is because of the extraordinary wealth and variety of talent.'

Perkins brought the two men into contact with each other and in June 1930 they met in Paris. By this time Fitzgerald felt he was a fading star – burdened by alcoholism and his wife's schizophrenic illness – while Wolfe was the great new figure in the American literary landscape. Like Fitzgerald, Wolfe was a heavy drinker, but he disliked his colleagues' concern with the lives of the rich and his obsession with his self-destructive weaknesses. He also felt inhibited by Fitzgerald's essential elegance. 'When I am with someone like Scott', Wolfe wrote to Perkins after the first Paris meeting, 'I feel that I am morose and sullen – and violent in my speech and movement part of the time. Later, I feel that I have repelled them.' Wolfe also found the notion of a 'Lost Generation' defeatist and decadent, preferring his own vision of American vitality.

GENNARO CONTI

Honoré de Balzac, *Béatrix* (1839)

Franz Liszt (1811–86)

Further reading:
Ernest Newman, *The Man Liszt* (1934)

Béatrix concerns the rivalry between the authoress, Camille Maupin, and the society blue-stocking, Beatrice de Rochefide, for the love of the Italian tenor, Gennaro Conti (see CAMILLE MAUPIN and BEATRICE DE ROCHEFIDE). By dint of her fashion, style and glamour, Beatrice wins Conti's affections, and Camille retires to a convent. In this novel Balzac is recounting the triangle which existed between George Sand, Maria d'Agoult and the composer and virtuoso pianist, Franz Liszt. Balzac transfers Liszt's musicianly and performing-star qualities from keyboard-performer to Italian tenor. Beatrice leaves her husband and children for Gennaro and they travel in Europe together, enjoying a passionate love affair in which Beatrice positively luxuriates. But love wanes and Gennaro forsakes her. This sad and cautionary satire on the world of fashion and artistic circles is seen through the eyes of Beatrice's rival, Camille. The risk-taking, demonic and enchanting qualities of Liszt's character are well portrayed in Gennaro. When Madame Hanska (1801-82) found herself attracted by Liszt, she reminded him of his past amorous escapades, particularly that with Madame d'Agoult. He replied: 'Have no fear. I have learned reason. This time . . . I shall take her husband too.' Eveline Hanska wrote in her diary: 'Liszt is of average height . . . His nose is straight . . . but the best thing about him is the shape of his mouth; there is something particularly sweet . . . seraphic, about that mouth . . . There are sublime things in him, but also deplorable ones. He is the human reflection of what is splendid in Nature – but also, alas, of what is terrible. There are sublime heights, but bottomless depths and abysses. . .' Liszt was a child prodigy, but when he heard Paganini play in 1831 he resolved to become the Paganini of the piano. He conquered Paris with his performances and was at the height of his powers between 1838 and 1848. He played throughout Europe. He retired to Weimar in 1849 to direct operas and concerts. He premiered Wagner's *Lohengrin* and Berlioz's *Benvenuto Cellini*. He later conducted at Budapest and Rome. In 1865 he received minor orders and was known as Abbé Liszt. He visited London in 1886 and was fêted. His amorous proclivities were phenomenal. By Madame d'Agoult he had three children, one of whom (Cosima, who married the German conductor Hans von Bülow) married Wagner. Liszt lived with Princess Carolyn zu Sayn-Wittgenstein from 1847 until his death. His influence as performer, teacher and composer has been considerable.

HAMISH CORBIE

John Davenport and Dylan Thomas, *The Death of the*

In *The Death of the King's Canary*, which John Davenport and Dylan Thomas wrote in 1940, the newly appointed Poet laureate, Hilary Byrd, holds a spectacular 'Laureate-Warming Party' at Dymmock Hall, Suf-

King's Canary (1976)

Aleister Crowley
(1875–1947)

folk. Planning the evening as a shock to the senses of his guests, Byrd invites various personalities including Hamish Corbie, who arrives with a 'long, black, coffin-like box' and drags his funereal luggage behind him: 'He wore a suit of yellow, check plus-fours, green woollen socks, and sandals.' Corbie, a self-styled magician and man of 'obscene bulk', is vividly described at the banquet: 'There was the noise of a man coming out of a pit; a wrenching and scraping, a rattle of chains in the throat: and Hamish Corbie, silent as the grave for two hours, released, slowly, the dust-dry torments of his profound and uneviable wisdom. "Man Aga Mem by the Seven Dams of Sheba's Toad", he cried. "In the thirteenth genital layer of the Sphinx a navel speaks through a priest dipped in nightshade. Logos Six Am. By Horus's last star. Yo, Yo", making a cross of his arms. Everyone at the table stopped quarrelling and stared at the Black Master. Ancient blessings and curses poured from his lips. He clapped his huge hands in a forgotten rhythm, and brought out a glass ball from his pocket. He looked like an absconding bank manager.'

Corbie (Scots for crow) is a caricature of the Scottish Satanist Aleister Crowley (also the original of Oliver Haddo in Somerset Maugham's *The Magician*). Calling himself the Great Beast or 666 or Lord Boleskine, Crowley convinced several members of the London literati that he had occult powers. By 1937 he was – according to Constantine FitzGibbon's *The Life of Dylan Thomas* (1965) – 'a gross old man in a kilt sponging drinks and babbling drivel about pentagrams and elementals'. Though Dylan Thomas realized that Crowley was a charlatan, he also had a terror of the supernatural. Around 1941 (that is, after the composition of the Davenport/Thomas satire) Thomas was drinking in the Swiss Pub in London, with FitzGibbon's wife Theodora. In an apprehensive mood, because Crowley was lurking at the far end of the pub, Thomas started doodling. Crowley walked over to the poet and placed in front of him a duplicate of his doodle. According to FitzGibbon, 'Dylan was extremely frightened. He insisted that Theodora and he leave the pub immediately, without waiting for the man they were supposed to meet.'

JONAS CORD

Harold Robbins, *The Carpetbaggers* (1961), film, *The Carpetbaggers* (1964), written by John Michael Hayes, starring George Peppard

Howard Hughes
(1905–76)

Further reading: Michael Drosnin, *Citizen Hughes* (1985)

The theme of *The Carpetbaggers* is the price paid for worldly success, and the sacrifice of love for ambition and power. Jonas Cord is a young playboy who inherits an aircraft business and develops into a megalomaniac and giant of industry, finally attempting to move into the Hollywood film industry in his search for even more worldly power. The search for ultimate power is ultimately self-destructure. Jonas Cord is based on Howard Hughes. He was born in Houston, Texas, and at the age of eighteen inherited the Hughes Tool Company, which made oil-drilling equipment. Within two years he was investing some of his profits in Hollywood films. Among the films he produced were *Two Arabian Knights*, *The Front Page* and *Scarface* (see TONY CAMONTE). His most celebrated film was *Hell's Angels*, which he co-produced, and which launched the career of Jean Harlow. He had a reputation as a Casanova, and among his conquests are reputedly Ava Gardner, Lana Turner, Ginger Rogers and Katharine Hepburn. He wanted to branch out into aircraft design and under an assumed name (Charles Howard) he took a job as a co-pilot with American Airways. In two months he had learned from the inside what he wanted to know, and by 1935 was flying machines of his own design. In 1936 he broke the transcontinental speed record, and broke it again the following year. In 1938 he flew round the world in ninety-one hours, earning a ticker-tape welcome in New York and Congressional medal in Washington. He produced and directed *The Outlaw* (1943), which made Jane Russell's uplift famous. He continued to experiment in aircraft design throughout the war, his unsuccessful Hercules seaplane earning valuable technical insight for future developments. He suffered severe injuries when he crashed his own photo-reconnaissance plane in 1946. In later years he became a recluse, still interested in the film business to the extent of having a controlling interest in RKO studios, which he sold for $10 million profit. He sold his holdings in TWA for over half a billion dollars in 1966. When he died he held a vast empire including Hughes Tool, Hughes Aircraft, Hughes Medical Institute, hotels, casinos and much land in Las Vegas, as well as interests in airlines and TV stations. In 1966 he cut himself off from the world in his exclusive penthouse suite in the Desert Inn Hotel, Las Vegas, cared for by five male Mormon nurses.

VITTORIA COROMBONA

John Webster, *The White Divel* (1608)

Vittoria Accoramboni (1557–85)

Further reading: Countess E. Martinengo-Cesaresco, *Lombard Studies* (1902), Gunnar Boklund, *The Sources of 'The White Divel'* (1957)

Webster's tragedy, *The White Divel*, is a wild, thrilling and rhetorical drama of adultery, murder, bloodshed and betrayal, which has the sound and fury of early Verdi opera. The Duke of Brachiano is married to Isabella, who is the sister of the Duke of Florence. He is tired of her and lusts after Vittoria who is already married to Camillo. Vittoria's brother, Flamineo, helps Brachiano in his sister's seduction, and assists in the killing of her husband, Camillo. In the meantime, Brachiano gets Isabella poisoned. Vittoria is accused of adultery and murder and sentenced to be confined. Her escape is effected and she is married to Brachiano. Flamineo and his brother, the virtuous young Marcello, quarrel, and Flamineo kills him. Isabella's brother, the Duke of Florence, avenges the death of his sister by poisoning Brachiano. Lodovico and Gasparo, dependants of the Duke of Florence, finally kill Vittoria and Flamineo. A significant aspect of the play's great fascination is Webster's exploitation of the tension which exists between the heroine's fair-seeming exterior and the black wickedness of which she is the centre. Monticelso, the cardinal, at her trial says: 'You see, my lords, what goodly fruits she seems;/Yet like those apples travellers report/To grow where Sodom and Gomorrah stood,/I will but touch her, and you straight shall see/She'll fall to soot and ashes.'

The real Vittoria Accoramboni was also famous for her great beauty and the violence and tragedy of her life. She was born in Rome and married Francesco Peretti in 1573. He was the nephew of Cardinal Montalto, who was expected to become Pope. She was admired by many men, in particular by Orsini, Duke of Bracciano. Her brother Marcello, hoping to see his sister married to Bracciano, had Peretti murdered in 1581. Bracciano and Vittoria were then married. Orsini was already suspected of murdering Vittoria's husband, as his name was associated in the murder of his first wife, Isabella de Medici. Vittoria was imprisoned and there was pressure to have the marriage annulled. In 1585 Cardinal Montalto became Pope and was determined to have vengeance on Bracciano and Vittoria for the death of Francesco Peretti, his nephew. They fled to Salo, where Bracciano died. Here Vittoria was put to death in December 1585 by Lodovico Orsini, a relation of Bracciano, who hoped to gain from the division of the property. This terrible story was also used by Ludwig Tieck in his novel *Vittoria Accoramboni* (1840).

RICHARD CRAUFORD

Edward Bulwer Lytton, *The Disowned* (1828)

Henry Fauntleroy (1785–1824)

Further reading: *The New Newgate Calendar*, edited with an Introduction by Lord Birkett (1960)

Bulwer Lytton's splendid melodrama *The Disowned* is, on the surface at least, the story of the young hero – Clinton L'Estrange – who is rejected by his father, Lord Ulswater. Ulswater believes that the boy is not really his son. In the end, father and son are reconciled, and Clinton's legitimacy established. But the most fascinating character in the book is the villain, Richard Crauford, swindler, forger and master of disguise. He nearly escapes justice and flees to Paris, under the successfully assumed identity of the Revd Dr Stapyton. Immediately before his arrest we find him at an inn in Dover, eating and drinking like a true *gourmand*, unconscious of the fact that the detective is on his tail. 'A pleasant trip to France!' he cries, filling a bumper, 'That's the land for hearts like ours . . . we will leave our wives behind us, and take, with a new country, and new names, a new lease of life. What will it signify to men making love at Paris what fools say of them in London? Another bumper . . . a bumper to the girls!' But, his triumphs are over: 'On the very day on which the patent for his peerage was to have been made out – on the very day on which he had afterwards calculated on reaching Paris – on that very day was Mr Richard Crauford lodged in Newgate, fully committed for a trial of life and death.' He is brilliant at his trial, having become a figure of public admiration and fame, he fully exploits these qualities. And the whole audience dissolve into tears. It is to no avail, he is sentenced to death and executed.

Crauford is based on the banker and forger Henry Fauntleroy. He was a partner in his father's bank. Marsh, Sibbald and Company in London, from 1807 until his arrest in 1824. He was accused of fraudulently selling stock in 1820 and for forging the trustees' signatures to a power of attorney. He defended his actions by claiming they were motivated by his desire to maintain the credit of the banking house. Many petitions were signed to gain him clemency, but Fauntleroy was executed in 1824.

REVD JOSIAH CRAWLEY

Anthony Trollope, *Framley Parsonage* (1861), *The Last Chronicle of Barset* (1867)

Thomas Anthony Trollope (1774–1835)

Further reading: Lucy Poate Stebbins and Richard Poate Stebbins, *The Trollopes – The Chronicle of a Writing Family* (1946)

The Revd Josiah Crawley makes his first appearance in Trollope's *Framley Parsonage*. He is the curate of Hogglestock, and a man burdened by failure and tribulation which combine to make him wretched, though he is acknowledged to be a pious and excellent clergyman: 'A man known by all who knew anything of him to be very poor, – an unhappy, moody, disappointed man, upon whom the troubles of the world aways seemed to come with a double weight. But he had ever been a respected clergyman, since his old friend Mr Arabin, the dean of Barchester, had given him the small incumbency which he now held. Though moody, unhappy, and disappointed, he was a hard-working, conscientious pastor among the poor people with whom his lot was cast; for in the parish . . . there resided only a few farmers higher in degree than field labourers, brickmakers, and such like . . . he had worked very hard to do his duty, struggling to teach the people around him perhaps too much of the mystery, but something also of the comfort, of religion. That he had become popular in his parish cannot be said of him. He was not a man to make himself popular in any position. I have said that he was moody and disappointed. He was even worse than this; he was morose, sometimes almost to insanity. There had been days in which even his wife found it impossible to deal with him otherwise than as with an acknowledged lunatic . . . the farmers . . . talked about their clergyman among themselves as though he were a madman. But among the very poor . . . he was held in high respect; for they knew that he lived hardly, as they lived; that he worked hard, as they worked; and that the outside world was hard to him, as it was to them...' Crawley is wrongfully accused of misappropriating a check [cheque] for £20, which he cashes to pay his bills. He claims it was in payment for his stipend, then that it was a gift from Dean Arabin. He is brought before the magistrates. He is persecuted particularly by Bishop Proudie's wife and is eventually deprived of his incumbency. His innocence is finally established and he is appointed to the living at St Ewold's. This is a portrait of the novelist's father, a hard working, though unsuccessful, barrister, who was a moody and somewhat tyrannical figure (see PLANTAGENET PALLISER, and ORLEY FARM).

CRISPINUS

Ben Jonson, *Poetaster* (1601)

John Marston (1576–1634)

In *Poetaster* Ben Jonson transfers the rivalries of the so-called War of the Theatres which raged between 1599 and 1602 (see CHRYSOGANUS, HORACE, VIRGIL and DEMETRIUS) to the golden age of Roman literature, the age of the Emperor Augustus. In his attempt to deal with his rivals, Ben Jonson portrays himself in the role of the great Horace. Crispinus is one of those who conspire against him, and who – after the matter has been brought before the Emperor for judgement – is sentenced to endure a light vomit, which will rid him of the long words which he is wont to use. His crime is that he practised as a 'poetaster and plagiary', and his punishment will purge him of these follies. This is a portrait of Jonson's opponent, John Marston. Jonson particularly disapproved of Marston's coarse, vigorous, cynical and strongly melancholy satiric style, which, he thought, was unharmonious, harsh and scathing. Marston confessed that his aim was to use: '. . . sharp mustard rhyme/To purge the snottery of our slimy time'. Marston's stance and style was antagonistic to the self-consciously learned and classical mode of Jonson. Among the words which poor Crispinus spews up in his punishment are: '*Spurious, snotteries, chilblain'd, clumsie*' – which are all characteristically hard and unpleasant words, typical of the satiric verse of John Marston. Crispinus claims earlier in *Poetaster*: 'We are a scholar, I assure thee. . . We are new turned poet, too, which is more; and a satirist too, which is more than that . . . We are a gentleman, besides. . .' Marston was the son of a lawyer, who graduated from Oxford and studied at the Middle Temple. He gave up his career in the law to become a writer, and composed two violent satires, *The Metamorphosis of Pygmalion's Image* and *The Scourge of Villainy*, which were burned by order of the Archbishop of Canterbury. By 1599 he was writing plays. The conflict with Jonson seems to have ended by 1604, as he dedicated his finest drama, *The Malcontent* to Ben Jonson, and collaborated with him on *Eastward Ho*! (1605). Marston's other plays included *The Dutch Courtezan* (1605) and *Parasitaster* (1606), *Sophonisba* (1606), *What You Will* (1607) and *The Insatiate Countess* (1613). There are interesting parallels in Marston's works with scenes in Shakespeare (*Antonio and Mellida* and the closet scene in *Hamlet*; *The Malcontent* and Gloucester's suicide attempt in *King Lear*). Marston entered the church, and became the rector of Christchurch in Hampshire, near Bournemouth, where he lived until three years before his death.

Further reading:
B. Gibbons, *Jacobean City Comedy* (1967)

LOTTIE CRUMP

Evelyn Waugh, *Vile Bodies* (1930)

Rosa Lewis (1867–1952)

Further reading:
Daphne Fielding, *The Duchess of Jermyn Street* (1964)

Waugh's novel of the escapades of the smart set in Mayfair of the 1920s features several memorable characters. Among them is Lottie Crump, proprietress of a fashionable Edwardian-style hotel in Dover Street, who was: 'attended invariably by two Cairn terriers' and was 'a happy reminder to us that the splendours of the Edwardian era were not entirely confined to Lady Anchorage or Mrs Blackwater. She is a fine figure of a woman, singularly unscathed by any sort of misfortune and superbly oblivious of those changes in the social order which agitate the more observant *grandes dames* of her period. When the war broke out she took down the signed photograph of the Kaiser and hung it in the menservants' lavatory; it was her one combative action, since then she has had her worries – income tax forms and drink restrictions and young men whose fathers she used to know, who gave her bad cheques . . . one can go to Shepheard's parched with modernity any day, if Lottie likes one's face, and still draw up, cool and uncontaminated, great, healing draughts from the well of Edwardian certainty . . . Lottie's parlour . . . contains a comprehensive collection of signed photographs. Most of the male members of the Royal families of Europe are represented . . . There are photographs of young men on horses riding in steeple-chases, of elderly men leading in the winners of 'classic' races, of horses alone and young men alone, dressed in tight, white collars or in the uniform of the Brigade of Guards . . . There are very few writers or painters and no actors, for Lottie is true to the sound old snobbery of pounds sterling and strawberry leaves'.

This is a portrait of Rosa Lewis, founder of the Cavendish Hotel (see MRS TROTTER). Waugh wrote to Daphne Fielding, biographer of Rosa Lewis: 'I really put all I knew about her into that sketch. I was never allowed back. The last time I set foot in the Cavendish . . . Rosa was having some trouble . . . over a cheque with a man called Lulu Water–Welch . . . She fixed me with fierce eyes and said: "Lulu Waters–Waugh take your arse off my chair" . . . As you know, Rosa had no liking for writers . . . I think it was after *Vile Bodies* that writers started to try to get into the Cavendish. They were driven out at once unless they were Americans'(letter dated 30 July 1962). Thornton Wilder, Aldous Huxley and Cyril Connolly stayed there, which gave the latter unhappy memories he could never speak of (see EVERARD SPRUCE), caused, Waugh said, by his regrets at 'not looking exactly like a cornet of the Blues (and, as you know, c of Bs were what Rosa really accepted).'

ROBINSON CRUSOE

Daniel Defoe, *The Life and Strange Surprising Adventures of Robinson Crusoe* (1719), *The Farther Adventures of Robinson Crusoe* (1719)

Alexander Selkirk (1676–1721)

Further reading: John Howell, *The Life and Adventures of Alexander Selkirk* (1829)

Defoe's masterpiece describes, to cite the full title of the first part of the novel published on 25 April 1719, 'The Life and Strange Surprising Adventures of Robinson Crusoe of York, Mariner.' Defoe narrates the book in the first person and comes alive as the resourceful young sailor cast away on an island in the Caribbean Sea where he survives thanks to his ingenuity and the devotion of 'My man Friday'.

The extraordinary narrative was based on the life of Alexander Selkirk, a Scotsman from Largo in Fife. As sailing master of the *Cinque Ports* galley. Selkirk sailed from the Downs to Brazil in 1703. When the captain of the *Cinque Ports* died in Brazil he was replaced by Thomas Stradling whose authority was undermined by Selkirk's hostility. After many quarrels Selkirk was, at his own request, put ashore in September 1704 on the island of Juan Fernandez where he lived, alone, for more than four years. Captain Woodes Rogers anchored the *Duke* off the island on 2 February 1709 and took Selkirk aboard as mate before returning to England.

Later Rogers published his journal, *A Cruizing Voyage round the World* (1712), and described Selkirk's life on the island: 'After he had conquered his melancholy, he diverted himself sometimes with cutting his name on the trees, and the time of his being left, and his continuance there... he came, at last, to conquer all the inconveniences of his solitude, and to be very easy.' From this principal source Defoe built up his adventure which is full of brilliantly inventive touches and so Selkirk the celebrity became Crusoe the hero of a classic fiction.

William Cowper was also inspired by the story of Selkirk and wrote 'Verses Supposed to by Written by Alexander Selkirk' beginning 'I am monarch of all I survey,/My right there is none to dispute.'

SERGEANT CUFF

Wilkie Collins, *The Moonstone* (1868)

Chief Inspector Jonathan Whicher

Further reading: Yseult Bridges, *Saint with Red Hands* (1954), J. Rhodes, *The Case of Constance Kent* (1928)

The Moonstone is the precious diamond which had once stood in the forehead of a Hindu moon-god. It has passed into the possession of Miss Verinder on her eighteenth birthday as a result of the disposition of its original possessor, John Herncastle, an English officer serving at Seringapatam. The diamond mysteriously disappears the same night. It has been taken by Franklin Blake, her lover, while in an opium trance. Three Indian jugglers, recently seen in the vicinity, are suspected. The villain, Godfrey Ablewhite, who is Blake's rival for Miss Verinder's love, manages to gain the Moonstone. He is murdered in mysterious circumstances, while engaged in a contest of cunning with the three Indians. The novel is complicated by the use of several differing points of view in the narration, and by the fact that Blake does not realize what he has done while in a trance. Suspicion is thrown on various innocent people in the household and the whole complication is finally resolved by the brilliant detective work of Sergeant Cuff.

Cuff is based on Jonathan Whicher, who had become famous as a result of his solving of the Roadhill House mystery, in Wiltshire in 1860. The three-year-old son of Samuel Kent was found murdered in the outside privy at Roadhill House and Whicher when called in to solve the crime concluded that it must have been committed by someone in the household. His theory was based on the fact that no bloodstained garment was found, yet the murderer must have been stained with the crime which was a very bloody one. A nightdress belonging to Constance Kent, the boy's sister, aged sixteen, was missing. Constance Kent later confessed to the crime in July 1865, was found guilty and sentenced to life imprisonment. She was released in 1885. She stated that she had committed the murder of the child on her own and 'unaided'. What made Whicher's reputation was the fact that he had suspected Constance Kent initially on the basis of the missing bloodstained garment, and had applied for a warrant to have her arrested as early as 19 July 1860, but the girl was discharged for lack of evidence. Bungling by the local police had allowed the bloodstained nightdress to be disposed of. Early in the case Whicher and his theories were ridiculed but the subsequent confession and trial fully vindicated him. Collins makes use of the missing garment incident and portrays Whicher as Cuff.

JULIA CUNNINGHAM

D.H. Lawrence, *Aaron's Rod* (1922)

Hilda Doolittle (1886–1961)

Daughter of a coal-owner in the midlands, Julia Cunningham first appears in D.H. Lawrence's *Aaron's Rod* as 'a tall stag of a thing'. It is Christmas Eve in her father's house, and she sits near the fire hunched up in her chair: 'She wore a wine-purple dress, her arms seemed to poke out of the sleeves, and she had dragged her brown hair into straight, untidy strands. Yet she had real beauty.' For six years Julia has been married to Robert Cunningham, a lieutenant about to be demobilized before resuming his career as a sculptor. At the Christmas party, however, she shows more interest in her friend Cyril Scott than in her husband. Scott, a composer, has a house in Dorset, and it is well known in Julia's circle that he wants her to go down and stay with him. During a night at the opera in London, Julia ponders whether she should go to Scott: 'She had carried on a nervous kind of *amour* with him, based on soul sympathy and emotional excitement... She was in that nervous state when desire seems to evaporate the moment fulfilment is offered.' Later it is made clear that 'Julia's gone with Cyril Scott'.

Hilda Doolittle – the author H.D. – lent a room to D.H. Lawrence in 1917. In the same house at 44 Mecklenburgh Square, Bloomsbury, H.D.'s husband Richard Aldington was having an affair with Dorothy Yorke (JOSEPHINE FORD in *Aaron's Rod*) who lived in the attic. Depressed by these circumstances, H.D. turned to Cecil Gray, the composer and original of Cyril Scott in Lawrence's novel. H.D. did go to live with Cecil Gray, in Cornwall, and gave birth to his child Perdita in 1919. Gray then abandoned H.D. and she eventually went to live in Switzerland with Bryher – the Lesbian writer Winifred Ellerman. Richard Aldington and H.D. were eventually divorced in 1937, and her version of the breakdown of their marriage was published in 1960 as the novel *Bid Me to Live*. Lawrence disapproved of H.D.'s decision to leave Aldington in order to live with Cecil Gray, even though Aldington's affair with Dorothy Yorke led to the break.

Further reading:
Harry T. Moore, *The Priest of Love* (1974)

ROBERT CUNNINGHAM

D.H. Lawrence, *Aaron's Rod* (1922)

Richard Aldington (1892–1962)

In D.H. Lawrence's *Aaron's Rod*, Robert Cunningham is introduced as a lieutenant about to be demobilized, a young man keen to resume his career as a sculptor. It is Christmas Eve in Shottle House, home of Cunningham's coal-owner father-in-law. Cunningham 'drank wine in large throatfuls, and his eyes grew a little moist. The room was hot and subdued, everyone was silent. "I say", said Robert suddenly, from the rear, "anybody have a drink? Don't you find it rather hot".' Stoutish Cunningham is also romantic Robert; though his wife Julia is present he takes an obvious interest in Josephine Ford, also at the Christmas party. During a conversation one night at the opera, Robert makes it clear he is quite happy to see his wife going to stay with another man. Married for six years, Robert Cunningham is obviously interested in an adventure with Josephine Ford. When one of his friends asks another what Cunningham will do about the news that his wife Julia has gone off with her lover, the answer is 'Have a shot at Josephine, apparently.'

This is Lawrence's interpretation of events involving his friend Richard Aldington who was married to Hilda Doolittle, the writer H.D. In 1917 H.D. lent Lawrence a room at 44 Mecklenburgh Square,

Further reading:
Richard Aldington, *Life for Life's Sake* (1941), Harry T. Moore, *The Priest of Love* (1974)

Bloomsbury, a house in whose attic Dorothy Yorke lived. Aldington and Dorothy Yorke became lovers and H.D. sought friendship from Lawrence himself and love from Cecil Gray, the composer. In *Aaron's Rod,* Aldington is Robert Cunningham; H.D. is Julia, Robert's wife; Dorothy Yorke is JOSEPHINE FORD; Cecil Gray is Cyril Scott. The same sexual circumstances are told from Aldington's viewpoint in *Death of a Hero* (1929) and from H.D.'s in *Bid Me to Live* (1960).

Born in Hampshire, and educated at London University, Richard Aldington married H.D. in 1913. During the First World War he fought in France and spent his periods of leave at 44 Mecklenburgh Square making conversation with H.D. and love to Dorothy Yorke. Lawrence was sympathetic to Aldington when H.D. went to live with Cecil Gray, and annoyed when, after being with Dorothy Yorke for more than a decade, Aldington turned to another woman. Aldington compiled *The Spirit of Place* (1935), an anthology of Lawrence's prose, and wrote an influential book – *Portrait of a Genius, But...* (1950) – about Lawrence.

WILLIAM ARTHUR CURRY

John Ehrlichman, *The Company* (1976)

John Fitzgerald Kennedy (1917–1963)

35th President of the USA

Further reading: David Halberstam, *The Best and the Brightest* (1973)

In *The Company* Richard Monckton, a lawyer with keen political ambitions, finds he has a powerful rival for the presidency in the person of William Arthur Curry, the Democratic candidate (see RICHARD MONCKTON). Curry has several advantages, including charm and money, he is described as a 'handsome, wealthy and articulate young Senator... as a political newcomer Curry had bucked the New York Democratic organization and won the Governor's seat. His storybook upset victory made him the youngest Governor in New York history. Although the son of a rich and conservative capitalist, Billy Curry spoke movingly of the poor, the disenfranchised and the hungry. And he promised change.' He is soon made a Senator and then begins to campaign actively in the Presidential primary states, gathering delegates. His Democratic rival Esker Scott Anderson is also campaigning and the convention is deadlocked until: 'in a secret meeting with Curry's father, Esker Anderson blinked first. Some said the elder Curry paid Anderson a lot of money. Others said he just bluffed Anderson out of the balloting.' Anderson supports Curry and he becomes President. The glamour of his presidency was considerably tarnished by the Bay of Glass fiasco – a CIA initiative in Dominica which went disastrously wrong; but he is only President for two years and eight months: 'On a Friday evening in September a weary manufacturer's representative flying his single engine Cessna home from Boston to Rochester collided with Air Force One as the President's aeroplane began its descent to Glens Falls, New York... The tail was torn from his great silver-and-blue aircraft and he died in a field of cornstalks near Cobleskill, New York... Within minutes of Billy Curry's death, Esker Scott Anderson was sworn in as President of the United States.'

John Fitzgerald Kennedy was the son of the wealthy Democrat Joseph P. Kennedy, one time ambassador to Britain. After graduating at Harvard, and serving in the US Navy, he was elected to the House of Representatives in 1946, and in 1952 he defeated Republican incumbent Henry Cabot Lodge for the Senate, representing Massachusetts. In 1956 he failed in a bid for the Democratic Vice-Presidential nomination, but after a careful campaign, he gained the Presidential nomination for the Democratic party in 1960. He defeated Richard M. Nixon (see RICHARD MONCKTON) for the Presidency in 1960 by 112,000 regular votes and 84 electoral votes. His politics were those of the liberal Democrats, but were considerably opposed by a rather conservative Democratic Congress. In foreign affairs his reputation was tarnished by the Bay of Pigs fiasco – a CIA inspired adventure in Cuba – though he triumphed in the Cuban missile crisis of 1962. He was assassinated in Dallas, Texas, on 22 November 1963.

ADOLPHUS CUSINS

George Bernard Shaw, *Major Barbara* (1905)

Gilbert Murray (1866–1957)

Further reading: Gilbert Murray, *Unfinished Autobiography* (1960)

Adolphus Cusins, engaged to the heroine of Shaw's *Major Barbara*, ends the play by changing his name to Andrew Undershaft and, as befits a foundling, inheriting a hugely profitable armaments business from Barbara's father. Throughout the play Adolphus, a professor of Greek, argues morality with Undershaft who calls him 'Euripides'. Shaw describes Adolphus in a typically precise stage-direction: 'His sense of humour is intellectual and subtle, and is complicated by an appalling temper. The lifelong struggle of a benevolent temperament and a high conscience against impulses of inhuman ridicule and fierce impatience has set up a chronic strain which has visibly wrecked his constitution. He is a most implacable, determined, tenacious, intolerant person who by mere force of character presents himself as – and indeed actually is – considerate, gentle, explanatory, even mild and apologetic, capable possibly of murder, but not of cruelty or coarseness.'

Shaw created Cusins as a caricature of his friend Gilbert Murray who was something of an irascible pedagogue. Murray was highly respected as a professor of Greek (in the universities of Glasgow and Oxford) who produced scholarly editions of the Greek classics. More influentially, and controversially, he produced popular verse translations of the tragedies of Sophocles, Aeschylus and Euripides. Shaw admired Murray's erudition and political tenacity and has Cusins declare at the end of the play: 'As a teacher of Greek I gave the intellectual man weapons against the common man. I now want to give the common man weapons against the intellectual man.'

Murray's political interests led him to become Chairman of the League of Nations Union from 1923 to 1938 and to publish books on pacifism. Although best known for his advocacy of Euripides his international reputation was broadly based and in 1926 he was Professor of Poetry at Harvard.

MR CYPRESS

Thomas Love Peacock, *Nightmare Abbey* (1818)

Lord Byron (1788–1824)

Further reading: H. Mills, *Peacock – His Circle and His Age* (1969)

Mr Cypress calls at Nightmare Abbey to bid farewell to Scythrop Glowry, before leaving the country. They had been friends since college days and he is now a famous poet. He is described as 'a lacerated spirit' – brooding, melancholy, disillusioned, slightly Satanic with a strong affection for the Greek world: 'The mind is restless.' he says, 'and must persist in seeking, though to find is to be disappointed. Do you feel no aspirations towards the countries of Socrates and Cicero? No wish to wander among the venerable remains of the greatness that has passed for ever?' He affects the fashionable pessimism of the time: 'I have no hope for myself or for others. Our life is a false nature; it is not in the harmony of things; it is all-blasting upas, whose root is earth, and whose leaves are the skies which rain their poison dews upon mankind. We wither from our youth; we gasp with unslaked thirst for unattainable good; lured from the first to the last by phantoms – love, fame, ambition, avarice – all idle, and all ill – one meteor of many names, that vanishes in the smoke of death.'

This is a comically exaggerated picture of Byron, in Wordsworth's phrase, 'the mocking bird of our Parnassian ornithology', It contains direct quotation from Byron's *Childe Harold*, which had made him famous throughout the land ('I awoke one morning and found myself famous' he wrote after the poem first appeared).

Byron created an alien and mysterious persona – gloomy, passionate, and world weary. He was born in London and educated at Aberdeen, he succeeded to the title and estates in 1798, was sent to Harrow and Cambridge, where he lived wildly and extravagantly. He travelled widely in Europe and achieved fame as satirist and poet. But it was *Childe Harold* which put before the public that personality forever associated with him. He separated from Lady Byron and left England, never to return, in 1816. He lived in Italy and died fighting with Greek insurgents against the Turks in 1824.

THE GRAND CYRUS

Madeleine de Scudery, *Artamène, ou le Grand Cyrus* (1653)

Louis Bourbon, Prince de Condé (1621–86)

Further reading: Henri Eugene Philippe Louis d'Orleans, Duc d'Aumale, *Histoire des princes de Condé (1897)*

Artamène, ou le Grand Cyrus, which appeared in ten volumes between 1649 and 1653, was one of the most widely-read and influential works of the day. In its English translation, by Dorothy Osborne, Lady Temple and Mrs Pepys, it was greatly admired in Restoration England, and influenced John Dryden and Thomas Killigrew. John Banks produced a play based on the novel in London in 1696. Samuel Pepys records in his diary for 12 May 1666 that he had to ask his wife to put a stop to her interminable stories from the novel. It is the ultimate French heroic romance, set in ancient Persia, and recounts the adventures of the young Cyrus, grandson of the King of Media, who travels under the assumed name of Artamène. He is in love with Mandane, daughter of his uncle, Cyaxares. Mandane is also sought in marriage by the King of Pontus and the King of Assyria. The chivalric action is endless and boundless; there is a multiplicity of sieges, battles and encounters, as the mysterious Artamène pursues his attempts to rescue Mandane, who is carried off by the Prince of Assyria. One of the great set pieces is the burning of the city of Sinope, where Mandane has been held captive. Cyrus has been compelled to conceal his identity as a result of his uncle's hostility, and hopes that by his bravery and chivalry he could demonstrate that he deserves the love of Mandane. In the end, hero and heroine are united. Undoubtedly one of the reasons which made this tarradiddle so hugely popular was the fact that it was a *roman à clef*, and that beneath all the trappings of ancient Persian history several distinguished contemporaries could clearly be discerned. Artamène, the Grand Cyrus, is in reality Louis, Prince of Condé, known as the Great Condé; Mandane is Anne-Geneviéve de Bourbon, Duchess de Longueville (1619-79), his sister. The character of Sapho is Madeleine de Scudery herself. Condé was generalissimo of the French forces, and achieved notable victories over the Spaniards (Rocroi, 1643) the Bavarians (Freiburg, 1644 and Nördlingen, 1645) and captured Dunkirk in 1646. He was disgraced and imprisoned by Mazarin, but popular feeling caused Mazarin to flee Paris and Condé was released. He served as commander in the Spanish army against France, and despite defeat was so formidable that he was pardoned and restored to his estates. In 1675 he was commander of the French army on the Rhine. He retired to Chantilly and associated with Molière, Racine, La Bruyère and Boileau.

D

CAPTAIN DUGALD DALGETTY

Sir Walter Scott, *The Legend of Montrose* (1819)

Sir James Turner (1615–86)

Further reading:
Sir James Turner, *Memoirs* (1683)

The Legend of Montrose is set in 1644 during the period when the Highland clans rose against the Covenanters and supported Charles I. They were led by the Earl of Montrose, and the Covenanters by the Marquess of Argyle, head of the clan of the Campbells. Against this gloomy historical background Scott weaves a Romeo and Juliet love story concerning the love of two rivals – Allan and Monteith – for the same beauty, Annot Lyle. The crisis of the narrative is reached when it is revealed that Annot is the daughter of Sir Duncan Campbell, and Allan stabs his rival at the marriage ceremony. But it is the character of the Scottish soldier of fortune, the talkative, pedantic and conceited Dugald Dalgetty of Drumthwacket, who dominates the story. He makes a great display of the scholarship he gained from his years at Marischal College at Aberdeen, but he loved fighting. The thirty years war in Europe had been a blessing to him as it enabled him so completely to realize himself, giving him ample scope for his love of military service, travel and companionship. Scott based this splendid figure on two celebrated Scottish mercenaries whose memoirs he studied. General Robert Monroe, who died in Ireland in 1680, served on the continent and sided with the Scots against Charles I. In the Irish rebellion he was a major general and achieved notable victories for the parliamentarian armies at Moira, Newry, Antrim and Belfast, but was defeated at Benburb in 1646. He came to an understanding with the Royalist party but was imprisoned and sent to England in 1648. He spent his declining years in Ireland. Scott seems to have taken most of the details for the character of Dalgetty from the life of Sir James Turner. He was educated at Glasgow and Edinburgh (MA 1621) and enlisted in the service of Gustavus Adolphus, serving in Germany between 1632–34. He joined the Scottish army and served in the invasion of England in 1645. Two years later he was adjutant-general and joined Hamilton's ill-fated expedition to England in 1648, returning to Scotland two years later. He was now a supporter of Charles II, who had been crowned at Scone in January 1651 and supported him at Worcester, fleeing with him to France in October. He was employed in several Royalist missions and (like Dalgetty) was knighted at the Restoration. He was given command of the forces which were sent to crush the Covenanters in south-west Scotland in 1666. He himself opined: 'So we serve our master honestlie, it is no matter what master we serve.'

MRS DALLOWAY

Virginia Woolf, *The Voyage Out* (1915), *Mrs Dalloway* (1925)

Kitty Maxse (1867–1922)

Further reading:
Quentin Bell, *Virginia Woolf* (1972), Bernard Blackstone, *Virginia Woolf – A Commentary* (1949)

Virginia Woolf's novel *Mrs Dalloway* was born when Kitty Maxse died after a fall at her London home. In her diary for 8 October 1922 Virginia wrote about 'visualising her – her white hair – pink cheeks – how she sat upright – her voice – with its characteristic tones [and] her earrings, her gaiety, yet melancholy; her smartness: her tears, which stayed on her cheek.' Six days later she wrote that 'Mrs Dalloway has branched into a book'.

In the novel, Clarissa is preparing for an evening party at her home when a series of coincidences brings back vivid memories of her life before her marriage to Richard Dalloway, MP. Whereas the past unfolds dynamically, her present life seems devoid of surprises: 'She had the oddest sense of being herself invisible [making] this astonishing and rather solemn progress with the rest of them, up Bond Street, this being Mrs Dalloway; not even Clarissa any more; this being Mrs Richard Dalloway.'

Virginia's mother Julia Stephen was friendly with Kitty's mother and Julia was responsible, in 1890, for matching Kitty in marriage with Leopold Maxse, owner-editor of *The National Review*. After Julia's death, in 1895, Kitty took a maternal interest in Virginia and her sister

Vanessa and helped to bring them on in smart London society. Virginia respected Kitty but could never feel at ease with her and her cultivation of the social graces. For her part Kitty had reservations about Virginia and she was not amused when the Stephen sisters moved from fashionable Kensington to bohemian Bloomsbury. Towards the end of the novel it is suggested that 'Clarissa was at heart a snob – one had to admit it, a snob' but also that 'Clarissa was pure-hearted'. After the book was published Virginia wrote in her diary (for 18 June 1925) that the distaste she felt for Mrs Dalloway was 'true to my feeling for Kitty'.

DAN

Rudyard Kipling, *Puck of Pook's Hill* (1906), *Rewards and Fairies* (1910)

John Kipling (1897–1915)

Further reading: Charles Carrington, *Rudyard Kipling* (1955)

From the west side of Bateman's, their home in Burwash (Surrey), the Kipling family – Rudyard, his wife Carrie, the children Elsie and John – could see Perch Hill. Kipling renamed the hill Pook's Hill (that is, Puck's Hill) in the ten stories he published in the *Strand Magazine* in 1906 before collecting them in *Puck of Pook's Hill*. In this book, and its sequel *Rewards and Fairies*, the human link between the tales, is provided by the presence of the children Dan and Una, modelled on Kipling's own children Elsie (1896–1976) and John. After Puck introduces himself to Dan and Una, 'the children stretched out beside him, their bare legs waving happily in the air. They felt they could not be afraid of him any more than of their particular friend old Hobden the badger . . . Dan handed over his big one-bladed knife, and Puck began to carve out a piece of turf from the centre of the Ring.'

Kipling's only son, a tall and myopic individual, greatly enjoyed the entertainments – charades, domestic productions of plays, games – organized by his father. John was not scholastically outstanding at his public school, Wellington College, and not at all inclined to follow in his father's literary footsteps. John's ambition, rather, was to pursue a career in the Navy, but he had to decline a naval cadetship because of his poor eyesight. In September 1914 he enlisted in the Irish Guards and was reported missing after the Battle of Loos (October 1915).

Although Carrie Kipling persisted in believing that her son had survived, Kipling was more realistic. In January 1916 he wrote to a friend, 'John was wounded as well as missing. We have no word of him and I fear there is but little to hope.' In his poems he conveyed something of his grief. 'Epitaphs of the War 1914–18' contains a couplet on 'A Son': 'My son was killed while laughing at some jest. I would I knew/What it was, and it might serve me in a time when jests are few.' More directly, he expressed his sorrow in 'My Boy Jack', a poem published in the *Daily Telegraph* of 19 October 1916. it begins: '"Have you news of my boy Jack?"/*Not this tide.*/"When d'you think that he'll come back?"/*Not with this wind blowing and this tide.*' Kipling never forgot the sacrifice of his only son and for many years he helped pay for the Last Post to be sounded every night at the Menin Gate Memorial at Ypres.

MONSIGNOR DARCY

F. Scott Fitzgerald, *This Side of Paradise* (1920)

Cyril Sigourney Webster Fay (1875–1919)

Further reading: Andrew Turnbull, *Scott Fitzgerald* (1962)

F. Scott Fitzgerald's first novel is an account of an autobiographical hero, Amory Blaine, as he passes through school and Princeton University and simultaneously pursues his quest for love and self-knowledge. In 'Book One: The Romantic Egotist', Amory comes under the influence of Monsignor Darcy, a loveable man with a lively intellect: 'Monsignor was forty-four then, and bustling – a trifle too stout for symmetry, with hair the colour of spun gold, and a brilliant, enveloping personality. When he came into a room clad in his full purple regalia from thatch to toe, he resembled a Turner sunset, and attracted both admiration and attention . . . Children adored him because he was like a child; youth revelled in his company because he was still a youth, and couldn't be shocked . . . He and Amory took to each other at first sight – the jovial, impressive prelate who could dazzle an embassy ball, and the green-eyed, intent youth, in his first long trousers, accepted in their own minds a relation of father and son within a half-hour's conversation.' Thereafter Amory tests experience against Darcy's ideals; when the Monsignor dies, Amory recalls his friend's gift of 'making all light and shadow merely aspects of God'.

This Side of Paradise is dedicated to Sigourney Fay, the model for Monsignor Darcy. In September 1911 Fitzgerald entered the Newman School, Hackensack, New Jersey – a Catholic institution that prepared its students for secular universities. Here Fitzgerald met Father Cyril Sigourney Webster Fay, a trustee who subsequently became headmaster of Newman. Describing the first meeting, in November 1912, between the thirty-seven-year-old priest and the sixteen-year-old student, Matthew J. Bruccoli writes as follows in *Some Sort of Epic Grandeur: The Life of F. Scott Fitzgerald* (1981): 'Fay soon became Scott's surrogate father . . . Fay was the first important person who responded to Scott and encouraged his aspirations.' Father Fay quickly realized that Fitzgerald's rebellious nature could lead to the rejection of Roman Catholic dogma, though he felt Fitzgerald had the ability to help the Catholic cause in America. When Father Fay was appointed head of a Red Cross mission to Russia, he asked Fitzgerald to go as his aide, with the rank of Red Cross Lieutenant. Fitzgerald agreed, but the Bolshevik Revolution of 1917 made the trip impossible. Fitzgerald kept in contact with his mentor and when Fay, by then a Monsignor, died of pneumonia on 10 January 1919, Fitzgerald wrote in a letter: 'now my little world made to order has been shattered by the death of one man . . . I feel as if his mantle had descended upon me – a desire, or more, to some day recreate the atmosphere of him'.

THE DARK LADY

William Shakespeare, *Sonnets* (1609)

Luce Morgan (1570–c1610) or **Emilia Lanier** (born 1570)

Further reading: Leslie Hotson, *Mr W. H.* (1964), A. L. Rowse, *Shakespeare The Man* (1973)

In his *Sonnets*, Shakespeare contrasts the love he has for the young man of the sequence with the lust he feels for the dark lady in his life. She is described in Sonnet 127: 'Therefore my mistress' brows are raven black,/Her eyes so suited, and they mourners seem/At such who, not born fair, no beauty lack,/Sland'ring creation with a false esteem.' In Sonnet 130, too, she is vividly evoked; 'My mistress' eyes are nothing like the sun;/Coral is far more red than her lips' red;/ If snow be white, why then her breasts are dun;/If hairs be wires, black wires grow on her head.' Inevitably, the identity of this dark lady of the sonnets has been the subject of endless speculation.

Leslie Hotson argues that the dark lady was a courtesan called Luce Morgan. She was (says Hotson) 'no more an Ethiop than the Black prince' but 'a raven-haired beauty, with irresistible black eyes'. Some time before 1588 she married a man called Parker (of whom nothing more is known) and, as one of the Queen's gentlewomen, is mentioned in the Accounts of the Great Wardrobe of 1579–81. For some indiscretion she was banished from the Queen's company and became a prostitute, eventually running her own bawdy house in Clerkenwell. Known professionally as Black Luce, she was sent to Bridewell prison in January 1601, and (Hotson notes) from a 'lewd epitaph printed 1656 no [precise date of death] can be gathered [as] it simply relates that she turned Roman Catholic and died diseased'.

A.L. Rowse, who holds the young man of the sonnets to be the Earl of Southampton, and dates the sequence to the period 1592–5 (whereas Hotson establishes the earlier dating of 1587–9 and identifies Mr W.H. as William Hatcliffe), has another candidate for the role of dark lady. Scrutinizing the puns in the sonnets – which gives lines like 'Wilt thou, whose will is large and spacious,/Not once vouchsafe to hide my will in thine?' (135) a sexual connotation since 'will' means both desire and sexual organs – Rowse pursues a path to Emilia Lanier, née Bassano. The daughter of one of the Queen's court musicians Emilia was, according to the astrologer Simon Forman, 'very brown in youth'. From 1588 Emilia had been mistress to Henry Carey, first Lord Hunsdon, Lord Chamberlain and first cousin to the Queen, and it was his child she carried when she married Will Lanier in 1593. Two years before the Lord Chamberlain died (in 1596) the company of the Chamberlain's Men was formed and members of the company, including Shakespeare, would have been presented to him. 'It is a piquant thought,' writes Rowse, 'that William Shakespeare should have succeeded him for a time with his mistress'.

D'ARTAGNAN

Alexandre Dumas, *The Three Musketeers* (1844), *Twenty Years After* (1845), *The Man in the Iron Mask* (1848–50)

Charles de Batz de Castelmore (1623–73)

Further reading: Henri d'Almèras, *Alexandre Dumas and the Three Musketeers* (1929)

D'Artagnan, the swashbuckling hero celebrated by Alexandre Dumas, makes an ungainly first entrance on a pony in *The Three Musketeers* though his quality still shines through: 'face long and brown; high cheek-bones, a sign of sagacity; the maxillary muscles enormously developed . . . the eye open and intelligent; the nose hooked, but finely chiselled'. He soon meets the three musketeers Athos, Porthos, Aramais whose 'appearance, although it was not quite at ease, excited by its carelessness, at once full of dignity and submission, the admiration of D'Artagnan, who beheld in these two men demigods, and in their leader [Athos] an Olympian Jupiter, armed with all his thunders'. Subsequently D'Artagnan becomes the greatest musketeer of all.

Dumas came across his hero in the fanciful *Mémoirs d'Artagnan, capitaine, lieutenant des grands Mousquetaires* (1700) by Gatien Courtilz de Sandras. With the assistance of historian Auguste Maquet. Dumas recreated the career of D'Artagnan in a spectacular manner. The historical D'Artagnan was born Charles de Batz de Castelmore in 1623 and inherited the estate of Artaignan. Commissioned in the Grey Musketeers he was entrusted with various daring exploits such as the arrest of Fouquet, the Finance Minister, in 1661. By 1667 D'Artagnan had become a captain and gradually he became involved in administrative work, first as Marshal of the Royal Camps and Armies then as military governor of Lille. He returned to active service in 1673 when, on behalf of the Duke of Monmouth, he led the storming of Maestricht. The action was illadvised and D'Artagnan was killed along with more than a hundred of his musketeers. His three stout-hearted companions in the Dumas novels were also historically based – on the Gascon noblemen Armand Athos d'Auterielle, Isaac de Portau and Henri d'Aramitz.

CLARA DAWES

D.H. Lawrence, *Sons and Lovers* (1913)

Alice Dax

Further reading: Harry T. Moore, *The Priest of Love* (1974)

Shortly after winning first prize at an autumn exhibition of paintings at the Nottingham Castle gallery, Paul Morel – the autobiographical hero of D.H. Lawrence's *Sons and Lovers* – is walking up Castle Gate, when he meets his girlfriend Miriam (based on Jessie Chambers) with 'a rather striking woman' called Clara Dawes. She has an aura of independence, a sullen expression, 'a defiant carriage' and no longer lives with her husband Baxter Dawes – a smith at Jordan's Surgical Appliance factory, where Paul is employed as a junior spiral clerk, and where Clara herself once worked as spiral overseer. When Paul Morel enters her life, Clara is devoted to the cause of Women's Rights; she returns to work at Jordan's and becomes friendly with Paul. Convinced that Miriam's love is too spiritually demanding, Paul turns to the more earthy passion of Clara Dawes: 'She kissed him fervently on the eyes, first one, then the other, and she folded herself to him. She gave herself. He held her fast. It was a moment intense almost to agony . . . Now she radiated with joy and pride again. It was her restoration and her recognition.' This affair with Clara arouses the fury of Baxter Dawes who attacks Paul. Later Paul is instrumental in bringing Baxter and Clara together again.

The character of Clara Dawes was suggested by Lawrence's relationship with Alice Dax, who is identified by Harry T. Moore, as 'the married woman in Eastwood who introduced Lawrence to physical love'. Married to a pharmacist, Henry Dax, Alice was one of the most liberated women in Eastwood and in nearby Mansfield (where she and her husband settled in 1912). She was known as an advanced thinker, a champion of women's rights, and an advocate of educational reform. It was she, apparently, who initiated Lawrence into sex, for as she told Mrs Sallie Hopkin: 'Sallie, I gave Bert sex. I had to. He was over at our house [in Eastwood, Lawrence's birthplace], struggling with a poem he couldn't finish, so I took him upstairs and gave him sex. He came downstairs and finished the poem.' In 1935 Alice Dax wrote to Frieda Lawrence saying that Lawrence had found the right woman for him: 'I was never *meet* for him and what he liked was not the me I *was*, but the me I might-have-been'. In 1928, writing to Enid Hilton, Lawrence wrote: 'Wonder what Alice Dax thought of *Lady C[hatterley's Lover]*!'

JEANIE DEANS

Sir Walter Scott, *The Heart of Midlothian* (1818)

Helen Walker
(1712–91)

Further reading:
Edgar Johnson, *Sir Walter Scott – The Great Unknown* (1970)

The source of the sentimental story that is at the heart of Sir Walter Scott's *The Heart of Midlothian* came to him in a letter from an admirer. Mrs Helen Goldie, who told the tale of Helen Walker: 'She had been left an orphan, with the charge of a sister considerably younger than herself, and who was educated and maintained by her exertions. Attached to her by so many ties, therefore, it will not be easy to conceive her feelings, when she found that this only sister must be tried by the laws of her country for child-murder, and upon being called as principal witness against her.' Scottish law stipulated that, in the case of a child being dead or missing, a woman who gave birth without seeking assistance should be charged with infanticide and executed if found guilty. Helen Walker could have spared her sister the death sentence if she had testified to her preparation for the birth but she declared 'It is impossible for me to swear to a falsehood; and, whatever may be the consequence. I will give my oath according to my conscience.' When her sister was duly sentenced to death Helen had a petition drawn up, then set out on foot to London to present herself (as Mrs Goldie told Scott) 'in her tartan plaid and country attire, to the late Duke of Argyle, who immediately procured the pardon she petitioned for, and Helen returned with it, on foot, just in time to save her sister'.

From this moral tale Scott fashioned the character of plain Jeanie Deans who, by a similar strategy, saves her beautiful half-sister from execution in Edinburgh in whose Tolbooth prison (known as the Heart of Midlothian) Effie is confined at the beginning of the book. Jeanie, daughter of the staunchly presbyterian Douce Davie Deans, rises to the moralistic occasion by saying 'I will bear my load alone – the back is made for the burden.'

Towards the end of his life Scott provided – in Irongray churchyard. Dumfriesshire – a tombstone to the memory of Helen Walker.

DEMETRIUS

Ben Jonson, *Poetaster* (1601)

Thomas Dekker (1572–1632)

Further reading:
C.G. Thayer, *Ben Jonson – Studies in the Plays* (1963), R.A. Small, *The Stage Quarrel Between Jonson and the So-called Poetasters* (1899), A.C. Swinburne, *The Age of Shakespeare* (1908)

In *Poetaster*, one of Jonson's most vigorous contributions to the so-called 'War of the Theatres' (see CRISPINUS, HORACE, VIRGIL and CHRYSOGANUS) Demetrius, 'a play-dresser and plagiary' is accused, together with Crispinus, of having ignorantly, foolishly and maliciously 'gone about to deprave, and calumniate the person and writings of Quintus Horatius Flaccus . . . poet, and priest of the Muses', and to that end to have plotted with Crispinus 'at sundry times, as by several means, and in sundry places, for the better accomplishing your base and envious purpose; taxing him falsely, of self-love, arrogancy, impudence, railing, filching by translation etc.' Demetrius's defence is that the cause he had for such action was that Horace: ' . . .kept better company, for the most part, than I; and that better men loved him than loved me; and that his writings thrived better than mine, and were better liked and graced: nothing else . . .' Horace is so moved by this, that he forgives him.

This is a portrait of the rivalry between Ben Jonson and Thomas Dekker, Jonson obviously believing that it had been aggravated by Dekker's envy of his success. Dekker was born in London, possibly of Dutch descent. Very little is known about his early life. His output was considerable; while employed writing for the Rose and the Fortune theatres, he worked on forty-four plays, many of them single-handedly, some in collaboration. He also brought several older plays up to date. This may well have earned him the reputation of a 'play-dresser' and a 'plagiary'. Few of his plays survive, but among them are the brilliant comedy of Elizabethan London, *The Shoemaker's Holiday* (1599), which contains the well-known drinking song: 'Cold's the wind, and wet's the rain,/Saint Hugh be our good speed;/Ill is the weather that bringeth no gain,/Nor helps good hearts in need.' He collaborated with John Marston on *Satiromastix* (1601) and produced the romance, *Old Fortunatus*. With Thomas Middleton he wrote *The Honest Whore* (1604) and also wrote a considerable number of prose pamphlets, many of them in the tradition of social satire associated with Thomas Nashe (see MOTH). *The Wonderful Year* (1603) concerns the death of Elizabeth I and the London plague and *The Belman of London* (1608) describes sharpers and rogues. *The Gul's Horne-Book* (1609) is a brilliant account of London life in the early sixteenth century. With Michael Drayton and others, Dekker collaborated on the play *Sir John Oldcastle*, an attempt to defend Oldcastle from the accusations of *Henry IV, Part Two* (see FALSTAFF)

JOHN DERRINGHAM

Elinor Glyn, *Halcyone* (1912)

George Nathaniel Curzon, Marquess Curzon of Kedleston (1859–1925)

Further reading: Leonard Mosley, *Lord Curzon* (1960). Anthony Glyn, *Elinor Glyn – A Biography* (1955)

John Derringham is the hero of Elinor Glyn's sentimental and poignant romance *Halcyone*. He is a brilliant and ambitious politician who meets and falls in love with Halcyone and agrees to marry her. The marriage will have to be kept secret for the time for political reasons. At the same time a cunning rich American widow is scheming to capture his attentions. Before they can marry, he suffers an accident and is separated from Halcyone. His engagement to Mrs Cricklander is announced in the papers and Halcyone is brokenhearted. His party falls from office and Mrs Cricklander, not wishing to marry an opposition leader, passes him over for a radical. After much tension on the heart strings, Derringham and Halcyone are reunited. Derringham is described as a tall, 'lanky, rather distinguished young Englishman'. He is brilliant, and got a double first at Oxford. He is 'full of ambitions in the political line, and he has a fearless and rather caustic wit'.

This is a portrait of Curzon. Derringham, like Curzon, was a fine scholar, and had been captain of the Oppidans at Eton. They shared an aristocratic descent obscured by poverty as well as tearing political ambition. Derringham, like Curzon, had already been Foreign Under-Secretary. They have less attractive qualities in common; both are selfish egotists who put their own ambitions above everything else. Elinor Glyn knew Curzon personally; in fact, he was a fan of hers, and made her a gift of the celebrated tiger skin, immortalized in the lines: 'Would you like to sin/with Elinor Glyn/on a tigerskin?/Or would you prefer/to err/with her/on some other fur?' Curzon was an intensely ambitious Conservative politician, a brilliant scholar and master of foreign affairs. A distinguished Viceroy of India, he was bitterly disappointed not to have been Prime Minister. He acknowledged his copy of *Halcyone* by pointing out two spelling mistakes in the author's accompanying letter.

DES ESSEINTES

Joris-Karl Huysmans, *A Rebours* (1884)

Count Robert de Montesquiou (1855–1921)

Further reading: George D. Painter, *Marcel Proust* (1959, 1965)

Contemptuous of humanity, Duc Jean Floressas des Esseintes conceives the idea of retreating from human society, of 'shutting himself up in some snug retreat, and deadening the thunderous din of life's inexorable activity' (as Robert Baldik translates Huysmans in his *Against Nature*, 1959). Buying a villa at Fontenay, on the outskirts of Paris, he luxuriates in his own decadence, convinced that artifice is the distinctive mark of human genius, and that Nature has had her day. This connoisseur of exquisite sensations creates his home as a temple to his aesthetic taste. In his dining-room, for example, is a 'collection of liqueur casks he called his mouth organ . . . Des Esseintes would drink a drop here, another there, playing internal symphonies to himself, and providing his palate with sensations analogous to those which music dispenses to the ear.' Having run the gamut of solitary pleasures – with books, paintings, interior decorations, drinks, perfumes, drugs – Des Esseintes is eventually overwhelmed by his self-indulgence: 'the solitude he had longed for so ardently and finally obtained had resulted in appalling unhappiness'. After further bouts of sensual experimentation Des Esseintes is told by his doctor that he must choose between 'a good recovery on the one hand and insanity speedily followed by tuberculosis on the other'. Finally, Des Esseintes goes back to Paris to satisfy his 'hunger for religion'.

Whereas Oscar Wilde, in *The Picture of Dorian Gray* (1891), enthused over *À Rebours* it caused some irritation to Count Robert de Montesquiou who (as Baldick notes) recognized himself as the prototype of Des Esseintes. A member of one of France's oldest aristocratic families, and a man wealthy enough to indulge his passion for elaborate interior decoration, Count Robert was friendly with writers such as Mallarmé and Proust, and considered himself a poet. In 1883 Mallarmé visited his house in the Rue Franklin and reported the details of his extraordinary lifestyle to Huysmans, who used them in *À Rebours*. For example, Count Robert inlaid the shell of a pet tortoise with turquoises (thus causing the death of the animal); Des Esseintes likewise has precious stones 'mounted on the actual shell of [his] tortoise'. Though he had gone to bed with Sarah Bernhardt, Count Robert's penchant was for young men. Count Robert was used by Proust as an original of Baron de Charlus in *Remembrance of Things Past*.

DIDO, QUEEN OF CARTHAGE

Virgil, *Aeneid* (circa 29 BC)

Cleopatra, Queen of Egypt, Cleopatra VII (69–30 BC)

Further reading: Jack Lindsay, *Cleopatra* (1971)

Virgil's masterpiece narrates the story of Aeneas, the Trojan hero, after the destruction of Troy. Aeneas and his followers are luxuriously entertained by Dido after they are shipwrecked at Carthage, and Aeneas returns to her after escaping from Troy. Here occurs the deep love between them. He is summoned to return to establish Rome and deserts the Queen, who takes her own life: 'Deep entered in her side/The piercing steel, with reeking purple dyed,/Clogged in the wound the cruel weapon stands,/The spouting blood came streaming on her hands./Her sad attendants saw the deadly stroke,/And with loud cries the sounding palace shook.'

Virgil's life spanned a period of considerable political upheaval, and his aim in the *Aeneid* was to portray the destiny of Rome as a civilizing and law-giving power, fully realized under the Emperor Augustus. He was twenty-five when Julius Caesar was assassinated. Then followed civil wars, the triumvirate of Antony, Lepidus and Octavius, the tension brought about in international stability by the relationship between Antony and Cleopatra, and the terrible threat posed to Roman power from the east which was ended by the battle of Actium in 31 BC.

The theme, so stressed in Virgil, of the need for a powerful central authority in the Mediterranean world, finds its parallel in the triumphant career of Octavius, who became the Emperor Augustus. The luxury of Carthage, Aeneas's fascination with Dido, the tension between love and duty, the suicide of the Queen, are all echoes of the exotic world of Egypt, Antony's infatuation with Cleopatra, his neglect of Roman duties and the suicide of the Queen of the Nile. It was while Antony was enamoured to Cleopatra that Octavius was able to consolidate his power in the western part of the Roman world. Cleopatra had already fascinated Julius Caesar, and now enchanted Antony. After they met in 41 BC she bore him three sons. The war between Octavius and Antony was decided at Actium, a sea battle fought in 31 BC off the West of Greece. Cleopatra fled with sixty of her ships and Antony followed. When besieged in Alexandria, Antony stabbed himself and Cleopatra died of the sting of a serpent.

DANDIE DINMONT

Sir Walter Scott, *Guy Mannering* (1815)

Willie Elliot (1755–1827)

The plot of *Guy Mannering* concerns the attempts made by the rascally and corrupt lawyer, Glossin, to lay hands on the Ellengowan estate by dispossessing its rightful heir, Harry Bertram, son of the laird of Ellengowan. Eventually the conspiracy is unmasked by Meg Merrilies, an old gipsy (see MEG MERRILIES) and the sturdy lowland farmer, Dandie Dinmont, who leaves a Cumberland alehouse with the young hero, Harry. Dandie is on his horse, Dumple, and Harry goes on foot. They have been warned about the dangers from assault by border bandits

Further reading: John Gibson Lockhart, *The Life of Sir Walter Scott* (1838)

on the Waste of Bewcastle, but Dandie has discounted these warnings. Dandie is attacked and saved only by the timely appearance of Harry, who is making his way into Dumfriesshire. They drive the bandits away and then both continue the journey on the back of Dandie's sturdy mount: 'Descending by a path towards a well-known ford, Dumple crossed the small river, and then, quickening his pace, trotted about a mile briskly up its banks, and approached two or three low thatched houses, placed with their angles to each other.' This is Dandie Dinmont's farmstead, where Harry is welcomed hospitably. Dandie's horse finds its own way to its stable and the good farmer is welcomed by all his numerous dogs, three generations of them, all called either Mustard or Pepper. Dandie Dinmont is based largely on the figure of Willie Elliot, a lowlands farmer, whom Scott got to know between 1792 and 1799, while he was a young advocate researching the traditions and balladry of the Border country at Liddesdale. His companion was Robert Shortreed, the son of a farmer in the area, who was himself to become a Sheriff-Substitute in the county. Shortreed was a scholar and authority on ballads and well known in the area. He introduced Scott to many people, among them Willie Eliot, whose farm was at Millburnholm (now Millburn) which Scott calls Charlieshope in *Guy Mannering*. When Scott first visited Eliot in Shortreed's company, he was virtually surrounded by Willie's dogs. Willie was the son of Robert Elliot, a tenant farmer. He married Elizabeth Laidlaw, of Falnash. One who knew the couple well said: 'Willie was the good and generous soul that Dandie was, and Mrs Elliot . . . was a pleasant woman.' Willie Elliot's grave may be seen in the kirkyard of Unthank in the Ewes valley.

THOMAS PARKE D'INVILLIERS

F. Scott Fitzgerald, *This Side of Paradise* (1920)

John Peale Bishop (1892–1944)

Further reading: Andrew Turnbull, *Scott Fitzgerald* (1962)

Amory Blaine, the autobiographical hero of Scott Fitzgerald's first novel, begins to glimpse the rich possibilities of his life while at Princeton University. 'From the first,' says Fitzgerald, '[Amory] loved Princeton – its lazy beauty, its half-grasped significance, the wild moonlight revel of the rushes'. After wrenching his knee in freshman football practice, Amory turns from athleticism to aestheticism, with the encouragement of Thomas Parke D'Invilliers, who contributes passionate love poems to the *Nassau Lit*. D'Invilliers introduces Amory to the work of Oscar Wilde and encourages his literary gifts: 'He was, perhaps, nineteen, with stooped shoulders, pale blue eyes, and, as Amory could tell from his general appearance, without much conception of social competition and such phenomena of absorbing interest . . . In a good-natured way [D'Invilliers] had almost decided that Princeton was one part deadly Philistines and one part deadly grinds, and to find a person who could mention Keats without stammering, yet evidently washed his hands, was rather a treat.' The two students become close friends.

Fitzgerald met John Peale Bishop, the original of D'Invilliers, in April 1914 at Princeton. Three years older than Fitzgerald, Bishop had started Princeton late because of a boyhood illness. As Matthew J. Bruccoli notes, in *Some Sort of Epic Grandeur: The Life of F. Scott Fitzgerald* (1981): 'Bishop was the first friend who fully shared Fitzgerald's commitment to writing, and under his influence Fitzgerald began to develop more serious literary ambitions.' Although the two remained friends, Bishop was sometimes critical of Fitzgerald's work, accusing him, for example, of 'flaws of vulgarity' in a review of *The Beautiful and Damned* (1922) in the New York Herald of 5 March 1922.

Bishop was a first lieutenant of infantry in the First World War. In New York he succeeded Edmund Wilson as managing editor of *Vanity Fair* and worked on the staff of Paramount Pictures. After a period at Cape Cod he returned to New York in 1941 as Publications Director of the Office of the Co-ordinator of Inter-American Affairs. He died of heart failure and is remembered for the grandiose tone of poems such as 'The Hours': 'I cannot animate with breath/syllables in the open mouth of death.' Fitzgerald was stung by Bishop's suggestion (in the *Virginia*

Quarterly of Winter 1937) that he had been a 'suck around the rich'. In a requiem for Fitzgerald, however, Bishop wrote: 'I have lived with you the hour of your humiliation./I have seen you turn upon the others in the night/And of sad self-loathing'.

NICOLE DIVER

F. Scott Fitzgerald, *Tender Is The Night* (1939, revd. version 1948)

Zelda Fitzgerald (1900–48)

Further reading: Nancy Milford, Zelda Fitzgerald (1970)

F. Scott Fitzgerald drew much of his literary material from his turbulent life with Zelda Sayre, the woman he married in 1920. Together Scott and Zelda became social celebrities whose drunken exploits were the subject of much gossip, and whose lives were vicariously shared by readers of Fitzgerald's fiction. Zelda is, for example, the belle Sally Carroll Happer in 'The Ice Palace'; Jonquil Cary in 'The Sensible Thing'; Rosalind Connage in *This Side of Paradise* (1920) and Minna, Monroe Stahr's dead wife, in *The Last Tycoon* (1941). Fitzgerald's most profound portrait of Zelda, however, is through the character of Nicole in *Tender is the Night*.

Zelda, a chronic schizophrenic, had her first serious breakdown in Paris in April 1930. After being treated in the Malmaison clinic, near Paris, she entered the Valmont clinic in Switzerland; on 5 June 1930 she was transferred to the Prangins clinic at Nyon, Switzerland. She was released from Prangins on 15 September 1931, and the Fitzgeralds returned to the USA. Zelda's father, Judge Sayre, died at the end of 1931, and in February 1932 her second serious breakdown led to hospitalization in the Phipps Psychiatric Clinic of Johns Hopkins Hospital, Baltimore. When Fitzgerald began to work on *Tender is The Night* in the summer of 1932 he made notes on the heroine, Nicole; 'She is an innocent, widely read but with no experience and no orientation except what [the hero Dick Diver] supplies her. Portrait of Zelda – that is, a part of Zelda.' Dick Diver is an autobiographical projection of Fitzgerald as he saw himself: a brilliant man brought down by the emotional instability of a beautiful woman.

The novel (in the author's revised version) begins with a 'Case History 1917-19'. In a Swiss clinic Dick Diver – a young psychiatrist apparently with a brilliant future ahead of him – treats Nicole Warren, a wealthy young lady traumatically shocked as a result of being raped by her father (an invented detail with no foundation in Zelda's life). Diver marries Nicole, uses her family's money to set himself up professionally, but deteriorates as he increasingly seeks refuge in drink to cope with the pressure of life with Nicole. While Nicole surfaces as an individual, the appropriately named Diver goes down in a sea of alcohol. At the end of the book we learn that 'Nicole kept in touch with Dick after her new marriage . . . Dick opened an office in Buffalo, but evidently without success . . . In the last letter she had from him he told her that he was practising in Geneva, New York'. In actuality, Fitzgerald – an alcoholic – died of a heart attack; Zelda died in a fire in a sanatorium in Asheville, North Carolina.

LUCKY JIM DIXON

Kingsley Amis, *Lucky Jim* (1954)

Philip Larkin (1922–85)

Further reading: Anthony Thwaite, *Larkin at Sixty* (1982)

English fiction was treated to a new sense of irreverant fun when Kingsley Amis presented the adventures of *Lucky Jim* as a university lecturer in a Department of History presided over by the pompous Professor Welch. The reader sympathizes with Jim Dixon as he endures the absurd pretensions of the academic establishment around him. Professor Welch's idea of a musical event is not, for example, Jim's: 'he disclosed that the local composer and the amateur violinist were going to "tackle" a violin sonata by some Teutonic bore, that an unstated number of recorders would then perform some suitable item, and that at some later time Johns might be expected to produce music from his oboe'.

The dread of cultural bores is something Kingsley Amis shared with his friend Philip Larkin who combined a great poetic gift with an enthusiasm for traditional jazz. *Lucky Jim* is dedicated to Larkin who was Amis's contemporary at wartime Oxford where they both read English at St John's College. In a tribute to the poet, included in

Anthony Thwaite's *Larkin at Sixty* (1982). Amis wrote: 'Jim Dixon's surname has something to do with ordinariness, but at the outset had much more to do with Dixon Drive, the street where Philip lived [in Leicester]. Yes, for a short time it was to be his story.' As Amis points out, Jim Dixon differed from Larkin. Whereas Larkin was tall and lean, Dixon is 'on the short side, fair and round-faced'. Moreover, Larkin worked as a librarian not a lecturer. Lucky Jim Dixon retains, though, some Larkinesque attitudes for he distrusts those in authority, dislikes stuffiness and is temperamentally inclined to endorse Larkin's dread (in 'Vers de Société') of 'Asking that ass about his fool research.' For a sample of Larkin's sceptical views on high culture, see his volume of essays *Required Writing* (1983).

WILLIAM DOBBIN
William Makepeace Thackeray, *Vanity Fair* (1848)

Archdeacon John Allen

Further reading: Ann Monsarrat, *An Uneasy Victorian – Thackeray the Man* (1980)

Thackeray described *Vanity Fair* as a novel without a hero, but if it has a hero, that hero is William Dobbin. He is a gangling, awkward boy at school, and hero-worships George Osborne. He falls in love with Amelia (see AMELIA SEDLEY) but keeps his love a secret to himself so as not to stand in the way of the happiness of his admired George and his beloved Amelia. As a character he barely develops, and the description we are given of him as a boy gives us William Dobbin as he appears throughout *Vanity Fair*: '(He) was the quietest, the clumsiest, and, as it seemed, the dullest of Dr Swishtail's young gentlemen. His parent was a grocer in the City: and it was bruited abroad that he was admitted . . . upon what are called "mutual principles" – that is to say, the expenses of his board and schooling were defrayed by his father in goods, not money; and he stood there – almost at the bottom of the school – in his scraggy corduroys and jacket, through the seams of which his great big bones were bursting – as the representative of so many pounds of tea, candles, sugar . . . The jokes were frightful, and merciless against him. "Hello, Dobbin", one wag would say, "here's good news in the paper. Sugar is ris, my boy". Another would set a sum – "If a pound of mutton-candles cost sevenpence-halfpenny, how much must Dobbin cost?" ...' He is so poor at Latin that he is compelled to remain the very last of Dr Swishtail's scholars, while boys much younger shoot ahead, but he makes the best of it: 'with downcast stupefied look, his dog's-eared primer, and his tight corduroys. High and low, all made fun of him. They sewed up those corduroys, tight as they were. They cut his bed strings . . . They sent him parcels, which, when opened, were found to contain the paternal soap and candles . . . and he bore everything quite patiently and was entirely dumb and miserable.' The quality which is stressed time and again is his humility in the face of all that life has to offer. He is a more admirable character than his beloved Amelia. Thackeray told a friend, while composing *Vanity Fair,* that Dobbin would marry Amelia: 'and when he has got her, he will not find her worth the having.' This is a portrait of John Allen, Thackeray's friend at Cambridge, who had tried to console him during periods of religious doubt. His simple devotion, and assurances that he would pray for him, with tears streaming down his simple, honest face, impressed Thackeray for life. Allen was a tall, gangling man, who pursued a successful career in the Anglican church, who later stood in the way of William Henry Brookfield's church preferment, remembering his days of undergraduate levity (see LORD CASTLEWOOD).

DOC
John Steinbeck, *Cannery Row* (1945)

Edward F. Ricketts
(died 1948)

John Steinbeck's *Cannery Row* is dedicated to 'Ed Ricketts who knows why or should' since, as the central character Doc, he dominates the book and gives it its human warmth. All the life that thrives on Cannery Row is drawn to Doc, owner and operator of the Western Biological Laboratory. Doc's existence is an example to others: 'He wears a beard and his face is half Christ and half satyr and his face tells the truth ... He became the fountain of philosophy and science and art ... Doc would listen to any kind of nonsense and change it for you to a kind of wisdom.

His mind had no horizon – and his sympathy had no warp. He could talk to children, telling them very profound things so that they understood. He lived in a world of wonders, of excitement. He was concupiscent as a rabbit and gentle as hell.'

In 1930 John Steinbeck and his wife Carol moved to a cottage in Pacific Grove on the Monterey Peninsula. There, on Cannery Row in Monterey, Steinbeck met Ed Ricketts, owner of the Pacific Biological Laboratory. Steinbeck's wife worked in the laboratory, which collected and sold West Coast biological specimens, and Steinbeck himself became fascinated by the ecological implications of Ricketts's research into marine biology. He adopted Ricketts as his guru and collaborated with him on a book *The Sea of Cortez* (1941).

Driving across the Southern Pacific tracks in 1948 Ricketts was killed when his car was struck by the evening train from San Francisco. Steinbeck wrote to a friend: 'there died the greatest man I have known and the best teacher. It is going to take a long time to reorganize my thinking and my planning without him. It is good that he was killed during the very best time of his life with his work at its peak and with the best girl he ever had. I am extremely glad for that.'

Further reading:
F.W. Watt, *Steinbeck* (1962)

DODO

E.F. Benson, *Dodo* (1893)

Margot Asquith (1864–1945)

Dodo, the eponymous heroine of E.F. Benson's satire on English society, is a young woman pursued by various men (including a prince) in search of the perfect wife. Jack Broxton, for example, is jealous when he hears that Dodo is contemplating a marriage to Lord Chesterford. Dodo tells him: 'I must have lots of money. Yes, a big must *and* a big lot . . . My husband must be so devoted to me that anything I do will seem good and charming . . . I must have everything I want. It is what I live on.' Jack reflects on Dodo's character: 'Stimulating she certainly was – what lovable woman is not – and personally he had known her long, and she did wear well. The hidden depths and unsuspected shallows were exactly what he loved her for; no one ever fell in love with a canal; and though the shallows were commoner than the depths, and their presence was sometimes indicated by a rather harsh jarring of the keel, yet he believed, fully and sincerely, in the dark, mysterious depths for love to lose itself in.'

When the novel appeared it was a popular success and readers recognised Dodo as a portrait of Emma Alice Margaret – 'Margot' – Tennant. Daughter of Sir Charles Tennant, the Glasgow ironmaster, Margot was a woman of character who became one of the leading lights of English society. A year after *Dodo* appeared she married Herbert Henry Asquith, then Home Secretary in Gladstone's government, and later Prime Minister (1908-16). Margot was as well known for her sardonic wit as for her bright personality. Of the fashionable hostess Lady Desborough she said 'Ettie is an ox, she will be made into Bovril when she dies.' Of Lady Diana Cooper she said: 'Diana's main faults are that she takes money from men and spends her day powdering her face till she looks like a bled pig.' Diana's response to this was: 'As bridge twelve hours in the twenty-four cannot really make the brain active, she [Margot] should keep her comments in her pocket.' *The Autobiography of Margot Asquith* (1922) gave Margot's often indiscreet observations on the English society she knew so well.

MEG DODS

Sir Walter Scott, *St Ronan's Well* (1823)

Marion Ritchie (died 1822)

St Ronan's Well, Scott's only novel set in contemporary times, concerns the marital and financial intrigues of two half-brothers. Lockhart recalls that it was based on 'a tale of dark domestic guilt' which Walter Scott had learned as part of his duties as Sheriff, the details of which 'were not of a kind to be dwelt upon'. Even so, Scott's publisher persuaded him to tone down some of the more salacious aspects of the story and his original intention of including seduction had to be abandoned. The novel is situated in the fictitious Scottish spa of St Ronan's Well. The most striking and memorable character in the book is the tyrannical landlady of the Cleikum Inn, Meg Dods. He took the name from Mrs Margaret Dods, who ran an inn at Howgate, Moorfoots, which was well known to Scott and his companions, but the personality of Meg has its sources elsewhere. Meg has hair of a brindled colour, between black and grey: 'which was apt to escape in elflocks from under her mutch [cap] when she was thrown into violent agitation; long skinny hands, terminated by stout talons; grey eyes, thin lips, a robust person, a broad though flat chest, capital wind, and a voice that could match a choir of fish-women'. *Chamber's Journal* for June 1833 identified her original as Marion Ritchie, daughter of the Provost of Peebles. She was a gentlewoman and well-connected, but had considerable independence of mind, which she was seldom averse to expressing. When treated with respect by her customers she was civility itself, but was always outspoken 'and could never conceal her real sentiments when either provoked or – as she thought – injured'. She succeeded her father as inn-keeper of the Cross Keys in Peebles, though 'she rather appeared as the obliging than as the obliged party in her transactions; and if any indulgence or comfort was expected . . . it was necessary, in the first place, to use all soothing terms of speech'. She was able to lord it in this fashion in the first place as hers was for many years the only hostelry in the town nor for twenty miles distance. She once served some French officers barley broth and hearing them declare it to be '*bon, bon*!' she burst out: '*Banes*! d'ye say there's *banes* in *my* kail? Get out o' my house, ye hallan-shaker-lookin' scoundrels!' She tolerated no excesses in her household, and whenever she thought a man had enough she would say: 'You have had plenty now. Gae awa hame to your mother.' Scott himself was a victim of her wrath when he broke a bowl there and secretly took it with him to have it mended, to be met when he returned it with a shower of abuse for 'leaving her decent house in such a clandesteen manner . . . a 'boot a bit of crockerie-ware that wasna worth fashin' ane's thoomb aboot'.

MR DOMBEY

Charles Dickens, *Dombey and Son* (1848)

Thomas Chapman

Further reading: Edgar Johnson, *Charles Dickens – His Tragedy and Triumph* (1953)

Paul Dombey is a proud London merchant, father of Florence and Paul (see PAUL DOMBEY), whose wife dies in childbirth bringing young Paul into the world. He neglects Florence (who is about ten) and concentrates all his efforts on making Paul into a son who will be worthy of him (Mr Dombey). When Paul dies, Mr Dombey marries the proud Edith, daughter of Mrs Skewton (see MRS SKEWTON), but she has an affair with his manager, James Carker, and the couple run away to France. Carker has been defrauding Dombey's business for a long time and the firm goes bankrupt. At the crisis of his emotional, social and financial life Florence returns to him they are reconciled: 'Dombey was about eight-and-forty years of age . . . rather bald, rather red, and though a handsome well-made man, too stern and pompous in appearance to be prepossessing . . .' Dickens was very particular, suspiciously so, in his directions to his illustrator, Hablot Browne, and congratulated him on the exactness of the portrayal. This is because he had in mind a man well known to him – Thomas Chapman, the chairman of Lloyd's, in whose Leadenhall Street company Augustus Dickens, the novelist's younger brother, was employed. This is an obvious reference in *Dombey*: '. . . the offices of Dombey and Son were within the liberties of the City of London, and within hearing of Bow Bells . . . the Royal Exchange was close at hand; the Bank of England . . . was their magnificent neighbour. 'Respect for persons still living no doubt compelled John Forster in his biography of Dickens to write that it was most unlikely that Dickens based Mr Dombey on Thomas Chapman. Edgar Johnson records that: 'when the book began to appear there were readers who were sure they recognized the character of Thomas Chapman' *(Charles Dickens – His Tragedy and Triumph*, 1952). There are other more striking pieces of evidence. The original plan of the novel, before Dickens started to write it, encompassed the idea that Mr Dombey's firm would go bankrupt, but he had not worked up the idea that Dombey would be defrauded by a colleague who would also seduce his wife. But in Thomas Chapman's firm a fellow clerk of Augustus Dickens's, named Thomas Powell, by a series of forgeries gained £10,000 from his employers. Thomas Chapman informed Dickens of these events himself. Chapman forgave Powell out of compassion for his wife and family, but he came before the law for other forgeries and pleaded insanity. He was confined at an asylum in Hoxton. When released he went to New York where he practised further forgeries and published an article in the *Evening Post* in which he said Mr Dombey was a literal portrait of Thomas Chapman. Powell's activities must have sparked off in Dickens's imagination the idea of James Carker's defalcations.

PAUL DOMBEY

Charles Dickens, *Dombey and Son* (1848)

Harry Burnett (died 1848)

Little Paul Dombey is his father's son and heir. Mr Dombey thought the world of his son. His mother died in bringing him into the world and he is cared for by Polly Toodle and Mrs Wickham. He is sent to Mrs Pipchin's establishment at Brighton and then on to Dr Blimber's academy. His father always had great plans for him and was all for pushing him forward and setting him great tasks. But Paul is a thoughtful and 'old fashioned' child, devoted to his sister Florence, the unwanted and neglected daughter of Mr Dombey, who is about ten when the novel opens. He is naturally delicate, and often in frail health: 'Every tooth was a breakneck fence, and every pimple in the measles a stone wall to him. He was down in every fit of the whooping-cough, and rolled upon and crushed by a whole field of small diseases. . . . Some bird of prey got into his throat instead of the thrush; and the very chickens turning ferocious – if they have anything to do with that infant malady to which they lend their name – worried him like tiger-cats.' But he is always wise beyond his years and has a disconcerting way of cutting right through cant and artifice with a directness and ruthlessness which adults find quite unstoppable. He tells Mrs Pipchin that there is nobody like his sister Florence. 'Well!' retorted Mrs Pipchin, shortly, 'and there's nobody like me, I suppose'. 'Ain't there really though?' asked Paul, leaning forward in his chair, and looking at her very hard. 'No,' said the old lady. 'I am glad of that,' observed Paul, 'that's a very good thing.' Paul is taken seriously ill when he is nine and dies soon afterwards, in one of the most famous of Dickens's child-death scenes.

The episode was written in January 1847. Paul was based on the frail and crippled son of Dickens's sister, Frances, who married Henry Burnett, the musician and actor. Frances was to die some months before her son, and she spoke to Charles Dickens 'about an invention she had heard of that she would like to have tried on the deformed child's back'.

Further reading:
E.W.F. Tomlin, *Charles Dickens 1812–70 (1970)*

DON ARMADO

William Shakespeare, *Love's Labours Lost* (1598)

Sir Walter Raleigh (1552–1618)

Don Adriano de Armado is a fantastical Spanish warrior and self-consciously romantic figure of great pomposity and arrogance. The major element in his comicality lies in his grandiloquent and extravagant language. He is in love with the country wench Jaquenetta and is rivalled by Costard. A love letter he writes to her is given by mistake to Rosaline, the clever young lady-in-waiting to the Queen of France. He portrays Hector in the pageant of the Nine Worthies in Act V (see HOLOFERNES). It has been suggested that this is a satiric portrait of Gabriel Harvey (see MOTH) but the parallels and references to Sir Walter Raleigh are more convincing.

Raleigh was a soldier, poet, navigator, explorer and the Queen's leading favourite until he made the tragic mistake of marrying one of her ladies-in-waiting. He was a court rival to the Earl of Essex, who was supported by Shakespeare. Raleigh was a major figure in the group known as the School of the Night, a fellowship of intellectuals who had ambitions similar to those of the King of Navarre and his friends in *Love's Labours Lost* – to abjure the company of women and to spend their time in study and pursuits of the mind. Raleigh's associates included Thomas Harriot, Henry Percy, Matthew Roydon and George

Further reading:
M.C. Bradbrook, *The School of Night* (1936)

Chapman, whose poem *The Shadow of Night* (1594) glorified the life of contemplation and study in contrast to the shallow entertainments of society and female company. Shakespeare's comedy contains a direct reference to the group: 'Black is the badge of hell,/The hue of dungeons and the school of night' (Act IV, Scene 3, lines 254-5).

Raleigh was tried for conspiracy against James I, found guilty but reprieved in 1603. He undertook an expedition up the Orinoco in 1616 when he was given strict orders not to make war against the Spanish. The Spanish settlement at San Tomas was burned and his punishment was demanded by the Spanish minister. He was executed in 1618. He wrote: 'What is our life? a play of passion;/Our mirth, the music of division;/Our mothers' wombs the tiring-houses be/Where we are dressed for this short comedy./Heaven the judicious sharp spectator is,/That sits and marks still who doth act amiss;/Our graves that hide us from the searching sun/Are like drawn curtains when the play is done,/Thus march we playing to our latest rest;/Only we die in earnest – that's no jest.' Raleigh may also be portrayed as Tarquin in the *Rape of Lucrece*, 'for his excessive pride surnamed Superbus'.

DON GIOVANNI

Opera, *Don Giovanni* (1787) music by Wolfgang Amadeus Mozart, libretto by Lorenzo da Ponte

Giovanni Jacopo Casanova (1725–98)

Further reading: Bonamy Dobree, *Life of Casanova* (1933)

Although the Don Juan story is widely spread in European literature, the figure was definitively placed in Western consciousness by Mozart's opera. When the composer and his librettist wanted expert advice they called in Casanova. Not only do they share first names, there are other fundamental and unmistakable parallels. The existence of an original person, Don Juan Tenorio, has long been discredited, but what is certain is Don Juan's first appearance in European literature in a play attributed to Tirso de Molina, *El Burlador de Sevilla y convidado de piedra*, printed in Barcelona in 1630. The story of the blaspheming profligate who invites a dead man to supper and is dragged off to hell is found much earlier and seems to be a universal type.

The opera opens with the Don attempting to seduce Donna Anna, daughter of the Commendatore. Giovanni is disturbed by Anna's father and then kills him in a sword fight. Giovanni flees with his servant, Leporello. Donna Elvira, Giovanni's discarded mistress, now appears only to be told – in the famous 'catalogue' aria – by Leporello, that she is wasting her time in pursuing Giovanni, as the Don has numerous conquests and is always seeking new game. Giovanni further attempts to seduce the peasant girl Zerlina, already betrothed. Mockingly Giovanni invites the statue of Anna's father, which stands on his grave, to supper. It arrives at the banquet and drags him to hades.

Casanova's autobiography, *Histoire de ma vie* (in twelve volumes!), catalogues amours in strikingly similar vein to Leporello's 'catalogue' aria. Leporello tells Elvira his master's adventures number 2,065: 640 in Italy, 231 in Germany, 100 in France, 91 in Turkey and in Spain some 1,003. Casanova claimed well over 130 women, including conquests of Italian, French, Swiss, German, English, Greek, Spanish, Polish, Dutch, Russian, African and Portuguese women of all ranks of society from the ages of eleven to over fifty, married, single and widowed, dark, blond and brown, involving sexual activities of all imaginable kinds. He was, like Don Giovanni, a connoisseur, genuinely believing in the passion of love. 'I was not born a nobleman,' he asserted, 'I achieved nobility.'

DON JUAN

Lord Byron, *Don Juan* (1819–24)

Lord Byron (1788–1824)

Although Byron believed his satiric poem *Don Juan* might have been 'too free for these very modest days' it is in fact a parody, or an inversion of the Don Juan legend – far from being an arch seducer from whose advances no woman is secure, Byron's hero is a naive and Candide-like innocent who is constantly seduced almost against his will. Juan is given a strictly academic education by his mother, Donna Inez (a satiric portrait of Byron's wife, Annabella) which totally fails to equip him for the moral complexities of life. In his teens he is seduced by Donna Julia, a young married woman: 'Juan she saw, and, as a pretty child,/caressed him often – such a thing might be/Quite innocently done, and harmless styled,/When she had twenty years, and thirteen he;/But I am not so sure I should have smiled/When he was sixteen, Julia twenty-three.' This is followed by exploits in Seville, the Greek islands, Constantinople, Russia and England.

To a very large extent *Don Juan* is self-confessional. Juan's precocious sexuality is a reflection of Byron's own. A very close friend, John Cam Hobhouse, related that when Byron was nine, 'a free Scotch girl used to come to bed to him and play tricks with his person'. His amours continued at Harrow and Cambridge and in seemingly inexhaustible profligacy in London, Greece, Albania and Asia Minor. He enjoyed a tempestuous affair with Lady Caroline Lamb, wife of the future prime minister, Lord Melbourne, and a liaison with Jane Elizabeth Scott, the wife of the Earl of Oxford. As well as numerous whores, he seduced his half-sister, Augusta Leigh, who bore him a daughter. His astonishing personal magnetism worked like enchantment. Women seemed to throw themselves at him – which is an experience shared by his hero Don Juan. Such a sacrificial victim was Claire Clairmont, half-sister of Shelley's wife, who gave him a daughter. 'I never loved nor pretended to love her,' Byron wrote, 'but a man is a man, and if a girl of eighteen comes prancing to you at all hours, there is but one way . . .' (letter dated 12 January 1817). Scandal forced him into exile in Italy, where his free-wheeling sexuality found free rein. He said that he had enjoyed some two hundred women. 'Perhaps more, for I have not kept count.' His affair with the nineteen-year-old Countess Guiccoli, whose husband he cuckolded in his own house (closely paralleled in the poem) dates immediately prior to its composition.

Further reading:
Leslie Marchand, *Byron – A Biography* (1957)

LITTLE DORRIT

Charles Dickens, *Little Dorrit* (1857)

Mary Ann Cooper (née Mitton)

Amy Dorrit is a classic realization of the child-as-parent in Dickens's work. She recognizes that her father has been broken by his long imprisonment and she – who was born in the Marshalsea prison – takes over the role of parent to the family. She looks after John Clennam while he is imprisoned there and eventually marries him: 'A pale, transparent face, quick in expression, though not beautiful in feature, its soft hazel eyes excepted. A delicately bent head, a tiny form, a quick little pair of busy hands, and a shabby dress.' This is based on Mary Ann, the sisterof Thomas Mitton, whom Charles Dickens got to know when they were clerks together at Lincoln's Inn and who became in later life the novelist's solicitor. In an interview in the *Evening Times* of 26 November 1910, when she was ninety-eight, she recalled the days when she was a friend and playmate of young Boz: 'I marvelled at the facility with which this old lady . . . set back the hands of time,' the journalist recorded. 'A short pause, a slight lifting of the forefinger, a roll of the eyes, and a puckering of the brow were all the external evidence of how the retrospect was being prepared . . . She lived again in the thirties and forties, and was able to roll out the drama of the past . . . She took me back to the days of imprisonment for debt, and to scenes in the Marshalsea prison, in which Dickens's father was lodging at the time she became acquainted with the family. Mrs Cooper's family were farmers at Sunbury, but owing to the illness of her mother, much of her youth was spent under the care of a nurse at a farm in Somers Town (north London, where John Dickens lodged his family in the 1820s). It was here . . . that the friendship with Dickens was established, and here that she was given the sobriquet of 'Little Dorrit' long before the name was immortalised . . . Dickens had a fondness for nicknames, some of which were created without the slightest regard to relation or applicability . . . Dickens, who was four or five years her senior, used to visit her home at Sunbury for rest and recuperation. After hard work in the gallery of the Commons or long hours in the chambers he shared with young Mitton (Thomas Mitton, her brother) he would rush off each Saturday for the

Further reading:
Edwin Pugh, *The Charles Dickens Originals* (1912)

Sunbury coach, and would spend a delightful weekend in ruraldom. It was at such times he gave full play to the mischievous instincts of his boyhood . . . "Little Dorrit" was the co-partner in most of his antics . . .'

DRACULA

Bram Stoker, *Dracula* (1897), *Dracula's Guest* (1914)

Prince Vlad Dracula (1431–76)

Further reading: H. Ludlam, *A Biography of Dracula – The Life Story of Bram Stoker* (1962)

In Bram Stoker's novel *Dracula* the Count is seen, in his coffin, as a being bloated with the blood of others: 'the mouth was redder than ever, for on the lips were gouts of fresh blood, which trickled from the corners of the mouth and ran over the chin and neck ... It seemed as if the whole creature were simply gorged with blood; he lay like a filthy leech, exhausted with his repletion.' Stoker's Dracula is a vampire who terrorizes Transylvania with his nocturnal habits. The historical Dracula was, if anything, more bloodthirsty than the fictional Count; he was not, however, a vampire.

Prince Vlad Dracula was the ruler of Wallachia at a time when the land that is now Romania was occupied by Wallachia, Moldavia and Transylvania; Vlad's father was called Dracul, or Dragon, so the name Dracula means 'son of the dragon'. As a child Vlad was imprisoned by the Turks and would bribe his guards to bring him birds which he first mutilated then impaled on sticks. As an adult he refined this practice and earned the name Vlad Tepes (*tzepa* = spike) or Vlad the Impaler. In his campaign against the infidel Turk he indulged in his favourite torture; his victims were pressed on to the oiled point of a stake and left as the weight of their bodies forced the point through them in an agonizing death that could take hours. After one triumph against the Turks, in 1456, Vlad impaled twenty thousand prisoners. Vlad Dracula's reputation was embellished in Romanian folklore and he was accused of unspeakable acts of cruelty such as forcing mothers to eat their babies and of being a 'wampyr'. In recreating Vlad as a vampire, Stoker seized on the images associated with Dracula and gave him an aura of elegant evil: 'The mouth, so far as I could see under the heavy moustache, was fixed and rather cruel looking, with peculiarly sharp white teeth.'

RICHARD DRITTER

Wyndham Lewis, *The Roaring Queen* (1973)

Walter Richard Sickert (1860–194

Most of the action of Wyndham Lewis's satirical novel *The Roaring Queen* takes place at a weekend party given by Mrs Wellesley-Crook at Beverley Chase, her Oxfordshire mansion. The principal guest is SAMUEL SHODBUTT (Arnold Bennett), the most influential book-reviewer in the land; the other guests are mainly involved in the commercial exploitation of literature. In the context of this company of careerists, Richard Dritter appears as a man of integrity. He is a great painter with an uproarious laugh, a burly physique and a coarse grey beard. Dritter, one of the guests explains, 'was reputed to be the most brilliant talker of all those gathered about Oscar [Wilde] . . . He is a painter, of course, but like his master, Whistler, he has a tongue to his credit as well as a brush.'

The character (as Walter Allen notes in his introduction to the book) is clearly based on the painter Walter Richard Sickert. Born in Munich, the son of a Danish painter, Sickert came to London and studied at the Slade School and with Whistler. Working in an Impressionist idiom, he created atmospheric interiors through broad brushwork. He became president of the Royal Society of British Artists and in 1934 was elected Royal Academician. Lewis, in *Blasting and Bombardiering* (1937), describes how Sickert praised Lewis's *Tarr* (1918) to Arnold Bennett at a London dinner-party: 'I could see Bennett didn't like it. I think Sickert saw that too, for he went on talking about it more and more, at every moment in more ecstatic terms . . . Naturally it was aggravating of Sickert to make Bennett talk about a "young author's" book for half an hour . . . I knew Sickert had made me an enemy though he had not meant to, for he is the kindest man in the world.' Sickert's low opinion of Bennett becomes, in *The Roaring Queen*, Dritter's condemnation of Samuel Shodbutt as a philistine and 'an old ruffian . . . a wicked old ruffian'.

Sickert's personality continues to fascinate writers. In *Jack the*

Ripper: The Final solution (1976) Stephen Knight names Sir William Gull as the Ripper and claims that Sickert was one of his associates: 'Sickert was not a helpless bystander but actually one of the Rippers. He may or may not have killed, but he was an accomplice to the most savage crimes of his generation'.

HENRY DRUMMOND

Film, *Inherit the Wind* (written by Nathan E. Douglas and Harold Jacob Smith, based on the play by Jerome Lawrence and Robert E. Lee, directed by Stanley Kramer, 1960)

Clarence Darrow (1857–1938)

Further reading:
I. Stone, *Charles Darrow for the Defence* (1941)

A schoolmaster in a small town in the southern United States is accused of teaching the theory of evolution to his pupils. The fundamentalists get him put on trial. The prosecution is led by a supporter of the Old Style Religion, Martin Harrison Brady, and the schoolmaster is defended by a brilliant liberal advocate Henry Drummond. The whole trial becomes a *cause célèbre* and public interest is fanned by its regularly being reported by E.R. Hornbeck, a cynical newspaper reporter, who is sent to cover the proceedings. The film provided starring roles for Frederick March (Brady), Spencer Tracy (Drummond) and Gene Kelly (Hornbeck).

This was based on the infamous Scopes trial in Tennessee in 1925, in which the courtroom confrontation of William Jennings Bryan (1860-1925) and Clarence Darrow was reported by H.L. Mencken in the *American Mercury*. Clarence Darrow was a famous defence attorney. His defence of Eugene Debs and the American Railway Union in 1894 made his name a household word. He represented the coalminers in the anthracite strike of 1902. William Haywood and other 'Wobblies' on the charge of murdering a former governor of Idaho. 'Wobblies' was the popular name for the Industrial Workers of the World, a labour organization founded in 1905, a coalition of left-wing trade unionists and political theorists. Their policy was the destruction of capitalism by direct action, similar to syndicalism in Europe. Darrow was a long-term opponent of capital punishment, and secured life imprisonment for Richard Loeb and Nathan Leopold in the Chicago youth-slaying case. This case was the basis of the film *Compulsion* in which the role of the defence lawyer, a portrait of Clarence Darrow, was played by Orson Welles. Darrow once said: 'I don't believe in God because I don't believe in Mother Goose.' This would hardly endear him to his opponent, William Jennings Bryan, who was a devout supporter of Protestant fundamentalism. Scopes was convicted, but Bryan died at the end of the trial. Darrow went on to defend eleven blacks who were accused of the murder of a Klu Klux Klansman in Detroit, and in 1934 was chosen by Franklin D. Roosevelt to head a commission to study the operation of the National Recovery Administration.

THE DUCHESS OF MALFI

John Webster, *The Duchess of Malfi* (1614)

Giovanna, Duchess of Amalfi (died 1513)

Further reading:
Gunnar Boklund, *The Duchess of Malfi – Sources, Themes, Characters* (1962), A. Lisini and A. Liberati, *Albero della famiglia Piccolomini* (1899)

Webster's *Duchess of Malfi* is one of the greatest Jacobean tragedies. The Duchess has recently been widowed. She reveals her love for Antonio, the steward of her court. Her two brothers – one of them a cardinal, the other the Duke of Calabria, insist that she should not marry again. Their motives are to get their hands on her property. The Duchess and Antonio secretly marry. The Cardinal and the Duke of Calabria employ espionage to watch her every move. Antonio and the Duchess separate for the time being. She is captured by Calabria, tortured and finally strangled together with her children. There is a strong suggestion of incestuous feelings by the Duke of Calabria for his sister, the Duchess of Malfi. He exclaims when he learns that she has married, contrary to his injunction: 'Whate'er thou art that hast enjoy'd my sister,/For I am sure thou hear'st me, for thine own sake/Let me not know thee. I came hither prepar'd/To work thy discovery; yet am now persuaded/It would beget such violent effects/As would damn us both.' He is overcome with grief when he has her murdered: 'Cover her face; mine eyes dazzle: she died young.' Her husband, Antonio, is also killed. The Duke of Calabria is driven mad and his brother, the Cardinal, is killed by the murderer who was hired by the two brothers to kill the Duchess and her husband.

The story is a true one which Webster read in William Painter's *Palace of Pleasure* (1566-67.) The historical facts are these; Enrico of

Aragona, half-brother of Federico, King of Naples, had three children. Lodovico was the eldest, and he became a cardinal. The younger son, Carlo, took the title Marquis of Gerace when Lodovico became a cardinal. Giovanna, their sister, was married in 1490 to Alphonso Piccolimini. Alphonso became Duke of Amalfi in 1493 but he died in 1498. Their son, Alphonso, was born in 1499, and Giovanna was to rule Amalfi during his minority. But she has secretly married Antonio Bologna, former master of her household. Both Antonio and the Duchess are killed, the latter together with her children at Amalfi in 1513. The Duchess is a truly tragic figure in the Shakespearean mould, proclaiming the stature of her soul at the moment of her death: 'I am Duchess of Malfi still.' She stands out in the gloomy, melancholy and revengeful atmosphere of the play as a generous and powerful spirit.

DUESSA

Edmund Spenser, *The Faerie Queene* (1589, 1596)

Mary Queen of Scots (1542-87)

Further reading: Antonia Fraser, *Mary Queen of Scots* (1969)

Duessa is the daughter of Deceit and Shame, and represents falsehood in general in Spenser's allegorical epic, *The Faerie Queene*. In Book I, after the enchantments of Archimago have convinced Redcrosse that Una came to seduce him while he slept, the knight runs away and meets Sansfoy, the Saracen, and his paramour, Fidessa – who is in reality Duessa. She turns herself into the likeness of Una in order to deceive Redcrosse, and she lures him into drinking from an enchanted pool, which causes him to lose his strength. He is thus easy prey for the wicked Orgolio. The latter then takes Duessa as his mistress. Her wickedness is exposed by Prince Arthur (see PRINCE ARTHUR). In Book V Prince Arthur and Sir Artegall (see SIR ARTEGALL) attend the court of Mercila (see UNA), where they are present at the trial of Duessa, who is found guilty of adultery, murder and treason. Nevertheless, Mercila does not have her executed.

This portrait of Mary Queen of Scots, caused much offence north of the border: 'Then there was brought, as prisoner to the barre,/A Ladie of great countenance and place,/But that she it with foule abuse did marre;/Yet did appeare rare beautie in her face,/But blotted with condition vile and base,/That all her other honour did obscure,/And titles of nobilitie deface:/Yet in that wretched semblant she did sure/The peoples great compassion unto her allure.' She is accused of 'many haynous crimes' which had brought 'mickle mischiefe unto many a knight', and in partnership with other villains of having practised to deprive Mercila of her crown. Mary was the daughter of James V of Scotland and Mary of Guise. She was Queen before she was a week old, following her father's defeat at Solway Moss. Promised in marriage to the English King Edward VI, she married the dauphin of France, later Francis II. He died 1560, and when she returned to Scotland the next year she found the Reformation in full flood, led by John Knox. She married her cousin Darnley, who died in mysterious circumstances in 1567. She then married the Earl of Bothwell, who had been implicated in the death of Darnley, in a Protestant ceremony. She abdicated rather than face a trial in Scotland, and fled to England, where she spent nineteen years a prisoner at various strongholds. Implicated in various Catholic conspiracies, it was the Babington plot of 1586 which brought her life to an end. She was tried and condemned, though Elizabeth postponed signing her death warrant. She was a renowned beauty and a woman of great charm and intelligence. She was beheaded at Fotheringhay.

DUNCAN

William Shakespeare, *Macbeth* (1606)

Macbeth, one of King Duncan of Scotland's most honoured commanders, urged on by the prediction of the three weird sisters that he shall be Thane of Cawdor and King thereafter, as well as by his own ambition and that of his wife, murders King Duncan while he is a guest at his castle (see MACBETH). He allays suspicion by committing the murder with daggers belonging to the King's servants, who are drunk and asleep. The historical King Duncan was killed in battle by Macbeth in 1040.

King Duff of Scotland (died 972), **Henry Stewart, Lord Darnley** (1545–67)

Shakespeare based *Macbeth* partly on the career of the real Macbeth, but for the act of regicide he went back to Holinshed's *Chronicles of England, Scotlande and Irelande* (1577) to the murder of King Duff by the ambitious Donwald. Here the King's chamberlains are drugged, Donwald has an ambitious wife and witchcraft plays a part in the story. Shakespeare was really compelled to alter the account of Macbeth's career found in the chronicles, for this details the complicity of Banquo in the crime, and King James I was supposedly descended from Banquo. *Macbeth* was performed before King James I and King Christian of Denmark in 1606. This alteration of the story was also made in order to alter the crime so that it resembled the murder of Lord Darnley, the father of James I, by Bothwell in 1567. Darnley was the Earl of Ross and Duke of Albany, and second husband of Mary, Queen of Scots, and through his mother, Lady Margaret Douglas, was the great-grandson of King Henry VII. His mother was ambitious that he should marry Mary, and for this purpose she sent him to France in 1560. He married Mary in 1565, but was refused the crown matrimonial and removed from political influence by David Rizzio, Mary's Italian favourite. Darnley was party to the murder of Rizzio by several Scottish nobles. Flattered and cajoled by Mary, he betrayed his associates to her and aided her escape to Dunbar from Holyrood. He refused to be present at the baptism of his son, James (who was to become King of England) and several Scottish nobles plotted to rid Mary of her husband. It is not clear what part she had in the Craigmillar conspiracy. Darnley got wind of the scheme and fled from Stirling to Glasgow, where he was taken ill, possibly from poisoning. Mary came to visit him and there was an apparent reconciliation. Darnley was persuaded to travel to Edinburgh where they stayed for a few days at Kirk o'Field, a house on the outskirts of Edinburgh. On 9 February 1567 Mary left him to attend some gaieties at Edinburgh. The house was blown up with gunpowder and Darnley was found strangled in the grounds. James Hepburn, Fourth Earl of Bothwell, was generally suspected of this murder. He married Mary on 15 May 1567. Since Darnley was the father of James I, he is the direct ancestor of all the sovereigns of England since 1603.

Further reading:
W.H. Thomson, *Shakespeare's Characters – A Historical Dictionary* (1951)

DUNCE

Dunce – noun, a very dull child at school; a stupid person

Johannes Duns Scotus (1265–1308)

The original 'Dunce' was one of the greatest of medieval schoolmen. Scotus was born in Roxburghshire and joined the Franciscan order. He was educated at Oxford and lectured there on theology and philosophy, to numerous students – legend has it that his teaching attracted some thirty thousand. He also taught at Paris and Cologne. He was the founder of a new type of scholarship – a critique of the existing union which had been maintained between Aristotelian philosophy and theology, the powerful tradition inherited from scholars such as Thomas Aquinas. Scotus maintained that Aquinas was in error in subordinating the practical to the theoretical, and seeking in speculation the foundation of faith, instead of realizing Christianity in practical work. It was here that true theology was based. Scotus urged that theology rests in faith, which is practical, not speculative. It is an act of will.

Because he subjected the vast apparatus of theology built up by Aquinas and his followers to the most thorough and searching critical analysis, he earned the name 'Doctor Subtilis'. He supported the doctrine of the Immaculate Conception against the teaching of the Dominicans (Aquinas's order). Scotus's work in turn became the basis of a new orthodoxy, and his followers became the dominating sect, the Scotists or Dunsemen. In the 16th century they were attacked by the New Humanists and reformers, as merchants of a farrago of hair-splitting sophistry. The term Duns became synonymous with a dull obstinate person, impervious to the New Learning. In 1530 Tindale wrote: 'Remember ye not how . . . the old barking curs, Dunces disciples and like draffe called Scotists . . . raged in every pulpit against Greek, Latin

Further reading:
C.R.S. Harris, *Duns Scotus* (1960)

and Hebrew.' (*Answer to More*). In 1728 Alexander Pope published the first version of his verse satire, *The Dunciad*, the epic of the Dunces.

MISS JOAN HUNTER DUNN
John Betjeman, 'A Subaltern's Love-song' (1940)

Joan Hunter Dunn
(born 1916)

At the beginning of the Second World War the poet John Betjeman was enjoying his lunch at the Ministry of Information canteen. When he noticed the deputy catering manageress of the canteen, he is said to have exclaimed: 'Look at that marvellous girl. Gosh, I bet she comes from Aldershot.' The young lady was Joan Hunter Dunn, a doctor's daughter from Farnborough, three miles north of Aldershot. She had been head of house at school and excellent at games. Betjeman took Miss Dunn out to lunch in 1940, and asked her permission to use her name in a poem. She agreed, and 'A Subaltern's Love-song' was ready to begin its literary life as one of Betjeman's most enduringly popular poems. The subaltern of the poem is in love with his fiancée's name as well as her personality, as the opening stanzas show: 'Miss J. Hunter Dunn, Miss J. Hunter Dunn,/furnish'd and burnish'd by Aldershot sun,/What strenuous singles we played after tea,/We in the tournament – you against me!//Love-thirty, love-forty, oh! weakness of joy,/The speed of a swallow, the grace of a boy,/With carefullest carelessness, gaily you won,/I am weak from your loveliness, Joan Hunter Dunn.//Miss Joan Hunter Dunn, Miss Joan Hunter Dunn,/How mad I am, sad I am, glad that you won./The warm-handled racket is back in its press,/But my shock-headed victor, she loves me no less.'

In 1945 Miss Dunn invited Betjeman and his wife Penelope to her wedding to H. Wycliffe Jackson (who died of a heart attack at the age of forty-two). Betjeman, who became Poet Laureate in 1972, kept in touch with Mrs Jackson over the years. When he died in 1983 she was invited to his memorial service at Westminster Abbey. Though Mrs Jackson disliked any publicity about her connexion with the poem – which has been frequently anthologized as well as being one of the most admired items in *John Betjeman's Collected Poems* (1958) – she agreed to send her photograph for inclusion in Bevis Hillier's *John Betjeman: A Life in Pictures* (1984).

MR EAMES

Norman Douglas, *South Wind* (1917)

John Ellington Brooks

Further reading:
Ian Greenlees, *Norman Douglas* (1957)

One of the most extraordinary characters in Norman Douglas's *South Wind* is Ernest Eames who spends his life annotating a book on the antiquities of the island of Nepenthe, where the action of the novel takes place. Although he is absolutely dedicated to his scholarly work he still attracts the gossip that sweeps round the island like the sirocco. Yet Mr Eames is safe and secure in his scholarship: 'He had taken a high degree in classics, though Greek was never much to his taste . . . But Latin – ah, Latin was different! Even at his preparatory school, where he was known as a swot of the first water, he had displayed an unhealthy infatuation for that tongue; he loved its cold, lapidary construction; and while other boys played football or cricket, this withered little fellow used to lark about with a note-book, all by himself, torturing sensible English into its refractory and colourless periods and elaborating, without the help of a Gradus, those inept word-mosaics which are called Latin verses. "Good fun," he used to say, "and every bit as exciting as algebra," as though that constituted a recommendation.'

Norman Douglas was born at Tilquhillie, on Deeside, of distinguished Scottish and German ancestry but found his spiritual home when he settled in Capri. There he came to know John Ellington Brooks who lived on his own and never travelled to the mainland. He was apparently a contented man who had his cat for company, his piano for amusement and his scholarly pursuits for passion. Brooks, the model for Mr Eames, spent his time writing original prose and poetry and translating work from the Greek and Latin. Yet he had no interest in publishing any of this work; scholarship was for him a fine end in itself. When Douglas published *Birds and Beasts of the Greek Anthology* (1927), an annotated list of the animals mentioned by the Greek poets, he used translations by Brooks and dedicated the book to him. That, and a sonnet he once sold, comprised the complete published work of John Ellington Brooks.

HUMPHREY CHIMPDEN EARWICKER

James Joyce, *Finnegans Wake* (1939)

John Stanislaus Joyce (1848–1931)

Further reading:
Richard Ellman, *James Joyce* (1959, 1982)

James Joyce designed *Finnegans Wake* as the dream of Finn MacCool, the legendary Irish hero, as he lies beside the River Liffey and lets the history of Ireland and the world flow through his mind. Finn's modern representative is Humphrey Chimpden Earwicker, keeper of a public house at Chapelizod, on the Liffey outside Dublin. Married to Anna Livia Plurabelle, Earwicker is father of the twins Shem and Shaun and their sister Isabel. Earwicker is also, as Joyce makes clear, an Everyman who has the nickname Here Comes Everybody: 'An imposing everybody he always indeed looked, constantly the same as and equal to himself and magnificently well worthy of any and all such universalisation'. He is, thus, both man and myth: 'To anyone who knew and loved the christlikeness of the big cleanminded giant H.C. Earwicker throughout his excellency long vicefreegal existence the mere suggestion of him as a lustsleuth nosing for trouble in a booby trap rings particularly preposterous.'

As Richard Ellman points out in his biography of Joyce, 'John Joyce is the chief model for Earwicker'. John Stanislaus Joyce, an exuberant Irishman who loved to sing and drink, fathered ten children including the author of *Ulysses*. Born in Cork, John Joyce attended Queens College, Cork, where he excelled at sports. With his fine voice and features he contemplated a musical career, but eventually invested £500 in a new distillery at Chapelizod, on condition that he became the company's secretary with a salary of £300 a year. When the company collapsed the eternally optimistic Joyce became secretary of the United Liberal Club, Dublin. In the general election of 1880 the Liberal candidates Brooks and Lyons succeeded in ousting Sir Arthur Guinness and James Stirling, the Tory MPs for Dublin. The Liberal triumph, partly organized by John Joyce, duly passed into *Finnegans Wake*: 'the grinning statesmen, Brock and Leon, have shunted the grumbling countedtouts, Starlin and Ser Artur Ghinis.'

As a reward for John Joyce's campaigning, the new Lord Lieutenant of Ireland made him the Collector of Rates for Dublin, at a salary of £500 per annum. Nevertheless, Ellman says he 'filled his house with children and debts'.

HARRY EAST

Thomas Hughes, *Tom Brown's Schooldays* (1857)

William Patrick Adam (1823–81), or possibly **William Stephen Raikes** (1821–58)

Further reading: Sydney Selfe, *Chapters From the History of Rugby School* (1910)

Harry East is Tom's mentor right from the first moment that he arrives at Rugby (see TOM BROWN). Even though Tom finds him slightly patronizing, he can't help but admire his assurance and maturity: 'A boy of just about his own height and age, but gifted with the most transcendent coolness and assurance, which Tom felt to be aggravating and hard to bear, but couldn't for the life of him help admiring and envying . . .' He advises Tom on choice of headgear and how to behave when he meets other boys: 'There's nothing for candour like a lower-school boy, and East was a genuine specimen. Frank, hearty and good-natured, well satisfied with himself and his position, and chock full of life and spirits, and all the Rugby prejudices and traditions which he had been able to get together . . . And Tom, notwithstanding his bumptiousness, felt friends with him at once, and began sucking in all his ways and prejudices, as fast as he could understand them . . .' This is one of the immortal friendships of school fiction, and the two boys spend happy hours together and are involved in all manner of scrapes and heroic escapades at Rugby. It is through Tom's influence that the knowing, worldly East eventually becomes a confirmed Christian.

One candidate for the original of the 'good-hearted and facetious Harry East' was the cavalry officer William Stephen Raikes Hodson, who was at Rugby, and graduated at Trinity College, Cambridge in 1844. He served in the Indian Army, giving distinguished service in the Sikh war and the Punjab. He was removed from commanding the Guides in 1855 on a charge of dishonesty, but was cleared by an enquiry. He raised 'Hodson's Horse' during the Mutiny, was commended for outstanding bravery at Delhi, but was killed at Lucknow. Hodson was not at School House, but at Price's. Also he did not go to Rugby until he was sixteen, and therefore the youthful escapades of Harry and Tom were unlikely to have involved him. A more convincing candidate is William Patrick Adam, who was at School House in 1835, and was nicknamed 'Scud' for his prowess in running (this is also East's nickname). Adam was a friend of Thomas Hughes at Rugby, went on to graduate from Trinity College, Cambridge and was called to the bar in 1849. He was secretary to Lord Elphinstone in India 1853-58, and MP for Clackmannan and Kinross 1859-80. At various stages of his distinguished career in public office he was lord of the treasury, commissioner of public works, privy councillor and Liberal whip 1874-80. He was appointed Governor of Madras in 1880, where he died. Other qualities may have been taken from one John Sayer, as Thomas Arnold, younger son of Dr Arnold, wrote in his autobiography, *Passages in a Wandering Life*: 'Among the characers . . . East must have been identified by many Rugbeians with Sayer, a strong, thick-set boy, rather low down in the School.' Sayer and Hughes were good friends after Rugby and Oxford.

EDDIE

Elizabeth Bowen, *The Death of the Heart* (1938)

Goronwy Rees

At the age of sixteen, Portia Quayne, an orphan, goes to live in London with her half-brother Thomas and his wife Anna. Thomas is a partner in Quayne and Merret, an advertising agency which employs Eddie, a somewhat caddish young man: 'Everyone seemed to get a kick out of their relations with Eddie; he was like a bright little cracker that, pulled hard enough, goes off with a loud bang. He had been the brilliant child of an obscure home, and came up to Oxford ready to have his head turned . . . His appearance was charming; he had a proletarian, animal quick grace. His manner, after a year of trying to get the pitch, had become bold, vivid and intimate. He became a quite frank *arriviste* – at the same time, the one thing no one, so far, knew about Eddie was quite how he *felt* about selling himself.' Eddie has had a satirical novel published, has worked on a newspaper, and has a charm that delights Portia. She falls in love with him and romantically dwells on him in her diary. When he eventually rejects her she is appalled and has to be coaxed back home by her half-brother Thomas who regards Eddie as 'a little rat'.

The original of Eddie is identified in A.L. Rowse's *Glimpses of the Great* (1985). Rowse describes how Elizabeth Bowen 'fell in love with Goronwy [Rees], a lower-class irresistible some eight or ten years younger – apt to be a humiliating situation, as it turned out to be. His character, or lack of it, is recognizably rendered in [*The Death of the Heart*] . . . Goronwy was . . . something of a cad.' Son of a Welsh Calvinist minister, Rees was a gifted student who became a Fellow of All Souls College, Oxford. However he was unable, according to Rowse, to pursue any research project with the necessary sense of dedication. He wrote two novels, worked as assistant literary editor of the *Spectator*, and became Principal of Aberystwyth University. When *The Death of the Heart* appeared he recognized himself and pronounced the book brilliant. Later (writes Rowse) he 'changed his mind completely, wrote to Elizabeth [Bowen] bitterly, threatening libel.' He was subsequently persuaded to drop his threat of legal action. Rowse says that when Rees's wife Margie died 'he went off [the rails], and took to drink as such people are apt to do'.

Further reading:
V. Glendinning, *Elizabeth Bowen: Portrait of a Writer* (1977)

MARTIN EDEN

Jack London, *Martin Eden* (1909)

Jack London (1876–1916)

Martin Eden is the story of an unsuccessful writer who is rejected at first by the wealthy woman that he loves. Only Russ Brissenden, a socialist poet, really understands and properly evaluates what Martin Eden is trying to do in his writings. Eden eventually achieves success and as he becomes rich and famous the self-same people who had previously neglected him now come flocking to him and try to court his favour. He is totally disgusted and leaves civilization on a voyage to the South Seas. Totally demoralized and lacking a sense of his bearings, his personality disintegrates and he commits suicide. The writer comments: 'Had Martin Eden been a socialist, he would not have died – he would have been able to find a meaning in life.'

Martin Eden is a self-portrait. Jack London was born in San Francisco, the illegitimate son of one W.H. Chancey, an astrologist and spiritualist, and Flora Wellman, who later married John London. Jack's early days were spent in poverty and upheaval. He worked on the waterfront, sailed to Japan, prospected at the Klondike and read voraciously – Darwin, Marx, Nietzsche, Huxley, Flaubert, Kipling, Melville, Hardy, Conrad and Zola. His stories began to appear in 1900 and *The Call of the Wild*, which made him rich and famous was published in 1903. He was war correspondent in the Russo-Japanese conflict, lived in the slums of London (*The People of the Abyss* 1903) earned and spent large sums and continually undermined an iron physique with drinking. He wrote some fifty books all told – including *The Sea-Wolf* (1904). *White Fang* (1906), *The Iron Heel* (1907), *John Barleycorn* (1913). *The Valley of the Moon* (1913) and *The Star Rover* (1915). He tries to reconcile his obsession with rugged individualism in a struggle against the world, with his fundamental belief in the Marxist concept of human collective cooperation. Like Martin Eden, he committed suicide while at sea.

Further reading:
Joan London, *Jack London and his Times* (1968)

FOXHALL EDWARDS

Thomas Wolfe, *You Can't Go Home Again* (1940)

Thomas Wolfe's posthumously published *You Can't Go Home Again* is an autobiographical novel about George Webber, reluctant college teacher of English and literary hopeful longing for fame. The crucial event in Webber's life is the news that comes to him, in New York, of the

Maxwell Perkins (1884–1947)

Further reading: Andrew Turnbull, *Thomas Wolfe* (1968)

acceptance of his novel *Home to Our Mountains* by Foxhall Edwards, the distinguished editor of the great publishing house of James Rodney & Co. Wolfe's narrative explains that *Home to Our Mountains* 'was a young man's first book . . . it had a good many of the faults and virtues of the kind of thing it was'. Though Webber has his share of insecurities, he is certain of one thing in his life, namely his relationship with Foxhall Edwards: 'During all these desperate years in Brooklyn, when George lived and worked alone, he had only one real friend, and this was his editor, Foxhall Edwards . . . Edwards, the reserved New Englander, with his deep sense of family and inheritance, had always wanted a son but had had five daughters, and as time went on he made of George a kind of foster son.' After describing 'the Fox' as 'great editor and father-confessor and true friend', Wolfe portrays him admiringly: 'A man of five and forty years, not really seeming younger, yet always seeming something of the boy . . . Eyes pale blue, full of a strange misty light, a kind of fair weather of the sea in them, eyes of a New England sailor long months outbound for China on a clipper ship, with something drowned, sea-sunken in them.'

Wolfe's first novel *Look Homeward, Angel* was (like George Webber's *Home to Our Mountains*) published in 1929. It was accepted by the celebrated publishing firm of Scribners, whose perceptive editor Maxwell Perkins helped prepare it for publication. Perkins was determined to encourage a selfconsciously American tone in fiction and became a legendary figure for his encouragement of F. Scott Fitzgerald, Ernest Hemingway and Thomas Wolfe – his three most distinguished, and difficult, Scribners authors. Wolfe relied enormously on Perkins's opinion and editorial skills, and in 1935 took an apartment at 865 Third Avenue, Midtown, New York, two blocks from his editor's home. Though Perkins had just seen Wolfe's *Of Time and the River* (1935) through the press, Wolfe continued to make great demands on his time – usually pressing him to come for a drink and often turning up for meals or a night on the couch.

ELEONORA

Edgar Allan Poe, *Eleonora* (1842)

Virginia Clemm (1823–47)

Further reading: Julian Symons, *The Tell Tale Heart* (1978)

Poe's *Eleonora* is a study of the torture of separation felt between two who truly love each other. It is one of those stories – so characteristic of its author – which extends the frontiers of experience from anguish even unto madness: 'I am come of a race noted for vigour of fancy and ardour of passion. Men have called me mad. . . . We will say, then, that I am mad. I grant, at least, that there are two distinct conditions of my mental existence – the condition of lucid reason . . . and a condition of shadow and doubt.' In the story Eleonora returns after death and forgives the narrator for breaking his vow of eternal love for her by marrying Ermengarde. He had loved Eleonora in his youth. She was the only daughter of his mother's only sister: 'Eleonora was the name of my cousin ... The loveliness of Eleonora was that of the Seraphim; but she was a maiden artless and innocent as the brief life she had led among the flowers.'

Eleonora was based on Poe's first cousin, Virginia Clemm, whom he married when she was only thirteen, on 16 May 1836. He was never able to bear the thought of parting from her, and the torture of separation at the core of *Eleonora* was the real emotion Poe experienced. It was once suggested that Virginia should leave home for a while and stay with a relative, Neilson Poe, who had married Virginia's half-sister, where she could be accommodated and have her schooling paid for. He could not bear it: 'I cannot express in words the fervent devotion I feel towards my dear little cousin – my own darling.' he wrote in a letter. She died when barely twenty-four, after a long and painful illness. It drove him nearly insane and he took to drink and often behaved in a manner friends and colleagues thought insane. The oscillation between hope and despair, sanity and madness, intoxication and sobriety, characteristic of his mood when under the stress of Virginia's illness and death, he had anticipated in the story written five years before. 'We will say, then, that I am mad.'

ELIZA
Mary Wollstonecraft, *Mary, A Fiction* (1788)

Lady Caroline Kingsborough

In her autobiographical *Mary, A Fiction*, Mary Wollstonecraft gives her heroine a mother who is both indolent and self-indulgent. Eliza, Mary's mother, reads romantic novels and dotes on her dogs, letting them share her bed. 'This fondness for animals,' the reader is informed, 'proceeded from vanity, it gave her an opportunity of lisping out the prettiest French expressions of ecstatic fondness, in accents that had never been attuned by tenderness.' After giving birth to several children, Eliza becomes ill: 'After the mother's throes she felt very few sentiments of maternal tenderness: the children were given to nurses, and she played with her dogs.' Eliza does not care for her daughter, and it is only when Mary becomes an heiress that 'her mother began to think her of consequence, and did not call her *the child*'. Though the character has qualities in common with Mary Wollstonecraft's own mother, the chief original of Eliza is Lady Caroline Kingsborough, for whom Mary Wollstonecraft worked as governess from 1786-7.

Caroline was nine when her mother died and left her heiress to huge estates, including Mitchelstown Castle, near Cork, Ireland. To secure the inheritance she was advised by her grandfather to marry her third cousin Robert King, who became Viscount Kingsborough in 1766. When the couple came of age they rebuilt Mitchelstown as a Palladian mansion where they brought up their many children. Caroline was confined to her room with a sore throat on Mary's arrival at Mitchelstown. Eventually Mary was summoned to the presence, a scene described by Claire Tomalin in *The Life and Death of Mary Wollstonecraft* (1974): 'The bed was a turmoil of satins and pet dogs; Mary perceived that the human occupant was a beauty and she established herself, through the yapping, as a woman to be reckoned with. She was clever – better read than her governess in fact; Mary was more intimidated by her than she had expected to be. There was friction from the beginning between the two women; Lady Kingsborough was jealous of Mary's popularity with her children and resentful of Mary's lack of humility. In August 1787, at Bristol Hot Wells, Lady Kinsgborough dismissed Mary.

ELLENORE
Benjamin Constant, *Adolphe* (1816)

Germaine Necker, Madame de Stael (1766-1817)

Further reading: J.C. Herold, *Mistress to an Age* (1959)

The hero of the novel is a brilliant young man who is the son of a member of the government of a small German principality. It is his father's ambition that Adolphe should be educated not only academically (he has just completed a splendid career at the university of Göttingen) but by the world. To this end Adolphe is dispatched to another small German state where it is hoped he will learn something of sophisticated court life. Here Adolphe meets Ellènore. She is the mistress of an aristocrat and has already borne him two children. Adolphe decides that he will seduce her and is successful. He almost convinces himself that he is in love with her, although he is conscious most of the time that his rational mind is in charge of his emotions and his activities. To some extent his feelings for Ellènore are the result of his pity for her, and these are the feelings which he sometimes mistakes for love. The dynamic tension in the novel is the result of the contrast Constant portrays between reason and emotions. He determines to leave her. At the same time Ellènore finally breaks with her lover, the count, and she is now free to follow Adolphe back to his home. His father disapproves of the relationship and make arrangements to have Ellènore sent away. Adolphe is now precipitated, partly by affection for her and partly by pity for her, to run away with Ellènore. They travel together to Bohemia and on to Warsaw. He has now seriously tired of her and plans to leave her. The truth dawns on Ellènore and she dies, brokenhearted.

Constant was a brilliantly intelligent civil servant, courtier and political journalist who had a great weakness for women older than himself. He was seduced by an older woman when he was eighteen. *Adolphe* seems to be based on his experiences with three women: Madame de Charrière, an older woman who greatly influenced him; Anna Lindsay, whom he seduced from another lover; and Madame de Stael, who was the daughter of Louis XIV's finance minister, and a critic, philosopher and novelist. She met Constant in 1794, and their relationship lasted until 1811. She had a great hold over him although their association was severely strained by jealousies and misunderstandings. It seems that *Adolphe* is an exploration of his affair with Madame de Stael in which he exploits the narrative framework of his association with Anna Lindsay.

ELSA

H.D., *Bid Me to Live* (1960)

Frieda Lawrence (1879–1956)

Further reading: Barbara Guest, *Herself Defined: The Poet H.D. and her World* (1984)

Bid Me to Live opens with the autobiographical heroine Julia Ashton living in Queen's Square, London, and brooding over the sexual affair between her husband RAFE (H.D.'s husband Richard Aldington) and Bella Carter (Dorothy Yorke). Julia is sustained by her correspondence with the novelist RICO (D.H. Lawrence), who comments on her poems. Having been ordered out of Cornwall, Rico and his German wife Elsa arrive at Queen's Square to stay with Julia. It is obvious to Julia that Elsa expects her, Julia, to sleep with Rico so she, Elsa, can make other arrangements. Elsa's chain-smoking, hearty Teutonic manner and guttural German grate on Julia who nevertheless acknowledges the influence Elsa has on her husband: 'Elsa was at-one in her straightforward manner... She had the flair and the indifference and the independence of her class; her pre-war German distinction seemed to send out waves of warmth, it was Rubens in a gallery. It was she really who had made a sort of aura round Rico, no one of his own people had been able to give him this confidence, it was the old-German attitude, that they jeered at in the daily papers, "kultur" really, if you come to think of it.' Elsa is a well observed impression of D.H. Lawrence's wife, Frieda.

In April 1912 – a month before the publication of his second novel *The Trespasser* – Lawrence went to Nottingham to see Professor Ernest Weekley, who had taught him French at Nottingham University. Weekley was married to Frieda von Richthofen – an aristocratic German girl fifteen years his junior – and they had three children. Some six weeks after their first meeting Lawrence and Frieda eloped to Germany, and married on their return to England in 1914. Henceforth, Frieda became part of the legend of Lawrence, the sexual saviour who preached an uninhibited message of erotic passion. In October 1917, probably on account of Frieda's German origins (she was the cousin of Manfred, Baron von Richthofen, the flying ace killed in action in 1918) Lawrence and Frieda were ordered out of Cornwall. Arriving in London, they moved to 44 Mecklenburgh Square, where H.D. lent them a room. In her memoir *Not I, But the Wind*... (1935) Frieda recalled that during this period at Mecklenburgh Square, 'Lawrence invented wonderful charades. Once we played the Garden of Eden. Lawrence was the Lord, H.D. was the tree, Richard Aldington waving a large chrysanthemum was Adam, and I was the serpent, and a little scared at my part.'

ELSHENDER THE RECLUSE

Sir Walter Scott, *The Black Dwarf* (1816)

David Ritchie (1740–1811)

Further reading: James Skene, *Series of Sketches of Existing Localities Alluded to in Waverley Novels* (1829)

The Black Dwarf concerns a deformed recluse whose small and crippled person is taken as an outward and visible sign of his evil nature, yet whose influence on others is for the good. Shunned as he is by society he has grown not only into a recluse but also into something of a misanthrope, embittered by the isolation brought upon him by his unacceptable physical appearance: 'His head was of uncommon size, covered with a fell of shaggy hair, partly grizzled with age; his eyebrows, shaggy and prominent, overhung a pair of small, dark, piercing eyes ... The rest of his features were of the coarse, rough-hewn stamp.' He has a wild, irregular and peculiar expression, and his body is thick and square: 'like that of a man of middle size... mounted upon two large feet; but nature seemed to have forgotten the legs and the thighs, or they were so very short as to be hidden by the dress which he wore. His arms were long and brawny, furnished with two muscular hands.' He lives in a lonely part of Scotland during the early 18th century, living in a hovel of stones he built himself. He has the reputation of a wizard, though as the tale develops the true benevolence of his powers is revealed. He saves Grace Armstrong from robbers and restores her to her beloved Hobbie Elliot. He intervenes in the forced marriage of Isabella Vere with Sir Frederick Langley – a marriage arranged by her father for his own advantage. It is eventually revealed that the recluse is really Sir Edward Manley, a close relative of Isabella's, who had been presumed dead but who has lived in isolation embittered by his deformities. Isabella's father is now deeply personally indebted to him for saving his daughter. Sir Walter Scott met David Ritchie, the original of the recluse, in 1797, at Hallyards in Peebleshire. He was on a journey with his brother up the Tweed valley to Moffat and Carlisle and the English Lakes. Ritchie was a celebrated local character, known as 'Bowed Davie' or 'Dauvit'. He was three feet six inches high, very ugly and ungainly. He always walked with a cane. A retired Peebles surgeon, Robert Craig, described Ritchie as having a narrow forehead, small, piercing and deep-set eyes, with pointed chin and nose, a body of normal size but diminutive legs. He was very strong and had a name for 'the poo'er' – the power (of magic). He was a misanthrope but was very fond of children and animals and was a capable gardener and bee-keeper. He worked as a mill-hand and brush-maker but eventually abandoned most human society and lived on charity in a house he built himself in Peebleshire. The laird later built him a stone house where he died in 1811.

EUGENIUS

Laurence Sterne, *Tristram Shandy* (1759)

John Hall Stevenson (1718–85)

Further reading: Henri Fluchère, *Laurence Sterne* (1961), Valerie Grosvenor Myer, *Laurence Sterne* (1985)

Eugenius is the sentimental friend of the Parson Yorick, in Sterne's comic masterpiece. The fond and tearful farewells as Yorick lies dying of a broken heart are among the immortal pages of *Tristram Shandy*: 'A few hours before Yorick breathed his last, Eugenius stept in with an intent to take his last farewell of him . . . he told him, he was within a few hours of giving his enemies the slip for ever. I hope not, answered Eugenius, with tears trickling down his cheeks, and with the tenderest tone that ever man spoke ... Eugenius was convinced ... that the heart of his friend was broke: he squeezed his hand . . . and then walked softly out of the room, weeping as he walked.'

John Hall met Sterne at Jesus College, Cambridge, and they became friends. He took his wife's surname – Stevenson – after 1738. He inherited Skelton Castle ('Crazy Castle') in Yorkshire from a maternal aunt, and there he formed, in imitation of John Wilkes and the Monks of Medmenham, a club of Demoniacs. He had probably been a member of Wilkes' circle, and certainly knew Wilkes and Horace Walpole. He published scurrilous libels about Sir Francis Dashwood (1701-81) – *Confessions of Sir F . . . of Medmenham* – which suggested the young lord had committed incest wih his stepmother and his sisters. He was also the author of *Crazy Tales* and *Monkish Epitaphs*, and writer and avid reader of erotic prose and poetry. Laurence Sterne was a member of Stevenson's Demoniacs, and as a result of black parsonic clothes was known as 'Blackbird'. The activities of this club seem to have been a strange mixture of shooting, fishing, racing their horses along Saltburn sands, drinking, black magic and erotic practices. He wrote a continuation of Sterne's *Sentimental Journey* (1769) as well as political pamphlets and imitations of coarse French *fabliaux*.

EUPHORION

Johann Wolfgang von Goethe, *Faust* (1808–31)

Lord Byron (1788–1824)

Further reading: Alan Bold (ed.), *Byron: Wrath and Rhyme* (1983)

In the Second Part of *Faust*, finished when he was eighty-one, Goethe presents the union of Faust and Helen, who is the embodiment of perfect beauty. Euphorion, the son of Faust and Helen, personifies poetry, and when he vanishes in a flame, the Chorus comments (in the 1959 translation by Philip Wayne): 'High in lineage and power,/Born for every earthly boon,/Snatched away in youthful flower/Lost to self and love so soon./Eyes the world so sharply proving,/Insight that all woes beheld,/ Heart for woman's ardent loving,/And a song unparalleled./Headlong yet your way pursuing/In the mesh that blinds the will,/Moral code and law eschewing,/You would ride a rebel still;/But at last a high aspiring/Gave pure courage worth and weight,/Glorious things all your desiring/Still, alas, denied by fate.' When Goethe wrote those lines he had Byron in mind.

Son of an English father and a Scottish mother, George Gordon Noel, Sixth Baron Byron, was both a literary celebrity and a social sensation. With his good looks and great charm he was, according to Lady Caroline Lamb's *Journal* of 25 March 1812, 'Mad – bad – and dangerous to know'. The publication of the first two cantos of *Childe Harold's Pilgrimage* in 1812 brought a dashingly romantic dimension to narrative poetry, and Byron 'awoke one morning and found myself famous'. He was soon infamous as well; his marriage to Anne Isabella Milbanke ended in separation, and the rumours of the poet's incestuous relationship with his half-sister Augusta Leigh led to his exile from England in 1816. Dedicated to the Greek struggle against an oppressive Turkish rule, Byron went to Missolonghi to train Greek soldiers. There he died of rheumatic fever. Byron's early death, in the cause of Greek independence, made him a symbol of romantic rebellion, and it is this quality, in addition to Byron's enthusiasm, that Goethe invokes. Euphorion is impulsive and forever urging action: 'Nay, not as a child was I appearing,/But an armed youth before your eyes,/Joined with the strongest, free, unfearing,/In spirit with their deeds he vies./Onwards I dare,/For there/The way to fame and honour lies.'

EVANGELIST

John Bunyan, *The Pilgrim's Progress* (1678)

John Gifford (died 1655)

Further reading: R. Sharrock, *Bunyan* (1954), Alexander Whyte, *Bunyan Characters* (ND), J. Brown, *John Bunyan – His Life, Times and Work* (1928), H.V. Brittain, *In the Steps of Bunyan* (1950)

At the beginning of the allegorical journey that constitutes *The Pilgrim's Progress*, Christian, 'greatly distressed in his mind', is turned towards the truth by Evangelist: 'Then said Evangelist, pointing with his finger over a very wide Field, Do you see Yonder Wicket-gate? The Man said, No. Then said the other, Do you see yonder shining Light? He said, I think I do. Then said Evangelist, Keep that Light in your eye, and go up directly thereto: so shalt thou see the Gate'. The spiritual trials and tribulations endured by Christian are a record of the various doubts and difficulties that assailed Bunyan in his own career.

Bunyan's mentor John Gifford, the original of Evangelist, provided Bunyan with inspirational assistance. Gifford's conversion to the Puritan cause was dramatic; he had been a major in the Royalist Army and a notorious womanizer and gambler. After losing a particularly large amount of money at cards he cursed God then suddenly felt himself reaching for religion. When he first associated with the Bedford Meeting (founded in 1650 as a rallying place for Puritans) he was a disruptive force. Gradually, though, his piety impressed others until he became an obvious candidate for the ministry: in 1653 he was presented with the living of St John's Church, Bedford. Gifford understood Bunyan's spiritual crisis and took him to his home to discuss the tenets of Puritanism and thus Bunyan was 'led from truth to truth'. Eventually Bunyan moved from Elstow to Bedford to be closer to Gifford who died in 1655. In his farewell to his flock Gifford urged Puritans to 'Salute the brethren who walke not in fellowship with you with the same love and name of brother or sister as those who do.' After Gifford's death Bunyan eloquently developed his own powers as a preacher and laid himself open to persecution and imprisonment; while a prisoner in 1675 he began work on *The Pilgrim's Progress*.

NANTY EWART

Sir Walter Scott, *Redgauntlet* (1827)

John Paul Jones (1747-92)

Redgauntlet, one of Scott's later novels (see SIR ROBERT REDGAUNTLET) contains a very colourful character in the person of Nanty Ewart, the sea-captain and privateer. 'His dress was what is emphatically termed the shabby genteel – a frock with tarnished lace – a small cocked hat, ornamented in a similar way – a scarlet waistcoat, with faded embroidery, breeches of the same, with silver kneebands, and he wore a smart hanger and a pair of pistols in a sullied sword-belt.' He is quite an able scholar, given to impromptu demonstrations of his acquaintance with Sallust and the scriptures as well as Juvenal and other classical authors: 'while, on the other hand, sea-phrases seldom chequered his conversation. He had been in person what is called a smart little man; but the tropical sun had burnt his originally fair complexion to a dusty red; and the bile, which was diffused through his system, had stained it with a yellowish black – what ought to have been the white part of his eyes, in particular, had a hue as deep as the topaz. He was very thin, or rather emaciated, and his countenance, though still indicating alertness and activity, showed a constitution exhausted with excessive use of his favourite stimulus.' John Paul Jones was born in the parish of Kirkbean, Kirkudbright. When he was twelve he went to sea, first to Virginia, and then to Jamaica and the Guinea coast, engaged in the slave trade.

Eventually he was trading on his own to Tobago as a merchant and during a mutiny he killed a fellow seaman who led the revolt. He then led the life of a privateer. In 1775 he entered the American navy, calling himself John Paul Jones, and performed brilliantly against the British in the American colonial war. In command of the *Ranger* he took the fort at Whitehaven, plundered the house of Lord Selkirk on St Mary's Isle and off Carrickfergus captured the *Drake*. He was now a hero in the eyes of the French. Through the efforts of Benjamin Franklin he obtained a new ship, which he called *Bon Homme Richard*, in deference to the author of *Poor Richard's Almanac*. An attack on Leith by a fleet under his command failed in 1779 but there was general concern about the safety of Edinburgh. He fought one of the most famous sea battles in history while returning, defeating a British merchant fleet, convoyed by two warships, *Countess of Scarborough* and *Serapis*. After three-and-a-half hours fighting by moonlight, Jones was victorious. He served in the French and Russian navies and died in Paris. Jones has always interested writers, and was the subject of books by Dumas, Fenimore Cooper, Melville and Churchill.

Further reading:
Don Seitz, *Paul Jones – His Exploits on English Seas* (1917)

F

FAGIN
Charles Dickens, *Oliver Twist* (1838)

Ikey Solomons
(1785-1850)

Further reading: Major Arthur Griffiths, *The Chronicles of Newgate* (1884), J.J. Tobias, *Prince of Fences – The Life and Crimes of Ikey Solomons* (1974)

Fagin is the Jewish fence and master criminal who runs a gang of young thieves into whose hands Oliver falls when he comes to London. Fagin hopes to train him as a pickpocket, and when this fails he sends him out to assist Bill Sikes in a burglary. Fagin is eventually betrayed by Noah Claypole and condemned and hanged: 'A very old shrivelled Jew, whose villainous-looking and repulsive face was obscured by a quantity of matted red hair. He was dressed in a greasy flannel gown, with his throat bare.' This is based on the famous criminal Ikey Solomons, who was imprisoned in Newgate in 1831. Major Arthur Griffiths in *The Chronicles of Newgate* (1884) wrote: 'Solomons began as an itinerant street vendor at eight, at ten he passed bad money, at fourteen he was a pickpocket and a seller of sham goods. He early saw the profits to be made out of purchasing stolen goods, but could not embark on it at first for want of capital. He was taken up while still in his teens for stealing a pocket-book, and was sentenced to transportation, but did not get beyond the hulks at Chatham. On his release an uncle, a slop-seller in Chatham, gave him a situation as 'barker' or salesman, at which he realized £150 within a couple of years. With this capital he returned to London and set up as a fence. He had such great aptitude for business and such a thorough knowledge of the real value of goods, that he was soon admitted to be one of the best judges known of all kinds of property, from a glass bottle to a five hundred guinea chronometer. But he never paid more than a fixed price for all the articles of the same class, whatever their intrinsic worth. Thus a watch was paid for as a watch, whether it was of gold or silver . . .' It made a fortune for Ikey. His system was infallible; he removed numbers and marks so goods were untraceable and shipped much out of the country: 'As a general rule Ikey Solomons confined his purchases to small articles, mostly jewelry and plate, which he kept concealed in a hiding place . . . just under his bed. He lived in Rosemary Lane, and sometimes had as much as £20,000 worth of goods secreted on the premises' (Griffiths). He also had an establishment at Lower Queen Street, Islington. He was eventually transported to Hobart. Griffiths estimated that in 1816 there were about two hundred dens of child thieves in London, employing some six thousand boys and girls. Dickens took the name from Bob Fagin, his companion at the blacking warehouse. Thackeray used the name 'Ikey Solomons, junior' as his pseudonym when he published his Newgate novel *Catherine* in 1840.

ALAN FAIRFORD
Sir Walter Scott, *Redgauntlet* (1827)

Sir Walter Scott (1771–1832)

Further reading: John Gibson Lockhart, *The Life of Sir Walter Scott* (1838)

John Gibson Lockhart, Scott's son-in-law and biographer, was of the opinion that 'Walter drew from himself in the younger Fairford' (see SAUNDERS FAIRFORD) in *Redgauntlet*. The relationship between father and son is portrayed very much as we know it was between the writer and his father. Mr Fairford had a very plain view of the tasks and duties of life and was ambitious that his son should *succeed* – and succeed in a worthwhile profession: 'He would have shuddered at Alan's acquiring the renown of a hero, and laughed with scorn at the equally barren laurels of literature; it was by the path of the law alone that he was desirous to see him rise to eminence. . . . The disposition of Alan Fairford, as well as his talents, were such as to encourage his father's expectations. He had acuteness of intellect, joined to habits of long and patient study, improved no doubt by the discipline of his father's house; to which generally speaking, he conformed with the utmost docility.' But he gradually neglects his studies as his heart is taken up with more romantic and adventurous thoughts than a career at the bar. He realizes himself as a young man by helping his friend-in-need, Darsie, who was abducted by Sir Robert Redgauntlet. Walter Scott's father was anxious that his son should be successful in the legal profession, but he did not shine at university preferring to read literature, history and poetry rather than law books, but he struggled and began to thrive at the trade towards which his father pushed him. He was sheriff-deputy of Selkirk before he was twenty-eight but by the first decade of the nineteenth century he was famous as the author of some of the most admired poetry of the day – *The Lay of the Last Minstrel, Marmion, The Lady of the Lake* – and he provided half the capital towards starting the publishing house of Ballantyne in 1812 and moved into the baronial splendours of Abbotsford. In 1812 *Waverley*, his first novel, was published anonymously. Before 1820 it was followed by *Guy Mannering, The Antiquary, Old Mortality, Rob Roy, The Heart of Midlothian, The Bride of Lammermoor, The Legend of Montrose, Ivanhoe*. His authorship was an open secret. He was elected President of the Royal Society of Scotland and was created a baronet. Abbotsford was the centre of literary pilgrimage. Then in 1826 catastrophe struck his publishing venture. He attempted to repay an outstanding debt to creditors of a quarter of a million pounds by writing – a stream of novels from *Woodstock* onwards, which includes *The Fair Maid of Perth, Anne of Geierstein, Count Robert of Paris, Castle Dangerous*, as well as a life of Napoleon and a collected edition of the Waverley novels. He died of apoplexy at his beloved Abbotsford.

SAUNDERS FAIRFORD

Sir Walter Scott, *Redgauntlet* (1827)

Walter Scott (1729–99)

In *Redgauntlet* (see SIR ROBERT REDGAUNTLET) Darsie Latimer is kidnapped as part of a scheme to further a Jacobite rebellion subsequent to the rising of 1745. The attempts to rescue him made by his loyal friend Alan Fairford (see ALAN FAIRFORD) form the basis of the novel. Alan's father, Saunders Fairford, is described by Scott as: 'a man of business of the old school, moderate in his charges, economical . . . in his expenditure, strictly honest in conducting his own affairs and those of his clients . . . wary and suspicious in observing the motions of others. Punctual as the clock of St Giles tolled nine the neat dapper form of the hale old gentleman was seen at the threshold of the Court hall . . . trimly dressed in a complete suit of snuff-coloured brown, with stockings of silk or woollen, as suited the weather; a bob-wig, and a small cocked hat; shoes blacked . . . silver shoe-buckles, and a gold stock-buckle. A nosegay in summer, and a sprig of holly in winter, completed his well-known dress and appearance. His manners corresponded with his attire . . . scrupulously civil, and not a little formal. He was an elder of the kirk, and, of course, zealous for King George and the government . . . . But then, as he had clients and connexions of business among families of opposite political tenets, he was particularly cautious to use all the conventional phrases which the civility of the time had devised . . . . Thus he spoke sometimes of the Chevalier, but never either of the Prince . . . or of the Pretender . . . Again, he usually designated the rebellion as the *affair* of 1745, and spoke of any one engaged in it as a person who had been *out* at a certin period.' This is a portrait of Sir Walter Scott's father, Walter Scott, who was a Writer to the Signet. In his autobiography the novelist says of him: 'He was the eldest of a large family . . . a singular instance of a man rising to eminence in a profession for which nature had in some degree unfitted him . . . in that sharp and intuitive perception which is necessary in driving bargains for himself and others . . . . Uncle Toby himself could not have conducted himself with more simplicity . . . . His person and face were uncommonly handsome, with an expression of sweetness and temper . . . his manners were rather formal, but full of genuine kindness, especially when exercising the duties of hospitality. His general habits were not only temperate, but severely abstemious . . . . His religion, in which he was devoutly sincere, was Calvinism of the strictest kind.' He was a most affectionate parent, even though – not understanding what literature meant to his son – he tried to discourage him from the pursuits which led him to the height of literary

Further reading:
John Gibson Lockhart, *The Life of Sir Walter Scott* (1838)

fame. It was said of him that he passed from cradle to grave without making an enemy or losing a friend.

FAITHFUL

John Bunyan, *The Pilgrim's Progress* (1678)

Richard Baxter (1615–91)

Further reading: H. Martin, *Life of Richard Baxter* (1954)

Vanity Fair is established by Beelzebub, Apollyon and Legion and pilgrims on their way to the Celestial City have to pass through it. It is lighter than vanity and all the vain things of the world – honours, kingdoms, houses, gold and a vast merchandise of trivia – are on sale there. Christian and Faithful have been warned by Evangelist (see EVANGELIST), and so they button their pockets and push by the booths and stalls in the hope of escaping by the upper gate before anyone speaks to them. But they are set upon by the men of the fair, who demand of them what it is they want to buy. 'We buy the truth only,' says Faithful, 'and we do not see any of that article of merchandise set out on any of your stalls.' There is then a riot and they are brought before the Judge (see HATE-GOOD). The three witnesses who appear against them are Envy, Superstition and Pickthank, and the jurymen are Blindman, No-good, Malice, Love-lust, Live-loose, Heady, High-mind, Enmity, Liar, Cruelty, Hate-light and Implacable. Faithful is condemned: 'Now I saw that there stood behind the multitude a chariot and a couple of horses waiting for Faithful who . . . was taken up into it, and straightway was carried up through the clouds, with sound of trumpet, the nearest way to the Celestial gate.'

This is an account of the persecution of Richard Baxter, the presbyterian divine, minister at Bridgnorth in Shropshire, who sided with the parliamentarian cause and recommended the Protestation of 1642. He was chaplain to the garrison at Coventry. After the Restoration he was compelled to retire after the passing of the Act of Uniformity, and was persecuted almost constantly between 1662-87. Baxter retired to Acton in Middlesex, but was taken to prison charged with keeping a conventicle. He was apprehended for preaching in London in 1672, when licences granted by the king were withdrawn. He was a peacemaker, and had used his influence during the Civil War to counteract the power of various sectarian groups and the republicans; his reward was endless legal harassment, the most famous of which was his appearance before Judge George Jeffreys on a charge of libelling the church in his *Paraphrase of the New Testament* (1685). Jeffreys called him 'a schismatical knave', 'an old hypocritical villain' and 'an old blockhead', and sentenced him to be whipped through London at the cart's tail, although he was a frail old man of seventy. He remained in prison for eighteen months, when his sentence was remitted. Baxter was a voluminous author of religious and devotional works.

SIR JOHN FALSTAFF

William Shakespeare, *Henry IV*, Parts 1 and 2; *The Merry Wives of Windsor*, (1597–1600)

Sir John Oldcastle (died 1417); **Sir John Fastolf** (1378–1459)

Further reading: Rudolph Fiehler, *The Strange History of Sir John Oldcastle* (1965), John Dover Wilson, *The Fortunes of Falstaff* (1943)

Falstaff is the cowardly companion of Prince Hal, who later rejects him when he becomes King Henry V. The fat knight may be seen as an alternative father-figure, a gross parody on the high-flown power-political themes of the history plays, though in other respects, he is Hal's tempter. We learn of Falstaff's death in *Henry V*. *The Merry Wives* is a droll account of Sir John's amorous escapades.

There are several clues in the plays which suggest Sir John Oldcastle as the original Falstaff, with many qualities from Sir John Fastolf. Sir John Oldcastle was a soldier and friend of Henry V, and served in the Welsh and French wars. He was a Lollard and a martyr to the cause, imprisoned and – after an escape – party to a plot to overthrow the King. He was executed in 1417. The Falstaff character was originally called 'Oldcastle' in the Henry IV plays, taken from Shakespeare's major source, the *Famous Victories of Henry V*. Oldcastle's descendants protested, and the name was changed to Falstaff, which was derived from a slight adjustment to the name of Sir John Fastolf, who served Henry V at Agincourt, was governor of the Bastille, regent in Normandy, governor of Anjou and Main, but was groundlessly accused of cowardice during the retreat at Patay in 1429. He was a friend of John

Paston and wrote a great number of the celebrated Paston letters and left funds towards the founding of Magdalen College.

The attempt to mollify the descendants of Oldcastle are apparent in the epilogue to *Henry IV Part Two*: 'if you be not too much cloy'd with fat meat, our humble author will make you merry with Fair Katherine of France; where . . . Falstaff shall die of a sweat, unless already he be killed with your hard opinions; for Oldcastle died a martyr and this is not the man'.

William Brooke, Seventh Lord Cobham, (descended from Oldcastle) a powerful Elizabethan nobleman, was nicknamed Falstaff. Essex wrote to the Earl of Salisbury and referred to Cobham as 'Sir Jo. Falstaff'. Hal calls Falstaff 'my old lad of the castle'. In *The Merry Wives* Master Ford originally assumed the name 'Brooke' when he seeks Falstaff's help in testing Mrs Ford's fidelity. Falstaff appears in operas by Nicolai, Vaughan Williams, Holst and Verdi, a symphonic work by Elgar and is the subject of a novel by Robert Nye.

MR FANG

Charles Dickens, *Oliver Twist* (1838)

Allan Stewart Laing, magistrate of Hatton Garden

Further reading:
Philip Collins, *Dickens and Crime* (1965)

Mr Fang is the magistrate who sentences Oliver to three months' hard labour on the charge of picking Mr Brownlow's pockets: 'A lean, long-backed, stiff-necked, middle-sized man, with no great quantity of hair, and what he had, growing on the back and sides of his head. His face was stern, and much flushed. If he were really not in the habit of drinking rather more than was exactly good for him, he might have brought an action against his countenence for libel, and have recovered heavy damages.' This is a portrait, done from the life, of Allan Stewart Laing, a notoriously bad-tempered and uncharitable magistrate in London. Dickens particularly wanted to expose the manner in which such functionaries discharged their duties – as he actually wrote in *Oliver Twist*: 'Although the presiding genii in such an office as this, exercise a summary and arbitrary power over the liberties, the good name, the character, almost the lives, of Her Majesty's subjects, especially of the poorer class; and although, within such walls, enough fantastic tricks are daily played to make the angels blind with weeping; they are closed to the public, save through the medium of the daily press.' John Forster attests in his *The Life of Charles Dickens* (1874) that this example is 'the only one known to me where a character in one of his books intended to be odious was copied wholly from a living original.' Dickens wrote to Mr Haines, who had general supervision over the police reports for the press, on 3 June 1837: 'In my next number of *Oliver Twist* I must have a magistrate; and, casting about for a magistrate whose harshness and insolence would render him a fit subject to be *shown up*, I have as a necessary consequence stumbled upon Mr Laing of Hatton-garden celebrity. I know the man's character perfectly well; but as it would be necessary to describe his personal appearance also, I ought to have seen him, which I have never done. In this dilemma it occurred to me that perhaps I might under your auspices be smuggled into the Hatton-garden office for a few moments some morning . . .' This was done, and in January 1838 Laing was removed from office six months after his appearance in the serial part of *Oliver Twist*. Serjeant William Ballentine, a lawyer of the time, said that notwithstanding his terrible temper, Laing was 'a thoroughly honourable man, a good lawyer, and accomplished scholar . . . though I never saw him without thinking of a shrivelled crab apple.'

DOCTOR FAUSTUS

Christopher Marlowe, *The Tragical History of Doctor Faustus* (1588)

Georg Faust (1480–1538)

Faustus is an academic and scholar who has mastered all that the law, philosophy, theology and medicine can offer. Believing that knowledge is power, he yearns to learn more, and dabbles in magic and necromancy. Not heeding heaven-sent warnings, he signs a pact with Mephistopheles. For twenty-four years of supreme power, he agrees to forfeit his immortal soul. At the end of the play, demons appear and drag him off to hell. Goethe also used the Faust legend as the basis for his *Faust* Part 1 (1808) and *Faust* Part 2 (1832), in which he introduces the Gretchen

Further reading: Carl Kiesewetter, *Faust in der Geschichte und Tradition* (1893)

story, and in which Faust is pardoned at the end of his life. Marlowe got the story from the popular Faust books, which spread the salutary tale of Faust, the magician who sold his soul to the devil.

The real Faust is first mentioned in a letter of 20 August 1507. A Benedictine, Johann Tritheim, abbot of Spanheim, writing to Johann Windung, the mathematician, refers with contempt to one Magister Georgius Sabellious Faustus, who is termed a mountebank. A further correspondent, the jurist and canon Konrad Mudt, calls this Faustus a charlatan. Philip Begardi, in *Index Sanitatis* (Worms, 1539) brackets Faustus along with Paracelsus, among: 'wicked, cheating, useless and unlearned doctors'. Faustus first earns a reputation for supernatural powers in the sermons of a Protestant minister in Basel, one Johann Gast, who asserted Faustus was in league with the devil, and that the horse and dog he went around with were his familiar spirits. Johann Mannel, court historian to the Emperor Maximilian II, in written evidence, speaks of Faustus as 'a disgraceful beast and sewer of many devils'. It seems that Faustus was born in Kundling, in Swabia, and studied magic at Cracow. He signed a pact with the devil, who appeared to him as a dog (he so appears in Marlowe's play), and after many years of wickedness and magic, the devil strangled him and stole his soul. Martin Luther, in the early Faust-books, records that he was able to ward off by prayer the many devils which Faustus had put upon him by sorcery. Johann Weiher, court physician to the Duke of Cleves, in his *De Praestigiis daemonum* (1563) writes of Faustus as a drunken vagabond who had practised magic that he had learned at Cracow.

MR FAX

Thomas Love Peacock, *Melincourt* (1817)

Thomas Robert Malthus (1766–1834)

Further reading: J. Bonar, *Malthus and his Work* (1885)

Melincourt features several long discussions on social, economic and philosophical topics involving Sylvester Forester and Mr Fax, who is described as: 'The champion of calm reason, the indefatigable explorer of the cold clear springs of knowledge, the bearer of the torch of dispassionate truth, that gives more light than warmth. He looks upon the human world, the world of mind, the conflict of interests, the collision of feelings, the infinitely diversified developments of energy and intelligence, as a mathematician looks on his diagrams, or a mechanist on his wheels and pulleys, as if they were foreign to his own nature, and were nothing more than subjects of curious speculation.' He is a 'tall, thin, pale, grave-looking personage'. There is not an emotion which crosses the human breast, or a thought which occurs to the human mind, which Mr Fax cannot discuss in an almost dismissive and detached scientific way. Forester happens to remark that mutations of fortune are often the inexhaustible theme of history, poetry and romance, and happen in daily life as often as on the stage of Drury Lane. Fax responds: 'That the best prospects are often overshadowed is most certainly true; but there are degrees and modes of well-grounded reliance on futurity, sufficient to justify the enterprises of prudence, and equally well-grounded prospiciences of hopelessness and helplessness, that should check the steps of rashness and passion, in their headlong progress to perdition'.

This is Peacock's sarcastic portrait of Thomas Malthus, the controversial economist. He was professor of history at Haileybury and was led to evolve his celebrated theories of population and subsistence by reading Godwin's *Enquiry Concerning Political Justice*. Godwin's theories were refuted by the facts of nature, Malthus believed. His *Essay on Population* (1798) caused tremendous controversy. Population ever treads on the limits of subsistence, surplus population was wiped out by misery, consequently checks on population were necessary.

MR FEATHERNEST

Thomas Love Peacock, *Melincourt* (1817)

Feathernest, one of the house-guests in *Melincourt*, is a reactionary poet and social-climber who began life as a political radical and supporter of the French Revolution, but becomes an *ami du prince*, who spends the morning writing odes to all the crowned heads of Europe. He is a parasite of Lord Anophel Achthar, who brings him to Melincourt Castle. Lord Anophel, in the course of a pleasant conversation, asks him 'what is the spirit of the age of chivalry?' This takes him by surprise: 'Since his profitable metamorphosis into an *ami du prince*, he had never dreamed of such a question. It burst upon him like the spectre of his youthful integrity, and he mumbled a half-intelligible reply about truth and liberty – disinterested benevolence – self oblivion – heroic devotion to love and honour – protection of the feeble, and subversion of tyranny.' He is naturally taken aback when his Lordship retorts: 'All the ingredients of a rank Jacobin, Feathernest, 'pon honour!' But he is not totally at a loss, his good friend Mr Mystic (see MYSTIC) had taught him the value of the mysterious of transcendental philosophy, and he calls on this for assistance, 'and overwhelmed his lordship with a volley of ponderous jargon, which left him in profound astonishment at the depth of Mr Feathernest's knowledge'.

Robert Southey (1774–1843)

Further reading:
J.I.M. Stewart, *Thomas Love Peacock* (1963)

This is Robert Southey, who became Poet Laureate. He was born in Bristol and educated at Oxford. As a young man he was sympathetic to the French Revolution and wrote his epic *Joan of Arc*, in 1793. He met Coleridge and the two of them planned to create an ideal democratic society, Pantisocracy, in north-east America. The scheme failed to get off the ground. Southey became an essayist and prolific poet, moving progressively to the right in politics, and received a government pension, augmented by his salary as Poet Laureate and a further pension of £300 in 1835, after he declined a baronetcy. He was attacked by Byron in *Don Juan*.

CARLOTTA FELL

D.H. Lawrence, 'Glad Ghosts' (1926)

Dorothy Brett (1883–1977) and **Lady Cynthia Asquith** (died 1960)

Further reading:
Sean Hiqnett, *Brett* (1984)

Mark Morier, the narrator of D.H. Lawrence's story 'Glad Ghosts' (first published in the *Dial*, July-August 1926) is invited to Derbyshire to see Carlotta Fell, an old friend now married to Lord Lathkill. Carlotta has been burdened by tragedy since her twin boys were killed in a motoring accident and her baby girl died of a sudden illness. Morier is put in the 'ghost room', for Lord Lathkill hopes he might tempt the ghost whose gifts restore the family fortune. When Morier goes to sleep, consumed by desire for Carlotta, he is visited by a ghost: 'I know she came even as a woman, to my man.' Later he reflects 'I shall never know if it was a ghost, some sweet spirit from the innermost of the ever-deepening cosmos; or a woman, a very woman, as the silkiness of my limbs seem to attest; or a dream, a hallucination!' The following autumn he receives a letter from Lord Lathkill who explains that Carlotta now has a son with 'yellow hair, like a little crocus'.

'Glad ghosts' was originally written for Cynthia Asquith's anthology *The Ghost Book* (1926): 'but am not sure if it's suitable', Lawrence told his agent, and *The Ghost Book* used 'The Rocking-Horse Winner' instead. The reason for Lawrence's doubts about the story's suitability was (so Lawrence scholars like Harry T. Moore reason) that he realized he had gradually made his heroine, Carlotta, into a portrait of Cynthia. As the story opens Carlotta is unmistakably based on the Honourable Dorothy Brett, Lawrence's disciple, and the daughter of Lord Esher. Carlotta studies art at the Thwaite (obviously the Slade, where Brett studied painting) and always wins the still-life prizes: 'They called it buttering the laurels, because Carlotta was Hon., and her father a well-known peer'. After her marriage to Lord Lathkill, Carlotta is transformed into the elegant Lady Cynthia Asquith: 'She was very still and remote, and . . . the touch of her was wonderful, like a flower that yields herself to the morning.' Lady Cynthia – who married Herbert Asquith, the Prime Minister's son, in 1910 – was one of the most admired women in Lawrence's life, and he wrote her some of his most revealing letters. After Lawrence Clark Powell first identified Carlotta with Cynthia in a bibliographical note of 1937, Richard Aldington commented that 'the finale of the story was a piece of reckless impudence'.

DR FELL

Nursery rhyme, 'I do not love thee, Dr Fell' – in Thomas Brown, *Collected Works* (1707)

John Fell (1625–86)

Further reading: Revd H.L. Thompson, *History of the University of Oxford* (1814), *Christ Church*

The English divine and distinguished dean of Christ Church, Oxford, is preserved in a traditional English nursery rhyme. John Fell was born in Longworth, Berkshire, and took holy orders at Christ Church. He was a deacon by 1647 and priest two years later. He supported the Royalist cause in the Civil War, and fell from favour during the Commonwealth. When Charles II was restored he was granted a succession of honours and preferments, including successively Canon of Christ Church, dean of Christ Church and chaplain to the King. In 1676 he was made bishop of Oxford and declined the primacy of Ireland.

His reforms at Oxford included the restoration of respect for authority and compulsory attendance at lectures and increasing the efficiency of the examination system. He also put in hand an extensive building programme, completing the quadrangle begun by Cardinal Wolsey – admired by John Aubrey who wrote: 'the brave designe whereof Dr John Fell hath deteriorated with his new device'. He also promoted the building of the theatre now named after Archbishop Sheldon. Fell was a considerable classical scholar and a formative influence in the creation of the university press at Oxford, bringing out authoritative editions of classical and theological texts.

While a student at Christ Church, John Locke earned the displeasure of the King by his friendship with Lord Shaftesbury. At the King's request, Fell suspended Locke and dismissed him without giving him a chance to defend himself. Fell later regretted his actions. Thomas Brown, author of the rhyme which immortalized Fell, was about to be expelled from Oxford when Fell set him the task of an impromptu translation of the thirty-third epigram of Martial: 'Non amo te, Sabidi, nec possum dicere quare;/Hoc tantum possum dicere, non amo te.' Brown responded immediately with his translation: 'I do not love thee, Doctor Fell,/The reason why I cannot tell;/But this alone I know full well,/I do not love thee, Doctor Fell.' Dr Fell pardoned him.

RICHARD DAVID FIDDES

James Kennaway, *Some Gorgeous Accident* (1967)

John Le Carré (1931–)

Further reading: Trevor Royle, *James and Jim: A Biography of James Kennaway* (1983)

In 1963, as Susan Kennaway explains in *The Kennaway Papers* (1981), her husband James Kennaway (who died in a car crash in 1968 at the age of forty) met a writer called David who had 'recently published a very successful novel'. When *The Kennaway Papers* appeared in print, journalists were not slow to identify David as David Cornwall who, under his pseudonym John le Carré, published *The Spy who Came in From the Cold* in 1963. Kennaway was impressed by Le Carré, writing to Susan 'I'm truly amazed by David. Believe me, he didn't get there by luck. The head is strong and the heart a much hunted one.' There was a hint of envy in Kennaway's tone, for Le Carré was not only a new friend; he was a literary rival whose international success threatened to eclipse Kennaway's reputation as a novelist and screenwriter. The two men went to Paris, in August 1965, for discussions on a film based on *The Looking Glass War* (1965), the novel Le Carré dedicated to Kennaway. There were some problems with director Karel Reisz, who resented Kennaway's presence; there was also (as Kennaway admitted) 'a good deal of late night drinking'. In November, Le Carré came to stay with the Kennaways in London and Susan fell in love with him, as she acknowledges in *The Kennaway Papers*: 'It was the first time that I had felt this way and I could hardly believe it when David expressed the very same emotion. We had arrived at the same point at the same time and what followed was inevitable. I never considered the rights or wrongs, it was just like coming home.'

Kennaway reacted hysterically to the affair, creating a scene that ended with him in tears at the Haus am Berg, a villa at Zell-am-See, the skiing resort south of Salzburg. Susan 'knew then that my little affair had ended'. Kennaway recreated the triangular relationship in *Some Gorgeous Accident*, in which Kennaway himself appears as James Link, a scheming Irish-American war photographer who falls in love with Susie Steinberg, a fashion editor with a successful magazine. Susie is Susan

Kennaway whose 'little affair' is recreated as the character comes into contact with Richard David Fiddes, a doctor modelled on Le Carré. Link's negative personality is contrasted with the positive appeal of his rival, for 'Fiddes was a very nice man'.

FLORA FINCHING

Charles Dickens, *Little Dorrit* (1855)

Maria Beadnell (1810–86)

Further reading: Christopher Hibbert, *The Making of Charles Dickens* (1967)

As a young man, Arthur Clennam had loved Flora. They meet in later life, when she has been widowed. Arthur now finds her to be a rather silly creature: 'Flora, always tall, had grown to be very broad too, and short of breath; but that was not much. Flora, whom he had left a lily, had become a peony; but that was not much. Flora, who had seemed enchanting in all she said and thought, was diffuse and silly. That was much. Flora, who had been spoiled and artless long ago, was determined to be spoiled and artless now. That was a fatal blow.' But in his youth he had ardently loved her and had heaped upon her 'all the locked up wealth of his affection and imagination. . . . Ever since that memorable time he had kept the old fancy of the Past unchanged, in its old sacred place.'

Dickens is here describing his youthful infatuation with Maria Beadnell, whom he had met in 1830, when she was pretty and petite with bright eyes and ringlets. Her father worked in a bank, and eventually became a bank manager. In fact, her family did not take very kindly to Charles, who was a young newspaper reporter at this time. Her father considered him to be an unsuitable match as he was inclined to be irresponsible. He was eventually not allowed to call and see her and she was sent abroad to finishing school. Their friendship was ended by Maria, and his pride was deeply wounded. He met her again after he had become a famous novelist, with *Copperfield* and *Hard Times* behind him, and was quite shocked at what an empty chatterbox she was. He caught a severe cold from her, which must have seemed the final blow. He felt so lowered by the whole experience that he said 'nothing would do me the least good, but setting up a balloon'. Maria also appears as Dora in *David Copperfield*.

PHINEAS FINN

Anthony Trollope, *Phineas Finn* (1869), *Phineas Redux* (1873), *The Prime Minister* (1875) and *The Duke's Children* (1880)

Sir John Pope-Hennessy (1834–91)

Further reading: Henry Sweet Escott, *Life of Anthony Trollope* (1913)

These are a series of political novels. Phineas is a charming but poor Irish MP who leaves behind the girl who loves him, Mary Flood Jones. In the whirl of parliamentary and social life in the metropolis he becomes associated with several society ladies, Violet Effingham, Lady Standish and the widow, Madame Goesler. He is made under-secretary for the colonies, falls out with the government, resigns, and comes back home to marry Mary. She dies and he returns to London life, nearly makes it to the Cabinet, is accused of killing a political rival but is exonerated and marries Madame Goesler who has supported him. He makes minor appearances in *The Prime Minister* and *The Duke's Children*, though the main focus of attention is on the political and social life of Plantagenet Palliser and Lady Glencora. Phineas is an elaborately created character, charming on the surface, but not strong-willed, and a man who tries to be honest and principled. The main impression is of an attractive man who learns and develops.

He is based on John Pope-Hennessy, who came from the same kind of drab social background in the middle-classes as Phineas, but shone in London society and in parliament. He was the first Roman Catholic Conservative to be elected. He was MP for King's County and a barrister at the Inner Temple in 1861. In 1867–71 he was governor of Labuan, and of the Gold Coast 1872–73, of the Windward Islands 1875–76, of Hongkong 1877–82 and Mauritius 1883–89. He was returned for Killkenny in 1890 as an anti-Parnellite home-ruler. Henry Sweet Escott, first biographer of Trollope, wrote of his 'fine presence, winning manners', and said his return to St Stephens after an interval of absence suggested Phineas Finn. (see LORD CHILTERN.)

MICHAEL FINSBURY

A tontine, as the authors explain in the first chapter of *The Wrong Box*, is a system in which 'A number of sprightly youths . . . put up a certain sum

Lloyd Osbourne and Robert Louis Stevenson, *The Wrong Box* (1889)

Charles Baxter
(1845–1919)

Further reading: D. Ferguson and M. Waingrow (eds.), *Stevenson's Letters to Charles Baxter* (1956), Jenni Calder, *R.L.S.: A Life Study* (1980)

of money, which is then funded in a pool under trustees; coming on for a century later, the proceeds are fluttered for a moment in the face of the last survivor.' As children, the brothers Masterman and Joseph Finsbury are made part of 'a small but rich tontine of seven-and-thirty lives', a thousand pounds being the entrance fee. Eventually the Finsbury brothers are the only members of the tontine left alive. As the tale commences Masterman Finsbury is seventy-three, living in seclusion with his son Michael, a well-known solicitor. Joseph, two years Masterman's junior, has become the guardian to three orphans: one Julia Hazeltine and two Finsburys, John and Morris (who regards the tontine as his rightful property). The pursuit of the tontine is described in a bizarre plot involving the mistaken identity of a corpse. If the story is complicated then Stevenson, who elaborated on an outline by his stepson Lloyd Osbourne, was quite clear about the character of Michael Finsbury: 'Michael was something of a public character. Launched upon the law at a very early age, and quite without protectors, he had become a trafficker in shady affairs. He was known to be the man for a lost cause; it was known he could extract testimony from a stone, and interest from a gold mine . . . In private life, Michael was a man of pleasure; but it was thought his dire experience at the office had gone far to sober him, and it was known that (in the matter of investments) he preferred the solid to the brilliant.'

Stevenson based the character of Michael Finsbury on his best friend, Charles Baxter. They were both pupils at the Edinburgh Academy and they both went to Edinburgh University, where Baxter read law. As students Baxter and Stevenson shared an appetite for drink and a penchant for prostitutes. Baxter became Stevenson's legal adviser and most loyal supporter. When Stevenson died Baxter – shattered by the death of his wife – was *en route* to Samoa to see his old friend. Stevenson said of Baxter: 'As a companion, when in spirits, he stands without an equal in my experience.' *Stevenson's Letters to Charles Baxter*, edited by D. Ferguson and M. Waingrow in 1956, indicate the depths of the relationship. In Bryan Forbes's fanciful 1966 film version of the *The Wrong Box*, Michael Finsbury was portrayed by Michael Caine.

MAX FISHER

William Gerhardie, *Pending Heaven* (1930)

Hugh Kingsmill
(1899–1949)

Further reading: Michael Holroyd, *Unreceived Opinions* (1973)

Of his friend Hugh Kingsmill, William Gerhardie observed in *Memoirs of a Polyglot* (1931), 'Kingsmill's habit, I regret to say, is to abscond and set up house with somebody in whom I have invested a good deal of emotion, and then to defend the purity of their hearth against my visits, though indulgent enough to consent to meet me outside his new home.' Son of Sir Henry Lunn, a proselytizing Puritan, Hugh Kingsmill Lunn (he dropped the surname for his books) was born in London. Reacting against his father's religious fanaticism, Kingsmill rejected orthodox Christianity at an early age. He was educated at Oxford and commissioned in the Royal Naval Volunteer Reserve; later, as a company commander, he was captured by the Germans at the Western Front. In 1927 his first marriage broke down and Kingsmill gave up his work in his father's tourist agency and settled down to sustained literary work, encouraged by his second wife Dorothy Vernon. His most popular book, an anthology of *Invective and Abuse*, appeared in 1929. He also published highly critical biographies of Matthew Arnold (1928); Frank Harris (1932), with whom he had worked on the ladies' journal *Hearth and Home*; Dickens (*The Sentimental Journey*, 1934); and D.H. Lawrence (1938). His reputation waned, though a revival of interest in his work was stimulated by Michael Holroyd's *Hugh Kingsmill: A Critical Biography* (1964). Holroyd also did much to draw attention to the neglected writings of William Gerhardie.

Kingsmill is portrayed as Max Fisher in Gerhardie's novel *Pending Heaven*. Max is an escapist, constantly seeking to obliterate life's difficulties with love's pleasures. He has had a bad year, he tells his friend

Victor Thurbon (Gerhardie), and wants to divorce his wife and settle down with a teenage girl, Sheila. Meanwhile, though, he takes advantage of Victor's relationship with his secretary Phyllis, sets up house with them in West Kensington, then makes his own emotional claims on Phyllis. This is typical of the lifestyle of Max, who is irritating but attractive: 'when Max was not bristling with nerves he was shaking with fun, he was trembling with laughter like a wet tree in the wind . . . And here was the very man for [Victor]; a great, sensitive, witty being, boisterous, tender, and refreshing like the sea breeze.'

ROWLEY FLINT

W. Somerset Maugham, *Up at the Villa* (1953)

Gerald Haxton (1892–1944)

Further reading: Robin Maugham, *Somerset and All the Maughams* (1966), Ted Walker, *Maugham* (1980)

In the First World War, Somerset Maugham served in a Red Cross ambulance unit in France and there met, in the same unit, the American Gerald Haxton. Maugham fell in love with Haxton who became his secretary–companion and the passion of his life. When Haxton was, in 1915, arrested on a charge of gross indecency he was acquitted but his reputation was ruined and in 1919 he was deported from England as an undesirable alien. The fact that Haxton could not return to England prompted Maugham's own decision to live in exile; in 1928 he bought the Villa Mauresque, on the French Riviera, and lived there with Haxton. Although Haxton's heavy drinking, gambling and sexual adventuring annoyed Maugham he reluctantly accepted these foibles because of the many compensations. When Maugham and Haxton travelled it was the gregarious Gerald who would make contact with the people subsequently used as raw material for the novels. When Haxton died Maugham was heartbroken.

Haxton appeared vividly in Maugham's *Up at the Villa* (1953) as Rowley Flint, an Englishman who helps a rich English widow to get rid of a body and then blackmails her into marrying him. The description of Rowley as a scoundrel is a detailed portrayal of Gerald: 'He had a tolerable figure, but he was of no more than average height, and in clothes he looked thick-set. He had not a single feature that you could call good: he had white teeth, but they were not very even; he had a fresh colour, but not a very clear skin; he had a good head of hair, but it was of a vague brown between dark and fair; his eyes were fairly large, but they were of the pallid blue that is generally described as grey. He had an air of dissipation and people who didn't like him said he looked shifty ... He was in short a young man with a shocking reputation which he thoroughly deserved.'

MR FLOSKY

Thomas Love Peacock, *Nightmare Abbey* (1818)

Samuel Taylor Coleridge (1772–1834)

Further reading: J.D. Campbell, *The Life of Samuel Taylor Coleridge* (1894), Donald Sultana, *New Approaches to Coleridge* (1981)

Nightmare Abbey puts before the reader a satiric portrait of some of the leading figures of English romanticism, who are friends and associates of the young Scythrop Glowry (see GLOWRY). Among the visitors to Nightmare Abbey is the poet and philosopher Ferdinando Flosky, 'a very lachrymose and morbid gentleman, of some note in the literary world, but in his own estimation of much more merit than name'. He has a very fine sense of the grim and the tearful: 'No one could relate a dismal story with so many minutiae of supererogatory wretchedness. No one could call up a *rawhead and bloody bones* with so many adjuncts and circumstances of ghastliness. Mystery was his natural element. He lived in the midst of that visionary world in which nothing is but what is not. He dreamed with his eyes open, and saw ghosts dancing round him at moontide.' As a young man, Flosky had been an enthusiast for Liberty, 'and had hailed the dawn of the French revolution as the promise of a day that was to banish war and slavery . . . from the face of the earth'. Because this faith had not been realized, he was convinced that nothing had been achieved, and became a reactionary, and wished to recreate the world of the past and ensure that there would be no loopholes such as had previously allowed in the light. To this endeavour he called on Kantian metaphysics 'and lay *perdu* several years in transcendental darkness, till the common daylight of common sense became intolerable to his eyes'.

This is an uncharitable thumbnail sketch of Coleridge, who, having earlier associated himself with radical causes and the hope of building utopia as Pantisocracy on the banks of the Susquehanna, failed in marriage, took to opium and soaked himself in the philosophy of Kant, notorious at the time for the obscurity of its terminology and style. Kant achieved a philosophical system which was an attempt to answer sceptism and empiricism. This was transcendental idealism, which made a prime distinction between *noumenon* (object of purely intellectual intuition) and *phenomenon* (object perceived or experienced). Coleridge's attempts to promulgate Kantian theory were considered by many incomprehensible. He was also associated with the Gothic and the gloomy – main targets in *Nightmare Abbey*. (See also MOLEY MYSTIC.)

FLUELLEN
William Shakespeare, *Henry V* (1600)
Sir Roger Williams
(1540–95)

Further reading: Geoffrey Bullough, *Narrative and Dramatic Sources of Shakespeare* Volume IV (1962)

Fluellen is a Welsh officer in the army of Henry V which goes to France and defeats the enemy in the battle of Agincourt. He is a thoroughly efficient and professional soldier and a colourful portrayal of what Shakespeare perceived as the Welsh character. He is very talkative, and the dramatist goes to a lot of trouble to get the sound and tone of his accent fully worked out – he repeats the phrase 'look you' and among his mannerisms in the tendency to pronounce b as p ('poys') but the general effect is of a loquacious, almost bullying character, without a shred of humour. He is frequently engaged in arguments with other officers, and has a very assertive manner which easily topples into the ridiculous. He makes out a case for Henry's similarity to Alexander the Great, though one was born in Macedon and the other in Monmouth: 'if you look in the maps of the 'orld. I warrant you sall find, in the comparisons between Macedon and Monmouth, that the situations, look you, is both alike. There is a river in Macedon; and there is also moreover a river at Monmouth; it is called the Wye at Monmouth, but it is out of my prains what is the name of the other river; but 'tis all one.'

Roger Williams was a Welsh soldier, who began his career as a page in the household of the First Earl of Pembroke, and served in Flanders in the army of Thomas Morgan, and was lieutenant to Sir John Norris. He later commanded with distinction under Leicester. He was knighted in 1586, and served at Zutphen and Sluys. During the threat of the Spanish invasion he was master of horse at the camp in Tilbury (1588). He served in France, accompanying Willoughby to Dieppe in 1589 and served in the cause of Henry of Navarre. He succeeded Essex when he was recalled to England in 1592 and Williams then became commander of the English troops before Rouen, and fought with great valour at the seige of Rue in the same year. His book, *A Brief Discourse of War*, was published in 1590. Some of Fluellen's Welsh regional characteristics may also be based on Lewis (or Ludowick) Lloyd (1573-1610) a well known figure at court, segeant-at-arms to Elizabeth I and James I, a classical scholar and author. The allusions to ancient history with which Fluellen colours his discourse may be an echo of Lloyd.

JULIA FLYTE
Evelyn Waugh, *Brideshead Revisited* (1945)
Olivia Plunket Greene
(1907–55)

Further reading: Alan Pryce Jones, *Waugh and his World* (1980)

Charles Ryder strikes up a close friendship with Sebastian Flyte at Oxford. During the first long vacation he is summoned to Brideshead by Sebastian, who has injured his foot playing croquet, and requires Charles's company. Julia, Sebastian's sister, meets him from the train: 'She so much resembled Sebastian that, sitting beside her in the gathering dusk, I was was confused by the double illusion of familiarity and strangeness . . . I knew her and she did not know me. Her dark hair was scarcely longer than Sebastian's, and it blew back from her forehead as his did; her eyes on the darkening road were his, but larger; her painted mouth was less friendly to the world. She wore a bangle of charms on her wrists and in her ears little gold rings. Her light coat revealed an inch or two of flowered silk; skirts were short in those days, and her legs . . . were spindly, as was also the fashion. Because her sex was the palpable difference between the familiar and the strange, it seemed to fill the space between us, so that I felt her to be especially female, as I had felt of no woman before.' After his entanglement with

Sebastian has passed, he and Julia become lovers, after her marriage (see REX MOTTRAM) has failed, but they are unable to marry.

Waugh is here describing Olivia, sister of Richard Plunket Greene, a contemporary of his at Oxford. She was the first girl with whom he had fallen in love; his previous close relationships had been with his male associates at Oxford – Richard Pares and Alastair Graham in particular. He was twenty-one when he realized he was falling for Olivia: 'I wonder whether I am falling in love with this woman' he noted in his diary on 24 December 1924, and in April the following year he recorded: 'the insistent sorrows of unrequited drink'. She was fond of drinking and dancing the Charleston. Harold Acton, in his *Memoirs of an Aesthete*, wrote of her: 'minute pursed lips and great goo-goo eyes'. There was always something wild in her character – 'Dined with Olivia . . . very depressing, stark crazy and roaring drunk' he noted on 15 Janauary 1937 and when he visited her in 1948 he wrote that she was one third drunk, one third insane and one third genius. Her strong attachment to Catholicism probably aided Waugh's conversion. She lived as a recluse on the Longleat estate with her mother, and developed a keen interest in Communism.

SEBASTIAN FLYTE

Evelyn Waugh, *Brideshead Revisited* (1945)

Hugh Lygon (1904–36)

Further reading: Alan Pryce Jones, *Waugh and His World* (1980)

When Evelyn Waugh arrived at Oxford in 1922 he was about to have the time of his life as his novel *Brideshead Revisited* affirms. Waugh became a member of the Hypocrites, an undergraduate drinking club presided over by Lord Elmley, son of Lord Beauchamp. Greatly impressed by Elmley's social credentials Waugh became friendly with the whole family, including Lord Beauchamp's second son Hugh Lygon who took him to the family seat of Madresfield Court in Worcestershire. After Oxford, Waugh and Hugh Lygon remained good friends. In a letter written to Hugh's sisters, Lady Mary and Lady Dorothy, in 1932 Waugh says, 'Well, I hate to say it but the truth is that Hugh had been at the bottle and he was walking about the house with a red candle saying he thought the lights might go out.' In 1934 Waugh visited Lord Beauchamp's London house, found Hugh 'in the library drinking gin', and decided to accompany his friend on an Arctic expedition to Spitzbergen. Two years later Hugh Lygon went to Germany on a motoring tour; when he got out of the car, probably weakened by sunstroke, he fell and fractured his skull. He died the same night, 19 August 1936.

Brideshead Revisited recreates Hugh as Sebastian Flyte who begins the novel as an irrepressible undergraduate clutching his teddy bear for comfort; and ends it as an irresponsible drunk in a North African monastery. Even then he is 'completely charming' and the narrator Charles Ryder conjures up an image of 'an arctic hut and a trapper alone with his furs and oil lamp and log fire' before the sun causes a block of ice to come down on the hut and obliterate the occupant. Although known for his cynicism there is no reason to doubt Waugh's sincerity when he wrote to Lady Mary Lygon, on hearing of Hugh's death, 'It is the saddest news I ever heard.. I shall miss him bitterly.'

PHILEAS FOGG

Jules Verne, *Le Tour du Monde en Quatre-vingts jours* (1873)

George Francis Train (1829–1904)

Further reading: Peter Costello, *Jules Verne – Inventor of Science Fiction* (1978), George Francis Train, *My Life in Many*

Around the World in Eighty Days was serialized in *Le Temps*, which more than tripled its circulation as a consequence. The novel was Verne's greatest success during his lifetime – its popular edition sold 108,000 copies and its illustrated edition over 300,000. The story opens in a London club where a recent scandalous robbery of the Bank of England is under discussion. What chances does the robber have of getting away with it? Fogg wagers that it was possible to go round the world in eighty days, basing his confidence on what he has read in the *Morning Chronicle*. To win his wager he sets out to do the trip himself with his servant Passepartout. Inspector Fix of Scotland Yard believes he is the robber and follows him. After an exciting circuit of the world Fogg comes back to London, believing he is a day late. He is ruined. His only consolation is that the beautiful Indian widow he saved from *suttee* wants to marry

States and in Foreign Lands (1902)

him. He goes to the club to face the music, only to find that he was wrong. He has won his bet – by travelling east round the world he gained twenty-four hours as a result of the cosmographical oddity of the international date-line. In his biography of his grandfather Jean, Jules Verne quotes the author's comment: 'I have dreams about it! I hope our readers enjoy it as much as I. You know, I must be a bit crazy: I fall for all the extravagant things my heroes get up to. There's only one thing I regret: not being able to get up to those things with them.'

The exploits of George Francis Train, the man who got up to it all, was the talk of Paris in the early 1870s. He was an American shipping magnate, transport speculator, author and famous traveller. He joined the French Communists in 1870, and organized the French Commune at Marseilles, Ligue du Midi, in October that year, while making his celebrated trip round the world in eighty days. He was born in Boston, and lost his mother and sisters from yellow fever when he was four. He worked as a clerk in his uncle's shipping office in Boston and came to Liverpool as manager of the shipping line in England. He made a fortune in Australia by 1855, built railroads in the USA, published considerably and lectured. He promoted tramways in Liverpool, London and Staffordshire, made four trips round the world, the first in two years, the second in eighty days (1870), the third in sixty-seven and a half days, and the fourth in sixty days (1892). Like Fogg he was eccentric – considered insane by many. He left a fascinating autobiography *My Life in Many States and in Foreign Lands* (1902). He was tall and dark and had much of the prankster in his character, running independently against Grant and Greeley for the US Presidency in 1872.

HARRY FOKER

William Makepeace Thackeray, *Pendennis* (1850)

Andrew Arcadeckne

Further reading: Clement K. Shorter, *Charlotte Brontë and Her Circle* (1896)

Harry Foker is a young man-about-town who befriends Arthur Pendennis. He plays an important part in the climax of the novel when Arthur, having learned of the economic catastrophe that has befallen Blanche Amory's father, goes to see her in order to offer to marry her in her hour of need, only to find that he has been pipped at the post by Harry Foker, who has just inherited a fortune from his father, the proprietor of 'Foker's Entire'–a fortune made from brewing beer. Arthur meets Harry at school, where he does not shine. Harry is always 'fast' and takes to cigar-smoking and inebriation at an early age, cutting a very fine figure in the eyes of his juniors. He precedes Arthur to Oxbridge. Arthur goes into Chatteris, where he is accosted by his old school friend, whom he has some difficulty in recognizing: 'under the broad-brimmed hat and the vast great-coats and neck-cloths ... the figure of his quondam schoolfellow . . . A year's absence had made no small difference in that gentleman. A youth who had been deservedly whipped a few months previously, and who had spent his pocket-money on tarts and hardbake, now appeared . . . in one of those costumes to which public consent . . . has awarded the title of "Swell". He had a bulldog between his legs, and in his scarlet shawl neck-cloth was a pin representing another bulldog in gold: he wore a fur waistcoat laced over with gold chains; a green cut-away coat with basket buttons, and a white upper-coat ornamented with cheese-plate buttons, on each of which was engraved some stirring incident of the road or the chase.' He strikes Arthur as either 'a boxer *en goguette*, or a coachman in his gala suit'. At school he was a duffer and continues in this way at Oxbridge, where he shows far more interest in prize-fighting and racing than the classics. He may be shallow and vulgar, but he has a heart of gold. This is a portrait of Andrew Arcadeckne, a plump man-about-town, whom Thackeray knew at the Garrick Club. He recognized himself in Harry Foker and teased the novelist about it, often striking matches to light his cigars on the soles of Thackeray's shoes as the writer sat at his ease in an armchair. He said 'he owed Thackeray one for using me in this way' and consoled him after his lectures on eighteenth-century writers had been criticized by saying: 'Ah! Thack my boy! You ought to ha' 'ad a pianner!'

JOSEPHINE FORD

D.H. Lawrence, *Aaron's Rod* (1922)

Dorothy Yorke

Further reading: Harry T. Moore, *The Priest of Love* (1974)

When Josephine Ford first appears in D.H. Lawrence's *Aaron's Rod*, she is engaged to the son of a coal-owner in a Midlands town. It is Christmas Eve in Shottle House as Josephine sits by the fire, her neat black hair done tight in the French style: 'She had strangely-drawn eyebrows, and her colour was brilliant . . . She wore a simple dress of apple-green satin, with full sleeves and ample skirt and a tiny bodice of green cloth.' When she is offered a cigarette she suddenly licks her 'rather full, dry red lips with the rapid end of her tongue. It was an odd movement, suggesting a snake's flicker . . . Her movements were very quiet and well bred; but perhaps too quiet, they had the dangerous impassivity of the Bohemian, Parisian or American, rather than English.' That night Josephine meets Aaron Sisson, secretary of the Miners' Union. Later, in London, Josephine is at the opera when she sees Aaron in his new capacity as flautist (the flute is Aaron's rod) in an opera house. Sisson has left his wife and children to make a new life. After Aaron collapses in Covent Garden market, he tells Rawdon Lilly (Lawrence by another name) that he has felt ill since Josephine seduced him: 'I gave in to her – and afterwards I cried, thinking of Lottie and the children. I felt my heart break, you know . . . I felt the minute I was loving her, I'd done myself. And I had.'

Dorothy Yorke, on whom Lawrence based the character of Josephine Ford, was a woman who made a great impact on other writers. She was the original of Fanny in Richard Aldington's *Death of a Hero* (1929), and of Bella Carter in H.D.'s *Bid Me to Live* (1960). John Cournos, the Kiev-born author, adored her, and described her as a woman of 'quiet restrained beauty, with an exotic flavour' in his *Autobiography* (1935). When Lawrence stayed at 44 Mecklenburgh Square, London, in 1917 he was lent a room by H.D. – Hilda Doolittle, then married to Richard Aldington. Installed in the attic of the same house was Dorothy Yorke, brought to London by John Cournos. Dorothy Yorke fell in love with Aldington and subsequently lived with him for a decade. She was born in Reading, Pennsylvania, and was twenty-six when Lawrence met her in 1917.

IRENE FORSYTE

John Galsworthy, *The Forsyte Saga* (1922)

Ada Galsworthy (1864–1956)

Further reading: H.V. Marrot, *The Life and Letters of John Galsworthy* (1935), D. Barker, *The Man of Principle – A View of John Galsworthy* (1963)

Describing the heroine of *The Forsyte Saga* John Galsworthy presented a seductive image of womanhood: 'A tall woman, with a beautiful figure, which some member of the family had once compared to a heathen goddess . . . Her figure swayed, so balanced that the very air seemed to set it moving. . . . But it was at her lips – asking a question, giving an answer, with that shadowy smile – that men looked; they were sensitive lips, sensuous and sweet, and through them seemed to come warmth and perfume like the warmth and perfume of a flower.'

So Galsworthy must have seen Ada, the wife of his first cousin Major Galsworthy, when they met in Paris in 1895. Later that year Galsworthy and Ada became lovers and for the rest of his life his work was made in the image of the woman who became his wife in 1905 and his Irene in *The Man of Property* (1906).

Ada Nemesis Pearson Cooper was born in 1864, the illegitimate child of Anna Julia Pearson and the adopted child of Dr Emanuel Cooper who delivered her. She married Major Galsworthy in 1891 but was unable to share his military enthusiasm and turned to the more compatible John Galsworthy. Ada was convinced that Galsworthy had great literary talent and made it her life's work to encourage him as a novelist. She also persuaded Galsworthy to see her as the embodiment of the long-suffering heroine and thus she appears in his fiction. Galsworthy was dependent on Ada and their marriage was an extremely close companionship rather than an intensely physical relationship. Ada's experience of Major Galsworthy had made her wary of men and one of her reasons for choosing to live with Galsworthy was undoubtedly her admiration for his undemanding nature. Galsworthy was eternally grateful to Ada and when he was briefly attracted to a young actres he was consumed by guilt at the thought of betraying Ada. At the end of his life he explored the possibility of making spiritual contact with Ada after his death.

SOAMES FORSYTE
John Galsworthy, *The Forsyte Saga* (1922)
Major Arthur Galsworthy

Further reading: R. Mottram, *John Galsworthy* (1953)

The Man of Property the first stage in *The Forsyte Saga* (which eventually comprised nine novels) is dominated by the figure of Soames Forsyte, a solicitor whose passion is for property. As a monument to his materialism he buys land at Robin Hill, outside London, and employs an architect to build a suitably impressive home. When the architect falls in love with Soame's beautiful wife Irene, Soames shows a rage for revenge. His appearance is as formidable as his personality: 'Soames Forsyte, flat-shouldered, clean-shaven, flat-cheeked, flat-waisted, yet with something round and secret about his whole appearance . . . the buttoned strictness of his black cut-away coat, conveyed an appearance of reserve and secrecy'.

Soames was modelled on Galsworthy's first cousin Major Arthur Galsworthy whose wife Ada was the woman the author eventually married. Major Galsworthy was a member of the Essex Yeomanry, not a professional soldier. He married Ada in April 1891 and the fact of her illegitimacy may well have hindered his hopes for a distinguished military career. Ada soon regretted her marriage to Major Galsworthy whose interests were confined to military matters. In 1900 Major Galsworthy had to accept the complete breakdown of his marriage and in 1904 he finally instituted divorce proceedings against Ada and John Galsworthy.

Soames as portrayed by Galsworthy is Major Galsworthy as seen by Ada, a version the author accepted as authentic. When Major Galsworthy died Ada wrote, in an undated letter to a friend, '[yesterday I had] news of the death of "Soames" (Major Galsworthy) [and heard] that two days before his death the local parson called and wished to ministrate. But the Major said: "No, and tell him the funeral will be at three." Witty to the last.' Despite Galsworthy's wish to make Soames a complete villain the character developed a life of its own and attracted the sympathy of readers.

HENRY FORTESCUE
Sir Compton Mackenzie, *Thin Ice* (1956)
Tom Driberg (1905-1976)

Further reading: Tom Driberg, *Ruling Passions* (1977)

Compton Mackenzie's *Thin Ice* is the story of a forty-four-years-long friendship between a homosexual politician Henry Fortescue (1879–1942) and the dilettantish George Gaymer, who narrates the novel. Innocent and easily shocked, Gaymer first gets to know Fortescue at Oxford in the 1890s, and thereafter watches his rise to political prominence as an enthusiastic imperialist with a special interest in the East. Henry becomes Unionist MP for Longcliff in 1906, and in the Bonar Law administration of 1922 is given an under-secretaryship. However, when the Conservatives return to power in 1924, Henry is 'passed over for office'. Henry's problem is his homosexual penchant for young men and he realizes, as he tells Gaymer, 'I'll never be in the Cabinet and therefore I refuse to spoil the rest of my life by crying for the moon. I intend to let discretion go hang.' Henry's habit of 'skating on thin ice' brings him to the brink of public disgrace several times, to the horror of the resolutely heterosexual Gaymer. During the Second World War, when Henry is no longer a Member of Parliament but head of the important Eastern Bureau, he is caught in the homosexual act by a police constable in Glasgow. Henry manages to talk his way out of this by imposing his impressive social credentials on the constable. When the policeman agrees to let him go, he refuses to shake hands with Henry. Henry eventually dies in the London blitz, though it is accepted that he really 'died long ago when he found himself passed over'.

In his posthumously published autobiography *Ruling Passions* (1977), Tom Driberg (Lord Bradwell) claims that his own circumstances provided Mackenzie with the notion of a novel about a politician suffering for his homosexuality. Unlike Henry Fortescue, Driberg was a leftwing Labour MP (1942–55 and 1959–74) and (as author of the *Daily Express* 'William Hickey' column in the 1930s) an influential journalist. Still, there are similarities. Driberg became Chairman of the Labour Party's National Executive Committee, but said he was never made a minister because 'both the Labour Prime Ministers with whom I served, Attlee and Wilson, knew of my reputation as a homosexual'. During the Second World War, Driberg had an encounter with a policeman in Edinburgh that provided Mackenzie with the material for Henry Fortescue's Glasgow experience. Driberg told the story of his narrow escape from the law to Robert Boothby, who then told it to Mackenzie. Driberg enjoyed *Thin Ice* but noted: 'at the end of [Henry Fortescue's] conversation with the policeman, the policeman refused to shake hands with him. This was inaccurate, and I found it deeply offensive.'

FRA DIAVOLO

Opera, *Fra Diavolo* (1830, music by Daniel François Esprit Auber, libretto by Eugène Scribe)

Michele Pezza

(1771–1806)

Further reading:
A. Luzio, *Profili et bozzetti storici*, Milan (1906)

Fra Diavolo was first performed at the Opera Comique, Paris, in January 1830, and remained for many years one of the most popular operas in the French repertory, with a leading role, the bandit chief, which was a favourite of Alessandro Bonci, Tito Schipa and Nicolai Gedda. Fra Diavolo is a kind of Robin Hood who operates round Naples. He is chivalrous and takes from the rich to give to the poor. The plot involves Fra Diavolo in duping an English milord, attempting to seduce his wife, stealing his money, hiding in his room in a country inn and making one miraculous escape after another. He is finally accidentally betrayed and is captured by the carabinieri and shot. There is an alternative ending in which he is forgiven and the opera ends in general forgiveness and rejoicing – happy endings are a requirement of *opera comique*. The tune of the carabinieri, featured in the overture, is the regimental call of the British dragoon regiment, the 3rd Carabiniers.

This almost Hollywood-style romantic tarradiddle is based on the life story of the Italian brigand and patriot, Michele Pezza. He was originally a monk who turned to the life of an outlaw – hence his nickname, Fra Diavolo ('Father Devil'). When Naples was invaded by the French in 1799, Pezza was appointed by Cardinal Ruffo to help in its recovery. Pezza organized 'bands of the Holy Faith' which were gangs of peasants, convicts, brigands and the poor. They were fully exploited by Pezza in a series of raids and expeditions to harass the French, cause them trouble and waste their time and effort. The complications in the plot of *Fra Diavolo* arise because a reward of ten thousand piastres is placed on his head, and then Lord Cockburn, whose wife's honour is liable to be compromised by Fra Diavolo, offers six thousand 'scudi' reward for him. In real life, when Joseph Bonaparte came to the throne of Naples he put a price on the head of Pezza, who was captured and shot in 1806.

VICTOR FRANKENSTEIN

Mary Shelley, *Frankenstein* (1818)

Konrad Dippel

(1673–1734)

Further reading:
Radu Florescu, *In Search of Frankenstein* (1975)
W. Bender, *Johann Konrad Dippel*, Bonn (1882)

According to Mary Shelley's account of 1831 the genesis of her novel *Frankenstein* was relatively simple. In the summer of 1816 Shelley and Mary lived near Lord Byron at Geneva. After reading a Gothic anthology, *Fantasmagoriana* (1812), Byron declared 'We will each write a ghost story.' At first unable to oblige, Mary was disturbed one night when Byron and Shelley discussed the principle of life; when she went to sleep she had a nightmare in which she saw 'the hideous phantasm of a man stretched out, and then, on the working of some powerful engine, show signs of life, and stir with an uneasy, half vital motion.' Mary omitted to say that when she eloped with Shelley in 1814 the couple sailed down the Rhine and probably spent the night somewhere near Castle Frankenstein near Darmstadt. Castle Frankenstein, which still stands, dates from the thirteenth century and was sold by the Frankenstein family in 1662.

When Konrad Dippel was born in the castle it was used as a hospital for the war-wounded. So the boy grew up, as Radu Florescu says in *In Search of Frankenstein* (1975), 'among the disfigured and amputated soldiers'. Dippel enrolled at the University of Giessen as 'Francken-steina' and went on to gain a formidable reputation as an alchemist in which capacity he was employed by the Landgrave of Hesse. Dippel was convinced (so Florescu records) that 'the body was an inert substance animated by an errant spirit that could leave it at any time to infuse life into another' and he offered to supply the Landgrave of Hesse with a vital secret in exchange for Castle Frankenstein which he wanted for his own experiments in distilling blood and bones. Negotiations broke down and Dippel died, but his audacious character was resuscitated by Mary Shelley in the person of Victor Frankenstein.

FRIEDA
Franz Kafka, *The Castle* (1926)
Milena Jesenská (1896–1944)

Further reading: Franz Kafka, *Letters to Milena* (1953)

Franz Kafka's novel *The Castle* confronts K., the central character, with a dilemma. K. is sure he has been summoned to the Castle by the Count, as an official Land Surveyor, but is unable to confirm this in a situation where reality dissolves into illusion and vice versa. K. is only certain of his own reality in the company of Frieda, a young girl who tells him she is the mistress of Klamm, the Castle's most powerful official. When K. meets Frieda he is impressed by her 'striking look of conscious superiority. As soon as her eye met K.'s it seemed to him that her look decided something concerning himself, something which he had not known to exist, but which her look assured him did exist.' K. suggests she should leave Klamm and become his sweetheart, and when she first embraces him he is transported 'into a strange country'. When Frieda, hearing Klamm call for her, says she will not obey the summons, K. (in the 1930 translation by Edwin and Willa Muir) 'wanted to object, to urge her to go to Klamm . . . but he could not bring himself to speak, he was too happy to have Frieda in his arms, too troubled also in his happiness, for it seemed to him that in letting Frieda go he would lose all he had'. Kafka wrote *The Castle* in 1922, two years after meeting the inspiration for Frieda – Milena Jesenská with whom he had, according to Ernst Pawel's *The Nightmare of Reason* (1984), 'perhaps the one true love affair of his life'.

Milena, a remarkable woman, whose heroic resistance to the Nazis led to her death at Ravensbrück, had an unusually eventful life. Her father, a surgeon and fanatical anti-Semite, was horrified when she had an affair with a Jew, Ernst Polak, and had her committed to the Veleslavin lunatic asylum, where she spent nine months (June 1917–March 1918) enduring a brutal therapy of beatings, straitjackets and solitary confinement. After this Milena went ahead with the marriage to Ernst Polak, a man capable of appalling mental cruelty. In 1919 Milena contacted Kafka with a view to translating some of his work in Czech. He responded enthusiastically and soon fell in love with her. Milena would not, however, leave her oppressive husband, and Kafka was too confused to act decisively. Although he adored Milena he could not take his passion to a physical conclusion; Milena, says Pawel, 'never forced the issue, but instead of coyly ignoring it, she brought it out into the open, made him face his fear of sex'. Kafka and Milena remained friends, and in October 1921 he gave her all his diaries with instructions to pass them to Max Brod, his friend, after his death (which occurred on 3 June 1924). Milena eventually left her husband and remarried in 1927.

BARBARA FRIETCHIE
John Greenleaf Whittier, *In War Time* (1864)
May Quantrell

John Greenleaf Whittier's celebrated Civil War poem 'Barbara Frietchie', from *In War Time*, describes the all-American spirit of the heroine who defies the might of the Southern troops. In Frederick town, 'by the hills of Maryland', General Lee's men ride in and take down all Union flags. Old Barbara, 'Bravest of all Frederick town', takes up a flag and flies it from her attic window. When Stonewall Jackson sees this he has it shot at but Barbara snatches the flag, shakes it defiantly and utters her famous lines: "'Shoot, if you must, this old grey head,/But spare your country's flag,' she said.' Deeply moved, Stonewall Jackson orders his men to march on and leave Barbara with her flag.

The story was told to Whittier by novelist Emma D.E.N. Southworth but she got it wrong: when the Southern troops entered Frederick on 6 September 1862 Stonewall Jackson was elsewhere, recovering from an injury; his troops did not pass Barbara's house. Moreover, Barbara was ninety-six and on her deathbed. The real heroine was May Quantrell who waved a Union flag at the Confederate troops led by General Ambrose P. Hill. Incensed, some of the soldiers broke the staff – whereupon Mrs Quantrell obtained another flag. Hill told his men to let the lady keep her flag and so, as in Whittier's poem, 'ever the stars above look down/On thy stars below in Frederick town'. The story quickly passed into folklore and fact became confused with fiction when Barbara was given credit for an act actually performed by her near-neighbour May Quantrell.

G

HEDDA GABLER

Henrik Ibsen, *Hedda Gabler* (1890)

Emilie Bardach (1873–1955)

Further reading: H. Koht, *The Life of Ibsen*, translated by R.L. McMohan and H.A. Larsen (1931)

When Ibsen's heroine makes her entrance in *Hedda Gabler* she is a sensuous image of self-assurance: 'Hedda . . . is a woman of twenty-nine. Her face and figure show breeding and distinction. Her complexion is pale and opaque. Her eyes are steel grey and express a cold, unruffled repose. Her hair is an agreeable medium brown, but not especially abundant. She wears a tasteful, somewhat loose-fitting negligee.' Despite her enticing appearance Hedda is unhappy – bored by her middle-class marriage and frustrated at her failure to achieve her potential. Her efforts to change her life end tragically – 'everything I touch becomes ludicrous and despicable' she cries – and she shoots herself just before the final curtain.

Ibsen wrote the play when he was still under the erotic influence of Emilie Bardach, an eighteen-year-old Viennese girl he met in Gossensass in 1889 at a reception to celebrate the naming of the Ibsenplatz after him. When she became ill Ibsen called on her and she recorded her feelings in her diary: 'The obstacles! How they grow more numerous, the more I think of them! The difference of age! – his wife! – his son! – all that there is to keep us apart! Did this have to happen?' There is no doubt that the sixty-one-year-old writer was infatuated with Emilie and even tempted to abandon everything for a new life with her. Still, he settled down to the reality of the situation and consoled himself through correspondence. On 30 December 1889 he wrote to Emilie 'I beg you, for the time being, not to write to me again. When conditions have changed, I will let you know. I shall soon send you my new play. Accept it in friendship – but in silence.' After the 'new play', *Hedda Gabler*, there was no further contact between Emilie and Ibsen until she sent him a telegram of congratulation on his seventieth birthday and he replied saying 'The summer in Gossensass was the happiest, most beautiful in my whole life.'

THE GREAT GATSBY

F. Scott Fitzgerald, *The Great Gatsby* (1926)

Max Gerlach

Further reading: Matthew Bruccoli, *Some Sort of Epic Grandeur* (1982)

F. Scott Fitzgerald's *The Great Gatsby* disturbs the American dream of innocent affluence. Installed in his Long Island mansion, Jay Gatsby seems the perfect symbol of success, having unlimited wealth to enjoy an endless round of parties: 'On weekends his Rolls-Royce became an omnibus, bearing parties to and from the city.' The great peacock display, however, is to attract one girl, for Gatsby is a romantic hopelessly in love with a married woman, Daisy Buchanan, whose cousin Nick narrates the novel. When Nick first meets Gatsby he is surprised by his 'elaborate formality of speech': Gatsby uses the old-worldly phrase 'old sport' which contrasts with the rumours of his criminal past.

From 1922 to 1924 Scott and Zelda Fitzgerald rented a house in Great Neck, Long Island, and Scott observed a convivial neighbour Max Gerlach. Shortly before her death, in 1948, Zelda recalled that Gatsby was modelled on 'a neighbour named Von Guerlach or something who was said to be General Pershing's nephew and was in trouble over bootlegging'. In the Fitzgeralds' scrapbook there is a newspaper photograph of Scott and Zelda with a note of 20 July 1923: 'En route from the coast – Here for a few days on business – How are you and the family old Sport? Gerlach.' As Matthew J. Bruccoli writes in *Some Sort of Epic Grandeur* (1982) 'Here is Gatsby's characterizing expression, *old sport*, from the hand of Gerlach. Attempts to fill in the history of Max Gerlach have failed; the only clue is a 1930 newspaper reference to him as a "wealthy yachtsman".' As 'yachtsman' was period slang for rum-runner Gerlach remains a shady, mysterious figure like the character he inspired.

MARGUERITE GAUTIER

Alexandre Dumas, fils, *La Dame aux camélias* (1852)

Rose Alphonsine Plessis, 'Marie Duplessis' (1824–46)

Further reading:
Andre Maurois, *Les Trois Dumas* (1957)

Alexandre Dumas's drama *La Dame aux camélias*, which was based on his novel of the same name (1848), has a straightforward plot. A young Parisian courtesan of great beauty, Marguerite Gautier, has many lovers from the top end of society. A young man of good family, Armand Duval, falls deeply in love with her and implores her to abandon her life in Paris and live with him in the country. They live blissfully together for some time and then Armand's father arrives and explains to Marguerite that the forthcoming marriage of his daughter is being seriously jeopardized by the scandal of the relationship between Armand and Marguerite. She now loves Armand and cannot really bear to lose him but his father tells her the boy is bound to tire of her and that the liaison is not blessed by heaven. She agrees to leave him. She returns to her life in Paris, knowing that she is dying of consumption. Armand misunderstands her motives, but they are briefly reconciled before she dies in his arms.

The real life Rose Alphonsine Plessis was the daughter of a pedlar, whose mother died when she was nine. By the age of thirteen she had been seduced by a man of seventy and later abandoned in Paris. She supported herself working as a corset maker, a messenger and street walker. By the age of sixteen she was in great demand, leading a life of luxury and supported by several wealthy lovers, among them the Count de Stackelberg, Russian ambassador to Vienna, who was eighty when they met. In *La Dame aux camélias* he appears as the Duc de Mauriac.

She met Dumas in 1842 and they fell in love. She was ill with consumption and he persuaded her to come and live with him in the healthier atmosphere of the countryside. She was not only a vital and attractive woman, but was also very intelligent. She had dark hair and a fine complexion. In appearance, her face was somewhat Asiatic, as she had long lacquer-like eyes. Dumas described her as 'à la virginité du vice'. Their affair was very passionate but brief. She left him to return to her life in Paris, but her illness worsened and she died at the age of twenty-three. Dumas came to see her body laid to rest in Paris in a monument engraved with marble camelias. He wrote a novel based on her life, but it was the play *La Dame aux camélias* which made her story famous. Verdi saw it in Paris in 1852 and based his opera 'La Traviata' on the story of 'Marie Duplessis'.

LUCIAN GAY

Benjamin Disraeli, *Coningsby* (1844)

Theodore Hook (1788–1841)

Further reading:
R.H. Dalton Barham, *The Life and Remains of Theodore Hook* (1843)

In Disraeli's political novel, *Coningsby*, we find this portrait of Lucian Gay: 'Nature had intended Lucian Gay for a scholar and wit; necessity had made him a scribbler and buffoon. He had distinguished himself at university; but had no patrimony, nor those powers of perseverance which success in any learned profession requires. He was good looking, had great animal spirits, and a keen sense of enjoyment, and could not drudge. Moreover, he had a fine voice, and sang his own songs with considerable taste, accomplishments which made his fortune in society, and completed his ruin. In due time he extricated himself from the bench and merged into journalism.'

This is a portrait of Theodore Hook, author, journalist and wit. He was the son of James Hook (1746-1827) who wrote many popular songs. Theodore's musical and literary gifts showed themselves at an early age, and he became the pet of green room circles. Educated at Harrow and Oxford, he did not graduate. Success came easily to him, and his comic opera *The Soldier's Return*, written when he was sixteen, made him famous and a leading socialite. He had peerless powers of mimicry and was an astounding raconteur. He perpetrated some of the most famous practical jokes in history: the Berners Street hoax which involved the Lord Mayor, regiments of cavalry, the Chancellor of the Exchequer and other dignitaries all foregathering at the same address in London at the same time; and bringing a production of *Hamlet* to a standstill by coming on stage in Elizabethan costume and handing Hamlet a letter during the grave-diggers' scene. Such was his esteem as a socialite that the Prince

Regent declared 'Something must be done for Hook!' and he was made Accountant General and Treasurer of Mauritius in 1813. He became the life and soul of the island but some £12,000 went missing and Hook was brought back home, for what he wittily termed: 'a disorder in his chest'. Journalism and miscellaneous writing sustained him for a time but he was eventually arrested for debt, whereupon he wrote a series of rollicking stories which still read well.

DAVIE GELLATLEY
Sir Walter Scott, *Waverley* (1814)
Daft Jock Gray
(1776–1837)

Davie Gellatley is a born innocent or simpleton who maintains himself as a member of the household of the Baron of Bradwardine (see BARON OF BRADWARDINE) as a fool or jester: 'Sometimes this mister wight held his hands clasped over his head . . . sometimes he swung them perpendicularly, like a pendulum, on each side; and anon he slapped them swiftly and repeatedly across his breast . . . . His gait was as singular as his gestures, for at times he hopped with great perseverance on the right foot, then exchanged that support to advance in the same manner on the left, and then, putting his feet close together, he hopped upon both at once. His attire also was antiquated and extravagant. It consisted in a sort of grey jerkin, with scarlet cuffs and slashed sleeves, showing a scarlet lining; the other parts of the dress corresponded in colour, not forgetting a pair of scarlet stockings and a scarlet bonnet proudly surmounted with a turkey's feather.' His facial expression was 'wild, unsettled and irregular' and his visage was 'naturally rather handsome' where 'the simplicity of the fool was mixed with the extravagance of a crazed imagination'. He often sings old Scottish songs with great earnestness and some good taste. This is a portrait of the celebrated innocent, Daft Jock Gray, whom Sir Walter Scott knew personally as a visitor to Ashestiel and in the early days of Abbotsford. He was the son of another famous Daft Jock Gray, who was bred a weaver but turned to peddling for his living. He was born at Ettrick and lived at Crosslee, where the original of Scott's Davie Gellatley was born. He was a very lazy boy and resisted all attempts to educate him. He wore knee-breeches, with stockings fastened in flashy red garters, his coat had buttons like cart-wheels and he wore a very tall hat. He was an astonishingly natural mimic and there is a reliable account of his taking a sermon at Ettrick Kirk. He was often seen wandering about the pews in Yarrow Kirk, munching a huge bread and cheese sandwich (dunt) and when one worthy admonished his indolence and recommended that he might at least herd cows he answered: 'Me herd cows! I dinna ken corn frae gersh.' His imitations of all the local preachers were notorious and students used to pay him a few pence to perform his clerical mimicries in the street at Selkirk. He was very fond of music and had a considerable repertory of songs and traditional ballads and composed many himself. There is an account of him and his father in Thomas Aird's *Old Bachelor*. Aird knew them both personally.

GEORGE
Jerome K. Jerome, *Three Men in a Boat* (1889)
George Wingrave

Further reading: Jerome K. Jerome, *My Life and Times* (1983)

George's main contribution to the venture of the famous three men in the boat up the Thames was his seeming practical wisdom. He points out that the only way they can resolve the problem of not being able to negotiate up the Thames a boat which will be large enough to take all that they believe they need is to look at the problem another way: 'We must not think of the things we could do with, but only of the things that we can't do without.' It has to be admitted that he 'comes out really quite sensible at times. You'd be surprised. I call that downright wisdom, not merely as it regards the present case, but with reference to our trip up the river of life generally.' George's recommendations include not taking a tent, but a boat with a cover, and among personal possessions a rug each, a lamp, some soap, a brush and comb (between us), a tooth-brush (each), a basin, some tooth-powder, some shaving tackle, and a couple of big towels for bathing. As for clothes, George says: 'two suits of flannel would be sufficient as we could wash them ourselves, in the river, when they got dirty. We asked him if he had ever tried washing flannels in the river, and he replied: "No, not exactly himself like, but he knew some fellows who had, and it was easy enough"; and Harris and I were weak enough to fancy he knew what he was talking about, and that three respectable young men, without position or influence, with no experience in washing, could really clean their own shirts and trousers in the River Thames with a bit of soap. We were to learn in the days to come, when it was too late, that George was a miserable impostor . . .'

In his autobiography Jerome says that he shared the ground floor of 19 Tavistock Place with George Wingrave, who eventually became a bank-manager. They used to go to 'the British Museum reading-room: the poor students' club, as it used to be called. We three (see HARRIS) would foregather on Sunday mornings, and take the train to Richmond. There were lovely stretches then between Richmond and Staines, meadowland and cornfields. At first, we used to have the river almost to ourselves; but year by year it got more crowded and Maidenhead became our starting-point. England in those days was still a Sabbath-keeping land. Often people would hiss us as we passed, carrying our hamper and clad in fancy "blazers". Once a Salvation Army lass dropped suddenly upon her knees in front of us and started praying.'

GILBERTE

Marcel Proust, *Remembrance of Things Past* (1913–27)

Marie de Benardaky

Further reading: George D. Painter, *Marcel Proust* (1959, 1965)

In 1882 Marcel Proust was sent to the Lycée Condorcet, in Paris, and after school took to playing in the Champs-Élysées with his fellow pupils. During the summer of 1886, when he was almost fifteen, Proust met two Polish sisters in the Champs-Élysées. They were Marie (who was the same age as Proust) and Nelly de Benardaky, daughters of the Polish nobleman Nicolas de Benardaky. Proust now contrived to be on Marie's side in the game of prisoner's base they played in the Champs-Élysées. Every evening, before going to sleep, he would tell himself 'I shall see her tomorrow'. The following February, when he was recovering from a bout of influenza, he was invited to Marie's house – which he regarded with awe since he considered Marie his social superior. Marie's parents felt that Marcel was a good influence on their daughter, and well placed to teach Marie about literature. Then, in the spring of 1887, Marcel stopped seeing Marie, probably because he felt she did not return his love. He contemplated suicide for some time, but recovered with a philosophical attitude towards the problems of heterosexual love for one of his temperament. Proust must have seen Marie subsequently, in the high society circles he entered, and George D. Painter notes that 'the grown-up Marie . . . was dark and pretty; she had the rosy cheeks, and features at once frank and foxy, of Gilberte Swann.' Marie married Prince Michel Radziwill in 1897, had a daughter Léontine in 1904, and saw her marriage dissolved in 1915. 'She was, perhaps without knowing it, the intoxication and despair of my childhood', said Proust, who saw Marie as 'one of the two great loves of my life'.

Gilberte, in Proust's novel, is the daughter of CHARLES and ODETTE SWANN who live at Tansonville on the outskirts of Combray (where the book begins). When young Marcel first sees Gilberte he is romantically stricken (in the C.K. Scott Moncrieff/Terence Kilmartin translation): 'I gazed at her, at first with that gaze which is not merely the messenger of the eyes, but at whose window all the senses assemble and lean out, petrified and anxious, a gaze eager to reach, touch, capture, bear off in triumph the body at which it is aimed, and the soul with the body; then . . . with another, an unconsciously imploring look, whose object was to force her to pay attention to me, to see, to know me.' Gilberte, however, is indifferent to Marcel's love and tells him so. She subsequently marries Robert de Saint-Loup and thus becomes a Guermantes, a development that would have delighted Charles Swann, although Gilberte is snobbishly ashamed of her dead father's Jewishness. Towards the end of the novel Marcel meets the daughter of the widowed Gilberte.

EDWARD MILLER GILLEY

John Ehrlichman, *The Company* (1976) and TV series *Washington Behind Closed Doors*, written by David W. Rintels and Eric Bercovici (Paramount 1977)

Hubert Horatio Humphrey (1911–83)

Further reading: H.R. Haldeman, *The Ends of Power* (1978)

Gilley is the Democratic Vice President to President Anderson (see ESKER SCOTT ANDERSON), and is nominated by Anderson to succeed him. He is defeated in the presidential election by Monckton, the Republican candidate (see RICHARD MONCKTON). Although opposed by the liberal wing of his party, Gilley's endorsement by Anderson and his support from his home-base delegation in Pennsylvania, as well as solid AFL-CIO support (labour unions) in the other industrial states ensure his endorsement in the first ballot at the convention. Gilley is sixty and was formerly a six-term Congressman from the Eleventh District of Pennsylvania and Chairman of the House Labour and Education Committee. He is married to Alice Mae Brown, from Denton, Texas, a housewife.

Hubert Humphrey was born in South Dakota, but is always associated with Minnesota, where he played a leading role in uniting the Democratic and Farmer-Labor parties. He early made a name for himself as a champion of liberal civil rights in the 1948 Democratic Convention. He was the first Democrat from his state to be elected for the US Senate in 1948, where he served until 1964 as a leading supporter of medical care for the aged, Food for Peace, the Peace Corps and nuclear arms limitation. He worked very closely and well with L.B. Johnson, who helped his selection as majority whip in 1961. He tried for high office several times. In 1956 Humphrey failed to get his party's nomination as vice presidential candidate and in 1960 he failed to get presidential nomination. He was selected as Johnson's running mate in 1964. He provided valuable service as Vice President, as his long career in public life had given him invaluable and numerous contacts in city and state governments, labour organizations and other minority groups. Unfortunately his loyalty to Johnson included his support of Johnson's Vietnam policies, and this cost him dearly in terms of liberal support. When Johnson suddenly announced that he would neither seek nor accept the Democratic nomination for the presidency it seemed to the 'Happy Warrior' (as Humphrey was called) that his moment had finally come; but he lost in a close-run election to Richard Nixon in 1968, probably because inflation was crippling the dollar in international markets, and it was felt that employment and wages should be held down and social services be cut back. The electorate possibly thought Nixon more likely to deliver the goods in these respects. Nixon also had the backing of big business. In 1970 Humphrey returned to the Senate and again sought the presidential nomination in 1972. Johnson said he always pictured Humphrey with 'tears in his eyes; he was always able to cry at the sight of something sad, whether it be a widow with her child or an old crippled-up man . . . the trouble is . . . he's never learned to put feelings and strength together, all too often he sways in the wind like a big old reed, pushed around by pressures of staff and friends and colleagues.' (Doris Kearns, *Lyndon Johnson and the American Dream*, 1976).

JOHN GILPIN

William Cowper, *The Diverting History of John Gilpin* (1782)

William Beyer (1692–1791)

Further reading: William Cowper, *Works*, edited with a Memoir by Robert Southey (1837)

John Gilpin is a citizen 'of credit and renown' who has devoted his life to a prosperous trade and to public service, and has neglected his wife of some twenty years. The 'linen-draper bold' of Cheapside resolves to celebrate the twentieth anniversary of their wedding with a trip to the 'Bell' at Edmonton. He is to travel there on a horse he borrows, while his wife, her sister and the children will go there in a chaise and pair. The bold burgher losses control of the horse: 'So "Fair and softly," John he cried,/But John he cried in vain;/That trot became a gallop soon,/In spite of curb and rein.' The more he tries to restrain the beast, the wilder the horse becomes: 'Away went Gilpin, neck or nought;/Away went hat and wig;/He little dreamt, when he set out,/Of running such a rig.' Dogs bark, children scream with excitement, crowds gather thinking it is a race or an event of some kind. He gallops on to Edmonton and ten miles beyond it, on to Ware, and back again. His wife sends after him, and a hue and cry is raised with people calling out: 'Stop thief! stop thief! – a highwayman!' He is the first to arrive back home again, at the end of an eventful wedding anniversary.

The story is a true one, and the events happened to William Beyer, a linen-draper, who lived at the Cheapside corner of Paternoster Row. He died in 1791 at a ripe old age. William Cowper was a religious maniac, who suffered recurring bouts of depression and melancholia. He was befriended by Lady Anne Austen, widow of Sir Robert Austen, in 1781. She was a neighbour of his at Olney. During one of his attacks of almost suicidal depression she told him the story of poor Mr Beyer, who owned land near Olney. She had heard the story as a child. It is said that on the night in 1782 when Cowper was entertained by Lady Austen's narrative of Beyer's wedding anniversary adventures, he was kept awake all night with laughter at it, and turned it into the famous ballad which was published first in the *Public Advertiser* on 14 November 1782.

SCYTHROP GLOWRY

Thomas Love Peacock, *Nightmare Abbey* (1818)

Percy Bysshe Shelley (1792–1822)

Further reading: H. Mills, *Peacock – His Circle and His Age* (1969)

Nightmare Abbey concerns the amorous entanglements of Scythrop Glowry, the young son of a gloomy misanthrope. One of his ancestors hanged himself, and Scythrop's father has the skull made into a drinking cup in his honour. Scythrop is sent to public school, 'where a little learning was painfully beaten into him,' and from there, to university: 'where it was carefully taken out of him; and he was sent home like a well threshed ear of corn, with nothing in his head.' But he did learn to drink deep. He is early disappointed in love, and is driven half distracted. It preys very deeply on his sensitive spirit. His father attempts to console him by enlarging on a text from *Ecclesiastes*: 'One man among a thousand have I found, but a woman amongst all those have I not found.' Scythrop asks why he should have expected it, when 'the whole thousand were locked up in his seraglio? His experience is no precedent for a free state of society like that in which we live.' They are always locked up, his father assures him, and vanity and interest keep the key. 'I am sorry for it,' retorts Scythrop. 'But how is it that their minds are locked up? The fault is in their artificial education, which studiously models them into mere musical dolls, to be set out for sale in the great toy-shop of society.'

These radical views of sexual politics had made Shelley notorious, and this is Peacock's portrait of young Shelley. He had been sent down from Oxford as a result of his atheism, had married Harriet Westbrook and left her for Mary Godwin. He believed in 'free love' and his poem, *Queen Mab*, published in 1813, put forward the theory that humankind was corrupted by human society, institutions and 'morality'. Peacock shows Shelley at heart a reformer: 'Scythrop now became troubled with the *passion for reforming the world*. He built many castles in the air, and peopled them with secret tribunals . . . As he intended to institute a perfect republic, he invested himself with absolute sovereignty over these mystical dispensers of liberty.' Shelley was by no means offended, but told Peacock he was 'delighted' with *Nightmare Abbey*.

GOLDBERRY

J.R.R. Tolkien, *The Lord of the Rings* (1954–55)

Mabel Tolkien (née Suffield) the author's mother (1860–1904)

Further reading: Humphrey Carpenter, *J.R.R. Tolkien – A Biography* (1977)

Goldberry is the wife of Tom Bombadil. She is a water-sprite of the Old Forest, daughter of the River-woman of Withywindle. Frodo and Sam meet Tom Bombadil and his wife, Goldberry, quite early in their epic journey in *The Lord of the Rings*: 'In a chair, at the far side of the room . . sat a woman. Her long yellow hair rippled down her shoulders; her gown was green, green as young reeds, shot with silver like beads of dew; and her belt was of gold . . .' But she is thoroughly domesticated and readily accepts it as her destiny to play a supporting role to the males: 'The hobbits sat down gladly in low rush-seated chairs, while Goldberry busied herself about the table; and their eyes followed her, for the slender grace of her movement filled them with quiet delight.' When her husband comes in, among the first words he addresses to her are: 'Is the table laden? I see yellow cream and honeycomb, and white bread, and butter; milk, cheese, and green herbs and ripe berries gathered. Is that enough for us? Is the supper ready?'

Tolkien's father died when he was four and he was brought up and educated by his mother. Mabel became a Roman Catholic in 1900 and taught the author and his brother the principles of the faith. Her attachment to the Catholic faith was deeply opposed by the rest of the family, and in the case of J.R.R. Tolkien it became a matter of very strong zeal. His biographer Humphrey Carpenter says: 'His religion took the place in his affections that she (his mother) had previously occupied.' He wrote: 'Though a Tolkien by name, I am a Suffield by tastes, talents and upbringing.' Mabel lived with her family at Sarehole, outside Birmingham, which was in the English countryside – the situation he idealized in the Bombadil and Goldberry sections of *The Lord of the Rings*. His mother taught him to read and to love languages. She also taught him a great deal of Botany and to love the natural world. His biographer records: 'he was good at drawing . . . particularly when the subject was a landscape or a tree. His mother taught him a good deal of botany . . . but he was more interested in the shape and feel of a plant than in its botanical details.' Mabel really sacrificed herself for her children. Tolkien wrote: 'My own dear mother was a martyr indeed, and it is not to everybody that God grants so easy a way to his great gifts as he did to Hilary and myself, giving us a mother who killed herself with labour and trouble to ensure us keeping the Faith.' Goldberry lives a pastoral life, by a forest, in a warm secure home, the provider of comfort, love and food. Mabel died at Oratory Cottage, a retreat in the country – all the places Tolkien associated with his mother – Sarehole, Rednal (Worcestershire) – were in his mind pastoral idylls.

EUGENIE GRANDET

Honoré de Balzac, *Eugénie Grandet* (1834)

Maria du Fresnay/ Madame Hanska

Further reading: F. Marceau, *Balzac et son monde* (1955), H.J. Hunt, *Honoré de Balzac* (1957)

The heroine of Balzac's *Eugénie Grandet*, a mixture of naivety and nobility, is deprived of love as a result of her father's appalling avarice. Eugénie is a portrait that combines two of the women in Balzac's life: Maria de Fresnay and Madame Hanska. In October 1833 Balzac wrote to his sister: 'I have fathered a child, that's another secret for you, the sweetest and most naive of beings who fell at my feet like a flower from heaven, who came to me secretly, refused to let me write to her, and asks for nothing from me except "Love me for a year. I will love you all my life".'

Little is known of Maria du Fresnay beyond the fact that she was married when she met Balzac; Marie, the child she had by Balzac, lived from 1834 to 1930. Still, Balzac dedicated his novel to Maria: 'May your name be set on this book, whose fairest ornament is your portrait.'

Physically, Eugénie is formidable, 'built on such a generous scale', and the description fits Madame Evelina Hanska, the Polish countess Balzac was to marry five months before his death. Madame Hanska first wrote anonymously to Balzac in 1832 then, encouraged by him to correspond, wrote a second letter telling him 'You elevate woman to her true dignity; love in her is a celestial virtue, a divine emanation.' This notion of nobility was in his mind as he composed *Eugénie Grandet* during 1833. Accustomed to the exercise of authority Madame Hanska, an enormously wealthy woman, demanded that Balzac write to her every week about his activities but he had, eventually, to put his work before this woman. When Mme Hanska's husband died in 1842 Balzac wrote to 'my angel, my heavenly flower' proposing marriage but she had turned against him on account of his infidelities. It was only when it became obvious that Balzac was dying that Madame Hanska agreed to marry him in a ceremony conducted at Berdichev on 14 March 1850.

GRANTORTO

Edmund Spenser, *The Faerie Queene* (1589, 1596)

Philip II, King of Spain (1527–98)

Philip II of Spain is several times portrayed allegorically in *The Faerie Queene*, as befits the Roman Catholic monarch who was seen as the arch-enemy of Britain during the period of Queen Elizabeth I's reign. He appears as the Souldan who threatens the kingdom but is cunningly slain by Prince Arthur and is destroyed by his own vicious chariot wheels. He also plays the role of Gerioneo, the vile oppressor of Belge (the Netherlands). As Grantorto, a tyrant with designs on the fair Irena (Ireland), he gets his come-uppance at the hands of the brave Sir Artegall (see SIR ARTEGALL), who discovers just in time that her only other defender has been forced to yield (see SIR BURBON). Grantorto is described as having a 'proud presumptuous gate' as if he was fearless: 'All armed in a cote of yron plate/Of great defence to ward the deadly feare;/And on his head a steele-cap he did weare/Of colour rustie-browne, but sure and strong;/And in his hand an huge Polaxe did beare,/Whose steale was yron-studded, but not long/With which he wont to fight to justifie his wrong:/Of stature huge and hideous he was,/Like to a Giant for his monstrous hight,/And did in strength most sorts of men surpas,/Ne ever any found his match in might;/Thereto he had great skill in single fight:/His face was ugly and his countenance sterne,/That could have frayd one with the very sight,/And gaped like a gulfe when he did gerne;/That whether man or monster one could scarse discerne.' After a terrible combat, Sir Artegall succeeds in beheading the dreadful Grantorto. Philip was heir to the huge empire of Charles V and saw as his task on earth the resistance of the Reformation and the New Learning. Against him were ranged the powers of England, France and the Netherlands. The threat from the Turks was ended by the battle of Lepanto, but he lost the Netherlands, and his attempted invasion of England with the Armada failed. He won Portugal and extended Spanish power in America. Philip was the son of the Emperor Charles V; he married Mary Tudor in 1554, and visited England, staying fourteen months, but failing to ingratiate himself here. The greatest danger to his European power was the series of alliances between England, France, the Netherlands and Pope Paul IV. He failed to gain Elizabeth I's hand in marriage and married Isabella of France in 1559. He was suspected in the deaths of William the Silent, Antonio Perez, and even his own son, Don Carlos. At one time he was the most powerful prince in Europe. It was said: 'When Spain stirs, Europe trembles'.

Further reading:
A.C. Hamilton, *The Structure of Allegory in the Faerie Queene* (1961)

DORIAN GRAY

Oscar Wilde, *The Picture of Dorian Gray* (1891)

Father John Gray (1866–1934)

Oscar Wilde's novel *The Picture of Dorian Gray* is a sumptuously told tale of a vain young man who exchanges his soul so he will retain his youth while his portrait ages instead. Gray is a collector of exquisite experiences and, for example, 'the Roman ritual had always a great attraction for him.... The fuming censers, that the grave boys, in their lace and scarlet, tossed into the air like great gilt flowers, had their subtle fascination for him... He had a special passion, also, for ecclesiastical vestments, as indeed he had for everything connected with the service of the Church.'

Although Dorian Gray never succumbs formally to the call of the Roman Catholic Church, John Gray – the friend Wilde referred to as 'Dorian' – eventually became Father John Gray of St Peter's Church, Edinburgh. Gray was introduced to Wilde in 1889 at a session of the Rhymers' Club. Wilde felt that Gray had all the makings of the perfect disciple for he was good-looking and wrote suitably decadent poems. After Wilde met Lord Alfred Douglas in 1891 he lost interest in John Gray but felt guilty enough about this to pay for the cost of publication of Gray's first collection of poems, *Silverpoints* (1892). Gray decided to enter the priesthood after the arrest of Oscar Wilde in 1895 and instructed a barrister to attend Wilde's trial to take action should his name be mentioned. In a letter, written to Lord Alfred Douglas from Reading Gaol, Wilde said 'When I compare my friendship with you with such still younger men as John Gray and Pierre Louys, I feel ashamed. My real life, my higher life was with them and such as they.'

Further reading:
Philippe Jullian, *Oscar Wilde* (1969), B. Sewell, *In the Dorian Mode* (1983), Hesketh Pearson, *The Life of Oscar Wilde* (1946)

GIDEON GRAY

Sir Walter Scott, *The Surgeon's Daughter* (1827)

Dr Ebenezer Clarkson (1763-1847)

The Surgeon's Daughter, one of the least credible of Scott's novels, has – for him – an unusual setting. Much of the action takes place in India, the local colour for which Sir Walter Scott got second hand from General Ronald Ferguson (1773-1841) of Huntlyburn, who compiled several pages of details about his experiences in Madras and Mysore. Scott's Indian scenes are set in the Court of Hyder Ali. Scott makes a major bloomer in describing Hindu India, where his narrative takes place, in

Further reading: John Gibson Lockhart, *The Life of Sir Walter Scott* (1838)

terms of the Mohammedan southern India he learned about from Ferguson, with its mullahs, fakirs and hajjis. However, it is a suitable background for the fantastic yarn which Scott weaves. Richard Middlemas is an illegitimate child brought up by the surgeon, Gideon Gray, in Middlemas village. Richard is a wilful, wayward, slightly sinister young man, and he and the surgeon's daughter, Menie, fall in love. Richard seeks his fortune in India, where he falls under the influence of the Begum Mootee Mahal, and goes along with her base scheme to lure Menie out to India under the promise of marriage, but really with the intention of selling her to a native Rajah, Tippoo Sahib. This dreadful plot is foiled by another pupil of surgeon Gray's – Adam Hartley – who has loved the surgeon's daughter himself for many years. Richard the unprincipled betrayer of the innocent Menie meets a terrible end: he is crushed to death by an elephant. This improbable farrago of pseudo-orientalism is rendered memorable by the splendid portrayal of the good, public-spirited surgeon, based on Walter Scott's own doctor, the virtuous Dr Ebenezer Clarkson of Selkirk: 'He was of such reputation in the medical world, that he had been often advised to exchange the village and its meagre circle of practice for Edinburgh,' Scott wrote, 'There is no creature in Scotland that works harder, and is more poorly requited, than the country doctor, unless perhaps it be his horse. Yet the horse is, and indeed must be, hardy, active, and indefatigable, in spite of a rough coat and indifferent condition; and so you will often find in his master, under a blunt exterior, professional skill and enthusiasm, intelligence, humanity, courage and science.' This was considered a fine portrait of Dr Clarkson, who was widely loved and respected. He was for many years Chief Magistrate of Selkirk and a credit to the medical profession. He was born in Dalkeith, was twice married, and had two sons; one was a physician to the King of Oude and the other in practice in Melrose. The latter son, in fact, had the sad task of laying out Sir Walter Scott after his death in September 1832.

GREEN-MANTLE

Sir Walter Scott, *Redgauntlet* (1824)

Williamina Belsches

(1775–1810)

Further reading: Edgar Johnson, *Sir Walter Scott – The Great Unknown* (1970)

When Alan Fairford, the autobiographical hero of Sir Walter Scott's *Redgauntlet*, comes face to face with the mysterious Green-Mantle, alias Lilias Redgauntlet, he is impressed: 'she was a very pretty young woman . . . and the slight derangement of the beautiful brown locks which escaped in natural ringlets from under her riding-hat, with the bloom which exercise had brought into her cheek, made her even more than usually fascinating.'

As a young advocate (called to the Scottish Bar in 1792) Scott felt he had found the love of his life in Williamina Belsches, an heiress whose father Sir John had squandered his own inheritance and was several thousand pounds in debt. Scott declared his love in a letter to Williamina in 1795 and her reply was ambiguous enough to give Scott hopes of an eventual match. Scott's father, however, felt Williamina too highly placed for the young advocate and wrote to Sir John to say so. In 1796 Williamina was shown a copy of Scott's first book, *The Chase, and William and Helen*, and was duly delighted though her praise of the author was dutiful not emotional. A rival had raised his financially irresistible head: William Forbes, son of a great banker. Since Sir John Belsches was becoming hopelessly in debt the marriage of Williamina and young Forbes, in 1797, solved his financial problems. Scott was shattered, 'broken-hearted for two years . . . but the crack will remain till my dying day.' On the rebound Scott married a French girl, Charlotte Charpentier, and embarked on thirty-nine years of marriage which was 'something short of love in all its fervour'. Scott never forgot his infatuation for Williamina and so portrayed her fondly as Green-Mantle. In his *Journal* of 1827 Scott confessed that the thought of Williamina was still enough to 'agitate my heart'.

When he met Williamina's mother in Edinburgh, the real Green-Mantle had been dead for seventeen years and Scott 'fairly softened myself, like an old fool, with recalling stories, till I was fit for nothing but shedding tears and repeating verses for the whole night'.

CLYDE GRIFFITHS

Theodore Dreiser, *An American Tragedy* (1925)

Chester Gillette
(1881–1908)

Further reading:
W.A. Swanberg, *Dreiser* (1965), Ellen Moers, *The Two Dreisers – The Man and the Novelist* (1969)

Early in Theodore Dreiser's *An American Tragedy* there is a glimpse of Clyde Griffiths as a twelve-year-old boy who seems apart from the little group he walks with: 'The boy moved restlessly from one foot to the other. . . . A tall and yet slight figure, surmounted by an interesting head and face – white skin, dark hair – he seemed more keenly observant and decidedly more sensitive than most of the others – appeared indeed to resent and even to suffer from the position in which he found himself.' Clyde longs to escape from the evangelical atmosphere associated with his parents who run a mission for misfits. After being involved in an accident resulting in the death of a child, Clyde goes to Chicago where he works as a bellboy in a club. There he meets his rich uncle Samuel who gives him a job in his shirt factory in Lycurgus. Two women now dramatically enter Clyde's life: Roberta Alden, who works in Clyde's department at the shirt factory; and Sondra Finchley, a beautiful society girl. When Roberta becomes pregnant Clyde attempts to simplify his life by drowning her – which he finally does more by accident than intention. He is found guilty of murder in the first degree and executed.

The story thus sticks closely to Dreiser's source in a murder case of 1906. Chester Gillette was brought up in the American West by his parents who ran a mission. He moved to Cortland, New York, where his uncle gave him a job as a supervisor in his skirt factory. Gillette seduced one of the factory girls, Grace 'Billy' Brown, and her pregnancy threatened his relationship with a local debutante. In July 1906 Gillette persuaded Billy to go on a holiday with him and, on Big Moose Lake, hit her over the head with a tennis racket and watched as she drowned. During the trial much was made of the heartbreakingly tender letters written by Billy to Gillette and these were integrated into Dreiser's novel. Gillette went to the electric chair in 1908 without ever acknowledging his guilt

CAPTAIN GRIMES

Evelyn Waugh, *Decline and Fall* (1928)

Captain Young

Further reading:
Evelyn Waugh Diaries edited by Michael Davie (1976), *Evelyn Waugh Letters* edited by Mark Amory (1980)

Captain Grimes, the one-legged schoolmaster colleague of Paul Pennyfeather, is a drunken fraud, permanently 'in the soup', who nevertheless always manages to pull through. He is, as Waugh writes, 'one of the Immortals'. Soon after Paul arrives at Llanabba Castle, Grimes tells him that another master, Mr Prendergast wears a wig: 'Very hard for a man with a wig to keep order. I've got a false leg, but that's different. Boys respect that. Think I lost it in the war. Actually . . . I was run over by a tram in Stoke-on-Trent when I was one-over-the-eight . . .' He is frequently fired from teaching posts but always manages to get a new job: 'I can always get on all right for about six weeks,' he says, 'and then I land in the soup. I don't believe I was ever meant by Nature to be a schoolmaster. Temperament . . . that's been my trouble, temperament and sex.' Paul asks him if it is quite easy to get another job after being in the soup: 'Not at first, it isn't, but there're ways. Besides, you see, I'm a public-school man. That means everything. There's a blessed equity in the English social system . . . that ensures the public-school man against starvation. One goes through four or five years of perfect hell at an age when life is bound to be hell, anyway, and after that the social system never lets one down.' He was expelled from his school at sixteen, but the housemaster helps him by writing him a letter of recommendation to any future employer, which has always helped him. He fails in business, spends the entire war drunk, and the old boy network saves his bacon at a court martial. His school career was similarly patchy, but, 'They may kick out, but they never let you down.'

Captain Young was the new usher at Arnold House, the school where Waugh taught in early 1925. In his journal for 5 May Waugh records: 'Young, the new usher, is monotonously pederastic and talks only of the beauty of sleeping boys.' On 3 July he records: 'Young and I went out and made ourselves very drunk and he confessed all his previous career. He was expelled from Wellington, sent down from Oxford, and forced to resign his commission in the army. He has left four schools precipitately, three in the middle of the term through his being taken in sodomy and one through his being drunk six nights in succession. And yet he goes on getting better and better jobs without difficulty. It was all very like Bruce and the spider.'

DR GULSON
Charles Reade, *It Is Never Too Late To Mend* (1856)
James Manby Gully (1808–83)

Further reading: Richard Metcalfe, *Rise and Progress of Hydropathy* (1906)

It is Never Too Late to Mend, one of Reade's most overtly reforming and campaigning novels, combines two narratives – the story of the young farmer who goes to Australia to achieve the £1,000 he needs to gain the approval of his beloved's father so that he may marry her; and the sorry tale of the thief sentenced to jail and transportation. The sequences in prison give Reade the chance to berate the British penal system and the barbarity of many of those who administer it. The system is exposed to us as we read things through the eyes of the prison chaplain, the Revd Eden. At one stage of the story Eden is stricken with a fearful bilious fever and is very likely to die, but is miraculously cured by water treatment, prescribed by Dr Gulson of Malvern, who is called in to the prison to treat the patient. Dr Gulson asks Eden for an account of his illness and details of the remedies applied by the medical staff. He then says: 'The old story . . . you were weak – therefore they gave you things to weaken you. You could not put so much nourishment as usual into your body – therefore they have been taking strength out. Lastly, the coats of your stomach were irritated by your disorder – so they have raked it like blazes. This is the mill-round of the old medicine; from irritation to inflammation, from inflammation to mortification, and decease of the patient. Now instead of irritating the irritated spot, suppose we try a little counter irritation.' He then cures the Revd Eden with water compresses and blankets.

This is a portrait of the celebrated pioneer of hydropathic treatment, James Manby Cully, who followed the work of Erasmus Wilson, in partnership with Edward Johnson. Gully was educated at Paris, and was awarded his MD at Edinburgh in 1829. He practised in London and Malvern, where he opened a clinic and pioneered the hydropathic treatment of disease, based on the availability of the pure spring water. Gully's reputation was at its height when it was severely damaged by the case of the strange death of Charles Bravo in 1876. He published *The Water Cure in Chronic Disease* (1846).

GUNGA DIN
Rudyard Kipling, *Barrack Room Ballads* (1892)
Juma

Further reading: Charles Carrington, *Rudyard Kipling* (1953), Bosworth Smith, *Life of Lord Lawrence* (1885)

Rudyard Kipling was born in Bombay and, after schooling in England, returned to India in 1882 to work on the Lahore *Civil Military Gazette*. In the course of his journalistic work he picked up many stories of local life which he was able to retell with soldierly slang. His poem 'Gunga Din', from *Barrack Room Ballads* (1892), is a tribute from a Cockney soldier to a low-caste water-carrier (or bhisti): 'Now in Inja's sunny clime,/Where I used to spend my time/A-servin' of 'Er Majesty the Queen,/Of all them blackfaced crew/The finest man I knew/Was our regimental bhisti, Gunga Din.'

Kipling based Gunga Din on Juma, the regimental bhisti, with the Corps of the Guides, a crack fighting unit comprising native soldiers and British officers. Low-caste Indians like Juma were excluded from actually joining the Corps on the grounds that experience of servility would prevent a man acquiring the necessary ferocity to fight. At the siege of Delhi in 1857 Juma distinguished himself over two months by disregarding his own safety in order to bring water to the wounded. As a result of this the soldiers themselves cited his humble heroism: 'This man is the bravest of the brave, for without arms or protection of any sort he is in the foremost line. If anyone deserves the star for valour, this man does.' On the recommendation of the fighting men of the Guides, Juma was himself enlisted and awarded the star for valour, the highest honour given to an Indian soldier. Subsequently Juma became an officer in the Guides and earned further honours for his displays of courage in the Afghan War of 1878.

MR W.H.
William Shakespeare, *Sonnets* (1609)

William Hatcliffe
(1568–1631)

Further reading:
Leslie Hotson, *Mr W.H.* (1964)

When Shakespeare's *Sonnets* were printed in 1609 the publisher, Thomas Thorpe, included the following dedication: 'TO.THE.ONLIE.BEGETTER.OF./THESE.INSUING.SONNETS./Mr. W.H.ALL.HAPPINESSE./AND.THAT.ETERNITIE./PROMISED./BY./OUR.EVER-LIVING.POET./WISHETH./THE.WELL-WISHING./ADVENTURER.IN./SETTING./FORTH.' As Shakespeare expresses his admiration for a youth of extraordinary beauty, generations of readers have puzzled over the identity of the Mr W.H. who inspired such lines as these, from Sonnet 20: 'A woman's face, with Nature's own hand painted,/Hast thou, the Master Mistress of my passion;/A woman's gentle heart, but not acquainted/With shifting change, as is false woman's fashion;/An eye more bright than theirs, less false in rolling,/Gilding the object whereupon it gazeth'. Several theorists assumed that Mr W.H. must be either William Herbert, third Earl of Pembroke; or Henry Wriothesley, Third Earl of Southampton (to whom *Venus and Adonis* and *The Rape of Lucrece* are dedicated).

In *Mr W.H.* (1964), however, the Shakespearean scholar Leslie Hotson comes up with an ingenious theory. Arguing that the line 'The mortal Moon hath her eclipse endur'd' (in the so-called 'dating sonnet', 107) is a reference to the defeat of the moon-shaped Spanish Armada, Hotson dates the composition of the sonnets to the period 1587-9 when Shakespeare was a young man in his twenties. The fact that Shakespeare adopts a tone of 'paradoxical senility' is, for Hotson, 'unmistakable *prima facie* evidence of a sonnetteer's youth'. Moreover, Shakespeare's references to his friend as 'my sovereign' (57), 'king' (63) and 'a king' (87) led Hotson to believe that Mr W.H. had once been chosen as a sovereign, or Prince of Purpoole, in one of the Elizabethan pageants devised by the Inns of Court. Such sovereigns had to play host to the Queen's greatest ministers and also converse with Elizabeth herself.

Hotson discovered, in Percival Vivian's 1909 edition of *Campion's Works*, a reference to William Hatcliffe, of Hatcliffe in Lincolnshire, who had been a Prince of Purpoole at Gray's Inn in 1586. Hatcliffe was twenty-one in September 1589 and had been admitted to Gray's Inn three years earlier, hence Shakespeare's reference in Sonnet 104: 'three winters cold/Have from the forests shook three summers' pride . . .' Hatcliffe was (says Hotson) 'the wealthy heir of an ancient line – and his aunt [was] the daughter of the Queen's Lord Admiral and Lord Steward'. He married Dorothy Kay in 1595 and the couple had two daughters before their son Thomas was born in 1606, so that eventually Mr W.H. had the heir Shakespeare urges on him in the sonnets.

OLIVER HADDO
W. Somerset Maugham, *The Magician* (1908)

Aleister Crowley
(1875–1947)

Further reading:
Ted Walker, *Maugham* (1980)

At the Chat Blanc, in Paris in 1905, Somerset Maugham met the notorious Satanist Aleister Crowley and soon began the process of transforming him into a fictional character. Oliver Haddo, as Crowley is called in Maugham's *The Magician*, is an unbearably arrogant individual with an aesthetic turn of phrase. When he arrives at the Chien Noir (as the Chat Blanc is renamed in the novel) he tells the waitress 'Marie, disembarrass me of this coat of frieze. Hang my sombrero upon a convenient peg.' Subsequently the story becomes more sinister as Haddo, whose activities include the making of test tube beings, pursues a young woman against her wishes and offers her as a human sacrifice.

Crowley, the Great Beast (as he called himself after the beast in Revelation), was attracted to the occult as a young man and formed his own secret society, the Astrum Argentinum (Silver Star) in London. As his infamy grew he began to travel in search of disciples and outrageous experiences. His *The Book of the Law*, dictated to him (so he said) by his guardian angel Aiwass, preached the message 'Do what thou wilt shall be the whole of the Law.' Drawing further on his fondness for Rabelais (who had used the motto in *Gargantua and Pantagruel*) Crowley founded, in 1920, his Abbey of Thelema on the northern coast of Sicily, but rumours of sexual perversion and sacrifice disturbed Mussolini who ordered Crowley out of the country in 1923. Crowley's career ended ingloriously with the Great Beast selling a patent medicine of his own concoction. Crowley was furious when Maugham's novel appeared, noting that the author had fictionalized 'some of the most private and personal incidents of my life, my marriage, my exploration, my adventures with big game, my magical opinions, ambitions and exploits [and] added a number of the many absurd legends of which I was the central figure'.

EDWARD HALLIN
Mrs Humphry Ward, *Marcella* (1894)
Arnold Toynbee (1852-83)

Further reading: Mrs Humphry Ward, *A Writer's Recollections* (1918)

Despite the various disagreements that trouble them in the course of their relationship Marcella Boyce, Venturist (Fabian socialist), and Aldous Raeburn, Tory and heir to Lord Maxwell's estate, are eventually united in their regard for Edward Hallin. A leading Christian Socialist, Hallin – Aldous's Cambridge mentor – is a formidable force in the Labour movement and an observer who realizes that Marcella and Aldous are meant for each other. Hallin stands for moderation, advocating collective action, but defending the principle of private property. As an individual he has great warmth: 'He had a singularly attractive voice, the voice indeed of the orator, which can adapt itself with equal charm and strength to the most various needs and to any pitch. As he spoke Marcella was conscious of a sudden impression that she already knew him and could be herself with him at once.' When he is clearly ill, Hallin decides to go ahead with his address on Land Reform to an audience of working-class Londoners. After being howled down by militants, he has a stroke – 'what a martyrdom!' Marcella comments. On his deathbed Hallin is visited by both Aldous and Marcella and Hallin reminds Aldous of what his life has amounted to; 'Land reform – Church Reform – Wages Reform – we have threshed them all out in this room . . . How full I was of it! – the Church that was to be the people – reflecting their life, their differences – governed by them – growing with them.'

Mrs Humphry Ward modelled the character of Hallin on the reformer Arnold Toynbee who devoted himself to economics and history at Oxford, and also went into industrial areas to speak on social problems. In 1875 he went to Whitechapel, where he was associated with the work of Canon Barnett. Toynbee Hall, the first of the social and educational settlements in east London, was named after him in 1885. Mrs Humphry Ward was sympathetic to Toynbee's social work, and she herself founded the Passmore Edwards Settlement (now bearing her name) to bring educational and recreational sustenance to working people.

PIED PIPER OF HAMELIN
Robert Browning, *The Pied Piper of Hamelin* (1845)
Nicholas, leader of the Children's Crusade (1212)

The town of Hamelin is plagued by rats. The mayor and corporation strike a bargain with a mysterious piper who has promised to rid them of the rats by means of a mysterious charm. He takes out a pipe, which he plays, and all the rats follow him to the River Weser where they are all drowned. When the piper returns to claim his reward the mayor then argues with him and offers him considerably less than he'd been promised. At this, the piper plays again and all the children run out into the streets and follow him: 'All the little boys and girls,/With rosy cheeks and flaxen curls,/And sparkling eyes, and teeth like pearls,/Tripping and skipping, ran merrily after/The wonderful music with shouting and laughter.' They follow him to the Koppenberg, here 'a wondrous portal opens wide' and the piper and the children go in, the door closes behind them, and they are never seen again. The poem ends by suggesting that the children come out in Transylvania, where their descendants still live.

There are several explanations for this story, variants of which are found in other parts of the world. One is that it is historically true and it happened in 1284; the man's name is given as 'Bunting' – on account of his parti-coloured costume (German, *bunte*, brightly coloured, cf bunting). Another explanation is that this is a mythological rendering of the German colonial settlement of Sudetenland in Bohemia during the Premyslid dynasty in the middle ages, when Germans settled in colonies near the German frontier formed by the Sudetic Mountains. Before the Second World War, Sudetan Germans numbered some four millions. Another explanation is that it is an account of the Children's Crusade of 1212 when a child called Nicholas, of Cologne, assembed 20,000 children as young crusaders. Many died on the way to the Italian coast, the rest boarded ship, but when they got to Alexandria they were sold into slavery.

Further reading:
Stephen Runciman, *A History of the Crusades* (1954), Ernest Barker, *The Crusades* (1923)

HAMLET

William Shakespeare, *Hamlet* (1602)

Robert Devereux, Second Earl of Essex
(1566–1601)

Hamlet is the classic tragedy of a young ill-advised prince who seems unable to make up his mind. A ghost resembling his late father appears to him and tells him that he was poisoned by his brother (Hamlet's uncle) who then married his mother and became king. After a series of delays and misadventures, in which his beloved is driven mad (see OPHELIA) and Hamlet kills her father in mistake for the king (see POLONIUS), Hamlet avenges his father, but is himself killed in the final climax. The story is ultimately based on an old Norse legend retold by Saxo Grammaticus (eleventh century) and the main ingredients are there – fratricide, incest, the antic disposition, the hero's association with Ophelia and so on. But the creation of character and many of the situations present clear parallels with the person and career of the Earl of Essex (see ACHILLES). Oscar James Campbell, editor of *The Reader's Encyclopaedia of Shakespeare* (1966) believes that Essex was the real-life model for Hamlet, and A.L. Rowse believes that the portrait owes much to Essex (*William Shakespeare: A Biography*, 1963) and writing that in the famous description of Hamlet; 'The courtier's, soldier's, scholar's eye, tongue, sword,/ The expectancy and rose of the fair state,/The glass of fashion . . .' etc. that is much of Essex. The eclipses of the sun mentioned refer to recent eclipses observed in England, the 'little patch of ground/That hath in it no profit but the name' refers to the siege of Ostend which began in the summer of 1601. There are political parallels – Dr Rowse comments on the dominant mood at the time: 'the cloud over the public scene . . . the people's hero in disgrace, withdrawn into an inner world of resentment, meditating treason . . . yet for long undecided on any course of action . . .', which is very like the atmosphere of *Hamlet*. Robert Naunton, in *Fragmenta Regalia* (1630), stresses Essex's 'most goodly' personality and his 'urbanity or innate courtesy' when he first came to court, a young lord. He also mentions his lack of good counsel: 'they blew the coles of his ambition, and infused into him too much of the spirit of glory, yea, and mixed the goodness of his nature with a touch of revenge . . .'. It is a fact that in 1600, the probable date of Shakespeare's composition of *Hamlet*, Essex was suffering from melancholia and depression, such as are portrayed in Hamlet's character. Also – even more striking – is the extraordinary coincidence that when Robert Devereux's father, Walter Devereux the First Earl of Essex, died of dysentery in the autumn of 1576, it was widely rumoured that he had been poisoned at the instigation of Robert Dudley, Earl of Leicester, who married his widow, Lettice, Countess of Essex, the eldest daughter of Sir Francis Knollys, thus paralleling the Hamlet/Claudio/Gertrude relationships quite closely.

Further reading:
A.L. Rowse, *Shakespeare – A Biography* (1963)

ROBERT HAND

James Joyce, *Exiles* (1918)

James Joyce's only play, *Exiles*, was written in Trieste and indifferently received for many years. In 1917 W.B. Yeats turned it down on behalf of Dublin's Abbey theatre and the first production – in German, at Munich,

Oliver St John Gogarty/Vincent Cosgrave/Thomas Kettle/Robert Prezioso

Further reading: Ulick O'Connor, *Oliver St John Gogarty* (1964)

on 17 August 1919 – was a flop. Although the New York production of 1925 ran for forty-one performances, the play was not highly regarded until Harold Pinter's sympathetic London production of 1970 revealed its psychosexual subtlety. In what Joyce described as 'three cat-and-mouse acts', the play contrasts the characters of two friends – the writer Richard Rowan (Joyce himself) who has come back to Dublin after years of exile in Italy and the plump journalist Robert Hand, who admires Richard's intellect and adores Richard's wife Bertha (modelled on Joyce's wife Nora Barnacle). Richard uses his charm on Bertha, and his journalistic position to help Richard get the chair of Romance literature. Though Richard and Robert are the best of friends, they appear as antagonists representing fundamentally different values. As Joyce explains in his Notes to the play, the title acknowledges that 'at the end either Robert or Richard must go into exile. Perhaps the new Ireland cannot contain both. Robert will go.' Though Joyce left Ireland, his native land is omnipresent in his creative work, so spiritually he remained.

In 1909 Joyce visited Dublin for the first time in almost five years, and his return from Italy was welcomed by his old friend Oliver St John Gogarty (the original of BUCK MULLIGAN in *Ulysses*) with whom he had shared several youthful adventures. Gogarty pressed himself on Joyce, praising the principle of friendship, but Joyce was suspicious of this plump and prosperous doctor. Another old friend, Vincent Cosgrave, took the opportunity of Joyce's Dublin visit to claim that he, Cosgrave, had once been intimate with Nora. Though this turned out to be a lie, Joyce was deeply distressed, and his awareness of his own jealousy found its way into *Exiles*. While Joyce was in Dublin, Thomas Kettle, the Nationalist MP, tried to get him a lectureship at the new National University, but when Joyce was offered only evening classes in commercial Italian he decided to return to Trieste, where he earned his living as an English, tutor. One of his pupils – Roberto Prezioso, editor of Trieste's main newspaper, the *Picollo della Sera* – admired Joyce's talents enormously, but also paid court to Nora, whom he attempted to seduce around 1911. Robert Hand is a composite, comprising elements of these four men; as Richard Ellman says, in *James Joyce* (1959, 1982), Joyce 'made Robert Hand out of Gogarty, Cosgrave, Kettle, and Prezioso'.

RICHARD HANNAY

John Buchan, *The Thirty-Nine Steps* (1915), *Greenmantle* (1916), *Mr Standfast* (1919), *The Three Hostages* (1924), *The Courts of the Morning* (1929), *The Island of Sheep* (1936)

William Edmund Ironside, First Baron Ironside (1880–1959)

Further reading: Janet Adam Smith, *John Buchan* (1965)

Richard Hannay, John Buchan's most popular hero, is a no-nonsense, get-up-and-go man of action who is at his best when on the move since, as he said in *Memory Hold-The-Door* (1941), Buchan was 'especially fascinated by the notion of hurried journeys'. Hannay is a Scotsman who has spent most of his life as a speculator and copper-engineer in South Africa. When *The Thirty-Nine Steps* opens he regrets leaving South Africa and reckons himself to be 'the best bored man in the United Kingdom' – at which point Franklin P. Scudder enters his life and then, with 'a long knife through his heart', leaves Hannay to save Britain.

Buchan went to South Africa in 1901 to work for Lord Milner, High Commissioner for South Africa; in this capacity he met Lieutenant Edmund Ironside who was doing Intelligence work in German South-West Africa. Ironically known as 'Tiny' because of his height of six foot four inches, Ironside was a brilliant operator with fourteen languages at his command. Using one of these languages – *taal* or Cape Dutch – Ironside disguised himself as a Boer transport-driver, accompanied a German military expedition against the Hereros (a nomadic Bantu-speaking people living in South-West Africa) and was awarded a German military medal before going back to British South Africa. When Buchan, confined to bed at Broadstairs in 1914 with a duodenal ulcer, wrote his 'shocker' *The Thirty-Nine Steps*, he made Hannay in the resourceful image of Ironside and gave him a similar combination of determination and panache. Ironside was Chief of the Imperial General Staff from 1938 until Dunkirk, and then for two months Commander-in-Chief, Home Forces. He was created Field Marshal in 1940 and a baron in 1941.

The name Hannay was familiar to Buchan from his boyhood holidays at his maternal grandfather's home in the village of Broughton (5 miles east of Biggar). In Broughton Free Church (now the John Buchan Centre), where Buchan's father preached in 1873-74, there is a stained glass window to the left of the pulpit commemorating the Hannay family.

GWENDOLEN HARLETH

George Eliot, *Daniel Deronda* (1876)

Miss Leigh, Lord Byron's grandniece

Daniel Deronda is a love story. Gwendolen Harleth is a vivacious, confident young woman, who marries Harleigh Grandcourt. He is a wealthy and sophisticated man, and she is attracted to him for the security he seems to offer. But she is aware that another woman exists and that there are children of this relationship. She learns to explore her own character and question her own motives when she comes under the influence of Daniel Deronda, a high-principled and noble character. She feels particularly guilty when Grandcourt is killed, as she has found herself wishing his death as she hopes to be able to turn to Daniel, but he marries Mirah, after discovering his Jewish origins and devoting himself to the ideal of a home for the Jewish race. Gwendolen learns to accept her life. We are first introduced to Gwendolen when she is in her mid-twenties, and she is in a gambling salon at Leubronn: 'one of those splendid resorts which the enlightenment of ages has prepared for the same species of pleasure at heavy cost of gilt mouldings, dark toned colour and chubby nudities. . . . There was deep stillness, broken only by a light rattle, a light chink, a small sweeping sound, and an occasional monotone in French.' Daniel looks at her, and asks himself: 'Was she beautiful or not beautiful?'

The seed which grew into *Daniel Deronda* was planted in George Eliot's imagination when, in September 1872, she watched Miss Leigh, Byron's grandniece, at the roulette table in Homburg. She wrote in a letter: 'The saddest thing to be witnessed is the play of Miss Leigh, Byron's grandniece, who is only twenty-six years old, and is completely in the grasp of this mean, money-making demon. It made me cry to see her young fresh face among the hags and brutally stupid men around her.' She had in fact lost £500, and looked hot and excited by her play. In the novel she wrote: 'the vice of gambling lay in losing money at it . . . while every single player differed markedly from every other, there was a certain uniform negativeness of expression which had the effect of a mask'.

Further reading:
Robert Rathburn and Martin Steinmann Jr., *From Jane Austen to Joseph Conrad* (1967)

GENERAL HARRAS

Carl Zuckmayer, play, *The Devil's General* (1946), film, starring Curt Jürgens (1954)

Lieutenant General Ernst Udet (1896–1941)

Carl Zuckmayer's play *Des Teufels General* is concerned with the inner torment of General Harras, a career officer in the German air-force during the Hitler years. His political conscience strengthens his resolve against the regime philosophically, but comes into conflict with all the social conditioning which makes him see his role as that of a servant of the state. His personality becomes the ideological battlefield of the conflict between duty and ideals. He manages to maintain the equilibrium by rationalizing his position. This is successful as long as matters can remain at the level of debate. But realities force his life to crisis point. He comes across a man, stricken with political conscience like himself, but who has resolved to act – a saboteur who has taken it into his own hands personally to wreck the Nazi war effort insofar as he is able, because he dreads the consequences for humanity should the Nazi war machine prove ultimately triumphant. General Harras realizes now that his own position is valueless. He deliberately destroys himself by flying an aeroplane which he knows has been sabotaged.

Harras is based on Ernst Udet, who was a flying ace in the First World War, and was made head of the Luftwaffe Technical Department. He was a close friend of Field Marshal Erhard Milch, but Milch recognized that, although Udet was a brilliant pilot, his technical insights

Further reading:
Carl Zuckmayer, *A Part of Myself*, translated by R. and C. Winston (1970)

and abilities were limited. Hitler's view of Udet as the great architect of the new Luftwaffe was a mistake. But gradually Udet was eased into the position where he controlled a vast military bureaucracy, responsible for aircraft production. Udet was the initiator of the programme which equipped the Luftwaffe with tactical rather than strategic aircraft, and favoured the development and production of the Messerschmitt 109. Udet was placed under considerable pressure to improve matters after the very serious decline in aircraft production in 1941. Udet became very suspicious of everybody, and after a disastrous conference with Field Marshall Milch, he committed suicide in November 1941. It was officially given out that he had died in an accident while testing a new aircraft, and he was given a hero's funeral.

HARRIS
Jerome K. Jerome, *Three Men in a Boat* (1889)
Carl Hentschel

Further reading: Jerome K. Jerome, *My Life and Times* (1983)

A classic of British comic writing, *Three Men in a Boat* recounts, with numerous digressions and interludes, the mishaps and adventures of three men and a dog as they voyage up the Thames. The famous dog, Montmorency, was an invention. In his autobiography Jerome wrote: 'There wasn't any dog. I did not possess a dog in those days.' But the travelling companions were real enough. Harris is phlegmatic: 'You can never rouse Harris. There is no poetry about Harris – no wild yearning for the unattainable. Harris never "weeps he knows not why". If Harris's eyes fill with tears, you can bet it is because Harris has been eating raw onions, or has put too much Worcester over his chop. If you were to stand at night by the seashore with Harris and say: "Hark! Do you not hear? Is it but the mermaids singing deep below the waving waters; or sad spirits, chanting dirges for white corpses, held by seaweed?" Harris would take you by the arm, and say: "I know what it is, old man; you've got a chill. Now, you come along with me. I know a place round the corner here, where you can get a drop of the finest Scotch whisky you ever tasted – put you right in less than no time." Harris always does know a place round the corner where you can get something brilliant in the drinking line. I believe that if you met Harris up in Paradise . . . he would immediately greet you with: "So glad you've come, old fellow; I've found a nice place round the corner here, where you can get some really first class nectar."'

Jerome first met Carl Hentschel 'outside a pit door. His father introduced photo-etching into England. It enabled newspapers to print pictures, and altered the whole character of journalism. The process was a secret then. Young Carl and his father, locking the back kitchen door, and drawing down the blind, would stir their crucibles far into the night. Carl worked the business up into a big concern; and we thought he was going to end as Lord Mayor. The War brought him low. He was accused of being a German. As a matter of fact he was a Pole. But his trade rivals had got their chance, and took it.' Jerome, Carl and George (see GEORGE) used to knock about together in London and spent many a happy weekend on the Thames. Carl's business activities eventually weaned him from these pastimes, and another young man, named Pett-Ridge, took his place, the bond being sealed by his marrying a sister of Carl's.

CAPTAIN HARVILLE
Jane Austen, *Persuasion* (1818)
Frank Austen (1774-1865)

One of the most persuasive moments in Jane Austen's *Persuasion* occurs when two characters, Captain Benwick and Louisa, are brought together in Lyme at the home of Captain Harville. Jane Austen's description of Captain Harville suggests a creature of infinite good will, which helps in his crucial discussion with the heroine towards the end of the novel. 'Captain Harville was a tall, dark man, with a sensible, benevolent countenance,' writes Austen, 'a perfect gentleman, unaffected, warm, and obliging.' With his wife he lives in a cottage near an old pier and, as a result of a wound, spends much time indoors where 'a mind of usefulness and ingenuity seemed to furnish him with constant employment within. He drew, he varnished, he carpentered, he glued, he made toys for the children, he fashioned new netting-needles and pins with improvements; and if everything else was done, sat down to his large fishing-net at one corner of the room.'

Captain Harville is Jane's affectionate portrait of her elder brother Frank Austen who was known to busy himself obsessively when indoors. As a boy of twelve, Frank entered the Royal Naval Academy in Portsmouth then served as a midshipman at home and abroad. He became Captain Austen in 1800 and helped blockade Boulogne in 1804 when Napoleon hoped to invade England. Subsequently he served as flag-captain to Nelson's second-in-command; diverted to Gibraltar for supplies he just missed the battle of Trafalgar and regretted losing 'all share in the glory'. After helping to defeat the French at St Domingo, Frank came home and in 1807 married Mary Gibson. He organized the disembarkation of Sir John Moore's troops in the Peninsular War, saw action against the French and Americans and was awarded the Companion of the Order of the Bath in 1815. After Jane's death (in 1817) Frank's career continued with distinction: he became Rear-Admiral in 1830 and Commander of the Fleet in 1863.

Further reading:
R.A. Austen-Leigh, *Jane Austen – Her Life and Letters* (1913), P.J.M. Scott, *Jane Austen – A Reassessment* (1981)

JUDGE HATE-GOOD

John Bunyan, *The Pilgrim's Progress* (1678)

George, First Baron Jeffreys of Wem (1648–89), **Lord Chancellor of England**

When Christian and Faithful refuse to purchase any of the vanities offered them as they pass through Vanity Fair (see FAITHFUL), there is a riot and they are arrested and brought for trial before the judge, Lord Hate-Good. He conducts the trial in a most brutal and unfair manner. The indictment reads: 'That they were enemies to and disturbers of their trade; that they had made commotions and divisions in the town, and had won a party to their own most dangerous opinions, in contempt of the law of their prince.' Envy, Superstition and Pickthank give biased evidence against them and Lord Hate-Good bullies and harangues them: 'Sirrah! Sirrah! Thou deservest to live no longer, but to be slain immediately upon the place; yet, that all men may see our gentleness towards thee, let us hear what thou, vile runagate, hast to say.' His advice to the jury is violent in the extreme, and the sentence appalling: 'first, they scoured him, then they buffeted him, then they lanced his flesh with knives; after that, they stoned him . . . and last of all they burned him to ashes at the stake. Thus came *Faithful* to his end.' This is a portrait of George Jeffreys, whose scathing tongue and brutal powers of cross-examination were honed to perfection with years of experience at the bar; terrorizing thieves, vagabonds and prostitutes. Through William Chiffinch he gained influence with the court party, and attached himself to James, Duke of York, brother of the king. He was knighted in 1677, and made recorder of London in 1678. His treatment of dissenters was notorious. He drank brandy and debauched all night, cursed and ranted at court and assizes all day. Religious persecution was rife. The Declaration of Indulgence of 1672 was withdrawn in the following year, and the Test Act, passed in 1673, aimed at oppressing Catholics and Presbyterians. As he sentenced one woman to whipping he said: 'Hangman, pay particular attention to this lady. Scourge her till the blood runs. It is the Christmas season; a cold season for madam to strip in. See that you warm her shoulders thoroughly!' He did not allow Richard Baxter's defence to speak (see FAITHFUL), and maintained a torrent of ribaldry and abuse throughout the proceedings. When James II fled the country Jeffreys fell from power, but he had achieved an undying reputation for cruelty and injustice.

Further reading:
Alan Bold and Robert Giddings, *The Book of Rotters* (1985)

MISS HAVISHAM

Charles Dickens, *Great Expectations* (1860)

Martha Joachim (1788–1850)

Miss Havisham is a former beauty and heiress. She was jilted by Compeyson and has lived ever since her bridal morning in complete seclusion in Satis House, Rochester. She has brought up an adopted child, Estella, to despise the male sex. Pip, the stepson of the local blacksmith, is called in to play with Estella, who is cruel to him. He longs to become a gentleman so that he may be worthy of her. When he is told

Further reading: E.W.F. Tomlin, *Charles Dickens 1812–1870* (1970)

he is a young man of great expectations and is to be sent to London to learn the *bon ton*, he assumes it is part of Miss Havisham's plans to bring him and Estella together. The first sight of Miss Havisham understandably greatly impresses young Pip: 'She was dressed in rich materials . . . all of white. Her shoes were white . . . she had a long white veil . . . her hair was white . . . everything within my view which ought to be white . . . had lost its lustre, and was faded and yellow . . . the bride within the bridal dress had withered like the dress.' In Satis House time has stopped. The hands of the clocks are stopped. No sunlight enters. Miss Havisham lives in the past

In January 1850 *Household Words*, a journal edited by Dickens, carried a report of the inquest on Martha Joachim, 'a wealthy and eccentric lady' who had died in York Buildings, Marylebone, aged sixty-two. 'It was shown in evidence that on the 1st. June 1808, her father, an officer in the Life Guards, was murdered and robbed . . . the murderer was apprehended. . . . In 1825, a suitor of the deceased, whom her mother rejected, shot himself. . . . From that instant she lost her reason . . . she had led the life of a recluse, dressed in white, and never going out.' There was another woman-in-white who fascinated Dickens, the White Woman of Berners Street, Oxford Street, whom he had seen in his childhood. He wrote about her in an essay, *Where We Stopped Growing*: 'she was constantly on parade in that street. . . . She is dressed entirely in white. . . . She is a conceited old creature, cold and formal in manner, and evidently went simpering mad on personal grounds. . . . This is her bridal dress. She is always walking up here, on her way to church.'

HEATHCLIFF

Emily Brontë, *Wuthering Heights* (1847)

'Welsh' Brunty

Further reading: William Wright, *The Brontës in Ireland* (1893), article by Jack Loudan in *The Listener* (18 December 1952)

The passionate love story of Catherine Earnshaw and the gipsy foundling taken in by her father is the main narrative thread of this wild and romantic novel. Heathcliff is brought back from Liverpool, 'a dirty, ragged, black-haired child, big enough both to walk and talk . . . its face looked older than Catherine's; yet when it was set on its feet it only stared round, and repeated over and over again some gibberish that nobody could understand'.

There is an interesting source for this story. Patrick Brontë, father of Emily, Charlotte and Anne, was born on the 17 March 1777, the son of Hugh Brunty and Alice Eleanor Brunty, in Drumballyroney, County Down. Hugh's grandfather had a farm near the Boyne. On a trip cattle-dealing to Liverpool, he picked up a dark, dirty and ragged foundling and adopted him. His dark complexion made them believe he was either Welsh or a gipsy, so he was named 'Welsh'. Though he was a morose and cunning lad, he learned the business and went everywhere with Mr Brunty and Brunty's own children grew very resentful of him. When Brunty died suddenly Welsh took over the farm, and made it clear he was determined to marry Brunty's daughter, Mary. He tried all his cunning to get the Brunty family in his grasp, but failed, though eventually he managed to manipulate Mary into marrying him. They were a childless couple and adopted Hugh Brunty, whose father lived in the south of Ireland, on condition that his father was never to communicate with him again. The journey was deliberately elongated so Hugh would never recall the way home. Hugh was badly treated by Welsh and made to work hard on the farm. Welsh had a second in command, a sullen bible-thumping peasant, similar to Joseph in *Wuthering Heights*, and Hugh's best friend was a farm dog, Keeper. Emily Brontë's favourite dog was called 'Keeper'. Hugh's aunt Mary, 'Welsh' Brunty's wife, told Hugh the whole story, as she was sorry for him. Hugh lived in Ireland and eloped with Alice McClory in 1776. Their son Patrick, passed on the story to the children of his marriage to Maria Branwell. It is echoed in Charlotte's story of Willie Ellin.

ETHEL HENDERSON

H.G. Wells, *Love and Mr Lewisham* (1900)

Isabel Wells (died 1931)

Further reading:
N. and J. Mackenzie, *The Time Traveller* (1973)

In 1884 H.G. Wells won a studentship to the Normal School of Science in South Kensington, London. After lodging in Westbourne Grove, he moved to 181 Euston Road where his aunt, Mary Williams, had rooms to let. On his first visit Aunt Mary introduced Wells to her daughter Isabel, who rapidly became the emotional obsession of his life. As he acknowledged in *Experiment in Autobiography* (1934) his imaginative and physical cravings were concentrated 'upon the one human being who was conceivable as an actual lover; my cousin Isabel . . . She was very pleasant to look upon, gentle mannered, kind and firm, and about her I realised all the pent up imaginations of my heart.' Isabel, a conventional girl, put marriage before sex. Wells returned to London in 1888, went to live with Aunt Mary and Isabel (now at Primrose Hill) and earned a living by teaching and tutoring until he married Isabel on 31 October 1891. On their wedding night Isabel was distressed by his sexual zeal and broke down in tears. In 1892, while teaching biology at the University Tutorial College, Wells fell in love with Catherine Amy Robbins, one of his students. He left Isabel in January 1894, set up house with Catherine (his future wife) in Mornington Road, London, and divorced Isabel in 1895. He did not forget Isabel, however, for five years after leaving her he visited her at her chicken-farm at Maidenhead where he tried to make love to her. When she refused, Wells was devastated: 'I felt like an automaton,' he said in *Experiment in Autobiography*, 'I felt as though all purpose had been drained out of me and nothing remained worth while. The world was dead and I was dead and I had only just discovered it.' A breakdown followed and it was several months before Wells could work again.

The failure of Wells's first marriage is recreated in *Love and Mr Lewisham*, in which Wells is the ambitiously intellectual Lewisham who abandons his intellectual ambitions when he marries Ethel Henderson on a guinea-a-week student's grant and accepts an existence dominated by economic difficulties. Though Ethel has little insight into his aspirations she is 'a very pretty girl' whose good looks distract Mr Lewisham.

MRS HEPBURN

D.H. Lawrence, 'The Thimble' (1917)

Lady Cynthia Asquith (died 1960)

Further reading:
Harry T. Moore, *The Priest of Love* (1974)

In 1910 Lady Cynthia Charteris, daughter of the eleventh Earl of Wemyss, married Herbert Asquith, second son of the Prime Minister. Three years later Cynthia got to know D.H. Lawrence and Frieda von Richthofen (whom Lawrence married in 1914). According to Harry T. Moore's *The Priest of Love* (1974) the novelist was enchanted by Cynthia: 'Lawrence, though he always loved Frieda, indicated again and again in his work a special kind of love for Cynthia Asquith [and] in his writing . . . he seems to have made love to her indirectly.' On the outbreak of the First World War, Cynthia's husband Herbert (or 'Beb' as she called him), a barrister by training, enlisted in the Royal Field Artillery and came home to convalesce after being slightly wounded. From this situation Lawrence created his story 'The Thimble' (an early version of 'The Ladybird') first published in *Seven Arts* (March 1917).

Mrs Hepburn is sitting in her room in her Mayfair flat waiting for her husband to come home from the war. A barrister by training, he has become a lieutenant in the artillery and has returned to England after being badly disfigured in a shellburst. Mrs Hepburn dreads the reunion, wondering what kind of personality will lurk behind his altered appearance. She considers her own appearance: 'She was a beautiful woman, tall and loose and rather thin, with swinging limbs, one for whom the modern fashions were perfect. Her skin was pure and clear, like a Christmas rose, her hair was fair and heavy. She had large, slow, unswerving eyes, that sometimes looked blue and open with a childish candour, sometimes greenish and intent with thought, sometimes hard, sea-like, cruel, sometimes grey and pathetic . . . She knew she was a beauty.' Sitting on a sofa, looking at 'her own large feet', Mrs Hepburn finds a thimble which her husband subsequently takes from her and throws into the street, a gesture symbolizing the disturbance in their domesticity.

In her diary of 31 October 1915, Cynthia noted the arrival of Lawrence's story and commented: 'I *was* amused to see the "word-picture" of me. He has quite gratuitously put in the large feet. I think some of his character hints are damnably good. He has kept fairly close to the model in the circumstances.'

MR HERBERT

William Hurrell Mallock, *The New Republic* (1877)

John Ruskin (1819–1900)

Further reading: Joan Abse, *John Ruskin – The Passionate Moralist* (1980), and Peter Quennell, *John Ruskin – The Portrait of a Prophet* (1949)

Among the most eloquent of the house-guests in *The New Republic* (see DR JENKINSON) is Mr Herbert, described by another guest, Robert Leslie, as: 'Almost the only man of these days for whom I feel a real reverence – almost the only one of our teachers who seems to me to speak with the least breath of inspiration. But he is too impressionable, perhaps – And now, as the years come, it seems that hope is more and more leaving him, and things look darker to him than ever . . .' This is a portrait of John Ruskin, art historian, author and social visionary, who expressed in prose of an unmatched intoxication, thoughts of a rarely equalled incomprehensibility. G.M. Young in *Victorian England* wrote of his profound intellect being yoked to the mind of a child. Mallock captures satirically the quality of Ruskin's utterances, which seem so deep and so brilliant, and yet are really unfathomably obscure: 'The real significance of life must be forever indescribable in words. But, in the present day, I fear also that for most of us it is not even thinkable in thought. The whole human race . . . is now wandering in an accursed wilderness, which not only shows us no hilltop whence the promised land may be seen, but which, to most of the wanderers, seems a promised land itself. And they have a God of their own, too, who engages now to lead them out of it if they will only follow him: who, for visible token of his Godhead, leads them with a pillar of cloud by day, and a pillar of fire by night – the cloud being the black smoke of their factory chimneys, and the fire the red glare of their blast-furnaces. And so effectual are these modern divine guides, that if we were standing on the brink of Jordan itself, we should be utterly unable to catch, through the fire and the smoke, one single glimpse of the sunlit hills beyond.'

Ruskin was the son of a wealthy wine merchant, educated privately and by much travel. He went up to Oxford in 1836. The first of five volumes of *Modern Painters* appeared in 1843. He also spread his ideas by lecturing, in many cases to colleges of working men, and his leading ideas were enshrined in *Sesame and the Lilies, The Crown of Wild Olive, Unto This Last, Flors Clavigera, The Seven Lamps of Architecture* and *The Stones of Venice*. He grew to loathe the consequences of unbridled capitalism and to adopt a position, confusing to many of his contemporaries, of something akin to Christian communism. He suffered several mental collapses.

PHILIP HERRITON

E.M. Forster, *Where Angels Fear to Tread* (1905)

Edward J. Dent (1876-1957)

Further reading: P.N. Furbank, *E.M. Forster: A Life* (1977–8)

Like Philip Herriton, his fictional counterpart, the musicologist Edward J. Dent believed that the cultural climate of Italy improved the individual. Herriton's Italian experience in E.M. Forster's first novel *Where Angels Fear to Tread*, however, turns out to be traumatic rather than triumphant: he becomes entangled in the aftermath of a marriage between his sister-in-law Lilia and Gino, a dentist's son. Philip is presented as an awkward man with the saving graces of aesthetic appreciation and good humour: 'The sense of beauty developed first. It caused him at the age of twenty to wear parti-coloured ties and a squashy hat. . . . At twenty-two he went to Italy with some cousins, and there he absorbed into one aesthetic whole olive-trees, blue sky, frescoes, country inns, saints, peasants, mosaics, statues, beggars.' As Dent, who knew Forster at Cambridge, spent his own holidays in Italy (in musical research) he encouraged his friend to follow suit, so in 1901 Forster visited San Gimignano, the model for the fictional Monteriano.

When he began to write the novel, Forster based Philip firmly on

Dent who (so Forster said in an interview) 'knew this, and took an interest in his own progress'. When the novel was accepted for publication Forster's original title, *Monteriano*, was rejected and Dent supplied the title Forster finally used. Dent went on to achieve great distinction as a scholar and brilliant translator of Italian opera into English; his superbly singable versions of Mozart made opera more accessible to English audiences. In 1919 Dent helped found the British Musical Society and in 1923 became the first President of the International Society for Contemporary Music. From 1926 to 1941 he was Professor of Music at Cambridge. On 22 March 1950 Forster wrote to Dent to say he was conscious 'of how much I owe you'.

HIAWATHA

Henry Wadsworth Longfellow, *Hiawatha* (1855)

Haion 'hwa 'tha and **'Manabozho'** (circa 1550)

Further reading: Henry Rose Schoolcraft, *The Myth of Hiawatha* (1856)

Longfellow's poem tells the story of the life and death of Hiawatha, an Indian chief of miraculous descent among the Iroquois. He was sent to earth to teach men the arts of peace and good civilization. He is the son of Wenonah, a beautiful Indian woman, and the West Wind. Hiawatha is brought up by his grandmother, Nokomis, the daughter of the Moon. From all his adventures Hiawatha accumulates great wisdom, and he is able to avenge his mother against the West Wind, his father. He becomes the leader of his people, teaching human-kind that maize is their food and teaching them the skills of navigation and the science of medicine. Tribes should live in peace with each other, and with the white man, was his message. In doing this people followed the wishes of the Great Spirit, Manitou, whom all Indians worshipped: 'On the Mountains of the Prairie/Gitche Manitou the mighty . . ./Stood erect and called the nations/Called the tribes of men together.'

Longfellow got his subject matter from the researches of Henry Rowe Schoolcraft (1793-1864) an American explorer (he discovered the source of the Mississippi), ethnologist and scholar. His six-volume work, *Information Respecting the Indian Tribes of the United States*, 1851-57, was the result of a commission by Congress. In 1839 he published *Algic Researches*, in two volumes, revised in 1856 as *The Myth of Hiawatha*. Schoolcraft married Jane D. Johnston, granddaughter of an Indian chief, who aided his researches into Indian myth and history. Schoolcraft confuses the Iroquois Hiawatha, Haion 'hwa 'tha, who was an historical figure, with the legendary hero of the Algongquin, 'Manabozho'. North American Indian culture was devoid of writing and time systems and consisted entirely of legendary traditions, which may have had factual bases. Schoolcraft encumbered the historical Hiawatha with the traditional exploits which accumulated round the name of Manabozho. Longfellow follows him in these errors, and sets the narrative on Lake Superior, but it belongs in central New York.

HENRY HIGGINS

George Bernard Shaw, *Pygmalion* (1912)

Henry Sweet (1845–1912)

In George Bernard Shaw's *Pygmalion* Professor Henry Higgins describes his apparently astounding powers of linguistic observation as perfectly logical: 'Simply phonetics. The science of speech. That's my profession: also my hobby. . . . You can spot an Irishman or a Yorkshireman by his brogue. *I* can place any man within six miles. I can place him within two miles in London. Sometimes within two streets.'

As Shaw acknowledged enthusiastically in his preface to the play, Higgins was based on the character and career of Henry Sweet the philologist who invented a phonetic shorthand. Sweet was born in London and studied for some time in Germany where he acquired an interest in the scientific study of language. His books, such as *A History of English Sounds* (1874) and *A Handbook of Phonetics* (1877), established him as the leading phonetist of his time. However his scorn for his colleagues made him an isolated figure and Oxford could accommodate him only by creating for him (in 1901) a special Readership in Phonetics. In Shaw's play Henry Higgins transforms Eliza Doolittle into a lady by linguistic methods. According to Shaw, Sweet too could have achieved stunning results had his personality been more practical: 'With Higgins's physique and temperament Sweet might have set the Thames on fire. As it was, he impressed himself professionally on Europe to an extent that made his comparative personal obscurity, and the failure of Oxford to do justice to his eminence, a puzzle to foreign specialists in his subject.' Shaw also noted that Sweet lacked 'sweetness of character: he was about as conciliatory to conventional mortals as Ibsen or Samuel Butler. His great ability as a phonetician (he was, I think, the best of them all at his job) would have entitled him to high official recognition . . . but for his Satanic contempt for all academic dignitaries and persons in general who thought more of Greek than phonetics.'

HIGGS

P.G. Wodehouse, *The Head of Kay's* (1905)

Sir William Seymour Hicks (1871–1949)

Further reading: Seymour Hicks, *Between Ourselves* and *Me and My Misses* (1939)

In 1904, after Wodehouse had published some five books, he was asked by an actor, Owen Hall, to write a lyric for a show called *Sergeant Brue*, to be performed at the Strand Theatre. It was a successful number and was encored. It was noticed by William Seymour Hicks, the noted actor-manager, who contracted Wodehouse for £2 a week to write additional songs for productions at the Aldwych. Hicks appears in *The Head of Kay's* when young Robert Fenn, the deposed House Captain of Eckleton School, goes to the local theatre to see a musical comedy written by his elder brother. The play has been mounted by Higgs, a locally celebrated actor-manager, whom Fenn discovers in his dressing room: 'A third of which was filled by a huge iron-bound chest, another third by a very stout man and a dressing-table, while the rest of the space was comparatively empty, being occupied by a wooden chair with three legs. On this seat his brother was trying to balance himself.' Higgs is far from satisfied with this accommodation for one so talented as himself, and complains: 'These provincial dressing-rooms. No room! Never any room! No chairs! Nothing!' But his appearance on stage is as magical as could be wished: 'Mr Higgs' performance sealed the success of the piece. The house laughed at everything he said. He sang a song in his gasping way, and they laughed still more.' Hicks was born in St Helier, Jersey, the son of an army officer, and made his first stage appearance at the Grand Theatre, Islington in 1887. He worked with William Hunter Kendal and his wife Madge (Dame Margaret Shafto) at the Court Theatre and St James's Theatre and in the USA. Hicks was the leading light comedian at the Gaiety from 1894. He married Ellaline Terriss, the actress, in 1902. He wrote several plays – *Bluebell in Fairyland* (1901), *The Catch of the Season* (1904) and *The Man in Dress Clothes* (1922). His mannered, clipped and 'gasping' style of delivery is well preserved in several films, notably *Vintage Wine*, *Scrooge* (1935) and *Busman's Honeymoon* (1940). He published readable volumes of reminiscences – *Twenty-Four Years of An Actor's Life* (1910), *Between Ourselves* (1930) and *Me and My Misses* (1939), as well as works on acting. He was knighted in 1935. Hicks was slim in his person and had a very pointed nose. He made an exemplary Scrooge, relishing the wickedness and latent comicality of the part.

HIGHLAND MARY

Robert Burns, *Poetical Works* (1904)

Mary Campbell (1763–86)

Further reading: Catherine Carswell, *Life of Robert Burns* (1930)

'Will ye go to the Indies, my Mary,/And leave auld Scotia's shore?/Will ye go to the Indies, my Mary,/Across the Atlantic's roar?': like many of his contemporaries Robert Burns frequently thought of seeking his fortunes overseas from Scotland. In 1786 he had good reason to contemplate a new life; he had got a girl, Jean Armour, pregnant and been rejected as a possible son-in-law by a man who disliked his behaviour and deplored his lack of prospects. Accordingly Burns accepted a job as a plantation book-keeper in Jamaica and turned his bruised affections to another girl – Mary Campbell, a Coilsfield dairymaid. On the second Sunday of May 1786, the couple met 'in a sequestered spot by the Banks of Ayr' and exchanged Bibles over the Faile stream. Then, as Burns put it, they 'spent the day in taking farewell, before she should embark for the West Highlands to arrange matters among her friends for our projected change of life'.

It seems that they intended to marry and emigrate to Jamaica together; the publication of Burns's first book would alleviate his financial worries for he was well on the way to raising the necessary subscriptions. *Poems, Chiefly in the Scottish Dialect,* published on 30 July 1786, was an immediate success. Burns was scheduled to meet Mary Campbell at Greenock in September so they could both sail for Kingston; meanwhile he went to Mossgiel farm where he heard that Jean Armour had given birth to twins. Then, from Greenock, came the shattering news of Mary Campbell's death – Burns claimed she died from a 'malignant fever' but there is a possibility that she died in childbirth. Suddenly the journey to Jamaica seemed pointless and Burns headed, instead, for Edinburgh where he was lionized as a cultural phenomenon. Burns, in 'Highland Mary', wrote: 'But still within my bosom's core/Shall live my Highland Mary.'

HOBBINOL

Edmund Spenser, *The Shepherd's Calendar* (1579)

Gabriel Harvey (1545-1630)

Further reading: C.S. Lewis, *English Literature in the 16th. Century* (1954), F.G. Harman, *Gabriel Harvey and Thomas Nashe* (1923)

The Shepherd's Calendar, is a pastoral poem in twelve eclogues (sections) which Spenser dedicated to Sir Philip Sidney. It has a prefatory letter addressed to Gabriel Harvey and detailed notes by 'E.K.' (generally identified as Edward Kirke 1553–1613, a friend of the poet's at Pembroke College, Cambridge). Spenser uses classical models – Theocritus, Virgil – as well as Mantuan, Sannarzaro, Marot and early Tudor poets such as Barclay and Googe. The eclogues are subdivided into three types – plaintive (love poems, with compliments to several persons); moral (satiric of religious abuses); and recreative (purely entertaining). The main theme holding the *Calendar* together is the narrative of the hopeless love of Colin Clout (= Spenser) for the cold and distant shepherdess, Rosalind (who has never satisfactorily been identified). Colin's close friend is Hobbinol, who is certainly the poet's dear friend Gabriel Harvey: 'the person of some his very special and most familiar friend, whom he entirely and extraordinarily beloved' as E.K. explains. In some ways there is a tension between Colin's affection for Rosalind and his love for Hobbinol: 'It is not Hobbinol wherefore I plaine,/Albee my love he seek with dayly suit; /His clownish gifts and curtsies I disdaine,/His kiddes, his cracknelles, and his early fruit./Ah, foolish Hobbinol! thy gyfts bene vayne;/Colin them gives to Rosalind againe.' As E.K. explains, the relationship might even seem somewhat of a homosexual nature: 'seemeth to be some savour of disorderly love, which the learned call *paederastice*'.

Harvey was a Cambridge scholar and met Spenser as a student. They became very good friends. Harvey was lecturer in Greek and professor of rhetoric, and became engaged in the celebrated Greene/-Harvey/Nashe controversy, which really was a debate about the changing role of the writer in Elizabethan society, with Harvey on the side of the academic, traditionalist and classical model. He was on the receiving end of Nashe's *Have With You to Saffron Walden*, and was notorious in hs efforts to dissuade Spenser from writing *The Faerie Queene*. With Philip Sidney the three formed the *Areopagus* – a literary club aimed at adapting classical metres to English verse.

PRINCE HOHENSTIEL-SCHWANGAU

Robert Browning, *Prince Hohenstiel-Schwangau, Saviour of Society* (1871)

Charles Louis Napoleon Bonaparte, Napoleon III (1808–73)

In Browning's monologue, the Prince is a deposed European autocrat, who picks up a girl in the Haymarket. In a tea-room he confides to the girl that he has seen better days: 'And worse too, for they brought me no such bud-mouth/As yours to lisp "You wish you knew me!"' He goes on to defend his political career, which was based on the principle of expediency, of taking things as they were, not seeking radical change, tolerating 'change' only insofar as the basic structure of society was not altered; though in terms of philosophy, the Prince was able to seem 'modern' by toying with fashionable ideas of the day, such as Darwinism. The shallow decadence of his empire is delineated, together with its

Further reading: B. Jerrold, *The Life of Napoleon III* (1882)

latent propensity for war: 'tired of the illimitable line on line/Of boulevard-building, tired o' the theatre/With the tuneful thousand in their thrones above,/For glory of the male intelligence,/And Nakedness in her due niche below,/For illustration of the female use.'

This is Louis Napoleon, then living in exile after the French defeat in the Franco-Prussian war. He was born in Paris, the third son of Louis Bonaparte and Hortense de Beauharnais, the brother and stepdaughter, respectively, of Napoleon I. He attempted to gain political power on two early occasions, and was imprisoned in 1840. He escaped in 1846 and lived in London but took advantage of the revolution of 1848 to return to France. He was elected President of the Republic and built up support by claiming to uphold stability and religion against the threat of revolution. He achieved a coup d'état in 1851 and within a year proclaimed himself Emperor. He perceived overseas war as a means of securing a sense of glory for his regime, and France entered the Crimean War, engaged in war against Austria in 1859 and attempted to create an imperial colony in Mexico 1863-67. At home, opposition forced him to make democratic concessions and corruption was rife. His *Vie de César* was not well received. Suspecting the loyalty of the army, he allowed himself to think war might rekindle national ardour and was pushed by Bismarck into the Prussian War in 1870. His empire collapsed after his surrender at Sedan, with 83,000 men.

SHERLOCK HOLMES

Sir Arthur Conan Doyle, *A Study in Scarlet* (1887), *The Sign of Four* (1890), *The Adventures of Sherlock Holmes* (1892), *The Memoirs of Sherlock Holmes* (1894), *The Hound of the Baskervilles* (1902), *The Return of Sherlock Holmes* (1905), *The Valley of Fear* (1915), *His Last Bow* (1917), *The Case-Book of Sherlock Holmes* (1927)

Dr Joseph Bell (1837–1911)

Further reading: Hesketh Pearson, *Conan Doyle* (1943), Owen Dudley Edwards, *The Quest for Sherlock Holmes* (1982)

When Arthur Conan Doyle settled down, in March 1886, to write *A Study in Scarlet* he determined to create a detective who would outdo in ingenuity his own favourite – Edgar Allen Poe's 'masterful detective, M. Dupin'. As a medical student in Edinburgh in the 1870s, Doyle had been hugely impressed by the deductive skills of Dr Joseph Bell who was consulting surgeon at Edinburgh Infirmary, professor at Edinburgh University, and editor of the *Edinburgh Medical Journal*. In creating Sherlock Holmes, so he writes in his *Memories and Adventures* (1924), Doyle 'thought of my old teacher Joe Bell, of his eagle face, of his curious ways, of his eerie trick of spotting details'. Writing to Dr Bell on 4 May 1892 Doyle declared 'It is most certainly to you that I owe Sherlock Holmes. . . . I do not think that his analytical work is in the least an exaggeration of some effects which I have seen you produce in the out-patient ward.'

Doyle served as Bell's out-patient clerk and prepared notes before each patient was presented to Bell for diagnosis. In one example recorded by Doyle, Bell deduced that a patient had recently served in a Highland regiment as a non-commissioned officer stationed at Barbados. 'You see, gentlemen,' Bell explained, 'the man was a respectful man but did not remove his hat. They do not in the army, but he would have learned civilian ways had he been long discharged. He has an air of authority and he is obviously Scottish. As to Barbados, his complaint is elephantiasis, which is West Indian and not British.' Bell himself, though flattered by the compliment Doyle had paid him, had a different view of the origins of the great detective and told Doyle 'You are yourself Sherlock Holmes, and well you know it.'

HOLOFERNES

William Shakespeare, *Love's Labours Lost* (1594)

Alexander Aspinall (died 1624)

Further reading: E.I. Fripp, *Shakespeare – Man and Artist* (1938)

In Shakespeare's early comedy *Love's Labours Lost*, the pedantic village schoolmaster, Holofernes, suggests that a dramatic presentation of the Nine Worthies is given for the entertainment of the Princess of France. He casts himself as Judas Maccabaeus, other village notables appear as Pompey, Alexander, Hector, Hercules etc. Holofernes is portrayed in the comedy as a pompous schoolmaster anxious to display his book-learning, who can never say anything directly, nor without showing off his command of the classics. Of a deer that is shot in the hunt he says: 'The deer was, as you know, sanguis, in blood; ripe as the pomewater, who now hangeth like a jewel in the ear of caelo, the sky, the welkin, the heaven; and anon falleth like a crab on the face of terra, the soil, the land, the earth.' He is admired for this, the curate, Nathaniel, answers: 'Truly, Master Holofernes, the epithets are sweetly varied, like a scholar at the least' and asserts that Holofernes' talent for learning and versifying are remarkable. Holofernes agrees with him: 'This is a gift that I have, simple, simple; a foolish extravagant spirit, full of forms, figures, shapes, objects, ideas, apprehensions, motions, revolutions. These are begot in the ventricle of memory, nourished in the womb pia mater, and delivered upon the mellowing of occasion. But the gift is good in those in whom it is acute, and I am grateful for it.' The elaborate masque of the heroes of the ancient world which Holofernes designed fails to give him the starring role he clearly had in mind for himself, and the audience constantly interrupt the performance and he is laughed off the stage.

Alexander Aspinall was the schoolmaster at Stratford grammar school from 1582 until the time of his death. He was born in Lancashire and educated at Brasenose, Oxford, where he gained his BA in 1575 and his MA in 1578. He was a notable citizen of Stratford, as he married a wealthy widow and went into trade while continuing as schoolmaster, later becoming successively burgess, alderman, and chamberlain of the ward where Shakespeare lived. The dramatist modelled Holofernes on Aspinall, who was a noted Stratford worthy, an 'ancient Master of Art and a man learned', according to one of his contemporaries. Shakespeare composed a posy for him when in middle age he went a-wooing with a pair of gloves for his beloved: 'The gift is small:/The will is all:/Alexander Aspinall.' This is recorded in Sir Francis Fane's commonplace book, with the comment: 'Shaxpaire upon a peaire of gloves that Master Aspinall sent to his mistris.'

FELIX HOLT

George Eliot, *Felix Holt the Radical* (1866)

Gerald Massey (1828–1907)

Further reading: Newman Flower, *Gerald Massey* (1895)

Felix Holt deals with the career, political ambitions and romantic complications of the lives of Felix Holt and Harold Transome. Holt is the son of a family which makes its living selling quack medicines. He develops into a noble young man with very high and sincere political ambitions to make the world a better place. He puts his ideas into practice by deliberately choosing a humble existence and the life of a working man in order to demonstrate to his fellows in the working classes that their amelioration lies in the direction of education and learning to think for themselves, rather than simply in hoping that improvement will come about in society as the result of the benevolence of the law-makers. He is contrasted with Transome, who is an honest enough young man, but a career politician who is not above using the system to get on. Romantic complications result from the choice that the heroine, Esther, has to make between them – either a life of ease, comfort and success with Transome, or hardship, poverty and good works with Holt. She chooses Felix Holt. Felix is a rough and ready man, with no trimmings. We first see him through the eyes of the minister of the town of Treby Magna: 'accustomed to the respectable air of provincial townsmen, and especially to the sleek well-clipped gravity of his own male congregation, felt a slight shock as his glasses made perfectly clear to him the shaggy-headed, large-eyed, strong-limbed person of this questionable young man, without waistcoat or cravat.'

This was based on Gerald Massey, of Tring, who worked from the age of eight, was self taught, became a poet and joined the Chartist movement and was a devout Christian Socialist, intimate of Maurice and Kingsley. He published much poetry and popular Egyptology, became a mystic and spiritualist. Massey was also a successful lecturer and journalist, and travelled in the USA.

BRIGADIER RITCHIE-HOOK

Evelyn Waugh, *Men at Arms* (1952)

Brigadier Ritchie-Hook is one of Waugh's finest portraits of the eccentric military genius. He has the kind of dotty-dangerous personality which, it is suggested, enabled the British to triumph in the Second World War. He is a mixture of schoolboy enthusiasm, sportiness, xenophobia and tyranny. He has only one eye, and has also lost much of his right hand: 'the

Major General Albert St Clair-Morford (1893–1945)

youngest company commander in the history of the Corps; the slowest to be promoted; often wounded, often decorated . . . where lesser men collected helmets Ritchie-Hook once came back . . . with the dripping head of a German sentry in either hand . . . Latterly he had wandered about the Holy Land tossing hand-grenades into the front parlours of dissident Arabs.' He believes in team games as a dry run for war: 'The men go for you and you go for them and there's no hard feelings when bones get broken. In my company at one time we had more casualties from soccer than from the enemy . . .' Tactics, as he interpreted them, 'consisted of the art of biffing. Defence was studied cursorily . . . Withdrawal was never mentioned. The Attack and the Element of Surprise were all.'

Waugh based this officer on his Brigade Commander, Albert St Clair-Morford. In his diary for 18 January 1940 he wrote that Morford: 'looks like something escaped from Sing-Sing and talks like a boy in the Fourth Form . . . teeth like a stoat, ears like a faun, eyes alight like a child playing pirates, "We then have to biff them, gentlemen." He scares half and fascinates half.' On 26 February he recorded: 'Most of the Brigadier's family reminiscences dealt with floggings he administered or with grave accidents resulting from various dangerous forms of holiday-making.' 'One has to play team games,' he told Waugh, 'Last war I was centre-half for my company . . . you get hold of your men that way . . . If a man was brought up before me for a crime, I used to say, "Will you have a court-martial or take it from me?" They always took it from me. I bent 'em over and gave 'em ten, as tight as I could. My company had the best record for crime in the regiment.' Morford was wounded four times and awarded the MC in the First World War. He commanded the Royal Marine Brigade 1940-41, and served in India 1942–3. He gave his recreations in *Who's Who* as 'Most games'.

HORACE

Ben Jonson, *The Poetaster* (1601), Thomas Dekker, *Satiromastix, or, The Untrussing of the Humorous Poet* (1602)

Ben Jonson (1572–1637)

Further reading: Marchette Chute, *Ben Jonson of Westminster* (1953)

At the court of the Emperor Augustus, two conspirators, Crispinus and Demetrius (see CRISPINUS and DEMETRIUS) attempt to discredit Horace. The matter is brought before Augustus, and Horace is cleared. The result of their efforts is that Crispinus and Demetrius have really defamed themselves. This play was one of Ben Jonson's contributions to the so-called War of the Theatres, which raged between 1599 and 1602 (see CHRYSOGANUS) and Jonson also fired off some heavy missiles in this conflict in *Cynthia's Revels* and *Every Man Out of his Humour*. In *Poetaster* Horace is flattered by lesser beings than he is. Crispinus, for example (=Marston) says to him: 'Horace, thou art exceeding happy in thy friends and acquaintance; they are all most excellent spirits, and of the first rank . . . I do not know that poet . . . has used his fortune more prosperously than thou hast . . .' But Horace can see through all these soft words and is ruthless in his exposure of the conspirators. This is, of course, a fairly generous portrait of Ben Jonson, as it was composed by him to place him in a good light. Thomas Dekker got his own back in *Satiromastix* for the drubbing he and Marston had received in *Poetaster*. In an early scene in Dekker's play Horace is discovered in his study, surrounded by books, working on another masterpiece: 'Damn me, if it be not the best that ever came from me' and he tiresomely reads it to a friend who comes to visit him, poring over the best bits. Horace says it is the will of the Muses: 'That we to learned ears should sweetly sing,/But to the vulgar and adulterate brain/Should loath to prostitute our virgin strain.' This is an echo from Jonson's lines in *Cynthia's Revels*: '. . . loath to prostitute their virgin strain/To ev'ry vulgar and adulterate brain'. Dekker also refers to Jonson's employment as a brick-layer, his service in the road company, his killing of a fellow actor, his pock-marked complexion, his slow manner of composition, the strange faces he pulled when he read his poetry aloud and his small stature. (see AJAX). William Drummond said of him: 'He is a great lover and praiser of himself, a condemner and scorner of others, given rather to lose a friend than a jest, jealous of every word and action of those about him, especially after drink . . .'

MR HORSFIELD

Jean Rhys, *After Leaving Mr Mackenzie* (1930)

Leslie Tilden-Smith
(1885–1945)

Further reading:
Francis Wyndham and Diana Melly (eds.), *Jean Rhys Letters, 1931–1966* (1984)

Jean Rhys's heroines are brittle women, easily broken by cynical men. When Julia Martin, the central figure in *After Leaving Mr Mackenzie*, is dumped by her lover Mackenzie she finds some solace in the attentions of George Horsfield, a young man who takes pity on her little-girl-lost appearance. Mr Horsfield first encounters Julia in Paris and watches her approach Mr Mackenzie in the Restaurant Albert and hit him on the cheek with her glove – a despairing gesture of dismissal. Mr Horsfield is first introduced as a thin, dark man with a bored expression, and Rhys later elaborates on his appearance: 'He looked very tidy and very precise. He looked the sort that never gives itself away and that despises people who do, that despises them and perhaps takes advantage of them . . . He was hollow-cheeked. His mouth drooped at the corners – not bad-temperedly, but sadly.'

Mr Horsfield is modelled on Leslie Tilden-Smith, the man Jean Rhys married in 1932 after her divorce from Jean Leglet. Leslie, who met Jean in 1927, worked as a literary agent and publisher's reader for Hamish Hamilton. During the Second World War, Leslie – who had been a pilot in the First World War – was too old for active duties but did para-military work in Norwich and Wales. On his return to London, in 1944, his health deteriorated. In a letter of 10 October 1945 Jean describes his death: 'He said that he had a terrible pain in his arm and chest . . . as I took Leslie's hand in mine he died . . . I loved Leslie too and I think he knew it. In spite of all the worry and all the strain which I cracked under so badly (and I won't ever forgive myself for that) still he was sometimes a little happy with me . . . I did love him though and knew all his generosity and gentleness – very well.' In another letter, written a few days later, she said 'he was a very gentle and generous man and oh Peggy I'd give all my idiotic life for an hour to say goodbye to him.' She married her third husband, Max Hamer, two years later.

HORTENSE

Charles Dickens, *Bleak House* (1852)

Maria Manning
(1821-49)

Further reading:
Philip Collins, *Dickens and Crime* (1962)

Hortense is a French maid, in the service of Lady Dedlock. She is thirty-two years old and from somewhere in the southern country about Avignon and Marseilles: 'a large-eyed, brown woman with black hair who would have been handsome, but for a certain feline mouth, and general uncomfortable tightness of face, rendering the jaws too eager, and the skull too prominent . . . she has a watchful way of looking out of the corners of her eyes without turning her head . . . especially when she was in an ill-humour and near knives.' She works for Lady Dedlock for five years and then is dismissed through becoming jealous of another servant, Rosa. But Hortense has found out something of Lady Dedlock's secret – that she had had a child by Captain Hawden – and tries to get money out of Tulkinghorn, the lawyer. She fails and murders him. She then tries to put the blame on Lady Dedlock. Inspector Bucket (see BUCKET) solves the crime and she is arrested.

Hortense was based on the Belgian murderess, Maria Manning. She and her husband George Manning murdered their lodger, Patrick O'Connor, for his money. The unfortunate O'Connor was invited to a dinner of roast goose. When he arrived they shot him and put his body in quicklime below the floor while they went on to enjoy their meal. At the trial she called out: 'There is no law nor justice to be got here!' – 'Base and degraded England!' In prison she was violent and abused the staff. She also attempted suicide. Dickens saw their execution on 13 November 1849, and subsequently wrote a letter to *The Times* about the harmfulness of public executions. Maria Manning had been lady's maid to the Duchess of Sunderland, and she was arrested by Inspector Field. He traced her to her lodging, tapped quietly on the door and said: 'Only me – Charley Field – so just open the door quietly, Maria.'

THE HOUSE OF THE SEVEN GABLES

Nathaniel Hawthorne, *The House of the Seven Gables* (1851)

Further reading: A. Robert Lee, *Nathaniel Hawthorne – New Critical Essays* (1981)

The first sentence of Nathaniel Hawthorne's *The House of the Seven Gables* describes the novel's central symbol: 'Halfway down a bystreet of one of our New England towns stands a rusty wooden house, with seven acutely peaked gables, facing towards various points of the compass, and a huge, clustered chimney in the midst.' Condemned as a wizard, Matthew Maule casts a curse from the scaffold on his tormentor, Colonel Pyncheon: 'God will give him blood to drink!' Still, Pyncheon builds the House of the Seven Gables over Maule's log-built hut: 'His home would include the home of the dead and buried wizard, and would thus afford the ghost of the latter a kind of privilege to haunt its new apartments, and the chambers into which bridegrooms were to lead their brides, and where children of the Pyncheon blood were to be born.' Colonel Pyncheon is found dead, his beard 'saturated' with blood, and Maule's curse hangs over the House for three generations.

Hawthorne was born and brought up in Salem, Massachusetts, and was a frequent visitor to the House of the Seven Gables which was owned by his cousin, Miss Susannah Ingersoll. Built in 1668 by Captain John Turner, the House was extended in the 1690s by John Turner II, so that it had the seven gables. Miss Susannah liked to tell Hawthorne tales of their ancestors, including Major William Hathorne (as the surname was spelt before Hawthorne altered it); among the Quakers he persecuted was one John Maule. In 1692, during the notorious witch hysteria, Hawthorne's ancestor John Hathorne acted as an examiner of persons accused. According to Salem folklore the curse 'God will give you blood to drink' was uttered in 1692 by a condemned witch. From his intimate knowledge of the House itself, and from stories of Salem, Hawthorne created his romance. In 1908 Caroline O. Emmerton bought the House and had it restored to the original design with the seven gables; since 1910 it has been open to the public.

WILL HUBBARD

Jack Kerouac, *Vanity of Duluoz* (1968)

William Burroughs (1914–)

Further reading: Ann Charteris, *Kerouac* (1973) and Barry Gifford and Lawrence Lee, *Jack's Book* (1979)

Jack Kerouac regarded his novels as sections in an autobiographical sequence, the Legend of Duluoz. *Vanity of Duluoz* chronicles the years 1939-46, and brings the hero, Jack Duluoz, from Lowell High School to New York on a football scholarship. Like Duluoz, Kerouac attended Horace Mann Prep School (1939-40), Columbia College (1940-1), and served in the Merchant Marine and US Navy (1942-3) before returning to New York to a life of artistry and abandon. In 1944 in New York, Kerouac first met fellow-novelist William Burroughs, who appears in the novel as Will Hubbard: 'Tall, 6 foot 1, strange, inscrutable because ordinary-looking (scrutable), like a shy bank clerk with a patrician thinlipped cold bluelipped face, blue eyes saying nothing behind steel rims and glass, sandy hair, a little wispy, a little of the wistful German Nazi youth as his soft hair fluffles in the breeze.'

Kerouac and Burroughs became great friends and shared an ambition to radicalize American prose by being both stylistically direct and thematically frank. For Burroughs this meant dealing with his experiences as a drug-addict. His *Junkie: Confessions of an Unredeemed Drug Addict* appeared in 1953 and *The Naked Lunch* (1959) explored the same disturbing territory with a brutal honesty. He was an addict for fifteen years and was cured in 1959 when he agreed to undergo apomorphine treatment in London. Subsequently he settled in Kansas City, not too far from his birthplace in St Louis, and continued to enjoy his reputation as the *enfant terrible* of American letters.

At a Writers' Conference, held during the Edinburgh Festival of 1962, Burroughs revealed that he wrote his books by a 'cut-up' method: some of his texts were cut up and reassembled, others were folded then juxtaposed. Burroughs was astonished at the shocked reaction of the audience, believing that the cut-up technique was not so much revolutionary as realistic: 'all it does is make the process of perception explicit with a pair of scissors. If you walk down the street your perception is cut up by objects. The random method is closer to the actual facts of perception.' Kerouac typed the first two chapters of *The Naked Lunch* for Burroughs in Tangiers, and the two men collaborated on a novel called *And the Hippos Were Boiled in Their Tanks*. It was not, however, published, and in a *Paris Review* interview of 1967, Kerouac said it was 'hidden under the floorboards, with Burroughs'. In the same interview, Kerouac said of Burroughs's *Junkie*: 'It's a classic. It's better than Hemingway'.

HUMBOLDT

Saul Bellow, *Humboldt's Gift* (1975)

Delmore Schwartz (1913–66)

Charlie Citrine, the playwright-narrator of Saul Bellow's *Humboldt's Gift*, finds that his life is inextricably connected with the rise and fall of the poet Von Humboldt Fleisher. Humboldt, Citrine explains, was a poetic sensation of the 1930s, an instant celebrity whose 'picture appeared in *Time* without insult and in *Newsweek* with praise'. He was good-looking, eloquent, erudite: 'The guy had it all.' After all his promise, though, Humbolt had degenerated into drunkenness, despair and madenss: 'He dropped dead in a dismal hotel off Times Square,' Citrine writes. At about 3 a.m. Humboldt had a heart attack: 'Fighting for breath, he tore off his shirt. When the cops came to take the dead man to the hospital his chest was naked. . . . At the morgue there were no readers of modern poetry. . . . So he lay there, another derelict.'

This description of the death of Humboldt is an exact account of the fate of Brooklyn-born Delmore Schwartz whose first volume of poems and stories, *In Dreams Begin Responsibilities* (1938), had been greatly applauded by the critics. Schwartz was, like Humboldt, a manic-depressive whose instability led to hospitalization in Bellevue. When Saul Bellow organized a collection to pay for psychiatric help, the disturbed poet turned against the successful novelist; this cycle of jealousy and love-hatred is recreated in Bellow's novel. Although Bellow stresses the comic aspects of Humboldt the book is a deeply felt tribute to Schwartz: 'He was a lovely man, and generous, with a heart of gold. . . . For after all Humboldt did what poets in crass America are supposed to do. He chased ruin and death even harder than he had chased women. He blew his talent and his health and reached home, the grave, in a dusty slide.'

MRS LEO HUNTER

Charles Dickens, *The Posthumous Papers of the Pickwick Club* (1836)

Mary Monckton, Countess of Cork and Orrery (1746–1840)

Further reading:
Edwin Pugh, *The Charles Dickens Originals* (1912)

Mrs Leo Hunter is the celebrated poetess of The Den, Eatanswill. Mr Pickwick is regaled by an account of her abilities by her husband: 'She dotes on poetry, sir. She adores it; I may say that her whole soul and mind are wound up, and entwined with it. She has produced some delightful pieces herself, sir. You may have met her "Ode to an Expiring Frog", sir . . . It created an immense sensation. It was signed with an 'L' and eight stars, and appeared originally in a Lady's Magazine. It commenced:

"Can I view thee panting, lying
On thy stomach, without sighing;
Can I unmoved see thee dying
On a log,
Expiring frog!"'

This is a caricature of the famous blue-stocking and lion-hunter (one who pursues celebrities), Lady Cork. Indeed, Dickens rather heavily puns on this in her name–Leo Hunter. She also figures in Disraeli's fiction (see VISCOUNTESS DOWAGER BELLAIR). Lady Cork was the daughter of the first Viscount Galway. As a result of her influence, her mother's house in London became the Mecca of literary and artistic England. Samuel Johnson was often there, as were also Sir Joshua Reynolds, Richard Brinsley Sheridan, Edmund Burke, Horace Walpole and Sydney Smith. Mrs Siddons was her closest friend. She knew everybody who was anybody, and if anybody was anybody she made a point of getting to know them. In 1786 she married the Seventh Earl of Cork and Orrery, who died in 1798. As Lady Cork she became an even more famous hostess. Among her guests she numbered Sir Walter Scott, George Canning, Lord Castlereagh, Lord Byron, Lord John Russell, Sir Robert Peel, Theodore Hook (see LUCIAN GAY) and others. Sydney Smith recorded that: 'Benevolence is a natural instinct of the human mind. When A sees B in grievous distress, his conscience always urges him to entreat C to help. Lady Cork was once so moved by a charity sermon that she begged me to lend her a guinea for her contribution. I did so. She never repaid me, and spent it on herself.'

RHODA HYMAN

Wyndham Lewis, *The Roaring Queen* (1973)

Virginia Woolf (1882–1941)

Further reading: Margaret Drabble, *Arnold Bennett* (1974)

Wyndham Lewis's satirical novel *The Roaring Queen* brings several disparate characters together at a weekend party at Beverley Chase, the Oxfordshire home of Mrs Wellesley-Crook. When SAMUEL SHODBUTT arrives, as the principal guest, he is appalled to behold one of his enemies Mrs Rhoda Hyman: 'And if the gaze of Samuel Shodbutt fell more ponderously in one place than another, it oppressed, if anything, more peculiarly that drooping intellect-ravaged exterior of the lanky and sickly lady in Victorian muslims . . . Yes! there, beneath his very eyes, wilted pretentiously the very woman who had but a few months ago written a vile supercilious pamphlet all about Shodbutt . . . The haughty Shodbutt eyed the little distant drooping image of best faded Victorian *chic* and he considered what remark, if any, he should make when they came face to face downstairs.' Mrs Rhoda Hyman is eligible for the Diploma for the Year's Cleverest Literary Larceny as she has successfully (she feels) produced a work of plagiarism. Walter Allen, introducing *The Roaring Queen*, identifies Rhoda Hyman as Virginia Woolf, whom Lewis considered a derivative writer. Comparing Joyce's *Ulysses* (1922) with Woolf's *Mrs Dalloway* (1925), in *Men Without Art* (1934), Lewis wrote 'the latter is a sort of undergraduate imitation of the former, winding up with a smoke-writing in the sky, a pathetic "crib" of the firework display and the rocket that is the culmination of Mr Bloom's beach ecstasy.'

The allusion to Rhoda Hyman's 'vile supercilious pamphlet all about Shodbutt' relates to the pamphlet *Mr Bennett and Mrs Brown* published by Virginia Woolf in 1924. Virginia Woolf found Bennett (who is caricatured as Shodbutt in *The Roaring Queen*) a vulgar man with a limited understanding of literature. Bennett, writing in the *Evening Standard* some two years later, claimed not to have read Mrs Woolf's pamphlet, then condemned her fiction for poor character-drawing, weak construction and a lack of vitality. On 1 December 1930 they met at a dinner-party; Bennett found Virginia Woolf 'all right' but she noted that she did not 'care a rap if I'm on terms with B[ennett] or not'. When Bennett died in 1928, however, Virginia Woolf was saddened: 'Queer how one regrets the dispersal of anybody who seemed – as I say – genuine: who had direct contact with life – for he abused me; and yet I rather wished him to go on abusing me; and me abusing him. An element in life – even in mine that was remote – taken away.'

J

ESTHER JACK

Thomas Wolfe, *Of Time and the River* (1935), *You Can't Go Home Again* (1940)

Aline Bernstein

Further reading: Andrew Turnbull, *Thomas Wolfe* (1968)

Eugene Gant, the autobiographical hero of Thomas Wolfe's first novel *Look Homeward, Angel* (1929), reappears in *Of Time and the River*. Gant leaves Altamont (Asheville, where Wolfe was born in 1900), goes to Harvard, teaches in New York and travels to Europe where he begins a novel. On the boat bringing him back to the USA he meets Esther Jack and is transformed by the encounter: 'From that moment on he never was again to lose her utterly, never to wholly repossess unto himself the lonely, wild integrity of youth which had been his . . . At that moment of their meeting she got into his life by some dark magic, and before he knew it he had her beating in the pulses of his blood . . . After all the blind, tormented wanderings of youth, the woman would become his heart's centre and the target of his life, the image of immortal one-ness that again collected him to one, and hurled the whole collected passion, power and might of his one life into the blazing certitude, the immortal governance and unity, of love.' In *You Can't Go Home Again*, George Webber (Wolfe by yet another name), broods about Esther Jack; 'much older than he, married and living with her husband and grown daughter. But she had given George her love, and given it so deeply, so exclusively, that he had come to feel himself caught as in a trap.'

After his first European trip Wolfe met Aline Bernstein on the *Olympic* when sailing home in August 1925. Eighteen years older than Wolfe, Aline was a Jewish actor's daughter married to Theodore Bernstein, a broker and father of her two children. She studied at the New York School of Applied Design, became a leading theatrical designer and in 1926 let Wolfe move into the loft of her studio of 13 East Eighth Street. Attracted by his immense energy and obvious artistic promise, she tried to help him realize his ambitions as a playwright, then, when she felt he was better suited to fiction than drama, assisted him with the Autobiographical Outline which formed the basis of *Look Homeward, Angel*. Wolfe depended on her (financially, at first, as well as emotionally), made trips to Europe with her and (when he resumed teaching) shared an apartment with her in 1927. After his first novel was accepted for publication he asserted his independence and in 1931 she took an overdose of sleeping pills. When she recovered she sent him love letters but he broke with her in 1932. They kept in touch as friends afterwards and Wolfe is supposed to have said, before his death, 'I want Aline . . . I want my Jew.'

PAUL JAGO

C.P. Snow, *The Light and the Dark* (1947), *The Masters* (1951), *The Affair* (1960)

Canon Charles Earle Raven (1885–1964)

Further reading: Philip Snow, *Stranger and Brother* (1982), John Halperin, *C.P. Snow – An Oral Biography* (1983)

The Masters by C.P. Snow is a study of a struggle for the control of a Cambridge college. In a claustrophobically close environment two candidates emerge as possible successors to the Master who is dying of cancer. Redvers Crawford represents the interests of science whereas Paul Jago, senior tutor, is a traditionalist devoted to Cambridge and 'the only one of the present college who had been born into the academic life'. Crawford triumphs in the interests of pragmatism but the reader's sympathy is directed towards Jago: 'Many [people] disliked his love of display. Yet they were affected by the depth of his feeling. Nearly everyone recognized that, though it took some insight to perceive that he was not only a man of deep feeling, but also one of passionate pride.'

According to the novelist's brother Philip Snow, Jago is 'a superbly drawn portrait' of Canon Charles Earle Raven who was Professor of Divinity at Cambridge from 1932 to 1950. Raven's greatest ambition was to become Master of Christ's College where C.P. Snow was a fellow from 1930. When the mastership election was held in 1939 Raven (unlike his fictional counterpart) was successful and C.P. Snow, who took a dim view of Raven's pacifism, wrote to his brother: 'I think if I had gone all out I could probably have kept him out. . . . You should have seen him on the morning of his election, when it was fairly certain that he would get it. He kept walking round the Court, only keeping himself from smiling by an effort; and, though he kept his mouth from smiling, he couldn't control his eyes.' Once Master, Raven basked in the glory of the position by dining almost every night and showing a proprietorial pride in fellows and furnishings. Snow's novel was resented by the college and for some time after the publication of the book the author was, in the words of his brother, '*persona non grata* among certain fellows'.

JARNDYCE v. JARNDYCE

Charles Dickens, *Bleak House* (1852)

The Jennings Case (1798)

Further reading: John Butt and Kathleen Tillotson, *Dickens at Work* (1957), Edgar Johnson, *Charles Dickens – His Tragedy and Triumph* (1952)

Bleak House is dominated by the prolonged case of Jarndyce v. Jarndyce, which has occupied the Court of Chancery for generations, which, in the words of one of the lawyers who has made such a good living out of it, is one of the greatest Chancery suits known, 'a monument of Chancery practice: In which (I would say) every difficulty, every contingency, every masterly fiction, every form of procedure known in that court, is represented over and over again. It is a cause that could not exist, out of this free and great country. I should say that the aggregate of costs in Jarndyce and Jarndyce . . . amounts at the present hour to from SIX-ty to SEVEN-ty THOUSAND POUNDS . . .' The lawyers at work are described: 'mistily engaged in one of the ten thousand stages of an endless cause, tripping one another up on slippery precedents, groping knee-deep in technicalities, running their goat-hair and horse-hair warded heads against walls of words, and making a pretence of equity with serious faces, as players might. On such an afternoon, the various solicitors in the cause, some two or three of whom have inherited it from their fathers, who made a fortune by it, ought to be . . . ranged in a line, in a long matted well (but you might look in vain for Truth at the bottom of it), between the registrar's red table and the silk gowns, with bills, cross-bills, answers, rejoinders, injunctions, affidavits, issues, references to masters, masters' reports, mountains of costly nonsense, piled before them.' The lawsuit arises from a will, and the question of how the trusts under the will are to be administered. As the case drags on one member of the Jarndyce family blows his brains out, Richard Carstone (a party to the suit) wears himself to death, and when a new will is discovered which settles the whole case, it is found that the entire fortune has been eaten up in the legal costs.

This is based on the notorious Jennings case. Jennings was an old miser who died intestate in 1798 at the age of eighty-seven leaving an estate of £1,500,000. He lived in a deserted mansion at Acton, in Suffolk. He made a will but neither of the executors could be located. At last an heir-at-law was traced in the person of the great-great-grandson of one C. Jennings of Gopsal, eldest uncle of the deceased, who then entered into the property. The case dragged on, and Edgar Johnson (*Charles Dickens – His Tragedy and Triumph*, 1952) records that when one of the claimants died in 1915 the case was still unresolved and the costs amounted to £250,000. As Dickens wrote: 'The one great principle of the English law is, to make business for itself. There is no other principle distinctly, certainly, and consistently maintained through all its narrow turnings.'

JEAN

Hugh MacDiarmid, *A Drunk Man Looks at the Thistle* (1926)

Peggy Grieve (1898–1962)

Further reading: Alan Bold, *MacDiarmid: The Terrible Crystal* (1983),

In Hugh MacDiarmid's long poem *A Drunk Man Looks at the Thistle* the hero undergoes a metamorphosis from spirit-sodden Scot to spiritual Scot possessed of a vision of a national rebirth. After drinking whisky with his cronies, the Drunk Man staggers off on his unsteady odyssey to the arms of his wife Jean – a figure corresponding to Homer's Penelope in the *Iliad* and James Joyce's Molly Bloom in *Ulysses*. Collapsing on a hillside, the Drunk Man wakes, under a full moon, to see a gigantic thistle, whose presence prompts him to a series of metaphysical speculations on Scotland and the universe. As he soars he is constantly brought back to earth with thoughts of Jean: 'For even Jean maun natter, natter, natter'. Jean's role is to anchor the Drunk Man to a domesticity he acknowledges and occasionally deplores: 'And Jean's nae mair my wife/Than whisky is at times,/Or munelicht or a thistle/Or kittle thochts or rhymes.//He's no a man ava',/And lacks a proper pride,/gin less than a' the warld/Can ser' him for a bride!' Towards the end of the poem the Drunk Man anticipates his homecoming: 'But aince Jean kens what I've been through/the nicht, I dinna doot it,/She'll ope her airms in welcome true,/And clack nae mair aboot it'. Ironically, Jean has the last word of the poem: 'O I ha'e Silence left,/– "And weel ye micht,"/Sae Jean'll say, "efter sic a nicht!"'

Christopher Murray Grieve – the poet used the pseudonym Hugh MacDiarmid from 1922 – met Margaret 'Peggy' Skinner in Cupar where she worked as a copyholder in a newspaper office. After serving in Salonika during The First World War, Grieve married Peggy in 1918. In 1921 the couple settled in Montrose, where Grieve was a journalist, town councillor, parish councillor, Justice of the Peace and author of several books – including *A Drunk Man* – that revolutionized Scots poetry. Peggy gave birth to two children, but disliked the smalltown atmosphere of Montrose and the poet's periodic bouts of drinking. When Grieve was offered a journalistic job in London, in 1929, Peggy was enthusiastic about the move. It was, however, disastrous for Grieve; the magazine *Vox*, of which he was London editor, collapsed; he had a bad fall from a bus, suffering severe concussion; and Peggy went off with a married man, William McElroy. After her divorce from Grieve, Peggy was taken to court by McElroy's wife since it was alleged that she, Peggy, had 'enticed' McElroy from his wife. Later Peggy emigrated to Canada and married a Canadian, Harry J. Tilar. She died at Deal in Kent. For a decade, though, she was the inspiration of some of MacDiarmid's greatest poems.

Alan Bold (ed.) *The Letters of Hugh MacDiarmid* (1984)

JEANIE WITH THE LIGHT BROWN HAIR

Stephen Foster, *'Jeanie with the Light Brown Hair'* (1854)

Jane McDowell

Stephen Foster's song 'Jeanie with the Light Brown Hair' expresses great tenderness: 'I long for Jeanie with the day-dawn smile,/Radiant in gladness, warm with winning guile.' It was composed at a time when Foster was living apart from his Jeanie – Jane Denny McDowell. Foster was born in Lawrenceville, Pittsburgh, and went to Cincinnati in the 1840s to work as a book-keeper for his brother Dunning Foster. He returned to his home town in 1850 and on 22 July married a beautiful local girl, Jane McDowell.

Like Foster, Jane was of Scottish-Irish pioneer stock; but as the daughter of a leading Pittsburgh physician she was accustomed to a higher standard of living than Foster could provide though in the first years of his marriage he produced such classic songs as 'Old Folks at Home'. On 18 April 1851 Marion, the only child of Stephen and Jane Foster, was born and the marriage seemed secure. Yet Stephen's drinking bouts distressed Jane and the couple separated in 1853. While his wife and daughter stayed in Pittsburgh, Foster went to New York so it was at an emotional and geographical distance from his wife that the self-taught songwriter created 'Jeanie with the Light Brown Hair'. The sentiment seemed to bring Stephen and 'Jeanie' together again and Foster returned to Pittsburgh to be with his family. In 1860 he brought his wife and daughter to New York but was unable to support them and Jane returned to work for the Pennsylvanian Railroad at Greensburg, near Pittsburgh. Alone in his room, in the Bowery of New York, Foster drank heavily; on 10 January 1864 he collapsed and seriously injured himself. He died in Bellevue Hospital seven days later and Jane, his 'Jeanie', came to New York to bring his body back to Pittsburgh.

Further reading:
J. Wheeler, *The Life of Stephen Foster* (1945)

JEANNE

Guy de Maupassant, *A Woman's life* (1883)

Guy de Maupassant's mother, Laure, played an enormously influential role in his life and art. Born Laure-Marie-Geneviève Le Poittevin, she was the daughter of Paul Le Poittevin, who owned two spinning mills at Rouen and was friendly with Dr Achille-Cléophas Flaubert, the surgeon

Laure Le Poittevin
(1821–1904)

Further reading:
Michael G. Lerner,
Maupassant (1975)

and father of the novelist Gustave Flaubert. Laure grew up with Gustave Flaubert and largely lived through literature. In 1846 Laure married Gustave de Maupassant at Rouen and after a honeymoon in Italy the couple lived mainly at Rouen, spending summers at Dieppe or Etretat. Laure had two children –Guy in 1851, Hervé in 1856– but her relations with her husband gradually deteriorated. He was fond of gambling and liked the company of his mistresses in Paris. When Guy was nine and staying with his father in Paris he wrote to Laure: 'Madame X took me to the circus along with papa. It appears she also gives papa some kind of reward too but I don't know exactly what sort.' By 1860 Laure and Gustave were living apart, and three years later they drew up a formal contract of separation (divorce not being legal in France until 1884). With her two sons, Laure settled at Etretat, in a house called 'The Orchards', and ensured that Guy's attention was drawn to literature in general and Flaubert – Laure's childhood friend – in particular. After Maupassant's death, in a Paris asylum, Laure's priority was to protect his reputation against the rumours about his insanity. Michael G. Lerner says, in *Maupassant* (1975), that Laure encouraged Maupassant along 'the road of ambition and sophistication that contributed, with the nervous temperament he inherited from her, to his undoing.'

Maupassant, however, adored his mother and transformed her into the character Jeanne who is martyred in his novel *Une Vie*. Jeanne leaves her convent school full of romantic dreams (in the translation by H.N.P. Sloman): 'radiant, bursting with life, thirsting for happiness, ready for all the joys and all the risks, which she had already anticipated in imagination in days of idleness and in the long hours of the night'. Her dreams, however, collapse when she marries Julien de Lamare, whose sexual drive disturbs Jeanne and who turns to other women with diasastrous consequences. Jeanne's only comfort, after all her suffering, is her relationship with her son Paul.

DR JEKYLL

Robert Louis Stevenson,
The Strange Case of Dr Jekyll and Mr Hyde (1886)

William Brodie
(1741–88)

Further reading:
Alan Bold and Robert Giddings, *The Book of Rotters* (1985)

In the summer of 1879 W.E. Henley stayed with Robert Louis Stevenson at Swanston village, Edinburgh, and the two men worked on a drama based on the life of William Brodie, Deacon of the Wrights (or cabinet-makers). By day, Deacon Brodie was a businessman, town councillor and prominent member of the Edinburgh establishment; by night he set his gang of burglars loose on the city. Brodie's most ambitious job, the break-in at the General Excise Office of Scotland, led to his downfall for the Brodie gang were caught in the act. Brodie, on hearing this, fled to Holland but he was brought back, put on trial, and hanged. After his escape from Edinburgh, Brodie wrote to a friend: 'Were I to write to you all that has happened to me and the hairbreadth escapes I made from a well-scented pack of bloodhounds, it would make a small volume.' The Henley-Stevenson play, *Deacon Brodie*, was not a success; it was privately printed in 1880 and produced in 1882.

However, in 1885 Stevenson had a nightmare about a man 'being pressed into a cabinet when he swallowed a drug and changed into another'. This insight into human duality was given an allegorical dimension, at the suggestion of Stevenson's wife Fanny, and written up as *The Strange Case of Dr Jekyll and Mr Hyde*. Though the novel is ostensibly set in London the townscape is unmistakably that of Deacon Brodie's Edinburgh while Henry Jekyll himself is, like the Deacon, a dangerously divided personality: 'I concealed my pleasures,' he says, 'I regarded and hid them with an almost morbid sense of shame. Though so profound a double-dealer, I was in no sense a hypocrite; both sides of me were in dead earnest.'

Brodie's bizarre personality is perhaps best conveyed by the will he made before he died: 'And lastly my neck being now about to be embraced by a halter I recommend to all Rogues, Sharpers, Thieves and Gamblers, as well in high as in low stations to take care of theirs by leaving of all wicked practices and becoming good members of society.' Incidentally, the heroine of Muriel Spark's *The Prime of Miss Jean Brodie* (1961), a woman divided between self-righteousness and romanticism, was proud to claim descent from Deacon Brodie.

JEMIMA, QUEEN TO KING MAGNUS

George Bernard Shaw, *The Apple Cart* (1929)

Charlotte Frances Payne-Townsend

Further reading: Hesketh Pearson, *Bernard Shaw – His Life and Personality* (1942)

Shaw described *The Apple Cart* as a political extravaganza. It concerns a political crisis brought about by a philosophic king who publishes brilliant newspaper articles and makes public pronouncements which annoy his elected government. The government threaten that he must put an end to these political posturings or else they will resign. The King counters by saying he will declare a state of political crisis, dissolve parliament and stand for election himself as candidate for the Royal Borough of Windsor–which he is bound to win. King Magnus's paramour, Orinthia, tries to persuade him that she would be a better queen for him than his wife, Jemima. Jemima is very businesslike and runs the royal household like an efficient housewife. When Magnus tells Orinthia that he must leave her, as the Queen does not like to be kept waiting, Orinthia says: 'Oh, bother Jemima!' Magnus says: 'My dear; I must' and adds: 'You are only trying to make me late to annoy my wife.' Magnus describes their relationship in these words: 'Now, if our limitations exactly corresponded I should never want to talk to anyone else; and neither would she. But as that never happens, we are like all other married couples: that is, there are subjects which can never be discussed between us because they are sore subjects. There are people we avoid mentioning to one another because one of us likes them and the other doesn't.' Their relationship is further detailed in this exchange between the King and his lover – '*Magnus:* But my wife? the Queen? What is to become of my poor dear Jemima? *Orinthia*: Oh, drown her: shoot her: tell your chauffeur to drive her into the Serpentine and leave her there. The woman makes you ridiculous. *Magnus*: I don't think I should like that. And the public would think it ill-natured. *Orinthia*: Oh, you know what I mean. Divorce her. Make her divorce you. It is quite easy... *Magnus*: But I can't imagine what I should do without Jemima. *Orinthia*: Nobody can imagine what you do with her.'

This is obviously a description of Shaw's married life with Charlotte Payne-Townsend, the daughter of an Irish landowning family. She had nursed him through illness and soon put the household in order. 'We are married,' he said, 'because we had become indispensable to one another.' At West Strand registry office the bridegroom was so scruffy that he was mistaken for a stray beggar hoping to profit from the general benevolence of these occasions. Mrs Shaw soon domesticated him.

DR JENKINSON

William Hurrell Mallock, *The New Republic* (1877)

Benjamin Jowett (1817–93)

Further reading: E.F. Benson, *As We Were – A Victorian Peep-Show* (1930), E.A. Abbott and Lewis Campbell, *The Life and Letters of Benjamin Jowett* (1897)

The New Republic is a satire in the manner of Thomas Love Peacock. It recounts the gathering at a weekend country-house party of several of the leading thinkers and intellectuals of the late Victorian era. They are foregathered at the household of Otho Laurence, who cherished a deep antipathy to the two things most admired by those of his time and order – Christianity and Feudalism. Among his guests is: 'Dr Jenkinson, the great Broad-church divine who thinks Christianity is not dead, but changed by himself and his followers in the twinkling of an eye.' He is described as: 'still full of vigour, though his hair was silver' with a sharp and restless sparkle in his eyes 'strangely joined with the most benevolent of smiles'. Mallock did not go to public school, but was introduced to books and society at a young age (he was a nephew of J.A. Froude) and went up to Balliol at a time when it was dominated by Jowett. John Squire described the intellectual world of this age as 'a sort of club with the ghost of the Prince Consort as a sort of perpetual President'. Benjamin Jowett, the formidable master of Balliol, was educated at St Paul's School and Balliol, where he was fellow from 1838. He was made Regius Professor of Greek at Oxford in 1855 and Master of Balliol 1870-93. He published numerous classical editions and translations and several influential liberal theological works which caused him to be suspected of heresy, and was for ten years deprived of the emoluments of his office. His learning was immense and his mastery of the verbal put-down notorious. H.C. Beeching's famous *The Masque of Balliol* has him intoning: 'First come I; my name is Jowett,/There's no knowledge but I know it./I am Master of this College:/What I don't know isn't knowledge.' When asked if he would sign the Thirty-nine Articles on being appointed to his professorship he replied he was willing to sign forty if so desired. He admonished a fastidious colleague who cut several passages in the production of a play by Aristophanes because they contained *double entendres* about boys: 'I hear you have been making cuts in the Greek play? Aristophanes wrote it. Who are you?' He told his intimates at Oxford once that there were three men to whom he owed a great deal – 'Gladstone, Homer . . .' There was a pause. 'Who was the third?' asked a colleague. 'I've forgotten the third,' Jowett answered. It was reputed that he was deeply in love with Florence Nightingale.

HERCULES JONES

John Davenport and Dylan Thomas, *The Death of the King's Canary* (1976)

Augustus John (1878-1961)

In 1940 John Davenport and Dylan Thomas collaborated on *The Death of the King's Canary*, a satirical fantasy about the bizarre banquet a new Poet Laureate arranges before he is murdered. The news of Hilary Byrd's appointment as Poet Laureate is the talk of the literary world and one poet asks 'the great painter' Hercules Jones for his opinion of the matter: 'Hercules Jones put his glass down. He raised his head. He set back his magnificent shoulder. There was a rumble as of an anchor being heaved from the ocean bed. His voice was rusty, and startlingly loud, as if he had not spoken for a year. "I knew his father before you were born", he said.' A formidable presence, Jones relishes drink and women as well as art: 'Inside the bar parlour of the White Swan Hercules Jones crumpled his tankard and beat with it upon the counter . . . Jones snorted contemptuously, a sardonic smile twisting under the ragged moustache, the stained beard jutting . . . [Then] he relapsed into a sombre reverie in which beautiful women and great men drank and made love prodigiously, and no one was less than a demigod at the very least.' At the 'Laureate Warming Party' given by Hilary Byrd, Jones is served by two women: 'The lovely blondes helped the great man. One to brandy, one to soda . . . Appeased, Jones leaned towards one as he pinched the other. "When are you going to seduce me?" His whisper was like tearing calico.' Later he asks a woman to pose for him: 'In a dress, naturally. In a low dress. No dress. No dress, naturally, I paint flesh and bone. Flesh and bone.'

Hercules Jones is a caricature of the painter Augustus John, one of the great bohemian figures of his time – a man famed for his sexual drive, his drinking and his painterly panache. A solicitor's son, he studied art at the Slade and rapidly established a reputation as a portrait painter. Dylan Thomas, whose portrait John painted, met John in 1935 – in the Fitzroy, a London pub – and a year later John introduced Dylan to Caitlin Macnamara (in the Wheatsheaf, another London pub). John, who liked to sleep with every girl he painted – including Caitlin – was jealous of Thomas's interest in Caitlin and knocked the poet down after an argument in a Carmarthen carpark. John then drove off with Caitlin. Next day Thomas arrived in Laugharne to make amends with Caitlin, whom he married in 1937. Augustus John was awarded the Order of Merit in 1942; ten years later he published his anecdotal autobiography *Chiaroscura*.

JUPIEN

Marcel Proust, *Remembrance of Things Past* (1913–27)

Albert Le Cuziat

In the lodger's wing of the Hôtel de Guermantes, in Paris, Jupien – an ex-tailor with a job in a Government office – has a shop where his niece operates as a seamstress. At first Marcel, the narrator, has an unfavourable impression of Jupien (in the C.K. Scott Moncrieff/Terence Kilmartin translation): 'From a few feet away, entirely destroying the effect that his plump cheeks and florid complexion would otherwise have produced, his eyes, brimming with a compassionate, mournful, dreamy gaze, led one to suppose that he was seriously ill or had just suffered a great bereavement. Not only was this not so, but as soon as he spoke (quite perfectly as it happened) he was inclined rather to be cold and mocking.' Soon the narrator observes in Jupien 'a rare intelligence, one of the most spontaneously literary that it has been my privilege to come across' and realizes that Jupien is 'kind and sympathetic [with] the most delicate and the most generous feelings.' Jupien meets the wealthy homosexual BARON DE CHARLUS and, through him, makes contact with the high society associated with the exalted Guermantes family. During the First World War, Marcel comes across a male brothel in Paris and discovers that it is run by Jupien largely to cater for the sadomasochistic urges of Charlus. When Charlus declines in health, Jupien remains his devoted friend and Marcel judges the ex-tailor turned brothel-keeper a man of 'intelligence and sensibility'.

Albert Le Cuziat – identified as the original of Jupien by George D. Painter – came to Paris from Brittany at the age of sixteen, and got a job as third footman to a Polish prince. Then Prince Constantin Radziwill (the original of Proust's Prince de Guermantes) was so impressed by Albert that he made him his first footman. Subsequently, Albert became footman to various members of the French aristocracy and developed such an exhaustive knowledge of their ways that Proust – who met Albert in 1911 and called him 'my walking *Almanach de Gotha*' – consulted him on details of etiquette for his novel. In 1917 Albert, then thirty-six, gave notice to the Duc de Rohan and – with money and furniture provided by Proust – set up a male brothel at the Hôtel Marigny, 11 Rue de l'Arcade, Paris. Proust was a frequent visitor to Albert's brothel and this period is, according to Painter, 'perhaps the only truly deplorable episode' in Proust's life when he was reduced to 'a sterile intercourse with professional catamites. He was experimenting with evil . . . and testing his power to associate with it unscathed'.

Further reading:
George D. Painter, *Marcel Proust* (1959, 1965)

K

LIZA KALITINA
Ivan Turgenev, *Liza* (1859)

Countess Lambert (1821–83)

Further reading: David Magarshack, *Turgenev* (1954)

Russians responded enthusiastically to the spiritually pure heroine of Ivan Turgenev's *Liza* (also known as *A Nest of Gentlefolk*). Liza Kalitina seemed to symbolize all that was noble in the Russian character and she was promoted as an example to all Russian women. In the novel Liza Kalitina falls in love with Lavretsky but sacrifices her own happiness because he is a married man. Rather than impinge further on his life she retreats to a convent in one of the most remote districts of Russia. Liza's religious zeal is noted by Lavretsky at a critical stage in the story for he sees her at morning service: 'She prayed fervently; her eyes shone with a quiet light; quietly she bowed and lifted her head . . . Her face seemed to him to be joyous, and once more he felt softened, and he asked, for another's soul, rest – for his own, pardon.'

Turgenev based the character on his friend Countess Elizaveta Egorovna Lambert, three years his junior. She was the daughter of Count Kankrin, Nicholas I's finance minister, and the wife of Alexander II's aide-de-camp. A deeply religious woman, Countess Lambert used her exalted position and aristocratic connections to do charitable work. From 1856 to 1867 Turgenev corresponded with Countess Lambert and he was deeply impressed by her warm personality and the clarity of her religious convictions. She was delighted by *Liza* and wrote to tell Turgenev that the novel 'is the visionary work of the pagan who has not renounced the worship of Venus, but who already understands a stricter form of worship towards which the strivings of his sick and relenting soul are bearing him a little against his will.' In an epilogue to the novel Turgenev imagines a last meeting between the autobiographical Lavretsky and Liza who 'passed onwards steadily, with the quick but silent step of a nun, and did not look at him. Only an almost imperceptible tremor was seen to move the eyelashes of the eye which was visible to him.'

CHARLES FOSTER KANE
Film, *Citizen Kane* (1941, directed by Orson Welles)

William Randolph Hearst (1863–1951)

Further reading: W.A. Swanberg, *Citizen Hearst* (1961), Pauline Kael, Herman J. Mankiewicz and Orson Welles, *The Citizen Kane Book* (1971), Robert L. Carringer, *The Making of Citizen Kane* (1985)

Citizen Kane is often cited as among the best ten films ever made, sometimes described as a cinematic box of tricks. Written by Herman J. Mankiewicz, it charts the extraordinary career of an American millionaire, who runs newspapers and radio stations, runs for high office but fails at the polls because a rival exposes his secret love-nest with a singer, and who dies wealthy and surrounded by ostentation but in his heart believing he is unloved. The leading theme of the story is the old truth that money cannot buy happiness, but along the way other social and political evils are explored. The narrative is framed within the context of journalists trying to piece together the important elements in Kane's life after he has died, and *Citizen Kane* is very much concerned with the manner in which the realities of the world are presented for consumption by the mass media. At one point a correspondent cables Kane from Cuba: 'Food marvellous-girls delightful-stop-could send you prose poems about scenery but don't feel right spending your money-stop-there's no war in Cuba.' Kane cables back: 'You provide the prose poems – I'll provide the war.'

Kane was quite closely based on the life and times of William Randolph Hearst. He was born in San Francisco and educated at Harvard and inherited the *Examiner* from his father. (Kane's paper is the *Enquirer*.) He jazzed up the paper with yellow journalism and brilliant picture journalism, specializing in sensation, violence and scandal. After this success on the West Coast, he invaded New York in 1895, purchasing the ailing *Morning Journal* and turning it into a success. He tried to enter high office, twice failing to become mayor of New York (Kane tries for the state governorship) and serving two terms in the US

House of Representatives. He was unsuccessful in winning nomination for US president. Like Kane he built exotic and expensive castles – Hearst built San Simeon in California – Kane had Xanadu. He had a long-standing love affair with Marion Davies, whom he tried to promote to film stardom, which parallels Kane's attempts to turn Susan Alexander into an opera singer. From Havana, Frederick Remington sent Hearst a cable: 'Everything is quiet. There is no trouble here. There will be no war. I wish to return.' Hearst cabled this answer: 'Please remain. You furnish the pictures and I'll furnish the war.'

KARMAZINOV

Fyodor Dostoevsky, *The Devils* (1871–72)

Ivan Turgenev (1818–83)

Dostoevsky's *The Devils* – also known as *The Possessed* – contains a bitter attack on his great Russian literary contemporary Ivan Turgenev. In the course of the novel the radical Peter Verkhovensky meets Karmazinov whose interest in political unrest is consistent with his virulently anti-Russian character. Like Turgenev, Karmazinov is a literary celebrity; when he receives Peter, he is wearing 'a kind of indoor wadded jacket with little mother-of-pearl buttons, but it was very short which was not becoming to his rather prominent belly and his firmly rounded thighs'. With aristocratic air and 'shrill voice' he announces his atheism to Peter and adds 'Russia, as she is now, has no future. I've become a German and I'm proud of it.' Dostoevsky had personal as well as political reasons for his dislike of Turgenev though he had admired him enormously when the two first met in 1845. Subsequently Dostoevsky turned to Turgenev in 1865 when he had lost all his money at the Wiesbaden roulette tables; he asked Turgenev for one hundred thalers and was given fifty thalers (which he paid back eleven years later). In 1867 Dostoevsky was in Germany again, still losing money through his gambling, and decided to call on Turgenev in Baden-Baden. Dostoevsky was determined to have an emotional showdown with his fellow author whose moral outlook he despised and whose work he now distrusted. Dostoevsky's verbal assault on Turgenev – for living outside Russia and thus attacking the homeland, in *Smoke* (1867), from a safe distance – provoked Turgenev into declaring that he felt 'more a German than a Russian'. This attitude was anathema to Dostoevsky who then pilloried Turgenev as the superficial and self-seeking Karmazinov. Turgenev did not take Dostoevsky's portrait seriously, regarding him as 'non compos mentis' and 'a madman'.

Further reading: David Magarshack, *Turgenev* (1954), Ivan Turgenev, *Literary Reminiscences and Autobiographical Fragments* translated by David Magarshack (1985)

KATH

Joe Orton, *Entertaining Mr Sloane* (1964)

Elsie Orton (1904–66)

Though it was praised by Sir Terence Rattigan, Joe Orton's *Entertaining Mr Sloane* was something of a shock to the critics who saw the first production at London's New Arts Theatre (6 May 1964). 'I feel as if snakes had been writhing round my feet', commented the *Daily Telegraph* reviewer. After he was murdered by his boyfriend Kenneth Halliwell, in 1967, Orton was acknowledged as one of the wittiest dramatists since Wilde. He was a homosexual with a boyish charm: the character of Sloane, with his arrogance and black-leather gear, is an autobiographical portrait of the author as a young rogue.

In the play Sloane comes to a 'house in the midst of a rubbish dump' where he is welcomed by his landlady Kath, a forty-one-year-old woman who wants to be his surrogate mother and sexually active mistress. Kath is presented as a dotty woman, with fantasies of gentility and phrases lifted from her light reading. 'Dont be embarrassed, Mr Sloane,' she tells her lodger after taking off his trousers. 'I'd the upbringing a nun would envy and that's the truth. Until I was fifteen I was more familiar with Africa than my own body. That's why I'm so pliable.' She also makes a comic spectacle of herself by admitting 'My teeth, since you mentioned the subject, Mr Sloane, are in the kitchen in Stergene. Usually I allow a good soak overnight.'

When Orton's sister Leonie Barnett saw Beryl Reid act the part of Kath in the 1975 Royal Court revival of *Entertaining Mr Sloane* she said: 'That's my mum. That's her. It's like seeing a ghost.' Quoting this

Further reading: John Lahr, *Prick Up Your Ears* (1978)

observation in his biography of Orton, John Lahr adds 'Even the plot of [the play] was built around a family memory of Elsie Orton taking in a much-despised lodger.' Elsie, who really did keep her dentures in bleach, married in 1931 and dominated her eight-stone husband (who features as Kemp in the play). She told her daughter Marilyn that she 'hated sex' but dressed garishly, enjoyed a good drink and sing-song at her local, and could be verbally flirtatious. Like Kath she was an eccentric with various pretentions. She doted on Orton and was the only mother on the Saffron Lane Estates, Leicester, to send her son to a private school (Clark's College). Orton's dramatic treatment of Kath is, characteristically, excessive: in the play she seduces Sloane, becomes pregnant, and ends up sharing him with her brother Ed.

ALROY KEAR

W. Somerset Maugham, *Cakes and Ale* (1930)

Hugh Walpole (1884–1941)

Further reading: Robin Maugham, *Somerset and All the Maughams* (1966), Ted Walker, *Maugham* (1980), Rupert Hart Davis, *Hugh Walpole* (1952)

The character Alroy Kear, in Somerset Maugham's *Cakes and Ale*, has come to epitomize the literary opportunist. Kear is intent on succeeding Edward Driffield (actually Thomas Hardy) as the Grand Old Man of English letters and intends, with the blessing of the second Mrs Driffield, to write the definitive life of the dead novelist by way of furthering his own career. Early in the novel Maugham takes Kear to task: 'His career might well have served as a model for any young man entering upon the pursuit of literature. I could think of no one among my contemporaries who had achieved so considerable a position on so little talent . . . It sounds a little brutal to say that when he had got all he could get from people he dropped them . . . He could use a man very shabbily without afterward bearing him the slightest ill-will.'

Before publication, *Cakes and Ale* was submitted to the Book Society and duly seen by Hugh Walpole, chairman of the selection committee. He instantly realized that Kear was a vicious portrait of himself and attempted, unsuccessfully, to stop publication of the book. He also wrote a letter of protest to Maugham who replied 'I certainly never intended Alroy Kear to be a portrait of you.' Walpole was distraught; Virginia Woolf notes, in her diary for November 1930, that she had seen Walpole writhing under Maugham's 'wincing & ridiculous & flaying alive story'. Walpole's bubble was effectively burst and he was never able to lord it over English letters again. Maugham's malice provoked some counterattacks: in 1931 the American writer Elinor Mordaunt published (under the pseudonym A. Riposte) *Gin and Bitters* in which Leverson Hurle (i.e. Maugham) is likened to 'a sick monkey'; and Walpole himself included a Maughamish novelist, Somerset Ball, in his *Captain Nicholas: A Modern Comedy* (1934).

SHIRLEY KEELDAR

Charlotte Brontë, *Shirley* (1849)

Emily Brontë (1818–48)

Further reading: Terry Eagleton, *Myths of Power* (1975), Phyllis Bentley, *The Brontës and Their World* (1969)

Shirley takes place in Yorkshire during the Napoleonic wars. The wool industry is suffering severely from lack of exports. Robert Gérard attempts to modernize his production by means of machinery and is threatened by Luddites. He needs capital and therefore proposes marriage to Shirley Keeldar, who has wealth. He is really loved by Caroline Helstone. Shirley rejects him, and he marries Caroline, after the end of the war terminates his business difficulties. Shirley marries Louis, Robert's brother, who – like her – is a proud and headstrong person with judgement of his own. Shirley is described as a handsome young woman, 'agreeable to the eye. Her height and shape were not unlike Miss Helstone's; perhaps in stature she might have the advantage by an inch or two. She was gracefully made, and her face, too, possessed a charm as well described by the word grace as any other. It was pale naturally, but intelligent, and of varied expression . . . Clear and dark were the characteristics of her aspect as to colour. Her face and brow were clear, her eyes of the darkest gray . . . and her hair of the darkest brown. Her features were distinguished . . . mobile they were, and speaking; but their changes were not to be understood nor their language interpreted all at once.'

Charlotte is describing her sister Emily, who together with Anne, made up that trio of extraordinary genius. Emily was a strong-willed young woman of tremendous and original imagination. Emily survived the rigours of Cowan Bridge school (see BROCKLEHURST) and became a governess in Halifax, went to the Heger Pensionat in Brussels and after 1845 devoted herself to writing. *Wuthering Heights* (1847) was her masterpiece and she wrote several outstanding poems. Her last poem opens: 'No coward soul is mine/No trembler in the world's storm-troubled sphere/I see heaven's glories shine,/And faith shines equal, arming me from fear.' She died of consumption, worsened by a cold caught at her brother Branwell's funeral, in September 1848.

KEITH OF RAVELSTONE

Wyndham Lewis, *The Apes of God* (1930)

Edwin Muir (1887–1959)

Further reading:
Alan Bold (ed.), *The Letters of Hugh MacDiarmid* (1984)

The satirical point of Wyndham Lewis's satirical masterpiece *The Apes of God* is to expose as 'the Apes of God', the London literati of the 1920s, those 'monied middleclass descendents of Victorian literary splendour'. To reveal the aesthetic Apes in their domestic environment, the innocent Dan Boleyn is taken, by Horace Zagreus, on a grand tour. At the home of Lionel Kein – actually Stephen Hudson (1869–1944), the novelist and translator – Zagreus points out Keith of Ravelstone, one of Kein's comrades. Lewis's description of Keith is extremely malicious. 'He is as you see,' Zagreus tells Dan, 'a very earnest, rather melancholy freckled little being – whose dossier is that, come into civilization from amid the gillies and haggises of Goy or Arran, living in poverty, he fell in with that massive, elderly Scottish lady next to him – that is his wife. She opened her jaws and swallowed him comfortably. There he was once more inside a woman, as it were – tucked up in her old tummy . . . And there in the remoter capitals of Europe the happy pair remained for some time, in erotic-maternal trance no doubt – the speckled foetus acquiring the German alphabet, learning to lisp Italian Greek and Portuguese . . . Keithie is a journalist, you must know, and develops a great deal of Scottish earnestness with traditional facility upon the slightest provocation. He is a "critic" you must know, too.'

Edwin Muir, the original of Keith of Ravelstone, was born on his father's rented farm in Orkney. In 1901 the Muir family settled in Glasgow, and Edwin was devastated by a series of family tragedies and by his experience of industrial squalor. Fortunately for him, Muir married (in 1918) Willa Anderson, a classics graduate of St Andrews, then working as a lecturer in a women's college in London. Muir was thirty-two, with no academic qualifications and little money, yet with Willa he was to recover his mental stability and sense of purpose: 'My marriage was the most fortunate event in my life', he said. In London Muir got a part-time job with the *New Age*, and by 1921 the Muirs were ready to leave London to spend four years abroad: in Czechoslovakia, Germany, Italy and Austria. Muir began to write the poems that established his reputation; back in London, in 1925, he and Willa worked at German translations, producing the definitive versions of the novels of Kafka. Recognized as a man of literary substance, Muir delivered the 1955–6 Charles Eliot Norton lectures at Harvard and subsequently settled in Swaffham Prior, outside Cambridge. Willa, a formidable woman, died in 1970.

KEMP

Joe Orton, *Entertaining Mr Sloane* (1964)

William Orton (1905–78)

Further reading:
John Lahr, *Prick Up Your Ears* (1978)

In *Entertaining Mr Sloane* the central character – an autobiographical projection of Orton himself – comes to a house in London where he is welcomed by his landlady Kath. Although Kath wants to be both surrogate mother and mistress to Sloane, her father, Kemp, is immediately suspicious of the lodger. Myopic and muddled, Kemp is sure he has met Sloane before. During the first Act, Kemp pulls Sloane towards him, scrutinizes him, then tells him: 'We have met before! I knew we had . . . I could still identify you.' As the play unfolds it is revealed that Sloane has killed a photographer who took pornographic pictures of him and that his murder victim was once Kemp's boss. As Kemp is now a threat to Sloane he is ripe for removal; Sloane constantly abuses him then kicks him to death at the end of Act Two.

Before his abrupt exit from the play, Kemp – the 'Dadda' – is seen as a wearisome old man. Sloane tells Ed, Kemp's son, 'I've nothing against him. But he's lived so long, he's more like an old bird than a bloke. How is it such a father has such a son? A mystery.' Kemp is a pathetic figure who seems a burden on everybody who knows him. He was, as John Lahr points out in *Prick Up Your Ears*, modelled on Joe Orton's father William. Orton's brother Douglas summed up the myopic William Orton by saying 'Dad was always an old man'.

William Orton found work in Leicester as a 'puller-over' in the boot and shoe trade. Later he took a job as a gardener for the Leicester Council, lost a finger pruning the trees of a public park but received no compensation. He married Elsie in 1931, settled with her on the Saffron Lane Estates and amused himself by getting away to his park garden. According to Lahr's biography of Orton, the dramatist perceived his eight-stone father as a moral and physical weakling. William was no match for Elsie – Kath in *Entertaining Mr Sloane* – who was taller and heavier than him. 'You look like a mouse!' Elsie would say to William: 'You eat like a bloody mouse!' Orton inherited this attitude. When his sister Leonie phoned him in 1966 to say that William had fractured his skull in a car accident, Orton said 'That won't make any difference to his brain.' When Joe Orton was murdered by his boyfriend Kenneth Halliwell, in 1967, William heard the news in an old people's home. John Lahr says: 'William wanted only one thing in life: a greenhouse. He never got it.'

JACK KETCH

'Punch and Judy' traditional British puppet entertainment

Jack Ketch (died 1686)

Further reading: Thomas Babington Macaulay, *History of England* (1861), Charles Whitehead, *The Autobiography of Jack Ketch* (1834)

Ketch became a generic name for the public hangman and appeared in *Punch and Judy* in the opening years of the 18th century. In this play he is fooled by Mr Punch, who claims he does not know how to put his head in the noose. When Ketch demonstrates the method, Punch hangs him instead.

John Ketch was appointed public executioner in 1663 and first appears in print in a broadside of December 1672, *The Plotters Ballad: Being Jack Ketch's Incomparable Receipt for the Cure of Traytorous Recusants and Wholesome Physick for a Popish Contagion*. Among his most famous victims were William, Lord Russell, executed for his alleged part in the Rye House Plot in 1683, and the Duke of Monmouth, executed after his part in the 'Monmouth rebellion' against James II in 1685. Ketch's beheading of Russell was typically clumsy and in a pamphlet published after the event, Ketch asserted that the victim did not 'dispose himself as was most suitable' and that he was in consequence interrupted in taking proper aim with his axe. When Monmouth was about to be executed he handed Ketch money and said: 'Here are six guineas for you. Do not hack me as you did my Lord Russell.' Monmouth felt the axe and said it was not sharp enough. Evidently unnerved by this, Ketch's first blow inflicted only a slight wound. Monmouth struggled to his feet, looked reproachfully at Ketch, and put his head on the block once more. Several subsequent strokes of the axe were badly aimed and the crowd began to shout angrily at Ketch, who threw down his axe, claiming: 'I cannot do it! My heart fails me!' The Sheriff said: 'Take up the axe, man!' and the crowd called: 'Fling him over the rails!' Ketch finished the job with two further strokes, but even so a knife had to be used finally to sever the head. The crowd was so angry that Ketch had to leave the scene strongly guarded. A year later he was turned out of his office for insulting one of the sheriffs and succeeded by a butcher named Rose. When Rose himself was hanged at Tyburn, Ketch regained his job. He died in 1686.

KING

Rudyard Kipling, *Stalky & Co* (1899)

In Rudyard Kipling's Stalky stories, the public schoolboy triumvirate of Stalky, M'Turk and Beetle (Kipling) take a malicious delight in embarrassing the rigidly conventional housemaster King. 'In Ambush', for example, develops as a struggle between Stalky & Co and King, who is humiliated at being taken for a poacher by Colonel Dabney. King has a conviction that boys are innately subversive and tries to deal with them with sarcasm and moral outbursts: 'Mr King desired no buts, nor was he interested in Stalky's evasions. They, on the other hand, might be interested in his poor views. Boys who crept – who sneaked – who lurked – out of bounds . . . Such boys, scabrous boys, moral lepers – the current of his words was carrying King off his feet – evil-speakers, liars, slow-bellies – yea, incipient drunkards . . . He was merely working up to a peroration, and the boys knew it'.

When Kipling was a public schoolboy – at the United Services College, Westward Ho!, Bideford, north Devon, from 1878–82 – William Carr Crofts, the original of King, taught him Latin and English literature. Educated at Oxford, Crofts was – according to Kipling's *Something of Myself* (1937) – 'a rowing-man of splendid physique, and a scholar who lived in secret hope of translating Theocritus worthily. He had a violent temper . . . and a gift of schoolmaster's "sarcasm" which must have been a relief to him and was certainly a treasure-trove to me . . . Under him I came to feel that words could be used as weapons.' As the only boy in the United Services College to wear glasses, Kipling was nicknamed 'Gig-lamps' or 'Gigger' and Crofts improved on this by calling Kipling 'Gigadibs, the literary man' and throwing a copy of Browning's *Men and Women* at his head so he could discover the source of the quotation. Charles Carrington says 'Of all Kipling's teachers, Crofts taught him most, by damping down his exuberance, by forcing him to study the classical writers, by ridiculing his more pretentious experiments in verse.' Kipling's indifference to hostile criticism was (suggests Carrington) a lesson he learned from Crofts, who was ruder than any literary commentators could be. After leaving the United Services College and going to Lahore (as sub-editor on the *Civil & Military Gazette*) Kipling kept up a correspondence with Crofts, who preserved the letters.

William Carr Crofts (1846–1912)

Further reading: Charles Carrington, *Rudyard Kipling* (1955)

KING OF SIAM

Richard Rodgers and Oscar Hammerstein
Operetta, *The King and I* (1956)

Mongkut (1804–68)

Further reading: W.A.R. Wood, *A History of Siam* (1926)

In 1862 an extraordinary English woman, Anna Leonowens, arrived in Bangkok. She had come to teach the sixty-seven children of the King of Siam. It is one of the accidents of history that she was also to teach the King himself some of the fundamental principles of civilization, as far as it may be understood that the Western world is 'civilized'. She wrote a fascinating autobiography which, in its turn, was to teach the West a great deal about what was then a little-known and even less understood part of the world. It was made into a successful film in 1946, with Rex Harrison as the King of Siam and Irene Dunne as Anna. It was turned into a stage musical and later filmed with Yul Brynner and Deborah Kerr in 1956.

Rarely can an Eastern potentate have become so widely known to the Western world, and rarely must the history of a public figure have become so distorted in its transformations – book, film and musical entertainment. Mongkut was even more extraordinary a character than the role associated with Yul Brynner has suggested. He was one of several royal children of the Siamese King. He married young and had two children. It was the tradition that at the age of twenty he became a Bhuddist monk, which meant he was to live a celibate life. His father died and his elder brother became King. When he was forty-six his brother died, and so in 1851 Mongkut became King of Siam. As a King he had a harem, estimated to number some three thousand women. He reigned seventeen years and fathered eighty-two children, sixty-six of whom survived him when he died in 1868. One of his most far-reaching reforms was his allowing his concubines to return to their families if they wished, even to marry other men if they wanted. This did not apply to the mothers of his children.

SIR IVOR KING
Nancy Mitford, *Pigeon Pie* (1940)

Mark Ogilvie-Grant
1905–69

Further reading: Harold Acton, *Nancy Mitford – A Memoir* (1975)

Pigeon Pie is the story of Sophia, who has a distaste for callow youths and fashionable balls, and longs to fulfil herself during the early years of the Second World War as a glamorous female spy. In the meantime, she works at a First Aid post. Among the characters she meets is a rather unusual Air Raid Warden, known as the 'Wonderful Old Songster of Kew Green', who was the idol of the British race and was loved universally by music-lovers: 'In his heyday he had been most famous as a singer of those sexy ballads which were adored by our grandparents . . . He was unrivalled, too, in opera. The unique quality of his voice was the fact that it could reach higher and also lower notes than have ever been reached before . . .Ivor King was knighted at an early age, he made a large fortune, gained an unassailable position and the nickname . . . "The King of Song" . . . Among particular achievements he was the only man ever to sing the name part in the opera *Norma*, the script of which had been re-written especially for him, and re-named *Norman*.' He had toured the world in what seemed like royal progresses: 'In remote parts of Africa the natives often mistook him for Queen Victoria's husband . . . he had done more towards welding the Empire in the cultural sphere than any other individual. Quite bald, although with a marvellous collection of wigs, and finally quite toothless, he still maintained a gallant fight against old age . . . "She wore a wreath of roses the day that first we met", he chanted . . . It was what the most vulgar of the many generations which had passed over his head would call his signature tune, and he sang it in a piercing soprano. Sophia poured out the tea, and asked after his Lesbian irises. "They were not what they seemed. Wretched things. I brought the roots all the way from Lesbos . . . and when they came up, what were they? Mere pansies. Too mortifying. And now I'm the Air Raid Warden for Kew Gardens, in a tin hat. And it will be years before I visit Greece again."'

This is Mark Ogilvie-Grant, friend of the Mitfords and Evelyn Waugh, cousin of the Countess of Seafield. He lived in Athens after 1945. His imitation of Dame Clara Butt singing *Land of Hope and Glory* was reputedly magnificent. This novel also contains a portrayal of Peter Rodd, to whom Nancy Mitford was married, as Rudolph Jocelyn (see BASIL SEAL).

COLONEL MIKE KIRBY
James Lee Barrett, Film, *The Green Berets*, based on the novel by Robin Moore, directed by John Wayne, and starring John Wayne (1968)

Colonel Charlie A. Beckwith

Further reading: Colonel Charlie A. Beckwith, *Delta Force* (1984)

The action of *The Green Berets*, in which John Wayne plays the ultimate Gung-ho role of Colonel Mike Kirby, concerns the intensive and extensive training given to two American army units prior to their service in the Indo-China War. In Britain the film did not get a good press, probably because of its unquestioning acceptance and support of the Johnson administration's Vietnam war policy, almost to the point of justifying the war on ideological grounds. In *The War Film* (1974), Ivan Butler commented that: 'Viewed away from partisan passion, the film appears no more and no less nauseating than the great majority of propaganda war pictures. The same bloody action scenes, the same loaded dialogue, the same contrived sentimental situations, the same dreadful soft-centred toughness. In fact, bearing in mind once more the climate of its time, it could be said that *The Green Berets* is a somewhat more courageous production than similar epics issued when all opposition is silenced or all public opinion in favour. At the very least, one can have little doubt as to its makers's sincerity.' This is true.

John Wayne based his portrayal of Colonel Mike Kirby on an American Colonel whom he greatly admired, Charlie A. Beckwith. Beckwith was a member of Special Forces. He was an exchange officer in the United Kingdom, serving the British SAS. The experience changed his life and came to dominate the rest of his military career. He came back to the USA with the ambition of starting an SAS-type unit in the US military but met considerable opposition from military bureaucracy. He served brilliantly and dangerously in the Vietnam war and was very badly wounded in the trunk while flying a helicopter. His life was considered beyond saving as he was losing so much blood, but when he heard doctors discussing this gloomy prognosis he grabbed one of them by the throat and demanded that his life be saved. He was successful in getting Delta Force created, which was the American answer to SAS, and he was given the task of rescuing the US Embassy staff who were hostages in Tehran during the Iranian revolution. His helicopters failed, and one of them crashed into a Hercules transport which was carrying fuel; thus eight of his soldiers were killed in the Iranian desert.

JULIUS KLESMER

George Eliot, *Daniel Deronda* (1876)

Anton Rubinstein
(1829–94)

Further reading:
Anton Rubenstein, *Autobiography* translated (1891)

The Jewish theme, so important to George Eliot's last novel *Daniel Deronda*, is initially orchestrated into the plot through the person of the musician Julius Klesmer: '"Ah, here comes Herr Klesmer," said Mrs Arrowpoint, rising: and presently bringing him to Gwendolen, she left them to a dialogue which was agreeable on both sides, Herr Klesmer being a felicitous combination of the German, the Slav and the Semite, with grand features, brown hair floating in artistic fashion, and brown eyes in spectacles.' Klesmer, who facetiously refers to himself as the Wandering Jew, has a devastating impact on all women who encounter him: his pupil Catherine Arrowpoint falls in love with him and Gwendolen Harleth, the self-assured heroine, confesses 'I feel crushed in his presence; my courage all oozes from me.'

The portrayal of the larger-than-life artistic temperament was inspired by Anton Rubinstein, the Russian pianist and composer. George Eliot was in Weimar in 1854 when Franz Liszt introduced her to Rubinstein whose opera *The Siberian Huntsmen* was about to be produced at the Court Theatre. Rubinstein, like Klesmer, rose from poverty to virtuosity and was supremely self-confident of his genius. When he came to London in May 1876 Mary Ann Evans (George Eliot) was in poor health and indisposed to interrupt her work on *Daniel Deronda* yet she accepted an invitation to have lunch with him. As her companion George Henry Lewes said, 'We shall so like to renew our acquaintance with Klesmer, whom we met at Weimar in '54.' On Rubinstein's return visit to London, the following year, Mary Ann was too ill to meet him but Lewes went to see him present duets from his opera *The Maccabees*.

DAVID KNIGHT

Zelda Fitzgerald, *Save Me the Waltz* (1932)

F. Scott Fitzgerald
(1896–1940)

Further reading:
Nancy Milford, *Zelda Fitzgerald* (1970)

After the 1920s, when they both ostentatiously and endlessly celebrated his literary success, F. Scott Fitzgerald and his wife Zelda found their married life coming apart in the 1930s. His alcoholism was a serious problem, and in February 1932 Zelda had her second serious breakdown which led to her being treated in the Phipps Psychiatric Clinic of Johns Hopkins Hospital, Baltimore. There, in six weeks, she wrote the first draft of *Save Me the Waltz*. In the novel Zelda is Alabama Beggs, southern belle and judge's daughter, who marries a successful painter, David Knight: 'So much she loved the man, so close and closer she felt herself that he became distorted in her vision . . . She felt the essence of herself pulled finer and smaller like those streams of spun glass that pull and stretch till there remains but a glimmering illusion . . . She felt herself very small and ecstatic. Alabama was in love.'

Zelda's hero was originally called Amory Blaine – the name Fitzgerald gave himself in his autobiographical *This Side of Paradise* (1920) – throughout the first draft. Fitzgerald was furious since he felt that Zelda was not only intruding into his personal life, but borrowing material he had reserved exclusively for use in *Tender Is The Night* (1939) – in which Scott and Zelda appear as Dick and Nicole Diver. After reading Zelda's draft, Fitzgerald wrote to Mildred Squires, the Phipps doctor to whom *Save Me the Waltz* is dedicated, in March 1932: 'Do you think that [my] turning up in a novel signed by my wife as a somewhat anemic portrait painter . . . could pass unnoticed . . . In short it puts me in an absurd and Zelda in a ridiculous position . . . My God, my books made her a legend and her single intention in this somewhat thin portrait is to make me a non-entity. That's why she sent the book directly to New York.'

Like Zelda, Alabama has ambitions for artistic recognition in her own right; unlike Zelda she has some success as a ballerina before an operation on her foot concludes her career. The description of Alabama and David invokes the intensity of the Fitzgeralds' existence: 'Alabama and David were proud of themselves and the baby, consciously affecting a vague *bouffant* casualness about the fifty thousand dollars they spent on two years' worth of polish for life's baroque façade. In reality, there is no materialist like the artist, asking back from life the double and the wastage and the cost on what he puts out in emotional usury.'

After the arguments over *Save Me the Waltz* the Fitzgeralds endured much personal distress; he died, of a heart attack, while she died in a fire at Highland Hospital, Asheville, North Carolina, in 1948.

LAURENCE KNIGHT

C.P. Snow, *Time of Hope* (1949), *Homecomings* (1956)

Francis Brett Young (1884–1954)

Further reading: Philip Snow, *Stranger and Brother* (1982)

A doctor's son, Francis Brett Young was born at Halesowen and educated at Birmingham University where he studied medicine. He worked as a ship's medical officer and as a doctor in Devon, before going to East Africa in the Medical Corps during the First World War. Before the war Young's novels *Deep Sea* (1914) and *The Dark Tower* (1914) established him as an outstanding young novelist. Later he had great success with *Portrait of Clare* (1927), *My Brother Jonathan* (1928) and *The House Under the Water* (1932). As he explains in his preface to Jessica Brett Young's biography *Francis Brett Young* (1962), C.P. Snow first met Young in 1938 when he went to Antibes for a holiday. The day of Snow's departure from Cambridge he read one of Young's books and found it 'much better than I had somehow assumed, or been told'. When the two men met, at the Antibes hotel they were both staying in, Snow was impressed by Young's intelligence and realized he was 'one of the most subtle and complex characters I have known. He looked, I often thought, like a colonial governor slightly down on his luck; not much like the GP he, following his father, had once been.' Snow and Young became good friends and kept in touch through correspondence when Young, and his wife Jessica, settled in South Africa.

Young appears as Laurence Knight, the clergyman father of Lewis Eliot's first wife Sheila, in two of the novels in C.P. Snow's *Strangers and Brothers* sequence – *Time of Hope* and *Homecomings*. Dealing with the period 1914–33 *Time of Hope* is thematically the first stage of Snow's narrative. Shortly after meeting Sheila, Lewis Eliot is taken to her home to meet her parents. When he arrives he is told that Laurence Knight is upstairs polishing a sermon. When Knight approaches the drawing-room there is an air of expectation: 'Mr Knight entered with an exaggeratedly languid step. He was tall, massive, with a bay-window of a stomach that began as far up as his lower chest . . . He was, at first glance, a good deal of an actor, and he was indicating that the virtue had gone out of him . . . Throughout his entry, which he enjoyed to the full, he had paid no attention to me . . . but as he lay back with heavy lids drawn down he was observing me from the corner of an eye that was disturbingly sly and shrewd.'

MRS KNOX

Edith Oenone Somerville and Martin Ross, *Some Experiences of an Irish R.M.* (1899), *Further Experiences of an Irish R.M.* (1908) *In Mr Knox's Country* (1915)

Mrs Martin of Co. Galway

Major Sinclair Yeates, Resident Magistrate at Skebawn, in the west of Ireland, lodges at Shreelane, 'a tall, ugly house, of three storeys high,' where he is a tenant of Mr Florence McCarthy Knox. Soon after he has arrived, he is invited to dine with Mr Knox's grandmother, 'old Mrs Knox of Aussolas'. She receives him in the library: 'where she was seated by a roaring turf fire, which lit the room a good deal more effectively than the pair of candles that stood beside her in tall silver candlesticks. Ceaseless and implacable growls from under her chair indicated the presence of the woolly dog. She talked with confounding culture of the books that rose all round her to the ceiling; her evening dress was accomplished by means of an additional white shawl, rather dirtier than its congeners. I took her into dinner, she quoted Virgil to me; and in the same breath screeched an objuration at a being whose matted head rose suddenly into view from behind an ancient Chinese screen . . . Dinner was as incongruous as everything else. Detestable soup in a splendid old silver tureen . . . a perfect salmon, perfectly cooked, on a chipped kitchen dish . . . sherry that . . . would burn the shell off an egg; and a bottle of port, draped in immemorial cobwebs, wan with age, and probably priceless.' Old Mrs Knox's conversation is flowing and full of literary and learned allusions. This is a portrait of Martin Ross's mother, who was born Violet Martin of Ross, and took her surname from her mother and the place of her origin as her *nom de plume*. Mrs Martin had a classical education and as a youth had translated into heroic couplets in English a poem composed in Latin by Lord Wellesley, the Viceroy of Ireland. A feature of the castle at Aussolas is a seat in the garden sheltered by laurels, which the chatelaine would use when hiding from the cook. In Mrs Martin's garden in Ross was a similar seat. When Major Yeates's bride, Philippa, first meets Mrs Knox she is invited to breakfast at Aussolas, where family prayers are interrupted readily when the passing hunt scent a fox. This incident occurred at the Martins' house in Ross, when family devotions were abandoned when the hunt came by in full cry. The story of the great gale at Shreelane, when the entire household shelter in the kitchen fearing the house would blow down, and narrated by Mrs Knox, refers to the Big Wind of 1839, and it was Martin's grandfather who sheltered his family in this way in their house at Ross.

Further reading:
Martin Ross, *Some Irish Yesterdays* (1906), *Strayaways* (1920)

KURTZ

Joseph Conrad, *Heart of Darkness* (1902)

Georges Antoine Klein
(died 1890)

Heart of Darkness is the story, narrated by Captain Marlow, of his adventures on a journey into the interior of the Congo to bring back an agent of a Continental trading company who was 'a first class agent . . . a very remarkable person' who was in charge of a distant trading post, 'a very important one, in the true ivory-country' who 'sends in as much ivory as all the others put together'. Marlow's journey takes on the nature of a nightmare. Information about the character and situation of Kurtz is assembled piece by piece, as the rescue party progresses up the river deeper into the jungle. The river-boat is attacked and several of the crew are killed by savages. After the dead have been buried they proceed and meet a European who has known Kurtz for a couple of years. He is living in the jungle almost like an emperor, ruling over his disciples, the local natives. Kurtz exerts his authority with barbaric rituals, including impaling human heads on posts. When they finally find Kurtz he is ill and carried in a stretcher. He is bald and very tall, as well as being physically emaciated. Kurtz is regarded as a universal genius, but to Marlow he seems insane and 'hollow at the core'. When Marlow tries to persuade him to return with them, Kurtz claims that he is on the threshold of 'immense plans' which would now be lost forever. To Marlow he seems rational, but his soul was mad. Kurtz is carried back to the river-boat for the two hundred mile journey back. The party leave amid scenes of violence and murder, and many native followers of Kurtz die. Kurtz tells Marlow his plans for the future, but realizes that he is dying. He says: 'The horror! The horror!' as he seems to glimpse life-after-death. Later that night one of the servants announces: 'Mistah Kurtz – he dead'.

When Conrad was thirty-three, he had been sent on the steamer *Roi des Belges* to Stanley Falls to bring back the trading agent Georges Antoine Klein, who was very ill. Klein died on the return journey. Conrad described *Heart of Darkness* as 'experience pushed a little (and only very little) beyond the actual facts of the case'. The story was used as the basis of Francis Ford Coppola's film *Apocalypse Now* (1979), in which Marlon Brando is a demented American officer who has to be eliminated as he is fighting his own renegade war in Vietnam.

Further reading:
Bernard C. Meyer, *Joseph Conrad – A Psychoanalytic Biography* (1967)

L

LADY OF QUALITY

Tobias Smollet, *The Adventure of Peregrine Pickle* (1751)

Frances Anne Vane (née Hawes), Viscountess Vane (1713–88)

Further reading: Lewis Melville, *The Life and Letters of Tobias Smollett* (1926) *Laura* (Petrarch)

It was the inclusion of the 'Memoirs of a Lady of Quality' which made *Peregrine Pickle* such a sensation when it was first published. The Memoirs are a catalogue of amorous activity, indiscretion, intrigue and infidelity which today read like a parody of eighteenth-century picaresque narrative. She was, she tells Peregrine, 'the only child of a man of good fortune, who indulged me, in my infancy, with all the tenderness of paternal affection . . . and sent me to a private school . . . carried me to all the places of public diversion, the court itself not excepted; and indulgence that flattered my love of pleasure . . . and encouraged those ideas of vanity and ambition, which spring up so early in the human mind'. She hopes that these memoirs will enable others to perceive: 'that howsoever my head may have erred, my heart hath always been uncorrupted, and that I have been unhappy, *because I loved and was a woman*'.

These are the memoirs of Viscountess Vane, nicknamed 'Lady Fanny'. In 1732 she married Lord William Douglas, who died in 1734. The next year she married William, Second Viscount Vane, and then embarked on her celebrated career of gambling and profligacy. Lord Vane was reputedly impotent, and so she left him. He advertised a reward of £100 for her discovery, in the words of Lord Egmont, as if 'he had lost some favourite spaniel bitch'. The advertisement, in the *Daily Journal* was quite specific: 'She is about 22 Years of Age, tall, well-shaped, has light brown Hair, is fair complexioned, and has her upper Teeth placed in an irregular manner . . .' A story circulated that Lord Vane found her reading *Peregrine Pickle*, which he craftily replaced with *The Practice of Piety*. She retorted: 'Nay, let our reformation go hand in hand, I beseech you; when you, my Lord, practice the Whole Duty of Man, then I'll read the Practice of Piety.' Lady Mary Wortley Montagu praised her patriotism: '. . . though she does not pique herself upon fidelity to any one man . . . she boasts that she has always been true to her nation, and notwithstanding foreign attacks, has always reserved her charms for the use of her own countrymen'. She was notoriously the lover of Lord Berkeley and others of the aristocracy, and was a favourite with the officer class. It was rumoured she followed the Brigade of Guards to Ghent in 1742, and brazenly walked about in the evenings with an officer on each side of her. Her husband unsuccessfully tried to get her back. From 1768 she lived in London as a permanent invalid.

CLAUDE LANTIER

Emile Zola, *L'Oeuvre* (1886)

Paul Cézanne (1839-1906), **Eduard Manet** (1832–83)

Further reading: E.A. Vizetelly, *Emile Zola – Novelist and Reformer* (1904)

Auguste Lantier is the lover of Gervaise Macquart in Zola's novel *L'Assommoir*. They have three sons, among them, Claude, the hero of *L'Oeuvre*. It deals with the career of the early Impressionist painter, Claude Lantier. He inherits money and becomes an artist in Paris. His fine painting, *Plein Air*, is exhibited at the *Salon des refusés*, instituted in 1863 at the express order of the Emperor Napoleon III, after the scandal and protests at the number of works rejected by the French Royal Academy, where among its fellows are works by Manet, Boudin, Fantin-Latour, Jongkind, Pissaro, Whistler and Cèzanne. His revolutionary style and technique arouses derision, but brings into being a new school of painting, the *Ecole de plein air*. His devotion to painting dominates his entire life, and he dissipates his fortune, and sacrifices his family to art. Eventually his own creative powers fail, and, realizing that he can no longer live up to the level of his own aesthetic theories, he commits suicide.

Claude Lantier is an amalgam of Manet and Cèzanne. Manet's wealthy middle-class father allowed his son to study painting under Thomas Couture, but he reacted strongly against the academic style, and made his debut as a revolutionary of a new style with the *Absinthe Drinker* in 1859. His technique was to work straight from the model and achieve effects from the opposition of light and shade, ignoring half-tone as much as possible, and using a narrow range of colours, in which black was important. He was frequently attacked by critics, but stoutly defended by his friend, Emile Zola. In spite of this he was always ambitious to be accepted by the establishment and resisted the idea of leading the 'Manet Gang'. Cézanne was the son of a banker and was at college with Zola, when studying law. He gave up law for painting in 1861, and lived in Paris until 1870. He associated with Pissaro, and contributed to the first Impressionist exhibition in 1874. His paintings often caused considerable scandal, both for their subject matter (which seemed erotic) and their technique. He worked slowly and laboriously, using colour to model the subject, which developed Impressionism towards the more solid. He was very sensitive to criticism and the publication of *L'Oeuvre* led to a breach with Zola, as he perceived it as a distortion of himself.

LARA

Lord Byron, *Lara, A Tale* (1814)

Lord Byron (1788–1824)

Further reading:
Peter Quennell (ed.) *Byron – A Portrait* (1950)

At the end of Byron's *The Corsair* Conrad disappears. He reappears in *Lara*, but he is disguised. He returns to the home of his ancestors in Spain, which he had left as a young man. His companion is a youthful page, Kaled, who is in reality the faithful Gulnare. Lara is usually taken as a portrait of a typically 'Byronic' hero – brooding, withdrawn and gloomy: ''tis quickly seen,/Whate'er he be, 'twas not what he had been:/That brow in furrow'd lines had fix'd at last,/And spake of passions, but of passions past:/The pride, but not the fire, of early days,/Coldness of mien, and carelessness of praise;/A high demeanour, and a glance that took/Their thoughts from others by a single look; And sarcastic levity of tongue,/The stinging of a heart the world hath stung.' He avoids contact with companions and neighbours, but is eventually caught up in a feud. He is killed and dies in the loyal Gulnare's arms.

Byron's sense that he has been abandoned by his father, Captain John Byron, a dissolute fortune-seeker, comes through very strongly in *Lara*: 'The chief of Lara is returned again:/And why had Lara cross'd the bounding main?/Left by his sire, too young such loss to know,/Lord of himself.' Lady Byron recounted that Byron once told her that Lara was based on a self portrait: 'There's more of me in that than any of them.' As he said this he shuddered and could not look her in the eye. He told Lady Blessington: 'I am so changeable, being everything by turns and nothing long – I am such a strange *mélange* of good and evil, that it would be difficult to describe me.' Reading his *Letters and Journals* after the poet died, Mary Shelley described the mercurial changes of character characteristic of Byron: 'the fascinating – faulty – childish – philosophical being – daring the world – docile to a private circle – impetuous and indolent – gloomy and yet more gay than any other'. As Byron wrote in *Lara*: 'they who saw him did not see in vain,/And once beheld, would ask of him again:/And those to whom he spoke remembered well,/And on the words, however light, would dwell:/None knew, nor how, nor why, but he entwined/Himself perforce around the hearer's mind.' (See also DON JUAN.)

LARA

Boris Pasternak, *Doctor Zhivago* (1958)

Olga Ivinskaia (born 1912)

In one of the poems appended to Boris Pasternak's novel *Doctor Zhivago* Zhivago reminds his beloved Lara 'You had come from Kursk to be a student': Olga Ivinskaia, daughter of a schoolteacher, spent her childhood in Kursk hence the reference.

Pasternak began to write his novel in 1945, a year before he knew Ivinskaia, but the creation of the character of Lara was a loving tribute to her. When Pasternak first met Ivinskaia, in the autumn of 1946, she ran the new-author's section of the Soviet periodical *Novyi mir* (New World). Like Pasternak, whose poetry she had worshipped for years, she had been married twice: her first husband had hanged himself in 1939, her

Further reading: Guy de Mallac, *Boris Pasternak – His Life and Art* (1983), Ronald Hingley, *Pasternak – A Biography* (1983)

second was killed in action in 1943 and she lived with her daughter Irina in a Moscow apartment. In 1949 Ivinskaia was arrested, confined in KGB headquarters (the Lubianka) and interrogated about Pasternak's alleged anti-Soviet activities. After a year in the Lubianka, during which time she refused to incriminate Pasternak, she was sent to a concentration camp.

Pasternak's reaction was to compose the description of Lara's disappearance in *Doctor Zhivago*: 'She vanished without a trace and probably died . . . in one of the innumerable mixed or women's concentration camps in the north.' Her misfortune was a form of torture for Pasternak who had heart attacks in 1950 and 1952. After the death of Stalin in 1953, Ivinskaia was released. Two months after Pasternak's death on 30 May 1960, however, Ivinskaia was arrested again and charged with currency offences relating to royalties from *Doctor Zhivago*, a novel banned in the Soviet Union. She was sentenced to eight years' imprisonment in Siberia but was released in 1964, whereupon she returned to Moscow to work as a translator.

SIR HUGO LATYMER

Noel Coward, *A Song at Twilight* (1966)

W. Somerset Maugham (1874–1965)

Further reading: Sheridan Morley, *A Talent to Amuse* (1969), Ted Walker, *Maugham* (1980)

Noel Coward's *A Song at Twilight* is the first in a trilogy of plays set in a Swiss hotel. Although he was sixty-seven and unwell at the time of the first production, Coward defied his doctors by himself taking the leading role of Sir Hugo Latymer. Described in the stage directions as 'an elderly writer of considerable eminence' Sir Hugo has kept a secret from his public. For twenty years he has played the part of the happily married man in order to conceal his homosexuality. The tension in the play is provided by the return of Sir Hugo's first female lover Carlotta who arrives unexpectedly to go over their early years together. Reminding him of the way he treated her as an experiment in heterosexuality, she reveals that she is in possession of homosexually incriminating letters written by Sir Hugo to the real love of his life.

When playing the part of Sir Hugo, Noel Coward made up to look like Somerset Maugham whose homosexuality was hidden from the public throughout his successful career. Maugham treated his wife Syrie abominably and had a well-deserved reputation for verbal cruelty and bitchiness. He admitted (to his cousin Robin) that his greatest mistake was that 'I tried to persuade myself that I was three-quarters normal and that only a quarter of me was queer – whereas really it was the other way round.' Nevertheless Maugham kept up the pretence of his heterosexuality and in his autobiographical writing referred in passing to his lover Gerald Haxton as 'a very useful companion'. Like Sir Hugo's lover in Coward's play, Gerald was an alcoholic; unlike Sir Hugo, though, Maugham did not abandon his lover but built his emotional life around Gerald. After Gerald's death, in 1944, Maugham was devastated. When Coward saw Maugham in 1965 he found him 'living out his last days in a desperate nightmare, poor beast. He rarely makes sense and, of course, he *knows* his mind has gone.'

LAURA

Francesco Petrarch, *Canzoniere – Rime in Vita e Morte di Madonna Laura* (1352)

Laura de Noves (1300–48)

Further reading: E.H. Wilkins, *Life of Petrarch* (1961)

Francesco di Petrarco was born in Arezzo in 1304, the son of a notary in Florence, who had to leave the court for political reasons and live in exile, where the poet was born. He studied law and classics and took orders. Then on 6 April 1327 occurred the most famous single event in his personal history – he saw the young woman with whom he fell passionately in love, and for whom he wrote one of the most overwhelmingly beautiful and influential sonnet sequences ever composed. The woman he saw in the church of St Clara at Avignon was already married. Petrarch kept her name a secret throughout his life, referring to her simply as 'Laura' in the sonnets. He poured forth his passionate love in verse addressed to his beloved, who could acknowledge his love but allow him no intimacy: 'It was the day when the sun's heavy rays/Grew pale in the pity of his suffering Lord/When I fell captive, lady, to the gaze/Of your fair eyes, fast bound in love's strong cord.' His love could not be measured: 'To be able to say how much you love, is to love but little.' His torment brought him its own tranquility: 'My soul has rest, sweet sigh! alone in thee.' On the evidence of the *canzoniere* this love filled the whole of his inner life, and Laura's death in the plague of 1348 brought both grief and yet a serene acceptance: 'A good death does honour to a whole life' and: 'You nightingale, whose strain so sweetly flows,/Mourning her ravish'd young or much loved mate,/A soothing charm o'er all the valleys throws/And skies, with notes well tuned to her sad state . . .' Petrarch claimed that this powerful platonic love alone inspired him to become a poet, and he attempted epic verse in Latin (*Africa*, unfinished (1338), which dealt with the second Punic War), twelve allegorical eclogues in which he emulated Virgil, and over sixty epistles in verse which are in the style of Horace. Mark Twain's opinion was not so romantic: 'Petrarch . . . the gentleman who loved another man's Laura, and lavished upon her all through life a love which was a clear waste of the raw material. It was sound sentiment, but bad judgement.' Laura was in fact the daughter of Audibert de Noves, and married Count Hugues de Sade, bearing him eleven children before dying of plague at the age of forty. Lord Byron's opinion was curt: 'Think you, if Laura had been Petrarch's wife,/He would have written sonnets all his life?'

LAURA

August Strindberg, *The Father* (1887)

Siri von Essen (died 1912)

Further reading:
E. Sprigge, *The Strange Life of August Strindberg* (1949)

Strindberg's play *The Father* is a grim account of a man being totally destroyed by the woman who has been his wife for twenty years. The Captain is an intelligent man, intent on his scientific research, and aware of the need to get his daughter away from the depressing atmosphere of his house. He wants her to become a teacher, but his wife Laura wants her to be a painter. Realizing that the only certainty of getting her own way is to have the Captain certified, she torments him by suggesting he is not the father of his daughter. She also tries to persuade the family doctor that the Captain's eccentricities are actually symptoms of insanity, and dwells on the fact that the Captain once wrote a letter expressing fears about his mental stability. Believing that 'Love between man and woman is war' (Michael Meyer's translation), Laura fights the battle to a catastrophic conclusion; the play ends with the Captain in a straitjacket and suffering a stroke.

In Stockholm, in 1875, Strindberg met a married couple who greatly admired his work: Baron Carl Gustaf Wrangel and his Finnish wife Siri von Essen. While continuing to be friendly with the Baron, Strindberg fell passionately in love with Siri. On the grounds that her desire to go on the stage compromised his social standing, the Baron agreed to divorce Siri (though he attended her marriage to Strindberg in 1877). Pregnant by Strindberg at the time of her marriage, Siri was distressed when the child died. However the marriage was reasonably successful until Strindberg's misogynist obsessions got the better of him. He was suspicious of Siri's motives in encouraging him to write to his family doctor about his mental health; he was convinced Siri was having affairs with men and with a young Danish girl; he was appalled when Siri wanted her two daughters to become actresses as he wanted them to train as nurses. By the spring of 1887, when he began to write *The Father*, the marriage was finished, and Strindberg recreated Siri as the frighteningly formidable Laura. Strindberg applied to Stockholm for a divorce, but could not get one while he and Siri were living abroad. Until the divorce was finalized in 1891 Strindberg and Siri lived apart in the same houses (in Lindau, Bavaria; then in Copenhagen). Siri died a few weeks before Strindberg who realized, in his final days, how much she had meant to him.

LAURENT

George Sand, *Elle et Lui* (1859)

George Sand's novel *Elle et Lui* is a classic study of the complex of personality failures which contribute to the strained relationship between a bohemian couple, Laurent and Thérèse. Laurent is a

Alfred de Musset (1810–57)

Further reading: Paul de Musset, *Biographie d'Alfred de Musset* (1877)

colourful, dandified, changeable young man, with a fatal weakness for drink, which takes the form of serious but periodic lapses. He suffers inner guilt from this inability to restrain himself. What seems on the surface an attractive and carefree quality, is – in contrast to Thérèse – in truth utter irresponsibility. Thérèse is a painter who works studiously at her canvasses as a means of bringing money into the house.

Laurent is a far-from-flattering portrayal of the French poet and dramatist Alfred de Musset, who met George Sand in 1833. The couple then proceeded to 'enjoy' what might with some considerable justice be described as a tempestuous relationship. He was born in Paris, studied law and medicine and finally discovered himself as a writer. He translated De Quincy's *Opium Eater* and achieved recognition with his first collection of poems, which were approved by Victor Hugo among others, in 1830. He tried stage plays and then wrote dramas for reading only. His output was considerable and his plays remarkable for character insight and the portrayal of love between the sexes with wit and sensitivity.

George Sand and Alfred de Musset set out to winter in Venice but split up and Alfred returned alone. He was beginning to take to drink in a big way, using a mixture of beer, brandy and absinthe. *Confessions d'un infant du siecle* (1835) is one of the key works of its time, a study of personal and political disillusionment. He continued to write extensively, was appointed Home Office Librarian in 1838, and was elected to the Academy in 1852. He died of heart failure, certainly hastened by drink.

His brother Paul de Musset was so angered by George Sand's *Elle et Lui* that he wrote a version of the story to defend Alfred, *Lui et Elle*, in which George Sand appears as Olympe, a vain but untalented songstress, and Alfred is a composer of genius named Edouard de Falconey. Louise Colet (see EMMA BOVARY) a later mistress of Alfred's, wrote yet a third version of the story, *Lui*. (see THÉRÈSE.)

ANNABEL LEE

Edgar Allan Poe, *'Annabel Lee'* (1849)

Virginia Poe (1822–47)

Further reading: Arthur Hobson Quinn, *Edgar Allan Poe* (1941)

Edgar Allan Poe's poem 'Annabel Lee' celebrates the author's love for a girl taken from him by death. 'She was a child and I was a child,/In this kingdom by the sea.' When Poe first met his cousin Virginia Eliza Clemm, in Baltimore in 1829, he was twenty and she was seven. At the time Poe was in need of some emotional stability and felt he had found it when he came to live with his widowed aunt Muddy (Maria Poet Clemm) and her two children Henry and Virginia. Little Virginia doted on her cousin Eddy and he not only treated her as a sister but called her 'Sis'. However in 1835, in a secret ceremony, Poe married the thirteen-year-old Virginia and then brought her and aunt Muddy to stay with him in Richmond where he worked on the *Messenger*. On 16 May 1836 a second, open, marriage was conducted in Richmond, the marriage bond recording the falsehood that Virginia was 'of the full age of twenty-one years'. Poe writes in 'Annabel Lee' that 'this maiden she lived with no other thought/Than to love and be loved by me'. It is unlikely that the marriage was ever consummated for Poe was fascinated by the notion of the eternally young female who was claimed by death.

He wrote, in *The Philosophy of Composition*, that 'the death, then, of a beautiful woman is, unquestionably, the most poetical topic in the world'; by 1841 Poe knew that Virginia was dying and by 1846 he had seen her coughing blood over her habitually white dress. Virginia's tubercular condition deteriorated and Poe wrote on 29 January 1847, the day before her death, 'My poor Virginia still lives, although failing fast and now suffering much pain.' She was buried in the graveyard of Fordham Dutch Reformed Church. When this cemetry was destroyed in 1875 Poe's biographer William F. Gill rescued the bones and eventually brought them to Baltimore where they were buried beside Poe: 'And so, all the night-tide, I lie down by the side/Of my darling – my darling – my life and my bride.'

ADRIAN LEVERKUHN

Thomas Mann, *Doctor Faustus* (1947)

Arnold Schoenberg (1874–1951)

'Leverkühn was not the first composer,' writes Thomas Mann in *Doctor Faustus*, 'who loved to put mysteries, magic formulas, and charms into his works.' Serenus Zeitblom, who narrates the novel, is friend and confidant to Adrian Leverkühn; when he becomes aware of the composer's 'intellectual passion for austere order' he begins to understand 'the idea of the daemonic'. Leverkühn's Faustian fantasy encourages him rigidly to systematize the principles of musical composition: 'you have four modes, each of which can be transposed to all the twelve notes of the chromatic scale, so that forty-eight different versions of the basic series may be used in a composition and whatever other variational diversions may present themselves'. Leverkühn sacrifices everything to his musical ambitions which are summed up in his last work, a symphonic cantata *The Lamentation of Dr Faustus* which the narrator calls 'the most frightful lament ever set up on this earth'.

Even before he had read the novel Arnold Schoenberg was furious that Mann had attributed to the fictional composer Leverkühn his own technical innovation – the twelve-note method of composition. Schoenberg even wrote to Mann with fabricated evidence suggesting that musicologists might credit Mann with the creation of the twelve-note technique. Mann replied, on 17 February 1948, 'In a novel that attempts to give a picture of an epoch as a whole, I have taken an enormously characteristic cultural phenomenon of the epoch and transferred it from its real author to a fictional artist, a representative martyr of the age.' He also appended a note to the novel acknowledging the twelve-note system to be 'the intellectual property' of Schoenberg.

Further reading:
H.H. Stuckenschmidt, *Arnold Schoenberg* (1943), R. Leibowitz, *Schoenberg and His School* (1949)

PROFESSOR LIDENBROCK

Jules Verne, *Journey to the Centre of the Earth* (1864)

Captain John Cleves Symmes, alias Captain Adam Seaborn, (died circa 1830)

In *Journey to the Centre of the Earth* the Danish Professor Lidenbrock and his nephew Axel go from Copenhagen to Iceland, on an expedition which takes them into the very heart of a dormant volcano, which in turn leads them into the dark hollow at the centre of the earth itself. The clue which sparked off this extraordinary adventure was found in a manuscript written in Old Norse by Arne Saknussemm, a sixteenth-century Icelandic alchemist: 'Go down into the crater of Sneffels Jokul over which the shadow of Scataris falls before the kalends of July, bold traveller, and you will arrive at the centre of the earth. I myself have done this . . .' Verne drew on several contemporary obsessions in writing *Journey to the Centre of the Earth*. The most important were the fascination and excitement aroused by recent attempts to explore the North Pole; the admiration for such geographers as Charles Sainte-Claire Deville (1818–81) who had explored the volcanoes at Stromboli and Teneriffe (and whom Verne got to know well in 1863); and the vogue for stories by Edgar Allan Poe, especially those of fantasy and discovery, such as '*MS Found in a Bottle*', '*The Unparallelled Adventures of One Hans Pfaal*' and the '*Narrative of Arthur Gordon Pym*'.

The man who really discovered this fertile field for the literary imagination, who opened up the territory and charted for later colonists, such as Poe and Verne and Rider Haggard, was Captain John Cleves Symmes, of the US Infantry, a hero of the War of 1812. He believed that the earth really was hollow in the middle, and that it was open at both Poles. Verne must have been aware of Symmes's ideas, for his character Dr Claebonny says: 'In recent times it has even been suggested that there are great chasms at the Poles; it is through these that there emerges the light which forms the Aurora, and you can get through them into the interior of the earth.' Symmes was convinced there were five concentric spheres, all with openings several thousand miles in diameter at the Poles. Symmes had lectured on these ideas since 1818. Symmes is the possible author, as 'Captain Adam Seaborn', of *Symzonia – Voyage of Discovery* (1820), about an expedition to the hollow centre of the earth. James McBride published *Symmes' Theory of Concentric Spheres* in 1826. There was an American expedition to the Antarctic in 1838, encouraged by a supporter of Symmes in Congress.

Further reading:
William Stanton, *The Great United States Exploring Expedition* (1975)

LILY OF KILLARNEY, THE COLLEEN BAWN

Gerald Griffin, *The Collegians* (1829)

Ellen Hanley (1803–19)

Further reading: Richard Fawkes, *Dion Boucicault – A Biography* (1979)

The Collegians is set in Killarney. Hardress Cregan, a young man of good family, is in love with a beautiful young girl, named Eily O'Connor, who comes from lower down the social scale. He is loved by a female of his own class. The Cregan family are hard up and Hardress's mother tries to pursuade him to marry the richer of his two loves. Eventually his mother connives at the murder of Eily, whom he has secretly married, so that he is free to marry the daughter of the wealthy landowner.

Griffin's novel was based on a real murder case, one of the sensations of its day – the murder of the pretty little sixteen-year-old peasant girl, Ellen Hanley. Ellen's body was found by the River Shannon at Limerick. She had been orphaned at the age of six and brought up by her uncle, a shoemaker. Her striking beauty had caught the eye of raffish Lieutenant John Scanlan, from Ballycahane Castle nearby. He promised to marry her and got her to run away from her uncle's house. With his boatman, Stephen Sullivan, dressed as a priest, a bogus marriage ceremony took place. Scanlan eventually tired of Ellen and resolved to rid himself of her encumbrance. She was last seen alive in the company of Scanlan and Sullivan at a farmhouse near the Shannon estuary. Her body was washed ashore weeks later. Scanlan and Sullivan seemed to vanish into thin air, but their crime assumed considerable political and social significance as it was perceived as an example of the brutal treatment of the Irish by the oppressive British. The Lieutenant was eventually discovered hiding in a pile of straw in his own castle. He was tried at Limerick, found guilty and hanged. Sullivan was found later, already in jail at Tralee, charged with uttering false banknotes. He confessed that he had murdered Ellen at Scanlan's request by beating her to death in his boat in the middle of the river. The trial at Limerick was attended by Griffin while he was a reporter for a local paper.

The novel was adapted for the stage by Dion Boucicault in 1860 and played to capacity audiences. His version, *Lily of Killarney*, has a happy ending – the attempted murder of Eily fails. This version of Ellen's story was used as the basis of the opera *Lily of Killarney*, music by Sir Julius Benedict and libretto by John Oxenham (1862), which contains the celebrated numbers 'The Moon has Raised her Lamp Above' and 'Eileen Mavourneen'.

LITTLE MISS MUFFET

Nursery rhyme, 'Little Miss Muffet'

Patience Muffet, daughter of Dr Thomas Muffet (1553–1604)

Further reading: Iona and Peter Opie; *The Oxford Book of Nursery Rhymes* (1951)

Little Miss Muffet is one of the most popular of all traditional English nursery rhymes: 'Little Miss Muffet/Sat on a tuffet,/Eating her curds and whey;/There came a big spider,/Who sat down beside her/And frightened Miss Muffet away.' Dr Thomas Muffet (or Moffet) was one of the most distinguished entomologists of his day, educated at Merchant Taylor's School and Trinity College, Cambridge. He studied at Basle and visited Italy, Spain and Germany 1579–82. He practised medicine at Ipswich and London, and published numerous works, including a lively one in verse: *The Silkworms and Their Flies* in 1599. He was patronized by Henry Herbert, Second Earl of Pembroke, who encouraged him to settle at Wilton in Wiltshire, for which constituency he was MP in 1597. Scientific works by Muffet were published several years after his death, an indication of his authority in his field.

It has been said that his 'admiration for spiders has never been surpassed' and even though no published record of the *Little Miss Muffet* verse earlier than 1805 has been located, his established interest in insects, his known exploitation of verse forms, and the fact that he had a daughter, Patience, as well as the well-attested durable oral traditions which exist in nursery and folk rhymes, would suggest Patience Muffet as an extremely likely original for the nursery rhyme. Other variants – *Little Mary Esther Sat upon a Tester – Little Miss Mopsey, Sat in the Shopsey* – and the similarities with such rhymes as *Little Tommy Tacket, Little Jack Horner*, as well as with singing games such as *Little Polly Sanders, Little Alice Sander*, all supply evidence of the long-standing existence and durable life of such tales. Miss Muffet probably originally sat on a grassy hillock, but tuffet has been glossed as a three-legged stool. Some versions have her sitting on a buffet, which is also a stool, especially in the North of England. The story may be associated ultimately with the cushion-dance custom, a May-Day ritual linked with mating and marriage, dating from pre-Christian times, which has someone sitting and waiting for something to happen – the appearance of the spider being a jocular parody of what should occur at the right moment.

LITTLE NELL

Charles Dickens, *The Old Curiosity Shop* (1841)

Mary Scott Hogarth (1819–37)

Further reading: Edgar Johnson, *Charles Dickens – His Tragedy and Triumph* (1953)

The Old Curiosity Shop is one of Dickens's most effective studies of the theme of inverted parent/child relationships. Grandfather Trent is determined that his daughter's child, Nell, should be brought up as a lady. To this end he spends all his money in gambling trying to win a fortune so that Little Nell shall want for nothing. To keep up his investment – for, like all compulsive gamblers, he believes it is only a matter of time before his luck will turn – he has to borrow large sums from Daniel Quilp, the dwarf. Nell tries to protect grandfather like a mother protecting her son, but in the end the two have to leave their house and flee from Quilp. Nell eventually succumbs to the strain, and dies. Old Trent goes mad with grief. Little Nell is one of Dickens's most pathetic divine children: 'For she was dead. There, upon her little bed, she lay at rest . . . No sleep so beautiful and calm, so free from trace of pain, so fair to look upon. She seemed a creature fresh from the hand of God, and waiting for the breath of life; not one who had lived and suffered death.'

Nell was based on the character of Mary, the younger sister of Dickens's wife, Catherine. She was a very pretty and lively girl and the novelist was deeply fond of her. She joined him and his wife when they set up home in 1836. One evening in May 1837 they had gone to the theatre. Mary was suddenly taken ill and died in Dickens's arms: 'sank under the attack and died – died in such a calm and gentle sleep, that though I had held her in my arms for sometime before, when she was certainly living . . . I continued to support her lifeless form, long after her soul had fled to Heaven', he wrote in a letter. He told her grandfather: 'Since our marriage she has been the grace and life of our home – the admired of all, for her beauty and excellence.' He took her ring from her finger and wore it himself for the rest of his life. He paid for her funeral at Kensal Green and hoped to be buried next to her himself one day. The tombstone bore an inscription which he composed: 'Mary Scott Hogarth. Died 7th May 1837. Young, beautiful and good, God in His Mercy Numbered her with his Angels at the early age of Seventeen.' He described her as: 'the dearest friend I ever had. Words cannot describe the pride I felt in her, and the devoted attachment I bore her . . . She had not a single fault.'

SOMERSET LLOYD-JAMES

Simon Raven, *Alms for Oblivion* (ten volumes, 1959–74)

Sir William Rees-Mogg (born 1928)

'Bristling with intellectual frills,' is how Somerset Lloyd-James is seen by the political powers-that-be in *Friends in Low Places* (1956), chronologically the fifth stage of Simon Raven's *Alms for Oblivion* sequence. Lloyd-James, who has been at the same school as Fielding Gray (the novelist based on Raven himself) is, by 1955, editor of the economic journal *Strix* and in a position to help old friends. He is enigmatic in appearance for 'As someone had once observed of Somerset, he derived much of his massive self-confidence from a poker-face which he thought he possessed but didn't. When Somerset was bluffing his eyes glazed over.' As one of his contributors tells him, when he declares his parliamentary ambitions, 'You are now a successful, even a powerful man, who need depend only on his own undoubted abilities. What can you possibly want in Parliament? Your abilities will go for nothing there.' Nevertheless Lloyd-James pursues his political career and is, by 1962, an MP; ten years later he is Parliamentary Under-Secretary of State at the Ministry of Commerce.

According to Simon Raven he originally modelled the character, in appearance and professional skill, on Sir William Rees-Mogg, editor of *The Times* from 1967 to 1981. Like Lloyd-James, Rees-Mogg was at school (Charterhouse) with Raven; like Lloyd-James he combined a brilliant career in journalism with parliamentary aspirations. He stood, unsuccessfully, as a Conservative in a by-election of 1956 and the general election of 1959.

There fact departs from fiction, for in Raven's series of novels Lloyd-James develops into an unscrupulous character who eventually – in *Bring Forth the Body* (1974) – kills himself when confronted by living proof of his disreputable past. When asked if he thought Sir William Rees-Mogg might be annoyed at having suggested such a character Raven replied 'I doubt if he's bothered to read it: I'm sure he's got better things to do.'

Commenting on the character, in a letter of 7 September 1983, Sir William Rees-Mogg said: 'There is no doubt that I was the starting point for the character, but apart from the development of the story there are substantial parts of the character which I suspect are drawn from other models.'

LORD JIM

Joseph Conrad, *Lord Jim* (1900)

Captain Clark of the *Jeddah*, Singapore (1880) and **Jim Lingard** (died 1917)

Further reading: Jocelyn Baines, *Joseph Conrad – A Critical Biography* (1960)

Jim is given no surname by Conrad. He trains as a seaman and becomes mate on the steamship *Patna*. The *Patna* puts out from an eastern port carrying eight hundred pilgrims to Mecca when it strikes a submerged object. The Europeans in charge of the ship believe it is doomed and decide to abandon ship. There are only seven lifeboats and the pilgrims are left to sink – as they suppose – on the *Patna*. When they are returned to shore Jim and the others learn that the *Patna* survived and reached Aden. Jim has to live with the terrible guilt that he did not live up to his responsibilities. He loses his certification and takes a succession of shore jobs. He becomes an agent at a trading post and is gradually accepted by the natives as a kind of ruler – Tuan Jim (Lord Jim). As the result of the intrigue of one Gentleman Brown, a pirate and freebooter, the leading native is killed and Jim is seen as morally responsible. His body is brought to his father and Jim says: 'I am come in sorrow . . . I come ready and unarmed.' The boy's father shoots Jim. Conrad writes: 'the white sent right and left . . . a proud and unflinching glance. Then with his hand over his lips he fell forward, dead.'

Conrad used a variety of sources for this story of a man in search of his own moral integrity. The *Patna* episode was based on the history of the steamer *Jeddah*, which left Singapore in the summer of 1888 bound for Mecca, met foul weather and was in danger of going down. Captain Clark abandoned the *Jeddah* off Cape Gardafui. He announced the *Jeddah*'s total loss at sea, only to learn later that she had reached Aden. The court of enquiry resulted in the loss of his certificate.

The episode of Jim's becoming a great white chief and marrying a native girl was based on the story of Jim Lingard, who was known as Tuan Jim and lived as a trader at Tandjong Redeb on the Berouw River. He died in 1917. Also Conrad may have used the story of Sir James Brooke (1803–68) who became Raja of Sarawak and put down piracy among Malays, Dayaks and other tribes in Bornean seas, and was adored by the natives.

THE LOST LEADER

Robert Browning, *Dramatic Romances and Lyrics* (1845)

William Wordsworth (1770–1850)

Browning's poem 'The Lost Leader' laments the loss of a man who has abandoned his principles for material gain: 'Just for a handful of silver he left us,/Just for a riband to stick in his coat –/Found the one gift of which fortune bereft us,/Lost all the others she lets us devote;/They, with the gold to give, doled him out silver,/So much was theirs who so little allowed:/How all our copper had gone for his service!/Rags – were they purple, his heart had been proud!/We that had loved him so, followed him, honoured him,/Lived in his mild and magnificent eye,/Learned his great language, caught his clear accents,/Made him our pattern to live and to die!/Shakespeare was of us, Milton was for us,/Burns, Shelley, were with us, they watch from their graves!/He alone breaks from the van and the freemen,/He alone sinks to the rear and the salves.' The Judas-figure in the poem is William Wordsworth, as Browning acknowledged in a letter of 1875 to Miss Lee: 'I undoubtedly had Wordsworth in my mind'.

An enthusiastic supporter of the French Revolution of 1789 – 'Bliss was it in that dawn to be alive,/But to be young was very heaven!' he later wrote in *The Prelude* – Wordsworth was also a revolutionary force in poetry. The *Lyrical Ballads* (1798) he produced with Coleridge encouraged an emotional approach to verse, and his preface to the second edition (1800) asserted that 'Poetry is the spontaneous overflow of powerful feelings; it takes its origin from emotion recollected in tranquillity.' Wordsworth, to the dismay of younger poets, gradually became more conservative in outlook and in 1813 was appointed Stamp Distributor by Lord Liverpool's reactionary government. In 1843 Wordsworth was appointed Poet Laureate and this position confirmed him as the voice of the English establishment.

Browning, then a young poet of twenty-four, met Wordsworth at a supper party on 26 May 1836. When a toast was proposed to the Poets of England, Wordsworth leaned across to Browning and said 'I am proud to drink your health, Mr Browning!' Despite this compliment, Browning was not at all impressed by Wordsworth's 'slow talk' and actively disliked his association with Toryism. It was shortly after Wordsworth's acceptance of the Poet Laureateship that Browning composed 'The Lost Leader' as a protest against the apostasy of a man who had once been an inspirational figure to the young.

EILERT LØVBORG

Henrik Ibsen, *Hedda Gabler* (1890)

Julius Hoffory (1855–97)

Further reading:
G. Grau, *Henrik Ibsen – Liv og Vergerker* (1918), B.W. Downs, *A Study of Six Plays by Ibsen* (1950)

Eilert Løvborg is first mentioned in Ibsen's *Hedda Gabler* as a man whose disreputable past has been eclipsed by his current celebrity as the author of a sensationally successful outline of civilization. He has been reformed, it seems, by Thea Elvsted whose children he tutors. When he arrives, in the second act, he is described as 'slim and lean. The same age as Tesman, he looks older, as though worn out by life.' He has brought with him the manuscript of his new work, a sequel to his outline, and come full of nostalgia for his time with Hedda – 'my days and nights of passion and frenzy, of drinking and madness'. Under the influence of Hedda he reverts to type and makes a dreadful exhibition of himself at a party. Hedda destroys his manuscript and encourages him to kill himself though she is devastated by the squalid manner of his death.

Julius Hoffory, the Dane who translated Ibsen into German, was delighted that Ibsen had modelled Løvborg on him. As Professor of Scandinavian Philology and Phonetics in Berlin he was respected as a scholar; in his private life he enjoyed wine and women and once lost a manuscript during a wild night of passion. When *Hedda Gabler* appeared Hoffory drew attention to himself as the original by adopting 'Løvborg' as his pseudonym. His own condition, however, increasingly alarmed Ibsen. Hoffory came to see Ibsen in 1890 and acted so erratically – forgetting names and finding difficulty with words – that he had to enter a sanitorium. Though he was released he never recovered and Ibsen noted: 'I am afraid he must be regarded as incurable . . . He continually sends me old, paid hotel bills, private letters and the like, with no indication of what he expects me to do with them.' Ibsen henceforth tried to avoid Hoffory who eventually died insane at an early age.

GEORGE LOWNDES

H. D., *Her* (1981)

Ezra Pound (1885–1972)

H.D.'s novel *Her*, written in 1927, and published posthumously, is the story of Hermione Gart (who shortens her first name to Her), and her relationships with the poet George Lowndes and the young woman Fayne Rabb. At the beginning of the novel Hermione is in Philadelphia with her family, brooding over her failure to pass her mathematics course at Bryn Mawr College. It is 1909 and she receives a letter from George Lowndes who tells her he is returning from Europe to 'Gawd's own

Further reading: Barbara Guest, *Herself Defined: The Poet H.D. and her World* (1984)

god-damn country'. George, with his literary self-confidence and passionate nature, represents an ideal for the neurotic Hermione: 'She wanted George as a child wants a doll, whose other dolls are broken. She wanted George as a little girl wants to put her hair up or to wear long skirts . . . George was the only young man who had ever kissed Her. George was the only person who had called her a "Greek goddess" . . . Her became almost Hermione as she looked at George with his collar torn open at the throat, turned-back Byronic collar, clean shirt, hot under-arms in great symmetrical patches . . . George in torn-open collar and throat long and angular rising out of torn-open collar and with throat flung back and square lean chin thrust out against a tree bole, made this almost the forest of Arden.' Hermione's parents at first oppose her decision to marry George, and by the time they change their mind about him, Hermione is determined to follow another road to her own selfhood.

In 1895 Hilda Doolittle's father became Professor of Astronomy at Pennsylvania University, in Philadelphia. Ezra Pound, a student of Romance languages at the university, first met Hilda when she was fifteen (in 1901) and subsequently became her fiancé for a brief period. Pound is vividly created as George Lowndes in *Her*. In 1912 both Pound and Hilda were in London. Reading some of Hilda's poems in the tea room of the British Museum, Pound cut down her 'Hermes of the Ways' and abbreviated her name to 'H.D. *Imagiste*' before submitting the poem to Harriet Monroe's magazine *Poetry*. When 'H.D. *Imagiste*' appeared in print in the January 1913 number of *Poetry*, Hilda had an identity and Pound's poetic aims had a label. Pound himself led the Imagist school of poetry and established the principles of pictorial clarity and verbal concision. One of the major poetic figures of the twentieth century, Pound eventually found himself on a treason charge for broadcasting on Italian radio during the Second World War, and was incarcerated in St Elizabeth's Hospital, Washington DC, until 1958 when he returned to Italy.

MR LUKE

William Hurrell Mallock, *The New Republic* (1877)

Matthew Arnold (1822–88)

Further reading: Lionel Trilling, *Matthew Arnold* (1963), Robert Giddings, *Matthew Arnold – Between Two Worlds* (1986)

Mr Luke is a distinguished author and critic who is a house-guest in *The New Republic* (see DR JENKINSON). He is described as a rather 'supercilious-looking man' who talks rather loudly and rather slowly, and who is 'the great critic and apostle of culture'. Without culture, he believes, 'We can never understand Christianity, and Christianity, whatever the vulgar may say of it, is the key to life, and is co-extensive with it . . . Culture is the union of two things – fastidious taste and liberal sympathy. These can only be gained by wide reading guided by sweet reason; and when they are gained . . . we are conscious, as it were, of a new sense, which at once enables us to discern the Eternal and the absolutely righteous, wherever we find it, whether in an epistle of St Paul's or in a comedy of Menander's . . .' He is asked by another guest why, if he has so clearly perceived the meaning of life, he is so melancholy? He answers that it is from the very knowledge that the melancholy springs: 'We – the cultured – we indeed see. But the world at large does not. It will not listen to us. It thinks we are talking nonsense. Surely that is enough to sadden us. Then, too, our ears are perpetually being pained and deafened by the din of the two opposing Philistinisms – science and orthodoxy – both equally vulgar, and equally useless. But the masses cannot see this. It is impossible to persuade some that science can teach them nothing worth knowing, and others that the dogmatic utterances of the gospels are either ignorant mistakes or oriental metaphors.' This is a portrait of Matthew Arnold, the distinguished son of Dr Thomas Arnold of Rugby (see TOM BROWN). He was educated at Rugby, Winchester and Balliol. He became a fellow of Oriel College and was from 1851 until 1883 an inspector of schools. He wrote several volumes of poetry, which included *The Forsaken Merman*, *Sohrab and Rustum* and *The Scholar Gipsy*. He published two volumes of *Essays in Criticism*, several volumes of reports on schools on the continent, and his celebrated polemic on the Condition of England Question, *Culture and Anarchy* in 1869. He opposed the mammonism, materialism and utilitarianism he saw all around him, believed that religious faith was permanently damaged by Darwinism, and that both science and religious orthodoxy were false gods. His faith was in culture, 'sweetness and light' as he termed it. He saw little hope in the aristocracy, whom he termed the 'barbarians', or the middle classes – the Philistines – or the working classes, whom he termed 'the populace'. Ironically enough he dropped dead running for a tramcar in a Liverpool street.

LUTHIEN TINUVIEL

J.R.R. Tolkien, *Lay of Leithian* and *The Silmarillion* (1977)

Edith Tolkien (née Bratt) (1889–1971)

Lúthien, the Elvan daughter of Thingol Greycloak of Doriath and Lady Melian of the Maiar, was the most beautiful maiden of all the world. She sacrifices her Elvan immortality in her love for Beren, son of Barahir of the Edain. There are strong echoes of the legend of Undine: 'As the stars above the mists of the world was her loveliness, and in her face was a shining light.' The story of the love of Lúthien and Beren is a complicated one. Their association is opposed by her father, Thingol, and Beren makes a vow in response to a challenge from him, then follows the Quest of the Silmaril (jewels-of-silima) and the fulfilment of the vow. Beren dies and his beloved soon follows him, but by the grace of the Valar (Angelic powers, the Ainur, Divinities created by The One before the Creation itself) they are granted life again. The story is told in full in the *Lay of Leithian*, and there is a prose version in *The Silmarillion*.

Tolkien's mentor, Father Francis Morgan, found him lodgings in Duchess Road, Birmingham, behind the Oratory. Here was another lodger, also an orphan, Edith Bratt. Tolkien's biographer, Humphrey Carpenter, writes: 'She was remarkably pretty, small and slim, with grey eyes, firm clear features and short dark hair.' There was something special about her birth, as she was illegitimate – traditionally there is frequently a mystery about the birth of heroes or heroines in myths and legends. Also, as the intensely romantic attachment developed, their relationship was opposed by their families. Edith was an Anglican, and in order to marry Tolkien, she had to renounce her faith and become a Roman Catholic. He wrote to her: 'I do so dearly believe that no half-heartedness and no worldly fear must turn us aside from following the light unflinchingly.' They married in 1916. She was a source of great support to him when he was recovering from trench fever in hospital in Hull. On leave he and Edith went for walks after the birth of their son at Cheltenham. They found a small wood near Roos, and Tolkien wrote of her at this time: 'Her hair was raven, her skin clear, her eyes bright, and she could sing – and *dance*.' She sang and danced for him in the wood, and – as Humphrey Carpenter points out – 'from this came the story of the mortal man Beren who loves the immortal elven-maid Lúthien Tinúviel, whom he first sees dancing among hemlock in a wood.' There was an undergrowth of hemlock in the wood at Roos. Tolkien wished to include the name Lúthien on her tombstone, and wrote to his son, Christopher: 'She was (and knew she was) my Lúthien' and recounted 'the dreadful sufferings of our childhoods, from which we rescued one another . . . we met in the woodland glade and went hand in hand many times to escape the shadows of imminent death before our last parting.'

Further reading: Humphrey Carpenter, *J.R.R. Tolkien – A Biography* (1977)

LYCIDAS

John Milton, 'Lycidas' (1637)

Edward King (1612–37)

When Milton was at King's College, Cambridge, from 1625–32, he sometimes kept the company of his fellow-student Edward King. Appointed to a college fellowship by royal mandate, King was apparently a young man destined for great things. His dedication to his religious calling impressed Milton and King had, like Milton, poetic ambitions. In 1637 King was appointed to a parish in Ireland and, while travelling from Chester to take up his new position in August of that year, drowned in the Irish Sea off the north coast of Wales. In 1632 Milton had retired to his father's estate at Horton, Buckinghamshire, in order to prepare himself as a poet. When he heard the news of King's death he was disturbed by the apparently pointless destruction of poetic promise. The year after

Further reading: E.M. Tillyard, *The Miltonic Setting* (1938), Frank Kermode (ed.), *The Living Milton* (1960)

King's drowning, Milton and other friends of King contributed to a memorial volume, *Justa Eduardo King*. The collection contains thirty-five poems, mainly in Latin; Milton's 'Lycidas' is the one work of genius prompted by King's death.

Milton's pastoral elegy begins by asserting that Lycidas (King in pastoral guise) was an outstanding poet: 'Who would not sing for Lycidas? He knew/Himself to sing, and build the lofty rhyme./He must not float upon his watery bier/Unwept, and welter to the parching wind,/Without the meed of some melodious tear.' Though Milton suggests that he is not yet equal to his poetic task, he prevails from a sense of loyalty to a lost friend: 'For we were nursed upon the selfsame hill,/Fed the same flock, by fountain, shade, and rill./Together both, ere the high lawns appeared/Under the opening eyelids of the morn,/We drove afield, and both together heard/What time the grayfly winds her sultry horn./Battening our flocks with the fresh dews of night,/Oft till the star that rose at evening bright/Toward Heaven's descent had sloped his westering wheel.'

Though the elegy develops into a meditation on the destiny of the poet, Milton never forgets the original impulse of the poem, and closes it by evoking King's spiritual immortality: 'Weep no more, woeful shepherds, weep no more,/For Lycidas your sorrow is not dead,/Sunk though he be beneath the watery floor . . . Now, Lycidas, the shepherds weep no more;/Henceforth thou art the genius of the shore,/In thy large recompense, and shalt be good/To all that wander in that perilous flood.'

TERTIUS LYDGATE

George Eliot, *Middlemarch* (1872)

Edward Clarke (died 1852)

Further reading: A.H. Paterson, *George Eliot's Family, Life and Letters* (1928)

Tertius Lydgate is an ambitious provincial physician, whose future is animated by dreams supported by his faith in the march of science and medical reform. He is in several important respects the 'hero' of the novel. The breadth of his vision is severely restricted by his marriage to the selfish Rosamond Vincy. George Eliot sums him up: 'He was but seven and twenty, an age at which many men are not quite common – at which they are hopeful of achievement, resolute in avoidance, thinking that Mammon shall never put a bit in their mouths and get astride their backs, but rather that Mammon, if they have anything to do with him, shall draw their chariot.' Of his faith in the future of his profession she wrote: 'He carried to his studies in London, Edinburgh, and Paris, the conviction that the medical profession as it might be was the finest in the world; presenting the most perfect interchange between science and art; offering the most direct alliance between intellectual conquest and the social good.' His wife's materialism is the destruction of his hopes.

Tertius is based on Edward Clarke, who married George Eliot's sister Chrissey, in 1837. Edward was the fifth son of Robert Clarke, of Brooksby Hall, Leicestershire. Edward's earnings as a physician in the country were never enough to run his family. He was helped by various members of the Eliot family; his wife's father bought from him a house at Attleborough that had been left by an uncle to Chrissey. He paid £250 for it. He later sent him a further £800. It was agreed that if the sum could not be repaid, it would be in order to take the debt from the estate he would inherit from his wife's family. However Edward went bankrupt in 1845. He had six children, and died suddenly in December 1852.

Tertius was always willing to show he was better born than most country doctors. He goes bankrupt with debts of £1,000.

M
Ian Fleming, *Casino Royale* (1953), *Live and Let Die* (1954), *Moonraker* (1955), *Diamonds Are Forever* (1956), *From Russia with Love* (1957), *Doctor No* (1958), *Goldfinger* (1959), *For Your Eyes Only* (1960), *Thunderball* (1961), *The Spy Who Loved Me* (1962), *On Her Majesty's Secret Service* (1963), *You Only Live Twice* (1964), *The Man With the Golden Gun* (1965), *Octopussy and the Living Daylights* (1966)

Mrs Valentine Fleming (1885–1964)

In the James Bond novels, secret agent 007 is always activated by M, Head of the British Secret Service. Behind his desk in the room at the end of a corridor in a 'gloomy building overlooking Regent's Park'. M supervises Bond who knows, as early as *Casino Royale* (1953), that 'one didn't argue with M'. Although M has been identified with Ian Fleming's Naval Intelligence boss Admiral John Godfrey and with Sir Stewart Menzies, once head of M16, the most plausible theory is put forward in John Pearson in his Life of Ian Fleming.

As a child Fleming called his mother 'M' and the fictional M, Pearson argues, is based on Fleming's mother Mrs Valentine Fleming. Born Evelyn St Croix Rose, she married Valentine Fleming in 1906 and assumed command of the four Fleming boys when, as Captain Fleming, their father went to fight in France in 1914 and was killed in action in 1917. Ian was nine when Mrs Val became acting head of the family and reigned supreme at home. She sent Ian away from home, to Eton and Sandhurst, and was disappointed at his lack of discipline and wayward nature. Her attitude to Fleming was to treat him as a gifted but spoilt child; exactly the way M treats Bond. Pearson writes: 'While Fleming was young, his mother was certainly one of the few people he was frightened of, and her sternness towards him, her unexplained demands, and her remorseless insistence on success finds a curious and constant echo in the way M handles that hard-ridden, hard-killing agent, 007. Never has a man who slaughtered so mercilessly taken orders so meekly.' The point, made in all the Bond books, is that 007 adores M, as is obvious in this extract from *Doctor No* (1958): 'Sitting here in this room opposite M was the symbol of normality he had longed for. He looked across through the smoke clouds into the shrewd grey eyes. They were watching him.'

Further reading:
John Pearson, *The Life of Ian Fleming* (1966)

MACBETH
William Shakespeare, *Macbeth* (1606)

Macbeth (1005–57)

Shakespeare's tragedy *Macbeth*, based on Holinshed's *Chronicle of Scottish History*, is great drama but bad history. In the play Macbeth is a madly ambitious man who, with the blessing of his bloodthirsty wife, murders his way to the crown of Scotland: 'I am in blood/Stepp'd in so far that, should I wade no more,/Returning were as tedious as go o'er.'

Duncan I (1001–40), the victim of Macbeth's regicide in the play, was founder of the royal House of Dunkeld and first monarch of a united Scotland. His marriage to a sister of the Danish earl Siward of Northumbria produced two sons, Malcolm Canmore and Donald Ban, whose hereditary right to the throne was threatened when Macbeth claimed the kingdom on the grounds of tanistry – succession by a previously elected member of the royal family. Like Duncan, Macbeth was a grandson of Malcolm II; his wife Gruoch – Shakespeare's Lady Macbeth – was granddaughter of Kenneth III. Macbeth was a formidable warrior and on 14 August 1040 defeated and killed his cousin Duncan I in battle. Five years later Duncan I's father Crinana challenged Macbeth in battle but he too was defeated and killed. Macbeth ruled Scotland for seventeen years with a good measure of success; he strengthened the position of the church and was confident enough to leave Scotland in 1050 and go on a pilgrimage to Rome. Macbeth had no children but Gruoch had a son, Lulach, by a previous marriage and he was regarded as the rightful successor. Yet Malcolm Canmore, Duncan I's son, was determined to destroy Macbeth and in 1054 he defeated the King at Scone. Three years later Malcolm avenged the death of his father when he defeated and killed Macbeth at Lumphanan on 15 August 1057. Malcolm III ruled Scotland until 1093.

Further reading:
Holinshed's Chronicles as Used in Shakespeare's Plays, edited by Allardyce and Josephine Nicholl (1927)

ROB ROY MACGREGOR
Sir Walter Scott, *Rob Roy* (1817)

Rob Roy MacGregor Campbell (1671–1734)

Further reading: see A A MacGregor, *Wild Drumalbain* (1927)

The hero of *Rob Roy*, Francis Osbaldistone, is banished by his father to the house of his boorish uncle in the north of England as a penance for not wishing to follow his father into business. He falls in love with his uncle's niece, Diana Vernon, and learns that Rashleigh, his uncle's son, is plotting his father's ruin and has evil designs on Diana. All is brought to a good end with the help of the bold, brave highland freebooter, Rob Roy. Rob Roy was once an honest drover but has been dispossessed of his land and proscribed by the government. He lives the life of an outlaw, a kind of highland Robin Hood – always working against the agents of the government, but gallant, honest and open towards those who need help. To aid Diana he gives his support to Francis against the deep plots of Rashleigh, whom he eventually kills. The family fortunes are restored and Francis marries Diana (see DIANA VERNON). Rob Roy MacGregor was originally a well-to-do grazier with a business which spread as far as the Tweed and Solway. He was involved in speculation which brought him great losses, and as well as this he misappropriated sums of money entrusted to him by the Duke of Montrose. Declared bankrupt he made a living from cattle-lifting and accepting money for affording protection against thieves. He was persecuted, along with members of his family, for conduct during the revolution of 1693 and this drove his clan further into lawlessness. He and his followers were in the wake of the rebel army in the 1715 Jacobite rebellion but they did not directly take part. He surrendered to the Duke of Atholl in 1717, but later escaped and continued his career as a bandit. He was arrested and sentenced to be transported to Barbados but was eventually pardoned in 1727. He was an educated and cultivated man and in fact was not simply a wild and lawless robber: his activities were very largely confined to the Graham country, associated with Montrose, as he had sworn to make Montrose rue the day that he had quarrelled with him. In later life he became a Roman Catholic. There is a traditional account of his death in which the priest urges him, as he expects forgiveness from God, to forgive all his enemies. The priest utters the Lord's Prayer, and Rob says: 'Ay, now ye ha'e gi'en me baith law and gospel for't. It's a hard law, but I ken it's gospel.' He turns to his son, saying: 'My sword and dirk lie there. Never draw them without reason, nor put them up without honour. I forgive my enemies; but see you to them, or may–' and at that point he expires. Scott drew considerably on oral traditions when composing *Rob Roy*. Rob's gun was a trophy at Abbotsford.

DENRY MACHIN
Arnold Bennett, *The Card* (1911)

H.K. Hales

Further reading: Margaret Drabble, *Arnold Bennett – A Biography* (1974)

The Card is a comic novel which details the career of a local lad who makes good. Edward Henry Machin – his mother calls him Denry for short – progresses from board school to become Bursley's youngest mayor. He 'wins' a scholarship by fiddling the results, loses his job as a solicitor's clerk after inviting himself to a municipal ball where he dances with the Countess of Chell (see COUNTESS OF CHELL) whose ball it was, becomes rent collector, estate agent, salvages sovereigns from a wreck, takes the Countess to the official opening of the Policemen's Institute she has donated in his mule-cart (after he has put her carriage out of action), and starts the Five Towns Universal Thrift Club. He earns considerable income, becomes a newspaper magnate, marries well, and rescues the local football team from financial ruin by buying them 'the greatest centre forward in England'. He is a complete joker, carrying into real life the classic attitudes and activities of the comedian – leg-pulling, trickery, double dealing, grabbing every opportunity which presents itself – and getting the applause of the world for his efforts.

Several incidents are based on Bennett's own life and experiences, such as his days of collecting rent for his father, and his father's experiences of newspaper rivalry. Denry is witty, quick on the draw, an exhibitionist with a real affection for his mother. The rise from obscurity to success and public acclaim Bennett took from his school friend H.K. Hales, who published *The Autobiography of 'The Card'*, and did enjoy a very successful career himself. He challenged Bennett with having based Denry on him, and demanded a share of the royalties! Bennett replied that the debt was paid as he had given Hales so much free publicity.

Bennett also used the character of Hales for Dick Povey in *The Old Wives' Tale*. Hales, like Povey, was a motor-car and cycle enthusiast and dealer, and made a successful balloon ascent – a feature of *The Old Wives' Tale*.

FERGUS MacIVOR VICH IAN VOHR OF GLENNAQUOICH

Sir Walter Scott, *Waverley* (1814)

Colonel Alexander Ranaldson MacDonnell of Glengarry (died 1828)

Waverley, Scott's first novel, took as its theme the second Jacobite rising in 1745. Detailed knowledge of these stirring events was transmitted to Scott by many who had actually participated in them or who had had expert hearsay evidence. The author's youth was passed in the shadow of these tragic events. Edward Waverley is an officer in the British army stationed with his regiment in Scotland. His father is a Hanoverian in politics, but he is also influenced by his uncle, a Jacobite landowner. He gets to know the Baron of Bradwardine (see BARON OF BRADWARDINE) who is also a Jacobite, and attracts the attention of Bradwardine's daughter, Rose. Curiosity leads him to meet the Jacobite freebooters, among them Fergus MacIvor Vich Ian Vohr of Glennaquoich. Edward falls in love with the Highland chieftain's beautiful sister, Flora. He is cashiered from his regiment and joins the Jacobites, and during the battle of Prestonpans he saves the life of a distinguished English officer, Colonel Talbot. This stands him in good stead and he is pardoned. Flora now rejects his love and he marries Rose Bradwardine. Fergus MacIvor is convicted of high treason against the crown and sentenced to death. Flora's farewell to Edward before she retires to the convent of Scottish Benedictine nuns in Paris is one of the finest scenes in Scott. 'Do you remember . . . you once found me making Fergus's bride-favours; and now I am sewing his bridal garments. Our friends here . . . are to give hallowed earth in their chapel to the bloody relics of the last Vich Ian Vohr.' She gives him a token of her regard for his betrothed, Rose Bradwardine – a chain of diamonds with which she used to decorate her hair. Fergus MacIvor is the prototype of the brave Highland chieftain, gallant, flamboyant and loyal to his cause. He was based on Colonel Alexander Ranaldson MacDonnell of Glengarry, who was a great personal friend of Sir Walter Scott's. His pride and his haughty temper were well-known. It was said of him that he was the last Highland chief who really kept up the customs and appearances of ancient gaeldom and always travelled with a full retinue of kilted attendants. He served as a Major in the Glengarry Fencibles Infantry 1795–1801 and lived thereafter in feudal style. Walter Scott always spoke and wrote of him in warm, admiring tones. He was killed attempting to get ashore from the wrecked steamer *Stirling Castle* on 14 January, 1828, and buried at Killionan.

Further reading:
John Gibson Lockhart, *The Life of Sir Walter Scott* (1838)

LADY RUBY MACLEAN

Enid Bagnold, *The Loved and the Envied* (1951)

Lady Diana Cooper (1892–1986)

As a young woman Lady Diana Manners was the favourite aristocratic personality of the British popular press, who kept their readers informed of her comings and goings in high society. Though she was born the daughter of Henry Manners, Lord Granby – later eighth Duke of Rutland – Diana believed her real father was Harry Cust, who had an affair with her mother Lady Violet. In 1910 Diana was presented at court, and came out to attend her first balls in London. She quickly acquired a reputation as a great beauty and colourful character, as Enid Bagnold noticed when she first saw young Diana descending a staircase: 'Her blind, blue stare swept over me. I was shocked – in the sense of electricity. Born to the city I wanted to storm, the Queen of Jericho swept past me.' Diana basked in the attention of the public and the adoration of the young men she met. One of these was Duff Cooper, then about to embark on his distinguished career in the Foreign Office, and known as a lover of wine and women. After working as a nurse at Guy's Hospital during the First World War, Diana married Duff Cooper in 1919. In 1923 she accepted the part of the Madonna in Max Reinhardt's revival of *The Miracle* and toured the play in the USA, Britain and Europe. Her husband, who became a Member of Parliament in 1924, progressed with his political life and was appointed British Ambassador to France in 1944. Diana adapted to this life with her usual panache.

By 1951, when Enid Bagnold's novel *The Loved and the Envied* appeared, Diana was almost sixty, and the character of Lady Ruby Maclean is intended as a sympathetic portrait of Diana as a mature woman: 'When she came into a room it was plain it was a spirited person who entered, a person with an extra dose of life. It was apparent on all sides how people were affected. They had a tendency to rise to their feet to be nearer her, not of course in her honour, but to be at the source of amusement, to be sure not to miss the exclamation, the personal comedy she might make of the moment of life just left behind.' According to Philip Ziegler's *Diana Cooper* (1981) Diana considered this a striking likeness but regretted that Ruby Maclean had 'no fears and frailties, panics and pains'.

KENNETH MACMAHON

Fred Urquhart, *A Diver in China Seas* (1980)

Robert Colquhoun (1914–62)/**Robert MacBryde** (1913–66)

Fred Urquhart's story 'Local Boy Makes Good' describes a celebrated Scottish artist's return from London to his native town – Glendownie – to perform the opening ceremony for the new Glendownie Reservoir. As the story opens, Kenneth MacMahon is involved in a four-day alcoholic event that starts in Soho and ends in a back-street pub in Pimlico. A typically wild Scot when under the influence of drink, MacMahon is delighted to receive the invitation from the Earl of Braesdale to open the reservoir: In his London flat he puts a kilt on, over his trousers, and dances a sword dance. In the company of his friend Davina, he gets the train from King's Cross, London, and reaches Glendownie and the 'wee cottage' of his mother. The ceremony goes well, to the relief of MacMahon's mother; 'Only she knew how sick he'd been that morning and how his hands had kept shaking until Geordie [his brother] had unearthed a half bottle of the hard stuff.' A week later MacMahon returns to London, drinking again for, as he tells Davina, 'I needed that after all I've been through these past few days. Opening a reservoir's a more strenuous job than folk would think.' In a letter of 28 November 1984, Fred Urquhart said that 'Kenneth MacMahon . . . could be called a twin-portrait as it is a mixture of the characteristics of my friends Robert Colquhoun and Robert MacBryde, the gifted Scottish artists known as "The Roberts" who died tragically in their early forties.'

In 1932 Colquhoun (from Kilmarnock, Ayrshire) and MacBryde (from Maybole, Ayrshire) met at Glasgow School of Art where both were students. From then, until Colquhoun's death (of heart disease, in MacBryde's arms) they were inseperable and became well-known figures in the artistic pubs of London in the 1940s. Both were talented painters and both were heavy self-destructive drinkers, MacBryde in particular becoming quarrelsome when intoxicated. Colquhoun was regarded as the finer painter of the two, influenced by Picasso and Wyndham Lewis. After his friend's death MacBryde felt his own life was hardly worth living. He drifted to Dublin where he lived with friends and spent most of his time drinking. He died after being knocked down by a car when making his way back to a basement couch in Lower Leeson Street.

REGAN MACNEIL

William Peter Blatty, *The Exorcist* (1972)

A boy from Mount Rainier

Further reading: Willam Peter Blatty, 'The

Demonic possession dominates William Peter Blatty's novel *The Exorcist* and the screenplay he wrote for the William Friedkin film of 1973. The story describes the hideous transformation of eleven-year-old Regan MacNeil from a charming all-American girl in Washington, DC, to a murderous foul-mouthed monster. Ironically, Regan's mother, Chris MacNeil, is an atheist who eventually requests an exorcism from a priest, Father Karras, who has lost his faith.

Blatty was educated by Jesuits and at one time considered training for the priesthood. When he was a student at Georgetown University in

Washington, DC, he read, in the *Washington Post* of 20 August 1949, a chilling account of exorcism concerning a fourteen-year-old Mount Rainier boy: 'Only after twenty to thirty performances of the ancient ritual of exorcism, here and in St Louis, was the devil finally cast out of the boy.' Fascinated by the case Blatty was able to read the exorcist's diary and collect details of levitation, rappings, telekinesis, paranormal strength, change of voice and brandings of words on the victim's flesh. To this situation Blatty added a plot involving murder (though there were no murders or deaths in the case of the Mount Rainier boy) and 'changed the boy in my story to a girl, although more to ease the exorcist's anxiety than from fear of doing any real harm to the boy'.

In a book about the making of the film of *The Exorcist*, Blatty mentions that the exorcist asked him never to reveal the boy's identity. Blatty also points out that he modelled the character of Regan's mother, Chris MacNeil, on actress Shirley MacLaine; and based Father Merrin, the exorcist, on Pierre Teilhard de Chardin (1881–1955), the Jesuit philosopher.

Exorcist' from Novel to Film (1974)

THE MAD HATTER

Lewis Carroll, *Alice In Wonderland* (1865)

Roger Crab (1621–80)

The Mad Hatter is one of the most memorable guests at the celebrated tea-party in *Alice in Wonderland*. He has been immortalized in Tenniell's brilliant illustrations, showing him in a loud check suit, wearing one of his hats with the price tag still in the hat-band. He asks Alice the famous riddle: 'Why is a raven like a writing desk?' to which there is no answer. Another guest at the table, the March Hare, tells Alice that she should say what she means. Alice answers: 'I do . . . at least – at least I mean what I say – that's the same thing, you know.' 'Not the same thing a bit,' says the Mad Hatter, 'Why, you might just as well say that "I see what I eat" is the same thing as "I eat what I see"!' He hospitably offers Alice some more tea. She retorts: 'I've had nothing yet . . . so I can't take more.' 'You mean you can't take *less*,' the Hatter answers, 'it's very easy to take *more* than nothing.' The Mad Hatter has an eccentric watch which tells the day but not the time. Further evidence of his bizarre behaviour is his pouring hot tea on the Dormouse so as to wake him. The phrase 'as mad as a hatter' was in popular use long before it was associated with such a celebrated creation as the Mad Hatter. It is recorded in the United States in the mid-1830s, and Thackeray uses it in *Pendennis* (1850). Sadly, mental instability and damage to the central nervous system was an occupational hazard of the hatters' trade. Mercurous nitrate, which can produce St Vitus's Dance and other kinds of nervous tremour, was used in the making of felt (a basic material in the hatters' trade) which is fabric produced by matting or felting together various fibrous materials – wools, furs and certain animal hairs. In fact the trade is very ancient. Felting is of an earlier date than weaving in the ancient civilizations of Asia. Roger Crab was a renowned eccentric who lived at Chesham. He was a successful hatter and by the early 1640s he had become a complete ascetic, living on water, dock leaves and grass. He gave all his worldly goods to the poor. He served in the Parliamentary Army 1642–9 and later practised as a quack physician at Uxbridge. It is reported of him that he predicted the Restoration and the accession of William of Orange. He published an interesting autobiography in 1655.

MAGGIE

Arthur Miller, *After the Fall* (1963)

Marilyn Monroe (1926–62)

The action of Arthur Miller's *After the Fall* 'takes place in the mind, thought, and memory of Quentin'. A lawyer, Quentin addresses the audience and confesses the sins and sensations of his life. Though he has married three times it is his second wife, Maggie, who brings out the best and worst in him. When he first meets her he is astonished by her beauty and aura of innocent sensuality. Later she becomes a famous singer noted for her sexually exciting interpretation of popular lyrics though Maggie insists 'it's not I say to myself, "I'm going to sound sexy", I just try to come *through* – like in love'. Quentin sees that success has not brought her security and reflects how 'she was chewed and spat out by a long line

Further reading:
Norman Mailer, *Marilyn – A Biography of Marilyn Mon-*

roe (1973), Anthony Summers, *Goddess – The Secret Lives of Marilyn Monroe* (1985)

of grinning men! Her name floating in the stench of locker rooms and parlour-car cigar smoke.' When he marries her he realizes that her great gifts include a talent for self-destruction and that she is too fragile to survive in a brutal world. Though Miller tried to focus attention on the play's issues, rather than the character of Maggie, the public responded to the drama for its insight into the nature of Marilyn Monroe.

Arthur Miller married Marilyn in 1956. He had won the Pulitzer Prize for *Death of a Salesman* but had never experienced anything like the public attention directed towards his wife. With the release in 1953 of *Gentlemen Prefer Blondes* and *How to Marry a Millionaire* she became America's greatest sex symbol; every detail of her life was devoured by the public and the strain affected the marriage. After Miller and Marilyn separated in 1960 she became less reliable as a person and performer though she turned in a fine performance in her last film – *The Misfits* (1961), scripted by Miller. She died in mysterious circumstances, from an overdose of pills, and was (as Miller said of Maggie in an article) 'a victim . . . of her exploitation as an entertainer'.

JULES MAIGRET

Georges Simenon, *Pietr-le-Letton* (1931, 'Maigret and the Enigmatic Lett'), *M. Gallet décédé* (1931, Maigret Stonewalled), *Le Pendu de Saint-Pholien* (1931, 'Maigret and the Hundred Gibbets'), etc..

Désiré Simenon
(1878–1921)

Further reading: Fenton Bresler, *The Mystery of Georges Simenon* (1983)

Between 1929 and 1972 Georges Simenon wrote eighty-four books featuring Jules Maigret, the French detective. The first full-length Maigret novel, *Pietr-le-Letton*, was written in four days in 1929 and the last one, *Maigret et M. Charles*, came out in 1972 as Simenon's farewell to fiction. Maigret appears, in *Pietr-le-Letton*, as a big, burly, pipe-smoking man: 'his frame was plebian – huge and bony. Strong muscles swelled beneath his jacket and soon took the crease out of even a new pair of trousers. He had a characteristic stance, too, which even many of his own colleagues found annoying. It expressed something more than self-confidence, and yet it was not conceit. He would arrive, massively, on the scene, and from that moment it seemed that everything must shatter against his rock-like form, no matter whether he was moving or standing still with feet planted slightly apart.' Citing this passage in *The Mystery of Georges Simenon*, Fenton Bresler suggests that Maigret was modelled on Simenon's father, Désiré: 'Maigret, like Désiré Simenon, loves his fellow men, understands and pities them.' Simenon himself said, in a radio interview of 1955, 'When I wanted to create a sympathetic person who understood everything, that is to say Maigret, I gave him without realising it certain of my father's characteristics.'

Désiré Simenon, whose father had a hat shop in Liège, was a tall handsome man of twenty-three when he married Hanriette Brull. He followed a career in fire insurance and was celebrated for his punctuality, leaving for his work at exactly the same time each day; Simenon says neighbours could tell what time it was without looking at their clocks and 'Shopkeepers taking down their shutters knew whether they were early or late'. He was a man of great patience, putting up with his wife's tantrums and accepting her decision to take in student lodgers. When Simenon was fifteen, the family doctor told him that Désiré – who suffered from angina – had only a few years to live. Simenon, who worshipped his father, was shattered by this news and by Désiré's subsequent death. 'On the afternoon of November 28, 1921,' writes Bresler, 'the day before Simenon was due to go into the Army, Désiré dropped dead standing at his high accountant's desk in his office.'

NORMAN MAINE

Film, *A Star is Born* (written by Dorothy Parker, Alan Campbell, Robert Carson and Moss Hart; directed by George Cukor in 1945)

A Star is Born, one of the most durable Hollywood narratives, was filmed in 1937 with Frederick March and Janet Gaynor, in 1954 with James Mason and Judy Garland, and again in 1979 with Chris Kristopherson and Barbara Streisand. In some ways it may well trace its origins back to the 1932 film *What Price Hollywood*. The story of *A Star is Born* is simple and direct – a study of the collapsing marriage between two film stars, one on the way down (Norman Maine) the other on the way up (Vicki Lester). As the young star's career ascends and she earns public and professional acclaim, her husband descends into alcoholism and suicide by drowning.

John Gilbert
(1895-1936)

Further reading:
Alexander Walker, *The Shattered Silents* (1978)

It is based on the real life career and professional eclipse of John Gilbert. He was the son of a theatrical family in Logan, Utah. Family connections made his entry into films a simple matter and by 1919 he was playing romantic leads with Mary Pickford. In the early 1920s he very nearly rivalled Valentino at the box office with a series of smash hits – *Monte Cristo, Arabian Love, Cameo Kirby, He Who Gets Slapped, The Merry Widow, The Big Parade* and *Bardlays the Magnificent*. He starred with Greta Garbo in *Flesh and the Devil* (based on *Anna Karenina*) and *A Woman of Affairs*. There was talk of an off-screen romance, which Garbo always denied. By 1928 he was the highest-paid star in the business.

His eclipse was almost instantaneous. At his height he was earning $10,000 a week, and married the star Ina Claire in 1929. Returning from his honeymoon he found he had lost a fortune in investments. Then came the talkies. He made *His Glorious Night*, his first talkie, but unfortunately his voice was rather prissy and contrasted so much with his established screen character of passionate romance that he was no longer to be taken seriously. At the same time as he fell out of fashion, Ina Claire made a great hit in *Talkie Heaven*, with her quality Boston tones. He took to drink in a big way, and died of a heart attack in 1936. The suicide by drowning was taken from the death of another failed actor, John Bowers, who walked into the waves at Malibu in 1936.

MALVOLIO

William Shakespeare, *Twelfth Night* (1601)

Sir William Knollys, Earl of Banbury
(1547-1632)

Further reading:
Leslie Hotson, *The First Night of Twelfth Night* (1954)

Malvolio is Olivia's steward. He is a pompous, puritanical prating ass, without a shred of humour. This makes him the butt of endless comicality from other characters. He fancies himself in love with Olivia, and her uncle, Sir Toby Belch and Maria, maid to Olivia, hatch a plot to make Malvolio think that Olivia loves him. The plot involves a forged letter, which Malvolio believes, and gulling him into wearing outlandish clothes which he thinks will impress the object of his passion. When he appears before Olivia smiling, wearing yellow crossgarters, quoting sections from the letter, she thinks he is mad. He has always taken delight in spoiling the fun and amusement of others so his ultimate exposure to such public ridicule seems justified. He accuses Toby and his companion Sir Andrew of turning Olivia's house into an ale-house: 'Is there no respect of place, persons, nor time, in you?' he demands. Sir Toby's retort is famous: 'Dost thou think, because thou art virtuous, there shall be no more cakes and ale?'

Shakespeare's portrait of Malvolio, Leslie Hotson believes (*The First Night of Twelfth Night*, 1954) is based on that of Sir William Knollys, comptroller of Queen Elizabeth's household. He had several of Malvolio's characteristics – he was strongly puritan in his sympathies, and was known to have interrupted revellers clad in his nightshirt. He was a supporter of Essex and declared a 'time-server' – which phrase is used by Maria to describe Malvolio. Knollys also pictured himself as a woman-slayer, and notoriously attempted the seduction of his ward, Mary Fitton (1578–1647) who was one of the Queen's maids of honour. Knollys began to take what at first seemed a fatherly interest in her, but his passion for Mary became one of the scandals of the day. Early in 1601 she began to associate with William Herbert, Third Earl of Pembroke, by whom she had a stillborn child. William Kempe, the comic actor who was a member of Shakespeare's company, dedicated his *Nine Days Wonder* (1600) to Mistress Anne Fitton 'Mayde of Honour to the Mayde Royal'. This must be intended for Mary, as she alone, and not her sister Anne, was maid of honour.

MANDERLEY

Daphne du Maurier, *Rebecca* (1938)

Menabilly

Rebecca is narrated by a heroine who is haunted by a house: Manderley, the de Winter family home, is strangely 'secretive and silent'. Daphne du Maurier first saw such a house in 1924, when she was seventeen and had come to Cornwall from London. First she read, in a guidebook, about an

Elizabethan house three miles from the harbour at Fowey. Then she asked the locals for information about the house and was told it was shut up and abandoned by an owner who lived in Devon. Intent on exploring it Daphne du Maurier rose one morning at 5 am and approached with a sense of expectancy which she records in *The Rebecca Notebook* (1981): 'I edged my way on to the lawn, and there she stood. My house of secrets. My elusive Menabilly . . . She was, or so it seemed to me, bathed in a strange mystery. She held a secret – not one, not two, but many – that she withheld from many people but would give to one who loved her well.'

In 1937 du Maurier found herself in Alexandria with her soldier husband; she was homesick for Cornwall and thought lovingly of Menabilly. Recalling a rumour that the owner 'had been married first to a very beautiful wife, whom he had divorced, and had married again a much younger woman', du Maurier began to write her novel. Five years after the publication of *Rebecca*, Daphne du Maurier learned that Menabilly was available for rent. At last it was to be lived in: 'I took a bold step and moved house on my own, with a nanny and three young children. I rented the old manor house Menabilly that I had written about in *Rebecca*, which had no electricity and no hot-water system, and was full of dry rot. My husband, in far-off Tunis, told his brother officers, "I am afraid Daphne has gone mad".' She lived in her 'house of secrets' for twenty-six years.

THE MAN IN KIPLING'S 'IF—'

Rudyard Kipling, *Rewards and Fairies* (1910)

Sir Leander Starr Jameson (1853–1917)

Further reading: Charles Carrington, *Rudyard Kipling* (1935), Norman Page, *A Kipling Companion* (1984)

Kipling's celebrated poem 'If—' is a catalogue of virtues considered manly by the author. The paragon in the poem can keep his head when all about 'Are losing theirs'; can 'wait and not be tired of waiting'; can 'meet with Triumph and Disaster/And treat those two imposters just the same'; can risk his winnings 'on one turn of pitch-and-toss'. In the final stanza, addressed to 'my son', Kipling eloquently reaches his conclusion: 'If you can talk with crowds and keep your virtue,/Or walk with Kings – nor lose the common touch,/If neither foes nor loving friends can hurt you,/If all men count with you, but none too much;/If you can fill the unforgiving minute/With sixty seconds' worth of distance run,/Yours is the Earth and everything that's in it,/And – which is more – you'll be a Man, my son!'

As an inspirational text the poem has become part of the English language. For example, after winning the General Election of 1964, Labour's Prime Minister Harold Wilson liked to quote the poem as a living presence in his mind. Kipling did not, however, conceive the poem as an abstract evocation of manhood for, it was firmly based on the character of Dr Jameson. Kipling first visited South Africa in 1891 and became friendly with Cecil Rhodes, Prime Minister from 1890. Rhodes made The Woolsack, a house on his own estate, available to the Kiplings, who visited it every year from 1900–8. Rhodes also introduced Kipling to Leander Starr Jameson, the Edinburgh-born statesman who, in 1896, led the Jameson Raid from Mafeking to Transvaal in support of the dissatisfied 'Uitlanders' (temporary mining settlers denied citizenship). Rhodes's complicity in this raid led to his resignation in 1896; Jameson himself was handed over to the British but, because of ill-health, served only part of his sentence of fifteen months' imprisonment. Succeeding Rhodes as leader of the Progressive Party, Jameson became Prime Minister in Cape Colony in 1904. After he was replaced by a Boer in 1908 Kipling never again visited South Africa. Jameson, however, visited Kipling at Bateman's, his home in Burshaw (Sussex), in October 1909, and it was this encounter that prompted Kipling to compose 'If—' which was first published in the *American Magazine* of October 1910.

MAN IN THE IRON MASK

Alexandre Dumas, père, *Vicomte de Bragelonne* (1847)

The man in the iron mask has always aroused romantic curiosity, even in his own lifetime. Several solutions have been offered as to the identity of the mysterious prisoner of the reign of Louis XIV who always wore an iron mask when being moved from one prison to another. He spent most of his time at Pignerol, but sojourned in other French prisons, dying finally at the Bastille on 19 November 1703.

The explanation given the most wide circulation, and which has certainly fanned popular interest in this figure, was that which Alexandre Dumas included in *Vicomte de Bragelonne*, that the 'Mask' was in reality the bastard elder brother of Louis XIV, the son of Anne of Austria (1601–66), wife of Louis XIII, and her minister, Cardinal Jules Mazarin (1602–61). When the prisoner was buried his name was given as 'Marchiali'. One widely accepted solution was that the 'Mask' was General du Bulonde who was imprisoned for raising the siege of Cuneo in 1691 contrary to orders of Nicolas Catinat, Marshall of France. This may be discounted as evidence indicates that the 'Mask' was imprisoned at Pignerol by 1666, and some twenty years later was transferred to the island of St Marguerite. This evidence predates the siege of Cuneo. Another candidate is the Duke de Vermandois, illegitimate son of Louis XIV and his mistress, Louise Francoise de Labaume Leblanc, Duchess de la Vallière (1644–1710). The Duke was imprisoned for life for giving the Dauphin a box on the ears. It has even been suggested that the 'Mask' was the Duke of Monmouth, who supposedly escaped beheading in 1685 after the failure of the Monmouth Rebellion against James II. Another candidate is Nicolas Fouquet, Vicomte de Melun et de Vaux and Marquis de Belle-Isle (1615–80), who had attempted to gain political power after the death of Mazarin, but who was conspired against by Colbert and arrested in 1661. His trials took three years and he was imprisoned for life at the fortress of Pignerol, where he died. Working on the private papers of Louis XIV and his ministers including Francois Michel le Tellier, Marquis de Louvois (1641–91), Franz Funk-Brentano has put forward the convincing explanation that the 'Mask' was in fact Count Giralamo Mattioli, leading minister to the Duke of Mantua. He acted treacherously to Louis XIV in 1678 as he had agreed by treaty to surrender to Louis the Fortress of Casale, the key to Italy, but later went back on his word. He was tricked into coming to France and there was imprisoned at Pignerol.

Count Giralamo Mattioli (1640-1703)

Further reading:
Franz Funk Brentano, *Lègends et archives de la Bastille* (1898)

MANON

Antoine-François Prévost, *Manon Lescaut* (1731)

Manon Porcher

Further reading:
Jean Sgard, *Prévost Romancier* (1968)

Manon is one of the great love stories of the world. A simple and moving narrative, harsh in its realities, but coloured with poignant and touching qualities which are emotive, often in spite of the resistance of sophisticated taste. André Gide, for example, placed it in his list of the ten best French novels. The Chevalier des Grieux is seventeen years old and is studying for the priesthood. He meets Manon Lescaut in a tavern and he believes her to be a girl who is being forced against her own wishes into entering a convent. She is fourteen years old but they fall passionately in love. He is conscious of the fact that although she is younger than he is, in many ways she seemed more mature: 'Love had already so enlightened me . . . I spoke to her in a way that made her understand my feelings; for she was far more experienced than I.' The only solution to the problems of their lives seem to them to lie in flight. With little money, they attempt a life together. But Manon constantly betrays him. She seeks a life of excitement and amusement, but each time – after abandoning him – she returns to be forgiven. He tries to put her out of his mind and to return to his studies, but she returns and captures him again. In their attempts to raise money he takes to gambling and she becomes a prostitute. Eventually she is deported to America but des Grieux determines to go with her to Louisiana. Here they hope to marry, but the son of the governor of Louisiana has fallen in love with her and he prevents the marriage. While trying to escape from Louisiana, Manon dies: 'I remained for more than twenty four hours with my lips pressed to the face and hands of my dear Manon . . . I formed the resolution to bury her and to wait for death on her grave.' He is discovered and tried for her murder, but is acquitted, and learns soon after that his father has died. He blames himself for this tragedy. The implication is that des Grieux is now a sadder but a wiser man.

Prévost based the novel on the true-life adventures of Manon Porcher who had been hounded by the French authorities for debauchery and prostitution and deported to the convict settlement in Louisiana where she was followed by her aristocratic young lover, Avril de la Varenne. They were married. The story has been the subject of several operas – by Auber, Massanet and Puccini.

THE DUKE OF MANTUA

Opera, *Rigoletto* (1851, music by Verdi, libretto by Piave)

Francis I (1494–1547)

Further reading: Julia Pardoe, *Life of Francis I* (1887)

'La donna è mobile/qual piume al vento,/muta d'accento/e di pensiero.' Woman is changeable, like a feather in the breeze, sings the Duke in Verdi's tragic opera *Rigoletto*. She changes her tune and her mind. We are always deceived as much by a pretty face, in tears or full of laughter. It is one of the most celebrated moments in 19th-century opera. It was one of Caruso's greatest roles. Among modern exponents of the part are Placido Domingo and Luciano Pavarotti. The Duke is master of a licentious court, and takes his pleasures where he wishes. Rigoletto, his jester, has a beautiful daughter, Gilda, whom he attempts to protect in purity by keeping her in secret. The Duke hears rumours of Rigoletto's 'secret' and believes the old man is keeping a mistress. He resolves to abduct her and unwittingly Rigoletto aids the conspiracy against his own daughter.

Rigoletto plots his revenge for the loss of Gilda's honour, intending to have the Duke murdered at an inn. Maddalena, the assassin's sister, smitten with the Duke herself, persuades the murderer to spare the Duke's life and to kill any man who may arrive and present the body in a sack to the waiting Rigoletto. Gilda overhears this plot and resolves to sacrifice herself for the Duke, whom she loves, and enters disguised as a man, to be stabbed to death. As Rigoletto gloats over what he supposes to be the body of the hated Duke, he hears his voice sing 'La donna è mobile' and tears open the sack to find the body of his own daughter.

Verdi and his librettist, Piave, based their opera on Victor Hugo's drama *La Roi s'amuse* (1832) and changed the names of the leading characters in accordance with the Austrian censorship in Italy at the time. Hugo's protagonist was based on Francis I of France, who was born at Cognac, the son of Charles, Comte d'Angoulème. In 1514 he married Claude, daughter of Louis XII, whom he succeeded that year. In war and foreign diplomacy he pursued vigorous policies, recapturing Milan and signing a concordat with the Pope. When the emperor Maximilian died in 1519, Francis challenged Charles of Spain for the Austrian imperial crown. Charles V was elected and in the ensuing war the French were driven out of Italy, eventually surrendering all Francis I's Italian possessions. He fostered arts and scholarship, maintained a lavish court, but Hugo's portrait of his licentiousness, followed in *Rigoletto*, has considerable basis in historical fact.

THE MAN WHO LOVED ISLANDS

D.H. Lawrence, *The Woman Who Rode Away* (1928)

Sir Compton Mackenzie (1883–1972)

Further reading: Compton Mackenzie, *My Life and Times* (10 vols, 1963–71), Harry T. Moore, *The Priest of Love* (1974)

While living on Capri in 1919, D. H. Lawrence became friendly with fellow writer Compton Mackenzie, a man – so Lawrence said – 'one can trust and like'. Mackenzie suggested that Lawrence consider coming with him on a writing trip to the South Sea islands but nothing came of the plan. Instead Mackenzie, at the suggestion of his publisher, went to the Channel island of Jethou which he leased from the British government at a cost of £1,000 a year. To Lawrence this insular passion was unwholesome so he satirized Mackenzie as 'The Man Who Loved Islands', a story included in the American, but not the British, edition of *The Woman Who Rode Away* (1928).

Mackenzie's search for absolute isolation is traced in a parable of antisocial escapism: 'There was a man who loved islands. He was born on one, but it didn't suit him, as there were too many other people on it, besides himself. He wanted an island all of his own: not necessarily to be alone on it, but to make it a world of his own.' Although the protagonist of the story has spiritual ideals, his pursuit of peace is achieved at the expense of others; each island he adopts is contaminated by human contact and so he moves on. Eventually he ends up on an island with only sheep for company: 'He was glad. He didn't want trees or bushes. They stood up like people, too assertive. His bare, low-pitched island in the pale blue sea was all he wanted.'

Mackenzie's own life was frequently a testing-ground for his fiction. After the success of *Sinister Street* (1913) he had a spectacular war career in the British Aegean Intelligence Service. After the First World War he lived on Capri, then Jethou and eventually settled on the little Hebridean island of Barra. There he wrote prolifically and conducted a campaign aimed at restoring political independence to Scotland. Towards the end of his life he divided his time between Edinburgh and the South of France.

IRIS MARCH

Michael Arlen, *The Green Hat* (1924)

Nancy Cunard (1896-1965)

Further reading: Anne Chisholm, *Nancy Cunard* (1979)

In 1920 Nancy Cunard, the unpredictable daughter of the celebrated Lady Cunard, met Michael Arlen who had been born Dikran Kouyoumdjian in Roustchouck, Bulgaria, and subsequently educated in England. He fell in love with Nancy, and saw her, as often as he could, in Paris and London. His first novel, *Piracy* (1922), portrayed Nancy and her mother as Virginia Tracy and Lady Carnal. His bestselling *The Green Hat* – which later became a film with Greta Garbo in the leading role – also evoked Nancy, as Iris March. Like Nancy, Iris acquires a risqué reputation on account of her disregard for concepts such as chastity. The narrator of the novel sees Iris as an extraordinary woman: 'You had a conviction, a rather despairing one, that she didn't fit in anywhere, to any class, nay, to any nationality. She wasn't that ghastly thing called bohemian, she wasn't any of the ghastly things called "society", "country", upper, middle and lower class. She was, you see, some invention, ghastly or not, of her own . . . You felt she had outlawed herself from somewhere, but where was that somewhere? You felt she was tremendously indifferent to whether she was outlawed or not.' The narrator goes to bed with Iris and the morning after notes 'She was like a tower of beauty in the morning of the world.'

Nancy Cunard was born at Nevill Holt, Leicestershire, the country home of her father Sir Bache Cunard. She was educated at home by governesses and later moved to London with her mother when Lady Cunard decided, in 1911, to leave her husband and live with Thomas Beecham. Nancy disliked her mother's snobbery and her use of money to establish power over others. Gradually Nancy began to make a literary reputation for herself, having seven poems published in 1916 in the Sitwells' anthology *Wheels*. In 1916, too, Nancy married Sydney Fairbairn but she soon tired of him and the marriage collapsed. When she met Michael Arlen – whom she called 'the Baron' because of his Bulgarian origins – she was waiting for a divorce, and could not take him seriously as a prospective husband. She later remembered her relationship with him, and how he told her he would marry her if he was rich enough. She, however, reflected: 'The vanity of some men! Marry the Baron indeed!' In 1928 Arlen married Countess Atalanta Inarcati.

LORD MARCHMAIN

Evelyn Waugh, *Brideshead Revisited* (1945)

William Lygon, Seventh Earl Beauchamp (1872–1938) and **Hubert Duggan** (1904-43)

Further reading: Alan Pryce-Jones, *Evelyn*

The theme of *Brideshead*, in the author's words, was 'the operation of divine grace on a group of diverse but closely connected characters'. Divine grace operates dramatically in the case of Lord Marchmain. Charles Ryder meets young Lord Flyte at Oxford (see SEBASTIAN FLYTE) and is a frequent house-guest at Brideshead, the family seat of the Marquis of Marchmain. The Marquis settles overseas with his mistress. The family is a Roman Catholic one, and Lord Marchmain is now removed from the bosom of the family and cannot share the fervent religious devotion of his wife. Charles and Sebastian visit him in his voluntary exile in Venice. Just before the outbreak of the Second World War, Lord Marchmain comes home to Brideshead. Cara, his mistress, tells Charles that he has come home to die. His elder son, Bridey, tries to reconcile his father to the faith, but Lord Marchmain dismisses the local

Waugh and His World (1980)

priest from his company. As his condition worsens while Bridey is absent, his elder daughter Julia (see JULIA FLYTE) summons the priest to give her father the last rites. As the priest anoints the dying man, Lord Marchmain gives acknowledgement of absolution, making the sign of the cross. Lord Marchmain is a composite character based on Lord Beauchamp and Waugh's friend Major Hubert Duggan. William Lygon was born in London, educated at Eton and Christ Church, Oxford, and succeeded his father to the title in 1891. He spent most of his life in public service. At twenty-three he was mayor of Worcester and at twenty-seven Governor of New South Wales. He married the daughter of the Duke of Westminster in 1902, and was a leading Liberal politician, a cabinet minister and leader of the Liberals in the Lords. Then, suddenly, in 1931, he resigned all offices and went to live abroad, as the result of a homosexual scandal. Waugh was a frequent visitor to the family seat at Madresfield. Hubert Duggan was another close friend of Waugh's. He was a lapsed Catholic, but Waugh got a priest to be present when his friend was dying. He anointed his head and Hubert crossed himself: 'so he knows what happened and accepted it,' Waugh recorded in his diary, 'So we spent the day watching for a spark of gratitude for the love of God and saw the spark.'

MARIA

Ernest Hemingway, *For Whom the Bell Tolls* (1941)

Maria

For Whom the Bell Tolls, Ernest Hemingway's celebrated novel of the Spanish Civil War, brings the hero Robert Jordan into contact with a beautiful and vulnerable Spanish girl Maria. She tells Jordan that she has been in prison at Valladolid and explains that her father was shot as a Republican. Jordan tells Maria that his father (like Hemingway's) shot himself and she feels that this brings them closer together. Later Maria comes to Jordon in the night. Jordan asks her if she has loved others and she replies 'Never. . . . But things were done to me. . . . Where things were done to me I fought until I could not see. I fought until – until – until one sat upon my head – and I bit him – and then they tied my mouth and held my arms behind my head – and others did things to me.'

During the Spanish Civil War, Hemingway visited Spain four times. On one of his visits, in the spring of 1938, he went to see a friend who was recovering from wounds at hospital in Mataró, north of Barcelona. There, in Mataró hospital, Hemingway met the nurse Maria who told Hemingway of her experiences of the war; she had been raped by Fascist soldiers and yet all those she nursed thought of her as the 'soul of serenity'. Hemingway used Maria's harrowing past and quietly courageous character as the basis for the Maria of his novel. He changed her appearance, however, to that of Martha Gellhorn, the woman who was to become his third wife and to whom *For Whom the Bell Tolls* is dedicated: 'She had high cheekbones, merry eyes and a straight mouth with full lips. Her hair was the golden brown of a grain field that has been burned dark in the sun.' Hemingway found the title of his novel, via *The Oxford Book of English Prose*, in a passage by John Donne.

MISS MARPLE

Agatha Christie, *Murder at the Vicarage* (1930), *The Thirteen Problems* (1932), *The Regatta Mystery* (1939), *The Body in the Library* (1942), *The Moving Finger* (1943), *A Murder is Announced* (1950), *Three Blind Mice* (1950), *They Do It With Mirrors* (1952), *A Pocket Full of Rye* (1953), *4.50 from Paddington* (1957), *The Adventure of*

In *The Murder of Roger Ackroyd* (1926) Agatha Christie took considerable care over the presentation of Dr Sheppard's sister Caroline, a lady she described in *An Autobiography* (1977) as 'an acidulated spinster, full of curiosity, knowing everything, hearing everything: the complete detective service in the home'. When the novel was adapted (by Michael Morton) as the play *Alibi*, Caroline was dropped and substituted by a much younger woman who could provide Hercule Poirot with a romantic interest. 'At that moment, in St Mary Mead,' Christie remembered, 'though I did not yet know it, Miss Marple was born.'

Miss Jane Marple, village gossip and amateur sleuth, first appeared in 1930 in the novel *Murder at the Vicarage* and the character was evidently inspired by Christie's grandmother, Mrs Miller, who brought up the author's mother at her home in Ealing. The main quality Mrs Miller had in common with Miss Marple was, Agatha Christie noted, a fatalistic outlook: 'though a cheerful person, she always expected the worst of everyone and everything, and was, with almost frightening accuracy, usually proved right'. Although her prophecies were of a mundane rather than a criminal nature they were taken very seriously indeed. Once she accurately predicted the escape, up the chimney, of a tame squirrel adopted by Agatha's brother and sister; on another occasion she warned that a disturbance would bring down a jar on a shelf over the drawing-room door and, sure enough, there was a thunderstorm that banged the door and brought down the jar. 'Anyway,' Agatha Christie remembered, 'I endowed my Miss Marple with something of Grannie's powers of prophecy. There was no unkindness in Miss Marple, she just did not trust people. Though she expected the worst, she often accepted people kindly in spite of what they were.'

the Christmas Pudding (1960), *Double Sin* (1961), *The Mirror Crack'd from Side to Side* (1962), *A Caribbean Mystery* (1964), *At Bertram's Hotel* (1965), *Sleeping Murder* (1976)

Mrs Miller

Further reading:
Agatha Christie, *An Autobiography* (1977)

RICHARD MARPLE

Edward Upward, *The Spiral Ascent* (1962–76)

Christopher Isherwood (1904–86)

Further reading:
Brian Finney, *Christopher Isherwood* (1979)

Edward Upward's trilogy *The Spiral Ascent* – comprising *In the Thirties* (1962), *The Rotten Elements* (1969), *No Home but the Struggle* (1976) – explores the infatuation of the hero, Alan Sebrill, with the Communist Party and the relevance, for an upper-class intellectual, of Marxist thought. The final volume recalls the unhappy years Sebrill spent at his public school (Repton, near Derby) and how his life was made more bearable through his friendship with fellow-pupil Richard Marple. At Cambridge, Alan and Richard encounter the Poshocracy (whose values are expressed by snobbish undergraduates) and concoct their own literary fantasy world by way of protection. Alan, who works as a teacher, constantly agonizes over the impact on his poetry of his commitment to Communism. When the trilogy opens he is spending a holiday on an island with Richard: 'Without any envy at all, and with happy admiration, Alan recognized that [Richard's poetic work] was far better than anything he himself had done or ever could do . . . He seemed to be able to see also, as from some slight distance away, both Richard and himself sitting there on the verandah, the two young poets; and he had the idea that the picture they formed would not disappear when they returned inside the house, was permanent, would continue to exist long after they were dead.' The two friends agree that the poor are doomed and that only the doomed are fine: 'Richard, excited by this conception, said, "Our duty is to live among the doomed and in our poetry we must record and celebrate what they are".'

The romantic opening of the trilogy is based on holidays Upward spent at Freshwater Bay, Isle of Wight in 1926 and 1928 with Christopher Isherwood – whose father was the second son of John Bradshaw-Isherwood of Marple Hall (hence Richard Marple) in Cheshire. Upward first met Isherwood, his junior by a year, in 1920 when they were both history students at Repton public school. Both boys wrote poetry – Upward winning the Howes Verse Prize with his 'The Surrender of the German Fleet at Scapa Flow' – and published poems in *The Reptonian*, the school magazine. At Cambridge, Upward and Isherwood concocted stories about Mortmere, an imaginary village on the edge of the Atlantic Ocean. Isherwood, who considered Upward his 'closest heterosexual male friend', made his name not as a poet but as a novelist. His first published novel, *All the Conspirators* (1928), is dedicated to Upward, who appears in it as ALLEN CHALMERS; in Isherwood's *Lions and Shadows* (1938) Upward is again Allen Chalmers. The sense of doom celebrated by Richard in Upward's trilogy is evident in the novels – such as *Mr Norris Changes Trains* (1935) – Isherwood based on his life in Berlin (1930–3).

MARTINET

Traditional term for one who practises a strictly disciplined adherence to rules and regulations – current

General Martinet's name has now passed into the language. At one time it was associated with the particular system of drill which he invented. In Wycherley's play *The Plain Dealer* a character exclaims: 'What! Do you find fault with Martinet? Tis the best exercise in the world!' So his name was associated with military drill as early as only four years after his from early 18th century

General Jean Martinet (died 1672)

Further reading: Francois Marie Arouet de Voltaire, *The Age of Louis XIV*, translated by Martyn Pollack (1926)

death. Gradually the word is used in a more general sense for a military or naval officer who is a stickler for precision and discipline. In France it was the name given to an instrument used in schools as a means of corporal punishment. Paul du Chaillu, writing in *Land of the Midnight Sun* in 1881 says: 'I saw what resembled a policeman's club, at the end of which was a thick piece of leather, the whole reminding one of a martinet.'

The term seems to have originated from the manner in which General Martinet habitually exercised his military duties and responsibilities during the middle years of the reign of Louis XIV. Jean Martinet was lieutenant-colonel of the King's Regiment of Foot and Inspector General of Infantry. He drilled and trained foot soldiers in the new model army of professional fighting men which was created by Louis and Francois Michel le Tellier, Marquis de Louvois (1641–91). Martinet won renown as a military engineer and pioneer tactician, devising forms of battle manoeuvre, pontoon bridges and a new type of assault boat with a copper bottom (used in Louis XIV's Dutch campaign), in the years 1660–70. Martinet played a significant role in making the French army the first and the best regular army in Europe. The key achievement of Martinet and his colleagues – Turenne, Condé, Luxemburg – was the introduction of a uniform system of drill and training. This was the period when the soldier of fortune, the man who joined a regiment with his own arms and equipment, and had learned his trade from his own (often varied) experience, began to be replaced by the professional, enlisted, full-time career soldier, recruited into permanent regiments which were trained by their own officers. Martinet, who had in large part made this possible, was ironically shot by accident by his own men when he led the infantry assault at the siege of Duisburg.

MASANIELLO

Eugène Scribe, Opera, *La Muette de Portici* (1828), libretto by Eugene Scribe, music by Daniel Francois Esprit Auber.

Tommaso Aniello (1623–47)

Further reading: August von Reumont, *Die Caraffa von Maddaloni*, Berlin (1849), Luigi Capasso, *La Casa e famiglia di Masanielo*, Naples (1893)

La Muette de Portici must be unique among operas, in the fact that its performance at Brussels on 25 August 1830 genuinely seems to have sparked off the revolt which led eventually to the independence of Belgium, recognized by the European powers in 1839. Auber felt at this stage of his career something a little more spectacular than his previous operas was called for. He could not have dreamed in his wildest moments that *La Muette de Portici*, written for a grand production at the Paris Opèra in 1828, would so dramatically realize his ambitions. He had chosen a sensational subject – the revolt of the Neapolitans against their Spanish oppressors in 1647 – and allied the action to another colourful event, the eruption of Mount Vesuvius in 1631. Masaniello, a humble young fisherman, has a sister, Fanella, who is dumb from birth. She is an attractive girl and is soon noticed by Alfonso, son of the Spanish Viceroy at Naples. She is seduced and abandoned by Alfonso, who is betrothed to be married to the Spanish Princess, Elvira. Masaniello's close friend, Pietro, tells him that Fanella has been ruined by Alfonso, and the two companions sing the celebrated patriotic duet, 'Amour sacré de la patrie', which became the theme song of the revolt in 1830. Fanella is imprisoned by Alfonso, but the people rise against the Spanish authorities, led by Masaniello, who becomes king of Naples. He is poisoned by Pietro, tells him that Fanella has been ruined by Alfonso, and the two Spanish rulers they have deposed. Nevertheless, he leads the rebels to victory and is slain in battle. Fanella commits suicide in her grief at hearing the news of her brother's death. She jumps from her window into the crater of Vesuvius. Masaniello is based on the story of Tommaso Aniello, the Neapolitan patriot, a fisherman at Amalfi. He led the revolt of July 1647 against the Spanish, and was successful in overthrowing Spanish rule. He ruled Naples for nine days, but was betrayed to agents of the Spanish Viceroy and was shot. His body was thrown into a ditch, but recovered by his companions, and he was given a hero's funeral. The actual cause of the rebellion was the heavy tax system levied by the Spanish. Tammaso's wife had smuggled flour and as a consequence his property had been confiscated (see FRA DIAVOLO). Ironically Auber was made Imperial Maitre de Chapelle in 1857, and he was deeply distressed by the events during the Paris Commune.

MASHA

Leo Tolstoy, *Family Hapiness* (1859)

Valeriya Arsyeneva (1836–1909)

Further reading: Henri Troyat, *Tolstoy* (1965)

In 1856 Leo Tolstoy met Valeriya Arsyeneva, an orphan who lived with her aunt on the estate of Sundakova, five miles from the Tolstoy family estate of Yasnaya Polyana. Initially, Tolstoy's attitude to Valeriya was critical: her smile, he noted, was 'sickly and submissive'; her arms, he lamented, were 'not pretty'; her 'frivolity about everything serious' dismayed him. Still, he began to find her attractive 'as a woman' and discussed marriage with her on 10 August 1856. Further exposure to Valeriya's personality, however, convinced Tolstoy she was too trivial for him. On 12 November he wrote to tell her that, whereas he was fundamentally serious, she was foolishly fascinated by 'the ball, the bare shoulders, the carriages and diamonds'. On 10 December Valeriya complained that she was bored by Tolstoy's preaching and he responded, two days later, with a letter ending any prospects of marriage: 'We are too far apart . . . Love and marriage would have given us nothing but misery'. Valeriya recovered from this rebuff and subsequently married A.A. Talysin, future magistrate at Orlov. Tolstoy pondered on what might have been and, as April FitzLyon says in her note on her translation (1953) of *Family Happiness*, 'wrote the novella in order to prove to himself that, if he had married Valeriya, the marriage would probably not have been a success.'

Family Happiness is narrated in the first person by Masha, the heroine, who describes her relationship with Sergey Mikhailovich. He, like Tolstoy, has a talent for candid conversation: 'He questioned me, provoked the frankest and most intimate discussions, gave advice, encouraged me, and would sometimes scold and restrain me . . . The fashionable hairstyles and dresses in which Katia liked to dress me up for smart occasions only provoked his mockery.' Just as Tolstoy was eleven years older than Valeriya, so Sergey Mikhailovich is the older man in Masha's life. When Masha marries Sergey she finds that romance atrophies into a dull rural routine at Nikolskoye. She becomes painfully aware of her husband's limitations and substitutes for conjugal love a maternal concern for her children. The novella ends ironically: 'From that day my romance with my husband was over, the old feeling became a dear, irretrievable memory, and a new feeling of love for my children and for the father of my children laid the foundation for another, this time completely different, happy life, which I am still living at the present moment . . .'

KATUSHA MASLOVA

Leo Tolstoy, *Resurrection* (1899)

Gasha (Agatha Mikhailovna Trubetskaya)

Before Tolstoy was two his mother died (on 7 March 1830) and her maternal place, on the family estate of Yasnaya Polyana, was taken by his 'Aunt Toinette' (actually his distant cousin Tatyana Alexandrovna Ergolskaya). As a young aristocrat in search of sexual adventure, Tolstoy felt that Aunt Toinette's servants were fair game, and he was particularly attracted to Gasha – Agatha Mikhailovna Trubetskaya – who was a virgin with a fine figure and eyes as 'black as wet currants'. Shortly before his death, Tolstoy told his biographer Biryukov of 'the crime I committed against Gasha, a maid-servant living in my aunt's house. She was a virgin. I seduced her, they turned her out, and she went to the bad.'

Haunted by this guilty memory, Tolstoy wrote his novel *Resurrection* in which Prince Dmitri Nekhludov has to judge Katusha Maslova, a prostitute on trial for murder, knowing she is the servant-girl he seduced. In the novel (as translated by Vera Traill) Katusha's beauty shines through her prison pallor. Like Gasha she has 'sparkling black eyes' and a good figure: 'She carried herself erect, her full bosom well forward, and her head thrown back.' In a flashback to Katusha's first encounter with a 'rich young prince', Tolstoy writes: 'Three years later [when Katusha was nineteen and the prince] was about to join his regiment, he paid his aunts a four-day visit. On the eve of his departure he seduced Katusha, and when he bade her good-bye handed her a hundred-rouble note. Within five months of this time it became clear to her that she was pregnant.' Katusha then drifts 'into a life of habitual sin against every commandment, divine and human' culminating in her trial for murder, ten years after her catastrophic seduction, before a jury that includes Prince Nekhludov who recognizes her as the girl 'whom he had seduced, forsaken, and forgotten. It had been an episode painful to remember, and he never allowed himself to think of it: he, who so prided himself on his good breeding, had proved to be anything but a gentleman.' Prince Nekhludov's moral dilemma supplies the substance of the novel which ends with Katusha's pardon and exile and his spiritual resurrection.

In recalling the story, Tolstoy had imagined what might have happened to Gasha. In fact, as Henri Troyat points out in his biography *Tolstoy* (1965), 'Gasha's fate had nothing in common with that of the Katusha Maslova of the novel. After her "fault", Gasha became a chambermaid to Marya Nikolayevna, Leo Tolstoy's sister, gained her confidence and raised her children.'

THE MASTER

H. D., *Collected Poems 1912–1944* (1984)

Sigmund Freud (1856–1939)

Further reading: Barbara Guest, *Herself Defined: The Poet H.D. and her World* (1984)

In 1913 the American poet Hilda Doolittle – or H.D. as she styled her literary self – married the English writer Richard Aldington; their joint volume *Images, Old and New* (1915) expressed their faith in the Imagist mode of poetry evolved by Ezra Pound. H.D. had been briefly engaged to Pound, but felt she could live in harmony with Aldington so, in 1917, she was distressed to discover that Aldington had become involved with another woman, Dorothy Yorke. H.D. turned for friendship to D.H. Lawrence, and for love to Cecil Gray, the Edinburgh-born composer with whom she went to Cornwall. After giving birth to Cecil Gray's daughter in 1919, H.D. went to Greece with her lesbian friend Bryher (Winifred Ellerman). On the voyage out she met Peter Rodeck, an architect on his way to India, and saw in him 'a symbol of everything I had not had, the perfect balance in my life'. However, H.D. and Rodeck parted abruptly in Athens and he subsequently married in India.

So many things had gone wrong, emotionally, for H.D. that she could not cope with the strain of her situation and went for psychiatric help to Sigmund Freud in Vienna. The great psychoanalyst treated her for three months in 1933 and for five weeks in 1934. Freud convinced H.D. she had to come to terms with her past and, as a result, she experienced what amounted to a resurrection of her psyche. For a decade, until the publication of *The Walls Do Not Fall* in 1944, H.D. published no new collections of verse (apart from a translation of the *Ion* of Euripides in 1937). Though she wrote a novel, *Bid Me To Live* (1960) about her personal crises during the First World War, she did not wish to publish her poem 'The Master'. It eventually appeared (twenty years after H.D.'s death) in *Feminist Studies* 7 (Fall 1981), and in Louis L. Martz's edition of H.D.'s *Collected Poems 1912–1944* (1984).

Freud, who developed the technique of free association as the basis of psychoanalysis and scrutinized the sexual impulse in such works as *Three Contributions to the Sexual Theory* (1905), is 'The Master' in H.D.'s poem. In the seventh section of the poem she pays tribute to Freud as prophet and healer: 'He will trouble the thoughts of men/yet for many an aeon,/they will travel far and wide,/they will discuss all his written words,/his pen will be sacred/they will build a temple/and keep all his sacred writings safe,/and men will come/and men will quarrel/but he will be safe;/they will found temples in his name,/his fame/will be so great/that anyone who has known him/will also be hailed as master,/seer/interpreter.'

GRAY MATURIN

W. Somerset Maugham,

In 1940 Somerset Maugham arrived in America for a speaking tour that would advocate American involvement in the Second World War. He was welcomed in New York by his American publisher Nelson Doubleday who had taken over the family firm in 1929 with spectacular success. Maugham liked Doubleday and appreciated all his efforts to further his reputation in the USA. When Maugham mentioned that he wanted to find somewhere to complete his new novel, Doubleday offered to build him a house, with a separate cottage for writing, on his South Carolina plantation. Accepting the offer, and gladly agreeing to contribute to the cost from future royalties, Maugham moved into Parker's Ferry, Yemassee, South Carolina in December 1940.

The Razor's Edge (1944)

Nelson Doubleday
(1889–1949)

Further reading:
Ted Walker, *Maugham* (1980)

As he worked on *The Razor's Edge* he saw Nelson Doubleday regularly as he used the plantation as a holiday home; inevitably Nelson appeared in the novel, as Gray Maturin. Gray is a big easygoing man: 'Though built on so large a scale he was finely proportioned, and stripped he must have been a fine figure of a man. He was obviously very powerful. His virility was impressive. He made Larry who was sitting next to him, though only three or four inches shorter, look puny.' Isabel the heroine of the novel, is in love with the spiritual Larry Darrell but marries the dependable Gray who 'was so kindly, so unselfish, so upright, so reliable, so unassuming that it was impossible not to like him'.

When Maugham heard that Doubleday was dying, in 1949, he came to New York to see him and spent weekends at his home in Oyster Bay. At Doubleday's funeral Maugham said 'It was touching to see the thoughtful tact with which the great big man sought for ways in which he could give pleasure to his friends. . . . For thirty years Nelson Doubleday gave me his constant and affectionate friendship. The recollection of it is a treasure that can never be taken away from me.'

DIANE DE MAUFRIGNEUSE

Honoré de Balzac, *Le Cabinet des Antiques* (1836), *Les Secrets de la Princesse de Cardignan* (1839)

Cordelia de Castellane

Further reading:
Andre Maurois, *Prometheus: The Life of Balzac* (1965)

Les Cabinet des Antiques covers the period 1822–24 and concerns the career of Victurnien, the weak-willed son of the Marquis d'Esgrignon. The Marquis has lost his estates and position but lives on the glories of the past. His salon has been wittily nick-named 'the cabinet of antiques' after a collection of coins, medals etc. begun by Francis I and completed by Louis XIV (now the Cabinet du Roi, in the Bibliothèque Nationale). Family hopes are centred on Victurnien, who is dispatched to Paris after sundry gallantries at Alençon, in the hope that he may prosper in a military and diplomatic career. He is corrupted by Parisian high-society and becomes a notorious dandy. He is seduced by the accomplished siren Diane de Maufrigneuse, who poses as an angel in religion and a high-priestess of romantic poetry and culture. He is lured into her net by her seraphic beauty and her complexion, which is as pure as the snow on the high Alps. She fleeces him of his fortune and in despair he turns to forgery. He is saved from condemnation to the galleys by the cunning of his mistress, who finally discards him. *Les Secrets de la Princesse de Cardignan* continues the amorous adventures of Diane, who has now become the Princesse de Cardignan on the death of her father-in-law. She seduces Daniel d'Arthez, a successful and fashionable man of letters and aspiring politician, and enjoys a succession of other lovers – thirteen are specified by Balzac not counting d'Arthez. She is an expensive mistress, and drains her lovers as well as her husband, who has joined Charles X in exile after the Revolution of July 1830.

This is based on the personality and career of Cordelia de Castellane, the mistress of Chateaubriand. Both were born into wealthy, aristocratic families, and both ended their lives in disaster. Cordelia de Castellane was separated from her husband and lived in the Faubourg Saint-Honoré. Diane lives in the Rue de Miromesnil, but both have small apartments. They were both astonishingly beautiful women, but beneath the surface corrupt and depraved. Diane de Maufrigneuse has a close confidant, the Marquise d'Espard, who supports her in her liaisons; and Cordelia de Castellane consorted with the Duchesse de Dino. 'Undoubtedly they knew weighty secrets concerning each other, and were not likely to quarrel over a man or a service to be rendered . . . When two women friends are capable of murdering each other,' wrote Balzac, 'they present a touching spectacle of harmony . . .'

CAMILLE MAUPIN
Honoré de Balzac, *Béatrix* (1839)
George Sand (1804–76)

Further reading: Curtis Cate, *George Sand – A Biography* (1975)

In Balzac's novel *Béatrix* two women of strong personality are rivals in love, Beatrice de Rochefide and Félicité des Touches, who both desire the romantic and successful Italian singer Gennaro Conti (see BÉATRICE DE ROCHEFIDE and GENNARO CONTI.) Beatrice is a shallow and pretentious member of the upper classes who wishes to shine in artistic circles. Her depth of character is given to us in the attention she pays to her hair styles and clothes. Felicité is an authoress, famous under her pen-name of Camille Maupin. The tenor is seduced by Béatrice's glamour and charm. Camille, who has genius but is self-effacing, loses out in the amorous game that is thus played out, though Béatrice's victory turns out to be a hollow success as love wanes. Camille retires to a convent, where her true genius pours itself out in successful authorship. The winner is the loser, and she who had lost has really triumphed; Balzac wrote in the preface: 'When certain women of high rank have sacrificed their position to some violent passion; when they have flouted the laws, do they not find in their pride of race, in the value they bestow upon themselves, and even in their own superiority, barriers as difficult to surmount as those already overcome? . . . All has not been said when a noble and generous woman has resigned her social and aristocratic sovereignty. She remains forever attached to the author of her ruin, like a convict to his chained companion.'

This is a portrayal of the rivalry between Marie d'Agoult and George Sand, who had both loved Franz Liszt, but who quarrelled after Marie had left her husband to join the composer. George Sand was married to Casimir, Baron Dudevant, but left him in 1829 to become the centre of literary and bohemian life, associating with Alfred de Musset, Chopin, Lemmennais, Leroux and Liszt. She was a prolific writer, her works consisting of over a hundred volumes, including novels, plays, autobiography and exquisite letters. Balzac makes Camille a celibate, of independent judgement and obvious superiority and not without altruism. She turns from the love of men to the love of God. This is a romantic and idealized portrait, but Balzac admired her to the end. He wrote in a letter to a friend: 'All the follies she has committed are titles to glory in the eyes of noble spirits . . . she is one of those people who are masterful at the writing-table but easily caught out in real life . . .'

MAZEPPA
Lord Byron, *Mazeppa* (1819)
Ivan Stepanovich Mazepa-Koledinsky (1644–1709)

Further reading: N.I. Kostomarov, *Mazepa and the Mazepanites*, St Petersburg (1885), R. Nisbet Bain, *The First Romanovs* (1905)

After the battle of Pultowa, a Ukrainian cavalry commander in the service of Charles II of Sweden is near to death. The King asks him to tell his story: 'Of all our band, Though firm of heart and strong of hand,/In skirmish, march, or forage, none/Can less have said, or more have done/Than thee, Mazeppa!' The old warrrior obliges with the narrative of seventy years' adventurous life, and tells his companions of his early life as page to Casimir V, King of Poland. He was discovered in his liaison with the wife of a local magnate and punished by being bound naked on the back of a wild horse. The horse was then whipped into madness and let loose. Mazeppa was carried on wild chase through forest and woodlands, through streams and finally to the plains of the Ukraine, where the horse drops dead. Mazeppa was released by peasants and brought back to health by the Cossacks.

Byron based this adventure on part of the life story of Mazepa-Koledinsky. He was educated at the court of the King of Poland, Casimir, and was punished for an intrigue with the wife of a Polish nobleman by being strapped on the back of a wild horse and sent into the steppe. The Dnieperian Cossacks rescued him and he became a Cossack leader. In 1687 he was made commander of the Cossacks and served under Peter the Great and was sufficiently honoured as to sit at the Tsar's own table. He changed to the service of Charles II of Sweden because he believed that Charles would defeat the Tsar. He was in touch with Charles's ministers when Peter ordered him to cooperate with his forces then mobilized in the Ukraine. This was in October 1708, and he had agreed with the Swedes to close the Ukraine to the Russians. Peter's wrath at Mazepa's treason was immense, and his effigy was burnt by the hangman and he was excommunicated. After the terrible defeat at Pultowa he went with Charles to Turkey with the remaining 1,500 horses of their original 80,000 cavalry and the Sultan refused to hand them over to Peter the Great, in spite of an offered ransom of 300,000 ducats. Mazepa died at Bender on 22 August 1709.

MR McGREGOR

Beatrix Potter, *The Tale of Peter Rabbit* (1902)

Mr Macgregor

Further reading:
Leslie Linder, *A History of the Writings of Beatrix Potter* (1971)

Beatrix Potter was sixteen when Annie Carter (1863–1950), then twenty, became her companion and German teacher in London. The two women became great friends and when Annie married, and became Mrs Moore, the close relationship continued. The first of Annie Moore's eight children, Noel, was born in 1887. He became ill as a child so Beatrix Potter sent him a letter, on 4 September 1893, about four little rabbits called Flopsy, Mopsy, Cottontail and Peter, who lived with their mother in a sand bank under the root of a big fir tree. As Mrs Rabbit explains to her children, they can go into the field or down the lane but not into Mr McGregor's garden. Peter, who was 'very naughty', ignores this advice and squeezes underneath the gate of Mr McGregor's garden: 'round the end of a cucumber frame whom should he meet but Mr McGregor! Mr McGregor was planting out young cabbages but he jumped up and ran after Peter waving a rake and calling out "Stop thief!"' The story delighted little Noel Moore who preserved the letter and lent it to Beatrix Potter when she decided to expand it into a book entitled 'The Tale of Peter Rabbit and Mr McGregor's Garden, by H.B. Potter'. As several publishers declined the story, the author had *The Tale of Peter Rabbit* privately printed and issued in a limited edition of 250 copies on 16 December 1901. This quickly sold out and the book became a children's classic.

In a letter in 1940 Beatrix Potter said 'I never knew a gardener named "Mr McGregor". Several bearded horticulturalists have resented the nickname; but I do not know how it came about.' In 1942, in another letter, she said 'Mr McGregor was no special person'. However the original Mr McGregor is identified in Leslie Linder's book on Beatrix Potter. The letter Beatrix Potter sent to Noel Moore was written in Eastwood, Dunkeld, a dower house on the Atholl Estate beside the river Tay in Perthshire; 'In actual fact the Peter Rabbit picture letter [of 4 September 1893] was written in Mr Macgregor's garden! For this was the name of the tenant who sub-let Eastwood to the Potters in 1893.' Peter Rabbit was Beatrix Potter's own pet rabbit Peter. She bought him in the Uxbridge Road, Shepherds Bush, for four shillings and sixpence in 1892 and he died on 26 January 1901.

LLOYD McHARG

Thomas Wolfe, *You Can't Go Home Again* (1940)

Sinclair Lewis (1885–1951)

Further reading:
Mark Schover, *Sinclair Lewis: An American Life* (1961), Andrew Turnbull, *Thomas Wolfe* (1968)

After Thomas Wolfe's *Look Homeward, Angel* (1929) appeared Sinclair Lewis, author of *Babbitt* (1922) and *Elmer Gantry* (1927), wrote to the young writer about the 'spacious power' of his first novel. When Lewis became the first American to win the Nobel Prize for Literature, in 1930, he made a speech naming Wolfe as a writer establishing a national literature worthy of the USA. In February 1931 Lewis met Wolfe in London and kept his company during a boozy week which culminated in a trip in a rented limousine to the English country house of a friend.

Wolfe recreated the circumstances in *You Can't Go Home Again*, the autobiographical story of George Webber's adventures as a published novelist. Webber's first novel is praised by Lloyd McHarg, 'one of the chief figures in American letters'. Awarded an honorary degree by a leading American university, McHarg makes a speech praising Webber as 'a future spokesman of his country's spirit . . . a man of genius'. The two writers arrange to meet in London, and Webber is astonished by his first sight of McHarg: 'McHarg was standing in the middle of the floor with a glass in one hand and a bottle of Scotch whisky in the other, preparing to pour himself a drink . . . The first and most violent impression was his astonishing redness. Everything about him was red – hair, large protuberant ears, eyebrows, eyelids, even his bony, freckled, knuckly hands . . . His face did not have that fleshy and high-coloured floridity that is often seen in men who have drunk too long and too earnestly. It was not like that at all. McHarg was thin to the point of emaciation. He was very tall, six feet two or three, and his excessive thinness and angularity made him seem even taller. George thought he looked ill and wasted.' Subsequently Webber accompanies an alcoholically exhausted McHarg on a trip, in a chartered Rolls-Royce, to Surrey.

Wolfe, a considerable drinker himself, joked that Lewis should have been given the Nobel Prize for his drinking abilities. No drinker he had met, he felt, was the equal of 'Red'. Lewis was a prolific author who shared with Wolfe great vitality and a tendency to value verbal energy more than form. Both writers created larger-than-life images of America and both wrote rapidly with little interest in literary finish. Lewis remains, though, a crucial figure in American literature whose best work was done in the 1920s before he reacted to the rigours of his life: like Lloyd McHarg, Lewis pushed his 'amazing reserves of energy and vitality' to the limit.

MR MERDLE

Charles Dickens, *Little Dorrit* (1857)

John Sadleir (1814–56)

Further reading: John Butt and Kathleen Tillotson, *Dickens at Work* (1957), Humphry House, *The Dickens World* (1941)

Mr Merdle MP is a swindler, banker, forger and thief whose enterprises flourish at a time when company law was in its infancy. His financial manipulations form the basis of the plot mechanism of the novel, and ruin Clennam, the Dorrits and others. 'Immensely rich; a man of prodigious enterprise; a Midas without the ears, who turned all he touched to gold. He was in everything good, from banking to building. . . . His desire was to the utmost to satisfy Society . . . and take up all its drafts upon him for tribute. He did not shine in company; he had not very much to say for himself; he was a reserved man, with a broad, overhanging, watchful head, that particular kind of dull red colour in his cheeks which is rather stale than fresh, and a somewhat uneasy expression about his coat-cuffs, as if they were in his confidence, and had reasons for being anxious to hide his hands.'

Dickens based Merdle on the Irish politician and swindler, Sadleir. He was educated at Clongowes College and became a solicitor in Dublin. He was a director of the Tipperary Joint Stock Bank, and chairman of the London and County Joint Stock Bank in 1848. He was MP for Carlow and for Sligo in 1853 and was made junior lord of the treasury in 1853. He committed suicide in 1856 on the failure of the Tipperary Bank, then managed by his brother James, which had been brought about by his fraudulent practices. Dickens had a long-standing interest in financial speculation and chicanery – with the exception only of *Barnaby Rudge* and *A Tale of Two Cities*, all his novels contain significant treatment of swindling and financial manipulation – but he confessed to his biographer, John Forster, that he shaped Mr Merdle himself out of the 'precious rascality' of John Sadleir, as early as the sixth episode of *Little Dorrit* (May 1856). It is the case that some aspects of the Merdle story are reminiscent of the escapades of George Henry Hudson, the Railway King, who fled to France in the financial panic of 1847–48, but Dickens says in the 'Preface' to *Dorrit*, 'If I might make so bold as to defend that extravagant conception, Mr Merdle, I would hint that it originated after the railroad-share epoch, in the times of a certain Irish bank.' Sadleir slit his throat on Hampstead Heath as his empire crashed in 1856.

DIANA MERION

George Meredith, *Diana of the Crossways* (1885)

Diana Merion, heroine of Meredith's novel, is the witty and lively daughter of a good Irish family. She marries the dull Warwick, who does not understand her or appreciate her true qualities. In a fit of jealousy he brings an action for divorce against her, in which he cites Lord Dannisburgh. Warwick loses his case. An ambitious young politician, Dacier, who is in love with her, finds that some important political confidences he has given her have been passed on to a national newspaper. Diana has done this because she was pressed for money. It leads to the end of the relationship between Dacier and Diana. Warwick dies, and Diana finally marries Redworth, a loyal admirer.

Caroline Norton (1808–77)

Further reading: David Cecil, *Melbourne* (1965), A. Woods, *George Meredith as Champion of Women* (1937)

Meredith based Diana on the beautiful Caroline Norton, daughter of Thomas Sheridan (1775–1817), a colonial administrator, who was the son of Sheridan the playwright. Caroline married the Hon George Chapple Norton in 1827, and enjoyed a literary career – *The Sorrows of Rosalie, With Other Poems* (1829), *A Voice From the Factories* (1836) – as well as miscellaneous pieces for journals. In 1836 her husband brought an action for divorce against her in which he cited William Temple, Lord Melbourne, the Prime Minister. The evidence was insubstantial, and many believed at the time that the action was brought to discredit Melbourne. Her husband died in 1875 and she married Sir William Stirling-Maxwell. Caroline was accused of obtaining a Cabinet secret from her lover and selling it to *The Times*.

Meredith knew her well and admitted to Robert Louis Stevenson that he had used her character and incidents from her life in composing *Diana of the Crossways*. After its publication several of Caroline's relatives expressed their shock and anger and fearing legal action Meredith published the 'Apology' reprinted in all subsequent editions: 'A lady of high distinction for wit and beauty, the daughter of an illustrious Irish house, came under the shadow of a calumny. It has latterly been examined and exposed as baseless. The story of *Diana of the Crossways* is to read as fiction.'

MERLIN

T.H. White, *The Once and Future King* (1958)

Terence Hanbury White (1906–64)

Further reading: Stephen P. Dunn, 'Mr White, Mr Williams and the Matter of Britain' in the *Kenyon Review*, XXIV (Spring 1962), Sylvia Townshend Warner, *T.H. White* (1967)

T.H. White's *The Once and Future King* is an eccentric reworking of the traditional Matter of Britain (see KING ARTHUR, MERLYN) which combines White's curious and peculiarly extensive knowledge of the medieval period, his gifts of comedy and pathos, and penchant for slangy modernism to produce an astonishingly original and compelling version of Malory's epic treatment of *Le Morte Darthur*. It is a quartet of four novels – *The Sword in the Stone* (1938), *The Witch in the Wood* (1940), *The Ill-Made Knight* (1941) and *The Candle in the Wind* (1958). The first meeting with Merlin is a classic moment of comic writing. He is dressed like a wizard and has a beard: 'Close inspection showed that he was far from clean. It was not that he had dirty finger-nails . . . but some large bird seemed to have been nesting in his hair . . . The old man was streaked with droppings over his shoulders . . .' He takes the future King Arthur to his study: 'It was the most marvellous room he had ever been in. There was a real corkindrill hanging from the rafters . . . When its master came into the room it winked one eye . . . although it was stuffed. There were thousands of brown books in leather bindings . . . Then there were stuffed birds, popinjays, and maggot-pies and kingfishers, and peacocks with all their feathers but two, and tiny birds like beetles . . . There were several boars' tusks and the claws of tigers and libbards mounted in symmetrical patterns . . . two young hedgehogs in cotton-wool, and a pair of badgers which immediately began to cry Yik-Yik-Yik in loud voices as soon as the magician apppeared . . . a gun case with all sorts of weapons which would not be invented for half a thousand years . . . a bunch of turkey feathers and goose-quills for making pens, an astrolabe, twelve pairs of boots . . . three dozen rabbit wires, twelve corkscrews . . . a medal for being the best scholar at Winchester . . . the fourteenth edition of the *Encyclopaedia Britannica* . . . and a complete set of cigarette cards depicting wild fowl by Peter Scott.' This is a self-portrait. White was born in Bombay, son of a senior police officer. He was educated at Cheltenham College and Cambridge University, was a schoolmaster who then turned to writing, using his immense knowledge of frequently obscure subjects. He really preferred his own company, but from time to time indulged in bouts of conviviality. He was an expert angler and hunstman, reviving the art of hawking. He lived on the isle of Alderney and kept a strange collection of domestic pets. He was an eccentric and eclectic scholar, who wrote valuable social history and several underrated novels as well as the monumental Arthurian cycle.

MERLYN

Nennius, *Historia Britonum* (circa 796), Geoffrey of Monmouth, *Historia Regum Britanniae* (circa 1150), *Arthour and Merlyn*, verse romance, (late thirteenth century), Robert de Boron, *Merlin* (thirteenth century), Sir Thomas Malory, *Le Morte D'Arthur* (1470) etc.

Merlin Ambrosius, or **Myrddin Emrys**

Further reading: Nikolai Tolstoy, *The Quest For Merlin* (1985)

In the traditional story of King Arthur (see KING ARTHUR) Merlyn is a wizard and enchanter who enables Uther Pendragon to sleep with Igraine, the wife of Gorlois of Cornwall, in which union Arthur is conceived. He is Arthur's guide, philosopher and friend during his youth and the early part of his reign. It is with Merlyn's help that the great stones are brought from Naas in Ireland to Stonehenge. In Malory's version of the legend it is Merlyn who makes the Round Table for Uther Pendragon. According to some versions of his story he is the son of a nun and the devil, and shows his powers of magic as a youth by solving the problem facing Vortigern, the British King, when he was building a citadel against Hengist and the Saxons. Merlyn demonstrated that the foundations kept falling in because beneath the ground are two dragons, one white and one red. The dragons then fight and the red dragon wins, thus predicting the triumph of the Britons. His gift of prophecy is particularly useful to King Arthur, but he meets his downfall through his infatuation with the sorceress Nimiane, who imprisons him in a cave. In Tennyson's version of this story, Vivian (as she is called by the Victorian poet) gets him to shelter from a storm by hiding in an oak-tree and there leaves him spell-bound.

Two traditions, both with strong bases in historical fact, combine to produce the figure of Merlyn. One is that of Merlyn Ambrosius, advisor to Vortigern and Aurelius, who is made ruler of the western part of Britain and aids the defeat of the Irish. Another tradition associates him with a historical figure who lived in the Scottish Lowlands around 600, who was a sage, druid and tutor, in touch with the darker mysteries of life and death. It is claimed that the Welsh Myrddin poems are by this Merlyn, and that shaman-druids constructed Stonehenge as an Omphalos, a magic stone circle. He is associated with the battle of Arderydd 573 (fought north of Carlisle) after which he went mad and lived wild in the woods. See Emma Jung: *The Grail Legend* and Nikolai Tolstoy: *The Quest for Merlin* 1985. He is the subject of a novel by Robert Nye and fully characterized in T.H. White's *The Once and Future King* (see MERLIN)

MERMAID ON A DOLPHIN'S BACK

William Shakespeare, *A Midsummer Night's Dream* (1595)

Mary Queen of Scots (1542–87)

Further reading: Antonia Fraser, *Mary Queen of Scots* (1969)

On 10 February 1567 Henry Stuart, Lord Darnley – the cousin and second husband of Mary Queen of Scots – was strangled in the grounds of the old provost's house at Kirk o' field, outside Edinburgh. Public opinion was probably correct in identifying the assassin as James Hepburn, Earl of Bothwell (who subsequently abducted Mary and married her, on 15 May 1567). The murder of Darnley ruined what remained of Mary's reputation, and on 1 March 1567 a placard appeared depicting the Queen of Scots as a mermaid and Bothwell (whose family crest was the hare) as a hare surrounded by swords. As Antonia Fraser writes, 'The implication behind the use of the mermaid was not romantic, as might appear to modern eyes, but deliberately insulting, since the word was commonly used in the sixteenth and seventeenth centuries to denote a siren, and thus, by analogy, a prostitute'.

Shakespeare certainly knew of the popular symbolism of the mermaid. Oberon, King of the Fairies in *A Midsummer Night's Dream*, addresses Puck (II.i.48); 'Thou rememb'rest/Since once I sat upon a promontory,/And heard a mermaid on a dolphin's back/Uttering such dulcet and harmonious breath/That the rude sea grew civil at her song,/And certain stars shot madly from their spheres/To hear the sea-maid's music.' Here the mermaid is Mary, whose arrival in England in 1568 did indeed cause 'certain stars' to shoot 'madly from their spheres'.

Although Mary spent the last nineteen years of her life as a prisoner of her cousin Elizabeth I, she was never allowed to meet the English queen. Elizabeth was well aware that they had a claim to the English throne; Elizabeth was the daughter of Henry VIII and his second wife Anne Boleyn, and, as the Pope had not recognised Henry VIII's divorce, Roman Catholics could not consider Elizabeth as a proper heir to the throne. In the first of a series of plots aimed at making Mary queen of England, the Duke of Norfolk planned to release Mary from her English captivity and marry her. In this he was supported by the Earls of Northumberland and Westmoreland – the northern stars who 'shot madly from their spheres/To hear the sea-maid's music'. Elizabeth discovered the plot, transferred Mary to Tutbury in Staffordshire, under the protection of five hundred men, drove the northern earls over the border, and imprisoned the Duke of Norfolk – he was eventually executed, in 1572, for his part in the Ridolfi plot to bring Mary to the English throne as his wife. (See DUESSA.)

MEG MERRILIES

Sir Walter Scott, *Guy Mannering* (1815)

Jean Gordon
(1670-1746)

Meg Merrilies, the gypsy queen whose 'eye had a wild roll that indicated something like real or affected insanity', is vividly present in Sir Walter Scott's *Guy Mannering* on account of her extraordinary appearance – six feet tall with 'dark elf-locks [that] shot out like the snakes of the gorgon' – and her ability to help Harry Bertram to recover his estate. Poignantly, Meg tells the hero: 'I've held you on my knee, Henry Bertram, and sung ye sangs of the auld barons and their bloody wars . . . and Meg Merrilies will never sing sangs mair, be they blithe or sad. But ye'll no forget her . . . For if ever the dead came back among the living, I'll be seen in this glen mony a night after these crazed banes are in the mould.'

Jean Gordon, Scott's prototype, was born in Kirk-Yetholm on the Scottish border and married Patrick Faa who was transported to the American Plantations after being found guilty of fire-raising. Misfortune ran in the family for one of Jean's sons was murdered and three were hanged for sheep-stealing at Jedburgh. She herself presented a petition, at Jedburgh in 1732, expressing her willingness to leave Scotland after being indicted as an Egyptian and common vagabond. When she entered England she embarked on a career of begging and petty crime but her character was still strong enough to cause trouble. After the failure of the 1745 uprising Jean, passing through Carlisle, was horrified to see the heads of Jacobite rebels on the Scotchgate. True to her Jacobite sympathies she protested so loudly that the mob decided to duck her to death in the Eden. She was stoned and ducked, yet every time she managed to get her head above water shouted 'Up wi' Chairlie yet!' She managed to drag herself out of the water but was found dead, the next day, from exposure.

Further reading:
James Reed, *Sir Walter Scott – Landscape and Locality* (1980)

MEURSAULT

Albert Camus, *The Outsider* (1942)

Pierre Galindo

Albert Camus's first novel *The Outsider* was received with international acclaim on account of its evocation of an absurd universe; its resistance to authority made it popular with the forces of the French Resistance and it circulated among inmates of Nazi concentration camps. It is narrated by Meursault, a French Algerian, who hears of his mother's death, buries her, befriends the loutish Raymond, then goes to the beach where he shoots an Arab who has quarrelled with Raymond. During his trial Meursault remains indifferent to the rule of law and to moralistic pressure. He ends by welcoming his imminent death: 'For all to be accomplished, for me to feel less lonely, all that remained was to hope that on the day of my execution there should be a huge crowd of spectators and that they should greet me with howls of execration.'

The character was based on Pierre Galindo whose sister Christiane was one of Camus's girlfriends. In 1938 Pierre came to Algiers for his summer holiday; his muscular appearance and terse talk greatly impressed Camus who warmed to Pierre as a complete contrast to his own introverted intellectuality. As well as being a pied-noir (Algerian-born Frenchman) who embodied Camus's ideal of proletarian toughness, Pierre had first-hand knowledge of the life that had eluded Camus. As an employee of an export firm he knew the sleazy areas of Oran and he also told Camus that he had been in a fight with some Arabs on the beach at Oran. Pierre's bravado and his anecdote about the encounter with Arabs provided Camus with enough material for *The Outsider*. When the novel was published Pierre was delighted, according to Patrick McCarthy's *Camus*: 'he recognised himself with enormous pride and he began acting the role of Meursault. Having become a character in a famous novel he transformed the novel into real life.'

WILKINS MICAWBER

Charles Dickens, *David Copperfield* (1850)

John Dickens (1785–1851)

Further reading: Christopher Hibbert, *The Making of Charles Dickens* (1967)

Micawber is improvidence personified. He is an agent for the firm of Murdstone and Grinby, and David lodges with him while he works there. He is pompous, long-winded and with genteel pretensions, and although he lives permanently beyond his income, he is buoyed up by an unquenchable optimism. He moves from debt to debt and job to job and spends some time in the Marshalsea prison for debt. He is a great friend to David, and finally unmasks the villainy of Uriah Heep ('You heap of infamy!') He is repaid by Betsy Trotwood who makes good his debts and he and his family sail for Australia. He is described in the novel: 'A stoutish, middle-aged person, in a brown surtout and black tights and shoes, with no more hair upon his head . . . than there is upon an egg, and with a very extensive face. . . . His clothes were shabby, but he had an imposing shirtcollar on. He carried a jaunty sort of a stick, with a large pair of rusty tassels to it.' His method of expressing himself is equally unique: 'My dear . . . your papa was very well in his way and heaven forbid that I should disparage him. Take him for all in all, we ne'er shall – in short, make the acquaintance probably, of anybody else possessing, at his time of life, the same legs for gaiters, and able to read the same description of print, without spectacles.'

John Dickens, the novelist's father, was a clerk in the Navy Pay Office at Portsmouth, where he married Elizabeth Barrow (see MRS NICKLEBY) and was later employed in similar circumstances at London, Chatham and later at Somerset House. He was arrested for debt in 1824. He later became parliamentary reporter for the *Morning Herald* and the *Mirror of Parliament*. His ability constantly to live beyond his means was a permanent source of concern to Charles Dickens, who nevertheless loved and admired his father dearly. Robert Langton, who knew John Dickens, described him as 'a chatty, pleasant companion . . . possessing a varied fund of anecdotes and a genuine vein of humour. He was a well built man, rather stout . . . a little pompous. . . . He dressed well, and wore a goodly bunch of seals suspended across his waistcoat.' His verbal prolixity was notorious. 'I do not think he will live long' from his lips became 'I must express my tendency to believe that his longevity is (to say the least of it) extremely problematical.'

DR MIDDLETON

George Meredith, *The Egoist* (1879)

Thomas Love Peacock (1785–1866)

Further reading: G. Beer, *Meredith: a change of masks* (1970), M. Butler, *Peacock Displayed*, A.B. Joung, *The Life and Novels of Thomas Love Peacock*

George Meredith married Mary Ellen Nicolls, a widow seven years his senior, in 1849 and for some time was financially obliged to her father Thomas Love Peacock. The established author (of, for example, *Nightmare Abbey*) and the aspiring writer did not have a harmonious relationship; Meredith disapproved of his father-in-law's politics and Peacock disliked Meredith's flamboyant personality and habit of smoking incessantly. Meredith's marriage was a difficult one and Mary Ellen left him in 1857 to live with the pre-Raphaelite painter Henry Wallis. When she eventually desired to return to her husband, Meredith rejected her. After her death, in 1861, he agonized over his inflexibility.

In *The Egoist* Meredith recalled his married life by portraying his father-in-law in the person of Dr Middleton, the rigidly reactionary father of his heroine Clara Middleton. Preposterously, Dr Middleton encourages the Egoist's courting of Clara on account of his social standing and the quality of his wine cellar. For Dr Middleton has a passion for port: 'Port is deep-sea deep. It is in its flavour deep. . . . It is like a classic tragedy, organic in conception.' Meredith's description of the prejudiced classical scholar is unmistakably Peacockian: 'The Rev Doctor was a fine old picture; a specimen of art peculiarly English; combining in himself piety and epicurism, learning and gentlemanliness, with good room for each and a seat at one another's table: for the rest, a strong man, an athlete in his youth, a keen reader of facts and no reader of persons, genial, a giant at a task, a steady worker besides, but easily discomposed. He loved his daughter and he feared her. However much he liked her character, the dread of her sex and age was constantly present to warn him that he was not tied to perfect sanity while the damsel Clara remained unmarried.'

(1904), Mark Van Doren, *Life of Thomas Love Peacock* (1911)

OSWALD MILLBANK

Benjamin Disraeli, *Coningsby* (1844)

William Ewart Gladstone (1809–94)

Many of Disraeli's parliamentary contemporaries are portrayed in *Coningsby*, notably the young Gladstone, who appears as Oswald Millbank: 'the son of one of the wealthiest manufacturers of Lancashire. His father sent his son to Eton, though he disapproved of the system of education pursued there, to show that he had as much right to do so as any duke in the land. He had, however, brought up his only boy with a due prejudice against every sentiment or institution of an aristocratic character. . . . The character of the son . . . tended to the fulfilment of these injunctions. Oswald Millbank was of a proud and independant nature; reserved, a little stern. . . . His talents were considerable, though invested with no dazzling quality. . . . But Millbank possessed one of those strong industrious volitions whose perseverence amounts almost to genius. . . . Millbank was not blessed with the charm of manner. He seemed close and cold; but he was courageous, just and flexible.' (*Coningsby*, Book I, ch. ix)

William Ewart Gladstone was born in 1809, the son of a successful Liverpool merchant, who traded successfully in the East and West Indies and defended the slave trade against the attacks of the reformers. An opponent of Corn Law Reform, he was Canningite MP for Lancaster. William was educated at Eton and Christ Church, Oxford. He took a double first in classics and mathematics and was president of the Union. He entered politics as Conservative MP for Newark in 1832, the seat he held between 1841–45. His first important speech, advocating a gradual winding down of the slave trade, was made in 1833. Peel made him Junior Lord of the Treasury in 1834, and he was later Under-Secretary for War and the Colonies in the same government. He opposed the Opium War with China in 1840 and was Vice-President of the Board of Trade and Privy Councillor in 1841. Peel made him President of the Board of Trade in 1843, and he introduced the first general railway bill in 1844. In 1845 he resigned over the Maynooth grant issue. He did not re-enter parliament until the struggle for the repeals of the Corn Laws was concluded. In 1847 he was elected MP for Oxford University, and was Chancellor of the Exchequer in Aberdeen's ministry. He became prime minister of the Liberal government in 1868–74, again in 1880 and again in 1886 and 1892–94. He died in May 1894 and was buried in Westminster Abbey.

Further reading: Philip Magnus, *Gladstone* (1954), Richard Shannon, *Gladstone 1809–1865* (1980)

COUNT ALCIBIADES DE MIRABEL

Benjamin Disraeli, *Henrietta Temple – A Love Story* (1837)

Alfred Guillaume Gabriel D'Orsay, Count

The plot of *Henrietta Temple* is simple, but the situation very complex. Armine, an impetuous and glamorous youth, son of an impoverished family, hopes to restore the family fortunes by marrying a wealthy cousin, Katherine. He is accepted, but, realizing his heart is not truly engaged, the marriage is put off for a year. In the meantime he meets and falls in love with Henrietta Temple, and becomes engaged to her. When news of his previous attachment to Katherine is revealed, Henrietta finds solace with the admirable Lord Montfort and agrees to marry him. Armine and Henrietta now realize they are still in love, but separated by very strong

D'Orsay (1801–52)

Further reading: Richard Madden, *Literary Life and Correspondence of the Countess of Blessington* (1855)

social conventions. The situation is saved by Count Mirabel, Montfort relinquishes Henrietta, and the lovers are united. Mirabel is portrayed as: 'The best dressed man in London, fresh and gay as a bird, with not a care on his sparkling visage, and his eye bright with bonhomie. As usual, the dappled light of dawn had guided him to his luxurious bed, that bed that had always afforded him serene slumbers. . . there was something in Count Mirabel's very presence which put everybody in good spirits. . .'

This is based on Disraeli's friend, Count D'Orsay, the 'Last of the Dandies'. He was an artist (he sketched Dickens and other contemporaries), and though of imperialist sympathies, he served in the Bourbons' bodyguard. He came to England at the coronation of George IV in 1821 and joined the Countess of Blessington, forming a fashionable coterie in London. Pressed by debts, he left for Paris in 1849, and was appointed director of fine arts by Louis Napoleon just before he died. In his memoirs Charles Greville says of him: 'He was extremely good looking, very quick, lively, good-natured, and agreeable, with considerable talent, taste for, and knowledge of art. . . His extravagance at one period had plunged him into inextricable difficulties. . . and for some years he made himself a prisoner at Gore House. . . to avoid being incarcerated in a more irksome confinement. Nothing, however, dampened his gaiety, and he procured the enjoyment of constant society. . . He was extremely hospitable, and managed to collect a society which was very miscellaneous, but included many eminent and remarkable men of all descriptions, professions and countries. . . Of course no women ever went there, except a few who were in some way connected with D'Orsay and Lady Blessington. . . There never was a foreigner who so completely took root in England as D'Orsay. . .'

MIRIAM LEIVERS

D.H. Lawrence, *Sons and Lovers* (1913)

Jessie Chambers (1887–1944)

Further reading: Harry T. Moore, *The Priest of Love* (1974), E.T. (Jessie Chambers) *D.H. Lawrence – A Personal Record* (ND), Anne Smith, *Lawrence and Women* (1981), Richard Aldington, *Portrait of a Genius But . . . The Life of D.H. Lawrence 1885–1930* (1950)

D.H. Lawrence's *Sons and Lovers* shows the anguish the hero, Paul Morel, feels as he tries to reconcile his love for his mother with his passion for other women. At Willey Farm he meets Miriam Leivers and is enchanted by her: 'The girl was romantic in her soul.' For the remainder of the novel Paul and Miriam agonize over their relationship and end by agreeing to part.

Miriam is a recreation of Jessie Chambers, whose early influence on Lawrence was profound. He first met her in 1901, on her father's farm at Haggs, near Eastwood. Lawrence liked to visit the Haggites (as he called Jessie's family) and he shared with her a love of literature: as Jessie wrote in her *D. H. Lawrence: A Personal Record* (1935) 'It was entering into possession of a new world, a widening and enlargement of life.' Lawrence told Jessie of his ambitions and added 'Every great man . . . is founded in some woman. Why shouldn't *you* be the woman I am founded in.' When the two met at Lawrence's mother's funeral in 1911 Lawrence admitted to Jessie he had loved his mother 'like a lover. That's why I could never love you.' Jessie resented the rivalry of Lawrence's mother and noted that in *Sons and Lovers* he had 'handed his mother the laurels of victory'.

Jessie Chambers helped Lawrence by writing out passages which he adapted for use in *Sons and Lovers*; when he informed her of his 'new attachment' to Frieda Weekley in 1912 she was stunned but not surprised. She later said that on what turned out to be the day of Lawrence's death (2 March 1930) she heard him say 'Can you remember only the pain and none of the joy?' Before she died she burned many of the letters Lawrence had sent to her.

GREGOR MITTENHOFER

Opera, *Elegy for Young Lovers* (1961), libretto by W.H. Auden and Chester Kallman, music by Hans

The original plan of the librettists of *Elegy for Young Lovers* was to have four or five characters, each of whom was mad in a different way. It is set in a mountain inn in the Austrian Alps. The great poet, Gregor Mittenhofer, stays here every year. He arrives with Carolina von Kirkstetten, his patroness, Elisabeth Zimmer, his mistress, Dr Reischmann, his physician and his son, Toni. The subject of the drama is the creation of a poem, from its gestation through to its final public reading. Mittenhofer has always relied on inspiration from the visions of the deranged widow, Hilda Mack, who lives at the inn. She believes she still lives at the time her husband was killed in the mountains, many years ago. His body is found preserved in a glacier. Frau Mack's visions are replaced by insights into the behaviour of neighbours. Elisabeth and Toni fall in love but they die in the same conditions which killed Herr Mack. Mittenhofer has lost the inspiration he used to have from Frau Mack, but he draws on the terrible tragedy of Toni and Elisabeth and the opera ends with the celebrated poet, Gregor Mittenhofer, in evening dress, reading his new poem to a fashionable audience.

Werner Henze.

W.B. Yeats (1865–1939)

Further reading: Humphrey Carpenter; *W.H. Auden – A Biography* (1981)

Auden and Kallman had W.B. Yeats in mind when they wrote *Elegy for Young Lovers*. Like Mittenhofer, Yeats wanted to be admired and, indeed, lionized in his own lifetime, and acted out the role of the 'great man'. Mittenhofer's reliance on the visions of Frau Mack is parallelled by Yeats's use of his own wife's alleged abilities as a medium. The medicines and hormones administered to Mittenhofer by his physician echo Yeats's own attempts to keep himself young by surgery. The librettists said in a programme note to the opera that its theme was summed up in W.B. Yeats's words: 'The intellect of man is forced to choose/Perfection of the life or of the work'. Gregor Mittenhofer chooses perfection of the work, and sacrifices life to see this achieved. There are elements of Auden himself in the portrait, and of Goethe, but the major model was certainly that of W.B. Yeats, who told John Singer Sargent that he wore a bow tie and had a loose lock of hair across his brow to remind himself of his own importance as an artist.

WALTER MITTY

James Thurber, *My World – and Welcome to It* (1942)

Charles Thurber (1867–1939)

Further reading: N. Yates, *The American Humanist Conscience and the Twentieth Century* (1964)

'The original of Walter Mitty,' said James Thurber, is every other man I have ever known. When the story was printed . . . six men from around the country, including a Des Moines dentist, wrote and asked me how I had got to know them so well.' Thurber's classic account of the little man who escapes from everyday defeats by daydreaming himself into heroic situations was a sensation on its first appearance in the *New Yorker* on 18 March 1939. During the war, servicemen formed Mitty clubs and adopted catchphrases from 'The Secret Life of Walter Mitty'. Thurber's family realized that Mitty was based on the author's father. Charles Thurber had a difficult early life, his father was killed in a fall from a horse so Charles had to help support the family by selling newspapers. Anxious to make a name for himself as an actor, or a lawyer, his circumstances made him settle for the less glamorous job of clerk. Despite his dreams he never achieved fame though when he married Mary Agnes Fisher in 1892 he found himself connected to one of the most prominent families in Columbus, Ohio. His wealthy father-in-law offered him a job but Charles valued his independence and worked his own way up to become secretary to the Chairman of the Republican State Committee. However he lost that job (and several others) and was often dependent on the income his wife received from stock given to her by her father. Charles Thurber had talent for defeatism: in 1912 he switched from the Republicans and became secretary of the Progressive Party's State Campaign thus ensuring he was unemployed come election day. On another occasion he inadvertently locked himself inside a rabbit pen for three hours. His fantasy life helped him win many newspaper competitions but he was unable to cope with the reality of his son's literary celebrity. Thurber used his father's idiosyncratic personality in several ways but never more memorably than as 'Walter Mitty, the undefeated, inscrutable to the last.'

MOBY DICK

Herman Melville, *Moby Dick* (1851)

Moby Dick concerns the hunt for a fierce and dangerous white whale. He has caused many disasters to whalers and has become legendary, an object of fear and superstition. Captain Ahab of the *Pequod*, who lost a leg to Moby Dick in a previous encounter, has vowed

Mocha Dick (circa 1820)

Further reading: Herman Melville, *Moby Dick*, The Norton Critical Edition, edited Hayford and Parker (1967), Jay Leyda, *The Melville Log – A Documentary Life of Herman Melville 1819–1891* (1969), A. Robert Lee, *Herman Melville: reassessments* (1983)

to take him. After a hunt which takes him three quarters round the globe, Ahab finds the white whale and the contest for his life lasts three days. Moby Dick triumphs in the end, Ahab's neck is broken and the *Pequod* sinks. Ahab has come up against the ultimate force of the universe in his own refusal to accept any limits to his humanity in striving against the ultimate: 'I own thy speechless, placeless power,' he says, 'Thou canst blind. . . . Thou canst consume.' But even this acknowledgement does not compel him to limit his search for Moby Dick: 'There is some unsuffering thing beyond thee, thou clear spirit, to whom all thy eternity is but time, all thy creativeness mechanical.' Melville seems to be using the colour white in a startling reversal of traditional symbolism. Moby Dick is the consummate evil, but Moby Dick had a real source.

Mocha Dick was legendary among whalers before Melville's novel. Jeremiah N. Reynolds (1799–1858) published *Mocha Dick* in 1839. It is a narrative about a fierce and cunning white whale, based on his own personal experience of sea adventure and polar exploration. Reynolds wrote of: 'an old bull whale, of prodigious size and strength . . . known by awe-struck whale hunters as "Mocha Dick" and also, because of his colour, he was white as wool, as the "White Whale of the Pacific".' Early in his career, Edgar Allan Poe was a journalist and reviewer, and he reviewed essays, journals and accounts of sea adventures, including Reynolds's and he incorporated several of these ideas and incidents into his own fiction – *Unparalleled Adventures of One Hans Pfaal* (1835) and *The Narrative of Arthur Gordon Pym* (1835).

RICHARD MONCKTON

John Ehrlichman; *The Company* (1976) and TV series *Washington Behind Closed Doors* written by David W. Rintels and Eric Bercovici (Paramount 1977)

Richard Milhous Nixon (1913-) **37th President of the USA**

Further reading: Carl Bernstein and Bob Woodward, *All the President's Men* (1974), *The Final Days* (1976)

The Company, a novel about corruption in high places, recounts the power struggle between an American president, Richard Monckton, and the CIA. Monckton is fifty-six and married to Amy Curtis; his lifestyle is rather square. He was Senator for Illinois for eighteen years, and Chairman of the Senate Foreign Relations Committee for four years. He became Vice President in the administration of James Dudley, but when he ran for the presidency he was defeated by the Democratic candidate, William Arthur Curry (John F. Kennedy). When Curry is killed in an air accident his Vice President, Esker Scott Anderson (Lyndon Johnson), becomes President. He is compelled to retire because of bad health, and this gives Monckton another crack at the presidency. After failing against Curry he had retired from public life and become a senior partner in a leading Chicago law firm. His victory over the former Democratic Vice President, Edward Miller Gilley (Hubert Humphrey) is the result of sheer political guile: 'When he decided to become President of the United States, Richard Monckton, characteristically, became an accomplished student of Presidential elections. He read everything he could find. There were lessons in history and Monckton was determined to know them better than anyone else . . . Ed Gilley's Congressional career had been a lacklustre snail creep to seniority. But at the hands of Richard Monckton and T.T. Talford it was displayed as a rape of the public purse, characterized by slothful absenteeism and consistent pandering to the Special Interests.' Monckton wins the election in a landslide, but his career ends amid accusations of corruption and dirty tricks, including bugging and telephone-tapping redolent of the Watergate scandal.

John Ehrlichman was a lawyer before being appointed White House Counsel and then President Nixon's Assistant for Domestic Affairs in 1969. Monckton is clearly based on Nixon, who, like Monckton, was born in rural poverty in California, was a lawyer, and served in the US Navy before entering Congress. He gained a national reputation for his part in the investigation of Alger Hiss, and was Vice President in the administration of Dwight Eisenhower. He was defeated by Kennedy in the presidential elections of 1960 and became a partner in a New York law firm. He defeated Hubert Humphrey to become 37th. President of the USA in 1968, after Johnson announced he would not stand again. Nixon's landslide victory for a second term, over George McGovern, in

1972 was overshadowed by the Watergate scandal, which disgraced him and compelled his resignation in 1974. Monckton was played by Jason Robarts in *Washington Behind Closed Doors*.

LORD MONMOUTH

Benjamin Disraeli, *Coningsby* (1844)

Francis Charles Seymour-Conway, Third Marquis of Hertford (1771–1842)

Further reading: Charles Greville, *A Journal of the Reign of Queen Victoria From 1837 to 1852* (1885)

Lord Monmouth is a wildly reactionary Tory parliamentarian, with ambitions for a dukedom and a lavish social life. Far from seeing the 1832 Reform Act as an obstacle to his ambitions, it spurs him on: 'While all his companions in discomforture were bewailing their irretrievable overthrow, Lord Monmouth became almost a convert to the measure, which had furnished his devising and daring mind, pallid with prosperity, and satiated with a life of success, with an object, and the stimulating enjoyment of a difficulty. . . . Lord Monmouth, even to save his party and gain his Dukedom, must not be bored. He therefore filled his castle with the most agreeable people from London, and even secured for their diversion, a little troop of French comedians. Thus supported he received his neighbours with all the splendour befitting his immense wealth and great position . . . as he was extremely good-natured, and for a selfish man even good-humoured, there was rarely a cloud of caprice or ill-temper to prevent his fine manners having their fair play. . . . Lord Monmouth, whose contempt for mankind was absolute . . . who never loved anyone, and never hated anyone except his own children was diverted by his popularity, but he was also gratified by it. . . . Lord Monmouth worshipped gold, though, if necessary, he could squander it like a caliph. He had even a respect for very rich men; it was his only weakness, the only exception to his general scorn for the species. Wit, power, particular friendships . . . public opinion, beauty, genius, virtue, all these could be purchased; but it does not follow that you can buy a rich man; you may not be able or willing to spare enough. A person or a thing that you could, perhaps, not buy, became invested, in the eyes of Lord Monmouth, with a kind of halo amounting almost to sanctity.'

This is a portrait of the third Marquis of Hertford, Francis Charles Seymour-Conway, who was known as Lord Yarmouth before he took his title, was a friend of the Regent's, moved in sporting circles, and entertained lavishly. (See LORD STEYNE).

CHARLES MOREL

Marcel Proust, *Remembrance of Things Past* (1913–27)

Léon Delafosse (1874–1955)

Further reading: George D. Painter, *Marcel Proust* (1959, 1965)

At Doncieres (based on Orleans, where Proust did his military service in 1889) the narrator of the novel meets a young bandsman and recognizes him as Morel, the son of his uncle's valet. To Marcel's surprise, Morel has changed (in the C.K. Scott Moncrieff/Terence Kilmartin translation): 'He had become an intense "poseur" and evidently the sight of myself, reminding him of his father's profession, was displeasing to him.' It transpires that the wealthy homosexual BARON DE CHARLUS is besotted by Morel, and for his sake climbs down the social ladder to attend the salon of Mme Verdurin, whose passion for art endears her to Morel's virtuosity on the violin. For all his physical beauty and musical talent, Morel is an unscrupulous manipulator of other people. He courts the niece of Jupien, Charlus's friend, then calls her a 'whore'; he spends a night with the Prince de Guermantes for a payment of fifty francs; he repudiates Charlus, after using him, thus driving the Baron to despair; he has a relationship with ALBERTINE, with whom the narrator Marcel is (for a while) in love; he is arrested, during the First World War, as a deserter but is released and does well in the war, surviving as usual. 'I do not wish,' says the narrator, 'to leave the reader under the impression that Morel was entirely wicked. He was, rather, a mass of contradictions, capable on certain days of being genuinely kind.'

In order to gain favour with the influential (and homosexual) Count Robert de Montesquiou (original of Charlus) Proust introduced the Count, in 1894, to the young virtuoso pianist Léon Delafosse – the chief original of Morel. Delafosse, as ambitious as Proust, had set some of Count Robert's poems to music, and the delighted Montesquiou told the pianist 'your settings of my poems will last as long as the poems themselves' – a statement full of unintentional irony. Count Robert contributed poems on Delafosse's piano-playing to *Le Figaro* of 10 April 1897, but was furious when, later that same year, Delafosse attempted to get a new patron, this time (in Montesquiou's words) 'an aged spinster of Swiss origin'. The end of the relationship between Montesquiou and Delafosse was, as Painter says, different from the break between Charlus and Morel: 'Far from being heartbroken, Montesquiou dismissed the unhappy young man with vengeful delight'. Montesquiou also transferred Delafosse's portrait from his drawing-room to his lavatory, and took to referring to the pianist as 'the Scrambled Egg'. Delafosse enjoyed some musical success after the fall from Montesquiou's favour; after the Second World War, however, he was neglected and died in poverty.

GERTRUDE MOREL

D.H. Lawrence, *Sons and Lovers* (1913)

Lydia Beardsall Lawrence (1852–1910)

Further reading: Harry T. Moore, *The Priest of Love* (1974)

Daughter of an engineer, Lydia Beardsall was born in Nottingham and became a schoolmistress at Sheerness. Her maternal grandfather, John Newton, was a gifted writer of nonconformist hymns, and Lydia herself wrote verse. After being jilted by a man who opted for an older – and richer – woman, Lydia met the miner Arthur Lawrence, and, attracted by his vitality, married him at Sneinton on 27 December 1875. When Arthur went back to the pits at Brinsley, he and Lydia took a cottage in the valley below Eastwood. Although Arthur had taken a teetotal pledge, he lapsed and began drinking on his way home from work; thus friction led to the fights that characterized the marriage. Soon Lydia and her husband rented a small brick house in Victoria Street, Eastwood, and there D.H. Lawrence ('Bert' to the family) was born in 1885, the fourth of five children. At the age of two Lawrence moved, with his family, to Walker Street, at the north of Eastwood, and in this house many domestic battles were fought. As Harry T. Moore observes, Lydia 'hated her husband and, just as extravagantly, she loved her children. These children became a battleground in the parents' war . . . The Walker Street house was never a house of peace [as the] children in bed at night could hear their father and mother arguing in the kitchen. Sometimes their voices rose even above the wind as it roared through the ash tree that then stood across the street.'

Lydia Lawrence adored her three sons, especially 'Bert' the youngest, whose intelligence and sensitivity reflected what she felt was best in herself. After Ernest Lawrence, the novelist's brother, died (of erysipelas) in 1901 Bert (whom she nursed through a serious illness) became the obsession of Lydia's life, and her overpowering presence made it almost impossible for him to love another woman, though he formed relationships with Jessie Chambers and Alice Dax (respectively MIRIAM LEIVERS and CLARA DAWES in *Sons and Lovers*). Eventually Lydia died a lingering death from cancer, an experience that exhausted Lawrence emotionally.

This autobiographical situation provided Lawrence with the plot for *Sons and Lovers*, in which Paul Morel (Lawrence) is overwhelmed by the love of his mother, an intelligent woman distressed by the coarse ways of her husband, Walter Morel, a Nottinghamshire miner. At the end of the book, Morel reflects on his mother: 'She was the only thing that held him up, himself, amid all this. And she was gone, intermingled herself. He wanted her to touch him, have him alongside with her.' However, he decides he will 'not take that direction, to the darkness, to follow her. He walked towards the faintly humming, glowing town, quickly'.

HUGH MORELAND

Anthony Powell, *Casanova's Chinese Restaurant*

The compositionally bright and conversationally brilliant Hugh Moreland, who appears in Anthony Powell's twelve-volume novel-sequence *A Dance to the Music of Time* (1951–75), is an affectionate portrait of the author's great friend Constant Lambert. Moreland first appears in

Casanova's Chinese Restaurant as the embodiment of music: 'He was formed physically in a "musical" mould, classical in type, with a massive, Beethoven-shaped head, high forehead, temples swelling outwards, eyes and nose somehow bunched together in a way to make him glare at times like a High Court judge about to pass sentence.' In *The Kindly Ones* Moreland explains his intense approach to music: 'The arts derive entirely from taking decisions. . . . Having taken the decision music requires, I want to be free of all others.'

Powell met Lambert in 1927 and immediately formed a close friendship with him. At that time Lambert was already established as the outstanding young British composer; his ballet *Romeo and Juliet* had been commissioned for the Russian Ballet by Diaghilev and produced at Monte Carlo in 1926. Nevertheless Lambert was depressed at Diaghilev's authoritarian methods and there was always a melancholy side to his apparently outgoing nature. He scored a great success with his choral work *The Rio Grande* (1929) and was instrumental in encouraging the development of British ballet. His forthright opinions were entertainingly aired in his book *Music, Ho!* (1934) which discussed jazz and classical music with equal enthusiasm. Powell and Lambert liked to discuss literature and painting – as well as music – in pubs and at parties. In his autobiographical *Messengers of Day* (1978) Powell recalls 'Towards the end of his life especially, the laughter and talk of Lambert's light-hearted moods had an obverse side of periodical grumpiness and ill humour.'

(1960), *The Kindly Ones* (1962), *The Valley of Bones* (1964), *The Soldier's Art* (1966), *The Military Philosophers* (1968), *Books Do Furnish a Room* (1971), *Temporary Kings* (1973), *Hearing Secret Harmonies* (1975)

Constant Lambert (1905–51)

Further reading: Anthony Powell, *Messengers of Day* (1978), John Pearson, *Facades – Edith Osbert and Sacheverell Sitwell* (1978)

CANDIDA MORELL

George Bernard Shaw, *Candida* (1895)

Dame Ellen Alice Terry (1848–1928)

Further reading: Frank Harris, *Bernard Shaw* (1931)

Frank Harris considered that Shaw was not convincing or successful in his portrayal of women characters: 'Though derived in much from Ibsen, Shaw's women do not resemble the human heroines of the great Norwegian . . . Where are the Noras and the Hedda Gablers in the plays of Shaw? . . . His are the sexless dolls which Ibsen threw out of the doll's house.' (*Bernard Shaw – An Unauthorised Biography based on Firsthand Information*, 1931). Harris made very few exceptions to this assertion; among them was the character of Candida. She is married to the Revd James Morell, a hearty Christian Socialist. She is loved by Eugene Marchbanks, a *fin-de-siècle* mystic, romantic and attitudinizing young poet of eighteen. The Revd Morell's idealism has shown itself in his objection to sweated labour, which unfortunately has upset his father-in-law, Burgess. Burgess blames Morell for the fact that he lost the contract for workhouse clothing on account of Morell's objections to exploitation. Candida tells her husband that he is a successful preacher because all women are in love with him. Marchbanks tells him that he simply has the gift of the gab, adding for good measure that Candida despises him secretly. When she has to choose between the two of them, Candida chooses her husband; she stays with the Revd Morell because he needs her.

Frank Harris bears witness that Ellen Terry was unquestionably 'the original living model' of this character. She was the leading actress of her day, with a melting voice, described by Henry James as having: 'a husky thickness which is extremely touching' and a countenance 'very happily adapted to the expression of pathetic emotion'. She married the painter Frederic Watts when she was sixteen, and then lived with Edward Godwin, the architect (see CAPTAIN SHOTOVER). She was Henry Irving's leading actress at the Lyceum, where she was particularly impressive in various Shakespearean roles – Beatrice, Lady Macbeth, Viola, Cordelia, Desdemona and Olivia. Shaw said of her that she was exceedingly innocent: 'When Watts kissed her, she took for granted she was going to have a baby.' The final, brilliant, speech given to Candida, with its mixture of pathos, innocence and comicality, must have been a direct imitation of Ellen Terry's natural manner. Choosing Morell she says: 'I make him master here, though he does not know it, and could not tell you . . . how it came to be so. And when he thought I might go away . . . his only anxiety was – what should become of me!' (see LADY CICELY WAYNFLETE).

DEAN MORIARTY
Jack Kerouac, *On the Road* (1957)
Neal Cassady (1926–68)

Further reading: Barry Gifford and Lawrence Lee, *Jack's Book* (1979)

Jack Kerouac's *On the Road* is the restless story which narrator Sal Paradise tells as he takes off on a series of trips across America with his friend Dean Moriarty: 'With the coming of Dean Moriarty began the part of my life you could call my life on the road. . . . Dean is the perfect guy for the road because he actually was born on the road, when his parents were passing through Salt Lake City in 1926, in a jalopy, on their way to Los Angeles.' Dean Moriarty is a new kind of American hero: totally uninhibited and open to all sorts of outrageous experiences as he experiments with drink, drugs and sex. As Sal Paradise sees it, 'Dean just raced in society, eager for bread and love.'

After the two men met, in New York in 1946, Kerouac became fascinated by Cassady as the embodiment of the beat generation. Cassady, the 'Adonis of Denver', had the kind of experience Kerouac needed for his books: he had served reformatory terms, had a powerful physical presence, and was a great talker. He also wrote lively letters as Kerouac acknowledged: 'The discovery of a style of my own based on spontaneous get-with-it came after reading the marvellous free-narrative letters of Neal Cassady, a great writer who happens also to be the Dean Moriarty of *On the Road*.' Living with the legend Kerouac had created for him, Cassady survived into the 1960s as a prophet of hippieness. In 1968 he was found unconscious near the railroad tracks outside San Miguel de Allende in Mexico and died in the local hospital from heart failure caused by exposure. Kerouac died one year later.

PETER MORRISON
Simon Raven, *Alms for Oblivion* (ten volumes, 1959–74)
James Prior (born 1927)

When he appears in *Sound the Retreat* (1971) – chronologically the second stage of Simon Raven's ten-volume *Alms for Oblivion* sequence – Peter Morrison is 'a large and slightly shambling Cadet with a huge round shining face . . . a young man of intelligence and iron will-power . . . a good-humoured boy who could take a joke at his own expense'. In *Friends in Low Places* (1965) he is 'Six foot two inches tall, broad both at chest and waist but giving no impression of overweight, carrying his huge round head thrown back like a guardsman's'. During the various stages of the story he rises step by step on the political ladder. By 1955 he is Conservative MP and leader of 'The Young England Group'; he returns to Parliament in a by-election of 1968 in a seat he retains at the general election two years later. On the death of his rival Somerset Lloyd-James he becomes, in 1972, Parliamentary Under-Secretary at the Ministry of Commerce. *The Survivors* (1976), the last novel of the series, has him as Minister of Commerce. Morrison is bright, if slightly devious, and tenacious.

Simon Raven has admitted that he based the character on James Prior, his contemporary at Charterhouse public school. Prior took a degree in Estate Management at Cambridge, was commissioned in the Royal Norfolk Regiment in 1946 and (like Morrison) looked after his East Anglian estate. He became an MP in 1959 and was closely associated with the rise to power of Edward Heath who (after winning the general election of 1970) made him Minister of Agriculture. Under Margaret Thatcher's premiership he served as Secretary of State for Employment and Secretary of State for Northern Ireland. His hobby is cricket and, in *Friends in Low Places*, he is seen – in a rare moment of relaxation – as he 'lumbered easily to the bowling crease and placed the ball just where he had told his son'.

Commenting on the character, in a letter of 16 January 1984, James Prior said: 'I have always been very fond of Simon and found him an engaging and loyal friend . . . [Peter Morrison] does not seem to have been a bad chap although obviously did not improve with age.'

SIR ROBERT MORTON
Terence Rattigan, *The Winslow Boy* (1946)

Terence Rattigan's *The Winslow Boy* was, as the dramatist acknowledged, 'inspired by the facts of a well-known case'. George Archer-Shee (Ronnie Winslow in the play) was, in 1908, removed from the Royal Naval College at Osborne after being accused of stealing and cashing a five-shilling postal order belonging to Terence Back, a fellow cadet. The case against George rested on the memory of the local postmistress and the opinion of a handwriting expert, but George's elder brother, Major Martin Archer-Shee, was convinced of George's innocence. Accordingly he persuaded his father to consult Sir Edward Carson then widely regarded (as George's father puts it in the play) as 'the best advocate in the country [and] certainly the most expensive'. After interrogating George for three hours, Sir Edward decided to take the case and proceeded by Petition of Right and then, when this was initially dismissed, by going to the Court of Appeal. All his efforts, including his devastating cross-examination of the postmistress, resulted in the Crown accepting George's innocence and awarding his father £7,120 compensation. Four years after this legal victory of 1910 George died of wounds recieved in the first battle of Ypres.

Rattigan portrays Sir Edward as Sir Robert Morton who is 'a man in the early forties; tall, thin, cadaverous and immensely elegant. He wears a long overcoat and carries his hat. He looks rather a fop and his supercilious expression bears out this view.' Sir Edward Carson was a member of both the English and Irish Bars and his career as a lawyer was spectacularly successful. He played a major part in the downfall of Oscar Wilde and featured in many criminal and civil cases. He was also active politically and, as a leader of the Ulstermen, urged Ulster to support the British Government during the First World War. He was an MP from 1892 to 1921 and served as Attorney-General, First Lord of the Admiralty and member of the War Cabinet.

Sir Edward Carson
(1854–1935)

Further reading:
E. Marjoribanks and I. Colvin, *The Life of Sir Edward Carson* (1934)

HENRIETTE DE MORTSAUF

Honoré de Balzac; *The Lily of the Valley* (1835)

Louise-Antoinette-Laure, Comtesse de Berny, (**née Hinner**)
(1777–1836)

Further reading:
André Marois, *Prometheus – The Life of Balzac* (1965)

The Lily of the Valley is set in the valley of Touraine during the period 1809–36, and deals with the passionate but unfulfilled love between a respectable married woman, Madam de Mortsauf, the wife of a returned *émigré*, and Fèlix de Vandenesse, an ambitious youth who is considerably younger than she is. Henriette gives herself entirely to her two sickly children and to her attempts to disguise from the outside world her husband's shortcomings and weaknesses. Fèlix is a frequent visitor to their *chateau* and their mutual attraction becomes obvious to them both, but although Henriette senses her passion truly at fever pitch she is restrained from surrendering herself but remains devoted to him. It is the strength of society and moral pressure which keeps her back, a mixture of the worldly and the spiritual: 'Straightforwardness, honour, loyalty and courtesy are the most sure and speedy instruments of fortune . . . But true courtesy implies Christian thinking; it is like the flower of charity . . . When something is asked of you that you cannot do, you should refuse plainly without encouraging hopes which are false. Do not be too confident, or commonplace, or over-zealous, these are common mistakes . . . The most important rule in the science of behaviour is to preserve complete silence regarding oneself . . . Cultivate influential women. Influential women are old women . . . They will give you their hearts, and protection is the last expression of love . . .' Henriette writes this to Fèlix when he is about to leave for the Court, and it distils her experience of life. Fèlix has a love affair with a young Englishwoman which brings him little happiness. On hearing of his affair with Lady Arabella Dudley, Henriette loses the will to live and dies from a painful illness. In a letter she leaves Fèlix learns of the love she always bore for him but refused to give in to.

Henriette is a portrait of the Comtesse de Berny, whom Balzac passionately loved, though she was some twenty years older than he was. They were neighbours in Villeparisis, where she was married to a Counsellor at the Royal Court. She was the daughter of a German musician and a lady-of-the-bedchamber to Marie Antoinette, and she and her husband barely escaped the Terror during the Revolution. It was an unhappy marriage, though it yielded nine children. She was forty-five when Balzac fell in love with her, and he was twenty-two. She was not a conventional beauty, but her face reflected her kindness and generosity of soul. He declared his love, but his family saw to it that he was separated from the object of his desire. Her death caused him great distress.

MOTH
William Shakespeare, *Love's Labours Lost* (1598)
Thomas Nashe (1567-1601)

Further reading: G.R. Hibbard, *Thomas Nashe* (1962)

Love's Labours Lost is, of all Shakespeare's comedies, probably the one most full of topical and contemporary references and allusions. Moth is the cheeky and delicately witty page to Don Armada – himself based on a celebrated contemporary (see DON ARMADO). His name amply suggests the felicitous and aerial nature of his ripostes. In the presentation of the Nine Worthies in Act V Moth plays the infant Hercules (see HOLOFERNES), but the general impression we carry away from the play is of his gossamer-like fanciful badinage: 'to jig off a tune at the tongue's end, canary to it with your feet, humour it with turning up your eye-lids, sigh a note and sing a note, sometimes through the throat, as if you swallowed love with singing love . . . with your hat penthouselike o'er the shop of your eyes . . . These are complements, these are humours; these betray nice wenches.'

There are several references in the play to identify Moth with Thomas Nashe, who was a brilliant and witty controversialist and pamphleteer who associated with William Shakespeare. He was the son of a minister, educated at Cambridge and was publishing books and pamphlets by the 1580s in which he identified himself with the University Wits and made caustic and satiric attacks on actors and dramatists who were not university educated. Nashe collaborated with John Lyly to answer the attacks made by the anonymous puritan pamphleteer Martin Marprelate, and a paper war ensued which contained some of the best satiric writing of the period. Nashe's association with Greene and Lyly brought him up against Gabriel Harvey, the friend of Edmund Spenser, and a further flurry of savage pamphleteering followed which was finally ended as a public scandal in 1599 when Nashe's pamphlets were among those ordered to be burned. These controversies may well be the basis for the disputes between Moth and Don Armado. Moth is named 'juvenal' in *Love's Labours Lost*, and as a satirist Nashe was equated with Juvenal in his own day, notably in Robert Greene's *Groats-Worth of Wit* (1592), see *Love's Labours Lost* Act I, Scene 2, line 8 and Act III, Scene 1, line 67. Nashe's replies to Harvey were widely read and frequently reprinted in his day. He also wrote *The Unfortunate Traveller*, a picaresque novel (1594) and it has been suggested that he collaborated with Shakespeare on the Henry VI plays and *The Taming of the Shrew*. There are also echoes of Nashe in *Hamlet* and *Titus Andronicus*.

REX MOTTRAM
Evelyn Waugh, *Brideshead Revisited* (1945)
Brendan Bracken, First Viscount Bracken (1901–58)

Further reading: A.J.P. Taylor; *English History 1914–1945* (1965)

Rex Mottram is the young, pushy, go-getting and wheeler-dealing Canadian-born politician who marries Julia Flyte. He exerts himself to make a good impression: 'He was a handsome fellow with dark hair growing low on forehead and heavy black eyebrows. He spoke with an engaging Canadian accent. One quickly learned all that he wished one to know about him, that he was a lucky man with money, a member of parliament, a gambler, a good fellow; that he played golf regularly with the Prince of Wales and was on easy terms with "Max" and "F.E." and "Gertie" Lawrence and Augustus John and Carpentier – with anyone, it seemed, who happened to be mentioned. Of the University he said: "No, I was never here. It just means you start life three years behind the other fellow." His life, so far as he made it known, began in the war, where he had got a good MC serving with the Canadians and had ended as ADC to a popular general.' Julia is rather patronizing to him at first, and when he starts to talk 'very big' she apologizes for him, saying: 'Remember, he's a colonial' (see JULIA FLYTE). Her marriage to him, a worldly round of political manipulation, parties, socializing and the pursuit of power, is a failure.

This is a portrait of the Irish-born politician Brendan Bracken, who was born in Kilmallock and educated at Sedbergh School, Yorkshire. He became a journalist and was associated with the *Financial News* and the *Economist*. He was elected to Parliament in 1929, and in A.J.P. Taylor's words became 'Churchill's most stalwart supporter in the lean years.' He served as Churchill's parliamentary private secretary and was appointed Minister of Information in July 1941. In May 1945 he became First Lord of the Admiralty. He was a vivid and witty character and in his capacity of Minister of Information he granted Waugh relief from military duties in January 1944 to write *Brideshead*. This unflattering caricature was his reward, and Waugh may have been repaying Bracken for not backing him up over a crisis which had arisen when the novelist had written an article on the Commandoes for the American magazine *Life* in 1941. The personal qualities which Waugh so chillingly records – an outsider who makes good in public life – are accurate enough, if uncharitable. Bracken was one of the most distinguished Conservatives to lose his seat in the Commons in the election of 1945.

MICKEY MOUSE

Walt Disney; *Plane Crazy*, film animated cartoon (1928), *Steamboat Willie* (1929) and numerous following cartoon films

Mortimer, the mouse

Further reading: Christopher Finch, *The Art of Walt Disney* (1973)

Mickey Mouse was probably the world's most famous cartoon character. In France he was named Michael Souris. Italians know him as Topolino. To the Japanese he is Miki Kuchi. His alias in Spain is the rather grand sounding Miguel Ratoncito, while in South America he glories in the name of El Ratón Miguelito. The Swedes rather prosaically call him Muse Pigg. In USSR he appears barely disguised in the name Mikki Maus. He first appeared in Disney's short silent animated cartoon *Plane Crazy* in 1928, where he was originally called Mortimer. A year later he was renamed Mickey and was provided with his famous high squeaky voice, vocalized by Walt Disney himself, in *Steamboat Willie*. Walt Disney's wife had suggested the name Mickey as much more suitable for the character Walt had created. He soon became a star in his own right, and gathered a supporting cast around himself, which included his paramour Minnie Mouse, his goony housedog Pluto, and his rival, the villainous Pegleg Pete. The personality he projected was that of the innocent nice-guy, often imposed upon, but who won through in the end. Although his popularity was soon overshadowed by the more dynamic creation of Donald Duck, Mickey was considered a sufficiently international star to play the lead in *L'Apprenti Sorcier* episode of Disney's feature film *Fantasia* (1940). He was probably at his most impressive in the 'Silly Symphony' series, where the screen animation was created to match the prerecorded film sound-track. Often in spoofs of well-known classics, such as *Danse Macabre* and the *William Tell* overture. He enjoyed a big revival as a result of TV in USA as the main attraction in the children's programme 'The Mickey Mouse Club'. Mickey Mouse watches are still valued, and he features in many games and toys. He is to be found in Madame Tussaud's waxworks in London.

Disney based his immortal rodent on a real-life mouse he trapped in a waste-paper basket and kept and trained as a pet in 1919 while working at the Newman Laugh O'Gram studio in Kansas City. As a living creation he was paid the considerable compliment by Graham Greene who wrote of Fred Astaire that he 'Is the nearest we are ever likely to get to a human Mickey . . . a touch of pathos, the sense of a courageous and impromptu intelligence, a capacity for getting into awkward situations . . .'

MISS MOWCHER

Charles Dickens; *David Copperfield* (1850)

Mrs Seymour-Hill

The character of Miss Mowcher caused Dickens considerable personal embarrassment, and is an example of a writer's basing a character on a real person, and the real person recognizing themselves – and disapproving. Miss Mowcher is a manicurist who visits James Steerforth (see JAMES STEERFORTH). She exposes the servant Littimer as a thief. She is a deformed dwarf: 'There came waddling round a sofa which stood

Further reading: Edgar Johnson, *Charles Dickens – His Tragedy and Triumph* (1952)

between me and it, a pursy dwarf, of about forty or forty-five, with a very large head and face, and a pair of roguish grey eyes, and such extremely little arms, that, to enable herself to lay a finger archly against her snub-nose as she ogled Steerforth, she was obliged to meet the finger half-way and lay her nose against it. Her chin, which was what is called a double-chin, was so fat this entirely swallowed up the strings of her bonnet, bow and all. Throat she had none; waist she had none; legs she had none, worth mentioning; for though she was more than full-sized down to where her waist would have been, if she had had any, and though she terminated, as human beings generally do, in a pair of feet, she was so short that she stood at a common-sized chair as at a table, resting a bag she carried on the seat.'

Dickens had used Mrs Seymour-Hill, a dwarf, and chiropodist and manicurist, whom he had observed going about her business on her short legs in the Devonshire Terrace area where he lived while composing *David Copperfield*. She wrote to the novelist on 18 December 1849 after reading this description of herself in the monthly serial part: 'I have suffered long and much from my personal deformities but never before at the hands of a Man so highly gifted as Charles Dickens.' He replied that he had her only partly in mind, and was deeply sorry for causing her such distress. A great portion of the character was based on somebody else altogether and in appearance Miss Mowcher was quite unlike Mrs Seymour-Hill: 'Pray consider all these things and do not make yourself unhappy,' he wrote. She had written to him that her nights had become sleepless and her daily work tearful. Dickens was so pained by her unhappiness that he said he would alter the entire design of the character: 'and oblige the reader to hold it in pleasant remembrance'. To Forster he admitted that 'there is no doubt one is wrong in being tempted to such a use of power'.

M'TURK

Rudyard Kipling, *Stalky & Co* (1899)

George Beresford (1865–1912)

Of the triumvirate known as Stalky & Co in Rudyard Kipling's collection of that name, M'Turk is the one most easily roused to indignation and thus a character in contrast to Stalky the practical joker, and Beetle (Kipling) the literary member of the group. 'In Ambush' has the three public schoolboys joining the College's Natural History Society and venturing onto Colonel Dabney's land. When Dabney's keeper shoots at a fox, M'Turk, an Irish landowner's son, is outraged and decides to confront the Colonel, despite the protests of his pals. M'Turk's Irish blood is up: 'Forgotten – forgotten was the College and the decency due to elders! M'Turk was treading again the barren purple mountains of the rainy West coast, where in his holidays he was viceroy of four thousand naked acres, only son of a three-hundred-year-old house, lord of a crazy fishing-boat, and the idol of his father's shiftless tenantry. It was the landed man speaking to his equal – deep calling to deep – and the old gentleman [Colonel Dabney] acknowledged the cry.'

When Kipling was twelve (in 1878) he went to public school at the United Services College, Westward Ho!, Bideford, north Devon, and on his first day befriended an Irish boy, George Beresford. In 1880 the two boys shared a room with Lionel Charles Dunsterville, known as Stalky in the school, and thus began their exploits as Stalky & Co. From Beresford's Irish origins, Kipling created M'Turk the Irish aristocrat. After College, Beresford became a civil engineer in India, and he was in England when *Stalky & Co* appeared. Charles Carrington comments, in *Rudyard Kipling* (1955): 'Since the characters, if not the events, were real, the book led to an immediate investigation for origins . . . "M' Turk" came to light as Beresford, and gave an interview about "Stalky" to a Cambridge newspaper, with a consequence that was no fault of Beresford; the editor was sued for damages, soon after, on a charge of fabricating news-items, and one question asked in court was whether the "Stalky" stories were fact or fiction. The Judge ruled them fiction, whereupon that part of the charge collapsed, except in the sense that it stimulated publicity.' When the Kipling Society was formed in 1927, Beresford became a committee member. In 1936 he published *Schooldays with Kipling*.

BUCK MULLIGAN
James Joyce, *Ulysses* (1922)

Oliver St John Gogarty (1878–1957)

Further reading: Richard Ellman, *James Joyce* (1959, 1982), Ulick O'Connor, *Oliver St John Gogarty* (1964)

In September 1904 James Joyce stayed with Oliver St John Gogarty in the Martello Tower at Sandycove, near Dublin. For a lease of eight pounds per year Gogarty had taken the tower in order to write and he put up with his difficult and demanding friend on condition that Joyce did the housework. Joyce and Gogarty soon found it impossible to live in the same place and Joyce left the Martello Tower. However, he returned to it imaginatively for the opening of *Ulysses*. In contrast to the sensitive, searching Stephen Dedalus (Joyce), 'Stately, plump Buck Mulligan' (Gogarty) is crude and complacent: 'Buck Mulligan at once put on a blithe broadly smiling face. He looked at them, his wellshaped mouth open happily, his eyes, from which he had suddenly withdrawn all shrewd sense, blinking with mad gaiety. He moved a doll's head to and fro, the brims of his Panama hat quivering, and began to chant in a quiet happy foolish voice.'

Like Joyce, Gogarty was born in Dublin but whereas Joyce chose 'Silence, cunning and exile' Gogarty acquired status, success and respectability. His wealthy parents sent him to Trinity College and, like Mulligan, he studied medicine. Because of his financial advantages he tended to patronize Joyce and encourage him to drink heavily; yet he sensed that Joyce's literary talent was greater than his own. After Joyce left Ireland, Gogarty pursued a distinguished career as a surgeon. In 1922 he was made a Senator of the Irish Free State but the same year *Ulysses* appeared and Gogarty was jealous of Joyce's international literary celebrity. When his country adopted the name Eire in 1936 Gogarty expressed his disapproval of new political developments and three years later he moved to the USA. His own works include the witty prose of *As I Was Going Down Sackville Street* (1937), *Tumbling in the Hay* (1939) and the verse of *Collected Poems* (1952).

JENNY MULLION
Aldous Huxley, *Crome Yellow* (1921)

Dorothy Brett (1883–1977)

Further reading: Sean Hignett, *Brett* (1984)

Denis Stone, the young novelist of Aldous Huxley's *Crome Yellow*, goes to see Anne Wimbush at her Uncle Henry's country house at Crome – modelled on Lady Ottoline Morrell's cultural haven at Garsington Manor on whose land Huxley worked during the Second World War. In one of the little summer houses at Crome a tea party is taking place, and Denis scrutinizes his companions. Among them is Jenny Mullion, separated from the world by her deafness: 'She was perhaps thirty, had a tilted nose and a pink-and-white complexion, and wore her brown hair plaited and coiled in two lateral buns over her ears. In the secret tower of her deafness she sat apart, looking down at the world through sharply piercing eyes . . . In her enigmatic remoteness Jenny was a little disquieting.' Later in the novel Denis discovers Jenny's notebook and is disturbed by her caricature of him: 'It was masterful . . . the expression of the face, an assumed aloofness and superiority tempered by a feeble envy'. Denis now sees himself objectively and is depressed by the experience. He contemplates suicide, but at the end of the novel leaves Crome to go to London. As Sean Hignett notes, in his biography of Dorothy Brett, Huxley used an eccentric aristocratic artist as the model for Jenny Mullion.

Daughter of Lord Esher and sister of the Ranee of Sarawak, the Hon Dorothy Brett visited Garsington in 1917 and found the conscientious objectors there 'awful', while the intellectuals made her 'feel very sick inside'. Aldous Huxley, a non-combatant (rejected on medical grounds) and an intellectual, asked Brett to illustrate his poem 'Leda and the Swan'. After a couple of sample drawings, says Hignett, 'Brett's employment as Huxley's illustrator seems to have died. Her only further artistic endeavour on his behalf was to help him paint his sitting room when he married Maria Nys the following August.' Brett subsequently became a faithful member of D.H. Lawrence's entourage in New Mexico, where she eventually settled for the last half-century of her long life. Huxley visited Brett in New Mexico in 1937, and found her 'odder than ever in a Mexican 10-gallon hat with a turkey's feather stuck in it, sky blue breeks, top boots and a strong American accent'.

MOLEY MYSTIC

Thomas Love Peacock, *Melincourt* (1817)

Samuel Taylor Coleridge (1772–1834)

Further reading: J. Charpentier, *Coleridge – The Sublime Somnambulist* (1929), J. Dykes Campbell, *The Life of Samuel Taylor Coleridge* (1894)

Moley Mystic is the 'poeticopolitical, rhapsodicoprosaical, deisidaemoniaco-paradoxogeaphical, pseudolatreiological, transcendental-meteorosophist . . . of Cimmerian Lodge.' His Christian name, he believed, was improperly spelt with an 'e', and was in truth: 'nothing more nor less than/That Moly,/Which Hermes erst to wise Ulysses gave', and which was, in the mind of Homer, *a pure anticipated cognition* of the system of Kantian metaphysics, or grand transcendental science of the *luminous obscure*; for it had a *dark root*, which was mystery; and *a white flower*, which was abstract truth; *it was called Moly by the gods*, who then kept it to themselves; and was *difficult to be dug up by mortal men*, having, in fact, lain *perdu* in subterranean darkness till the immortal Kant dug for it *under the stone of doubt*, and produced it to the astonished world as the *root of human science*. Other persons, however, derived his first name differently; and maintained that the 'e' in it showed it very clearly to be a corruption of *Mole-eye*, it being the opinion of some naturalists that the *mole* has *eyes*, which it can withdraw or project at pleasure, implying the faculty of wilful blindness, most happily characteristic of a transcendental metaphysician since, according to the old proverb, *None are so blind as those who won't see*.

This portrait of a pretentiously intellectual poet and philosopher whose discourse is almost totally incomprehensible, is Peacock's view of Coleridge. As Byron said in *Don Juan*, Coleridge explained Metaphysics to the nation, 'I wish he would explain his Explanation.' Hazlitt said he 'talked on for ever; and you wished him to talk on for ever'. Coleridge was a brilliant student but left Cambridge without graduating, introduced England to German metaphysics and the brilliant Shakespeare criticism of Schlegel, Lessing and Tieck, and became an influential lecturer and critic. A friend and collaborator of Wordsworth's, much of his own poetry was not completed, but is nevertheless powerful and moving. The *Ancient Mariner* is justifiably regarded as a classic, and *Biographia Literaria* a landmark in English romanticism. (See also FLOSKY.)

N

NAMBY-PAMBY

Henry Carey, *Namby-Pamby* (1726)

Ambrose Phillips (1675–1749)

Further reading: Samuel Johnson, *The Lives of the Poets* (1779)

Ambrose Phillips was a poet and fellow of St John's College, Cambridge, and a member of Joseph Addison's literary circle. His version of Racine's *Andromaque* (1712) entitled 'The Distressed Mother' was lauded in the *Spectator*. Pope and Addison were initially on good terms, but after their split, any friend of Addison's was a fair target for the satiric barbs of Alexander Pope (see ATTICUS) and so Phillips' *Pastorals*, in which he took Edmund Spenser as his model, were savagely received by Pope, who published his *Pastorals* a few years later. Pope took Virgil as his model and strove for elegance and harmony – he considered Ambrose Phillips' efforts were weak and simpering, especially as Phillips' verses were adulatory of public figures and politicians whom Pope despised. Phillips described Robert Walpole, manipulator of the system Pope decried, as 'steerer of the realm', for example. Henry Carey wrote: 'So the Nurses get by heart, Namby-Pamby's little rhymes.' But what put poor Phillips' cruel nickname into general circulation was a section in the 1733 version of Pope's *Dunciad*: 'Beneath his reign, shall Eusden wear the bays,/Cibber preside Lord Chancellor of Plays,/Benson sole judge of architecture sit,/And Namby Pamby be prefer'd for wit.'

By the middle of the 18th century, Ambrose Phillips' nickname had passed into the language as a term to describe anything weakly sentimental or affectedly childish. The quarrel between Phillips and Pope was a violent one, fanned by their deep political differences, and at one stage Phillips hung up a rod at Button's Coffee House, with which he threatened to chastise Pope. He tried, with success, to write dramas, and hoped for advancement when the Whigs came to power. He was in fact made a Justice of the Peace. Samuel Johnson's verdict: 'The pieces that please best are those which . . . procured him the name of Namby Pamby, the poems of short lines, by which he paid court to all ages and characters.'

NANA

Emile Zola, *Nana* (1880)

Cora Pearl (1835–86)

Further reading: *The Memoirs of Cora Pearl*, edited by William Blatchford (1981)

The heroine of Emile Zola's sensationally successful *Nana* is a harlot who wants to use her stunningly erotic beauty to take revenge on the sex that she feels has ruined her. At the Variety Theatre in Paris, where the book begins, Nana is due to appear in an operetta, 'The Blonde Venus'. Although she has no acting ability and no singing voice her presence electrifies the audience. When she flaunts her flesh a shiver goes round the house: 'She was wearing nothing but a veil of gauze; and her round shoulders, her Amazon breasts, the rosy points of which stood up as stiff and straight as spears, her broad hips, which swayed to and fro voluptuously, her thighs – the thighs of a buxom blonde – her whole body, in fact, could be divined, indeed clearly discerned, in all its foamlike whiteness, beneath the filmy fabric.' Nana is a woman with sexual power over men and attracts admirers like Count Muffat; yet she contrives to misuse her natural possessions and, after contracting smallpox, is ironically alone in her final disintegration.

Zola based Nana on the celebrated courtesan Cora Pearl, a woman whose erotic expertise earned her a fortune which she eventually squandered. Born Emma Elizabeth Crouch, the daughter of a popular composer, Cora became one of the most sought-after prostitutes in London. She transferred her business to Paris in 1858 and rapidly acquired what she referred to as her 'Golden Chain' of affluent and aristocratic clients. Her promotional activities were extraordinary; she once appeared naked on a silver platter as if being served to her dinner guests; she also bathed naked, before an invited audience, in champagne in her silver tub. Despite her many influential contacts Cora eventually lost her friends, and her fortune, when she lost her looks. She died of cancer in poverty and alone.

PEGGY NASH-BELMONT

Pierre Rey, *The Greek* (1973), film, *The Greek Tycoon*, written by Mort Fine, directed by J. Lee Thompson, starring Jacqueline Bisset, Anthony Quinn, (1978)

Jacqueline Lee Bouvier Onassis (born 1929)

Further reading: John Sutherland; *Bestsellers – Popular Fiction of the 1970s* (1981)

Peggy Nash-Belmont is the beautiful daughter of a well-to-do family on the east coast of the USA, who has all the social grace and charm that money can buy. She is a reporter for a glossy magazine read by the smart set. She meets and falls in love with Scott Baltimore, a young and ambitious career politician. He is the son of a vastly rich Catholic father, who is determined that his son shall be the President of the USA. His elder brother has already died, and the family hopes are all pinned on Scott (who has two younger brothers). Peggy and Scott are married, but just before he comes up for the Presidential nomination of his party, she resolves to divorce him. She is compelled to change her mind by Scott's father's 'gift' of a million dollars. Scott Baltimore is assassinated in New Orleans. He is driving in an open-air motorcade through the city when he is shot by a rifleman. The assassin is himself killed soon after, as he is the patsy in a conspiracy of a group of the most financially powerful men in the nation who fear that Scott Baltimore's liberal policies would seriously damage their interests if he came to power. Peggy then marries the Greek of the novel's title, Socrates Satraoulos, a shipping tycoon. Socrates was previously engaged in a liaison with a concert pianist named Menelas, a woman of genius but highly temperamental. Public opinion in America is outraged when Baltimore's widow marries the Greek millionaire.

The events this novel thinly disguises are the main elements in the story of Jacqueline Kennedy, who married John F. Kennedy (see WILLIAM ARTHUR CURRY) and then married Aristotle Onassis in 1968, after his tempestuous affair with the opera singer, Maria Callas. Jacqueline Lee Bouvier was born in July 1929, and educated at Vassar College, George Washington University and the University of Paris. She married John Fitzgerald Kennedy in 1953. He was assassinated in a motorcade in Dallas, Texas, in November 1963. She married Aristotle Onassis in 1968. He died in 1975. She was for a time a photographer for the Washington *Times-Herald*, before she married John F. Kennedy. She initiated and supervised the historical reconstruction of the decor of the White House between 1961–63, and represented the President on a tour of India in 1962.

ETHEL NEWCOME

William Makepeace Thackeray, *The Newcomes* (1853–55)

Sally Baxter (1833–62)

Further reading: Margaret Forster, *William Makepeace Thackeray – Memoirs of a Victorian Gentleman* (1978)

Ethel Newcome, the heroine of *The Newcomes*, is one of Thackeray's most attractive characters: 'Her eyes were grey; her mouth rather large; her teeth as regular and bright as Lady Kew's own; her voice low and sweet; and her smile, when it lighted up her face and eyes, as beautiful as spring sunshine; also they could lighten and flash often, and sometimes, though rarely, rain.'

Thackeray met Sally Baxter in New York, during his American tour of 1852, and knew immediately she would make a splendid heroine. All his romantic impulses soared at the sight of Sally and he wrote, in a letter, 'I have been actually in love for 3 days with a pretty wild girl of 19 (and was never more delighted in my life than by discovering that I could have this malady over again).' Sally teased Thackeray, whose work she admired enormously and told him how she expected to exploit her nubility. He was well aware of the dangers of his infatuation and did his best to control himself, writing to Sally 'My heart was longing and yearning after you full of love and gratitude for your welcome of me – but the words grew a little too warm. . . . When the destined man comes, with a good head and a good heart fit to win such a girl, and love and guide her; then old Mr Thackeray will make his bow and say God bless her.' When he returned to America, in 1855, he met Sally just after her marriage to Frank Hampton of South Carolina. He accepted the situation philosophically and was disturbed when the American Civil War meant that Sally's husband was actually fighting the part of the country that had produced Sally. While Frank Hampton was at war

Sally, with fond memories of New York, was dying of tuberculosis on his plantation. Distraught by the news of Sally's death Thackeray wrote to her mother: 'What a bright creature! What a laugh, a life, a happiness! And it is all gone.'

COLONEL THOMAS NEWCOME

William Makepeace Thackeray, *The Newcomes* (1853–55)

Henry Carmichael-Smyth (1778–1861)

The romantic aspects of Thackeray's novel *The Newcomes* literally begin and end with the character of Colonel Thomas Newcome who enters the book comically and leaves it tragically. Unable to marry the woman he loves, the Colonel settles for a life in India and marriage to a woman he wishes to help. As portrayed by Thackeray, Colonel Newcome is a paragon: 'Besides his own boy, whom he worshipped, this kind Colonel had a score, at least, of adopted children, to whom he chose to stand in the light of a father. . . . On board the ship in which he returned from Calcutta were a dozen of little children, of both sexes, some of whom he actually escorted to their friends before he visited his own.'

The Colonel is a tribute to the author's stepfather Henry Carmichael-Smyth. Thackeray's mother Anne Becher was sixteen when, in 1808, she fell in love with Lieutenant Henry Carmichael-Smyth who was staying in England after ten years' active service in India. As Grandmother Becher disapproved of his prospects she told Anne that the Lieutenant had died of a fever; Anne then went to Calcutta where she met and married Richmond Thackeray. A year after the birth of William Makepeace (on 18 July 1811) Anne discovered that her Lieutenant (now a Captain) was in fact alive and well and also living in India. The situation was only resolved when Richmond Thackeray died in 1815 and Anne married Henry Carmichael-Smyth. Three years after William Makepeace had been sent to England, his mother and stepfather came home. Major (as he now was) Carmichael-Smyth was a short man of military bearing and patriotic politics. Thackeray greatly admired his integrity and, when the Major was buried in his native Scotland, put on his gravestone the words with which the Colonel makes his exit in *The Newcomes*: '*Adsum* – And lo, he whose heart was as that of a little child, had answered to his name, and stood in the presence of The Master.'

Further reading:
Ann Montsarrat, *An Uneasy Victorian – Thackeray the Man* (1980)

COLONEL NICHOLSON

David Lean, *The Bridge on the River Kwai* (1957)

Colonel Philip Toosey

In one of his greatest film roles, Alec Guinness played Colonel Nicholson, a British POW of the Japanese, who collaborates with the enemy and supervises the construction by allied prisoners of a railway bridge in Burma. He begins by defying the camp commandant, General Saito, but after being punished he returns triumphantly to build an even better bridge than the Japanese had originally designed, sited in a better place. The bridge becomes an obsession to him, and represents the full realization of the purpose of his life. Meanwhile British commando agents train to destroy the bridge. In the final moments of the film, the bridge is blown up and Nicholson dies of mortar fire, falling on one of the plungers which detonates his own bridge.

The film was written by Carl Foreman, based on Pierre Boulle's novel, *Le Pont de la Rivière Kwai*. Boulle placed the bridge near the Burmese border, though it was in fact constructed at Tha Makham, three miles west of Karnburi, Thailand, across the Khwae Yai. It was constructed to carry the railway from Bangkok to Rangoon. After the surrender of Singapore, the Dutch East Indies and the Philippines in 1942 the Japanese had over 200,000 POWs to look after. The inefficiencies and brutalities of POW camp life at Tha Makham were brought to an end by the extraordinary personality of Philip Toosey. He was not a professional soldier, but businessman and administrator with considerable industrial experience. Immediately before the war he had been a merchant banker and cotton merchant. He realized that escape was impossible and open defiance simply led to insufferable physical punishment. His negotiating skills enabled him to bargain with the Japanese and he effected an exchange of better living and working conditions, increased food and medical supplies, for the prisoners' organization of

Further reading:
Steven Jay Rubin, *The Combat Film* (1981), Ian Watt, *The Bridge on the River Kwai as Myth*, *Berkshire Review*, (Winter 1971)

themselves to achieve work on the bridge. Toosey's aim was to work to guarantee the survival of as many POWs as possible. He was never accused by his fellow POWs of being 'Jap happy', but was considered, simply, as the one who could best handle the Japanese. Boulle never knew Toosey, was never a prisoner of the Japanese and had never been near the railway. His version of events is part based on the French stereotypical view of the British officer class and on the attitudes of French officers who collaborated with the Vichy government. The film version adds further distortions.

MRS NICKLEBY

Charles Dickens, *Nicholas Nickleby* (1839)

Mrs John (Elizabeth) Dickens (1789–1863)

Further reading: Norman and Jeanne Mac-Kenzie, *Dickens – A Life* (1979)

Mrs Nickleby is the widow of Nicholas Nickleby, father of the hero of the novel, and of his sister Kate. She is a scatterbrained person, whose mind is a total jumble of inconsequential memories on which she has instant and copious recall. She is hopeless with money and when her irresponsible husband dies, she throws herself at the mercy of Ralph Nickleby, her husband's brother, a rich and miserly money-lender, whose machinations and their effect on Nicholas and Kate form the basis of the novel. Mrs Nickleby's character is bodied forth in a wild and brilliant profusion which, although to a large extent is meaningless to all but herself (and, occasionally, to members of her family), has a poetry all its own. She carries her gift for uncontrolled fancy into real life when she imagines she is wooed by the Gentleman in Small-clothes. 'I don't know how it is, but a fine warm summer day like this, with the birds singing in every direction, always puts me in mind of roast pig, with sage and onion sauce, and made gravy. . . . Roast pig; let me see. On the day five weeks after you were christened, we had a roast – no, that couldn't have been a pig, either, because I recollect there were a pair of them to carve, and your poor dear papa and I could never have thought of sitting down to two pigs – they must have been partridges. Roast pig! I hardly think we ever could have had one . . . for your papa could never bear the sight of them in the shops, and used to say that they always put him in mind of very little babies, only the pigs had much fairer complexions; and he had a horror of little babies, too, because he couldn't very well afford any increase to his family. . . . I recollect dining once at Mrs Bevan's, in that broad street round the corner by the coachmaker's where the tipsy man fell through the cellar flap of an empty house nearly a week before the quarter-day, and wasn't found till the new tenant went in – and we had roast pig there.'

She is based on Dickens's mother, who married John Dickens (see MICAWBER) in 1809 and became the mother of eight children, including the novelist. She seems to have been a loving mother who spent much time teaching Charles and encouraging his mental development and imagination, but she was rather shallow and vain. She read *Nickleby* and asked her brilliant son whether he thought anyone as silly as Mrs Nickleby could ever have existed.

NICHOLAS NICKLEBY

Charles Dickens; *Nicholas Nickleby* (1839)

Henry Burnett (1811–93)

Further reading: Arthur L. Hayward, *The Dickens Encyclopaedia* (1924), Norman and Jeanne MacKenzie, *Dickens – A Life* (1979)

Nicholas is the son of Mrs Nickleby (see MRS NICKLEBY) and her husband who has just died as the novel opens; he is Kate's brother and nephew to the wicked Ralph Nickleby. He is a charming, open and honest young man, somewhat innocent of the world and its ways, but whose naiveté is compensated for by the heart of a lion: 'His figure was somewhat slight, but manly and well formed; and, apart from all the grace of youth and comeliness, there was an emanation from the warm young heart in his look.' He works at Dotheboys Hall, where he befriends Smike and thrashes Squeers (see SQUEERS). The pair then travel in the company of actors run by Vincent Crummles, later working for the Cheerybles (see CHEERYBLE BROTHERS). He saves Kate from the machinations of Sir Mulberry Hawk, falls in love with Madeline Bray, and exposes Ralph Nickleby.

The model Dickens used for this worthy character was his brother-in-law Henry Burnett, husband of his sister Fanny, father to little Harry

Burnett (see PAUL DOMBEY). He is also the original of Edward Chester in *Barnaby Rudge*, Tom Pinch in *Martin Chuzzlewit* and Walter Gay in *Dombey and Son*, but in *Nickleby* he is given the fullest treatment. Edwin Pugh in *The Charles Dickens Originals* 1912 commented: 'it is hard to believe that any young man of this type ever existed – even in those stilted times – except as a gorgeous figment of a raw young novelist's imagination . . . And yet Dickens was at all times so eager to justify the extravagances and excesses into which his buoyant fancy did so often betray him that even in the description of his preposterous heroes he must draw from some living model that he could point to as the prototype of his most improbable character . . . he copied the features, the manner, the style and the tone of his brother-in-law, and in the ardour of creation lost sight of the real man.' Henry Burnett's character was deeply influenced by his grandmother, who was very religious. He was a musician and vocalist, and while living with his father in Brighton, he sang before George IV at the Pavilion at the age of ten. He studied music with the organist at the Chapel Royal, and in 1832 went to the Royal Academy of Music. Here he met Dickens's sister, Fanny, and they sang together in several concerts, marrying in 1837. He sang the role of Norton in Dickens's *The Village Coquettes*, and joined Macready's company in 1838. He left the stage in 1841 for religious reasons, and never entered a theatre again. He was an immensely personable young man.

MR NIXON

Ezra Pound, *Hugh Selwyn Mauberley* (1920)

Arnold Bennett (1867–1931)

Further reading: Margaret Drabble, *Arnold Bennett* (1974)

Ezra Pound's poetic sequence *Hugh Selwyn Mauberley* expresses, in carefully controlled and allusive verse, the author's attitude to what he felt was the triviality of pre-war English literary life. It traces the career of the poet Mauberley, and begins ironically with a dismissive summary of Pound's own achievement, how he 'strove to resuscitate the dead art/Of poetry . . . Wrong from the start'. After a powerful evocation of trench warfare on the Western front, Pound describes the literary civilization Englishmen died for as he condemns the state of English culture and includes a number of portraits of literary personalities he knew when he lived in London from 1908–20. 'Brenbaum', with his 'skylike limpid eyes', is modelled on Max Beerbohm (1872–1956), the writer and caricaturist; 'the stylist', of section X, is based on the novelist Ford Madox Ford (1873–1939), whose artistic integrity impressed Pound; the affluently aesthetic Lady Valentine (section XII) is Lady Ottoline Morrell (1873–1939).

As a dedicated artist (and champion of fellow modernists such as T.S. Eliot and James Joyce) Pound concentrates his contempt on 'Mr Nixon', a literary mercenary. Mr Nixon has a steam yacht and grandly dispenses advice. 'Take a column,/Even if you have to work free', he says; and 'Butter reviewers'. Advising against a poetic career since 'There's nothing in it', Mr Nixon explains his own formula for success: 'I never mentioned a man but with the view/Of selling my own works./The tip's a good one, as for literature/It gives no man a sinecure.' Hugh Kenner, in *The Poetry of Ezra Pound* (1951) convincingly suggests that Mr Nixon is a portrayal of Arnold Bennett.

Bennett, a solicitor's son, left Hanley (one of the Five Towns he made famous in his fiction) and came to London, at the age of twenty-one, to shape a successful literary career. He wrote a weekly column on London topics and established himself as a novelist with *Anna of the Five Towns* (1902), *The Grim Smile of the Five Towns* (1907) and *The Old Wives' Tale* (1908). Thus when Pound arrived in London, in 1908, Bennett was a celebrated representative of the literary Establishment; one, moreover, rich enough by 1913 to own a yacht, *Velsa*. In a letter of May 1936 to Laurence Pollinger, Pound said that 'Bennett knew his eggs . . . he never showed the public anything but his AVARICE. Consequently they adored him.' In another letter, of July 1937, to Michael Roberts, Pound referred to 'nickle cash-register Bennett'.

NEWMAN NOGGS

Charles Dickens, *Nicholas Nickleby* (1839)

Newman Knott

Further reading: Christopher Hibbert, *The Making of Charles Dickens* (1967)

Newman Noggs is Ralph Nickleby's clerk, a broken down figure of a man, one who has clearly seen better days. There is the strong suspicion that he has been ruined by an addiction to drink. Ralph believes that he has him completely under his thumb, but the reverse is the case, for Newman Noggs takes very good care to ensure he knows everything that his master is up to, and in fact the villainy of Ralph could not have been finally exposed had it not been for the patient observation of Noggs. He is also a good friend to Nicholas. He is: 'A tall man of middle age, with two goggle eyes whereof one was a fixture, a rubicund nose, a cadaverous face, and a suit of clothes (if the term be allowable when they suited him not at all) much the worse for wear, very much too small, and placed upon such a short allowance of buttons that it was marvellous how he contrived to keep them on.'

This is a portrait of Newman Knott, who was a broken down never-do-well and failed tenant farmer who used to call at the offices of Ellis and Blackmores, the firm of solicitors at 5 Holborn Court, Gray's Inn, where Charles Dickens was employed as a clerk from March 1827, when he was sixteen, up to the time he became a reporter early in 1829. He found his day's work tedious, but as Christopher Hibbert points out in *The Making of Charles Dickens* (1967), between visits to offices and shops on behalf of the firm Charles derived his main pleasure in his working life from observing the people around him, the lawyers, clerks and the clients: 'One of the oddest of the regular visitors to the firm's offices, the broken-down black sheep of a respectable family named Newman Knott, was easily recognisable by those who knew him as being represented in the character of Mr Newman Noggs . . . ' Newman Knott used to have seven shillings weekly dole from a relative and he called to collect it from Ellis and Blackmores. Noggs is down-at-heel when we first meet him, but he had once kept his own hounds in the North. He has fallen into the hands of moneylenders and is reduced to enslavement to Ralph Nickleby. Nott came from Barnard Castle, a market town in Durham. This is where Noggs lived before he was ruined. When Nicholas Nickleby goes to Yorkshire, Noggs recommends to call at the King's Head, 'where there is good ale'. Dickens and his illustrator, Hablot Browne, stayed at this inn when they went to investigate the Yorkshire schools in preparation for writing *Nicholas Nickleby* in 1838 (see SQUEERS).

NORA

Henrik Ibsen, *A Doll's House* (1879)

Laura Kieler

In 1870 Henrik Ibsen was sent a copy of Laura Petersen's *Brand's Daughters*, a feminist novel presented as a sequel to his play *Brand*. Ibsen replied on 11 June telling Laura 'The main thing is to be true and faithful to oneself. It is not a question of willing to go in this direction or that, but of willing what one absolutely must, because one is oneself and cannot do otherwise. The rest is only lies.'

Laura first visited Ibsen in Dresden in 1871 and he was attracted to her, calling her his 'skylark'. Again, after her marriage to Danish schoolteacher Victor Kieler, she called on Ibsen in 1876 and told him of her personal problem: since her tubercular husband needed an Italian holiday to improve his health Laura had secretly borrowed the money to pay for it. Two years later she was obliged to return the money and hoped that Ibsen would help her by recommending her new novel to a publisher. He declined, telling her 'In a family where the husband is alive it can never be necessary for the wife to sacrifice her heart's blood as you have done.' Distressed by Ibsen's attitude Laura burned her manuscript and forged a cheque to repay the debt; when she was found out her husband rejected her and, when she suffered a nervous breakdown as a result, had her placed in a public asylum while he sought a separation. Reluctantly he took her back when she implored him to do so.

Laura was appalled at *A Doll's House* because she realized how closely Ibsen had modelled his drama on her own trauma. Her connection with the play continued to disturb her and in 1891 a critical article suggested she was less idealistic than Ibsen's heroine Nora. Ibsen refused to issue a public denial that Nora was indeed Laura and told a friend: 'she herself or her husband, preferably both are the only people able to kill these rumours by an open and emphatic denial. I cannot understand why Herr Kieler has not long since taken this course, which would immediately put an end to the gossip.'

ARTHUR NORRIS
Christopher Isherwood, *Mr Norris Changes Trains* (1935)

Gerald Hamilton (1890–1970)

Set in Berlin, during the critical period 1930-3, Christopher Isherwood's novel *Mr Norris Changes Trains* (US title: *The Last of Mr Norris*) is a portrait of a rogue permanently on the lookout for sources of personal profit, which is why, paradoxically, he joins the Communist Party for example. Arthur Norris's confidence trickery and comically corrupt nature is not immediately apparent to the naive English narrator William Bradshaw (Isherwood's full name is Christopher William Bradshaw Isherwood). When Bradshaw first meets Arthur Norris on a train his first impression is of schoolboy naughtiness. He then looks more closely: 'He had a large blunt fleshy nose and a chin which seemed to have slipped sideways. It was like a broken concertina. Above his ripe red cheeks, his forehead was sculpturally white, like marble. A queerly cut fringe of dark grey hair lay across it, compact, thick and heavy. After a moment's examination, I realized, with extreme interest, that he was wearing a wig.' As Isherwood acknowledges, in *Christopher and his Kind* (1976) the character was modelled on his friend Gerald Hamilton, with one important difference; whereas Norris is a masochist who visits dominant women, Hamilton was a homosexual.

In Berlin, in 1930, Isherwood first met Hamilton who was then sales representative of *The Times* in Germany. Of Irish extraction, Hamilton was born in Shanghai and became a communist sympathizer and promoter of liberal causes (legalized abortion, prison reform, the abolition of capital punishment). His *Desert Dreamers* (914) – which becomes *Miss Smith's Torture Chamber* in Isherwood's novel – is a homosexual story of the love of an Englishman for an Arab guide. During the First World War, Hamilton was twice imprisoned – first for a homosexual offence, then for anti-British activities. As Brian Finney writes, in *Christopher Isherwood* (1979), 'By the time Isherwood met [Hamilton] he had helped steal a Greek millionaire's wife's jewel case from the Blue Train, been arrested and imprisoned by the Italians for fraud in connection with a pearl necklace, and become an associate both of Willi Münzenberg [Bayer in the novel], the leading Communist organiser in Berlin and prominent Nazis.' Both Hamilton and Isherwood left Berlin in 1933. Two years later Isherwood, worried about his boyfriend Heinz being conscripted into the German army, asked Hamilton to obtain a change of nationality for Heinz. Though Hamilton did very little to help, he collected £1,000 for his efforts. Isherwood and Hamilton remained friends, and Isherwood contributed a preface to Hamilton's book *Mr Norris and I* (1956).

PROFESSOR NORTH
Rhoda Broughton, *Belinda* (1883)

Mark Pattison (1813–84)

Further reading:
Mark Pattison, *Memoirs* (1885)

Rhoda Broughton's *Belinda* shows a vital Victorian heroine being dragged down by the dreary old academic she marries. Professor North (of the Chair of Etruscan at Oxbridge) is the embodiment of intellectual aridity: 'a fur-coat wrapped about his thin figure, a skull-cap on his head, his feet aloft upon a hot water bottle, a writing-case upon his meagre knees and an ink-horn in his left hand'. Before he actually dies, at the end of the novel, he shows little love of life.

In 1878 the popular novelist Rhoda Broughton and her widowed sister Mrs Newcome moved to Oxford, where they became friendly with Mark Pattison. Following years of frustration, he had been appointed Rector of Lincoln College in 1861, the year of his marriage to Emilia Francis Strong, a woman almost thirty years younger than him. Pattison was known as a pedant who avoided undergraduates, neglected his administrative duties, published little, and had a penchant for young women. One of his girlfriends, Meta Bradley, came to his Rectory in 1880 and openly flirted with him to the annoyance of Rhoda Broughton, who told Pattison he was acting foolishly. Rhoda did not know Pattison and Meta were lovers, but when an anonymous letter referred to the affair, Pattison assumed it had been written by Rhoda. When Rhoda learned, on 11 March 1881, of his groundless suspicions, she began to brood on Pattison's fictional possibilities. As Tammie Watters writes, in her introduction to the 1984 reprint of *Belinda*, 'We can be pretty sure that the caricature [of Pattison as Professor North] began to take form on that fateful day, 11 March 1881. Rhoda might have felt that she was also settling accounts for [Pattison's wife Emilia], who confessed to a friend that her husband's pettiness and tendency to place an evil construction on the most innocent behaviour had provoked a passionate resentment in her and "poisoned so many years of my young life and drove me to desperation and the verge of utmost folly".' After the publication of *Belinda*, Pattison called on Rhoda and announced himself as Professor North, though he never apologized for his error in assuming that Rhoda had written the anonymous letter. A year after *Belinda*'s appearance Pattison died from cancer, and Emilia subsequently married the Liberal politician Sir Charles Dilke. In the novel Belinda (a composite based on Emilia and the author herself) is in love with the student David Rivers, but persuaded by conventional morality to marry Professor North. She is soon trapped in his scholarly routine and exasperated by his cold mind and 'chill-blooded' body.

NOSEY PARKER

Popular/folk expression for one of over-zealous curiosity of others' business

Matthew Parker (1504–75), **Second Protestant Archbishop of Canterbury**

Further reading: John Strype, *Life of Matthew Parker* (1821)

There are several claimants for the original of the term 'nosey parker'. Among them are Richard Parker (1767–97), who was hanged as leader of the Sheerness Mutiny. He had certainly poked his nose too deeply into military affairs to be tolerated by the authorities, as during the height of the mutiny he had thirteen ships of the line as well as frigates under his orders. But use of the term dates back to earlier times. The term was used abusively of Oliver Cromwell, for example. The most likely candidate seems to be Matthew Parker. He was born at Norwich and graduated at Cambridge in 1525. In the same year he was ordained deacon in April and priest in June 1527. He found favour with Wolsey, but resisted the Cardinal's promises as he had come under the influence of the Cambridge reformers. When Anne Boleyn became queen he was made her chaplain. He was also dean of a college at Stoke in Suffolk, canon of Ely, Master of Corpus Christi and later Vice-chancellor of the University of Cambridge. He courted a minor scandal by being associated with a play performed by Cambridge students, *Pammachius*, which mocked the old ecclesiasticism, but his reputation emerged unscathed. He was responsible for preserving the university from the spoliation with which they seemed threatened. He supported Lady Jane Grey and was deprived of his preferments by Queen Mary and lived quietly in retirement. When Elizabeth I came to the throne Parker was made Archbishop of Canterbury and identified himself wholly with the main church party, between Romanism and Puritanism, which was to become the Anglican church. He exercised his considerable powers over church preferments to prevent the spread of doctrines he considered obnoxious – puritanism and Romish tendencies – thus earning the dislike of the two opposing extremes of religious faction. He had a long nose, and his active, often interfering, nature earned him his famous sobriquet. He expended enormous energies on achieving general church conformity – the Thirty Nine Articles were passed by Convocation in 1562 – and he is associated with other influential measures for the regulation of services. He supported the revised translation of the scriptures (the Bishops' Bible) and edited several learned texts. His collection of manuscripts, bequeathed to his college at Cambridge, was priceless.

NOSTROMO

Joseph Conrad, *Nostromo* (1904)

Dominic Cervoni (born 1834)

Further reading: Jocelyn Baines, *Joseph Conrad – A Critical Biography* (1960), Bernard C. Meyer, *Joseph Conrad – A Psychoanalytic Biography* (1967)

Nostromo is the captain of the dock workers at the port of Sulaco in Costaguana. He is handsome, proud and a born leader of men, but he has one fatal flaw – vanity. The dictator of Costaguana dies and there is a power struggle which really centres on the power represented by the Sant Tomé silver mine. At one stage the struggle is won by the forces of Ribera, backed by the mine owner, Gould. There is then a further revolution, led by General Montero, which aims to drive Europeans out of this South American nation. The Europeans then support a counter revolution aimed at keeping Montero from gaining control of the San Tomé mine. The silver has to be hidden and contact has to be made with forces outside. The venture is entrusted to Nostromo and a French boulevadier, Decoud. Under strain of this mission, Decoud's nerve snaps and he shoots himself. Nostromo is corrupted by the silver and resolves to hide it and preserve it as a means to his own advancement. Later to his horror he learns that a lighthouse is to be built on the island where he has hidden the silver. To gain access to his hoard he affects to be courting one of the two daughters of old Viola, the lighthouse keeper. Nostromo begins to realize that he is really in love with the younger daughter and they agree to run away together. But on the night when he goes to regain his hoard, Violo shoots him in mistake for someone else – a former suitor of his younger daughter. The gallant, flamboyant exterior personality of Nostromo has always hidden his essential foolishness, which is now tragically rewarded.

Nostromo was based on Dominic Cervoni, the Corsican first mate of the *Saint Antoine*, a vain and colourful forty-two year old, whom Conrad described in these words: 'His thick black moustaches, curled every morning . . . seemed to hide a perpetual smile. But nobody, I believe, had ever seen the true shape of his lips. From the slow, imperturbable gravity of that broad-chested man you would think that he had never smiled. . . . In his eyes lurked a look of perfectly remorseless irony . . . the slightest distension of his nostrils would give to his bronzed face a look of extraordinary boldness.' Conrad sailed with him to the West Indies in 1876.

EDIE OCHILTREE
Sir Walter Scott, *The Antiquary* (1816)
Andrew Gemmels (1687–1793)

Sir Walter Scott's third novel *The Antiquary* is one of his warmest thanks to the presence of Edie Ochiltree who, as a bedesman, receives the royal bounty to beggars. Scott describes Edie's extraordinary appearance thus: 'A slouched hat of huge dimensions; a long white beard, which mingled with his grizzled hair; an aged, but strongly marked and expressive countenance, hardened, by climate and exposure, to a right brick-dust complexion; a long blue gown, with a pewter badge on the right arm; two or three wallets, or bags, slung across his shoulder, for holding the different kinds of meal, when he received his charity in kind from those who were but a degree richer than himself, – all these marked at once a beggar by profession, and one of the privileged class which are called in Scotland the King's Bedes-men, or, vulgarly, Blue-gowns.'

As a child Scott stayed with his aunt in Kelso and thus saw some of the colourful characters who moved back and forwards over the Scottish Border. One of these was Edie's original – Andrew Gemmels from Old Cumnock near Ochiltree in Ayrshire. After serving in the army, and fighting at Fontenoy, Andrew found himself penniless and so naturally took to begging since there was no shame attached to the practice at that time. As the most celebrated mendicant, or gaberlunzie, of his day Andrew was a welcome figure in Border towns like Galashiels where he was once observed playing cards with the Laird of Gala. Through the power of his personality and his entertaining ability to sing and spin stories he was well rewarded and became affluent enough, on his death at the age of 106, to leave a tidy sum of money to a nephew. As Edie says, in Scott's novel, 'what wad a' the country about do for want o' auld Edie Ochiltree, that . . . kens mair auld sangs and tales than a' the barony besides, and gars ilka body laugh whereever he comes?'

ODETTE
Marcel Proust, *Remembrance of Things Past* (1913–27)
Laure Hayman (1851–1932)

Further reading: George D. Painter, *Marcel Proust* (1959, 1965)

As a youth the narrator of Proust's novel visits his Uncle Adolphe in Paris and finds him keeping the company of his latest mistress. Of this 'lady in pink' Marcel says (in the translation by C.K. Scott Moncrieff and Terence Kilmartin): 'I had difficulty in believing that she was a courtesan, and certainly I should never have believed her to be an ultra-fashionable one, had I not seen the carriage and pair, the pink dress, the pearl necklace, had I not been aware, too, that my uncle knew only those of the top flight.' This, it later transpires, is his first glimpse of Odette de Crécy who becomes one of the central characters in Proust's novel. Odette, 'a young woman almost of the demi-monde', frequents the salon of MME VERDURIN and is there courted by CHARLES SWANN, a wealthy man accustomed to higher society. The narrator sees Swann and Odette, now married with a daughter GILBERTE, at their mansion (Tansonville) on the outskirts of Combray; and attends the salon Swann has established for his wife in Paris. Inevitably, Swann's love for the sexually promiscuous Odette fades and she settles into her increasingly fashionable salon: 'Nowadays it was rarely in Japanese kimonos that Odette received her intimates, but rather in the bright and billowing silk of a Watteau housecoat whose flowering foam she would make as though to rub gently over her bosom'. Rising up the social scale, Odette marries the Comte de Forcheville after Swann's death and later becomes the mistress of the Duc de Guermantes. For the narrator, though, she is perceived as an essentially vulgar woman, unworthy of the love she once inspired in Swann.

When Proust was seventeen, in 1888, he met Laure Hayman, the mistress of his great-uncle Louis Weill. Daughter of an engineer who died when she was a child, Laure was raised as a courtesan by her mother. Laure's lovers included the Duc d'Orléans, the King of Greece, and Karageorgevitch, the pretender to the Serbian throne. George D. Painter, who identifies Laure as the chief original of Odette, says Proust 'was attracted not only by Mme Hayman's beauty but by her salon, which was full of dukes, club-men, writers and future academicians'. Laure was an intelligent woman who warned Proust's father of Marcel's careless attitude to money, for he liked to take her to expensive restaurants and buy her masses of her favourite flowers – chrysanthemums. When Proust first met Laure she was (says Painter) 'plump but wasp-waisted, and wore an extremely low décolletée with festoons of pearls dangling, three a side, from what little of her bosom was hidden from view. Her hair was . . . tied with a pink ribbon'.

JONATHAN OLDBUCK

Sir Walter Scott, *The Antiquary* (1816)

George Constable
(1719–1803)

Further reading:
Edgar Johnson, *Sir Walter Scott – The Great Unknown* (1970)

Jonathan Oldbuck, Laird of Monkbarns, is *The Antiquary* in Sir Walter Scott's novel. He is a fussy old bachelor of radical views and a forceful turn of phrase ('his Scottish accent predominating when in anger'), a figure of some importance in Fairport (actually Arbroath). 'The country gentlemen,' writes Scott, 'were generally above him in fortune, and beneath him in intellect.' He had, however, the usual resources, the company of the clergyman, and of the doctor, when he chose to request it, and also his own pursuits and pleasures, being in correspondence with most of the virtuosi of his time, who, like himself, measured decayed entrenchments, made plans of ruined castles, read illegible inscriptions, and wrote essays on medals in the proportion of twelve pages to each letter of the legend.'

Scott acknowledged that Oldbuck was derived from George Constable, 'an old friend of my father's, educated to the law, but retired upon his independent property and generally residing near Dundee'. As a child Scott saw Constable as a man anxious to escape his bachelor status as he was in the habit of calling on Scott's Aunt Jenny when she was over fifty and he almost sixty, but the romance came to nothing. When Constable visited the Scotts he would expound his antiquarian interests, to the delight of young Walter, and also told the story that Scott later shaped into 'The Two Drovers'. Constable bought the estate of Wallace-Craigie near Dundee and held court there. Scott was fascinated by the man and once watched Constable dispute with the female proprietor of a stagecoach, a scene he subsequently fashioned into the opening of *The Antiquary* in which Oldbuck appears as 'a good-looking man of the age of sixty [whose] countenance was of the true Scottish cast, strongly marked, and rather harsh in features, with a shrewd and penetrating eye, and a countenance in which habitual gravity was enlived by a cast of ironical humour'.

OLD MORTALITY

Sir Walter Scott, *Old Mortality* (1816)

Robert Paterson
(1715-1801)

By the framing format of Scott's 'Tales of My landlord' series of novels, *Old Mortality* is narrated by Peter Pattieson, who bases his text on anecdotes told him by the wandering inscription-carver Old Mortality. Pattieson's favourite walk, from the village schoolhouse of Gandercleugh, ends in a deserted burial-ground where stand stones to the Covenanters (those Scots who supported the National Covenant of 1638 since it protected the Church of Scotland from English interference).

One summer evening, Pattieson sees Old Mortality: 'An old man was seated upon the monument of the slaughtered presbyterians, and busily employed in deepening, with his chisel, the letters of the inscription, which, announcing, in scriptural language, the promised blessings of futurity to be the lot of the slain, anathematized the murderers with corresponding violence. A blue bonnet of unusual dimensions covered the grey hairs of the pious workman . . . I had no difficulty in recognising a religious itinerant whom I had often heard talked of, and who was known in various parts of Scotland by the title of Old Mortality . . . In the language of Scripture, he left his house, his home and his kindred, and wandered about until the day of his death, a period of nearly thirty years. During this long pilgrimage, the pious enthusiast regulated his circuit so as annually to visit the graves of the unfortunate Covenanters, who suffered by the sword, or by the executioner, during the reigns of the two last monarchs of the Stewart line . . . Their tombs are often apart from all human habitation, in the remote moors and wilds to which the wanderers had fled for concealment. But wherever they existed, Old Mortality was sure to visit them when his annual round brought them within his reach.'

In his introduction to the 1830 'Magnum Opus' edition of the novel, Scott explained that he had met the original Old Mortality, Robert Paterson, in Dunnotar churchyard around 1800. Paterson was born at Burnflat, or Haggisha', near Hawick. At the age of thirteen he was apprenticed to his brother Francis of Corncockle Quarry, Lochmaben, where he studied stonecraft. In 1743 he married Lizzie Gray and obtained a lease of Gatelawbridge Quarry in the parish of Morton. As an ardent member of the religious sect known as Hill-men or Cameronians (after their Covenanting founder Richard Cameron), Paterson took it upon himself to repair the Cameronian monuments in Galloway, even though this responsibility led to the neglect of his wife and children. Gradually he extended his work throughout the Lowlands and beyond, hence Scott's meeting with him at Dunnotar churchyard.

THE OLD STRAIGHT TRACK

Alfred Watkins, *The Old Straight Track* (1925)

Blackwardine hills

Further reading: Tom Williamson and Liz Bellamy, *Ley Lines in Question* (1983)

The image of the Old Straight Track – along which ley lines are linked by archaeological landmarks – is a powerful one in literature. Alan Garner writes, in *The Moon of Gomrath* (1963): 'There was the old straight track, dipping and flowing over the rounded fields, and rising a silver thread like a distant mountain stream, up the face of the hills to the peak of shining Tor, and behind it the broad disc of the moon, white as an elven shield.' W.H. Auden, in 'The Old Man's Road,' explains: 'Under their noses, unsuspected,/The Old Man's road runs as it did//When a light subsoil, a simple ore/Were still in vogue: true to His wherefore,//By stiles, gates, hedge-gaps it goes/Over ploughland, woodland, cow meadows,/ Past shrines to a cosmological myth/No heretic today would be caught dead with,//Near hill-top rings that were so safe then,/Now stormed easily by small children.'

As expounded by Alfred Watkins, in his influential *The Old Straight Track*, the notion has obvious attractions. Acknowledging the appeal of the image though dismissing its archaeological accuracy, Tom Williamson and Liz Bellamy describe Watkins's theory as follows: 'He [Alfred Watkins] believed that ancient man tended to travel in exactly straight lines, and that, in order to progress in this way through foreign terrain, he set his eyes on a distant hilltop and then made straight for it. He would then head for the next hill, and so on . . . [The straight lines] were marked between natural sighting points by artificial "mark points", in order to keep the walker on the right track. These have now become "ancient monuments" and, because they were constructed to mark a straight path, can be found to be in exact alignment . . . Again and again the lines passed through villages, farms and hamlets which had the element "ley" in their names, and it was this that led Watkins to believe that the tracks had once been called leys.'

Watkins's theory had an enormous impact, though it was ignored by professional archaeologists. Enthusiastic amateurs formed the Straight Track Club in 1926, and in 1962 a Ley Hunter's Club came into being (complete with a journal *The Ley Hunter*). Though Williamson and Bellamy argue persuasively that ley theory amounts to a romantic quest for evidence of a Golden Age, and that archaeology had a 'depth and complexity that is entirely negated by ley theory', Watkins's work retains its appeal. It was in the Blackwardine hills, in June 1921, in his native Herefordshire, that Watkins first had the revelation of how the past had left its ley lines on the present.

OPHELIA
William Shakespeare, *Hamlet* (1602)

Katharine Hamlet (died 1579)

Further reading: A.L. Rowse, *Shakespeare – A Biography* (1963)

Ophelia is the daughter of Polonius, and sister to Laertes. She is loved by Hamlet and in turn, loves him. Polonius and his son are suspicious of Hamlet's attentions to her, and Laertes attempts to warn Ophelia off him, and to suggest that the liaison is a dangerous one. On the other hand, Polonius is quite prepared to use Ophelia to find out things about Hamlet and to report back his findings to Claudius. Hamlet's behaviour towards Ophelia also confuses her, and this complex of stress and contradiction is too much for her and she loses her reason, goes mad, and drowns herself. This is reported by Queen Gertrude: 'There is a willow grows aslant the brook/That shows his hoar leaves in the glassy stream;/Therewith fantastic garlands did she make/Of crowflowers, nettles, daisies, and long purples ... There, on the pendent boughs her coronet weeds/Clamb'ring to hang, an envious sliver broke;/When down her weedy trophies and herself/Fell in the weeping brook.'

Katharine Hamlet was a resident of Tiddington, which lay some two miles from Stratford. She was drowned in the Avon on 17 December 1579. At the inquest held at the offices of the Stratford town clerk, it was declared that her death was accidental and not suicide. The gravediggers in Hamlet Act V, Scene I debate whether Ophelia's death was suicide or an accident, and the priest who conducts the burial service says that: 'Her obsequies have been as far enlarg'd/As we have warrantise. Her death was doubtful.' The coincidences between Katharine's death and the death of Ophelia, as well as the astonishing coincidence of the name Hamlet, are very striking.

SIR ORAN-HAUT-TON
Thomas Love Peacock, *Melincourt* (1817)

Orang-outang owned by James Burnett, Lord Monboddo (1714–99)

Further reading: James Boswell, *Journal of a Tour to the Hebrides*, edited by Frederick A. Pottle (1936), Walter Jackson Bate, *Samuel Johnson* (1978), James Burnett, Lord Monboddo, *Origin and Progress of Language* (1792)

Sir Oran-Haut-ton is an orang-outang owned by Mr Sylvan Forester, a wealthy young philosopher. He has educated it, taught it manners and how to move in high society and has bought him a baronetcy and a seat in parliament. Unfortunately, it has not mastered human speech.

This is a satiric attack on the social standards of the day, the wildness of some theories then current in the sciences, and the political system of the time, with rotten boroughs, etc. Although he is an animal, he has all the surface qualities which would make him a gentleman, hence the essential punning nature of his name. As Forester says of him, when he is first seen sitting under a tree in a green coat and nankeens, looking 'very thoughtful', he is of a 'very contemplative disposition . . . you must not be surprised if he should not speak a word . . . The politeness of his manner makes amends for his habitual taciturnity.' One of the visitors, though too polite to laugh, 'could not help thinking there was something very ludicrous in Sir Oran's physiognomy, notwithstanding the air of high fashion which characterized his whole deportment'. His manners at table are exemplary, though he shows a weakness for wine. He was liable, without warning, having taken too much, to rise from the table and take a flying leap through the window, and go 'dancing along the woods like a harlequin'. Forester asserts that he is a specimen of 'natural and original man'. He learns to play the flute and the French horn by ear 'with great exactness and brilliancy of execution'.

This extraordinary creature is a portrait of Lord Monboddo's orang-outang. Monboddo was a Scottish judge and scientist whose ideas to some extent predated Darwin's origin of species. His ape could play the flute, but never learned to speak. Human language, Monboddo believed, was the outcome of man's social needs. If he lived in a natural state, his language would disappear. Apes, he held, showed intelligence, affection, gentleness and 'a perception of numbers, measure and melody'.

ORIANE, DUCHESSE DE GUERMANTES

The narrator of Proust's novel is obsessed, from an early age, with the glamour of the name Guermantes. For him, the Guermantes way (or walk) from Combray represents the road to an ideal aristocratic world that always seems out of reach: 'Nor could we ever get as far as that other goal which I so longed to reach, Guermantes itself. I knew that it was the

Marcel Proust, *Remembrance of Things Past* (1913–27)

Comtesse Laure de Chevigné (1860–1936)

Further reading: George D. Painter, *Marcel Proust* (1959, 1965)

residence of the Duc and Duchesse de Guermantes.' Marcel dreams of Oriane, Duchesse de Geurmantes, so is fascinated when his parents rent a flat in a wing of the Hôtel de Guermantes, the Paris home of his goddess Oriane. One night at the opera Marcel gazes adoringly at Oriane, and is astonished by her response (in the C.K. Scott Moncrieff/Terence Kilmartin translation): 'the Duchess, goddess turned woman, and appearing in that moment a thousand times more lovely, raised towards me the white-gloved hand which had been resting on the balustrade of the box and waved it in token of friendship'. Convinced he is 'genuinely in love' with Oriane, Marcel dogs her footsteps and generally insinuates his way into her glittering social circle and prestigious salon. Towards the end of the novel Marcel has become Oriane's 'oldest friend' and the older and wiser man knows she is not without faults; that she was always both bitchy and beautiful, both arrogant and enchanting.

In 1892, when he was twenty-one, Proust was attracted to the Comtesse Laure de Chevigné, *née* de Sade. Every morning during March of that year he waited on the Avenue de Marigny so he could watch her take her daily walk. One day he approached her in the Avenue Gabriel hoping to open a conversation, but the Comtesse cut him abruptly with the phrase 'FitzJames is expecting me' (a reference to Comte Robert de FitzJames). Proust was humiliated and, though he subsequently became friendly with the Comtesse, he took his revenge on her by creating Oriane in her image. Proust made sure that the Comtesse knew about her role in his novel. In a letter of 1921, to Duc Armand de Guiche, Proust said: 'Except that the Duchesse de Guermantes is virtuous she resembles a little the tough hen whom I mistook long ago for a bird of paradise, and who could only repeat like a parrot: "FitzJames is expecting me!", when I tried to capture her under the trees of the Avenue Gabriel. By changing her into a mighty vulture, I at least prevent people from thinking her an old magpie.' Painter says that 'Mme de Chevigné was goaded to make the only completely effective retort: she declined to read his book. "When I was twenty she refused to love me," he lamented to their mutual friend [Jean] Cocteau, "will she refuse to read me now I am forty" (in fact he was now just fifty) "and have made from her all that is best in the Duchesse de Guermantes?"'

ORGILIO

Samuel Johnson, *London: A Poem* (1738)

Sir Robert Walpole (1676–1745)

Further reading: J.P. Hardy, *Reinterpretations – Essays on Poems by Milton, Pope and Johnson* (1971)

In Johnson's *London* the persona, Thales, is shocked by the squalid materialism and political jobbery of the metropolis, and tries to escape the uncongenial atmosphere by fleeing to Wales. The core of the poem is to be found in Thales's speech to a friend as he embarks at Greenwich: 'Here let those reign, whom Pensions can incite/To vote a Patriot black, a Courtier white;/Explain their Country's dear-bought Rights away,/And plead for Pirates in the Face of Day;/With slavish Tenets taint our poison'd Youth,/And lend a Lye the Confidence of Truth./Let such raise Palaces, and Manors buy,/Collect a Tax, or farm a Lottery . . . To such, a groaning Nation's spoils are giv'n,/When publick Crimes inflame the Wrath of Heav'n . . . Well may they rise, while I, whose Rustic Tongue/Ne'er knew to puzzle Right, or varnish Wrong,/Spurn'd as a Beggar, dreaded as a Spy,/Live unregarded, unlamented die./For what but social Guilt the Friend endears?/Who shares *Orgilio*'s Crimes, his Fortune shares . . .' Thales feels that he has been treated with indifference by Orgilio, and that the civilizing mission of poetry and the creative arts is swamped by trade, commerce and materialism.

Sir Robert Walpole is undoubtedly caricatured in the figure of Orgilio, the proud and pompous statesman, who maintained himself and his faction in power by a complex system of bribery and pocket boroughs, manipulating public opinion in his attempts to control the press and using a well oiled political machine which involved lies, pensions, vote-buying and various other 'public Crimes' (see JONATHAN WILD, COCK-ROBIN). Those who go along with the system, Johnson suggests, enjoy the benefit: 'Who shares Orgilio's Crimes, his Fortunes shares'. The reference to raising palaces is directed at the lavish extensions which Walpole undertook at his country house at Houghton (see TIMON'S VILLA). Lord Chesterfield recorded of him: 'He would frequently ask young fellows at their first appearance in the world, while their honest hearts were yet untainted, "Well, are you to be an old Roman? A patriot? You will soon come off of that and grow wiser." And thus he was more dangerous to the morals than to the liberties of his country . . . his ambition was subservient to his desire of making a great fortune . . . He would do mean things for profit, and never thought of doing great ones for glory.' Johnson's *Dictionary* defines 'orgilous' as 'proud, haughty'.

ORLANDO

Virginia Woolf, *Orlando* (1928)

Vita Sackville-West (1892–1962)

Further reading: Quentin Bell, *Virginia Woolf* (1972), Victoria Glendinning, *Vita – The Life of Vita Sackville-West* (1983)

Orlando's adventures through time in Virginia Woolf's prose fantasy *Orlando* range from a sixteenth-century encounter with 'the great Queen herself' to a sudden realization that 'It was the eleventh of October. It was 1928. It was the present moment.' Initially, Orlando is a boy but after a seven-day trance in the seventeenth century he changes into a woman: 'Orlando stood stark naked. No human being, since the world began, has ever looked more ravishing. His form combined in one the strength of a man and a woman's grace.' In her diary for 5 October 1927 Virginia Woolf recorded her plans for 'a biography beginning in the year 1500 & continuing to the present day, called Orlando: Vita.'

Vita Sackville-West, Lord Sackville's daughter, was born at Knole, Sevenoaks, Kent; this ancestral home of the Sackvilles is duly celebrated in *Orlando*. Although well aware of her lesbian inclinations, Vita married Harold Nicolson in 1913; their son Nigel Nicolson called *Orlando* 'the longest and most charming love-letter in literature'. Virginia Woolf, who married Leonard Woolf in 1912, was undoubtedly in love with Vita though Virginia's frigidity probably prevented the affair from coming to a physical conclusion. Other literary women came closer.

Vita's passionate involvement with novelist Violet Trefusis features in the intimate diary kept by Vita and incorporated in *Portrait of a Marriage* (1973) by Nigel Nicolson. Vita's lesbian affair with Mary Campbell, wife of the poet Roy Campbell, is the subject of her verse-collection *King's Daughter* (1929). Campbell retaliated furiously in *The Georgiad* (1931) by setting the satire in the Nicolsons' half-timbered house Long Barn (two miles from Knole) and describing Vita as 'Too gaunt and bony to attract a man/But proud in love to scavenge what she can.'

ORLEY FARM

Anthony Trollope, *Orley Farm* (1862)

Julians Hill, Harrow

Orley Farm is a complex novel which concerns itself with unravelling the problems posed by legacy of Sir Joseph Mason and Orley Farm, which is dealt with in a codicil to his will. This codicil bequeaths the estate to his baby son, Lucius, and it is disputed by other members of the family. It was a novel of which its author was especially proud. Trollope wrote in his autobiography that although it was not his finest work, it had an excellent plot: 'The plot of *Orley Farm* is probably the best I have ever made,' but it gives itself away too early. He perceived that it had other merits: 'Independently, however, of this the novel is good. Sir Peregrine Orme, his grandson, Madeline Stavely, Mr Furnival, Mr Chaffanbrass, and the commercial gentlemen are all good. The lawyer's talk is good. The hunting is good . . . I do not know that there is a dull page in the book. I am fond of *Orley Farm*, and am especially fond of its illustrations by Millais . . .'

What Trollope has portrayed in *Orley Farm* is the estate and farm bought by his father at Harrow on land which runs up to the foot of the hill on which the school and church stand 'on the side towards London'. This was actually drawn by Millais. The Trollope family lived there in some comfort after his mother had returned from America in 1831 and published a book on her experiences which was a pecuniary success and enabled them to live in better financial security in the house in Harrow 'which has since been called Orley Farm, and which was an Eden as compared to our abode at Harrow Weald'. Mrs Trollope refurnished the farmhouse, 'and surrounded us again with moderate comforts. Of the mixture of joviality and industry which formed her character, it is almost impossible to speak with exaggeration. The industry was a thing apart, kept to herself . . . but the joviality was for all others. She could dance with other people's legs, eat and drink with other people's palates, be proud with the lustre of other people's finery . . . Even when she was at work, the laughter of those she loved was a pleasure to her . . . We continued this renewed life at Harrow for nearly two years, during which I was still at the school, and at the end of which I was nearly nineteen.' Then financial ruin struck the family again. Looking back at these happy days spent at the farmhouse in his early years, it was no wonder Anthony Trollope maintained such a lively interest in recapturing qualities he associated in his memory and transferred to the pages of *Orley Farm*.

OSMIN

Opera, *Die Entführung aus dem Serail* (1782), music by Wolfgang Amadeus Mozart, libretto by Gottlob Stephanie, altered from Christopher Friedrich Bretzner's libretto, *Belmont und Constanze* (1781)

Hieronymus Colleredo, Archbishop of Salzburg (1732–)

Further reading: Otto Jahn, *Life of Mozart* (1859), translated (1882)

Constance has been captured by the Pasha Selim, and is held, together with her maid and Pedrillo, a manservant, in his palace in Turkey. Her betrothed, Belmonte, arrives to rescue them. The first person he meets is Osmin, the head of the seraglio. Osmin rejects all Belmonte's attempts to gain admittance to the palace, and tells Belmonte in no uncertain terms what he thinks of him and of the captives held in the palace. His utterances are seasoned with violence and abuse; he says he'd like to break people's necks, or that they are suitable for the gallows, or their heads stuck on poles. In a quarrel with Pedrillo, the imprisoned servingman, Osmin says he'd like to behead him, then hang him, then spear his head on a pole, then burn him, then bind him and drown him, and finally flay him alive. In order to effect their escape, they get Osmin drunk, and are about to flee from the palace grounds when they are discovered. Osmin is now in his hour of triumph, and Mozart rose to the occasion, composing one of the finest bass display numbers in the operatic repertory, *Ha, wie will ich triumphieren*. He says he will dance and leap for joy when they are led to execution, and laugh when the nooses are tied round their necks. The hero and heroine, much to Osmin's chagrin, are spared by the merciful Pasha.

This wonderful portrait of barbarism and cruelty carried to the level of gross comedy is based on Mozart's employer, the notoriously hateful Archbishop of Salzburg, whose tyranny has thus been enshrined in glorious music. Mozart was a member of the Archbishop's court at Salzburg, but was treated like a base servant. He had composed an opera, *Il Sogno di Scipione* for his installation, and much other occasional and ceremonial music, as well as the *Missa Brevis* in F. His fame as an opera composer and *konzertmeister* at Munich and Paris angered the Archbishop, who reduced his salary by one-fifth. When Mozart's patience was finally exhausted and he resigned, the language of the Archbishop was unprintable and Mozart was physically kicked out. When the Emperor commissioned him to write *Die Entführung* the following year he himself created the part of Osmin, and he insisted that his librettist do exactly what he told him, 'to a T.' In the great *buffo* role of Osmin he immortalized his dreadful employer in Salzburg, from the safe distance of Vienna, where it was first performed on 16 July 1782.

LORD OTTERCOVE

William Gerhardie, *Doom* (1928)

Lord Beaverbrook (1879–1964)

William Gerhardie's second novel *The Polyglots* (1925) established the twenty-nine-year-old author as an important new force in fiction. One of the book's greatest admirers was Lord Beaverbrook (Max Aitken), the Canadian newspaper tycoon who controlled the *Daily Express*. Gerhardie was summoned to Beaverbrook's presence and acclaimed, as he explains in *Memoirs of Polyglot* (1931): 'When a powerful newspaper proprietor . . . writes of his own accord inviting you to come and see him and then says: "Look here, you're enormously brilliant and haven't had the success which you deserve. We must do something about it," you melt, you shed tears of self-reproach, and you begin to love him. I was immediately fascinated by the man.' Beaverbrook championed Gerhardie's work and introduced him to his influential friends. When they dined together, Beaverbrook would say 'I will provide the champagne, and you the conversation' to which Gerhardie would reply 'You will provide both'. When Gerhardie asked Beaverbrook if he was a multi-millionaire he replied 'No, a Maxi-millionaire'. As a Conservative MP Max Aitken had impressed the leaders of his party, and had received a peerage in 1917, the year before he was appointed Minister of Information. His newspapers – the *Sunday Express* and the *Evening Standard* as well as the *Daily Express* – expressed his outlook and campaigned, for example, on behalf of Empire Free Trade in 1929–31.

In Gerhardie's novel *Doom*, Lord Beaverbrook is portrayed as Lord Ottercove, owner of the *Daily Runner*. Frank Dickin, a literary hopeful, goes to see Lord Ottercove in the *Daily Runner* building in Fleet Street: 'In a vast radiant space of yellow and blue, at an octagonal table surrounded by chairs, sat a slim middle-sized figure in a dark-blue suit, a negligent lock over the brow . . . The visitor sat hushed and abashed, slowly taking in the surroundings, and Lord Ottercove went on with his work . . . From time to time Lord Ottercove would take up the receiver and say, "Give me the Prime Minister," or "Give me the Duke of Liverpool," and, incredible as it seemed, the Prime Minister or the Duke of Liverpool was already talking – and not from Liverpool . . . The visitor had a feeling of sharing in Lord Ottercove's multifarious activities and interests, and when he smiled – his eyes were grey and full of mischief – the visitor smiled too.'

Further reading:
A.J.P. Taylor, *Beaverbrook* (1972), Michael Holroyd, *Unreceived Opinions* (1973)

CLAY OVERBURY

Gore Vidal, *Washington D.C.* (1967)

John Fitzgerald Kennedy (1917–63) **35th President of the USA**

Washington D.C. is a novel which describes in detail the unwholesome goings-on behind the scenes in power struggles in Washington, the way in which the machinery of democratic government can be manipulated by those who can pay for it. It portrays presidential power politics as the sport of the rich. Eric Mottram described it as 'an appalling picture of those who might control the world'. It is set in the period 1937 to 1952. Senator Burden Day is an old fashioned and rather 'moral' politician, whose hopes for presidential office in 1940 make him accept money raised by doing a favour to a persistent lobbyist. The senator has young and ambitious Clay Overbury as his assistant. Overbury is handsome and – at the opening of the novel – unassuming and charming – but he becomes worldly and ambitious. Burden Day is demoralized by his crime, but, as Gore Vidal himself wrote: 'The young senator was very much in the Kennedy tradition, and so was able to take without a second thought anything that was not nailed down because that's the way you play the game around here: that's what the word "pragmatism" means. At the end of the book it was fairly plain that he was presidential material.' Backed with cash from the rich press baron Balise Delacroix Sanford, it is obvious that Clay Overbury is destined for the highest office in the most powerful nation on earth. Gore Vidal's novel sharply points up the great changes that take place in Clay as he begins to ascend to power. Early in the book he is described thus: 'Although he was only a senatorial assistant, Clay was often invited to great houses, largely because of the way he looked: tight blond curls, violet eyes and a short nose somewhat thickened as the result of a fall during a Warrenton hunt. An excellent athlete and a good listener, he was expected to go far, if only as the future husband of Diana Day.' Later in the book Burden Day notices he has changed remarkably: 'gone the soft curve to the jaw, the smooth cheeks, the red lips. Now a man's face looked upon the world. Most striking of all, beneath pale brows, thicker than he recalled, a stranger's eyes reflected unnatural light and in their brightness Burden saw the glory to come. He shuddered . . .'

Further reading:
Gore Vidal, *Matters of Fact and Fiction* (1977)

John Kennedy was born into a wealthy Boston family, educated at Harvard and groomed for high office, his political ambition supported by a well-oiled organization that led to his becoming the youngest man to become President of the USA, in 1960, and the first Roman Catholic to hold this office. He was assassinated in 1963. Herb Gold wrote in the *New York Post* June 1962 '. . . undoubtedly talented, but ever since he was a tiny boy he's had one idea – succeeding' (see WILLIAM CURRY).

SIR GILES OVERREACH

Philip Massinger, *A New Way to Pay Old Debts* (1622)

Sir Giles Mompesson (1584–1651)

Further reading: R.H. Ball, *The Amazing Career of Sir Giles Overreach* (1939)

Sir Giles Overreach is one of the finest comic roles in English drama. He is a cunning trickster who is motivated by the desire for riches, and there is much of Shylock in his make-up, as well as echoes of Ben Jonson's money-grabbing comic villains, such as Volpone or Subtle (see SHYLOCK, SUBTLE). He has no time for Christian morality, as his god is money: 'I would be worldly wise; for the other wisdom, That does prescribe us a well-governed life,/And to do right to others, as ourselves,/ I value not an atom.' The essence of the comedy lies in Overreach's attempts to gain a fortune by making the right marriage, but he is out-witted at every step of the way by the cunning Frank Wellborn, who so contrives it that Sir Giles pays out a fortune – as he thinks to pave the way to a greater one for himself – only to end up with neither the wife nor the money he had conspired for. His vast confidence in himself makes him an outrageously comic and grotesque figure: 'Now all's cocksure:/ Methinks I hear already knights and ladies/Say, Sir Giles Overreach, how is it with/Your honourable daughter! has her honour/Slept well tonight? or, will her honour please/To accept this monkey, dog, or paroqueto,/(This is state in ladies,) or my eldest son/To be her page, and wait upon her trencher?/My ends, my ends are compass'd – then for Wellborn/And the lands; were he once married to the widow –/I have him here – I can scarce contain myself,/I am so full of joy, nay, joy all over.'

Massinger is here satirizing the activities of Sir Giles Mompesson, and his accomplice, Sir Francis Michell, who appears as Justice Greedy. They were two notorious extortionists who had recently been tried and convicted. Mompesson was a politician, MP for Great Bedwin. He suggested the creation of the licensing commission in 1616, and became a commissioner and was knighted in 1616. He charged exorbitant fees and exacted heavy fines. He was gold and silver thread commissioner in 1618, and surveyor of the New River Company profits in 1619. The next year he was awarded the charcoal licence. But in 1621 the House of Commons ordered an investigation of the licensing patent and he fled to France. He was deprived of his knighthood and fined £10,000. He lived in retirement in Wiltshire. Michell was involved in peculation and corruption in the matter of monopolies and the gold and silver thread patents, and he too was investigated and degraded from his knighthood.

P

LADY GLENCORA PALLISER

Anthony Trollope, *The Small House at Allingham* (1864), *Can You Forgive Her?* (1864), *The Prime Minister* (1876), *The Duke's Children* (1880)

Frances Trollope (née Milton) (1780–1863)

Lady Glencora is the wife of the successful politician Plantagenet Palliser (see PLANTAGENET PALLISER), and is strongly contrasted with him in the series of novels in which they appeared from the mid 1860s. Plantagenet's aim was to render his country good and loyal service. Lady Glencora's ambitions are to advance her husband, for whom her hopes and ambitions are bottomless. She is ambitious, too, for her children. Often these ambitions led Plantagenet into embarrassing situations. He is cold, glittering, uncomfortable, saturnine, silent and takes everything very seriously. Glencora is probably cleverer than he is and 'kind-hearted, bustling, ambitious', with a great capacity for public and social life. She is not above intrigue, making friends with dubious political adventurers, often disobeying her husband, and even when punished and repentant, she was 'too full of vitality to be much repressed by any calamity', even when the Duke accuses her of vulgarity.

This is a portrait of the novelist's mother, Frances Milton, who married Thomas Anthony Trollope in 1809. She visited America between 1827–30, and published *The Domestic Manners of the Americans* (1832) and other travel books about Belgium, Paris and Vienna. When the family fell on hard times she wrote a series of novels, including *The Vicar of Wrexhill* (1837) and *The Widow* (1838). Anthony Trollope wrote in his autobiography that she had always loved society: 'affecting a somewhat liberal *role*, and professing an emotional dislike of tyrants . . . an Italian marquis who had escaped with only a second shirt from the clutches of some archduke whom he had wished to exterminate, or a french *proletaire* . . . were always welcome . . . In after years, when marquises of another caste had been gracious to her, she became a strong Tory . . . But with her politics were always an affair of the heart . . . Of reasoning from causes, I think that she knew nothing . . . she was emotional . . . The poets she loved best were Dante and Spenser. But she raved also of him of whom all such ladies were raving then, and rejoiced in the popularity and wept over the persecution of Lord Byron. She . . . seized with avidity on the novels . . . of the then unknown Scott . . . Of the mixture of joviality and industry which formed her character it is almost impossible to speak with exaggeration . . .' (see ORLEY FARM).

Further reading:
T.H.S. Escott, *Anthony Trollope – His Works, Associates and Literary Originals* (1913)

PLANTAGENET PALLISER

Anthony Trollope, *The Small House at Allingham*, *Can You Forgive Her?* (1864), *Phineas Finn* (1869), *The Prime Minister* (1876), *The Duke's Children* (1880)

Thomas Anthony Trollope (1774–1835)

Plantagenet Palliser makes his first appearance in Trollope's fiction almost as an after-thought at the end of *The Small House at Allingham*, but he was developed in the later political novels as a figure of some considerable stature and importance. He is the nephew and heir of the Duke of Omnium, he becomes Prime Minister to Her Majesty Queen Victoria, and in the author's own words, he is: 'a very noble gentleman, such a one as justifies to the nation the seeming anomaly of an hereditary peerage and of primogeniture'. Although he is a fine figure of an English gentleman and an admirable character, he is not likable, or even lovable. He is deeply virtuous, but unattractive as a personality. He finds it impossible to get on with people. His obsession with trifles causes his wife, Glencora, (see GLENCORA PLANTAGENET) to laugh at him. He pedantically quotes Latin. In his own way he loves his children, and they try to love him, though respect might be a better word, as they keep their secrets from their father and tend to be much closer to their mother. Plantagenet is a tireless worker whose devotion to duty and energy seem inexhaustible. He is patient with his wife's behaviour, and overlooks her follies, even though he finds her ambitions rather crude and worldly.

This is a portrait of the novelist's father in which the writer has compensated for the failure which dogged all his father's efforts by

Further reading:
Anthony Trollope, *An Autobiography* (1883)

making him at least successful in worldly terms, in picturing him as the well born, wealthy and professionally fulfilled Plantagenet Palliser. Trollope's father was a Wykehamist and a fellow of New College. He became a barrister in Chancery cases who had: 'dingy, almost suicidal chambers, at No. 23 Old Square, Lincoln's Inn, chambers which on one melancholy occasion did become absolutely suicidal (a pupil killed himself in one of the rooms). He was . . . an excellent and most conscientious lawyer, but plagued with so bad a temper, that he drove the attorneys from him. In his early days he was a man of some small fortune and higher hopes. These stood so high . . . that he was felt to be entitled to a country house . . . Things there went much against him; the farm was ruinous . . . My father's clients deserted him . . . as a final crushing blow, an old uncle, whose heir he was to have been, married and had a family!' Thus wrote the novelist in his autobiography (see JOSIAH CRAWLEY).

PETER PAN

J.M. Barrie, *Peter Pan* (1904), *Peter and Wendy* (1911)

Peter Llewelyn Davies (1897–1960)

Further reading: Janet Dunbar, *J.M. Barrie* (1970), Andrew Birkon, *J.M. Barrie and the Lost Boys* (1979), J. Dunbar, *J.M. Barrie – The Man Behind the Image* (1970)

At a New Year's Eve dinner party of 1897 J. M. Barrie met a lady he considered 'the most beautiful creature' he had ever seen. Sylvia's husband Arthur Llewelyn Davies was a barrister and her father was George du Maurier. Sylvia had named her youngest son Peter (born in 1897) after her father's novel *Peter Ibbetson* and Barrie, when walking through Kensington Gardens with his dog Porthos (named after the dog in *Peter Ibbetson*), had seen this baby boy with his brothers George and Jack and their nurse Mary. Barrie, though impotent, adored children; Sylvia produced two more boys, Michael and Nicholas, and Barrie attached himself to the family, lavishing his attention on the five boys.

Peter Pan portrays Arthur and Sylvia as Mr and Mrs Darling and, as he told the boys, 'I made Peter by rubbing the five of you violently together, as savages with two sticks produce a flame. That is all he is, the spark I got from you.' After the death of Arthur Llewelyn Davies (from sarcoma in 1907) and Sylvia (from cancer in 1910) Barrie adopted the five boys and was twice devastated by tragedy: in 1915 George was killed in action and in 1921 Michael was drowned at Oxford in what was possibly a suicide pact with a friend. Peter Llewelyn Davies, then a successful publisher, killed himself in 1960 by throwing himself under a train in the London underground. He suffered for his namesake for he was ragged at Eton as the real Peter Pan. 'What's in a name?' Peter asked in the family *Morgue* he kept from 1945 onwards, 'My God, what isn't? If that perennially juvenile lead, if that boy so fatally committed to an arrestation of his development, had only been dubbed George, or Jack, or Michael, or Nicholas, what miseries would have been spared me.' He thought the play he had helped to inspire was a 'terrible masterpiece'.

DR PANGLOSS

François-Marie Arouet Voltaire, *Candide* (1759)

Johann Christian von Wolff (1679–1754)

Further reading: C. Joesten, *Johann Christian von Wolff-Grundlegung der Praktischen Philosophie* (1931), Johann Christian von Wolff, *Eigene Lebens-beschreibung* edited by H. Wuttke (1841), W. Arnsperger, *Christian Wolffs Verhältnis zu Leibnitz* (1897)

Candide, a philosophical tale by Voltaire, satirizes the optimism of Rousseau and Leibnitz. Candide is the illegitimate son of the sister of the Baron Thunder-ten-tronckh. He is brought up in the Baron's household with Dr Pangloss, an incurable optimist whose motto is 'All is for the best in this best of all possible worlds', as his tutor. Catastrophe after catastrophe happens to the pair on their journey through life. Candide experiences the brutality of war, the Lisbon earthquake, the drowning of dear friends and Pangloss contracts syphilis, which rots his nose, covers him in sores and blackens his teeth. Dr Pangloss is finally hanged for heresy.

Voltaire was not attacking the philosophy of Leibnitz, but the popular notion of it, a kind of senseless optimism which accepted the belief that a benevolent providence was in command of the world. Pangloss teaches Candide: 'Metaphysico-theologo-cosmolonigology. He proved admirably that there is no effect without a cause and that . . . things cannot be otherwise; for, since everything is made for an end, everything is necessarily for the best end . . . noses were made to wear spectacles and so we have spectacles. Legs were visibly instituted to be breeched, and we have breeches.'

Christian von Wolff was the influential popularizer of the philosophy of Leibnitz. He was born at Breslau and educated at Jena. He taught at the universities of Leipzig and Halle and his system of philosophy soon spread. He was attacked by pietistic colleagues and expelled from Prussia in 1723 but got a chair at Marburg. In 1740 Frederick the Great recalled him and he became Professor of the Law of Nations and Chancellor of the University of Berlin in 1743. His most influential publication was his *Theologica Naturalis* of 1737.

Pangloss survives hanging, finishes up serving in the galleys and experiences many hardships, but even then will not recant, for – as he tells Candide – 'after all I am a philosopher; and it would be unbecoming of me to recant, since Leibnitz could not be in the wrong.' *Candide* was made into a comic operetta with book by Lillian Hellman, lyrics by Richard Wilbur and music by Leonard Bernstein.

PAOLO AND FRANCESCA

Dante Alighieri, *Divina Commedia, Inferno* (1314)

Paolo Malatesta da Verrucchio (died 1285) and **Francesca da Rimini** (died 1285)

Francesca is the daughter of the Count of Ravenna, and she is given in marriage by her father to Giovanni Malatesta (who is known as Sciancato, the Lame) for political and military reasons. But she falls in love with her husband's handsome younger brother, Paolo. They were reading together the story of Launcelot and Guinevere. Dante, at the end of the fifth canto of the *Inferno*, tells of Paolo's meeting with Francesca, who rehearses to him her temptation and sin as a result of reading the illicit love story of Launcelot and Arthur's Queen: 'The bitterest woe of woes,' she says in her torment, 'is to remember in our wretchedness/Old happy times.' Her fall was such a casual thing: 'One day we read for pastime how in thrall/Lord Launcelot lay to love, who loved the Queen; We were alone – we thought no harm at all./As we read on, our eyes met now and then,/And to our cheeks the changing colour started,/But just one moment overcame us – when/We read of the smile, desired of lips long-thwarted,/Such smile, by such a lover kissed away,/He that may never more from me be parted/Trembling all over, kissed my mouth.' They are discovered by Francesca's husband, who kills them both, and now they suffer endless torment in the howling darkness of helpless discomfort.

Francesca was the daughter of Guido Vecchio di Polenta of Ravenna, and aunt to Guido Novella di Polenta, who was a friend of Dante, and his host at the end of his life. Francesca was married to Gianciotto, son of Malatesta da Verrucchio, Lord of Rimini. The marriage was an arranged one, in return for military services. She fell in love with his younger brother, Paolo. The lovers were discovered by Gianciotto, who stabbed them both to death. Dante had the story, therefore, at first hand.

Further reading:
M. Barbi, *Life of Dante* (1954), Dorothy L. Sayers, *Introductory Papers on Dante* (1954), Dorothy L. Sayers, *Further Papers on Dante* (1957), U. Limentani, *The Mind of Dante* (1965)

MR PAPERSTAMP

Thomas Love Peacock, *Melincourt* (1817)

William Wordsworth (1770–1850)

Paperstamp is one of the Lake poets. He is 'chiefly remarkable for an affected infantine lisp in his speech, and for always wearing waistcoats of a duffel grey'. He hears Mr Feathernest give vent to self-praise at dinner at Melincourt Castle, and this is too good an example to be thrown away: 'and Mr Paperstamp followed it up with a very lofty encomium on his own virtues and talents, declaring he did not believe so great a genius, or so amiable a man as himself, Peter Paypaul Paperstamp, Esquire, of Mainchance Villa, had appeared in the world since the days of Jack the Giantkiller, whose *coat of darkness* he hoped would become the costume of the rising generation.' He strongly supports Mr Antijack's case that the wise man is he who appropriates as much of the public money as he can, 'saying to those from whose pockets it is taken: "I am perfectly satisfied with things as they are. Let *well* alone!".' To this he adds some useful political sophistry: 'you must not forget to call the present public distress an awful dispensation: a little pious cant goes a long way towards turning the thoughts of men from the dangerous and jacobinical propensity of looking into moral and political causes for moral and political effects.'

Further reading:
Hunter Davis, *William Wordsworth* (1979), F.W. Bateson, *Wordsworth – A Reinterpretation* (1954), Dorothy Wordsworth, *Journals*, edited by E. de Selincourt (1941)

This is Wordsworth, who in earlier days had supported radical causes but grew reactionary in direct proportion to his public success, despite affecting to choose his poetical subject matter among the poor and the humble. He was made Distributor of Stamps for the County of Westmoreland in 1813 (a post he held until 1842) hence his name 'Paperstamp'. Browning immortalized the turncoat in Wordsworth: 'Just for a handful of silver he left us;/Just for a riband to stick in his coat.' Keats wrote (letter 3 February 1818): 'Every man has his speculations, but every man does not brood and peacock over them till he makes a false coinage and deceives himself.'

PAROLLES
William Shakespeare, *All's Well That Ends Well* (1603)
Barnabe Barnes
(1571–1609)

Further reading:
C.J. Sissons, *Thomas Lodge and Other Elizabethans* (1933)

Parolles is a lovable coward and fraud. He is variously described in *All's Well That Ends Well* as 'a notorious liar', 'vile rascal', 'counterfeit lump of ore', and 'owner of no one good quality'. He is a braggart who disguises his lack of valour beneath his bluster, but he is brilliantly exposed in Act IV, when his fellow officers play a trick on him. He has claimed that he is so brave that he will recapture a drum which has been stolen by the enemy. When he leaves the camp his colleagues, in disguise and pretending to speak a foreign language, seize him and blindfold him. He is then interrogated, and willingly blabs out military secrets and slanders his superiors. He displays little embarrassment when the deception is revealed to him, merely being excited by the fact that he is still alive: 'Yet am I thankful. If my heart were great,/'Twould burst at this. Captain I'll be no more;/But I will eat, and drink, and sleep as soft/As captain shall. Simply the thing I am/Shall make me live. Who knows himself a braggart,/Let him fear this; for it will come to pass/That every braggart shall be found an ass./Rust, sword; cool, blushes; and, Parolles, live/Safest in shame. Being fool'd, by fool'ry thrive./There's place and means for every man alive.'

This is a portrait of Shakespeare's fellow poet Barnabe Barnes, who was a coward, intriguer and braggart. He was the son of the bishop of Nottingham, educated at Oxford, but left without taking his degree. He joined the service of the Earl of Essex (see ACHILLES) and published his first volume of verse in 1593. Five years later he was accused of attempted murder, but escaped from the Marshalsea prison and fled to the north. He then turned to play-writing, and in 1607 his tragedy *The Devil's Charter* was played by Shakespeare's company. Parallels have been found between this play and sections of *The Tempest* and *Cymbeline*. Like Parolles, Barnes was essentially a man of words, rather than deeds, a living representation of the *Miles Gloriosus* figure beloved of Plautus, full of strange oaths and tales of war, battles, sieges, victories and his own splendid deeds. Barnes actually served in Essex's army which accompanied the French against Parma in 1591. His published works include *Parthenophil and Parthenophe, Sonnets, Madrigals, Elegies, and Odes* and *A Divine Century of Spiritual Sonnets*. Marc Eccles identifies Barnes as Parolles in C.J. Sisson's *Thomas Lodge and Other Elizabethans* (1933).

DON PARRITT
Eugene O'Neill, *The Iceman Cometh* (1946)
Louis Holliday

Further reading:
Arthur and Barbara Gelb, *O'Neill* (1962), J.H. Raleigh, *The Plays of Eugene O'Neill* (1965)

Eugene O'Neill's *The Iceman Cometh* deals with various personal, political and philosophical 'pipe dreams' as embodied in the assembled drinkers at Harry Hope's saloon-hotel. Whereas the regulars betray themselves, the newcomer Don Parritt has committed an archetypal act of treachery by going to the police and informing on his anarchist mother who is then imprisoned. Ironically, Parritt says to Larry Slade, his mother's old lover, that to her the anarchist movement is like a religion and 'Anyone who loses faith in it is more than dead to her; he's a Judas who ought to be boiled in oil.' Parritt, the Judas of the piece, is 'eighteen, tall and broad-shouldered but thin, gangling and awkward. . . . There is a shifting defiance and ingratiation in his light-blue eyes and an irritating aggressiveness in his manner.' At the end of the play Parritt kills himself by jumping off a fire escape.

O'Neill gradually evolved the character out of a traumatic memory of his drinking friend Louis Holliday, a young New York radical who was one of the first intellectuals to frequent Greenwich Village bars. After meeting a girl he wanted to marry Louis stopped drinking and began to make himself a career in the West as a fruit grower. In January 1918 he told his friends he was coming to New York to celebrate the fact that he had saved enough money to get married; so the evening started at the Hell Hole (the real Harry Hope's). After a while Holliday succumbed to despair and admitted that his girlfriend had left him for another man. Holliday asked his friend Terry Carlin (the prototype of Larry Slade) for enough heroin to kill himself and Terry obliged. Louis died in Romany Marie's cafe at six-thirty in the morning of 23 January. O'Neill's histrionic version of the tragic evening made Don Parritt a man determined to die and Larry Slade his judge and executioner who tells him to 'Get the hell out of life'.

ELIZABETH PASTON

Richard Aldington, *Death of a Hero* (1929)

Hilda Doolittle (1886–1961)

Before he is killed in the First World War, George Winterbourne – the 'hero' of Richard Aldington's *Death of a Hero* – is a man whose attentions are divided between the two women in his life. He marries Elizabeth Paston, after she experiences a phantom pregnancy, but he finds Fanny 'a marvellous lover'. Like George, Elizabeth Paston is a painter. He first meets her at a cultural party in London: 'The women lit cigarettes. George looked at Elizabeth Paston. A slender figure in red silk; black, glossy hair drawn back from a high, intellectual forehead; large, very intelligent dark eyes; a rather pale, rather Egyptian-looking face with prominent cheek-bones, slightly sunken cheeks, and full red lips; a nervous manner. She was one of those "near" virgins so common in the countries of sexual prohibition. Her hands were slender, the line from her ear to her chin exquisitely beautiful, her breasts too flat. She smoked cigarettes too rapidly, and had a way of sitting with a look of abstraction in a pose which showed off the lovely line of her throat and jaw . . . George was greatly attracted.' Elizabeth has liberal views of love and, though she marries George, insists on her right to keep the company of other men.

Richard Aldington married Hilda Doolittle – the poet H.D. and original of Elizabeth Paston – in 1913. In the USA she had been friendly with Ezra Pound, and when she arrived in England was interested in like-minded intellectuals such as Aldington. In 1915 H.D. had a miscarriage which caused complications in her relationship with her husband. Later the Aldingtons had a house at 44 Mecklenburgh Square, Bloomsbury, London, and when Aldington came home from France on leave the main object of his sexual interest was not H.D. but Dorothy Yorke, who lived in the attic in the same house. H.D. naturally resented Dorothy (the original of Fanny in *Death of a Hero*) and herself had an affair with Cecil Gray, whose child, Perdita, she gave birth to in 1919. After the war Aldington and H.D. separated, though they were not divorced until 1937. H.D. settled in Switzerland with Bryher (Winifred Ellerman, the Lesbian writer) while Aldington lived with Dorothy Yorke, then Brigit Patmore, and then Netta McCullough, whom he married in 1938. H.D.'s version of her life with Aldington and Dorothy Yorke is told in her novel *Bid Me to Live*, in which Aldington appears as RAFE ASHTON.

Further reading:
Richard Aldington, *Life for Life's sake* (1941), Barbara Guest, *Herself Defined: The Poet H.D. and her World* (1984)

PATROCLUS

William Shakespeare, *Troilus and Cressida* (1602)

Henry Wriothesley, Third Earl of Southampton (1573–1624)

As the war between the Trojans and Greeks drags on, Achilles loses interest in military matters, and spends his time in his tent with his closest friend, Patroclus (see ACHILLES). Both Homer and Shakespeare portray in Patroclus a man who tries to get Achilles to take up arms again, act the role of a commander, and assist the ultimate Greek victory. Even when Achilles receives a direct and taunting challenge from Hector, he does not respond. He is only roused when his dear friend Patroclus is killed in battle by Hector. Robert Kimbrough in *Shakespeare's Troilus*

Further reading: A.L. Rowse, Shakespeare – A Biography (1963), Robert Kimborough, *Shakespeare's 'Troilus and Cressida' and Its Setting* (1964), A.L. Rowse, *Shakespeare's Southampton* (1965)

and Cressida and its Setting (1964) argues that there are direct parallels between the way Shakespeare presents Homer's story and recent contemporary events in Elizabethan politics, war and diplomacy, and that the drama contains several recognizable portraits. A.L. Rowse argues in *William Shakespeare – A Biography* (1963) that there is something in the relationship of Essex and Southampton 'imagined in that of Achilles and Patroclus': we have seen them skulking in their tent together, sulkily withdrawing themselves from action and the life around them; and their relationship was an emotional one, particularly on Southampton's side'.

The Earl of Southampton was Shakespeare's patron, and early in his career became an admirer of the Earl of Essex, attaching himself to him and taking part in his expedition to the Azores in 1597. When Essex tried to overthrow the government in 1601, Southampton supported him. He was captured and sentenced to death, but Lord Burghley (see POLONIUS) interceded on his behalf (Burghley had been Southampton's guardian) and the sentence was commuted to imprisonment. He was released on the accession of James I. He was a strikingly handsome man. In Sonnet 20 Shakespeare wrote of him: 'A woman's face with Nature's own hand painted/Hast thou, the master-mistress of my passion;/A woman's gentle heart, but not acquainted/With shifting change, as is false women's fashion; An eye more bright than theirs, less false in rolling,/ Gilding the object whereupon it gazeth:/A man in hue, all hues in his controlling,/Which steals men's eyes and women's souls amazeth.' Southampton helped to equip the expedition to Virginia in 1605, and was a member of the East India Company. He died of fever at Bergen-op-Zoom while in command of a troop of English volunteers in the Low Countries. He ordered a performance of Shakespeare's *Richard II* at the Globe in 1601 to incite public feeling with the presentation of the deposition of a monarch on the eve of the Essex rebellion (see ACHILLES).

PROVOST JAMES PAWKIE

James Galt, *The Provost* (1822)

Bailie Fullerton

Set in Gudetown – that is, John Galt's birthplace of Irvine, Ayrshire – *The Provost* was an immediate success; the first run of 2,000 copies sold out in a fortnight and Coleridge wrote (in his own copy of the book): 'in the unconscious, perfectly natural, irony of Self-delusion, in all parts intelligible to the intelligent Reader, without the slightest suspicion on the part of the Autobiographer, I know of no equal in our Literature . . . In the provost a similar *Selfness* is united with a *Slyness* and a plausibility eminently successful in cheating the man himself into a happy state of constant Self-applause.' The novel is narrated by Provost James Pawkie ('pawkie' being Scots for sly or shrewd), a merchant who sits on the Town Council and becomes Dean of Guild, then Bailie, then three times Provost.

As a man who has 'thrice reached the highest station of life' Pawkie recalls, with immense self-satisfaction, his successful career and ability to 'wind the council round my finger'. Although he acknowledges, in passing, a 'sinister respect for my own interests', he argues that in looking after his commercial interests he is merely acting in accordance with the spirit of the age. At the end of the book (shortly after the battle of Waterloo) Pawkie reflects: 'it will not be found, I think, that, one thing weighed with another, I have been an unprofitable servant to the community. Magistrates and rulers must rule according to the maxims and affections of the world . . . Posterity, therefore, or I am far mistaken, will not be angered at my plain dealing, with regard to the small motives of private advantage of which I have made mention'.

When Galt began to write *The Provost* he took, as the model for Pawkie, Bailie Fullerton who had thrice been Provost of Irvine. Assuming that Fullerton was dead, Galt (then resident in London) made full use of his memories of the former Provost. On 7 September 1825 Galt was back in his birthplace to be given the Freedom of the Burgh of

Irvine. He was astonished when Bailie Fullerton, now a man in his nineties, came forward to make the presentation. He was also impressed by the quality of Fullerton's speech. Mentioning the incident in his *Literary Life* (1834), Galt said 'Provost Pawkie himself could never have said anything half so good.'

SETH PECKSNIFF

Charles Dickens, *Martin Chuzzlewit* (1844)

Samuel Carter Hall (1800–89)

Further reading: Percy Fitzgerald, *The Life of Charles Dickens as Revealed in His Writings* (1905)

Pecksniff is the most monumental hypocrite in Dickens. A widower, with two daughters, Charity and Mercy, he comes before the world as a model of virtue and righteousness. But secretly he schemes to lay hands on Martin Chuzzlewit's money: 'He was a most exemplary man: fuller of virtuous precept than a copybook. Some people likened him to a direction post, which is always telling the way to a place, and never goes there: but these were his enemies; the shadows cast by his brightness; that was all. His very throat was moral . . . It seemed to say, on the part of Mr Pecksniff, "There is no deception, ladies and gentlemen, all is peace, a holy calm pervades me." So did his hair, just grizzled with an iron-grey, which was all brushed off his forehead, and stood bolt upright, or slightly drooped in kindred action with his heavy eyelids. So did his person, which was sleek though free from corpulency. So did his manner, which was soft and oily. In a word, even his plain black suit, and state of widower, and dangling eye-glass, all tended to the same purpose, and cried aloud: "Behold the moral Pecksniff!"' His character is splendidly exposed in his dialogue: 'It was once said of him by a homely admirer, that he had a Fortunatus's purse of good sentiments in his inside. In this particular he was like the girl in the fairy tale, except that if they were not actual diamonds which fell from his lips, they were the very brightest paste, and shone prodigiously.' He is an architect at Salisbury, and young Martin Chuzzlewit goes to him as a pupil. His villainy is finally exposed by Martin's grandfather.

Several originals have been proposed for Pecksniff, including Sir Robert Peel, who was considered unctuous by some (his smile was likened to the silver handles on a coffin by Daniel O'Connor) and Peel was certainly caricatured as Pecksniff many times. Augustus Welby Northmore Pugin, the architect and champion of the gothic style, has also been put forward as the original Pecksniff. He built St Mary's Grange, on the Salisbury – Southampton road, which is certainly Pecksniff's house. But the most likely is Samuel Carter Hall, a frequent guest at Dickens's house in Devonshire Terrace. Born in County Waterford, he studied law, became a reporter, became editor of *New Monthly Magazine*, worked on *John Bull*, and founded the *Art Journal* in 1839. He was an indefatigable compiler; works by him and his wife exceed five hundred volumes. Percy Fitzgerald (*The Life of Charles Dickens as Revealed in his Writings*, 1905) says: 'Having heard the novelist speak of this writer I might be inclined to think the theory of his being the original Pecksniff not so far fetched.' In 1880 Hall received a Civil List pension of £150 a year.

CLARA PEGGOTTY

Charles Dickens, *David Copperfield* (1850)

Mary Weller (1804–88)

Further reading: Angus Wilson, *The World of Charles Dickens* (1970)

Clara Peggotty was Mrs Copperfield's servant, and a loving nurse to young David Copperfield. When Mrs Copperfield marries the baneful Mr Murdstone, Peggotty takes David to her brother Daniel's house at Yarmouth. During Mrs Copperfield's second marriage, when she has become Mrs Murdstone, Peggotty is her only friend, solace and support. When her mistress dies, she is dismissed. She marries Joe Barkis, the carrier, who had always told David he was 'willin', and after Joe dies she goes to live with David and Aunty Betsy (see BETSY TROTWOOD). She is always known simply as 'Peggotty', and Miss Trotwood cannot believe this to be her real name: 'Peggotty? Do you mean to say, child, that any human being has gone into a Christian church and got herself named Peggotty?' Though far from a beauty, she is truly a saint: 'Peggotty, with no shape at all, and eyes so dark that they seemed to darken their whole neighbourhood in her face, and cheeks and arms so hard and red that I wondered the birds didn't peck her in preference to the apples.'

This is an affectionate portrait of Mary Weller, who was a nurse to the Dickens family when they lived at Ordnance Terrace, Chatham, in 1817 and the next few years. Her comments about the young Charles Dickens are preserved in Robert Langton's *The Childhood and Youth of Charles Dickens* (1891). She recalled how fond he was of fun and games and reading: 'Little Charles was a terrible boy to read and his custom was to sit with his book in his left hand, holding his wrist with his right hand, and constantly moving it up and down, and at the same time sucking his thumb.' Charles could remember Mary putting him to bed at night and humming the evening hymn to him while he cried on his pillow, stricken with remorse for having kicked somebody else or because somebody else had hurt his feelings that day, according to his *Dullborough Town*, in *Reprinted Pieces*. She fostered his imagination in all manner of ways, taking him to see the lying-in of the four children ('I am afraid to write five, though I fully believe it was five', he wrote) born at a green-grocer's shop, and by telling him truly blood-curdling stories, last thing at night, of ghosts, murderers, bloody vengeances and the like. She is also the model of Mary, the pretty house-maid at Mr Nupkins's house in *Pickwick*, where she and Sam Weller fall in love and marry – so she actually becomes Mary Weller. The real Mary Weller married Thomas Gibson, a shipwright, of Mount Row, Ordnance Place, Chatham.

ARTHUR PENDENNIS

William Makepeace Thackeray, *Pendennis* (1850)

William Makepeace Thackeray (1811–63)

Further reading: Anne Thackeray Ritchie, *Chapters From Some Memoirs* (1894)

Arthur's father, who comes from a good family, dies when the boy is sixteen. His mother, Helen, is a saintly character, but has little influence on him. His main mentor in early life is his uncle, Major Pendennis, who is able to get him out of the amorous entanglement he contracts with Emily Costigan, 'Miss Fotheringay', an actress, the daughter of the drunken Irishman, Captain Costigan. Captain Costigan was all for the marriage, as he is sure that young Arthur will inherit a considerable fortune. Arthur is sent to Oxbridge, where he is seduced into idle and extravagant ways (see BLOUNDELL BLOUNDELL), and is only saved from total ruin by the generosity of Laura Bell, the daughter of a previous friend of his mother's, whom she has adopted. Arthur then goes to London and embarks on a career as journalist and author, under the beneficial influence of Warrington (see GEORGE WARRINGTON). Mrs Pendennis hopes that Arthur will marry Laura, but he next falls into the clutches of the shallow and wiley Blanche Amory (see BLANCHE AMORY). Arthur and Laura are finally united. Arthur is not a wicked person, but foolish, and one who slowly learns the ways of the world only from his own experiences, by trial and error, often not aware of the distress his actions cause to others: 'As a boy, he was in no ways remarkable either as a dunce or as a scholar. He never read to improve himself out of school hours, but, on the contrary, devoured all the novels, plays, and poetry, on which he could lay his hands. He never was flogged, but it was a wonder how he escaped . . . When he had money he spent it royally . . . when he had no funds he went on tick. When he could get no credit he went without . . . He seldom if ever told lies, and never bullied little boys . . .' Many of the upper boys smoked and drank strong liquors, many of them were in love and boasted of locks of hair, but Pen was not yet beyond 'the theory . . . the practice of life was all to come.'

This is a self portrait, admitted by the author. His daughter, Annie, said it was like hearing her father talk, and when a lady in New York excaimed disbelief in the portrait: 'Surely not, Pendennis was so weak!' he replied: 'Ah well . . . your humble servant is not very strong.' Thackeray admitted he was feckless with money, easily tempted, and frequently naive, and the portrayals of his days at Charterhouse and Cambridge are considered particularly fine.

ISABEL PERVIN

D.H. Lawrence, *England,*

In 1918 D.H. Lawrence visited the Forest of Dean, where Donald and Catherine Carswell lived in a vicarage. This house became the Grange,

My England (1922)

Catherine Carswell
(1879–1946)

Further reading:
Catherine Carswell, *Lying Awake* (1950)

near Oxford, in Lawrence's story 'The Blind Man', which portrays Catherine Carswell as the heroine Isabel Pervin. Isabel's husband has been blinded in Flanders, and she is caught between respect for him and regard for her closest friend, Bertie Reid, a Scotsman, barrister and man of letters. The tension between the two men is sustained throughout the story, with Isabel as witness to their rivalry. A book-reviewer for a Scottish newspaper, Isabel tries to cope with difficult circumstances: 'Her face was oval and calm, her nose a little arched. Her neck made a beautiful line down to her shoulder. With hair knotted loosely behind, she had something of a warm, maternal look. Thinking this of herself, she arched her eyebrows and her rather heavy eyelids, with a little flicker of a smile, and for a moment her grey eyes looked amused and wicked, a little sardonic, out of her transfigured Madonna face.'

Catherine Carswell, one of Lawrence's closest friends, and the author of *The Savage Pilgrimage: A Narrative of D.H. Lawrence* (1932), was born Catherine Roxburgh Macfarlane, in Glasgow. She experienced an unhappy first marriage to H.P.M. Jackson (annulled 1908), and made a reputation as dramatic and literary critic of the *Glasgow Herald*, beginning in 1907. She reviewed Lawrence's *The White Peacock* favourably in 1911, and in 1915, the year she married the barrister and man of letters Donald Carswell, the *Glasgow Herald* dropped her after she wrote a piece praising Lawrence's *The Rainbow*. Lawrence encouraged her to complete her Glasgow novel *Open the Door* (1920), and also urged her to do justice to the passionate nature of Robert Burns in her book *The Life of Burns* (1930). In Harry T. Moore's *The Priest of Love* (1974) Catherine Carswell's response to the character of Isabel Pervin is cited: 'There was nothing superficially like me in her that could not easily be refuted. Yet somewhere the truth smote me . . . Here was little of portraiture, still less of summing up. But what an inescapable reading of the pulse of a life!' Catherine Carswell's husband Donald was killed in a motor-car accident shortly after the outbreak of the Second World War.

HARALD PETERSEN

Mary McCarthy, *The Group* (1963)

Harold Johnsrud

Further reading:
D. Grumbach, *The Company She Kept – a Revealing Portrait of Mary McCarthy* (1967)

One week after graduating from Vassar College in 1933 Mary McCarthy married the actor Harold Johnsrud. As the first sentence of McCarthy's *The Group* puts it: 'It was June, 1933, one week after Commencement, when Kay Leiland Strong, Vassar '33, the first of her class to run around the table at the Class Day dinner, was married to Harald Petersen, Reed '27, in the chapel of St George's Church, P.E., Karl F. Reiland, Rector.' The novel spans seven years (from Kay's marriage to her funeral, both services taking place in the same church) in the lives of eight girls from Vassar and in this excessively feminine world Harald stands as the representative of his sex. As such he is a failure: unimaginative, unpleasant and unfaithful to Kay (Mary McCarthy).

Like his fictional counterpart Harold Johnsrud was conditioned to failure; his father, a school administrator, had been involved in an academic scandal and Harold protected himself through a cynically hard exterior. His ambitions as a dramatist came to nothing but when Mary McCarthy first saw him, in Seattle in 1929, he impressed her as an actor – a career she herself considered. When she came to New York, Johnsrud befriended her and kept in touch when he went, briefly, to Hollywood in 1932 to work as a scriptwriter for MGM. During her three years of marriage to Johnsrud, Mary McCarthy was influenced by his leftist political sympathies but disturbed by his violent moods of depression. Perhaps partly on account of his odd appearance – prematurely bald, with a broken nose – he was unsuccessful as an actor. In the novel he is fired from a musical show by a homosexual director, which is probably a colourful version of the truth. In 1936 Mary McCarthy decided to divorce Johnsrud. After leaving her, Johnsrud's life continued towards catastrophe: he wrote plays that were never produced and was burned to death in the Hotel Breevort fire during the war. Apparently he had returned to the burning building to rescue some of his manuscripts.

JASPER PETULENGRO

George Borrow, *Lavengro: the Scholar, the Gipsy, the Priest* (1851)

Ambrose Smith (1804–78)

Further reading: W.I. Knapp, *The Life, Writings and Correspondence of George Borrow* (1899), G.A. Stephen, *Borrow House Museum – A Biographical Account of the Life of George Borrow and His Norwich Home* (1927)

Lavengro combines fiction with autobiography. The hero is the son of an officer in the army, who spends much of his military career guarding French prisoners, and moving from one station to another. The son develops a wandering nature and *Lavengro* is the story of his travels, adventures and the characters he meets. Among the most memorable people he gets to know is a family of gipsies, with a son, Jasper, slightly younger than himself: 'A queer look had Jasper; he was a lad of some twelve or thirteen years, with long arms, unlike the singular being who called himself his father; his complexion was ruddy, but his face was seamed.' His face was 'roguish enough' without being evil, and he 'wore drab breeches, with certain strings at the knee, a rather gay waistcoat, and tolerably white shirt; under his arm he bore a mighty whip of whalebone with a brass knob, and upon his head was a hat without either top or brim'.

Borrow was almost an adopted member of the Romany race, having learned the language and the way of life from personal experience, and his works – *Lavengro and Romany Rye* in particular – put into circulation a great deal of the initial information on which British conception of the Romany life was based.

Jasper is one of his finest portraits. He was based on Borrow's friend Ambrose Smith, son of Faden and Mirella Smith, gipsies of East Anglia. Ambrose's uncle, also called Ambrose, was transported for stealing. This episode is also used in *Lavengro*, though it is transferred to Jasper's father. After the publication of *Lavengro* Ambrose Smith became something of a celebrity. The *Athenaeum* reviewer had written that Borrow 'is never thoroughly at his ease except when among Gipsies'. Ambrose Smith was, in fact, presented to Queen Victoria at Knockenhair Park in 1878, the year of his death.

SAMUEL PICKWICK

Charles Dickens, *The Posthumous Papers of the Pickwick Club* (1836)

John Foster

Further reading: Walter Dexter and J.W. Ley, *The Origin of Pickwick* (1936)

Pickwick is one of the immortals of literature, a figure instantly and universally recognizable by his 'bald head and circular spectacles . . . gigantic brain beneath that forehead . . . beaming eyes . . . twinkling behind those glasses' and his enviable tights and gaiters. He is described, when we first see him in action standing on a Windsor chair to address the Club which he had founded, as presenting a subject suitable for the study of an artist with one hand gracefully concealed behind his coat tails, and the other waving in air, to assist his glowing declamation; his elevated position revealing those tights and gaiters, which, had they clothed an ordinary man, might have passed without observation, but which, when Pickwick clothed them – if we may use the expression – inspired voluntary awe and respect'.

The figure of Pickwick, now so familiar to us, was made from a description of one John Foster, who was a friend of the book's publisher, Edward Chapman. Robert Seymour, the original illustrator, first sketched a long thin man, but, as Chapman recorded: 'The present immortal one was made from my description of a friend of mine at Richmond, a fat old beau, who would wear, in spite of the ladies' protests, drab tights and black gaiters. His name was John Foster.' Thus was born the short and plump Pickwickian prototype. As Dickens says: 'I thought of Pickwick and wrote the first number, from the proof sheets of which Mr Seymour made his drawing of the Club, and that happy portrait of its founder by which he is always recognised.' Writer and illustrator seemed harmonious and in accord with their creation. Dickens took the name from Moses Pickwick, a coach proprietor at Bath. Sam Weller, in the book, is somewhat indignant to see the name on the outside of a coach at Bath, taking it to be a personal reflection upon his employer.

PIERROT

Traditional character in pantomime, seaside con-

Pierrot is still immediately recognizable in his traditional white ill-fitting silk suit and conical cap. He is usually wholly untrustworthy and unreliable, kleptomaniacal in tendency, mendacious, greedy, and severely lacking in moral scruple. His main weapon in earning the indulgence and affection of the audience is his exploitation of pathos, in which he is aided by his unmistakable whitened face. The tradition is still strongly present in Marcel Marceau's character, Bip, and the comic mime featured in the Kenny Everett television shows. Pierrot derives ultimately from the commedia dell'arte character, Pedrolino, the comic servant (compare Pedrillo, in Mozart's opera *Die Entführung aus dem Serail*). Pierrot became popular in Britain at the end of the nineteenth century as a result of the success of his appearance in a mime-play, *L'Enfant prodigue*. Concert parties of 'pierrots' – dressed in the traditional pierrot costumes – were a feature of British holiday resorts and sea-side towns, and in London established their popularity in the long running revue, *The Co-Optimists*, which packed them in in the West End between 1921 and 1927. The show was revived in 1928 and again in 1935.

cert parties etc.

Jean Baptiste Gaspard Deburau (1796–1846)

This entire tradition is based on Jean Deburau, who was born in Bohemia in 1796 into a poor family, and earned a living in a variety of travelling troupes of players and entertainers. His was a very harsh apprenticeship, but in it he learned to master all the tricks of his trade; among his specialities were phenomenal powers of creative farce, the ability to balance a ladder on his nose, and a mastery of *le saut périlleux*. He created the Pierrot character, and went to the *Théatre des Funambules*, on the Boulevard du Temple, Paris, famous for pantomimes, vaudevilles and melodramas, where with his face whitened with flour, wearing baggy white silk clothes and the famous dunce's cap, his genius was recognized by Charles Nodier. His role as Pierrot became the rage of Paris, Théophile Gautier thought he was the greatest actor of the day. He died tragically after a fall on stage (which features in *Les Frères Zemganno* (1879) a novel of circus life). His son, Charles Deburau, was a well-known Pierrot at the *Funambules*. He died in 1873. Jean Deburau was played by Jean-Louis Barrault in Marcel Carné's film *Les Enfants du Paradis* (1945), written by Jacques Prèvert.

MRS PIPCHIN

Charles Dickens, *Dombey and Son* (1848)

Mrs Roylance

Mrs Pipchin is the formidable widowed lady who is the proprietor of the children's boarding house in Brighton where Paul (see PAUL DOMBEY) and Florence were sent by their father: 'A marvellous ill-favoured, ill-conditioned old lady, of a stooping figure, with a mottled face, like bad marble, a hook nose, and a hard grey eye, that looked as if it might have been hammered at an anvil without sustaining any injury. Forty years at least had elapsed since the Peruvian mines had been the death of Mr Pipchin; but his relict still wore black bombazeen, of such a lustreless, deep, dead, sombre shade, that gas itself couldn't light her up after dark, and her presence was a quencher to any number of candles. She was generally spoken of as "a great manager" of children; and the secret of her management was, to give them everything that they didn't like, and nothing that they did – which was found to sweeten their dispositions very much.' Her husband had broken his heart in pumping the water out of the mines in Peru. She kept Paul and Florence and her niece, Berinthia, in awe. Mr Dombey (see MR DOMBEY) employs her as his housekeeper later in the novel.

Further reading:
John Forster, *The Life of Charles Dickens* (1874)

This is a vivid portrait of Mrs Roylance, who was the landlady of the boarding house in Little College Street, Camden Town, where Charles Dickens stayed when his father was committed to the Marshalsea prison for debt in 1824. Dickens gave an account of this harrowing period of his life to his friend and biographer John Forster: 'I (small Cain that I was, except that I had never done harm to any one) was handed over as a lodger to a reduced old lady, long known to our family, in Little College Street . . . who took children in to board, and had once done so in Brighton; and who, with a few alterations and embellishments, unconsciously began to sit for Mrs Pipchin in *Dombey* when she took in me. She had a little brother and sister under her care then; somebody's natural children, who were very irregularly paid for; and a widow's little son. The two boys and I slept in the same room. My own exclusive breakfast, of a penny cottage loaf and a pennyworth of milk, I provided for myself. I kept another small loaf, and a quarter of a pound of cheese . . . to make my supper when I came back at night (from the blacking factory where he worked) . . . I suppose my lodging was paid for by my father . . . I certainly had no other assistance whatever from Monday morning until Saturday night. No advice, no counsel, no encouragement, no consolation, no support, from any one that I can call to mind. Sundays, Fanny [his sister] and I passed in the prison.' When the family left the Marshalsea they all went to lodge for a time with Mrs Roylance.

PAUL PLEYDELL
Sir Walter Scott, *Guy Mannering* (1815)

Adam Rolland (1734–1819); **Andrew Crosbie** (1736–85)

Further reading: Henry Thomas, Lord Cockburn, *Memoirs* (1856)

Paul Pleydell, the Sheriff of the county who conducts the enquiry into the murder of Kennedy, is a complex character based by Sir Walter Scott on two originals. By day he is an upright and formal representative of the Scottish legal profession, and by night a reveller of great capacity and fortitude. He is described as 'well born and well educated; and, although somewhat pedantic and professional in his habits, he enjoyed great respect'. He is a veteran of the profession and of an old-fashioned cast of mind who believed the old ways were the best and that modern times had lapsed into degeneracy. His positive qualities are strongly marked – he is a sound scholar, an outstanding lawyer and a most genuine person. But there is another dimension to his character: 'His professionalism, like his three-tailed wig and black coat, he could slip off on a Saturday evening, when surrounded by a party of jolly companions, and disposed for what he called his altitudes.' He may then be found at his favourite tavern: 'enthroned as a monarch in an elbow-chair placed on the dining-table, his . . . wig on one side, his head crowned with a bottle-slider, his eye learing with an expression betwixt fun and the effects of wine with his "court" all around him. Scott drew on two personages for the character of Pleydell. Adam Rolland was the original of the formal lawyer. He was over eighty when the novel appeared. He was the son of the Laird of Luscar and Gask, Fifeshire, and was educated at Dunfermline and Edinburgh University. He was called to the bar in 1757. He was not a brilliant advocate as far as court appearances went but had an immense reputation in written pleadings and giving opinions. When he retired in 1799 he was made Deputy Director of the Bank of Scotland. He was a devout Presbyterian, was always elegantly attired and spoke and wrote English with precision and charm. Lord Cockburn said he was like a dried butterfly, 'crisp in his mulberry-coloured kerseymere coat, single-breasted . . . black satin breeches . . . bright morocco shoes with silver or blue steel buckles . . . copious frill and ruffles'. Andrew Crosbie was born in Dumfries, son of the Provost and was a brilliant lawyer who rose to the top of his profession and was Vice Dean of the Faculty of Advocates by 1784. He probably died from an excess of high living as most of his business was conducted in taverns and coffee houses in the Lawnmarket and High Street of Edinburgh. He met Dr Johnson when the Great Cham visited Edinburgh in 1773. He was said to have died of a broken heart when the Douglas and Heron Bank failed, in which he had invested his fortunes.

MATTHEW PLUNKETT
Wyndham Lewis, *The Apes of God* (1930)

Lytton Strachey (1880–1932)

One of the main subjects of Wyndham Lewis's satirical scorn in *The Apes of God* is the collective mentality of the Bloomsbury Group of writers (named after Bloomsbury, in west-central London). Lewis disliked the aesthetic affectations of the Bloomsberries, their sexual ambiguity, their tendency to promote each other as geniuses, their combination of cultural power and social prestige. In this novel, Lewis describes the Bloomsbury Group as 'a select and snobbish club [whose] foundation-members consisted of monied middleclass descendants of Victorian literary splendour'. Matthew Plunkett is a typical Bloomsberry, with his 'dropped, limp, swan-wristed hand' and 'lovesick face'. When he walks into the 'public-air' of Bloomsbury, 'Matthew thrust his hands brutally into his trouser-pockets and assumed an expression of aggressive imbecility, half scowling tramp-comedian, half baby-boy. It was a rhythmic tramp-tramp-tramp, with every third step or so a stumble, that took him to the end of the square.' Plunkett is a poseur, a ridiculous creature to behold – he wears outsize shoes so is 'too small for his boots'. He is a man bogged down in petty details as he ponders on 'a few scraps of a feast of reason of Eminent Victorian giants', an allusion to *Eminent Victorians*, the best-known book by Lytton Strachey.

Strachey was one of the central figures of the Bloomsbury Group – a writer who cultivated an ironical style, a homosexual who lived with a woman (Carrington, the artist who nursed him at the end of his life), a friend of the famous (such as John Maynard Keynes, the economist), an oddly elongated figure (especially in the portrait by Henry Lamb in the National Portrait Gallery, London). The son of General Sir Richard Strachey, Lytton was educated at Cambridge and became a contributor to the *Spectator*. His *Landmarks in French Literature* (1912) had little impact, but the iconoclastic tone of *Eminent Victorians* – with its debunking treatment of Cardinal Manning, Florence Nightingale, Matthew Arnold and General Gordon – was widely admired and imitated. Strachey published *Queen Victoria* in 1921 and *Elizabeth and Essex* in 1928. His articles were collected in *Books and Characters* (1922) and *Characters and Commentaries* (1933).

Further reading:
Michael Holroyd, *Lytton Strachey* (1967, 1968)

MR PODSNAP

Charles Dickens, *Our Mutual Friend* (1865)

John Forster (1812–76)

John Podsnap is a complacent businessman, firm-handed and very self-opinionated: 'Mr Podsnap was well-to-do, and stood very high in Mr Podsnap's opinion. Beginning with a good inheritance, he had married a good inheritance, and had thriven exceedingly in the Marine Insurance way, and was quite satisfied. He never could make out why everybody was not quite satisfied, and he felt conscious that he set a brilliant social example in being particularly well satisfied with most things, and, above all other things, with himself.' He was intolerant of the opinions of others about anything, and developed mannerisms and gestures for sweeping others' opinions aside, in which he 'settled that whatever he put behind him he put out of existence: "I don't want to know about it; I don't choose to discuss it; I don't admit it!" Mr Podsnap had even acquired a peculiar flourish of his right arm in often clearing the world of its most difficult problems by sweeping them behind him (and consequently sheer away) with those words and a flushed face.'

He is modelled on Dickens's close friend and biographer, John Forster. A barrister at the Inner Temple by 1843, he developed a distinguished literary career, as drama critic for the *Examiner*, editor of several journals and contributor to learned publications. He was a friend of Lamb, Bulwer Lytton, Landor, Tennyson, Carlyle, Leigh Hunt and others of the Dickens circle. He wrote *The Life of Charles Dickens*, a valuable, detailed and influential biography of the novelist, which excludes any breath of scandal or blemishes on Dickens's life or character. He was a bossily loquacious man, who would not brook interruption or contradiction, and would literally shout down all opposition with loud explosions of 'Don't tell me!' – 'Incredible!' – 'Monstrous!'. Having beaten opponents into the ground, he would then simply reiterate his own assertions and opinions in his loud sarcastic tones, seasoned with mocking laughter and dismissive snorts. Robert Browning commented on his 'rhinoceros-laugh', and William Macready termed it a 'horse-laugh'. All the same, this pompous and dominating character aroused deep and lasting affection amongst a wide group of sensitive and intelligent people. At table on one occasion he demanded carrots, only to be told by the maid that there were none. With a wave of his hand he exclaimed: 'Mary! Let there be carrots!'.

Further reading:
R. Renton, *John Forster and His Friends* (1912), M. Elwin, *Victorian Wallflowers* (1934)

CYRIL POGES

Sean O'Casey, *Purple Dust* (1940)

Billy McElroy

Further reading: Eileen O'Casey, *Sean* (1971), Alan Bold (ed.), *The Letters of Hugh MacDiarmid* (1984)

O'Casey's play *Purple Dust*, first performed in Liverpool in 1945, sets up a satirical situation. Two English businessmen, Stoke and Poges, have acquired an old Tudor mansion in the west of Ireland. Converts to the countryside, they hope to create a self-supporting Irish Eden as a haven from the war engulfing England. Both men have Irish mistresses, on whom they have settled five hundred pounds a year for life. Basil Stoke, a thin man of thirty, has Avril, a pretty girl of twenty-one. Cyril Poges's mistress Souhaun is half his age. Though convincingly drawn, Stoke and Poges are clearly emblems of a reactionary England attempting unsuccessfully to absorb romantic Ireland. Poges (O'Casey explains in his stage directions) is a man of sixty-five. 'He was, when young, a rather good-looking man, but age has altered him a lot. He is now inclined to be too stout, with a broad chest and too prominent belly; his face is a little too broad, too ruddy, and there are perceptible bags of flesh under his eyes . . . He has a fussy manner [and] wants his way at all times.' At the end of the play the river rises symbolically to drown the foreign din of Stoke and Poges – who have come to the conclusion that Ireland is 'a waste land; a wilderness'.

O'Casey modelled the character of Poges on Billy McElroy, some seven years his senior. McElroy was a wealthy coal-merchant and a friend of various writers, including O'Casey, whose best man he was when the dramatist married Eileen in London in 1927. When the Scottish poet Hugh MacDiarmid (C.M. Grieve) came to London in 1929 he and his wife Peggy – the original of JEAN in *A Drunk Man Looks at the Thistle* – got to know McElroy. The relationship between McElroy and Peggy led to the collapse of MacDiarmid's marriage and, by 1932, Peggy was not only living with McElroy, but had become a director and secretary in his firm. McElroy, who had married in 1895, left his wife Kate, by whom he had nine children, five of whom were still living in 1932. On 9 October 1949 O'Casey wrote to tell MacDiarmid that 'When I came first to England, I was just a gaum, having practically no experience . . . McElroy was, I knew, something of a business rascal, but he was a character, and, in my mind then, a friend to artists.' Later, however, O'Casey felt that 'McElroy was the most egoistic & selfish mortal that ever crossed my path'.

AUNT POLLY

Mark Twain, *The Adventures of Tom Sawyer* (1876)

Jane Clemens (née Lampton)

Further reading: Van Wyck Brooks, *The Ordeal of Mark Twain* (1920)

'The old lady pulled her spectacles down and looked over them, about the room; then she put them up and looked out under them. She seldom or never looked *through* them for so small a thing as a boy, for they were her state pair, the pride of her heart, and were built for 'style' not service; she could have seen through a pair of stove lids as well . . .' Tom Sawyer is brought up by his Aunt Polly, one of the immortals of American literature. On the surface she is strict and unyielding, and always unwilling to admit to any merit in Tom's behaviour. Beneath this exterior, she has a loving heart. When she congratulates him on the fine job of work he has done in painting the famous white fence, she says: 'Well, I never! There's no getting round it; you *can* work when you've a mind to, Tom.' But she dilutes the compliment by adding: 'But it's powerful seldom you've a mind to, I'm bound to say. Well, go 'long and play; but mind you get back some time in a week, or I'll tan you.' She gives him his reward: 'She was so overcome by the splendour of his achievement that she took him into the closet and selected a choice apple, and delivered it to him, along with an improving lecture upon the added value and flavour a treat took to itself when it came without sin through virtuous effort . . .'

This is a portrait of the writer's mother, Jane Clemens, who was regarded as a character by all the town (Hannibal, Missouri), and who was reputed to have been the handsomest girl and the wittiest, as well as the best dancer, in all Kentucky, where she met the writer's father, John Marshall Clemens. She lived to be eighty-seven and directed her children with considerable firmness. She was always scolding her son, Sam (whom the world now knows as Mark Twain) and then comforting him, punishing him and pleading with him. In later life Twain wrote: 'I have been abroad in the world for twenty years and have listened to many of its best talkers . . . in the matter of moving and pathetic eloquence none of them was the equal of that untrained and artless talker out there in the western village, that obscure little woman with the beautiful spirit and the great heart and the enchanted tongue.'

POLONIUS

William Shakespeare, *Hamlet* (1602)

William Cecil, Lord Burghley (1520–98)

Polonius is the Lord Chamberlain of Denmark, and father to Laertes and Ophelia. He is a complex character, a wily and mature politician who has grown old and whose acumen is affected by senility. At the same time he is a man of considerable – if rather worldly – experience and insight. His long-windedness and pomposity make him an easy butt of the comedy of others, of Prince Hamlet in particular. His most famous speech is the advice he gives his son as he leaves to return to France: 'Neither a borrower nor a lender be;/For loan oft loses both itself and friend,/And borrowing dulls the edge of husbandry,/This above all – to thine own self be true,/And it must follow, as the night the day,/Thou canst not then be false to any man.' He diagnoses the cause of Hamlet's supposed madness – his unrequited love for Ophelia. He and Claudius attempt to overhear Hamlet and Ophelia conversing. He is slain by Hamlet, in mistake for the King, while hiding behind the curtains in the Queen's room. Here he had hoped to spy on Hamlet as he spoke with his mother. Hamlet sums him up, as a 'rash, intruding fool'.

Burghley had a reputation for investigating the conspiracies of others, and organized what was in effect a secret police to detect plots against Queen Elizabeth, tracking down all the clues and threads in the labyrinthine entanglement of intrigues surrounding Mary Queen of Scots. His main opponent at Elizabeth's court was the Earl of Essex, whom Shakespeare supported. The evidence for the dramatist's satirizing Burghley in the character of Polonius is considerable. Burghley was the author of *Certaine Preceptes, or Directions*, which he wrote for his son and which Shakespeare may have had privy sight of in manuscript. Polonius begins his advice to Laertes by saying: 'these few precepts in thy memory/Look thou character'. And the nature of Burghley's precepts is close to those trotted out by Polonius. Hamlet is deliberately rude to Polonius and mistakes him for 'a fishmonger' – an obvious reference to Lord Burghley's celebrated attempts while treasurer to foster and stimulate the fish trade. He was a renowned busybody. One of his household described him as 'never less idle than when he had most leisure to be idle' and Robert Naunton (1563–1635) commented on his ability to 'unlock the counsels of the Queen's enemies'.

Further reading:
A.L. Rowse, *Shakespeare – A Biography* (1963), C. Read, *Lord Burghley and Queen Elizabeth* (1960)

ALETHA PONTIFEX

Samuel Butler, *The Way of All Flesh* (1903)

Mary Ann Savage (1836–85)

The only human warmth which Ernest Pontifex experiences in his schooldays is that lavished on him by his good aunt, Aletha. His father has attempted to beat scholarship, obedience and the Christian religion into him, ably assisted by his hypocritical wife, Christina, and at boarding school he experiences the commendable harshness of school discipline. Aunt Aletha moves from London to be near her favourite nephew, as she recognizes Ernest's qualities and encourages his love of music. With her active support he constructs an organ, which shows his skill in carpentry as well as music. His father holds music to be sinful and degenerate. On her death she leaves him £15,000 which he is to inherit when he is twenty-eight. Aletha represents the qualities of good sense and good nature in a world frequently dominated by the hard and the unyielding.

This is an affectionate portrait of Butler's life-long friend Mary Ann Savage, whom he met at Heatherley's Art School in 1870. She had been a governess and was professionally associated with several clubs for young ladies. She was an intelligent and witty person and a brilliant letter-writer. They corresponded until her death and he consulted her about all

Further reading:
A.T. Bartholemew, *Butleriana* (1932), M. Garnett, *Samuel Butler and His Family Relations* (1926)

his writings. He wrote of her after her death: 'I never knew any woman to approach her at once for brilliancy and goodness.' After her funeral he said: 'I felt that I was attending the funeral of incomparably the best and most remarkable woman I have ever known.' He was asked if he had been in love with her, and he replied: 'I never was and never pretended to be. I valued her, and she perfectly understood that I could do no more. I can never think of her without pain.' He wrote several extraordinary sonnets inspired by their relationship, one of which contains the honest lines: 'I liked, but like and love are far removed;/Hard though I tried to love I tried in vain./For she was plain and lame and fat and short,/Forty and over-kind. Hence it befell/That though I loved her in a certain sort,/Yet did I love too wisely but not well.'

THEOBALD PONTIFEX

Samuel Butler, *The Way of All Flesh* (1903)

Thomas Butler (1806-86)

Further reading: See ALETHA PONTIFEX

Samuel Butler's novel was written between 1873 and 1885 and not published until 1903, a year after the author's death. The novel deals with the life and career of Ernest Pontifex, the son of the Revd Theobald Pontifex and his wife Christina. Ernest's father is the rector of Battersby on the Hill and is brought up on strict Victorian middle-class and religious principles. The constant and harsh discipline inflicted on the boy by his father successfully crushes any affection he might have for his father, who crams him with Greek and Latin and the scriptures, driven home by frequent thrashings. On one occasion he is beaten within an inch of his life for mispronouncing a word. He is sent away to a boarding school which is almost as harsh as his home and his love of music is his sole consolation apart from the warmth and affection he has from his aunt, who encourages him in his music and his ambitions to build an organ (see ALETHA PONTIFEX). The nadir of the father/son relationship is reached when Ernest witnesses his father's dismissing a pregnant servant girl. Overcome with compassion for her, Ernest gives her his watch and his pocket-money, and his father immediately suspects Ernest to be responsible for Ellen's condition.

This dreadful picture of a Victorian pater familias is based on Butler's own father, Thomas Butler, who was educated at Shrewsbury, under his father, Dr Samuel Butler, and at St John's College, Cambridge. Thomas Butler taught at Shrewsbury and was later rector at Langar-with-Bramston and eventually made Canon of Lincoln. The novelist wrote of him in his notebooks: 'He never liked me, nor I him; from my earliest recollections I can call to mind no time when I did not fear and dislike him . . . no matter whose [fault] it is, the fact remains that for years and years I have never passed a day without thinking of him . . . as the man who was sure to be against me, and who would see the bad side rather than the good of everything I said and did.'

ALISON PORTER

John Osborne, *Look Back in Anger* (1956)

Pamela Lane (born 1930)

John Osborne's *Look Back in Anger* brought a sense of excitement to the complacent English theatre. In the play Jimmy Porter often imposes his opinions on a captive audience of two comprising his submissive wife Alison and his friend Cliff Lewis. Jimmy resents the fact that Alison's background is more privileged than his: whereas his upbringing has been drab and his education undistinguished ('not even red brick, but white tile'), she has been raised by affluent upper-class Colonel and Mrs Redfern. In a typical outburst against Alison's mother Jimmy explains that he has long hair because he likes it: 'But that obvious, innocent explanation didn't appeal to Mummy at all. So she hires detectives to watch me, to see if she can't somehow get me into the *News of the World*. All so that I shan't carry off her daughter on that poor old charger of mine.'

Before his dramatic success with the play, John Osborne was an obscure actor who, in 1951, found himself playing in Bridgwater in a family comedy opposite Pamela Lane. She was a Bridgwater girl who had made good at the Royal Academy of Dramatic Art and had returned to perform before the suspicious locals. Pamela's parents, who ran a draper's business, disapproved of Osborne and hired a private detective to probe into his supposedly disreputable life. In his autobiography *A Better Class of Person* (1981) Osborne says 'Mr and Mrs Lane were much coarser characters than Alison's mother and father, but their tactics were similar. They were certainly farther down in the class scale, firmly entrenched in trade for generations.' Still, Osborne married Pamela and took her to live with him in London; she brought 'her twenty-first birthday present from her parents, a portable typewriter on which I was to type *Look back in Anger*'. The couple separated in 1954.

SIR JOSEPH PORTER, KCB, FIRST LORD OF THE ADMIRALTY

Opera, *HMS Pinafore* (1878, music by A.S. Sullivan, libretto by W.S. Gilbert)

William Henry Smith (1825–91)

The portrait of the First Lord of the Admiralty is a satiric attack on the political system which allowed those to be in charge of departments of government who had little or no professional experience of their affairs. Sir Joseph sings a celebrated patter song which describes his brilliant career from office boy in a lawyer's firm, through junior clerk, articled clerk, legal partnership, on to a seat in the Commons by means of a pocket borough, party stalwart and finally to the position of First Lord: 'I grew so rich that I was sent/By a pocket borough into Parliament./I always voted at my party's call,/And never thought of thinking for myself at all./I thought so little, they rewarded me/By making me the Ruler of the Queen's Navee!'

Although Gilbert made some efforts to deny it, this was clearly a portrait of W. H. Smith. Gilbert wrote to Sullivan in 1877: 'Among other things there is a song for the First Lord – tracing his career as office boy in a cotton broker's office, clerk, traveller, junior partner, and First Lord of Britain's Navy. I think a splendid song can be made of this. Of course there will be no personality in this – the fact that the First Lord in the opera is a Radical of the most pronounced type will do away with any suspicion that W. H. Smith is intended.' But the character who sang urging those who wished to follow his success should stick close to their desks 'and never go to sea' was all too obviously based on W. H. Smith. He entered his father's news agency business in the Strand in 1841 and was a junior partner in 1846. By securing the railway bookstall monopoly he developed the profits of the firm enormously and later developed a circulating library. In 1868 he was elected MP for Westminster and was a member of the first London School Board in 1871. In 1877, only a year before the premier of *HMS Pinafore*, he entered Disraeli's Cabinet as First Lord of the Admiralty. Gilbert commented: 'You would naturally think that a person who commanded the entire British Navy would be the most accomplished sailor who could be found, but that is not the way in which such things are managed in England.'

Further reading:
Herbert Maxwell, *Life of William Henry Smith* (1893), Hesketh Pearson, *Gilbert and Sullivan* (1935)

MR POTT

Charles Dickens, *The Posthumous Papers of the Pickwick Club* (1836)

Henry Peter Brougham, Lord Brougham and Vaux (1778–1868)

Mr Pott is the pompous, self-important editor of the *Eatanswill Gazette*: 'A tall, thin man, with a sandy-coloured head inclined to baldness, and a face in which solemn importance was blended with a look of unfathomable profundity.' During the Eatanswill election, Pickwick and Mr Winkle lodge with Mr Pott, who comes to suspect a liaison between Winkle and Mrs Pott. Mr Pott calls Winkle a serpent much to his surprise: 'Serpent, sir!' he repeats when Winkle expresses his disbelief, 'I said, Serpent, sir – make the most of it.' Mr Pott resolves to be calm: 'in proof of his calmness, Mr Pott flung himself into a chair, and foamed at the mouth.' The quarrel blows over, for such is Mr Pott's terror in the face of his wife, that his rage melts when he attempts to confront her with the evidence, such as it was.

Dickens is here picturing his contemporary Lord Brougham, whom he would have observed in his days as a parliamentary reporter. Brougham was brilliantly intelligent and a man of vast energies, but was renowned for his short temper, mercurial shifts of mood, and sudden animosities towards colleagues. Justin McCarthy in *A History of Our Own Times* wrote: 'The comic literature of more than a generation had no subject more fruitful than the vanity and restlessness of Lord Brougham . . . Brougham's was an excitable and self-assertive nature . . .

Further reading:
Charles New, *The Life of Lord Brougham* (1961)

his personal vanity was immense . . . his eccentricities and his almost savage temper made him intolerable . . .' He was educated at the University of Edinburgh, a lawyer and journalist before entering public life, and became MP for Camelford and later for Winchelsea. He defended Queen Caroline at her trial in 1820. He later became MP for Knaresborough and then for Yorkshire, was tireless as an advocate of reforms in the law, education, charities, and was vociferously anti-slavery. He was one of the most influential lord chancellors of the nineteenth century, an anonymous commentator saying: 'If the Lord Chancellor only knew a little law he would know something of everything.' Dugald Stewart, his professor at Edinburgh, said Brougham was the ablest man he had ever known: 'but that even then (forty years ago) he considered his to be a mind that was continually oscillating on the verge of sanity' (*The Greville Memoirs* 1837).

TOM POWERS

Film, *The Public Enemy* (1931), written by Kubec Glasmon and John Bright, directed by William Wellman, starring James Cagney.

Earl 'Hymie' Weiss (died 1927)

Further reading: Carlos Clarens, *Crime Movies* (1980)

Tom Powers was one of James Cagney's most famous roles, and *The Public Enemy* was one of the most influential of the early gangster *genre*. The scene where Tom shoves half a grapefruit into the face of his moll, Mae Clarke, is one of the truly memorable moments in film history. The story is simplicity itself, and concerns two brothers, born in the slums, who break into organized crime and the bootlegging business, and are finally destroyed by the system that made them big-time guys. Tom is born into an Irish family; his father is a stern figure, a policeman, his mother a weak and ineffectual character who dotes on him and his brother a morally orthodox young man. Tom begins in petty crime and graduates to minor robberies. He then gets his first revolver, and in one stroke has metamorphosed from street urchin to potential killer. His apprenticeship is over. Prohibition gives him what he is looking for – the chance for money, glamour and power. The price that has to be paid is the readiness to kill, and the awareness that you may be killed. He is prepared to pay this price. In a gang war he begins to move triumphantly to the top of his trade. As an example of his ruthlessness, he kills the horse that accidentally killed his friend, 'Nails'. He is merciless to his women, saying to Mae Clarke: 'I wish you were a wishing well so that I could tie a bucket to you and sink it.' The violence is unremitting. His friend is machine-gunned in broad daylight, yet when he himself is wounded, his mother cuddles him and calls him: 'My baby'. The final dreadful irony is that he is delivered wrapped as a package by the gang who have wiped him out, after his mother has been given a message to the effect that her beloved Tom is being 'brought home'. He is; as a corpse.

This is based on the career of the Earl 'Hymie' Weiss, a rival of Al Capone's. During the gang wars in Chicago, Weiss, Bugs Moran and their mobsters drove eight cars blazing machine-gunners past the Hawthorne Hotel, in which Capone and friends barely escaped with their lives. Weiss himself stood in the road and fired from the hip. This was Weiss's revenge for the killing of Dion O'Bannion. He also attempted to kill Capone's right-hand man, Johnny Torrio. Weiss was himself gunned down outside O'Bannion's flowershop. The grapefruit episode was based on an incident between Weiss and a girlfriend; the weapon was not a grapefruit, but an omelette.

GEORGE PRIMROSE

Oliver Goldsmith, *The Vicar of Wakefield* (1766)

Oliver Goldsmith (1728–74)

Further reading: John Forster, *Life of Oliver Goldsmith* (1854), Andrew

George Primrose is the eldest son of the Vicar of Wakefield, who lives a vagabond life in search of a living, and finally joins the army after trying his hand at all manner of careers. As he says: 'travelling after fortune, is not the way to secure her; and, indeed . . . I have desisted from the pursuit'. But throughout it all he is buoyantly optimistic: 'No person ever had a better knack at hoping than I. The less kind I found fortune at one time, the more I expected from her another.' His early attempts take him to London, where he hopes to prosper as an usher in a school. He then tries authorship. He fails to earn recognition, lacking influential friends. He tries hack writing. He becomes a family servant. He attempts to move into a grand household, but fails to gain entrance and nears despair. Then he hears of opportunities for British citizens to be transported as slaves to America, but he is saved from this fate and given the chance to sail for Amsterdam, where he is assured of a living teaching English. He then finds that he needs to learn Dutch first: 'How I came to overlook so obvious an objection, is to me amazing.' A fellow Irishman tells him there is a need for professors of Greek, and being a scholar, he tries this. To no avail. He manages to earn his bed and food by singing, and makes his way to France. In Paris he is involved in buying and selling paintings. For a time he is a travelling tutor, but is abandoned by his charge at Leghorn. He gets back to England and joins a troop of players.

This is a comic version of Goldsmith's own life. His father was a curate of Kilkenny West, and he ran away from college, returned and graduated, was rejected for holy orders, resolved to go to America but got no further than Cork. He was given £50 to study in London, but gambled this away in Dublin. He went to Edinburgh to study medicine, but excelled socially rather than academically. He drifted to Leyden and again gambled his funds. He attempted the Grand Tour on foot but returned penniless in 1756. He was then successively poor doctor, proofreader, teacher, hack-writer and failed to leave the country. After pawning his clothes he was nearly imprisoned for debt until finally he succeeded as a writer, after Dr Johnson got a publisher to accept *The Vicar of Wakefield*.

Swarbrick, *The Art of Oliver Goldsmith* (1983)

PRINCESS OF FRANCE

William Shakespeare, *Love's Labours Lost* (1594)

Marguerite de Valois (1553–1615)

Ferdinand, King of Navarre, and three of his courtiers – Berowne, Longaville and Dumain – have sworn to live a life of study and retirement away from society, and have sworn to forgo the company of women: 'Our court shall be a little Academe,/Still and contemplative in living art./You three, Berowne, Dumain and Longaville,/Have sworn for three years term to live with me/My fellow scholars . . .' They are soon compelled to yield up this resolve, as the Princess of France arrives in their rural retreat, together with several ladies of her court. She is on an embassy. Her wit, cultivation, charm and spirit soon enchant Ferdinand, who falls in love with her. His three lords likewise fall for the Princess's three ladies. The courtship is delightfully handled as a mixture of flirtation, merriment, buffoonery and disguises, as a civil war of wits. When Ferdinand yields to her charms and invites her to his court, she teases him with having broken his oath: 'This field shall hold me, and so hold your vow:/Nor God, nor I, delights in perjur'd men.' He protests that the virtue of her eye has made him break his oath: but she replies: 'You nickname virtue; vice you should have spoke;/For virtue's office never breaks men's troth./Now by my maiden honour, yet as pure/As the unsullied lily, I protest,/A world of torments though I should endure,/I would not yield to be your house guest.' Their wooing is interrupted by news of the death of the Princess's father, and the ladies impose a year's ordeal of waiting on their lovers. The situation and the character of the princess have their basis in Marguerite of Navarre and her ladies. She was the daughter of Henry II of France. She married Henry of Navarre in 1572. In 1578, separated from her husband, she accompanied her mother, Cathérine de Médici, as ambassadress of France during the negotiations with Henry of Navarre. It is a fact that Marguerite, who was a witty and charming person, attempted to influence the diplomatic outcome of these negotiations by using the charms of her ladies-in-waiting on Henry and his courtiers. The names of the courtiers were marèchal de Biron (in Shakespeare – Berowne), the duc de Longueville (in Shakespeare – Longaville) and the duc de Mayenne (in Shakespeare – Dumain). Biron was to become the military associate and advisor of the Earl of Essex, who led the English force which supported Henry of Navarre. The original princess was renowned for her beauty, wit, learning and the looseness of her conduct. She left some of the finest letters and most interesting memoirs of the sixteenth century.

Further reading:
H.N. Williams, *Queen Margot* (1907), J.H. Mariéjol, *La Vie de Marguerite de Valois* (1928)

RUPERT PSMITH

P.G. Wodehouse, *The Lost Lambs* (serialized 1909), *Enter Psmith* (1909), *Leave it to Psmith* (1923) etc.

Rupert D'Oyly Carte

Further reading:
Benny Green, *P.G. Wodehouse – A Literary Biography* (1979)

Mike Jackson, the hero of a series of school stories Wodehouse wrote early in his career, is transferred from Wrykyn to Sedleigh, a minor public school. Here he meets: 'A very long, thin youth, with a solemn face and immaculate clothes,' who fumbles in his top waistcoat pocket and produces 'an eyeglass attached to a cord, and fixed it in his right eye. With the help of this aid to vision he inspected Mike in silence for a while.' He flicks an invisible speck of dust from his sleeve and then speaks in a tired voice: 'Hullo . . . Take a seat. If you don't mind dirtying your bags, that's to say. Personally I don't see any prospect of ever sitting down in this place. It looks to me as if they meant to use these chairs as mustard-and-cress beds.' In the course of their conversation he explains his name: 'If you ever have occasion to write to me, would you mind sticking a P at the beginning of my name? P-s-m-i-t-h. See? There are too many Smiths, and I don't care for Smythe. My father's content to worry along in the old-fashioned way, but I've decided to strike out a fresh line. I shall found a new dynasty. The resolve came to me unexpectedly this morning. I jotted it down on the back of an envelope. In conversation you may address me as Rupert (though I hope you won't), or simply Smith, the P not being sounded.'

Wodehouse wrote about the creation of this character: 'The character of Psmith . . . is the only thing in my literary career which was handed to me on a plate with watercress around it.' Psmith, he said, came to him 'ready-made'. He learned of this original from a cousin of his at Winchester, who told him about Rupert D'Oyly Carte, a schoolmate of his: 'Rupert . . . was long, slender, always beautifully dressed and very dignified. His speech was what is known as orotund, and he wore a monocle. He habitually addressed his fellow Wykehamists as "Comrade" . . .' (*The World of Psmith*, 1974). Benny Green (*P.G. Wodehouse – A Literary Biography*, 1981) also finds traces of Henry Mayers Hyndman (1842–1921), the British Marxist. This would account for the affectation of Socialism, which is a characteristic of Psmith's, adopted after his father transferred him to Sedleigh from Eton, which ensured his being unable to represent Eton against Harrow at cricket – Hyndman was a keen cricketer, and scored two centuries for Sussex, but was passed over for his cricket blue. Barbara Tuchman (*The Proud Tower*, 1966) writes that Hyndman had 'adopted Socialism out of spite . . . because he was not included in the Cambridge eleven'.

R

DON RAMON

D.H. Lawrence, *The Plumed Serpent* (1926)

José Vasconcelos (1882–1959)

The Plumed Serpent, D.H. Lawrence's Mexican novel, brings the Irish widow Kate Leslie into contact with a revolutionary movement based on the Aztec snakebird god Quetzalcoatl. Calling themselves the men of Quetzalcoatl, the rebels are led by Don Ramón, an archeologist and historian who regards himself as the living Quetzalcoatl. Ramón is a man of immense will and impressive appearance: 'He was handsome, almost horribly handsome, with his black head poised as it were without weight, about his darkened, smooth neck ... With the blue sash round his waist, pressing a fold in the flesh, and the thin linen seeming to gleam with the life of his lips and his thighs, he emanated a fascination almost like a narcotic, asserting his pure, fine sensuality against her [his wife, Doña Carlota]. The strange, soft, still sureness of him, as if he sat secure within his own dark aura . . . He emitted an effluence so powerful, that it seemed to hamper [his wife's] consciousness, to bind down her limbs.'

Don Ramón is partly a romantic projection of the author, but Lawrence also borrowed details from the career and personality of José Vasconcelos, a man he disliked. Lawrence met José Vasconcelos, then Secretary of Public Education, in the government of Alvaro Obregón, on 26 April 1923. Shortly after this meeting, Lawrence was furious when Vasconcelos had to postpone a luncheon to deal with a crisis. As *The Plumed Serpent* shows, Lawrence disapproved of the propagandist murals of Rivera and Orozco, which Vasconcelos had commissioned. For his part, Vasconcelos thought Lawrence was 'a second-rate idiot' whose Mexican novel was a work of fantasy.

One of the intellectual leaders of the Mexican Revolution, Vasconcelos was a supporter of Madero, and a Minister of Education in one of the revolutionary governments. He subsequently served as Obregón's minister of education, and attempted to raise the cultural consciousness of the people, through a policy of making art more accessible. In 1929 he fought an election campaign against Plutarcho Calles, and went abroad when he lost it. His autobiography, *Ulises Criollo* ('Creole Ulysses') appeared in 1935, and in his theoretical works he advanced the theory that Mexico and Latin America would lead the human race to an advanced level.

Further reading: Harry T. Moore, *The Priest of Love* (1974)

MARK RAMPION

Aldous Huxley, *Point Counter Point* (1928)

D.H. Lawrence (1885–1930)

Although it has a plot involving political assassination the point of Aldous Huxley's *Point Counter Point* is the satirical treatment of various aspects of life in the 1920s when intellectual ideals were treated as playthings by the privileged. Huxley constructed the story round a series of portraits of recognizable characters: JOHN BIDLAKE, for example, is the painter Augustus John: 'handsome, huge, exuberant, careless; a great laugher, a greater worker, a great eater, drinker, and taker of virginities'. EVERARD WEBLEY, the Fascist leader who is murdered in the book, is based on Sir Oswald Mosley.

The most incisive portrait, however, shows D. H. Lawrence as the writer Mark Rampion: 'His profile was steep, with a hooked fierce nose like a cutting instrument and a pointed chin. The eyes were blue and piercing, and the very fine hair, a little on the reddish side of golden, fluttered up at every moment, every breath of wind, like wisps of blown flame.' Rampion's affirmative utterances provide the novel with a visionary alternative to the mental confusion of the other characters. As Rampion tells the evil Spandrell: 'You hate the very source of your life, its ultimate basis – for there's no denying it, sex *is* fundamental. And you hate it, *hate* it.' At the end of the book, when Spandrell is about to be shot by members of Webley's Brotherhood of British Freemen, Rampion is still hammering home his opinions on life and art. Lawrence was aware of

Further reading: E. Nehls, *D.H. Lawrence – A Composite Biography* (1959), Harry T. Moore, *The Intelligent Heart* (1960), Jocelyn Brooke, *Aldous Huxley* (1954), P. Bowering, *Aldous Huxley – A Study of the Major Novels* (1969)

Huxley's use of his opinions as an important part of *Point Counter Point* but wrote to the writer William Gerhardi on 14 November 1928: 'I refuse to be Rampioned. Aldous' admiration for me is only skin-deep, and out of a Mary Mary quite contrary impulse.' Mary was Maria Huxley who was devoted to Lawrence and typed parts of his novels.

Writing to Huxley, though, Lawrence said: 'I do think you've shown the truth, perhaps the last truth, about you and your generation, with really fine courage. It seems to me it would take ten times the courage to write *P. Counter P.* than it took to write *Lady C.*; and if the public knew *what* it was reading, it would throw a hundred stones at you, to one at me.'

MRS RAMSAY

Virginia Woolf, *To the Lighthouse* (1927)

Julia Stephen (1846–95)

Further reading: Herbert Marder, *Feminism and Art – A Study of Virginia Woolf* (1968), Bernard Blackstone, *Virginia Woolf* (1949), Noel Annan, *Leslie Stephen: The Godless Victorian* (1984)

The central figure and source of the emotional light in Virginia Woolf's *To the Lighthouse* is Mrs Ramsay who copes with her idiosyncratic husband and with eight children. On the Isle of Skye, Mrs Ramsay holds out hopes that a trip to the lighthouse might be possible whereas Mr Ramsay, who 'never altered a disagreeable word to suit the pleasure or convenience of any mortal being', insists that the weather will make a journey impossible. Mr Ramsay, the prominent writer, is correct but it is Mrs Ramsay who provides human warmth and comfort: 'Flashing her needles, confident, upright, she created drawing-room and kitchen, set them all aglow . . . there was scarcely a shell of herself left for her to know herself by; all was so lavished and spent'.

In her novel Virginia Woolf drew Mr and Mrs Ramsay as portraits of her father Leslie (who was also the model for VERNON WHITFORD in Meredith's *The Egoist*) and her mother Julia. When her first husband, Herbert Duckworth, died in 1870 Julia (née Jackson) was a young woman of twenty-four with three children to care for. In 1875 she met Leslie Stephen, a literary journalist whose wife died that year. Widow and widower found they first had sorrow, and then love, in common and were married on 26 March 1878. Between them, like Mr and Mrs Ramsay, they were responsible for eight children though Julia always felt her greatest duty was to protect her sensitive husband from his worries. While he exhausted himself in his work on the *Dictionary of National Biography* (which he began in 1882, the year of Virginia's birth) she bore the family's emotional burdens. On 5 May 1895 she died, after an attack of rheumatic fever, and for Virginia this was 'the greatest disaster that could happen'. As well as sustaining a personal shock she had to endure the sight of her father suffering as he succumbed to the grief that overwhelmed him.

After Julia's death, Stephen was inconsolable. 'The rest of his life,' writes Noel Annan, 'he decided to consecrate as a memorial to Julia. Unfortunately in remembering her he forgot everyone but himself. His grief cut to the bone, but he luxuriated in the pain.'

RASKOLNIKOV

Fyodor Dostoevsky, *Crime and Punishment* (1866)

Pierre-François Lacenaire (1800–36)

Further reading: Donald Fanger, *Dostoevksy and Romantic Realism* (1965)

Raskolnikov is a poor student of jurisprudence in St Petersburg, who is compelled to abandon his studies and leave the university. He murders an old pawnbroker and also – by accident – the old woman's half-sister. He has a mixture of motives for his crime. One is that the old woman is a cruel and unsavoury character who may soon die in any case; he would be able to use her money to do good, since he would be able to help his mother and improve the lot of his fellow citizens. It would also enable him to save his sister, Dunya, from a marriage which she does not want with a lawyer she does not love. A further motive is Raskolnikov's belief (which predates the Nietzschean theory of the superman) that there are two kinds of man: those who obey the rules laid down by society, and those who are above the law because they are superior beings and thereby entitled to make their own laws. In the event, he bungles the crime and only escapes by sheer luck. His grand crime results in his taking possession of just a few odds and ends, which are of little value. He betrays himself by his own foolishness. He is sent to Siberia, where he is followed by Sonia, a prostitute, who plays a part in Raskolnikov's redemption through his discovery of God, and that all life is sacred. This is a truth he had half-realized earlier in the novel, when he reflects on the squalor of city-life: 'Only to live, to live and live! Whatever sort of life. Only life! Man is a scoundrel! And a scoundrel is the man who calls him one for that.'

Prior to his composition of *Crime and Punishment*, Dostoevsky published a series of articles in journals on murder, crime and legal punishment, many of them dealing with French criminals. Among them was an account of Lacenaire, whom Dostoevsky described as: 'a phenominal, enigmatic, fearful and interesting figure'. Lacenaire was an unsuccessful French criminal who left a fascinating series of memoirs, unfortunately interrupted by the executioner. He spent six years in prison, and his one major crime, the robbery of a bank messenger, was a failure. He traced his criminality back to childhood and his lack of parental love and social status. At his trial he assumed the role of prosecutor so as to ensure that the accomplices who had betrayed him would receive their deserts. He rationalized his position by asserting he was a duellist against society.

REBECCA

Sir Walter Scott, *Ivanhoe* (1819)

Rebecca Gratz (1781–1869)

Rebecca, the daughter of Isaac of York in *Ivanhoe*, is one of Sir Walter Scott's most compelling female characters as she displays both physical and moral beauty: 'Her form was exquisitely symmetrical, and was shown to advantage by a sort of Eastern dress, which she wore according to the fashion of the females of her nation . . . The brilliancy of her eyes, the superb arch of her eyebrows, her well-formed aquiline nose, her teeth as white as pearl, and the profusion of her sable tresses which, each arranged in its own little spiral of twisted curls, fell down upon as much of a lovely neck and bosom as a simarre of the richest Persian silk, exhibiting flowers in their natural colours embossed upon a purple ground, permitted to be visible – all these constituted a combination of loveliness, which yielded not to the most beautiful of the maidens who surrounded her.'

Scott conceived the character after a meeting, at Abbotsford in 1817, with Washington Irving. In one of their many conversations the American author told Scott about a tragedy that dominated his life: in 1809 his fiancée, Mathilda Hoffman, had died of consumption at the age of eighteen. On her deathbed Mathilda had been looked after by her close friend Rebecca Gratz and the devotion of this lady – known as 'the good Jewess' and 'the beautiful Jewess' in Philadelphia – deeply impressed Scott. Irving further revealed that Rebecca Gratz had renounced a financially and emotionally tempting offer of marriage rather than compromise her religion. Instead she dedicated herself to philanthropic pursuits and died (as she said) 'believing with firm faith in the religion of my fathers'. When Scott's medieval romance was published he sent a copy to Irving with the question 'How do you like your Rebecca? Does the Rebecca I have pictured, compare well with the pattern given?'

Further reading:
Alan Bold, *Sir Walter Scott – The Long Forgotten Melody* (1983), David Brown, *Sir Walter Scott and the Historical Imagination* (1979)

SIR ROBERT REDGAUNTLET

Sir Walter Scott, *Redgauntlet* (1824)

Sir Robert Grierson of Lag (*c* 1655-1736)

In *Redgauntlet*, Scott's genius is most evident in'Wandering Willie's Tale', the story told to Darsie Latimer (modelled on Scott's friend Will Clerk) by the blind fiddler, Willie Steenson, as they walk along the shore of the Solway. It is a supernatural tale whose climax in hell – where Steenie Steenson gets a receipt for his rent from Sir Robert – is artistically appropriate, given the diabolical reputation of the historical character on whom Scott based Sir Robert Redgauntlet.

Sir Robert Grierson of Lag was a sworn enemy of the Covenanters – those Scots who supported the National Covenant of 1638, as it protected the institution of the Church of Scotland from the English liturgy. In 1667, on his cousin's death, Grierson succeeded to the estate of Lag (in Dunscore), and from 1681 he presided over the Kircudbright Military Court which dispensed summary justice in Galloway. Grierson's sadistic acts made his name synonymous with cruelty; he had prisoners tortured with the thumbscrew, had men hanged on an iron hook, and rolled some of his victims down hillsides in barrels spiked with knife-blades. In recognition of his gift for persecution, Grierson was made a baronet by King James II and VII, and elevated to the post of Lord-Justice of

Wigtonshire. One of his most notorious judgements, in his new position, was to condemn the Wigtown martyrs (Margaret MacLachlan and Margaret Wilson) to death by drowning. After the downfall of James II, Grierson was imprisoned in Edinburgh, but managed to obtain his release on the payment of £1,500 bail. He died in his Dumfries house, the Turnpike, suffering from gout.

Wandering Willie vividly presents the character of a villain: 'Ye maun had heard of Sir Robert Redgauntlet of that Ilk, who lived in these parts before the dear years. The country will lang mind him; and our fathers used to draw breath thick if ever they heard him named . . . He was knighted at Lonon court, wi' the King's ain sword; and being a red-hot prelatist, he came down here, rampauging like a lion, with commissions of lieutenancy (and of lunacy, for what I ken), to put down a' the Whigs and Covenanters in the country. Wild wark they made of it; for the Whigs were as dour as the Cavaliers were fierce, and it was which should fire tire the other. Redgauntlet was aye for the strong hand . . . Glen, nor dargle, nor mountain, nor cave, could hide the puir hill-folk when Redgauntlet was out with bugle and bloodhound after them, as if they had been sae many deer . . . Far and wide was Sir Robert hated and feared. Men thought he had a direct compact with Satan . . .'

UNCLE REMUS

Joel Chandler Harris, *Uncle Remus – His Songs and his Sayings* (1881), *Told by Uncle Remus – New Stories From the Old Plantation* (1905), *Uncle Remus and Brer Rabbit* (1907)

Remus, black gardener at Forsyth, Georgia

Further reading: Stella B. Brookes, *Joel Chandler Harris – Folklorist* (1950), Julia F.C. Harris, *The Life and Letters of Joel Chandler Harris* (1918)

Uncle Remus, an old black slave on a plantation in Georgia, tells the son of his white master a series of humorous and pathetic tales which narrate the life and adventures of the irrepressible Brer Rabbit in his endless conflicts with Brer Fox. The stories reveal the story-teller as one with a shrewd view of the world, a bottomless affection for the underdog, and an admiration for the cunning, cheek, and duplicity which so often enable the weak to triumph over the strong. Brer Rabbit may be seen as the embodiment of the patience, humility and endurance of the black slaves themselves. The author of the Uncle Remus stories wrote: 'It needs no scientific investigation to show why the negro selects as his hero the weakest and most harmless of all animals, and brings him out victorious in contests with the bear, the wolf, and the fox. It is not virtue that triumphs, but helplessness; it it is not malice, but mischievousness.' Cunning and luck always enabled Brer Rabbit to triumph over the stronger animals who oppressed him. As Remus says: 'Brer Rabbit wuz a mighty man fer luck.' The major personality which emerges from these stories is that of Uncle Remus himself. It is true that many feature Brer Rabbit's tricks – such as dropping his foes into boiling water, setting fire to burdens of hay as they carry them on their shoulders, or getting them to stick their heads in holes in trees from which they cannot escape – but the overwhelming character is Remus himself, one of nature's philosophers, with a complex view of man and his world. He is no stereotype 'darky', but the philosopher of the poor, the gentle and the defenceless.

Joel Chandler Harris was born in Eatonton, Georgia, and began his career as a journalist, writing eventually for the *Atlanta Constitution*. He was born into a poor white family himself, and had great sympathy with the downtrodden. He collected negro folk tales, which he wove into the subtle and elaborate narratives of these famous stories, many of which may well have African origins. Among the ex-slaves who helped him with this fund of tales was an old black gardener in Forsyth, Georgia, whose name was Remus.

ARCHIE RICE

John Osborne, *The Entertainer* (1957)

Max Miller (1894–1963)

John Osborne's second play, *The Entertainer*, takes place in an English coastal resort. As young Mick Rice is fighting in Suez the political crisis impinges on the whole Rice family and Osborne arranges his play as a domestic drama interrupted by Archie Rice's stage-act. At home Archie is an obvious failure but when he performs he comes alive with his music-hall patter: 'I bet you think I have a marvellous time up here with all these posing girls, don't you? . . . You're dead right! You wouldn't think I was sexy to look at me, would you! No, lady.'

Archie's act, consisting of sexual innuendo aimed at the audience, is a deliberate parody of the outrageous approach of the Cheeky Chappie, Max Miller. Archie is, however, third-rate; a pathetic version of Miller who was, in John Osborne's opinion, a genius – 'flashiness perfected'. In *A Better Class of Person* (1981) Osborne compares his fictional failure with the real thing: 'Archie was a man. Max was a god, a saloon bar Priapus. Archie never got away with anything properly. Life cost him dearly always. When he came on, the audience was immediately suspicious or indifferent. Archie's cheek was less than ordinary. Max didn't have to be lovable. . . . His humanity was in his cheek.'

Archie's father, Billy Rice, is an old performer of some style; he is a 'part-portrait' of William Crawford Grove, Osborne's maternal grandfather. Grandpa Grove managed a pub in London 'but unlike Billy Rice he could not be regarded as having been a star, except in a very small way at the height of his career as a publican, when there were hansom cabs, cigars and his famous breakfast'. The sheer vulgar energy of working-class entertainment delighted Osborne and of Max Miller he says 'hardly a week passes when I don't miss his pointing star among us'.

RICO

H.D., *Bid Me to Live* (1960)

D.H. Lawrence (1885–1930)

Further reading: Harry T. Moore, *The Priest of Love* (1974), Barbara Guest, *Herself Defined: The Poet H.D. and her World* (1984)

The dominant figure in H.D.'s *Bid Me to Live* is Rico, the novelist who comes from Cornwall with his wife Elsa to live in Queen's Square, Bloomsbury, in a room lent by the heroine Julia Ashton. Depressed because of her husband's involvement with another woman, Julia is kept alive through Rico's interest in her poetry and personality. It soon becomes clear to Julia that Elsa, who has her eye on another man, expects her (Julia) to sleep with Rico. However, 'things worked out differently, she and Rico had not been intimate as Elsa had expected'.

The novel is an imaginative transcription of the situation Hilda Doolittle (H.D.) found herself in in 1917, when her husband, Richard Aldington (Rafe in the novel), was having an affair with Dorothy Yorke (Bella Carter) during the period (October-December) D.H. Lawrence and his wife Frieda (Elas) stayed in the Aldingtons' room, at the front of the house at 44 Mecklenburgh Square. With his flaming red beard and brooding presence, Rico is the image of D.H. Lawrence: 'There he sat. He had poured himself, at volcanic heat, into his novels, those heady sex-expositions that nobody would publish, after his last novel [*The Rainbow*] had been suppressed. That had happened just at the beginning of the war. But anyhow, people weren't publishing that sort of novel now. His poems were written at the same state of molten-lava temperature, but now the lava was cool, ashes fell almost visibly upon them. He was tired out . . . Soon he would be white and drawn, as he had been the first time she saw him, visibly an invalid, with his narrow chest, his too-flaming beard, his blue eyes.'

Lawrence met Richard Aldington and his wife H.D. at a dinner party in 1914 and enjoyed their company. He corresponded with H.D., took an interest in her work, and diagnosed her depressive moods as evidence of suppressed hysteria. Writing to Amy Lowell on 23 March 1917, Lawrence noted 'Hilda Aldington is very sad and suppressed, everything is wrong. I *wish* things would get better.' When H.D. extricated herself from the situation of 1917 by going to Cornwall with the composer Cecil Gray (father of her child Perdita), Lawrence disapproved, since he regarded Aldington as a good friend. In 1929, after receiving a request from H.D. for poems and a meeting, Lawrence replied (10 August 1929): 'it's more than ten years since we met, and what should we have to say? God knows! Nothing really. It's no use saying anything. That's my last conviction.'

RIGOLETTO

Opera, libretto by Francesco Maria Piave, based on Victor Hugo's drama *La*

Verdi drew his librettist, Piave, to Victor Hugo's play as a suitable subject for an opera. Verdi described it as 'one of the greatest subjects and perhaps the greatest drama of modern times'. He was particularly impressed with Hugo's creation of the character Tribolet, the jester in

Roi s'amuse, music by Giuseppe Verdi (1851)

Fevrial Triboulet (died *c* 1536)

Further reading: *Kobbe's Complete Opera Book*

the court of King Francis I of France: 'Tribolet is a creation worthy of Shakespeare'. When the libretto was submitted to the Austrian censors, three months before the opera was to be premiered in February 1851, it was rejected for public performance as revoltingly immoral and obscenely trivial. In fact Victor Hugo's drama had caused a scandal when first performed in Paris in 1832, the authorities claiming that it was disrespectful to royalty. Hugo went to law, but lost his case; the judgement was that the work offended under the censorship laws, which had been abolished as far as printed literature was concerned after the Revolution of 1830, but still applied to the stage. Verdi and Piave had severely to alter their planned opera as a result of the Austrian censorship, which at that time applied in Venice, where the work was to be performed. Hugo's play, which Verdi wanted to use with little alteration, was set in the court in Paris in the sixteenth century, and concerned the licentious amours of the King of France, which were connived at by his jester, Tribolet. The latter has brought up his beautiful daughter in secret, to spare her the corruption of the court. The king discovers his secret and seduces her. Tribolet plans his revenge, plotting to have the king murdered while he is pursuing his amorous proclivities incognito in the bawdy house district of the city. Tribolet collects the king's body at midnight. Just before he throws the sack into the Seine, he discovers that it contains the body of his beloved daughter, who had resolved to take her seducer's place as victim, out of love for the king. Verdi's opera *Rigoletto* had to be set in Mantua, the King of France had to be transformed into the Duke (see DUKE OF MANTUA), and Tribolet had to be renamed. When Hugo heard of its immense success he was initially resentful, but when he heard the work, he admired its greatness. Rigoletto (or Tribolet) was based on the character of Triboulet, court jester to Louis XII and Francis I. He also figures in several chapters of Rabelais' *Gargantua and Pantagruel* (1533), where he is employed by Panurge as an oracle, to little benefit: 'We've been nicely caught . . . He's a fool alright. There's no denying that . . . and I am a fool for explaining my thoughts to him.'

ROBERT THE DEVIL

Robert le diable, French romance (1496), *Sir Gowther*, English romance, (fifteenth century), Thomas Lodge, *The History of Robert, Second Duke of Normandy, surnamed Robert the Divell* (1590), *Robert le Diable*, opera in five acts, libretto by Eugene Scribe, music by Giacomo Meyerbeer (1831)

Robert I, Duke of Normandy (died 1035)

Further reading: L.A. Hibbard, *Medieval Romances in England* (1924)

Robert the Devil occurs in several medieval romances, and was given the full romantic treatment in Meyerbeer's glamorous opera. The outline of the legend is that Robert was the son of a duke and duchess, and grew into an immensely strong young man, but devoted all his strength and endeavours to terrible crimes. Eventually he learns from his mother that she, being childless, had prayed to the Devil for a son. Seeking his salvation, he is sent to the pope, who in turn sends him to a hermit. The hermit assures him that he will be spared if he follows certain penances – he must maintain total silence, pretend to be mad, take his food from the mouth of a dog, provoke the common people into ill-treating him, and take this punishment without demur. He becomes court fool to the emperor at Rome, and three times saves this city from the Saracen invaders, disguised as an unknown knight. Each time he is called to the defence of Rome by a celestial messenger. The emperor has a daughter who has never been able to speak, but miraculously she gains the power of speech to declare the identity of the court fool with the knight who saves the city. Robert declines her hand in marriage and the imperial inheritance. He ends his days with the hermit who had saved him.

In Meyerbeer's sumptuous operatic version of the legend, first performed at the Paris Opera in 1831, the court is transferred to thirteenth-century Palermo, and Robert marries the beautiful Princess Isabella. The historical Robert was the younger son of Richard, Second Duke of Normandy. He succeeded his brother, whom he was suspected of having poisoned, in 1028. He gave shelter to the exiled English princes, Edward (later Edward the Confessor) and Alfred, and assisted them in their attempts to regain their inheritance, but the fleet he equipped was scattered in a storm. He was notoriously cruel and barbarous. It was widely reported that he had been advised to go on a pilgrimage to Jerusalem for the good of his soul. When returning from this pilgrimage, in July 1035, he died at Nicaea. William the Conqueror was Robert's illegitimate son.

ROBIN HOOD

Sir Walter Scott, *Ivanhoe* (1819), Francis James Child, *The English and Scottish Popular Ballads* (1882–98)

Robin Hood

'Call me no longer Locksley, my Liege,' says the Outlaw in Scott's *Ivanhoe* when the Black Knight reveals that he is Richard Coeur de Lion: 'I am Robin Hood of Sherwood Forest.' Scott adds that a full pardon was granted to Robin but that 'Richard's good intentions towards the bold Outlaw were frustrated by the King's untimely death. . . . As for the rest of Robin Hood's career, as well as the tale of his treacherous death, they are to be found in those black-letter garlands, once sold at the low and easy rate of one halfpenny.'

There are several Robin Hoods in the manorial rolls and court records of medieval England and any one of them might have been the original outlaw. However, as the great scholar Francis James Child points out in *The English and Scottish Popular Ballads* 'Robin Hood is absolutely a creation of the balladmuse'. Robin Hood is the only character who appears in a large number of ballads (Child Nos 117–54); he was the darling of the minstrels since his name was enough to sell a song. Robin is a simple soul piously devoted to Our Lady. He loves individual combat, is more than a match for his adversary the Sheriff of Nottingham, and is 'a gode yeoman' as the minstrels affirm. In the thirty-eight ballads that comprise the Robin Hood sequence the good yeoman assumes disguises, steals the king's deer but honours the king himself, abuses the clergy but respects the poor. He is an outlaw with a heart of gold: 'Cryst have mercy on his soule,/That dyed on the rode!/For he was a good outlawe,/And dyde pore men moch god.' So says 'A Gest of Robyn Hode'. The Robin Hood legend has circulated at least since the fourteenth century for Sloth, in the poem *Piers Plowman* (1362), mentions 'rymes of Robyn Hood'.

Further reading:
John Matthew Gutch, *Lytell Geste of Robin Hood* (1847), J.W. Hales, *Introduction* to *Bishop Percy's Folio Manuscript* edited by J.W. Hales and F.J. Furnivall (1867), Alan Bold, *The Ballad* (1979)

BEATRICE DE ROCHEFIDE

Honoré de Balzac, *Béatrix* (1839)

Marie de Flavigny, Comtesse d'Agoult (1805–76)

The theme of Balzac's *Béatrix* is that of amorous rivalry and waning love. Set in Paris, just after the revolution of 1830, the narrative moves to Brittany, and to Guérande, an old fortified town and the home of an ancient family. This stands for the values of the past which are destroyed by the degeneracy of modern times. Félicité des Touches and Béatrix de Rochefide are rivals for the love of Calyste du Guénic, only son of the Baron du Guénic. Béatrix is a pretentious and affected woman, who considers her social class has become effete. She is a woman of fashion and social ambition. She mixes in literary and artistic circles, and desires to become an important figure in the world of culture. She believes she may achieve this by a liaison with a distinguished artist, and steals the love of the musician, Conti, from Félicité des Touches, and runs away with him to Italy. Their ardour eventually wanes and they part. The women are then rivals for the love of Calyste du Guénic.

The character of Béatrix de Rochefide is seen mainly through the eyes of Félicité, and is a portrait of Marie de Flavigny, Comtesse d'Agoult, who had run away with the musician Franz Liszt to Geneva in 1835. George Sand had associated with them in Switzerland, and they stayed with her in Nohant in 1837, before they went on to Italy. Balzac got the story of the romance from George Sand, whom he visited in 1838. Conti is a portrait of Liszt and Félicité is George Sand (see CAMILLE MAUPIN and CONTI). The novel also contains a potrayal of Gustave Planché (1808–57), the noted literary and art critic, who appears as Claude Vignon, the lover of Félicité – Planché had, in fact, at one time been deeply enamoured of George Sand, who appears as Camille in BÉATRIX. Marie de Flavigny was born in Frankfurt-on-Main in 1805, the daughter of a French officer. In 1827 she married the Comte d'Agoult, and became a leading light of artistic circles in Paris, associating with Alfred de Vigny, Sainte-Beuve, Chopin, Meyerbeer,

Further reading:
Daniel Oliver, *Memoires de la comtesse d'Agoult* (1926)

Heine, Ingres and others. She left her husband and children for Liszt, by whom she had three children, among them Cosima, who eventually became the wife of Wagner. She was a distinguished author and journalist, and wrote several novels, including *Nèlida*. She supported the revolutionaries in 1848. Her drama *Jeanne D'arc* (1857), was a success in France and Italy. Under the name Daniel Stern she wrote significant political and historical essays. She died in Paris.

ROCKY

Sylvester Stallone, *Rocky* (1976), *Rocky II* (1979), *Rocky III* (1982)

Rocky Marciano (1923–69)

In *Rocky* an unknown Philadelphia club fighter, Rocky Balboa, gets the chance of a lifetime and decides to 'go for it' (the motto of the three *Rocky* films): through sheer determination and courage he becomes the first man to go the distance with fast-talking world champion Apollo Creed (modelled on the flamboyant Muhammad Ali). In *Rocky II* the 'Italian stallion' wins the title, in *Rocky III* he loses and regains it.

Although Sylvester Stallone (creator and star of the films) drew the loser-as-winner theme from his own life as a poor Italian attempting to break through to stardom in America – and partly from watching club fighter Chuck Wepner go fifteen rounds with Ali in March 1975 – the fighting character was suggested by the apparently indestructible Italian-American heavyweight champion Rocky Marciano. In the first *Rocky* film the hero is visited by Mickey, an old trainer, who wants to manage Rocky for the big fight. Pointing to a photograph of Marciano on the wall, Mickey says 'Ah, Rocky Marciano. You know, you kinda remind me of the Rock, you know that. You move like them, you got heart like he did.' Like Rocky Balboa, Marciano lacked technical skill but more than made up for this by his ability to take (as *Rocky II* has it) a 'terrific beating' before winning by the relentless power of his punching.

Marciano became heavyweight champion of the world on 23 September 1952 by defeating Jersey Joe Walcott. For twelve rounds Walcott completely outclassed Marciano. Then, in the thirteenth round, Marciano threw a short right-hand punch that caught Walcott coming off the ropes and floored him. Marciano defended his title six times and retired undefeated in 1956. He was killed in an aeroplane accident the day before his forty-sixth birthday.

HERMIONE RODDICE

D.H. Lawrence, *Women in Love* (1921)

Lady Ottoline Morrell (1873–1938)

Further reading: R.G. Hardy (ed.), *Ottoline; The Early Memoirs Of Lady Ottoline Morrell* (1963), Sybile Bedford *Aldous Huxley* (1973, 1974), Harry T. Moore, *The Priest of Love* (1974), *The Letters of D.H. Lawrence*, Volume II (1913–16), edited by George J. Zytaruk, Volume III 1916–21, edited by James T. Boulton (1985), Graham Housh, *The Dark Sun* (1956)

Women in Love brings D. H. Lawrence's heroines, the sisters Gundrun and Ursula Brangwen, to Willey Green. Here, Ursula is fascinated by Hermione Roddice: 'She was rich. . . . She was impressive, in her lovely pale-yellow and brownish-rose, yet macabre, something repulsive. . . . She was a *Kulturtrager*, a medium for the culture of ideas.' Later in the novel Gundrun and Ursula visit Breadalby where Hermione wilts before the presence of Rupert Birkin (a self-portrait of Lawrence): 'he caught her, as it were, beneath all her defences, and destroyed her with some insidious occult potency.

Lady Ottoline Morrell recognized herself as the ridiculous Hermione; felt Lawrence's wife Frieda was responsible for the malice of the portrayal; and called *Women in Love 'horrible* . . . a wicked chaotic spiteful book'. Lawrence had written to Lady Ottoline on 1 February 1915, urging her 'to form the nucleus of a new community which shall start a new life amongst us – a life in which the only riches is integrity of character'. Coincidentally her husband Philip Morrell, a Liberal member of parliament, had a 500-acre estate – Garsington Manor near Oxford – suitable for the cultural community Lawrence envisaged. Lady Ottoline brought to Garsington such celebrities as Bertrand Russell (Sir Joshua Mattheson in *Women in Love*) and Lawrence himself. At first grateful for Lady Ottoline's generosity, Lawrence turned on her in a letter of 23 April 1915: 'Why must you always use your *will* so much, why can't you let things be, without always grasping and trying to know and to dominate.' By 1929 Lawrence had re-established relations with Lady Ottoline who was (so he wrote to a friend) 'a queen, among the mass of women'.

After she and her husband moved into Garsington in May 1815, Lady Ottoline regarded the mansion as her own work of art and there were periods when it was regarded as a second home by such as Aldous Huxley and Russell (who had a love affair with Lady Ottoline).

RODOLPHE

Henry Murger, *La Vie de Bohème* (1849 play) and opera, *La Bohème* (1896, music by *Puccini*, libretto by Giacosa and Illica)

Henry Murger (1822–61)

Scènes de la Vie Bohème was a series of sketches of Bohemian life in Paris serialized in the journal *Corsaire* 1847–49. They catalogue the fortunes and misfortunes of a group of poverty stricken students and artists – would-be poets, painters, philosophers, writers – their loves, hopes, amusements and catastrophes. It was adapted for the stage by Murger with the assistance of Théodore Barrière and was a resounding success from its premier at the Variétiés on 22 November 1849. The operatic version, with libretto based on the stage version by Giacosa and Illica and music by Puccini, was premiered at Turin under Toscanini on 1 February 1896. The main thrust of the narrative is the tragic love affair between Rodolphe, the young poet, and Mimi. The relationship is always a difficult one and the quarrels are frequent, aggravated by the poverty in which they and their companions – Marcel, the painter, and his old flame Musette, Colline, the philosopher and Schaunard, the musician, live. Mimi is taken seriously ill with consumption, and Colline sells a precious overcoat to buy her medicine, but it is too late. Rodolphe realizes what the others have already seen – that Mimi is dead.

Murger based the character of Rodolphe on himself. He was born in Paris of German descent, and at one time was secretary to Count Alexei Tolstoy. He always lived in grinding poverty. Mimi was based on Lucile Louvet and Musette on Marie Christine Roux, famous for her wit and charming voice. Colline was based on Jean Wallon, who eventually became Directeur de l'Imprimerie Impériale. When his work had made him wealthy and secure Murger wrote of the Bohemians: 'The great family of poor artists, whose destiny is to be unknown, because they do not know . . . the means to attest their existence in art. . . . They are the race of stubborn dreamers, for whom art remains a faith and not a trade.'

Further reading: Joanna Richardson, *The Bohemians – La Vie de Bohème in Paris 1830–1914* (1969), Robert Baldick, *The First Bohemian – The Life of Henry Murger* (1961)

LORD ROEHAMPTON

Benjamin Disraeli, *Endymion* (1880)

Henry John Temple, Third Viscount Palmerston (1784–1865)

Endymion and Myra are two children of William Pitt Ferrars, an ambitious and rising politician, who dies in poverty after just failing to enter the Cabinet. Endymion plods away at a clerkship in Somerset House; his sister enters social eminence by marrying Lord Roehampton, then Foreign Secretary. She later marries a second time, Florestan, a parvenu king. The period Disraeli portrays in *Endymion* is the late 1830s and early 1840s, when he himself had failed to gain preferment under Robert Peel. Endymion rises as a result of his own efforts and the influence of his wife, rather than because of his powerful brother-in-law, Lord Roehampton, 'the strongest member of the government, except, of course, the premier himself. He was the man from whose combined force and flexibility of character the country had confidence that in all their councils there would be no lack of courage yet tempered with adroit discretion. Lord Roehampton, though an Englishman, was an Irish peer, and was resolved to remain so, for he fully appreciated the position, which united social distinction, with the power of a seat in the Commons. He was a very ambitious and . . . worldly man, deemed even by many to be unscrupulous, and yet he was romantic. A great favourite in society, and especially with the softer sex, somewhat late in life, he had married suddenly a beautiful woman, who was without fortune, and not a member of the enchanted circle in which he flourished . . . [he] was gifted with a sweet temper, and, though people said he had no heart, with a winning tenderness of disposition.'

This is Lord Palmerston, who was of the Irish branch of an ancient English family, educated at Edinburgh and Cambridge, a life-long parliamentarian, Foreign Secretary and a master of foreign affairs in several governments, and Prime Minister when he died in 1865. This kindly portrait is of the young Palmerston; later in life Disraeli said he

Further reading: A.E.M. Ashley, *The Life and Correspondence of Henry John Temple, Viscount Palmerston* (1879), H.F.C. Bell, *Lord Palmerston* (1936), Jasper Ridley, *Palmerston* (1971)

was 'at best only ginger beer and not champagne, and now an old painted Pantaloon'.

MARIE ROGET

Edgar Allan Poe, *The Mystery of Marie Roget* (1843)

Mary Cecilia Rogers (1820–41)

Further reading: John E. Walsh, *Poe the Detective* (1968), Raymond Paul, *Who Murdered Mary Rogers?* (1971)

Marie Roget is a pretty young *grisette* who works in a Parisian perfumery. She is popular with the customers, and good for trade. She disappears for a few days but when she returns she tells her widowed mother that she had been to stay with friends: 'It was about five months after this return home, that her friends were alarmed by her sudden disappearance for the second time. Three days elapsed. . . . On the fourth day her corpse was found floating in the Seine.' Poe's celebrated detective, Dupin, unravels the mystery, concluding that Marie had been killed by someone who knew her, and not a stranger; that he was probably a former lover; that the murder was committed to conceal a pregnancy. The murderer had a swarthy complexion and the knot tied in the bandage found with the body suggested a serving member of the navy. He was probably an officer and his position prevented his coming forward and identifying himself.

Poe based the story on that of the murder of the New York tobacconist's salesgirl Mary Cecilia Rogers, who worked at the counter in Anderson's shop on Broadway, where Poe was a customer. He read in the newspapers that her body had been found in the Hudson. She had apparently left home with a young man on the Sunday before the Thursday when her body was found. Like Marie, she had previously disappeared for a week, claiming that she had stayed with friends in Brooklyn. Poe transfers the story to Paris. John H. Ingram, whose biography of Poe was published in 1880, claimed that the naval officer responsible for Mary's death was named Spencer. William Kurtz Wimsatt Jr of Yale has examined the naval records of the time and has concluded that the suspect was one Philip Spencer, son of the Secretary of State for the US Navy, John Canfield Spencer. Philip Spencer had an unfortunate record of drunkenness and disorderly conduct and was expelled from several colleges. He was hanged for his part in a mutiny.

ROLAND

Chanson de Roland (*circa* twelfth century), Matteo Maria Boiardo, *Orlando innamorato* (1494), Ludovico Ariosto, *Orlando furioso* (1516)

Hruotland of Brittany (died 778)

Roland is the most famous of the paladins (peers) associated with Charlemagne. He is the son of a sister of Charlemagne, and a humble seneschal (steward) with whom she elopes. Roland grows up to become a hero, accomplishing great deeds with his sword, Durendal. He is usually portrayed as impetuous and proud, bordering on the arrogant. His companion is Oliver, and their friendship is one of the great fraternities of legend. Oliver's prudent valour contrasts with Roland's boastfulness. They meet at the siege of Viane, where Oliver is one of the defenders, with his beautiful sister, Aude, and Roland is one of the leaders of the attacking forces. Roland falls in love with Aude and attempts to carry her off, but she is rescued by her brother. The issue of the war is then to be decided in single combat between Roland and Oliver. This epic duel is fought with great chivalry on both sides, and is eventually ended by divine intervention. Roland and Oliver then swear eternal friendship. Roland marries Aude, which seals the bond between them. Charlemagne has conquered the whole of Spain from the Moors, with the exception of Saragossa. A meeting is arranged between Charlemagne and the Moorish leader, Marsile, to arrange for Charlemagne's departure from Spain. Roland suspects that this is a trap, but the King takes Ganelon's advice and sends a messenger to Marsile. Ganelon then betrays Charlemagne. Roland is appointed to lead the rearguard, but the route through the pass at Roncevalles is betrayed to Marsile, who descends on their twenty thousand men with an army of forty thousand. Roland is too proud to sound his horn to summon help from the main body of the army, in spite of Oliver's advice. Eventually when only sixty men are left, Roland sounds his horn, bursting his veins in the effort. All perish. Charlemagne defeats the Moors and executes the treacherous Ganelon.

In August 778 the rearguard of the French army was attacked by the

Basques as it returned from the Pyrenees through the valley of Roncevaux. All were slain, including Hruotland, a count of the Breton marches. This event is the basis of the much-elaborated stories of the great chivalric hero, Roland. Traditionally, Taillefer, a minstrel of William the Conqueror, sang a song of the battle of Roncevalles at the Battle of Hastings in 1066. Evidence of the historical Roland is found in Einhard's *Life of Charlemagne* (*c* 820).

ROMEO AND JULIET

William Shakespeare, *Romeo and Juliet* (1595)

Romeo Montecchi and Giuletta Cappelletto (died 1303)

Further reading: Robert Hendrickson, *The Literary Life and Other Curiosities* (1981), Kenneth Muir, *The Sources of Shakespeare's Plays* (1977)

In Verona an ancient feud between the two rival families of the Montagues and the Capulets bursts out once more in public brawls. The Prince of Verona is so angered that he decrees the death penalty for such acts in future. Romeo, son of Lord Montague, has not taken part in the fray because he is besotted with Rosaline. He is persuaded to go to a masque given by the Capulets so that he may compare Rosaline's beauty with other beauties there. Here he falls in love with Juliet, daughter of Lord Capulet. After the feast, he overhears Juliet confess that she loves him, and he gains her consent to their marriage. Friar Lawrence, Juliet's confessor, agrees to help them, as it may bring an end to the war between the families of the Montagues and the Capulets. They are secretly married the next day. Mercutio, a very close friend of Romeo's, is killed by Tybalt, a bully-boy of the Capulet clan. Romeo had tried to come between them as they were about to fight, but was unable to prevent the bloodshed. Romeo kills Tybalt, and is banished from Verona. He spends the night with Juliet, and then leaves for Mantua the next day. Capulet intends that his daughter should marry Count Paris, oblivious of the knowledge that she already has a husband, a member of the hated Montague family. Friar Lawrence proposes to reveal the marriage of Romeo and Juliet at an opportune moment, but meanwhile tells Juliet to drink a potion he provides for her on the night before her wedding day. It will render her seemingly lifeless for forty hours, which will enable him to get a message through to Romeo, who may then rescue her from the family vaults and return with her to Mantua till such time as the good friar can reconcile the two families. The plan goes tragically wrong, the message miscarries, and Romeo believes that Juliet has died. He comes to Verona to die with her, and at her tomb he meets Paris, whom he kills. He then discovers Juliet, apparently dead, and poisons himself. Juliet wakes, finds her beloved dead beside her, and stabs herself. In death they are united; grief reconciles the Montagues and the Capulets.

Shakespeare's tragedy contains the greatest of all Elizabethan love poetry. His main source was Arthur Brooke's *The Tragicall Historye of Romeus and Juliet* (1562), based on Italian versions by Luigi da Porto, Matteo Bandello and others, of the true-life tragic love story of a young couple in Verona who committed suicide in 1303, destroyed by the ancient grudge between their families.

FAIR ROSAMOND

Samuel Daniel, *The Complaint of Rosamond* (1592); Thomas Deloney, *Fair Rosamond* (1612); opera, *Rosamond* (libretto by Joseph Addison, music by Thomas Arne, 1733)

Rosamond de Clifford (died 1176)

Rosamond was the subject of several traditional and well-loved ballads, all of which told a fairly consistent story. She was the beloved mistress of King Henry II who was so desperate as to her safety that he had constructed a house which was impossible to get into unless one had the key to the labyrinth. Queen Eleanore gained access through the maze by means of a thread or a silk and was able to poison the beautiful damsel: 'But when the queene with stedfast eye/Beheld her beauteous face,/She was amazed in her minde/At her exceeding grace. Cast off from thee these robes, she said,/That riche and costlye bee;/And drink thou up this deadly draughte,/Which I have brought to thee. Then presently upon her knees/Sweet Rosamonde did falle;/And pardon of the queen she crav'd/For her offences all.' This is how Deloney gives us the climax of the story. There is strong historical evidence for the authenticity of this story.

Rosamond was the daughter of Walter de Clifford (died 1190) who inherited estates in Herefordshire and other counties and was Baron de

Further reading: R. Barber, *Henry II* (1964), Mrs. J.R. Green, *Henry II* (1888), J. Rees, *Samuel Daniel* (1964)

Clifford by 1138. He owned estates in Shropshire and fought against the Welsh. His daughter was acknowledged as mistress of Henry II by 1174. Ranulf Higden, the chronicler, has an account of the story in his *Polychronicon*, which would date the story certainly before 1364. This was translated by John Trevisa in 1387, and this was used as the basis of the version found in John Stow's *Chronicles of England*: 'Rosamond the fayre daughter of Walter Lord Clifford, concubine to Henry II (poisoned by Queen Elianor as some thought) dyed at Woodstocke where King Henry had made for her a house of wonderful working, so that no man or woman might come to her but he that was instructed by the King. This house was named by some Labyrinthus . . . wrought like unto a knot in a garden, called a maze, but it was commonly said that lastly the Queen came to her by a clue of thredde or silke.' Rosamond's body was buried in the choir of Godstow Abbey and her remains later removed to the chapter house in 1191.

MR ROSE

William Hurrell Mallock, *The New Republic* (1877)

Walter Pater (1839–94)

Further reading: A.C. Benson, *Walter Pater* (1904)

Mr Rose, the pre-Raphaelite, is one of the intellectual guests at the house-party in *The New Republic* (see DR JENKINSON). He is described as 'a pale creature' with a large moustache: 'He always speaks in an undertone, and his two topics are self-indulgence and art'. Life, he maintains, may be looked at as a chamber: 'Which we decorate as we would decorate the chamber of the woman or the youth that we love, tinting the walls of it with symphonies of subdued colour, and filling it with works of fair form, and with flowers, and with strange scents, and with instruments of music. And this can be done now as well – better, rather – than at any former time; since we know that so many of the old aims were false, and so cease to be distracted by them. We have learned the weariness of creeds; and know that for us the grave has no secrets. We have learned that the aim of life is life; and what does successful life consist in? Simply . . . in the consciousness of exquisite living – in the making our own each highest thrill of joy that the moment offers us – be it some touch of colour on the sea or on the mountains, in the early dew in the crimson shadows of a rose, the shining of a woman's limbs in clear water . . .'

This is a portrait of the celebrated scholar, critic and aesthete, Walter Pater, who had such a profound effect on Victorian Oxford. He was born in London and educated at King's School, Canterbury, and Queen's College, Oxford. He was made a fellow at Brasenose and lived the life of a scholar and aesthete, influenced deeply by the pre-Raphaelites. His *Studies in the History of the Renaissance* was published in 1873 and his philosophical-romance, *Marius the Epicurean* in 1885. He advocated hedonism as the true fulfilment of life, and towards the end of his career many had come to the conclusion that his influence was decadent. Henry James described him in a letter to Edmund Gosse as faint, pale and embarrassed, and said that he reminded him, 'in the disturbed midnight of our actual literature, of one of those lucent match boxes which you place, on going to bed, near the candle, to show you, in the darkness, where you can strike a light: he shines in the uneasy gloom – vaguely, and has a phosphorescence, not a flame.' His style was admired, by many, as fastidious, elegant, eloquent and charming; but Max Beerbohm believed he wrote English 'as a dead language, bored by that sedulous ritual wherewith he laid out every sentence in a shroud – hanging, like a widower, long over its marmoreal beauty or ever he could lay it in his book, its sepulchre.'

ROSETTA

W.H. Auden, *The Age of Anxiety* (1947)

Rhoda Jaffe

Auden's last long poem, *The Age of Anxiety* won the Pulitzer Prize in 1948, inspired Leonard Bernstein's Second Symphony 'The Age of Anxiety' (for piano and orchestra, 1947-9); and suggested Jerome Robbins's ballet 'The Age of Anxiety' (1950), which used Bernstein's score. Subtitled 'A Baroque Eclogue', and dedicated to John Betjeman, the poem features four characters who meet in New York on the night of

All Souls during wartime. In his biography of Auden, Humphrey Carpenter says that Malin, Rosetta, Quant and Emble respectively represent 'the four faculties of the personality as characterised by Jung: Thinking, Feeling, Intuition and Sensation'.

Further reading:
Humphrey Carpenter, *W.H. Auden* (1981)

Rosetta, 'a buyer for a big department store', is a romantic who daydreams of 'lovely innocent countrysides'. She drinks with the three men, in a booth in the bar, then – in a dream sequence – drives with Emble 'to the maritime plains' and sails eastward on a boat with Quant as the characters complete successive stages of their journey. Waking up, the four take a cab to Rosetta's apartment, where Emble passes out in her bedroom. Malin and Quant leave, while Rosetta looks at the sleeping Emble and soliloquizes: 'Blind on the bride-bed, the bridegroom snores,/too aloof to love. Did you lose your nerve/And cloud your conscience because I wasn't/Your dish really?'

When Auden came to New York in 1939, he fell in love with Chester Kallman, who became his lifelong companion. Although he acknowledged his homosexuality as crucial to his personality, Auden had a heterosexual affair in 1946 with Rhoda Jaffe, employment director for a New York chain of restaurants. Auden and Rhoda met in 1944, and she worked for a while as his secretary. In 1946 Rhoda and her husband Milton Klonsky were beginning the series of trial separations that eventually led to their divorce. As Carpenter observes, Auden was for some months 'involved domestically with Chester and sexually with Rhoda'. After an assignation in New York, Auden wrote to Rhoda: 'the weather is lovely here but the bed is lonely and I wish you were in it'. He also invited her to his summer beach house at Cherry Grove on Fire Island. Brought up in an orphanage, Rhoda was delighted by Auden, and insisted that 'Wystan was a real man in bed'. Subsequently Rhoda remarried, and after a period of illness, took her own life.

NUMA ROUMESTAN

Alphonse Daudet, *Numa Roumestan* (1881)

Lèon Michel Gambetta (1838–82)

Further reading:
H. Stannard, *Gambetta and the Foundations of the Third Republic* (1921)

Daudet's novel, *Numa Roumestan*, is the story of a brilliant politician who comes up against the south-north divide in the French nation. Numa is a characteristic young man of the south of France, outward-going, flamboyant, articulate and loquacious. He is sent to Paris to study law, and seems on the brink of a dazzling career. He enters politics, and attracts both attention and support, largely a result of his rhetorical powers and natural exuberance. He becomes minister of education, but both his private life and public career come to grief. He fails to realize that in public office he has to deal mainly with the cold, realistic northern temperament, and that words must be translated into deeds, and promises must be fulfilled. In his private life, his expansive character carries built-in flaws as well as advantages. His Provencal wit collides dramatically with Parisian pragmatism.

This is based on Leon Gambetta, who was born in Cahors in April 1838. He lost an eye as a youth, but did well at school, and in 1857 went to Paris to study law. His southern energies and charm soon gained him ascendancy over the Quartier Latin, and he was soon known as a staunch opponent of the imperial government. He was called to the bar in 1859, and became nationally famous for his defence of the journalist, Delescluze, who was prosecuted for promoting the erection of a monument to Baudin, who had lost his life resisting the coup d'etat in 1851. In 1869 Gambetta was returned for the Assembly, and constantly attacked the Empire. He opposed the war with Prussia, but when it became inevitable, he supported France vehemently. After the battle of Sedan he proclaimed the fall of the emperor and was minister of the interior in the government of national defence. He escaped from Paris to Tours by balloon, and continued in the government at Tours and later at Bordeaux. He resigned on the capitulation to Bismarck. Gambetta sat for the Assembly, representing Strasbourg, and when this was ceded to Germany he resigned, returned to France, and ran an influential journal, *La République Francaise*. He was now at the height of his oratorical powers, always opposing reaction; it was feared that he was aiming for a personal dictatorship. Gambetta held office in *Le Grand Ministère* for only sixty-six days, and died as the result of a shooting accident.

RUBASHOV

Arthur Koestler, *Darkness at Noon* (1940)

Nikolai Ivanovich Bukharin (1888–1939)

Further reading: Iain Hamilton, *Koestler* (1982)

Arthur Koestler, once a prominent Marxist intellectual who put his faith to the test in Germany and Spain (where the fascists kept him in a death cell for three months before releasing him), renounced communism in 1938 after recoiling from the spectacle of the Moscow show trials. Koestler believed that Marxist theory had been distorted in practice, and that in Stalin's Soviet Union communism had been reduced to a brutal creed willing to use the most appalling means in pursuit of some impossible end. *Darkness at Noon*, the author's most devastating critique of communism, portrays Rubashov, an old Bolshevik, as he undergoes arrest, imprisonment, interrogation and trial for treason. Rubashov realizes that the revolutionary means determine the political ends and that a revolution in the name of humanity has perpetrated the most atrocious offences against the individual who is seen as a unit – a millionth part of a million. Before he is shot in the back of the head Rubashov understands that the unprincipled use of expedients during the revolution has created the perfect conditions for Stalinism.

When Koestler started work on the novel he conceived Rubashov as 'a member of the Old Bolshevik guard, his manner of thinking modelled on Nikolai Bukharin's'. Nikolai Ivanovich Bukharin was a prominent Party member: theorist, author of the Soviet constitution, member of the Politburo, general secretary of Comintern, editor-in-chief of *Izvestia*. Despite his record of loyalty and his personal friendship with Stalin he was expelled from the Party, accused of treason at a show trial in 1938 and executed. In *The Gulag Archipelago*, Alexander Solzhenitsyn praises Koestler's 'talented inquiry' and points out that Bukharin constantly 'renounced his views in order to remain in the Party'.

Koestler, who had himself been under sentence of death during the Spanish Civil War, despaired at the triumph of ideology over the individual. Listing the limitations of Stalinism in *Darkness at Noon*, he declares that, for the Communist Party, 'The definition of the individual was: a multitude of one million divided by one million.'

RUDIN

Ivan Turgenev, *Rudin* (1856)

Mikhail Bakunin (1814–76)

Further reading: A. Yarmolinsky, *Turgenev* (1959), E.H. Carr, *The Life of Mikhail Bakunin* (1937), James Gaillaume, *L'Internationale* (1905), M. Nettlau, *Biographie von Mikhail Bakunin* (1898)

The tragi-comic hero of Ivan Turgenev's *Rudin* has been taken as a representative of the 'superfluous man' whose Hamlet-like indecision was a feature of the intellectual life of pre-revolutionary Russia. Rudin's arrival at a prominent Russian household is both fortuitous and forceful for he enters as 'a man of about thirty-five, tall, slightly round-shouldered, curly-haired, swarthy, with irregular, but expressive and intelligent features and a liquid brilliance in his lively dark-blue eyes, with a straight broad nose and finely chiselled lips'. Rudin impresses all by his faith in the future and his astonishing eloquence: 'Image after image poured out; analogies, now unexpectedly bold, now devastatingly apt, rose one after another. . . . He did not seek after words: they came obediently and freely to his lips and each word, it seemed, literally flowed straight from his soul and burned with all the heat of conviction.' Eventually Rudin is shot on the barricades during the 1848 Revolution in Paris.

As Turgenev acknowledged, Rudin is a portrait of Mikhail Bakunin, the celebrated Russian anarchist and once Turgenev's best friend. After meeting in Berlin in 1840 the two men shared a flat, read Hegel together and regularly went to listen to the music of Beethoven. In 1848 Bakunin was expelled from France; in 1849 he was sentenced to death for participating in a Dresden revolt and, when this sentence was commuted to imprisonment, was sent to Siberia in 1855. After escaping to Switzerland in 1861 Bakunin was recognized as the leader of the anarchist movement but Turgenev said, in a letter of 1862, that his old friend was simply a 'Rudin who was not killed on the barricades . . . a spent agitator'. Bakunin joined the First International in 1869 but was expelled in 1872 after ideological confrontations with Marx.

AGATHA RUNCIBLE

Evelyn Waugh, *Vile Bodies* (1930)

The Hon. Elizabeth Ponsonby (1900–40)

After he left Oxford in 1923, Evelyn Waugh found himself earning his living in several jobs, none of which he really liked. He missed the companionship he had enjoyed at Oxford, and attempted to fulfil himself socially by associating with the Bright Young Things in London (see LOTTIE CRUMP). Their existence was manifested mainly in parties, and *Vile Bodies* is an attempt to portray these curious lives and social rituals. One of the characters says there are such a lot of parties: 'Masked parties, Savage parties, Victorian parties, Greek parties, Wild West parties, Russian parties, Circus parties, parties where one had to dress as somebody else, almost naked parties . . . parties in flats and studios and houses and ships and hotels and nightclubs, in windmills and swimming-baths . . .' One of the leading lights in this set is Agatha Runcible, memorable in *Vile Bodies* for her turn of phrase. She describes hearing a religious service during a very rough Channel crossing: 'So like one's first parties, being sick with other people singing'. She is very knowing. One character says of her: ' . . . whenever I see Agatha Runcible I can't help thinking . . . girls seem to know so much nowadays. We had to learn everything for ourselves . . .' At one stage she is dressed in Hawaiian costume at a party and is the life and soul of the event. Then she hears something about 'an Independent Labour Party', and is furious that she has not been asked. Her political ambitions are in part realized when unwittingly she brings down a government. She also gets involved in a motor-car race, and establishes a record for the course, until it is discovered that she left the road and cut across country for five miles, rejoining the track towards the end of the circuit.

This is a portrait of the Hon. Elizabeth Ponsonby, daughter of the First Baron Ponsonby of Shulbrede, who was a distinguished politician and cabinet minister between the wars. At a dinner party in January 1926 Waugh recorded in his diary: 'Rather to my surprise but considerably to my gratification Elizabeth Ponsonby made vigorous love to me which I am sorry now I did not accept. She has furry arms.' She was one of the first of the Bright Young Things to have her hair shingled. She married John Denis Pelly in 1929, they were divorced in 1933. With several of Waugh's friends from the 1920s she joined a group called the Federal Union, which included Harold Acton (see ANTHONY BLANCHE) and John Sutro. She died in 1940.

Further reading: *Evelyn Waugh Diaries* edited by Michael Davie (1976), *Evelyn Waugh Letters* edited by Mark Amory (1980)

WILLIAM RUSSELL

Gore Vidal, *The Best Man* (1964, screenplay from his play of the same name; film directed by Franklin Schaffner)

Adlai Stevenson (1900–65)

Set in and around a US political convention, Vidal's *The Best Man* examines the two leading personalities engaged in a struggle for the presidential nomination of their party. William Russell is an affluent and idealistic intellectual concerned to keep politics clean; his rival, Joe Cantwell, is a self-made man who shrewdly attracts attention by exploiting anti-Communist hysteria. Ostensibly, Russell and Cantwell are hero and villain, though the situation subtly alters when Cantwell threatens to inform delegates that Russell once received psychiatric treatment for a breakdown. Urged on by his advisers, Russell considers an act of retaliation when he is informed that Cantwell was possibly involved in an army scandal over homosexuality. Sickened by the evidence of his increasing cynicism, Russell withdraws from the convention in a way that gives Cantwell no chance of nomination.

Vidal based the characters of Russell and Cantwell on Adlai Stevenson and Richard Nixon respectively. Like Cantwell, Nixon rose to political prominence as a scourge of liberal intellectuals: he became President of the USA in 1968, and resigned in 1974 over the Watergate affair. Adlai Stevenson, like Russell in Vidal's work, was a man of principle, unable to adjust to the ferocity of political in-fighting in America. Born in Los Angeles, Stevenson was educated at Princeton and Northwestern University Law School; he was admitted to the bar in

Further reading: Gore Vidal, *Matters of Fact and Fiction* (1977)

1926. In 1945 he was chief US delegate at the founding conference of the United Nations and gradually established a reputation as an eloquent advocate of liberal causes. From 1949–53 he was Governor of Illinois, and put the authority of his office behind a condemnation of poltical corruption. He was Democratic presidential candidate in 1952 and 1956, being twice defeated by Eisenhower. In 1959 he again contemplated the Democratic nomination, but his earnest approach was no match for the glamour and charismatic appeal of John F. Kennedy, who was nominated for the presidency on the first ballot at the Los Angeles Democratic Convention in 1960. Though he had a distinguished career, Stevenson was cast as a loser by comparison to men who actually won the presidential election; it is this defeatist quality that Vidal captures in his characterization.

S

MR SAMGRASS

Evelyn Waugh, *Brideshead Revisited* (1945)

Sir Maurice Bowra (1898–1971)

Further reading: Maurice Bowra, *Memories 1898–1939* (1967)

Mr Samgrass is a young history don of All Souls, Oxford, who is directed by Lady Marchmain to keep an eye on her son, Sebastian, and his progress at the university. He becomes almost a permanent fixture of the family's house, and Sebastian is taken on a tour of the Near East under his supervision. He is ridiculed by Charles Ryder and Sebastian, but seems to take it all in good part. He is described as: 'a short, plump man, dapper in dress, with sparse hair brushed flat on an over-large head, neat hands, small feet and the general appearance of being too often bathed. His manner was genial and his speech idiosyncratic'. He is generous in his help with others 'but he was himself the author of several stylish little books'. He is a painstaking and finicking scholar, a genealogist and legitimist: 'he was not a man of religious habit, but he knew more than most Catholics about their Church . . . he loved forgotten scandals in high life and was an expert in putative parentage; he claimed to love the past, but I always felt that he thought all the splendid company, living or dead, with whom he associated slightly absurd; it was Mr Samgrass who was real, the rest were an insubstantial pageant . . . And there was something a little too brisk about his literary manners; I suspected the existence of a dictaphone somewhere in his panelled rooms.'

This is a portrait of Maurice Bowra, an influential classical scholar and fellow of Wadham College, Oxford. He was born in Kiukiang, China, the son of an official at the Chinese customs. He was educated at Cheltenham College and New College, Oxford, was a fellow of Wadham College from 1922 to 1938, and warden from 1938 to 1970. He was professor of poetry at Oxford 1946–51, and Charles Eliot Norton Professor of Poetry at Harvard 1948–9, and Vice Chancellor of Oxford University 1951–4. His numerous publications included *Tradition and Design in the Iliad* (1930), *Ancient Greek Literature* (1932), *Greek Lyric Poetry* (1936), *The Heritage of Symbolism* (1943), *Sophoclean Tragedy* (1944), *From Virgil to Milton* (1945), *The Creative Experiment* (1949), *Heroic Poetry* (1952), *The Greek Experience* (1957), *Primitive Song* (1962) and *Memories* (1966). Waugh described him as an 'acquaintance' who became 'a friend' after he (Waugh) had attracted some attention 'as a novelist'. Christopher Sykes wrote that Waugh's relationship with Bowra was ambivalent, 'sometimes admiring and sometimes contemptuous'. (*Evelyn Waugh – A Biography*, 1975). Bowra took his appearance in *Brideshead* with a good grace, and commented on *Sword of Honour*: 'A Waugh to end Waugh'.

DOMINIE SAMPSON

Sir Walter Scott, *Guy Mannering* (1815)

George Thomson (1782–1838)

Further reading: John Gibson Lockhart, *The Life of Sir Walter Scott* (1838)

Dominie Sampson is the eccentric and uncouth tutor of the young hero of *Guy Mannering*, Harry Bertram. He is a rather simple and unworldly man, a considerable scholar but a simpleton in the ways of society. His favourite exclamation is: 'Prodigious!' He is based on George Thomson, who was tutor to Sir Walter Scott's children at Abbortsford. He had been educated at Melrose, Jedburgh and the University of Edinburgh and was licensed as a preacher by the Presbytery of Selkirk in 1816. He lost a leg as a schoolboy in a wrestling match with a fellow schoolboy, but notwithstanding this incapacity he was a sturdy pedestrian and considerable horseman and swordsman. His absentmindedness was notorious. It is claimed that he once walked from Edinburgh to Melrose in nine hours and ended the day by climbing to the top of the Eildons. He was very fond of children and by all accounts a good teacher. This is emphasized in *Guy Mannering*, where Harry says 'God bless him for it! He deserves the love with which I have always regarded even that dim and imperfect shadow of his memory which my childhood retained.' Sir Walter Scott attempted to gain preferment for George Thomson, and wrote to the Duke of Buccleuch in the hope of urging him to make Thomson preacher at the Kirk of Middlebie in 1819. His letter describes the good scholar as: 'nearer Parson Abraham Adams than any living creature I ever saw – very learned, very religious, very simple, and extremely absent. . . . He lost a leg by an accident in his boyhood, which spoiled as bold and fine-looking grenadier as ever charged bayonet against a Frenchman's throat. I think your Grace will not like him the worse for having a spice of military and loyal spirit about him. If you knew the poor fellow, your Grace would take uncommon interest in him, were it but for the odd mixture of sense and simplicity, and spirit and good morals.' Unfortunately his eccentricity always stood in the way of his advancement. It was reputed that the socket of his wooden leg contained a hundred sovereigns of his savings. His obituary in the *Edinburgh Advertiser* praised his classical scholarship and superior mathematics: 'He had a remarkable simplicity of character, indeed from a moral point of view he was the most amiable, downright, and honest of human beings . . . there was displayed in him an utter negation of anything like duplicity and malevolence.' He was buried at Melrose Abbey.

SAMSON

Jonh Milton, *Samson Agonistes* (1671)

John Milton (1608–74)

Further reading: Arthur Sewell, *A Study in Milton's Christian Doctrine* (1939), Edward Wagenknecht, *The Personality of Milton* (1970)

Samson, the great hero and wrestler, is a prisoner of the Philistines. He was betrayed to his enemies by the woman who loved him. He has been blinded: 'O dark, dark, dark, amid the blaze of noon,/Irrecoverably dark, total Ecipse/Without all hope of day!/O first created Beam, and thou great Word,/Let there be light, and light was over all;/Why am I thus bereav'd thy prime decree? The Sun to me is dark/And silent as the Moon.' He is visited by his friends and father who seek to comfort him and finally by Dalila, who hopes for his forgiveness. She finally taunts him. The tragedy ends when he is brought forth to entertain his captors at a feast to their god and realizing the purpose he has to fulfil Samson pulls down the pillars holding the roof and totally destroys his enemies.

Milton himself was blind by 1652. In writing *Samson* he is writing from personal experience of his affliction. Also strongly present in *Samson Agonistes* is Milton's awareness of the irresistible attraction of women, and the sense that the attraction was dangerous to full realization of a man's destiny. He had early resolved to remain celibate to devote himself to study, teaching and writing, but in 1642 he married Mary Powell, then less than seventeen. Milton was a passionate man. He wrote of feminine charm as a young man: 'I do not let spring time pass by me in vain' and he describes watching 'groups of girls stroll by, stars that breathe out tempting flames'. This marriage failed and Mary left him as they had deep political differences (her family were Royalist). He married Catherine Woodcock, who died in 1658, and in 1662 he married Elizabeth Minshull, who outlived him. He published pamphlets on divorce which were very advanced for their day. Also present in *Samson* is Milton's almost Calvinistic belief that whatever we are, however weak, or strong, we are all part of God's purpose, and that we should wait, and endure until that purpose be revealed. This is the same theme found in the sonnet on his blindness, which ends: 'they also serve who only stand and wait'. Samson waits. And he serves his moment.

SAPPHO

Alexander Pope, *On the Characters of Women* (1735)

Lady Mary Wortley Montagu (1689–1762)

Further reading: Lord Wharncliffe, *Life and*

Pope portrays Sappho as one who had been beautiful in her day but is now certainly past it. A former poetess, she is described as being none too careful about her appearance. Pope refers to her habit of wearing: 'diamonds with her dirty smock' and pictures her at her 'toilet's greasy task' in preparatin for a day's socializing which will conclude with her 'Fragrant at an evening masque;/So morning insects that in muck begun,/Shine, buzz and flyblow in the setting sun.'

This is a malicious portrait of Lady Mary Wortley Montagu, who – like Sappho – was a famous beauty and poetess, who grew somewhat slatternly of her appearance in later life. She was born in 1689, the daughter of Evelyn Pierreoint (later Duke of Kingston) and married Edward Wortley Montagu, MP for Huntingdon, in 1712. She travelled with him to Constantinople when he was in the diplomatic service, and on her return to England she introduced inoculation for smallpox, which she had observed being used abroad. She was a celebrated figure in the social life of the day, and was courted by Edward Young, the poet, and on good terms with Sarah, Duchess of Marlborough (see ATOSSA). It was said that she rebuffed Pope's amorous advances by laughing in his face. She lived in Brecia, Venice and Avignon, and published *Court Poems* and *Letters From the East*. Her beauty, when she was a young woman, was said by all to have been quite striking, and the carelessness of her appearance in later life equally famous. Horace Walpole said of her: 'She was always a dirty little thing. This habit has continued with her.' He met her during her exile in Rome and left this account of her: 'Her dress, her avarice and her impudence must amaze anyone that never heard her name. She wears a foul mob that does not cover her greasy black locks, that hang loose, never combed or curled, an old mazarine blue wrapper, that gapes open and discovers a canvas petticoat. Her face swelled violently on one side, partly covered with a plaster, and partly with white paint, which for cheapness she has bought coarse.' Pope alludes to her unfavourably also in *The Dunciad* and in his *Imitation of the First Satire of the Second Book of Horace*. Her verse was invariably accomplished and frequently witty and is often deservedly anthologized.

Works of Lady Mary Wortley Montagu (1887), Edith Sitwell, *Alexander Pope* (1930), R. Halsband, *Life of Lady Mary Wortley Montagu* (1956)

MR SAUNDERS

William Hurrell Mallock, *The New Republic* (1877)

William Kingdon Clifford (1845–79)

Mr Saunders, house-guest at Otho Laurence's in *The New Republic* (see DR JENKINSON) is a leading champion of the new scientific orthodoxy, whose infallible light will illuminate man's future progress down the ages. He is introduced as 'Mr Saunders from Oxford, supposed to be very clever and advanced' and he soon asserts that: 'Progress is the aim of life'. When challenged to define what he means by 'progress', he confidently replies that he has discovered a definition which will meet with general acceptance: 'There is nothing original in it – it is merely an abstract of the meaning of all our great liberal thinkers – progress is such improvement as can be verified by statistics, just as education is such knowledge as can be tested by examinations.' What will man do when total progress has been achieved? This can never be, Saunders opines, for: 'as long as the human race lasts, it will still have some belief in God left in it, and . . . the eradication of this will afford an unending employment to all enlightened minds'. The great enemy to clarity in human vision, Saunders believes, is sentiment: 'that dense pestiferous fog of crazed sentiment that still hides our view, but which the present generation has sternly set its face to dispel and conquer. Science will drain the marshy grounds of the human mind, so that the deadly malaria of Christianity, which has already destroyed two civilisations, shall never be fatal to a third.'

This is a portrait of the distinguished Victorian mathematician and philosopher, William Kingdon Clifford. This exemplar of the triumph of scientific certitude, who so warmly preached what Lionel Trilling termed: 'the irrefrangible commandments of scientific method which make a perpetual analytic laboratory of the mind', was educated at King's College, London, and Trinity College, Cambridge. He became professor of mathematics at University College, London, and was one of the most renowned intellectual scientists of his day. He married Lucy Lane, of Barbados, who became well known as a writer under her married name. Clifford was particularly interested in universal algebra, non-Euclidean geometry and elliptic functions. His major publications – *Seeing and Thinking*, *Lectures and Essays*, *The Common Sense of the Exact Sciences* – appeared after his death, in 1879, from consumption at Madeira. He coined two notable phrases – 'mind stuff' and 'the tribal self' – which were his insights to the functioning of society: each individual develops a self which prescribes the nature of the service he/she may render to the welfare of the tribe (see also STOCKTON).

CAPTAIN SAVAGE
Frederick Marryat, *Peter Simple* (1834)

Thomas Cochrane, Tenth Earl of Dundonald (1775–1860)

Further reading: Florence Marryat, *Life and Letters of Captain Marryat* (1872), H. Cecil, *A Matter of Speculation* (1965), J.W.P. Mallaliru, *Extraordinary Seaman* (1957)

Peter Simple is usually regarded as Marryat's masterpiece. It tells the story of a young man – the fool of his family – and his gradual maturity into becoming a first-class naval officer. The book is packed with notable characters, Chucks the boatswain, Swinburne, the quartermaster, O'Brien, the plucky Irishman, Captain Kearney, the habitual liar, and the incomparable Captain Savage: 'A sailor every inch of him. He knew a ship from stem to stern, understood the character of seamen and gained their confidence. He was besides a good mechanic, a carpenter, a rope-maker, sail-maker, and cooper. He could hand-reef and steer, knot and splice: but he was no orator. He was good-tempered, honest and unsophisticated, with a large proportion of common sense and free with his officers.'

Thomas Cochrane was the son of Archibald Cochrane, Ninth Earl of Dundonald, and originally held a commission in the army. He joined his first ship, the *Hind*, in 1793. He served in North America and on the French and Spanish coasts 1796–1800. As commander of the *Speedy* he captured several enemy vessels, and was captain by 1801. He was captured by the French but exchanged in 1801. He cruised in the Azores, Bay of Biscay and the Mediterranean. He put forward plans to destroy the French fleet in Aix in 1809, but this was ruined by petty jealousies among senior officers. His criticisms for a time got him placed on half-pay and after service with his uncle, Sir Alexander Forrester Inglis Cochrane, he was expelled from the navy, from his seat in parliament and other honours for his alleged part in a stock exchange fraud in 1814. He served with the Chilean navy, and became admiral in the Brazilian and Greek navies. He was a pioneer supporter of steam-power and an original naval strategist. By 1832 he was a rear-admiral in the British Navy, and admiral by 1851. Marryat had served with Cochrane from 1806 on the *Impérieuse*.

NAOMI SAVAGE
Anthony West, *Heritage* (1955)

Rebecca West (1892–1983)

Further reading: Anthony West, *Aspects of a Life* (1984)

Anthony West's novel *Heritage* describes the struggle of the narrator, Richard Savage, to establish his own identity in a world confused by the relationship between his extraordinary parents. Richard is the illegitimate son of Naomi Savage, an actress, and Max Town, a famous writer. Naomi's ambition to be the greatest actress of her day keeps her at a distance from her son; moreover, she does not want Richard to fall under the influence of his father, who has a house in Paris. At the beginning of the book Richard is a boy in London, duly puzzled by the complexity of Naomi: 'She was so many different people that it seemed impossible that she could be any one of them, much less all of them.' Later in the book, when Richard says he would like to write plays, Naomi – now the wife of the wealthy Colonel Jack Arthur – is furious: 'What have I done to deserve such a child? . . . This isn't one of Max's ideas, is it? He hasn't put you up to choosing this dreadful career, has he?' Eventually, when Richard has established a relationship with the Colonel, Naomi indicates that she intends to leave the Colonel. Tired of Naomi's selfish disregard for the feelings of others, Richard tells the Colonel that Naomi is 'an absolutely indifferent [mother] who had a child by mistake'.

Introducing the first British edition of *Heritage* in 1984, Anthony West acknowledges that Naomi Savage and Max Town are portraits of his parents Rebecca West and H.G. Wells. Rebecca West was born Cicely Isabel Fairfield, and educated in Edinburgh, where her acting in a charity performance led to her attendance at the Royal Academy of Dramatic Art in London. Unpopular at RADA, she began to write for the *Freewoman*, the feminist weekly for which she reviewed H.G. Wells's novel *Marriage* (1912). Wells was impressed by her writing, and captivated by her formidable character. Anthony West, the illegitimate child of West and Wells, was born on 4 August 1914, but as Wells grew apart from her, so Rebecca West resented his child (whom she adopted). According to Anthony West, his mother maliciously did her worst to ruin his life, making it difficult for him to make a career, and impossible for *Heritage* to appear in England while she was alive. 'She was minded to do me what hurt she could,' Anthony West says of his mother, 'and . . . remained set in that determination as long as there was breath in her body to sustain her malice.' West called his hero Richard Savage after the eighteenth-century poet whose mother did her best to have him hanged.

STEPHEN SAVAGE

Christopher Isherwood, *Lions and Shadows* (1938)

Stephen Spender
(born 1909)

In his autobiographical novel *Lions and Shadows* Christopher Isherwood is visited, in London, by the writer Stephen Savage, a tall youth of nineteen 'with a great scarlet poppy-face, wild frizzy hair, and eyes the violent colour of bluebells'. Savage, we learn, 'inhabited a world of self-created and absorbing drama, into which each new acquaintance was immediately conscripted to play a part . . . But if Savage compelled you to act in his life drama, he also rewarded you handsomely for your services. He was the slave of his friends . . . Even when, a couple of years later, we were living only a few streets away from each other in Berlin, and met several times a day, Savage would often arrive with a large specially chosen orange or a little bunch of flowers. His kindness was so touching and disarming that it sometimes made me quite irritable.' This is a verbal portrait of Stephen Spender, who was one of the leading English leftist poets of the 1930s, and subsequently co-editor of *Horizon* (from 1940–1) and *Encounter* (from 1953–65).

Son of Harold Spender (the political journalist and biographer), Spender was educated at Oxford, where he met Auden who, in the summer of 1928, introduced him to Isherwood. In August 1930 Isherwood spent a weekend in Hamburg with Spender, and that winter invited Spender to join him in Berlin. Spender took a bed-sitting-room in the Motzstrasse, and got into the routine of regular visits to Isherwood's flat in the Nollendorfstrasse. Following two years of close friendship, however, the two men quarrelled because Isherwood feared that Spender would be the first to use the Berlin material they had both examined. Spender abandoned Berlin as a result. In October 1935, when Isherwood was living with his boyfriend Heinz, in Brussels, they were joined by Spender and his boyfriend Tony, with whom Isherwood subsequently had a relationship. After divorcing Inez Pearn, Spender married (1941) the concert pianist Natasha Litvin, and Isherwood visited the couple in 1947. When Spender was working on his autobiography *World Within World* (1951), he came to California to see Isherwood, who advised his friend to complete the book, despite its indiscretions. Writing of his quarrel of 1932 with Isherwood, Spender drew some positive conclusions: 'It made me break with my habit of dependence on Christopher. Most important of all, it made me realize that at the age of twenty-four I had still succeeded in forming no intimate human relationship . . . Christopher went back to Berlin. We immediately made up the quarrel by writing to one another frequently, and by meeting often when we happened to be in the same place.'

Further reading: Christopher Isherwood, *Christopher and His Kind* (1976), Brian Finney, *Christopher Isherwood* (1979)

MARGARET SCHLEGEL

E.M. Forster, *Howards End* (1910)

May Dickinson

On hearing that her sister Helen has impetuously fallen in love with young Paul Wilcox of Howards End, Hertfordshire, Margaret Schlegel feels drawn to her 'at this crisis of her life'. Introducing Margaret in *Howards End* E. M. Forster describes her as 'not beautiful, not supremely brilliant, but filled with something that took the place of both qualities – something best described as a profound vivacity, a continual and sincere response to all that she encountered in her path through life'. Margaret is also impulsive – 'She did swing rapidly from one decision to another' – and lets her aunt go in her place and so the events of the novel are set in motion. Destined to inherit Howards End, Margaret is convinced she can improve the lot of those she encounters: 'Only connect! That was the whole of her sermon. Only connect the prose and the passion, and both will be exalted, and human love will be seen at its highest.'

Forster modelled Margaret on one of the three sisters of his great friend G. L. Dickinson. At the Dickinson family home near Langham Place in Londn, Forster observed May, Janet and Hester and noted their habit of slumming in order to uplift the so-called lower orders. May – as P. N. Furbank observes in *E.M. Forster: A Life* (1977–78) – was 'ugly, intelligent and something of an intellectual manqué'. Apparently she was in the habit of marking, in the margins of books she could not understand, the comment 'Some confusion of thought here.' Assured and eccentric, and yet alert enough to study Greek at the age of eighty, she was known as an accomplished hostess with an interest in cultural self-improvement. On 17 March 1931 Forster wrote to Dickinson about the genesis of his novel and acknowledged that 'May was, perhaps, more definitely Margaret than anyone else was anything else in those two worlds'.

MR SCOGAN

Aldous Huxley, *Crome Yellow* (1921)

Bertrand Russell (1872–1970)

Further reading: Ronald W. Clark, *The Life of Bertrand Russell* (1975)

At the beginning of Aldous Huxley's *Crome Yellow*, the young writer Denis Stone goes to see Anne Wimbush at her Uncle Henry's country house at Crome. After he arrives he joins a tea party in a little summer house, on the estate, and sees Mr Scogan, a former schoolfellow of Henry Wimbush, now in his fifties. Mr Scogan sits rigid and erect in his chair: 'In appearance Mr Scogan was like one of those extinct bird-lizards of the Tertiary. His nose was beaked, his dark eye had the shining quickness of a robin's. But there was nothing soft or gracious or feathery about him. The skin of his wrinkled brown face had a dry and scaly look; his hands were the hands of a crocodile. His movements were marked by the lizard's disconcertingly abrupt clockwork speed; his speech was thin, fluty, and dry.' The story of Denis's relationship with Anne is often punctuated by Mr Scogan's cynical monologues on many subjects. He has an opinion, it seems on everything and talks incessantly. Looking like 'an extinct saurian', Mr Scogan inflicts his advice on Denis Stone at every available opportunity.

Russell never really forgave Huxley for portraying him as a garrulous cynic, and had another reason for his grudge. In 1911 Russell fell in love with Lady Ottoline Morrell, who appears in *Crome Yellow* as Priscilla Wimbush. Henry Wimbush's home at Crome is modelled on Garsington Manor, the Elizabethan house outside Oxford, which Lady Ottoline recreated in 1915 as a cultural haven. After her move to Garsington, Russell recalled, Lady Ottoline 'gave me less and less while at the same time she gave more and more to others. For instance, I was never allowed to enter her bedroom but Aldous Huxley was habitually present while she undressed.' Huxley may well have resented Russell's intellectual arrogance, for when he first began to frequent Garsington, he was known as an aspiring poet, whereas Russell was already known as an important philosopher, the author of *The Philosophy of Leibniz* (1900) and co-author (with A.N. Whitehead) of *Principia Mathematica* (1910). Huxley suggested, in a *Paris Review* interview, that Scogan also contained a touch of the Scottish novelist Norman Douglas (1868–1952) who would 'talk about almost nothing but drink and sex. He became quite boring after a time'.

SIR ROGER SCRATCHERD

Anthony Trollope, *Doctor Thorne* (1858)

Sir Joseph Paxton (1801–65)

Further reading: V. Markham, *Life of Sir Joseph Paxton* (1935)

Roger Scratcherd, a stonemason, takes to drink but nevertheless becomes a 'great man in the world' by dint of his own efforts. His sister, Mary, is seduced by Thorne's brother, and Dr Thorne brings up the child which results from this union. No one in the community is aware of her origins. Meanwhile Roger Scratcherd becomes a contractor, 'first for little things, such as half a mile or so of a railway embankment, or three or four canal bridges, and then a contractor for great things, such as Government hospitals, locks, docks, and quays, and had latterly had in his hands the making of whole lines of railway'. He becomes a very rich man. But he gains more than wealth: 'There had been a time when the Government wanted the immediate performance of some extraordinary piece of work, and Roger Scratcherd had been the man to do it. . . . He went up one day to Court to kiss Her Majesty's hand, and came down to his new grand house . . . Sir Roger Scratcherd, Bart.' But he does not change in essentials: 'he was the same man at all points that he had been when formerly seen about the streets of Barchester with his stone-mason's apron tucked up round his waist'.

The character of Scratcherd was based on Joseph Paxton, who was a gardener and architect, and an example of a man who rose from humble origins and manual work to a position of wealth and public acclaim. He was born at Milton Bryant, near Woburn. He worked in the arboretum at Chiswick and became intimate with the Duke of Devonshire, who made him superintendent of his gardens and grounds at Chatsworth. He became manager of his estates at Derbyshire. In 1836 he began work on the three-hundred-foot conservatory which became the prototype of the design of the Great Exhibition building in 1851, for which he was knighted. He also designed the mansion at Ferrières for Baron James de Rothschild. He was MP for Coventry from 1854 until his death. Ruskin considered the Crystal Palace simply a large greenhouse.

VICTOR SCRIASSINE

Simone de Beauvoir, *The Mandarins* (1954)

Arthur Koestler
(1905–83)

Further reading:
Jenni Calder, *Chronicles of a Conscience* (1968), J. Cruickshank, *The Novelist as Philosopher* (1962), Iain Hamilton, *Koestler* (1982)

At the beginning of Simone de Beauvoir's *The Mandarins* the heroine, Anne, is aware of the excitement associated with the liberation of France. Married to Robert Dubreuilh, a prominent intellectual interested in a united front with the communists, she functions as an observer of ideological ferment. She is flattered when approached by Victor Scriassine, a writer fiercely critical of communism: 'I liked his brusque manner. Like everyone else, I had read his famous book, *The Red Paradise*. But I had been especially moved by his book on Austria under the Nazis. . . . I studied his triangular face with its prominent cheekbones, its hard, fiery eyes, its thin, almost feminine mouth. It wasn't at all the face of a Frenchman. To him Russia was an enemy nation, and he did not have any great love for the United States. There wasn't a place on earth where he really felt at home.'

Scriassine is a political portrait of Arthur Koestler and his hostility to Dubreuilh's plans conveys Koestler's dislike of Sartre's political tolerance of communism. In the novel Scriassine's dogmatic anti-communism is reinforced by his clinically cold approach to human relationships and Anne finds his attempt at seduction distasteful. Everything Scriassine does is conceived in terms of confrontation as he is unable to compromise. As Simone de Beauvoir said: 'He always created the impression that everything happening where he chanced to be and even where he chanced not to be – was his personal concern.' Koestler got to know the French intellectuals–Sartre, Camus, de Beauvoir – after the liberation of France and alienated them by his assertive manner and vanity. In her autobiography Simone de Beauvoir wrote of Koestler: 'we were a bit embarrassed by his self-taught pedantry, by the doctrinaire self-assurance and the scientism he had retained from his rather mediocre Marxist training'.

BASIL SEAL

Evelyn Waugh, *Black Mischief* (1932), *Put Out More Flags* (1942)

The Hon. Peter Rodd
(1904–68)

Basil Seal is a brilliant product of Oxford who is invariably involved in some racket or other. In *Black Mischief*, the once prosperous African empire of Azania has become a backward country. Seth, whom Basil knew at Oxford, ascends to the throne as 'Emperor of Azania, Lord of Wanda, Tyrant of the Seas and Bachelor of Arts of Oxford University'. Basil goes to his court to help the young monarch reform and restore his nation, with surprising results. Early in the novel we are shown Basil's extraordinary understanding of affairs, as he explains to an old clubman in Mayfair, who has not been following the Azanian crisis very closely, 'I never thought things would turn out quite in this way . . . fundamentally it is an issue between the Arabs and the christianized Sakuyu . . . I think the mistake was made to underestimate the prestige of the dynasty . . . As a matter of fact, I've never been satisfied in my mind about the legitimacy of the old Empress . . .'

Peter Rodd was educated at Wellington and Balliol College, Oxford. During the Spanish Civil War he worked with refugees, and he served in the Welsh Guards in the Second World War. He married Nancy Mitford in 1933 (marriage dissolved 1958). In *A Little Learning* (1964) Waugh refers to Rodd's sulky arrogance, but all who knew him agreed on his intellectual brilliance. Christopher Sykes wrote that he possessed: 'intellectual abilities which can be compared with those of the greatest minds' (*Evelyn Waugh – A Biography*, 1975). Harold Acton, who also knew him at Oxford, recorded that he was 'a very superior con-man' (*Nancy Mitford – A Memoir*, 1975). Waugh believed him capable of any mischief, and wrote to Nancy Mitford, on 29 August 1949, that he supposed he was correct in believing that Peter Rodd had a hand in starting the forest fires south of Bordeaux in which eighty-two people died. Waugh admitted to Lady Diana Cooper in a letter dated 28 August 1962 that Basil Seal was based on Peter Rodd, and on Basil Murray, a young man with an unsavoury reputation whom he met at Oxford in 1922. In 1963 he published a short story which delineated Basil Seal's adventures at the age of sixty, *Basil Seal Rides Again or The Rake's Progress*. He jokingly suggested to Nancy Mitford that the Labour government elected after the war believed in euthanasia, and that the health centres were really gas-chambers for cripples, lunatics and undesirables, and that Peter Rodd should be sent to one to be dealt with.

AMELIA SEDLEY

William Makepeace Thackeray, *Vanity Fair* (1848)

Jane Octavia Brookfield (née Elton) (1821–96)

Further reading: John Carey, *Thackeray – Prodigal Genius* (1977)

Vanity Fair concerns the two parallel careers of deeply contrasting heroines, Becky Sharp, the orphaned daughter of a French opera dancer (see BECKY SHARP), who is selfish and worldly, and the innocent, kind-hearted Amelia Sedley, daughter of a rich London businessman. Amelia is worthy of all the praises lavished upon her by her teachers, and more: 'For she could not only sing like a lark . . . and embroider beautifully . . . but she had such a kindly, smiling, tender, generous heart . . . as won the love of everybody who came near her . . . she was a dear little creature; and a great mercy it is, both in life and in novels, which (and the latter especially) abound in villains of the most sombre sort, that we are to have for a constant companion so guileless and good-natured a person; indeed, I am afraid that her nose was rather short than otherwise, and her cheeks a great deal too round and red for a heroine; but her face blushed with rosy health, and her lips with the freshest of smiles, and she had a pair of eyes which sparkled with the brightest and honestest good-humour, except indeed when they filled with tears, and that was a great deal too often; for the silly thing would cry over a dead canary-bird; or over a mouse, that the cat had haply seized upon; or over the end of a novel, were it ever so stupid; and as to saying an unkind word to her, were any persons hard-hearted enough to do so, why, why so much the worse for them. Even Miss Pinkerton, that austere and god-like woman, ceased scolding her after the first time, and though she no more comprehended sensibility than she did Algebra, gave all masters and teachers particular orders to treat Miss Sedley with the utmost gentleness, as harsh treatment was injurious to her.' She is loved at a distance by the loyal William Dobbin, who gallantly steps aside when she is courted and won by the more dashing George Osborne. George is killed at Waterloo, and Amelia eventually marries Dobbin.

This is a picture of Jane Brookfield, the wife of Thackeray's contemporary at Cambridge, William Brookfield, who became a minister. The minute he saw her, the novelist fell in love with her. She was the youngest of eleven children of Charles Elton, scholar and author, of Clevedon, near Bristol. She was five-foot nine inches tall, and a great beauty. Loyalty to his friend compelled Thackeray to behave sensibly, but his passion for Jane endured. The couple remained childless, and Jane developed into a beautiful semi-invalid. She wrote several novels.

MR POPULAR SENTIMENT

Anthony Trollope, *The Warden* (1855)

Charles Dickens (1812–70)

The basis of the plot in *The Warden* is the controversy over Hiram's Hospital, a charitable foundation. The property of the charity has increased in value and now yields an income of £800 a year to the warden, the Revd Septimus Harding. This sinecure is attacked by a journalist, John Bold, who writes for the *Jupiter* (*the Times*, which was nicknamed the 'Thunderer'). The theme of the almshouse controversy is taken up and used as the basis of a sensational 'reforming' novel, published in monthly instalments, by Popular Sentiment.

This was a satiric attack by Trollope on his contemporary radical, reforming and humanitarian novelist, Charles Dickens, who attacked one social abuse after another. Trollope writes of Popular Sentiment: 'In former times great objects were attained by great work. When evils were to be reformed, reformers set about their heavy task with grave decorum and laborious argument. . . . We get on now with a lighter step, and quicker: ridicule is found to be more convincing than argument, imaginary agonies touch more than true sorrows, and monthly novels convince, when learned quartos fail to do so. If the world is to be set right, the work will be done by shilling numbers. Of all such reformers Mr Sentiment is the most powerful. It is incredible the number of evil practices he has put down: it is to be feared he will soon lack subjects, and that when he has made the working classes comfortable, and got bitter beer put into proper sized pint bottles, there will be nothing further for him left to do. Mr. Sentiment is certainly a very powerful man, and perhaps not the less so that his good poor people are so very good; his hard rich people so very hard; and the genuinely honest so very honest. . . . If his heroes and heroines walk upon stilts, as heroes and heroines, I fear, ever must, their attendant satellites are as natural as though one met them in the street.' (See DR PESSIMIST ANTICANT.)

Further reading: Robert Giddings, *The Changing World of Charles Dickens* (1983), Tony Bareham, *Anthony Trollope* (1980)

JUSTICE SHALLOW

William Shakespeare, *Henry IV*, Part 2, *The Merry Wives of Windsor* (1597-1600)

Sir Thomas Lucy (1532-1600) **or perhaps William Gardner** (1531-97)

Robert Shallow is a country justice. In *Henry IV* he recruits a group of bumpkins for service of the King under Sir John Falstaff. Falstaff lodges with him and borrows £1,000 from him. He is a foolish old fellow who constantly harps on the exploits and daring of his youthful days: 'Jesu, Jesu, the mad days that I have spent! And to see how many of my old acquaintance are dead!' In *The Merry Wives of Windsor* he is even more grotesquely senile, but brags of the days when he could make 'fellows skip like rats' and claims that his fingers itch whenever he sees a sword drawn. Falstaff has fallen into his bad books for killing his deer, breaking open his lodge and assaulting his servants. He is also engaged in some complex love intrigue with Anne and his cousin, Slender.

It was traditionally assumed that Robert Shallow was based on Sir Thomas Lucy, who owned the great estate of Charlcote, near Stratford, where the young Shakespeare – legend has it – was caught poaching deer. Lucy was educated by John Foxe, the martyrologist and became a puritan. He rebuilt the great manor house at Charlcote 1558–59. He was knighted in 1565 and was MP for Warwick in 1571 and 1584. He is reputed to have prosecuted Shakespeare in 1585. Shallow threatens to make Falstaff's deer-poaching episode a matter for the Star Chamber, and following his outburst in *Merry Wives* there is a reference to the 'dozen white luces' in the coat-of-arms of Shallow's family. The Lucy coat-of-arms shows three luces (pike fish) in each quarter, that is to say, a dozen luces. Shallow is also fond of archery, as was Sir Thomas Lucy himself.

Leslie Hotson argues, however, that Shallow is really a satiric attack on another justice, William Gardner (Hotson, *Shakespeare versus Shallow*, 1931). Gardner's coat-of-arms had three luces, as he had married into the family of Sir Robert Luce. Gardner became justice of the peace for Brixton Hundred (which included Southwark) and high sheriff of Sussex and Surrey. Shakespeare lived at Southwark and was an associate of one Langley, owner of the Swan theatre. Langley and Gardner were engaged in acrimonious litigation and the portrait of

Further reading: Leslie Hotson, *Shakespeare versus Shallow* (1931)

Shallow may be interpreted as a satiric squib at Shakespeare's part in their quarrel.

MRS ELIZABETH SHANDY
Laurence Sterne, *Tristram Shandy* (1760–67)

Mrs Elizabeth Sterne (1714–73)

Further reading: J. Traugott, *Tristram Shandy's World* (1954)

In Sterne's *Tristram Shandy* Walter Shandy habitually amuses himself at the expense of his wife who 'knew no more than her backside what my father meant' (as the narrator puts it). Mrs Elizabeth Shandy is portrayed as a wearisome wife: 'A temperate current of blood ran orderly through her veins in all months of the year, and in all critical moments both of the day and night alike; nor did she superinduce the least heat into her humours from the manual effervescencies of devotional tracts.'

The only wife in Sterne's fiction is based on his own wife. Sterne was a clergyman when he met Elizabeth Lumley, a vicar's daughter, in York; when the couple married on 30 March 1741 she was already aware of his amorous reputation. When word of the match reached her relatives they had reservations and Mathew Robinson wrote to his sister that 'our cousin Betty Lumley is married to a Parson who once delighted in debauchery, who is possessed of about £100 a year in preferment, and has a good prospect of more. What hopes our relation may have of settling the affections of a light and fickle man, I know not, but I imagine she will set about it not by means of the beauty but of the arm of flesh.' Sterne's delight in debauchery survived the marriage and Elizabeth's increasing irritability may well have been provoked by the frequency of her husband's extramarital affairs. She was known for being easily offended and for her quarrelsome nature; and she was generally considered to be dull, which she doubtless was in comparison to her brilliant and accomplished husband. Like many of the women of her time Elizabeth had problems with childbirth; one daughter, Lydia, survived but there were two miscarriages, the one of 1751 probably ending her sexual relationship with Sterne. Sterne left his widow in poverty and she and Lydia had to make the most of the famous author's literary remains.

TOBY SHANDY
Laurence Sterne, *Tristram Shandy* (1760–67)

Roger Sterne (1692–1731)

Further reading: J. Traugott, *Tristram Shandy's World* (1954)

'My uncle TOBY SHANDY,' declares the narrator of Laurence Sterne's *Tristram Shandy*, 'was a gentleman, who, with the virtues which usually constitute the character of a man of honour and rectitude,–possessed one in a very eminent degree, which is seldom or never put into the catalogue; and that was a most extreme and unparallel'd modesty of nature . . . which happening to be somewhat subtilized and rarified by the constant heat of a little family pride'. After being wounded in the groin at the siege of Namur, Toby begins to ride a hobby-horse by studying the science of attacking fortified towns.

With his military obsession and curious character, Toby is a caricature of Laurence Sterne's own father. Roger Sterne broke with family tradition by enlisting in Marlborough's army and serving as an ensign in the 34th Regiment of Foot. By the time he was ready for action the great battles (Blenheim, Ramillies) had been fought and the English army had settled down to a series of sieges. Roger Sterne was at the siege of Douay in 1710 and then at the sieges of Bethune, Aire, St Venant and Bouchaine – where he married Agnes Hebert, Laurence Sterne's mother. In 1727 Roger Sterne was with the 34th at Gibraltar and there he was (as his son recorded in a letter) 'run through the body by Captain Phillips, in a duel (the quarrel begun about a goose), with much difficulty he survived – tho' with an impaired constitution'. Weakened by the wound ensign Sterne nevertheless resumed active service and was posted, in 1731, to Jamaica where he died 'by the country fever, which took away his senses first, and made a child of him, and then, in a month or two, walking about continually without complaining, till the moment he sat down in an arm chair, and breathed his last.' Sterne remembered him as 'a little smart man – active to the last degree, in all exercises . . . he was in his temper somewhat rapid, and hasty – but of a kindly, sweet disposition.'

TAM O'SHANTER

Robert Burns, *Poetical Works* (1904)

Douglas Graham
(1738–1811)

Further reading:
Maurice Lindsay, *The Burns Encylopaedia* (1980)

In the summer of 1775 Robert Burns left the drudgery of Mount Oliphant farm in Ayrshire to go to school on the 'smuggling coast' of Kirkoswald; he later recalled that he did well at his studies and made even more progress in 'the knowledge of mankind'. Among scenes of 'swaggering riot and roaring dissipation', the sixteen-year-old found out how to 'mix without fear in a drunken squabble'.

One local who participated enthusiastically in the 'roaring dissipation' of Kirkoswald was Douglas Graham who rented the farm of Shanter (*seann tor* means 'old mound') and had a boat called the *Tam O'Shanter* for the purposes of smuggling. The village inn, adjacent to the church, was called the Kirkton; as the landlady Jean Kennedy affected airs her hostelry was known as 'The Leddies' House'. In Burn's poem about 'Tam O'Shanter' the hero 'at the Lord's house, even on Sunday . . . drank wi' Kirkton Jean till Monday'. As well as farming (and smuggling) Graham was a dealer in malt so every market day he would go to Ayr accompanied by his 'ancient, trusty drouthy crony', the shoemaker John Davidson (1728–1806) – Souter Johnny. These excursions were anathema to Graham's wife Helen (*née* M'Taggart) who thus became a 'sulky sullen dame' in his absence. Years after his visit to Kirkoswald, Burns leased Ellisland Farm in Dumfriesshire where he became friendly with the antiquarian Captain Francis Grose who was working on his *Antiquities of Scotland*. Burns asked Grose to include an illustration of Kirk Alloway (where his father was buried); Grose agreed on condition that Burns would provide a witch story to go with the picture. A letter to Grose beginning 'On a market day, in the town of Ayr, a farmer from Carrick . . .' contains the narrative germ of 'Tam O'Shanter', in which Douglas Graham's homeward ride from Ayr to Shanter Farm becomes a drink-induced nightmare vision.

BECKY SHARP

William Makepeace Thackeray, *Vanity Fair* (1848)

Theresa Reviss

Further reading:
Ann Monsarrat, *An Uneasy Victorian – Thackeray the Man* (1980)

Becky Sharp is the impoverished daughter of a ballet-dancer at the opera in Paris and a drunken English artist. She is taken on at Pinkerton's academy, where she becomes the companion of Amelia Sedley (see AMELIA SEDLEY) because she speaks such excellent French. She is a worldly, cunning and self-seeking coquette: 'She was small and slight in person; pale, sandy-haired, and with eyes habitually cast down; when they looked up they were very large, odd, and attractive . . .' She realizes very early in her life that she is able to exert an extraordinary power over men, causing the Revd Mr Crisp, fresh from Oxford, and a curate at Chiswick, where she is at school, to fall in love with her by a single glance of her eyes: 'fired all the way across Chiswick Church from the school-pew to the reading desk'. She might seem like a child, but she had been an adult all her life: '. . . she had the dismal precocity of poverty. Many a dun had she talked to, and turned away from her father's door; many a tradesman had she coaxed and wheedled into good-humour, and into the granting of one meal more. She sat commonly with her father, who was very proud of her wit, and heard the talk of many of his wild companions – often but ill-suited for a girl to hear. But she never had been a girl . . . she had been a woman since she was eight years old . . .' Becky is retained at the finishing school because she can teach the other girls good French. Her initial plan is to land Amelia's brother, Jos, but she is baulked by his sudden return to India. She is then employed as governess in the household of Sir Pitt Crawley, where she worms her way into the family and encaptures the heart of Rawden, Sir Pitt's son by a previous marriage. Rawden is a dashing officer. Becky nurses Sir Pitt's sister when she is ill, and, to her surprise, Sir Pitt then proposes to her. Becky has to admit that she has already secretly married Rawden. He develops into a gambler and she flirts with other rich men, among them Lord Steyne (see LORD STEYNE). She then has a liaison with Rawden's elder brother, and Rawden is arrested for debt. Her husband leaves her, and she circulates among various European spas. Jos returns from India and she becomes his mistress; when he dies she is a rich woman. There is some good in her as she is instrumental finally in bringing Dobbin and Amelia together. As Lady Crawley, she ended her days in Bath and Cheltenham: 'She has her enemies. Who has not? Her life is her answer to them.' This portrait of the cunning little Miss Reviss was recognized by those who knew her (see BLANCHE AMORY).

JAWSTER SHARP

Benjamin Disraeli, *Coningsby* (1844)

John Bright (1811–89)

Further reading: G.M. Trevelyan, *Life of John Bright* (1925), M.E. Hurst, *John Bright* (1946)

Jawster Sharp is a 'radical shopkeeper . . . who had taken what is called "a leading part" in the town on every "crisis" that had occurred since 1830; one of those zealous patriots who had got up penny subscriptions for gold cups to Lord Grey; cries for the Bill, the whole Bill, and nothing but the Bill . . . a worthy who makes speeches, passes resolutions, votes addresses, goes up with deputations, has at all times the necessary quantity of confidence in the necessary individual; confidence in Lord Grey; confidence in Lord Durham; confidence in Lord Melbourne; and can also, if necessary, give three cheers for the King or three groans for the Queen.'

This is an unflattering portrait of John Bright, who was no hero of Disraeli's. He was the son of a Rochdale miller and worked at his father's mill for a time. He gained a reputation as an orator in the temperance cause and in opposition to the principle of church rates in 1834. He supported the Reform Bill and abolition of capital punishment. He was friend and supporter of Richard Cobden in the Anti Corn Law struggle and by 1843 was MP for Durham. He opposed the Maynooth Grant and the Ten Hour Bill, the former as a non-conformist with no time for Catholicism, and the latter as a believer in leaving the management of industry to industrialists. As a Liberal-Whig Bright was inevitably bound not to appeal to Disraeli and their mutual opposition was to show itself during the Turkish crisis of 1876 and the Transvaal issue in 1881. He was a sincere anti-imperialist and resigned over British policy in Egypt in 1882. With Cobden he seemed to embody the ideology of the new manufacturing classes. His opinion of himself was rather more flattering than Disraeli's: 'I have seen so much intrigue and ambition, so much selfishness and inconsistency in the character of so-called statesmen, that I have always been anxious to disclaim the title. I have been content to describe myself as a simple citizen, who honestly examines such questions as affect the public weal and honestly offers his counsels to his countrymen.'

LADY HARRIET FINNIAN SHAW

Wyndham Lewis, *The Apes of God* (1930)

Edith Sitwell (1887–1964)

Further reading: V. Glendinning, *Edith Sitwell* (1981)

In Wyndham Lewis's satirical novel *The Apes of God* the idiotically innocent Dan Boleyn is sent in search of the Apes of God – those self-styled geniuses who imitate (ape) the artistic manners of genuine creators (Gods). Apes abound in London (in Chelsea, Bloomsbury and Mayfair) and also assemble in country homes – such as LORD OSMUND FINNIAN SHAW's weekend country estate, Jays Mill Manor Farm. Lord Osmund's sister is Lady Harriet, an 'old harpy' who listens to 'the little brassy tinkle of her verses for the grown-up nursery'. As Horace Zagreus explains to Dan Boleyn at Lord Osmund's Lenten Party, Lady Harriet Finnian Shaw 'is about forty and very bright in a stately cantankerous fashion'. She is also described as a 'flying harpy, in her embroidered gold, with a sinister tiara', and as the author of a book of verse 'All about arab rocking-horses of true Banbury Cross breed. Still making mudpies at forty!' This is Wyndham Lewis's verbal portrait of Edith Sitwell. He had already abandoned his visual portrait of her, after a quarrel, so that the painting now in the Tate Gallery has no hands.

Edith Louisa Sitwell, the eldest child of Sir George and Lady Ida Sitwell, was born in Scarborough and raised – with her brothers Osbert and Sacheverell – in the family home at Renishaw Hall, Derbyshire. Edith, who emphasized her resemblance to Elizabeth I, gained a reputation as an eccentric aristocratic aesthete, whose weird appearance was a substitute for real poetic talent. However, the poems in *Façade* (1922) revealed linguistic agility and a sophisticated wit. In June 1923

Façade, set to music by William Walton, was given its first public performance at the Aeolian Hall, London, and was angrily received by an audience who thought their legs were being pulled. As Edith Sitwell wrote in her autobiography *Taken Care Of* (1965): 'Never, I should think, was a larger and more imposing shower of brickbats hurled at any new work.' This sensation made Edith Sitwell fair game for sustained abuse in the popular press, and she became a figure of fun. Noel Coward parodied her as the absurd Miss Hernia Whittlebot, and she was cruelly caricatured by Lewis in *The Apes of God*. Her later work showed a concern for humanity: 'Still Falls the Rain' described the raids of 1940 as a modern crucifixion; *The Shadow of Cain* (1947) was an indignant reaction to the dropping of the atomic bomb on Hiroshima.

LORD OSMUND FINNIAN SHAW

Wyndham Lewis, *The Apes of God* (1930)

Sir Osbert Sitwell (1892–1969)

Wyndham Lewis's novel *The Apes of God* satirizes the artistic affectations of the English aristocracy who are condemned as Apes of God – 'those prosperous mountebanks who alternately imitate and mock at and traduce those figures they at once admire and hate'. As the novel moves towards its mock-heroic catastrophe the innocent Dan Boleyn is inexorably drawn towards the Lenten Party held by the supreme ape, 'the figurehead, the host, the famous Chelsea Star of "Gossip", Lord Osmund Finnian Shaw'. Lewis draws attention to Lord Osmund's 'carefully-contained obesity' and then describes him in some detail: 'In colour Lord Osmund was a pale coral, with flaxen hair brushed tightly back, his blond pencilled pap rising straight from his sloping forehead: galb-like wings to his nostrils – the goat-like profile of Edward the Peacemaker. . . . Eyes, nose, and lips contributed to one effect, so that they seemed one feature. It was the effect of the joissant animal – the licking, eating, sniffing, fat-muzzled machine – dedicated to Wine, Womanry, and Free Verse-cum-soda-water.'

When the novel was first published this was instantly recognized as a malicious portrayal of Sir Osbert Sitwell who – with his sister Edith and brother Sacheverell – escaped from the claustrophobic atmosphere of the family home at Renishaw Hall and created the rarefied English cultural climate of the 1920s which was anathema to a modernist such as Lewis. By way of revenge Sir Osbert printed copies of a picture postcard, showing two actors dressed in the sinister hat-and-cloak outfit favoured by Lewis, then had these mysteriously mailed to Lewis from various parts of Europe.

Further reading:
John Pearson, *Facades – Edith, Osbert and Sacheverell Sitwell* (1978), Osbert Sitwell, *Left Hand, Right Hand!* (1944), *The Scarlet Tree* (1945), *Great Morning* (1947), *Laughter in the Next Room* (1948), *Noble Essences* (1950)

HAMER SHAWCROSS

Howard Spring, *Fame is the Spur* (1940)

James Ramsay Macdonald (1866–1937)

Howard Spring's novel, *Fame is the Spur*, charts the career of a young man, born in humble life in Manchester, who gradually rises to political eminence. Initially he is spurred on by apparently sincere feelings motivated by his compassion for the poor and a burning sense of social injustice. He inherits a sword from a relative which was used at the Peterloo massacre, and this sword symbolizes for him the struggle against oppression which must never be abandoned until social equality and the dignity of life have been guaranteed to all. He is a brilliant and moving orator. Early in his career to public office he witnesses the tyranny of management and owners during the mining strike and he vows not to rest until his aims have been realized. However, as he becomes a successful politician and a writer, he gradually sheds his zeal, becomes cautious and compromising in his political stance, and betrays his original principles. He has forgotten his origins.

Hamer Shawcross was based on Ramsay MacDonald, who was born illegitimately in Morayshire of farming stock, experienced great poverty and hardship in his early days and became politically active in the Labour movement. He married Margaret Ethel Gladstone, daughter of a scientist and became gradually more middle-class and respectable himself. He was a natural parliamentarian, with greatly attractive eloquence. He was MP for Leicester 1906-18 and wrote several books of political theory. He gradually developed a sure instinct for moderation,

Further reading:
Lord Elton, *Life of Ramsay MacDonald* (1939), Claude Cockburn, *The Devil's Decade* (1973), A.J.P. Taylor, *English History 1914–1945* (1965)

and was actively anti-communist in the 1920s and by 1922 was leader of the opposition in the Commons as MP for Aberavon. He formed an all-party government with the Conservatives and Liberals in 1931 and a permanent breach with his own party was the cost. He was described by Winston Churchill as a 'boneless wonder' who had the gift of 'compressing the largest amount of words into the smallest amount of thought'.

SAMUEL SHODBUTT

Wyndham Lewis, *The Roaring Queen* (1973)

Arnold Bennett (1867–1931)

Further reading: Margaret Drabble, *Arnold Bennett* (1974)

Wyndham Lewis's satirical novel *The Roaring Queen* – suppressed in 1936 by a publisher fearful of libel – is built round the absurd figure of Samuel Shodbutt. A literary dictator who makes and breaks reputations, Shodbutt is chief reviewer of the *Morning Outcry* and chairman of the Book of the Week Club. He has a banal approach to literature, but absolute confidence in his opinions: 'Samuel Shodbutt's richly-tailored *embonpoint* was regal. Literature was the richer for Samuel Shodbutt's appearance, and S.S. was the richer for Literature. A lock of sallow leaden silver oppressed his right-hand temple – he had the constant frown of Power – the frown of the Power-of-the pen – to make and to mar, of course: the great critic's frown *in excelsis*. For this was a Literary Emperor. Or was not Shodbutt the dream of a literary emperor (or of a French literary pontiff) by a mid-Victorian haberdasher.'

Introducing the first edition of the book, Walter Allen points out that Shodbutt 'can only be Arnold Bennett'. Bennett not only established himself as one of the most successful English novelists of his time, but became an enormously influential reviewer, especially for Lord Beaverbrook's *Evening Standard*: His accessibility, combined with his fame, made him the favourite reviewer of a large public. Wyndham Lewis, like his friend Ezra Pound (who portrayed Bennett as the literary careerist Mr Nixon in *Hugh Selwyn Mauberley*) was a modernist temperamentally opposed to Bennett's assessment of books as commercial commodities. Lewis, always quick to make enemies, also held a personal grudge against Bennett because of a dinner-party in London in 1920. According to Lewis's *Blasting and Bombardiering* (1937) Bennett took offence because the painter Walter Richard Sickert made a point of praising Lewis's novel *Tarr* (1918) in extravagant terms: '*Tarr* had been made to stink in [Bennett's] nostrils . . . For a number of years Arnold Bennett was a kind of book-dictator. . . . He was the Hitler of the book-racket. The book-trade said that he could make a book overnight . . . The "author of *Tarr*" under this Dictatorship spent his time in a spiritual concentration camp – of barbed silence. No one ever heaved a heartier sigh of relief at the death of a Tyrant, than that the "author of *Tarr*" heaved when Bennett passed from this scene to a better and even more resplendent one.'

CAPTAIN SHOTOVER

George Bernard Shaw, *Heartbreak House* (1917)

Edward William Godwin (1833–86)

Further reading: John Ervine, *Bernard Shaw – His Life, Work and Friends* (1956)

Heartbreak House was begun by Bernard Shaw before the outbreak of the First World War, and first performed in 1920. Heartbreak House is a metaphor for modern England as Shaw perceived it – a nation in grave danger of running itself onto the rocks because its leaders were acting like a drunken sea-captain lying in his bunk while the hands waste their time playing cards for money, when they should be running the ship. The presiding spirit of the play is the brooding, Old-Testament-like figure of Captain Shotover, an eighty-eight-year-old retired master mariner, much given to gnomic utterances. In the midst of modern evils and confusions, he represents the voice of common sense. All the characters are emblems of the various qualities which Shaw feels have brought the world very nearly to its end, and they all have names which allegorically body forth their principles. The Sussex villa, where the action takes place, has been done up to resemble the interior of a ship such as Shotover had worked on board as a seaman. He lives here with his daughter, Hesione, and her husband, Hector Hushabye. A young friend of Hesione's – Ellie Dunn – arrives, in search of a husband. She represents the new generation, looking for a new way of life in the ruins of the old. At one point she intends to marry the capitalist millionaire, Boss Mangan; she is tempted because his money will give her security and buy her the things she wants out of life. Captain Shotover says to her: 'If you sell yourself, you deal your soul a blow that all the books and pictures and concerts and scenery in the world won't heal.' As the European war, the destruction of the old world, begins to affect Heartbreak House, when the first bombs fall and kill Boss Mangan, Ellie selects Shotover as her spiritual husband. The best of the old world is unified to the hope in the new. This is an affectionate portrait of Edward William Godwin, the lover of Ellen Terry, and father of Gordon Craig. Godwin was an architect who worked in Bristol and London. He restored Dromore Castle and Castle Abbey, and designed theatrical costumes and scenery. Ellen Terry lived in retirement with Godwin betwen 1868-74, after her separation from George Frederic Watts, in June 1865. On his deathbed Edward William Godwin refused the bread of supreme unction unless he could have cheese with it.

SHYLOCK

William Shakespeare, *The Merchant of Venice* (1597)

Roderigo Lopez
(died 1594)

Further reading:
A.L. Rowse, *Shakespeare – A Biography* (1963), Sidney Lee, *The Jews in England*, in *The Merchant of Venice*, New Variorum Edition, edited by F.H. Furness (1888)

Shylock, although he is one of Shakespeare's most impressive creations, appears in only five scenes of *The Merchant of Venice*. His character remains a puzzle. On one level he seems to be a characteristic Elizabethan stage-villain who out-Herods Herod and would have been hissed and hooted off the stage, but on another level the irony of his presentation and the pathos of his persecution at the hands of the Christians, make him seem almost more sinned-against than sinning. Our reaction to his treatment by the court is bound to be tinged with post-Nazi guilt and unease.

Shylock is abused by the businessmen and mechants of Venice, and long endures their taunts. Bassanio wants to borrow from Antonio in order to court Portia. To support his friend, Antonio, who hopes his trading enterprises are about to pay off, borrows 3,000 ducats from Shylock, the Jewish money-lender. If the debt is not repaid, then Antonio will have to repay the bond with a pound of flesh. Antonio's ships are lost and Shylock demands his pound of flesh. Portia, in disguise as a lawyer, appears in the court, begs for mercy for Antonio, and, when this fails, asserts that in payment of the bond Shylock must not spill one drop of blood. Shylock is defeated and loses his wealth – half to Antonio and half to the state. Antonio graciously declines the fortune provided that Shylock turns Christian and gives his property to his daughter Jessica, whom he had disinherited for eloping with a gentile. Anti-semitic feeling was strong in England at this time.

Roderigo Lopez was a Jewish doctor who settled in England and was house physician at St Bartholomew's Hospital and a member of the Royal College of Physicians before 1569. He became Elizabeth I's chief physician in 1586, but was implicated in a plot to murder the Queen and executed at Tyburn in 1594.

SIDONIA

Benjamin Disraeli, *Coningsby* (1844)

Benjamin Disraeli
(1804–81)

Further reading:
B.R. Jerman, *The Young Disraeli* (1960), W.F. Moneypenny and G.E. Buckle, *The Life of Benjamin Disraeli, Earl of Beaconsfield* (1929), John Holloway, *The Victorian Sage* (1953)

Sidonia is a central character in *Coningsby*, used by the author to put forward – often in dialogue form – the leading ideas of the Young England movement, a revival of the aristocracy and of the chivalrous ideas they represent, the support of the old social order which preceded the factory system and the Manchester school, a revitalizing of the Church and the consequent rebirth of the true and innate greatness of Britain. 'He was above middle height, and of a distinguished air and figure, pale, with an impressive brow, and dark eyes of great intelligence.' Harry Coningsby asks him whether he believes in the influence of the individual character, even though it may not be the Spirit of the Age. Sidonia answers: 'The Age does not believe in great men, because it does not possess any.... The Spirit of the Age is the very thing that a great man changes.... From the throne to the hovel all call for a guide.' Coningsby then asks him: 'What is an individual, against a vast public opinion?' and receives Sidonia's reply: 'Divine... God made Man in his own image; but the Public is made by Newspapers, Members of Parliament, Excise Officers, Poor Law Guardians. Would Philip have succeeded, if Epamanondas had not been slain? . . . Would Prussia have existed had Frederick not been born?'

Sidonia is Disraeli's portrait of himself. The name 'Sidonia' suggests Sidney, and Sir Philip Sidney (1554-86) evoked the chivalrous and aristocratic qualities which motivated the Young England movement. He was particularly bitter at not being given Cabinet office by Robert Peel and by 1842 he was leader of a new force in British conservatism, and he used the novels *Coningsby* and *Sybil*, which appeared in the mid-1840s, to put his faith in Tory radicalism before the public. He attacked Peel's policy of Corn Law repeal and led the Protectionist faction in the Commons. He was Chancellor under Derby in 1852 and again in the Cabinet in 1858 and 1866. Briefly Prime Minister in 1868 his great administration was from 1874-80, and among the measures associated with him are reform at home, expansion abroad, the purchase of the Suez Canal shares and his handling of the Balkan crisis.

AMBROSE SILK
Evelyn Waugh, *Put Out More Flags* (1942)
Brian Howard
(1905–58)

Further reading: Marie-Jaqueline Lancaster, *Brian Howard – Portrait of a Failure* (1978)

Put Out More Flags recounts the fortunes of the smart set from *Decline and Fall* and *Vile Bodies* in the dark days of the Second World War. Ambrose Silk's position in the Ministry of Information is almost the comic counterpart of Winston Smith's in Orwell's 1984 (see BIG BROTHER) – he is the sole representative of atheism in the religious department. His task consisted of demonstrating to British and colonial atheists that Nazism was at heart 'agnostic with a strong tinge of religious superstition'. It was uphill work: 'he served a small and critical public; but whenever he discovered in the . . . foreign newspapers . . . any reference to German church-going, he circulated it to the two or three magazines devoted to his cause. He counted the number of times the word 'God' appeared in Hitler's speeches and found the sum impressive; he wrote a pointed little article to show that Jew-baiting was religious in origin . . .' In some ways he feels he is an anachronism, he has lived to see the high camp style he affected in undergraduate days become the butt of low comedians: 'A pansy. An old queen. A habit of dress, a tone of voice, an elegant, humorous deportment that had been admired and imitated, a swift, epicene felicity of wit . . . these had been his, and now they were the current exchange of comedians . . . this was where Art had brought him . . . It had been a primrose path in the days of Diaghilev; at Eton he had collected Lovat Frazer rhyme sheets; at Oxford he had recited *In Memoriam* through a megaphone to an accompaniment hummed on combs and tissue paper . . . the primrose path led gently downhill to the world of fashionable photographers, stage sets for Cochrane, Cedric Lyne and his Neapolitan grottoes . . .'

This is a portrait of Brian Howard, whom Waugh met at Oxford. He was of American parentage, and educated at Eton and Christ Church, Oxford. Lady Cunard published his *First Poems* in her Hours Press in 1931. In 1929 Diana and Bryan Guinness put on a hoax exhibition of paintings by Howard, representing them as avant-garde work by the 'German emigré genius, Bruno Hat'. Many were fooled – Lytton Strachey bought a painting. Howard travelled in Europe and was an early and energetic anti-Fascist. During the Second World War he served as an aircraftsman. He was an overt aesthete homosexual. Waugh wrote in *A Little Learning* (1964): 'The characters in my novels often wrongly identified with Harold Acton (see ANTHONY BLANCHE) were to a great extent drawn from him'. He committed suicide and is buried at Nice.

LONG JOHN SILVER
Robert Louis Stevenson, *Treasure Island* (1883)

When Jim Hawkins, in *Treasure Island*, approaches the Spy-glass tavern he sees Long John Silver: 'His left leg was cut off close by the hip, and under the left shoulder he carried a crutch, which he managed with wonderful dexterity, hopping about upon it like a bird. He was very tall

W.E. Henley (1849–1903)

Further reading: Jenni Calder, *RLS – A Life Study* (1980), John Gross, *The Rise and Fall of the Man of Letters* (1969), John Connell, *W.E. Henley* (1949)

and strong, with a face as big as a ham – plain and pale, but intelligent and smiling.'

The description fits W.E. Henley who, at the age of sixteen, had his left leg amputated beneath the knee and thereafter walked with a crutch or a stick (and sometimes both). Stevenson admitted that Henley's 'maimed masterfulness gave me the germ from which John Silver grew'. Henley was born in Gloucester and, after English doctors recommended the amputation of his right leg when the tubercular infection became active, he moved to Edinburgh to be treated by Joseph Lister at the Royal Infirmary. Lister saved Henley's leg, and probably his sanity, by his expertise and his example. Henley idolized Lister and evolved, as a result of his triumph over mental anguish and physical agony, a heartily heroic attitude to life best summed up in the closing lines of his poem 'Invictus': 'I am the master of my fate;/ I am the captain of my soul.'

He acted as Stevenson's agent, collaborated with him on the play *Deacon Brodie* and in 1889 became editor of the *Scots Observer*. His positive attitude to life enabled him to surmount adversity and he can be well-imagined, like Long John Silver in *Treasure Island*, dreaming his dreams: 'Why, it makes me young again. I was going to forget my timber leg, I was. It's a pleasant thing to be young, and have ten toes, and you may lay to that. When you want to go a bit of exploring, you just ask old John, and he'll put up a snack for you to take along.'

JOCK SINCLAIR

James Kennaway, *Tunes of Glory* (1956)

Captain Jock Laurie

Further reading: Trevor Royle, *James and Jim: A Biography of James Kennaway* (1983)

James Kennaway's first novel *Tunes of Glory* opens atmospherically in Campbell Barracks (actually Queen's Barracks, Perth) with the snow sealing the soldiers in their own small world. In command of the battalion is acting-colonel Jock Sinclair, a war hero who intimidates friend and foe alike with his aggressive behaviour. In peacetime Jock is an anachronism with more muscles than manners and no sense of decorum: all the graces he lacks are supplied by the new colonel – Basil Barrow of Eton, Oxford and Sandhurst. Jock, by contrast, rose to command 'by way of Sauchiehall Street, Barlinnie gaol, and the band. I was a boy piper.' Campbell Barracks is not big enough for both men and Jock drives Colonel Barrow to suicide and himself to distraction.

James Kennaway did his national service with the Queen's Own Cameron Highlanders. In 1948 he was attached to the 1st Battalion, Gordon Highlanders, with the British Army on the Rhine at Essen. Since drink was cheap and the men were not allowed to fraternize with the Germans the evenings were spent in the barracks in alcoholic self-indulgence; occasionally the men ventured out to pick a fight with Germans just for the fun of it. One of the men Kennaway observed was Captain Jock Laurie, a tough character who had been a sergeant in the 8th Argylls. During the war his heroism earned him promotion and he was greatly admired for his courage. In peacetime, however, he undermined the authority of the senior officers with his belligerent behaviour and his insistence on hard competitive drinking. Laurie's activities caught up with him and he was eventually cashiered and ended his days in Barlinnie gaol. Kennaway found the whole atmosphere alarming and told his mother he would 'rather serve in the Argentine police than in this regiment'.

HUGH SKENE

Eric Linklater, *Magnus Merriman* (1934)

Hugh MacDiarmid (1892–1978)

Eric Linklater's comic novel *Magnus Merriman* describes the hero's experiences as a successful Orkney novelist at large in Scotland as he fights for national autonomy and loses his own independence to a farmer's daughter. In Edinburgh, where he mingles with the literati, he meets the poet Hugh Skene: 'In Scotland the chief exponent of literal revolution was Hugh Skene, and he . . . attempted to revive the ancient Scottish forms of speech. They had this advantage, at least, that they were fully as obscure as Joyce's neologisms or the asyntactical compressions of the young English poets. But as Skene's genius matured he discovered that the

Further reading: Alan Bold, *MacDiarmid: The Terrible Crystal* (1983)

Scots of Dunbar and Henryson was insufficient to contain both his emotion and his meaning, and he began to draw occasional buckets from the fountains of other tongues. At this time it was not uncommon to find in his verse, besides ancient Scots, an occasional Gaelic, German, or Russian phrase. The title-poem of his new volume, *The Flauchter-spaad*, was strikingly polyglot, and after three hours' study Magnus was unable to decide whether it was a plea for Communism, a tribute to William Wallace, or a poetical rendering of certain prehistoric fertility rites.'

Skene is Hugh MacDiarmid whose Synthetic Scots poems of the 1920s, particularly *A Drunk Man Looks at the Thistle* (1926), created a new style of Scottish poetry, international in range and modernistic in approach. MacDiarmid's volume *Scots Unbound and Other Poems* (1932) used what the poet called Aggrandized Scots to extend the idiom and this is the experiment Linklater satirizes – his description of Skene's title-poem refers to a MacDiarmid poem 'Tarras' with its line 'Nor wi' their flauchter-spades ettle to play'. MacDiarmid (who was born Christopher Murray Grieve and adopted the pseudonym in 1922) thoroughly approved of the fictional portrayal: 'That's me to a T' he said in his autobiography *Lucky Poet* (1943).

MRS SKEWTON

Charles Dickens, *Dombey and Son* (1848)

Mrs Campbell

Further reading: Arthur L. Hayward, *The Dickens Encyclopaedia* (1924)

Mrs Skewton, who is known as 'Cleopatra' from having had her portrait painted in that character, is a vain, shallow and artificial character, thoroughly worldly and materialistic. She is the mother of Edith Granger, who becomes Mr Dombey's second wife as a result of her mother's scheming (see MR DOMBEY). Her appearance is artificial: 'The discrepancy between Mrs Skewton's fresh enthusiasm for words, and forlornly faded manner, was hardly less observable than that between her age, which was about seventy, and her dress, which would have been youthful for twenty-seven. Her attitude in the wheeled chair . . . was one in which she had been taken in a barouche, some fifty years before, by a then fashionable artist, who had appended to his published sketch the name of Cleopatra; in consequence of a discovery made by the critics of the time, that it bore an exact resemblance to that princess as she reclined on board her galley. Mrs Skewton was a beauty then, and bucks threw wine glasses over their heads by dozens in her honour. The beauty and the barouche had both passed away, but she still preserved the attitude, and for this reason expressly, maintained the wheeled chair and the butting page: there being nothing whatever, except the attitude, to prevent her from walking.' She is a completely calculating person, who yet poses as one whose actions are dominated by feelings and emotions: 'What do we live for *but* sympathy! What else is so extremely charming! Without that gleam of sunshine on our cold cold earth . . . how could we possibly bear it?' Her curls are false, her face is painted, her body laced into shape – she has become so artificial that she has turned into something mechanical. In fact, when she suffers a stroke and has to be stripped of her finery and trimmings, what is left of her is put to be 'like a horrible doll'. This is a portrait of Mrs Campbell, a well-known character at Leamington. Dickens and Hablot Browne visited Leamington in the late autumn of 1838, and stayed at the Royal Hotel, where Mr Dombey and Major Bagstock put up in *Dombey and Son*. It is at Leamington that Mr Dombey is introduced to Mrs Skewton and her daughter, the former being an old flame of the Major's. A local jeweller at Leamington described Mrs Campbell as being 'laced up to the nines', and openly referred to her as 'Mrs Skewton'. She too, was a faded bloom who tried by all known means to keep up the appearance of youthfulness in defiance of chronology.

HAROLD SKIMPOLE

Charles Dickens, *Bleak House* (1852)

Harold Skimpole is a protégé of John Jarndyce, who hides his utter irresponsibility, especially of money matters, under the guise of an assumed childish innocence. He attacks Jarndyce, accusing him of selfishness: 'He was a bright little creature, with a rather large head, but a

James Henry Leigh Hunt (1784–1859)

Further reading: John Forster, *The Life of Charles Dickens* (1874), Edmund Blunden, *James Henry Leigh-Hung* (1930)

delicate face, and a sweet voice, and there was a perfect charm in him. All he said was so free from effort and spontaneous, and was said with such a captivating gaiety, that it was fascinating to hear him talk. . . . He had more the appearance, in all respects, of a damaged young man, than a well preserved elderly one. There was an easy negligence in his manner, and even in his dress (his hair carelessly disposed, and his neck-kerchief loose and flowing, as I have seen artists paint their own portraits), which I could not separate from the idea of a romantic youth who had undergone some unique process of depreciation.'

This is a rather unflattering portrait of Henry Leigh Hunt, brilliant essayist and friend of several distinguished men of letters, including Keats, Byron, Shelley and Lamb, as well as Dickens. He was a distinguished journalist and editor, who ran the *Examiner* and the *Reflector* at various times in his career. A man of great personal charm, he had been imprisoned in 1813 for making derogatory remarks about the Regent. He was distressed to realize Dickens had caricatured him as Skimpole, though Dickens's biographer, John Forster, claims that the novelist; 'erred from thoughtlessness only'. Dickens, Forster said: 'yielded to the temptation of too often making the character speak like his old friend'. Dickens tried to mollify Hunt and to justify the portrait, but the damage was done. At first the original had not recognized himself: 'but good natured friends in time told Hunt everything'.

LARRY SLADE

Eugene O'Neill, *The Iceman Cometh* (1946)

Terry Carlin

Further reading: Arthur and Barbara Gelb, *O'Neill* (1962), Edwin A. e Engel, *The Haunted Heroes of Eugene O'Neill* (1953)

In 1915 Eugene O'Neill, finding himself down and almost out in New York, began to drink heavily at the Hell Hole, as the regulars called the Golden Swan saloon-hotel in Greenwich Village. This alcoholically extreme period is recreated in *The Iceman Cometh* in which O'Neill appears as Willie Oban, one of the roomers at Harry Hope's saloon-hotel. Another is the 'grandstand philosopher' Larry Slade whose drunkenness is an attempt to escape from his Syndicalist-Anarchist past. 'He stares in front of him,' reads O'Neill's stage-direction on Larry, 'an expression of tired tolerance giving his face the quality of a pitying but weary old priest's.'

O'Neill met Terry Carlin, Larry's original, in the Hell Hole and instantly adopted him as friend, philosopher and surrogate father. Terry, who was born Terence O'Carolan, had an Irish peasant background (as had O'Neill's father) and had come to America as a child in the 1860s. He worked for ten years, as a tanner, then opted out of what he regarded as a rat race. He was brought back into the commercial world when his brother Jim, a stockholder in a tannery, persuaded him to advise the firm. Although Terry's suggestions were profitable the owner of the firm refused to reward him and this caused Jim to resign and thus bring financial ruin on himself and his family. Terry returned to his former poverty and dreamed of an art that would encompass his experience: 'Oh,' Terry wrote, 'that I might expand my written words into an Epic of the Slums, into an Iliad of the Proletaire!' O'Neill articulated this ambition for him and later went with Terry to Provincetown in search of theatrical fame and fortune. Terry had a powerful influence on O'Neill who felt responsible for him; when O'Neill left Provincetown he maintained an account for Terry at a general store. 'I am free and always drunk,' maintained Terry.

JULIUS SLINKTON

Charles Dickens, *Hunted Down* (1859)

Thomas Griffiths Wainewright (1794–1847)

Julius Slinkton is a murderer. He murders one of his nieces, and has designs on the other, Margaret. He stands to gain from their insurance money. His crimes are detected by Meltham, who is the actuary of the insurance company Slinkton had hoped to defraud. Meltham was in love with Slinkton's first victim, and uses various disguises in the pursuit of the criminal, including that of Major Banks and Alfred Beckwith. Slinkton assumes that Beckwith is what he pretends to be – a drunkard near to death – and insures him preparatory to his attempt to poison him. Slinkton's villainy is revealed, and he takes his own life. Dickens

Further reading: J. Curling, *Janus Weathercock – The Life of Thomas Griffiths Wainewright* (1938)

describes him as: 'About forty or so, dark, exceedingly well dressed in black, – being in mourning, – and the hand he extended with a polite air, had a particularly well fitting black-kid glove upon it. His hair, which was elaborately brushed and oiled, was parted straight up the middle; and he presented this parting to the clerk, exactly . . . as if he had said, in so many words: "You must take me, if you please, my friend, just as I show myself. Come straight up here, follow the gravel path, keep off the grass, I allow no trespassing".'

Dickens based Slinkton on the painter, art critic and forger Wainewright, who was also alleged to have murdered his uncle, mother-in-law, sister-in-law as well as other victims. His sister-in-law, Helen, he had insured for £16,000. The company refused to pay, and Wainewright took them to court and nearly won his case. He was sentenced to transportation in 1837 and continued to paint. Dickens may also have had the notorious William Palmer of Rugely in mind (1825-56) who was hanged for the murder of John Parsons Cook but probably poisoned his brother and his wife in order to collect insurance to finance horse-racing and gambling. Dickens followed these cases and wrote about Palmer in *Demeanour of Murderers* (*Miscellaneous Papers*).

DR SLOPER

Henry James, *Washington Square* (1881)

William James (1842–1910)

Further reading: R.B. Perry, *The Thought and Character of William James* (1935), Edmund Wilson, *The Triple Thinkers* (1948), Richard Poirer, *The Comic Sense of Henry James – A Study of the Early Novels* (1960), Leon Edel, *The Life of Henry James*, (4 vols, 1953–72)

Henry James discovered the plot of *Washington Square* in a conversation with the actress Fanny Kemble who told an anecdote about her brother jilting an Oxford heiress on hearing that her father would disinherit her rather than sanction the marriage. In the novel, Catherine Sloper's romance with Morris Townsend is destroyed by the arrogant actions of her distinguished father. Dr Austin Sloper is a famous New York physician who is faithful to the memory of his wife, a rich woman who died a week after giving birth to Catherine. He cannot accept that Catherine is attractive in herself and generally ridicules her efforts to be individual. Commenting on his daughter's prospects Dr Sloper says 'You must remember that she has the prospect of thirty thousand a year. . . . I don't mean that is her only merit; I simply mean that it is a great one. . . . Catherine is not unmarriageable, but she is absolutely unattractive.'

The relationship between the diffident Catherine and her father recalls the tension between Henry James and his brother William, sixteen months his senior. William James was, as psychologist and pragmatic philosopher, one of the most accomplished intellectuals of his time and, like Dr Sloper, 'a thoroughly honest man'. He was, however, easily irritated and given to pouring scorn on what he thought of as brother Henry's literary pretensions. He was astonished at Henry's stunning success as a novelist and eventually found himself in the disagreeable position of being eclipsed by his younger brother. In 1905 William was elected to the American Academy of Arts and Letters but the honour came two months after it had been conferred on Henry. Accordingly William refused the election – ostensibly because he felt the James' family influence would be excessive. He added, with typical sarcasm, 'I am the more encouraged in this course by the fact that my younger and shallower and vainer brother is already in the Academy.'

MR SLUDGE

Robert Browning, *Mr Sludge 'The Medium'* (1864)

Daniel Dunglas Home (1833–86)

Further reading: Donald Thomas, *Robert Browning – A Life Within a*

In this dramatic monologue the fraudulent medium, Sludge, defends the course of his career. He urges that we cannot blame him too fiercely, as a large part of the responsibility for what seems to be his guilt, is the fact that the public are so anxious to be deceived. They desperately want to believe what he attempts to fool them with: 'It's fancying, fable-making, nonsense work – /What never meant to be so very bad – /The knack of story-telling, brightening up/Each dull old bit of fact that drops its shine./One does see somewhat when one shuts one's eyes,/If only spots and streaks; tables do tip/In the oddest way of themselves; and pens, good Lord,/Who knows if you drive them or they drive you?'

This is a portrait of Daniel Dunglas Home, the doyen of Victorian spiritualism. He was at the height of his fame in the decade 1860-70. Browning was particularly distrustful of those who claimed to be able to contact the 'other world' – and regarded them as little better than magicians. Home was born near Edinburgh, and claimed to be related to the Earls of Home. His mother took him to the USA when he was quite young, and it was in America that he made his initial reputation. He came to Britain in 1855 and held numerous seances, which attracted large audiences and many of the famous, including the historian H.T. Buckle, who was present when Home caused a dining table to leave the floor and float in midair. In Florence he demonstrated his powers to English expatriots and the American sculptor, Hiram Powers, was present when he produced spirit hands. Lord Lyndhurst, Lord Dufferin, Landseer, Henry Grattan, the Duchess of Somerset, Lady Salisbury, Lady Londonderry and Lady Mitford were among other celebrities who saw Home in action. In 1867 he was taken to court by a wealthy widow, after claiming he had messages from her husband involving her handing over to him cash and property of considerable value. The case ruined his reputation, he had already been expelled from the Catholic church as a sorcerer. He died in France.

Life (1982), Ronald Pearsall, *The Table Rappers* (1972)

SMELFUNGUS

Laurence Sterne, *A Sentimental Journey through France and Italy* (1768)

Tobias Smollett
(1721–71)

Further reading:
Lewis Melville, *The Life and Letters of Tobias Smollett* (1926), Robert Giddings, *The Tradition of Smollett* (1967), Alan Bold, *Smollett – Author of the First Distinction* (1982)

A Sentimental Journey was to have consisted of four volumes, but Sterne lived to complete only two. They recount travels through Calais, Amiens and to Paris, through the Bourbonnais and on to Lyons, en route to Italy. The narrative is packed with sentimental adventures, and the narrator, presumed to be Mr Yorick, finds everything to his taste, unlike Smelfungus, whom he meets. Smelfungus travels from Boulogne to Paris, and from Paris to Rome, but sees everything through the distortions of his own irascibility and spleen: 'I pity the man who can travel from Dan to Beersheba, and cry: "Tis all barren" – and so it is; and so is all the world to him who will not cultivate the fruit it offers . . . was I in a desert, I would out wherewith in it to call forth my affection.' By contrast, Smelfungus writes an account of his travels which is 'nothing but the account of his miserable feelings'. Of the Pantheon he said: ''Tis nothing but a huge cockpit.'

This is a malicious portrait of Tobias Smollett, the Scottish novelist, journalist and historian, who had a rather jaundiced view and an acid wit. Sterne met Smollett at Montpellier in 1763. Smollett published his *Travels in France and Italy* in 1766, to which Sterne directly replies in *A Sentimental Journey*, at times echoing Smollett's own words, as he had written: 'I was most disappointed at sight of the Pantheon, which, after all that has been said of it, looks like a huge cockpit, open at top. . . . I cannot help thinking that there is no beauty in the features of Venus, and that the attitude is awkward and out of character.' It is true to say, however, that Smollett was in very poor health at this time, and no doubt this considerably coloured his view. The character Mundungus in *A Sentimental Journey*, is a characterization of Dr Samuel Sharp, who went across Europe 'without one generous connection or pleasurable anecdote to tell of'. He published *Letters From Italy* in 1766, and died in 1778. Smollett wrote on returning: 'You cannot imagine what pleasure I feel while surveying the White cliffs of Dover.'

GEORGE SMILEY

John Le Carré, *Tinker Tailor Soldier Spy* (1974), *The Honourable Schoolboy* (1977), *Smiley's People* (1980)

Revd Dr V.H.H. Green
(born 1915)

John Le Carré's subtle spymaster George Smiley has the appearance of an academic and the cunning of a vastly experienced operator. In *Tinker Tailor Soldier Spy* Le Carré mentions his 'Buddha-like inscrutability' and in *The Honourable Schoolboy* he is described with 'a sheet of notes before him. . . . As he spoke, he was actually marking something with his pencil.'

Interviewed on the subject of Smiley, Le Carré mentioned 'my mentor at Oxford' and in a letter of 24 January 1983 named the original as Vivian Green: 'it was Green's quiet, and shrewdness, which I liked'. When David Cornwell (John le Carré) went to read Modern Languages at Oxford in 1952 he was admitted to Lincoln College by Green, then Senior Tutor. The Revd Dr Vivian Hubert Howard Green is a historian who became Sub-Rector of Lincoln in 1970, and Rector in 1983. He has published books on *The Young Mr Wesley* (1961), *Martin Luther and the German Reformation* (1964) and *Religion at Oxford and Cambridge, c. 1160-1960* (1964). He names his recreation as 'mountain walking in Switzerland'. Smiley himself is an Oxford man though his interest is in philosophy rather than ecclesiastical history. In a letter of 30 January 1983 Dr Green commented on his connection with Smiley: 'I understand that such likeness as there is is in some facets of character, more especially, I am told, in being a good listener! Obviously Smiley is a compound of many ingredients, the author's among them, but it seems that somewhere there is at least a minimal something of myself. . . . I have known David Cornwell for a very long time, and been a close friend. . . . I remember reading the first Smiley MS as I came back from visiting him in London in the train from Paddington. . . . When David and his wife stayed with me last October, they brought a present of caviare and vodka with a card reading "With love from Karla".' (Karla is Smiley's Soviet opposite number.)

JULIEN SOREL

Stendhal, *Scarlet and Black* (1830)

Antoine Berthet (executed 1827)

Further reading: V. Brombert, *Stendhal – Fiction and the Themes of Freedom* (1968), F.W.J. Hemmings, *Stendhal* (1964)

Julien Sorel is an ambitious young Bonapartist, humbly born, but hoping to rise in society by adopting the priesthood. As a tutor to the Renal family, he seduces Madame de Renal. After returning to the seminary, he leaves to take up a post at the family of the de la Moles, where he has a love affair with their young daughter. He loses his post, believing that he has been betrayed by Madame de Renal. He attempts to shoot her out of vengeance, while she is attending church. He is condemned to death. While awaiting execution he is visited by the confessor who says to him: 'Your youth . . . the attractive face with which Providence has endowed you, the motive itself of your crime, which remains a mystery, the heroic efforts which Mademoiselle de la Mole has not spared on your behalf . . . have all combined to make you the hero of the young women of Besancon. . . . Your conversion would find an echo in their hearts and would leave a deep impression. . . . You can be of the greatest service, to religion.' Julien answers: 'And what shall I have left, if I despise myself? I have been ambitious, I am not going to blame myself for that; I acted then in accordance with the demands of the time. Now I live for the day, without thought of the morrow. . . . I should be making myself extremely unhappy if I allowed myself to slide into any act of cowardice.' He is beheaded.

Stendhal found the story in several issues of a newspaper, the *Gazette de Tribuneaux*, during December 1827. Antoine Berthet was the good-looking, ambitious son of a blacksmith at Grenoble. With the help of a priest he obtained the post of tutor in the family of a well-to-do lawyer, Michaud. Berthet seduced Madame Michaud. He got bored with her and left to enter the local seminary. He later took another post as tutor in the aristocratic family of de Cordet. Here he had an affair with their young daughter. He was dismissed from his post and was no longer able to continue in the priesthood. He was convinced that it was his former mistress, Madame Michaud, who had betrayed him. In revenge he shot her in church and later attempted suicide. At his trial he argued that his mistress, more worldly than he was, had corrupted him. All attempts to gain a reprieve failed, and he was executed.

SIR PATRICK SPENCE

Francis James Child, *The English and Scottish Popular Ballads* (1882–98)

Sir Patrick Spence

Traditional ballads that tell the story of the drowning of Sir Patrick Spence agree that Sir Patrick was reluctant to accept the King's commission for a sea voyage and that his fears were shared by his men, one of whom says prophetically: 'I saw the new moon late yestreen,/ Wi' the auld moon in her arms;/And if we gang to sea, master,/I fear we'll suffer harm.'

The King who sat in Dunfermline town drinking the blood-red

wine was Alexander III (1241-86) during whose reign Scotland enjoyed a golden age of prosperity. As his daughter Margaret (1261-83) was to marry King Erik of Norway in 1281 the King sent courtiers to attend the ceremony scheduled for August. The variant of 'Sir Patrick Spence' collected in Robert Jamieson's *Popular Ballads and Songs* (1806) duly sends Sir Patrick Spence on the voyage north: 'They mounted sail on Munenday morn,/Wi' a' the haste they may,/And they hae landed in Norraway,/Upon the Wednesday.' According to this version the Scots encountered hostility in Norway: 'They hadna been a month, a month/In Norraway but three,/Till lads of Norraway began to say,/"Ye spend a' our white monie".' Indignant at this insult Sir Patrick and his men make haste to return to Scotland; and it is an historical fact that courtiers who went with Margaret to Norway were drowned on the return voyage. Sir Patrick Spence's name does not appear in the chronicles but survives in the oral tradition, which underlines the contrast that distinguishes the ballad; the King drinks wine, Sir Patrick swallows salt water. Margaret died giving birth to the Maid of Norway who herself died of seasickness on a voyage from Norway to Scotland in 1290.

Further reading:
Alan Bold, *The Ballad* (1979)

RODERICK SPODE

P.G. Wodehouse, *The Code of the Woosters* (1938)

Sir Oswald Mosley
(1896–1980)

In P.G. Wodehouse's novel *The Code of the Woosters* there appears the fascist leader, Roderick Spode. In Bertie Wooster's words, Spode has 'succeeded in inducing a handful of half-wits to disfigure the London scene by going about in black shorts. . . . You hear them shouting "Heil Spode!" and you imagine it is the voice of the people. This is where you make your bloomer. What the Voice of the People is saying is: "Look at that frightful ass Spode swanking about in footer bags. Did you ever in your puff see such a perfect perisher?"' Jeeves later discovers that Spode is secretly a dealer in lingerie.

Roderick Spode is a satiric portrait of the British politician, Sir Oswald Mosley. He was educated at Winchester and the Royal Military College at Sandhurst. He was Conservative MP for Harrow between 1918 and 1922 and then sat as an Independent. Between 1924 and 1930 he sat as a Labour MP. In December 1930 he issued a manifesto which put forward his own plans for dealing with the economic crisis. His advice was not heeded and he and a few supporters left the Labour party to form a group of their own, as Ramsay MacDonald resigned and later became Prime Minister of a National government. In the election of 1931 Mosley's new party failed to win a single seat at the election. The British Union of Fascists, as it was called, held some of the biggest public political meetings in history, and occasioned mob riots and public disturbances in the run up to the Second World War. Under the Defence Regulations Mosley was arrested in May 1940 and he and a number of his fellow party members were interned during the war. He subsequently lived in exile in France. In 1968 he declared: 'I am not, and never have been, a man of the right. My position was on the left and is now in the centre of politics.' He published his political ideas in *My Answer* (1946) and *Mosley-Right or Wrong*? (1961).

Further reading:
A.J.P. Taylor, *English History 1914–1945* (1965), Benny Green, *P.G. Wodehouse – A Literary Biography* (1979)

SPORUS

Alexander Pope, *Epistle to Dr. Arbuthnot* (1735)

John Hervey, Baron Hervey of Ickworth
(1696–1743)

The *Epistle to Dr Arbuthnot* was written by Pope as an answer to his critics and a defence of his literary career. In addressing it to Dr Arbuthnot (1667-1735) the poet was able to establish some virtue by association, as Arbuthnot was a man of great respect and probity. Among the persons attacked in the *Epistle* is Sporus, whom the poet particularly chides for weakness and cowardice, and one who incites others to attack him. In the dialogue, Dr Arbuthnot asks why Sporus should be attacked, when he was a 'thing of silk' and a 'mere white curd of ass's milk'. What point is there in breaking 'a butterfly upon a wheel?' he asks. Pope answers: 'Yet let me flap this bug with gilded wings,/This painted child of dirt, that stinks and stings;/Whose buzz the witty and the fair annoys,/ Yet wit ne'er tastes, and beauty ne'er enjoys.' He hints strongly at Sporus's sexual ambiguity, and likens him to Milton's Satan, tempting

Further reading:
Basil Williams, *The Whig Supremacy 1714–1760* (1962), Robert Walcott, *English Politics in the Early*

18th. Century (1956), John Hervey, Baron Hervey of Ickworth, *Memoirs of the Reign of George II*, edited by J.W. Croker (1848), Earl of Ilchester, *Lord Hervey and His Friends* (1950)

Eve, beautiful to look upon yet vile in spirit: 'A cherub's face, a reptile all the rest./Beauty that shocks you, parts that none will trust,/Wit that can creep, and pride that licks the dust.' He is seen as the tempter of Queen Caroline, wife of George II.

This is a portrait of Lord Hervey, who acted in consort with Lady Mary Montagu (see SAPPHO) to attack Pope. The attacks on Pope had been no less personal and abusive: 'as thou hat'st, be hated by all mankind,/Marked on thy back, like Cain, by God's own hand,/Wander like him accursed through the land.' The allusion to Pope's deformity is particularly distasteful. As Pope wrote in a letter: 'There is a woman's war declared against me by a certain Lord. His weapons are the same which women and children use: a pin to scratch, and a squirt to bespatter.' The result of this quarrel has been Hervey's assured immortality in Pope's poetry. As Vice Chamberlain Hervey had particular influence over Queen Caroline. He was a close friend of Lady Mary Montagu. He had been granted a pension by George II when he deserted Frederick, Prince of Wales, and as a supporter of Robert Walpole and friend of Lady Mary soon fell foul of Pope, who attacked him as Lord Fanny in *Bathos, the Art of Sinking in Poetry* and in *The Duniciad*. Hervey's *Memoirs of the Reign of George II* remain a vivid portrait of the times.

EVERARD SPRUCE

Evelyn Waugh, *Sword of Honour* (1965)

Cyril Connolly (1903–74)

Further reading: Cyril Connolly, *Enemies of Promise* (1938), *The Modern Movement* (1965)

Everard Spruce is the founder and editor of *Survival*: 'A man who cherished no ambitions for the future, believing, despite the title of his monthly review, that the human race was destined to dissolve in chaos.' He is one of those intellectuals whom war brought to an eminence they might not otherwise have enjoyed: 'Those of his friends who had not fled to Ireland or America had joined the Fire Brigade.' In the years preceding the war Spruce had emphatically not been the most esteemed of his coterie of 'youngish, socialist writers'. His journal had announced itself devoted to 'the Survival of Values' and had been protected by the Ministry of Information, exempted its staff from other duties and granted it a generous allowance of paper. It had also been privileged by being exported in bulk to countries still open to British shipping. A chapter of accidents, then, created the literary persona of Everard Spruce, who: 'was in his middle thirties. Time was, he cultivated a proletarian, youthful, aspect; not successfully; now, perhaps without design, he looked older than his years and presented the negligent elegance of a fashionable don . . . he wore a heavy silk, heavily striped shirt and a bow tie above noncommittal trousers.'

This is a portrait of Cyril Connolly, seen by Waugh as one who created a legend of his own brilliance and then failed to live up to it. Waugh's friend Hubert Duggan described Connolly as one who looked as if he'd 'been kicked in the face by a mule'. He did have a snub nose and shaggy eyebrows, and his eyes were set rather far apart. Connolly and Waugh met at Oxford and remained friends, though Waugh constantly provoked and needled him. Connolly was one of the founders and editor of *Horizon*, a journal which was intended to 'give to writers a place to express themselves, and to readers the best writing we can obtain'. It lasted from 1940 until 1950. He was literary editor of *The Observer*, and author of several novels and a fascinating autobiography, *Enemies of Promise*. Waugh's *Black Mischief* has a character called General Connolly, and Apthorpe in *Sword of Honour* has a luxury portable lavatory, *Connolly's Chemical Closet*.

WACKFORD SQUEERS, SENIOR

Charles Dickens, *Nicholas Nickleby* (1839)

William Shaw

Squeers is the owner of the dreadful school, Dotheboys Hall in Yorkshire, where Nicholas is employed as a teacher (see NICHOLAS NICKLEBY). His barbarity is now part of British folklore. Nicholas canes him before the whole school, and Squeers is eventually transported. His appearance is appropriately villainous: he has but one eye, which is of unfortunate greenish-grey: 'The blank side of his face was much wrinkled and puckered up, which gave him a very sinister appearance, especially when he smiled. His hair was very flat and shiny, save at the ends, where it was brushed stiffly up from a low protruding forehead, which assorted well with his harsh voice and coarse manner'. Edgar Johnson in *Charles Dickens – His Tragedy and Triumph* (1952) identifies this as William Shaw, the notorious Yorkshire schoolmaster. Like Squeers, Shaw had only one eye. Dickens also used evidence from court cases where parents had taken Shaw to law for the ill-treatment of their children. Shaw's cards, like Squeer's, actually stated 'near Greta Bridge' as the location of his school, and offered to: 'teach young gentlemen Latin, English, arithmetic, geography and geometry, and to board and lodge them for £20'. These are also Squeers' terms. Shaw advertised the fact that the school party left from the Saracen's Head, Snow Hill, also stated in *Nickleby*. Boys in court deposed that there were nearly three hundred boys there, and that they had meat three times a week, with bread and cheese the rest of the time: 'When any gentleman came to see his children, Mr Shaw used to order the boys who were without trousers or jackets to get under the desks.' They washed in a trough, had no supper, just warm water and milk and dry bread for tea, slept on straw with one sheet to each bed, in which four or five boys slept. Fleas and maggots abounded and soap and towels were in short supply. A boy testified that young customers went blind from malnutrition: 'On one occasion I felt a weakness in my eyes, and could not write my copy; the defendant said he would beat me; next day, I could not see at all, and told Mr Shaw, who sent me, with three others, to the wash-house, as he had no doctor; those who were totally blind were sent into a room; there were nine boys in this room totally blind . . .' This boy was completely blind when he gave evidence. The local graveyard contained the bodies of twenty-five boys between the age of seven to eighteen who had died in Shaw's school between 1810 and 1834. Shaw was fined £500, but continued to run his establishment. Dickens and his illustrator personally researched the matter, and visited Shaw's school, Bowes Academy.

Further reading:
Philip Collins, *Dickens and Education* (1963)

SS CABINET MINISTER

Sir Compton Mackenzie, *Whisky Galore* (1947)

SS Politician

Compton Mackenzie's farce *Whisky Galore* opens in 1943 with the people of the Hebridean island of Little Todday lamenting the lack of whisky owing to wartime restrictions: there has not been a drop of whisky on the island for twelve days. Suddenly, like manna from heaven, whisky is delivered on (as it were) the islanders' doorstep when the SS *Cabinet Minister*, carrying a cargo of 50,000 cases of whisky, strikes a reef in the Minch. The islanders are quick to use all their native ingenuity to dispose of the hard stuff in the most suitable way. Mackenzie presents the treasure thus: 'Many romantic pages have been written about the sunken Spanish galleon in the bay of Tobermory. That 4,000-ton steamship on the rocks of Little Todday provided more practical romance in three and a half hours than the Tobermory galleon has provided in three and a half centuries. Doubloons, ducats, and ducatoons, moidores, pieces of eight, sequins, guineas, rose and angel nobles, what are these to vaunt above the liquid gold carried by the *Cabinet Minister*?' Put in that golden light the SS *Cabinet Minister* emerges as the heroine of Mackenzie's novel and she had an historical counterpart.

In February 1941 the SS *Politician*, a ship considered fast enough to outrun the U-boats in the Atlantic, foundered on a reef in the Sound of Eriskay with her cargo of 264,750 bottles of whisky. Inevitably, the men of Eriskay illegally salvaged the 'liquid gold'. Mackenzie, who settled in the Hebridean island of Barra in 1928, changed one local detail for comic effect: Eriskay is a Roman Catholic island whereas Little Todday is depicted as a Presbyterian stronghold. This causes some problems since the islanders are obliged to observe the Sabbath – the day on which the SS *Cabinet Minister* is wrecked.

Further reading:
Compton Mackenzie, *My Life and Times* (10 vols., 1963–71)

ELENA STAHOV

Ivan Turgenev, *On the Eve* (1860)

Elena Stahov, heroine of Ivan Turgenev's *On the Eve*, is an earnest woman in search of an heroic ideal: 'Weakness of character made her indignant, stupidity angered her, a lie she would not forgive "as long as

Anita Garibaldi (1821–49)

Further reading: A. Yarmolinsky, *Turgenev* (1959), R. Freeborn, *Turgenev – The Novelist's Novelist* (1960), H. Herschkowitz: *Democratic Ideas in Turgenev's Works* (1932)

she lived". . . . A person had but to lose her respect – and she passed judgement quickly, often too quickly – and at once he ceased to exist for her. Every impression was imprinted sharply on her soul; life, for her, was no light matter.' Elena finds the cause she is looking for when she falls in love with Insarov, a Bulgarian patriot exiled in Russia. Henceforth she devotes her life to him and, when he dies, takes his body to Bulgaria and prepares to participate in the war of liberation.

In creating Elena, Turgenev drew on the inspirational figure of Anita Garibaldi, wife of the great Italian patriot. Born in a Brazilian village (now named after her) Anita had been married for four years when Garibaldi noticed her in Laguna in 1839. In his memoirs he described the meeting: 'We both remained enraptured and silent, gazing on each other like two people who had met before, and seeking in each other's faces something which makes it easier to recall the forgotten past. . . . I had formed a tie, pronounced a decree, which only death could annul. I had come upon a forbidden treasure, but yet a treasure of great price!!!' Anita eloped with Garibaldi and married him, in Montevideo, in 1842. She was subsequently his most passionate supporter, insisting on being present in the most demanding and dangerous actions such as the defence of Rome, and the march to San Marino although at the time she was pregnant and suffering from fever. After her death she was celebrated as a great woman of the people. Turgenev's hero, Insarov, had nothing to do with Garibaldi: the prototype was Katranov, a Bulgarian poet, whose love story Turgenev learned about in a notebook given to him by Vassili Karatyeev, a landowner he knew at Spasskoye.

MONROE STAHR

F. Scott Fitzgerald, *The Last Tycoon* (1941)

Irving Thalberg (1899–1936)

Further reading: Andrew Turnbull, *Scott Fitzgerald* (1962), Matthew J. Bruccoli, *Some Sort of Epic Grandeur* (1981), Aaron Latham, *Crazy Sundays – F. Scott Fitzgerald in Hollywood*, Sergio Perosa, *The Art of F. Scott Fitzgerald* (1965)

Despite (or, as he thought, *because*) of his great literary style, F. Scott Fitzgerald was a failure in Hollywood terms; though he worked as a writer in Hollywood in 1927, 1931 and 1937 his only screen credit was for his work on the MGM movie *Three Comrades* (1938). Moreover, Fitzgerald's alcoholic excesses made him an embarrassing figure at Hollywood parties where one could be flamboyant but not frankly vulgar. At one party (described in his story 'Crazy Sunday') Fitzgerald offended the guests of producer Irving Thalberg and was dismissed by MGM a week later.

When Fitzgerald conceived what was to be his final novel, *The Last Tycoon*, he portrayed Thalberg as an artist carefully controlling his sensitivity in order to survive in a viciously competitive business. Monroe Stahr, the hero of the novel, is described in terms exactly applicable to Thalberg: 'He was a marker in industry like Edison and Lumière and Griffith and Chaplin. He led pictures way up past the range and power of the theatre, reaching a sort of golden age, before the censorship.' In fact Thalberg was the brains behind the MGM successes of the 1930s, bringing artistic quality to such films as *The Barretts of Wimpole Street* (1934) and *Romeo and Juliet* (1936).

In Fitzgerald's fiction the Thalberg-Stahr figure assumes certain of the author's own characteristics for he falls in love with a young English girl, Kathleen Moore, who is clearly an affectionate portrait of Sheila Graham, the woman Fitzgerald lived with at the end of his life. In a synopsis of his novel Fitzgerald said 'Thalberg has always fascinated me. His peculiar charm, his extraordinary good looks, his bountiful success, the tragic end of his great adventure. The events I have built around him are fiction, but all of them are things which might very well have happened.'

STALKY

Rudyard Kipling, *Stalky & Co* (1899)

Lionel Charles Dunsterville (1865–1946)

Most of the adventures in Kipling's 'Stalky' stories are intiated by Stalky himself – Arthur Lionel Corkran, whose greatest delight is in making the housemasters of his college look ridiculous. Stalky naturally assumes the role of leader, asking his two companions M'Turk and Beetle (Kipling) rhetorical questions: 'Did you ever know your Uncle Stalky forget you yet? . . . Isn't your Uncle Stalky a great man?' Stalky relishes situations that cause embarrassment to others (especially King, the moralistic housemaster), controls the funds of the triumvirate, and decides just how far they can go in a particular situation. He is a mischievous schoolboy, who dislikes organized school games, but constantly enlists his two chums in the games he contrives.

When Kipling went to public school at the United Services College, Westward Ho!, Bideford, north Devon – from 1878 to 1882 – he fell in with two other boys: George Beresford (the original of M'Turk), and Lionel Charles Dunsterville, known as 'Stalky' (in recognition of his stealth as a practical joker). After school, Dunsterville went to Sandhurst and served in Malta, Egypt, China, and the Northwest Frontier. In 1886, he met Kipling in India and made the first of many visits to Kipling's home – Bateman's, Burwash, Sussex – in 1904. During the First World War, General Dunsterville delighted Kipling with his activities, according to Charles Carrington's *Kipling* (1955): 'His audacious expedition to save North Persia from the Bolsheviks was an exploit surpassing anything the young "Stalky" could have imagined. Rudyard had been right and "Stalky" needed only scope.' After the war, however, Stalky was a retired major-general, with only a pension to sustain him. He decided (Carrington says) 'there was nothing for it but to cash-in on his reminiscences of Rudyard Kipling'. He helped form the Kipling Society, and became, in 1927, its first president. The following year he published *Stalky's Reminiscences*.

MAJOR GENERAL STANLEY

Opera, *The Pirates of Penzance* (1879, music by A.S. Sullivan, libretto by W.S. Gilbert)

Sir Garnet Wolseley
(1833–1913)

Further reading:
Sir Garnet Wolseley, *Story of a Soldier's Life* (1903), J.H. Lehman, *The Life of Garnet Wolseley* (1964)

Major General Stanley introduces himself with one of the most famous patter songs in the Savoy operas: 'I am the very model of a modern Major-General,/I've information vegetable, animal, and mineral,/I know the kings of England, and I quote the fights historical,/From Marathon to Waterloo, in order categorical;/I'm very well acquainted too with matters mathematical,/I understand equations, both the simple and quadratical,/About binomial theorem I'm teeming with a lot o' news –/With many cheerful facts about the square of the hypoteneuse.'

Stanley is based on Garnet Wolseley, the most renowned Victorian major-general and trouble-shooter of imperialism. When George Goldsmith appeared in the premier of *The Pirates* in this role he was made up to look like Wolseley, who was a household name after exploits in India, Burma, China, the Ashanti wars, Natal, the Transvaal and Cyprus. The general delighted in singing this song to entertain family and friends at his home, happy to declare himself 'the very model of a modern Major-General'. Indeed there was something of the braggart in Wolseley's character which Gilbert wholly captured. Disraeli wrote of him in a letter to Queen Victoria: 'It is quite true that Wolseley is an egotist and a braggart . . . men of action when eminently successful in early life are generally boastful and full of themselves.'

Wolseley was born in County Dublin, of a long line of military men. His early career was one long series of brilliant exploits, he was dangerously wounded during the Crimean war, and his promotion was rapid – Assistant Quarter Marshall General in Canada 1861, Colonel 1865, Deputy Quarter Master General 1867, Commander of the Red River expedition 1870, KCMG and CB 1870, Assistant Adjutant General at the War Office 1871, Commander of the Ashanti expedition 1873, Major-General GCMG and KCB 1874, General Commanding in Natal 1875, First Administrator in Cyprus 1878, sent to retrieve the situation in the Zulu wars in 1879 and Adjutant General by 1882, victor at Tel-el-Kebir 1882 and the leader of the expedition finally sent to relieve Gordon at Khartoum. A Viscount by 1885, he was Commander-in-Chief in Ireland 1890-95 and finally Commander-in-Chief of the British Army.

JUSTICE STARELEIGH

Charles Dickens, *The Post-*

Mr Justice Stareleigh is the judge presiding at the trial of the Bardell v. Pickwick case: 'A most particularly short man, and so fat, that he seemed all face and waistcoat. He rolled in, upon two little turned legs, and *humous Papers of the Pickwick Club* (1836)

Sir Stephen Gazelee

Further reading: Philip Collins, *Dickens and Crime* (1962)

having bobbed gravely to the bar, who bobbed gravely to him, put his little legs underneath his table, and his little three-cornered hat upon it; and when Mr Justice Stareleigh had done this, all you could see of him was two queer little eyes, one broad pink face, and somewhere about half of a big and very comical-looking wig.' As Philip Collins has pointed out (*Dickens and Crime*, 1962) Dickens's portraits of judges are generally quite favourable, but Stareleigh is an exception. The trial scene from *Pickwick* was one of Dickens's most successful reading extracts, and Rudolph Chambers Lehman (*Memories of Half a Century*, 1908) has left an account of his impersonation of Stareleigh, in which he had the impression that Dickens had left the stage and been replaced by: 'a fat, pompous, pursy little man, with a plump, imbecile face, from which every vestige of good temper and cheerfulness had been removed. The upper lip had become long, the corners of the mouth drooped, the nose was short and podgy, all the angles of the chin had gone, the chin itself has receded into the throat, and the eyes, lately so humorous and human, had become as malicious and obstinate as those of a pig.' Sir Alexander Cockburn, the Lord Chief Justice of England, was present at a reading where Dickens performed the trial scene and he 'pished' and 'psha'd' throughout the performance of Mr Justice Stareleigh, opining that it was: 'perfectly ridiculous, a mere broad farce or exaggerated pantomime'. Other experienced members of the legal profession thought that Dickens had immortalized Sir Stephen Gazelee, whose eccentricities, pomposities and comicalities had been a source of amusement to the bar for years. It has been claimed that Gazelee's retirement was expedited as a result of the ridicule which this treatment brought him. The case of Bardell v. Pickwick was based on the Norton-Melbourne case (see DIANA MERION), which Dickens covered for the *Morning Chronicle* in June 1836. Serjeant Buzfuz, Mrs Bardell's counsel, a lawyer 'with a fat body and a red face', was based on Serjeant Bompas, who was called to the bar in November 1815, and was a prominent member of the Inner Temple.

WILLIE STARK

Robert Penn Warren, *All the King's Men* (1946)

Huey Long (1893–1935)

Further reading: Allan P. Sindler, *Huey Long's Louisiana* (1956), Huey Long, *Every Man a King* (1933), Forest Davis, *Huey Long – A Candid Biography* (1935)

All the King's Men is the life story of an honest man from a small town background who gets involved in politics. He gets elected mayor and gradually develops ambition, which fuels his career. He is eventually elected governor of the state and gradually power begins to corrupt him, and he destroys his own personality and ruins the lives of friends and family who have supported him. He is eventually assassinated. It is a classic study of the 'gothic' politics of the Southern United States.

The leading character, Willie Stark, is based on the Louisiana politician, Huey Long, known as the 'Kingfish'. He combined an apparently genuine concern for the ordinary citizen, with demagogic political ruthlessness. He was born in Wingfield, Louisiana. He left high school before graduating, was a salesman, and then went to law school. He was called to the Louisiana bar in 1915. He was soon fascinated by politics. Elected as state railroad commissioner in 1918 he soon showed what he could do; he transformed it into a properly energetic public agency, the Public Service Commission. His attacks on big business and the monopoly tactics of the large corporations earned him considerable public support. He was seen as the champion of the Little Man against the likes of Standard Oil. He was elected governor in 1928 and pushed through an extensive series of legislative measures affecting education and public health, in the face of considerable conservative opposition, maintaining his political influence with a machine which he created. Initially he supported Roosevelt, but presidential ambitions of his own as well as feelings that Roosevelt was insufficiently radical caused Long to break with him. In 1934 he declared his 'Share Our Wealth' campaign. His spectacular career was brought to an end by his assassination on 8 September 1935, when he was shot by Dr Carl A. Weiss. Weiss was killed by Long's bodyguard and the assassination has never really been explained. It might have been personal revenge (Weiss believed Long had insulted him) or it might have been a conspiracy to end Long's power. The novel was filmed in 1949 with Broderick Crawford as Willie Stark. Long is also the basis of Hamilton Basso's *Sun in Capricorn* (1942) and John Dos Passos' *Number One* (1943).

CAPTAIN STARLIGHT

Rolf Boldrewood, *Robbery Under Arms* (1882)

Andrew George Scott, 'Captain Moonlight' (1842–76)

Further reading: C. Roderick, *An Introduction to Australian Fiction* (1950), and G. Dutton, *The Literature of Australia* (1964)

Thomas Alexander Browne was born in London in 1826 and went to Australia in 1830 with his parents. He was a squatter in Victoria, and later became a Goldfields Commissioner and a magistrate. He was also a prolific journalist, but the serialization of *Robbery Under Arms* in the *Sydney Mail* in 1882 made him famous, under the *nom-de-plume* of Rolf Boldrewood (a name he found in Sir Walter Scott, a key influence in his fiction). This is a novel of bushranging and banditry, about a father and his two sons who are unable to scrape much of a living together by legal means, and are tempted to a life of robbery by the romantic figure of Captain Starlight, whose aristocratic posings are a splendid mask for his life of crime. Captain Starlight successfully leads a double life – half of it spent as a seemingly respectable landowner and horseman, visiting local land auctions and cattle markets, the rest spent in daring armed robberies which supply the capital for his role as prosperous farmer.

Magistrate Thomas Alexander Browne heard all about the career of Andrew George Scott, 'Captain Moonlight', in the Australian bush. Scott was born in County Tyrone, the son of a parson. He was intended for the priesthood, but found the life dull. He was trained as an engineer, and hoped for a career in the British navy but was rejected. He went to America and fought on the Union side in the Civil War. Later he served with Garibaldi, and in New Zealand, where a wound in the leg gave him the limp he retained all his life. He returned to the priesthood in Melbourne, but found bank-robbery rather more fulfilling. In Sydney he passed himself off as Captain the Honourable George Scott, but was then imprisoned for passing a dud cheque. He attempted escape, but seemed to repent his life of crime, holding bible classes for other inmates. When released, he toured as a collector for charity relief, but then returned to robbery around Victoria. In November 1876, Captain Moonlight, as he was now called, raided the Wantabadgery Station with a gang of bushrangers. After a shoot-out with the police in which three died, he surrendered. At his trial, he pleaded guilty and manfully attempted to take all the blame upon himself; but he and his three remaining companions paid the supreme penalty at the end of the hangman's noose.

JAMES STEERFORTH

Charles Dickens, *David Copperfield* (1850)

George Stroughill

Further reading: Edgar Johnson, *Charles Dickens – His Tragedy and Triumph* (1952)

Steerforth is the head boy at Salem House, the school where David is a pupil. He is young Copperfield's hero. A colourful, striking personality, there was always a streak of the reckless and the dangerous in his character. David takes him to Yarmouth to meet Peggotty's family (see CLARA PEGGOTTY), and on the day that Emily Peggotty is to be married to Ham, she runs away with Steerforth. He tires of her and abandons her on the continent. Steerforth is drowned in a terrible storm off Yarmouth, and Ham – whom he had so wronged – was drowned in trying to save him. Steerforth dominates any company in which he finds himself by the sheer magnetism of his being: 'I was not considered as being formally received into the school, however, until J. Steerforth arrived. Before this boy, who was reputed to be a great scholar, and was very good looking, and at least half a dozen years my senior, I was carried as before a magistrate.' It seems for much of the time that David is actually hypnotized by Steerforth, and even when he knows the evil he has done in seducing Emily, David cannot find it in his heart to condemn him: 'What is natural in me, is natural in many other men, I infer, and so I am not afraid to write that I never had loved Steerforth better than when the ties that bound me to him were broken. In the keen distress of the discovery of his unworthiness, I thought more of all that was brilliant in him, I softened more towards all that was good in him, I did more justice to the qualities that might have made him a man of a noble nature and a great name, than ever I had done in the height of my devotion to him. Deeply as I felt my own unconscious part in his pollution of an honest home, I believed that if I had been brought face to face with him, I could not have uttered one reproach.'

When Charles Dickens was a child he lived with his family at 2 Ordnance Terrace, Chatham. Next door lived two friends of his, Lucy Stroughill, who was the same age as he was, and her brother George, who was several years older. They were all great playmates, but George was the ringleader. In *Nurse's Tales* Dickens writes of the games they played in the fields, in which 'I had been delivered from my dungeons of Seringapatam, an immense pile of (haycock), by my countrymen, the victorious British (the boy next door and his two cousins), and had been recognized with ecstasy by my affianced one (Lucy) who had come all the way from England (second house in the terrace) to ransom me, and marry me.'

STELLA

Sir Philip Sidney, *Astrophel and Stella* (1591)

Penelope Rich (1562–1617)

Further reading: Fulke Greville, *Life of Sir Philip Sidney* (1652), edited by David Nicholl Smith (1907), Kenneth Muir, *Sir Philip Sidney* (1960)

Astrophel and Stella is a sequence of 108 sonnets and eleven songs which Philip Sidney wrote between 1581 and 1583 to celebrate his love for Penelope Devereux, the 'Stella' of the sequence. The story which holds the work together is a simple and moving one. Astrophel loves Stella. But Stella marries another, who is despised by Astrophel, who is tortured by the struggle which takes place in his bosom between passion and reason: 'When I say "Stella", I do mean the same/Princess of beauty for whose only sake/The reins of love I love, though never slake,/And joy therein, though nations count it shame./I beg no subject to use eloquence,/Nor in hid ways to guide philosophy;/Look at my hands for no such quintessence;/But know that I in pure simplicity/Breathe out the flames which burn within my heart,/Love only reading unto me this art.' Sidney's beloved 'Stella' was to marry Sir Robert Rich, who became Second Earl of Warwick. Sidney constantly puns on his name: 'Towards Aurora's court a nymph doth dwell,/Rich in all beauties which man's eyes can see,/Beauties so far from reach of words, that we/Abase her praise saying she doth excell;/Rich in the treasure of deserved renown,/Rich in the riches of a royal heart,/Rich in those gifts which give the eternal crown;/Who, though most rich in these and every part/Which makes the patents of true worldly bliss,/Hath no misfortune but that Rich she is.'

Penelope was the daughter of Walter Devereux, First Earl of Essex. When she was fourteen years old Philip Sidney fell in love with her, and her father was anxious that they should marry. But in 1581, she married Robert Rich. The marriage was an unfortunate one and she encouraged the attentions of Philip Sidney. After Sir Philip Sidney died of wounds received at Zutphen, she became the mistress of Lord Mountjoy. The couple lived together in open adultery. Her husband finally abandoned her after her brother, the celebrated Second Earl of Essex, was executed for treason in 1601, and in 1605 she married Mountjoy, who had now become Earl of Devonshire.

STEPANIDA

Leo Tolstoy, *The Devil* (1911)

Aksinya Bazykina

Further reading: Henri Troyat, *Tolstoy* (1965)

Before he married Sonya Behrs, in 1862, Tolstoy sowed his wild oats on the family estate of Yasnaya Polyana ('Bright Glade'). Sonya bore him thirteen children and once sarcastically remarked of a vegetarian menu prepared by Tolstoy: 'I expect the person who wrote the menu practises vegetarianism as much as the author of the *Kreutzer Sonata* practises chastity.' Frequently possessed by sexual passion, Tolstoy regarded women as sensual beings who brought out the animal in man. It is this assumption that informs *The Devil*, in which the erotic power of a peasant girl drives a married man to suicide.

Before his death Tolstoy told his biographer Biryukov that he was tormented by his memory of 'a liaison with a peasant woman from our village before my marriage'. She was Aksinya Bazykina, whom Tolstoy first met in 1858. He was unable to forget his life with her, and wrote in his diary, a year before his death, 'Looked at bare legs, and remembered Aksinya, that she is still alive and, they say, Yermil is my son.' Sonia Tolstoy also noted in 1909 her husband's delight 'at a woman's *full* bosom and a girl's sunburnt legs, all that once so strongly tempted him; the same Aksinya, with shining eyes re-emerging almost unconsciously now, at the age of eighty, from the depths of his memory and the feelings of former years.'

Tolstoy wrote *The Devil* in less than two weeks, in November 1899 but it was not published in his lifetime, since Sonya saw the manuscript and was reduced to tears of jealous rage. She realized that Stepanida, in the novella, was a portrait of Aksinya: in *The Devil* (as translated by Kyril and April FitzLyon) Stepanida has 'black, shining eyes' and a 'high bosom lifting up the blouse'; an embodiment of sexuality, she is 'a devil! A real devil'. The plot, dominated by the devil of lust, was based on the true story of N.N. Friedrichs, a magistrate who lived with a peasant woman, before making a marriage based on respectability rather than love. Friedrichs (Evgeniy Irtyenev in *The Devil*) shot his mistress, was acquitted on medical evidence, then died when he was run over by a train (possibly as a result of a suicidal impulse). Tolstoy devised two endings to the story: in the first, Irtyenev shoots himself; in the second (composed as an alternative in 1909) he shoots Stepanida. 'If Evgeniy Irtyenev was insane,' Tolstoy concludes the 1899 text, 'then all men are just as insane.'

LORD STEYNE

William Makepeace Thackeray, *Vanity Fair* (1848)

Francis Charles Seymour-Conway, Third Marquis of Hertford (1771–1842)

Vanity Fair details the various adventures of two young girls of very different character. The virtuous Amelia, daughter of a wealthy businessman, and the crafty Becky, daughter of an artist and an opera dancer. Becky attempts to entrap Amelia's brother, is then employed as a governess at the household of Sir Pitt Crawley and secretly marries his second son and is then proposed to by Sir Pitt, whose wife dies suddenly. She seduces Amelia's husband, George, and gradually makes her way up in society, by manipulation and intrigue. Among her associates is Lord Steyne, with whom she enjoys a liaison which compromises her virtue. Steyne is one of the finest portraits of a society roué in Victorian fiction. He has a 'shining bald head, which was fringed with red hair. He had thick bushy eyebrows, with little twinkling bloodshot eyes, surrounded by a thousand wrinkles. His jaw was underhung, and when he laughed, two white buck-teeth protruded themselves and glistened savagely in the midst of the grin . . . he wore his garter and ribbon. A short man was his Lordship, broadchested and bow-legged, but proud of the fineness of his foot and ankle, and always caressing his garter-knee. . . . Lord Steyne in early life had been notorious for his daring and his success at play. He had sat up two days and two nights with Mr Fox at Hazard. He had won money of the most august personages of the realm; he had won his marquisate, it was said, at the gaming-table.'

This is a picture of the Third Marquis of Hertford, son of the Second Marquis. He was a BA of St Mary Hall, Oxford in 1796 and MP for Oxford, Lisburne and Camelford 1819-22. He was made a Knight of the Order of the Garter in 1822 and was an intimate friend of the Prince Regent and of the Duke of Wellington (see LORD MONMOUTH). Henry William Greville recorded of him: 'He was a *bon vivant*, and when young and gay his parties were agreeable . . . but he became puffed up with pride. . . . There has been . . . no such example of undisguised debauchery exhibited to the world.'

Further reading: Charles Greville, *A Journal of the Reign of Queen Victor-Victoria From 1837–1852* (1885)

MRS ALGERNON STITCH

Evelyn Waugh, *Scoop* (1938), and *Sword of Honour* (1965)

Lady Diana Cooper (1892–1986)

Mrs Stitch is the wife of the Cabinet minister, Algernon Stitch. The hero of *Scoop*, the writer and journalist John Boot, is proud of the fact that his novels sold 15,000 copies in their first year and were read by people whose opinions John Boot respected. Among them is 'the lovely Mrs Algernon Stitch'. She is a source of great comfort and support to him: 'Like all in her circle John Boot habitually brought his difficulties to her for solution.' She is a busy, involved and rather arty member of the

Further reading: Philip Ziegler, *Diana Cooper* (1981), *Evelyn Waugh Diaries*, edited by Michael Davie (1976), *Evelyn Waugh Letters*, edited by Mark Amory (1980).

upper-class so well portrayed by Waugh: 'she was still in bed although it was past eleven o'clock. Her normally mobile face encased in clay was rigid and menacing as an Aztec mask. But she was not resting. Her secretary . . . sat at her side with account books, bills, and correspondence. With one hand Mrs Stitch was signing cheques; with the other she held the telephone to which, at the moment, she was dictating details of the costumes for a charity ball. An elegant young man at the top of a step ladder was painting ruined castles on the ceiling.'

Evelyn Waugh met Diana Cooper at Lady Cunard's and they became life-long friends. She was the third daughter of the Eighth Duke of Rutland and married Alfred Duff Cooper (later Viscount Norwich) in 1919. She worked as a nurse at Guy's Hospital in the First World War and went on the stage after the war, mainly to finance her husband's political career. She scored a noted success in Max Reinhardt's production of *The Miracle*. She greatly amused Waugh by her imitations of Edward and Mrs Simpson, with whom she had enjoyed a sea voyage while her husband was in the government (Duff Cooper resigned as First Lord of the Admiralty during the Munich crisis, was Minister of Information and later British Minister in Algiers during the Second World War). When Waugh told her she was the original of Mrs Stitch she did not mind at all. When he apologized for having made her behave badly as Mrs Stitch in *Sword of Honour* in tearing up an official letter of Guy Crouchback's she told the novelist she did not mind at all, as she would have done the same. In old age she became absent-minded and vague and often acted true to her Mrs Stitch role. At the party to celebrate Sir Robert Mayer's 100th birthday she failed to recognize a lady who apparently knew her well. It was only when she recognized the diamonds she realized it was the Queen. She apologized, saying she did not recognize her without her crown.

MR STOCKTON

William Hurrell Mallock, *The New Republic* (1877)

John Tyndall (1820–93)

Further reading: A.S. Eve and C.H. Creasey, *The Life of John Tyndall* (1945)

Mr Stockton, a man 'with long locks' of hair, is first seen in *The New Republic* explaining a microscope to a dark-haired girl. His eager manner is immediately noticeable. This is natural, as he was one of the most zealous scientists of his generation (see STORCKS, SAUNDERS). He asserts that: 'the Alps looked grander, and the sky bluer than ever, to those who truly realized the atomic theory'. Religion was dead, but the immortality of man was assured in his intellect: 'Of course we don't waste time now in thinking about personal immortality. *We* shall not live; but the mind of man will; and religion will live, too, being part of the mind of man. Religion is, indeed, to the inner world what the sky is to the outer. It is the mind's canopy – the infinite mental azure in which the mysterious source of our being is at once revealed and hidden. Let us beware, then, of not considering religion noble; but let us beware still more of considering it true. We may fancy that we may trace in the clouds shapes of real things; and, as long as we know that this is only fancy, I know of no holier occupation for the human mind than such cloud-gazing. But let us always recollect that the cloud which to us may seem shaped like a son of man, may seem to another to be backed like a weasel, and to another to be very like a whale. What, then, can be a nobler study than the great book of Nature, or, as we used to call it, the works of God?' But in Stockton's religion men – and especially scientists – have become as gods: 'Consider the race of men, and note the truly celestial light that science throws on that. We have ascended, noble thought! We have not descended! We are rising towards heaven, we have not fallen from it. Yes – we, with attributes so like an angel's, with understanding so like a God's – to this height we have already risen. Who knows what future may not be in store for us? And then, on the other hand, when the awe-struck eye gazes, guided by science, through the "dark backward and abysm of time" and sees that all that is has unfolded itself . . . from a brainless, senseless, lifeless gas – the cosmic vapour, as we call it – and that it may, for aught we know, one day return to it – I say when we realize . . . this stupendous thought, must not our feelings at such moments be religious?' This is a portrait of John Tyndall, one of the leading Victorian physicists. Born in county Carlow, Ireland, he studied in Marburg, and became professor of natural philosophy at the Royal Institution. With Huxley he made important discoveries in Penrhyn and the Alps, published in the joint work, *The Glaciers of the Alps* (1860). He also made important discoveries in radiation and acoustics.

MR STORCKS

William Hurrell Mallock, *The New Republic* (1877)

Thomas Henry Huxley (1825–95)

Further reading: Leonard Huxley, *Life of T.H. Huxley* (1900)

One of the house-guests at the weekend party in *The New Republic* (see DR JENKINSON) is the distinguished scientist, Storcks. He is first seen turning over books by himself as the other guests arrive. He has black whiskers, spectacles and bushy eyebrows. He is introduced as: 'Mr Storcks of the Royal Society', and it is asserted that he 'is great on the physical basis of life and the imaginative basis of God'. Life, for him, is 'a solemn mystery' and 'matter, which, under certain conditions not yet fully understood, has become self-conscious'. He advises his fellows to look to the future, not to dwell in the past, and to allow the wisdom of science to guide them into a future of progress, enlightenment and improvement: 'I was going to claim for the present age,' he says, 'in thought and speculation (and it is these that give their tone to its entire conduct of life), as its noble and peculiar feature, a universal, intrepid, dogged resolve to find out and face the complete truth of things, and to allow no prejudice, however dear to us, to obscure our vision. This is the only real morality: and not only is it full of blessing for the future, but it is giving us 'manifold more in this present time' as well. The work of science, you see, is twofold; it enlarges the horizons of the mind, and improves the conditions of the body . . .'

This is a mildly satiric portrait of T.H. Huxley, the English biologist, who was the father of Leonard Huxley, the journalist and editor, who married a niece of Matthew Arnold (see MR LUKE), and whose son was Aldous Huxley, the novelist and man of letters (see MARK RAMPION). Originally an opponent of evolution, he was converted after reading Darwin's *Origin of Species*, and became Darwin's most avid champion in the face of opposition from the clergy as well as fellow scientists. He held several academic posts, and advocated science teaching in schools and colleges. H.G. Wells knew him and described him in his *Experiment in Autobiography* 1934: 'As I knew Huxley he was a yellow-faced, square-faced old man, with bright little brown eyes, lurking as it were in caves under his heavy grey eyebrows, and a mane of grey hair brushed back from his wall of forehead. He lectured in a clear firm voice without hurry and without delay, turning to the blackboard behind him to sketch some diagram, and always dusting the chalk from his fingers rather fastidiously before he resumed'. Huxley was zealous in Darwin's cause, and dubbed himself 'Darwin's Bulldog'. Huxley's essays were published in 1863 under the title *Man's Place in Nature*; he also published *Science and Education* (1899).

NIGEL STRANGEWAYS

Nicholas Blake, *A Question of Proof* (1935), *Thou Shell of Death* (1936), *There's Trouble Brewing* (1937), *The Beast Must Die* (1938), *The Smiler with the Knife* (1939), *Malice in Wonderland* (1940), *The Case of the Abominable Snowman* (1941), *Minute for Murder* (1947), *The Dreadful Hollow* (1953), *The Whisper in the*

Nigel Strangeways, the detective featured in novels by Nicholas Blake, is a highly literate man who solves the mystery in *Thou Shell of Death*, for example, by recognizing a quotation from the Jacobean dramatist Cyril Tourneur. Strangeways has a wife, Georgia, but after her death in the blitz of April 1941 he takes up with the talented sculptor Clare Massinger. When Strangeways appears in the first Nicholas Blake novel, *A Question of Proof*, he is introduced as a 'private inquiry agent' and nephew of the Assistant Commissioner of Scotland Yard. Although he has been dismissed from Oxford University for answering his Mods paper in limericks, he has a 'first-rate brain', and is well equipped to solve the mystery of a body discovered in a hay castle.

Nicholas Blake was the pseudonym of the poet Cecil Day-Lewis, whose second son was called Nicholas, and whose mother used the family name Blake. Originally, Day-Lewis based the character of Strangeways

Gloom (1954), *End of Chapter* (1957), *The Widow's Cruise* (1959), *The Worm of Death* (1961), *The Sad Variety* (1964), *The Morning After Death* (1966).

W.H. Auden (1907–73)

Further reading: Sean Day Lewis, *C. Day Lewis* (1980), Humphrey Carpenter, *W.H. Auden* (1981)

on his friend W.H. Auden. As Sean Day-Lewis writes in his biography of his father: 'When Strangeways arrives, emerging from a first-class railway compartment, he is recognizably Auden. He walks towards his hostess "with rather ostrich-like strides". He blinks at her short-sightedly and bows over her hand "with a courtliness a little spoilt by the angularity of his movement". He makes some "flat remarks, which his loud and exuberant voice somehow redeemed from banality" . . . Later he launches into Handel's *Israel in Egypt*, curses his poor sight and decides he is not a "proper, inhuman cold-blooded sleuth" as he would "always believe my friends sooner than the facts".' Auden himself said, in a *Sunday Times* interview of 4 June 1972, that he was 'proud to believe' Strangeways was based on himself. In the later novels, Strangeways became increasingly a self-portrait of Day-Lewis.

Day-Lewis first met Auden when they were both at Oxford in 1925. Though Auden was three years his junior, Day-Lewis became a disciple of his fellow-poet, and the poetry he wrote in the 1930s was obviously Audenesque. Though Day-Lewis developed as a distinctive poet, he was always categorized as a member of the Auden Generation.

CHARLES STRICKLAND

W. Somerset Maugham, *The Moon and Sixpence* (1919)

Paul Gauguin (1848–1903)

Further reading: Ted Walker, *Maugham* (1980), R. Cogniat, *Life of Paul Gauguin* (1947), *Paul Gauguin – Letters to His Wife and Friends*, edited by M. Malingue (1948)

Fascinated by the notion of artistic excess, W. Somerset Maugham decided in 1916 to write a novel based on the life of the painter Paul Gauguin who had (in 1881) given up a career in banking to dedicate himself to art. He worked in Brittany and with Van Gogh in Arles; then, in 1890, he left Paris for Tahiti where he executed a series of symbolically-charged compositions using scenes and figures from Tahitian life. As Maugham discovered, when he arrived in Tahiti in 1917 to research his novel, Gauguin's stay in Tahiti had been far from romantic. He was forty-two when he came to the island in bad health and without money; as usual he was obstreperous and had clashes with the local police and clergy. There was a suicide attempt in 1898 and he left Tahiti in 1901; he died of syphilis two years later in the Marquesas Islands. While on Tahiti, Maugham sent his friend Gerald Haxton round the bars picking up stories from people who had known Gauguin. He also discovered a house in which there was a door decorated by Gauguin, bought the door for two hundred francs, and sold it for $37,400 in 1962.

In Maugham's novel Charles Strickland, a London stock-broker, leaves his wife and goes to Paris to practise the art he knows is inside him. Despising domesticity he drives a woman, Blanche, to suicide and then heads for Tahiti where he marries a native girl. Now Strickland realizes pictorially his vision of the Garden of Eden: 'those nude men and women. They were of the earth, the clay of which they were created, and at the same time something divine'. Maugham commented on the title of his novel in 1923: 'It means reaching for the moon and missing the sixpence at one's feet.'

SUBTLE, THE ALCHEMIST

Ben Jonson, *The Alchemist* (1610)

Dr John Dee (1527–1608)

Further reading: *Aubrey's Brief Lives*, edited by Oliver Lawson Dick (1949)

Jonson's comedy concerns the attempts made by Subtle, an alchemist, and his assistant, Face, to dupe gullible people by promising to transform base metals into gold.

According to John Aubrey, a nigh-on-infallible literary gossip, Jonson based Subtle on the Elizabethan mathematician, geographer, astronomer and astrologer, Dr John Dee. He was educated at St John's College, Cambridge 1542-45, and was one of the original fellows of Trinity in 1546. During a production of a comedy by Aristophanes, Dee earned a reputation for wizardry, by his demonstration of a mechanical beetle which flew as if by magic. He earned a European reputation as a scholar and scientist – travelling and lecturing in centres of learning as distant as Poland and Bohemia, as well as neighbouring European academies. Edward VI gave him a pension, but he was imprisoned by Mary I on suspicion of attempting to murder her husband. He was released after examination by the Star Chamber. Elizabeth I showed him favour and frequently consulted him. He was involved in the search for the Northwest passage. In 1578 he was consulted during the Queen's illness. In the 1580s he began to work with Edward Kelley, a mountebank who claimed to consult the angels. They were partners on a Subtle and Face basis for some twenty years. Prince Albert Laski, a bankrupt ruler of Siradz (Bohemia) was duped by the two who claimed to be able to restore him to fortune. Laski passed them on to the emperor Rudolph at Prague and they later attempted to impress King Stephen Bathory of Poland. The partnership broke up when Kelley claimed divine instructions for the sharing of their wives.

Although Dee asserted he had found quantities of the elixir at the ruins of Glastonbury, he died in poverty in 1608. His library numbered 4,000 volumes, and he left a collection of charts, astronomical and scientific paraphernalia. His 'speculum', a mirror – a solid piece of pinkish glass the size of an orange – is held by the British Museum.

ANGUS SUTHERLAND

Neil M. Gunn, *Highland River* (1937)

Benjamin Gunn

(1888–1917)

Further reading:
F.R. Hart and J.B. Pick, *Neil M. Gunn: a Highland Life* (1981), Neil M. Gunn, *The Atom of Delight* (1956)

Neil M. Gunn's novel *Highland River* concerns the search for the source of a river running through his birthplace, the village of Dunbeath. The quest is symbolic as, after a struggle with a salmon, 'the river became the river of life for Kenn'.

Kenn Sutherland, who comes to maturity in the novel, is largely a self-portrait of the author who is encouraged in his adventures by his brother Angus. When Angus takes Kenn on to the moor, the 'immense distances drew Kenn's spirit out of him. He had come into the far country of legendary names. As Angus murmured them, pointing from under his nose with the heather stalk he nibbled, his excitement went out from Kenn like heat vibrations from a moor, and left him exposed to the feel of hidden watching eyes; and yet, for that very reason, his brother's companionship deeply warmed him'. Neil Gunn had six brothers. Benjamin, three years older than him, emigrated to Canada but then came home to join the army on the outbreak of the First World War, and died stranded on barbed wire in front of the trenches. In Gunn's novel Benjamin is represented as the 'good-natured and kind' Angus whose relationship with Kenn is close and crucial to the development of the central theme. Benjamin Gunn's death is recorded in the book when a Canadian soldier tells Kenn of the manner of Angus's death: 'Shrapnel in his back and legs. He was lying out in front of us. We could see him. We said to the officer we would go out for him. He said it meant death. Heavy machine-gun fire. We said we would go. He handled his revolver. He said he would shoot anyone who made a move to go. . . . We could have saved him. We should – have – saved him. . . . In the dark, I brought him in. But he had bled too much.' Angus represents Kenn's original ideal of physical courage, and the horrific facts of his death shock him into a greater understanding of his own life.

ŠVEJK

Jaroslav Hašek, *The Good Soldier Švejk* (1930)

Private Strašlipka

Further reading:
V. Menger, *Lidsky profil Jaroslav Hašek* (1946), G. Janouch, *Jaroslav Hašek – Der Vater des Braven Soldaten Schweyk* (1967)

Although he seems to be an unusually vulnerable individual in a cruel bureaucratic world, the hero of Jaroslav Hašek's *The Good Soldier Švejk* exists by imaginatively establishing his human rights in the most unlikely circumstances. For example when Švejk becomes batman to Lieutenant Lukáš, after being gambled away in a game of cards, he is told to look after a lady who comes to stay in his superior's apartment. When she sees Švejk she is described (in Cecil Parrott's translation) as wearing 'a transparent gown, which made her exceptionally alluring and attractive'; she orders him to do his duty 'And so it happened that the good soldier Švejk could report to the lieutenant when he returned from the barracks: "Humbly report, sir, I've fulfilled all the lady's wishes and served her decently according to your orders".' Švejk, in other words, is not as stupid as he looks so he survives war and what passes for peace in Czechoslovakia.

Jaroslav Hašek was known in Czechoslovakia as an anarchist and an eccentric who loved to play elaborate practical jokes on the authorities. He was called up in 1915 and drafted to Švejk's regiment – the 91st

Infantry – but was soon dropped when the army recalled his dangerous political opinions. While he was with the 91st Infantry, Hašek became friendly with his company commander, Lieutenant Lukáš, who appears in the novel under his own name: 'Lieutenant Lukáš was a typical regular officer of the ramshackle Austrian monarchy.' Lukáš's batman was a private named Strašlipka who displayed an endearing ingenuity. Thus this humble character was endowed, by Hašek, with the heroic qualities of the good soldier: 'His simple face, smiling like a full moon, beamed with enthusiasm. Everything was so clear to him.' In a surviving regimental photograph the face of Strašlipka conforms to the description of Švejk in the novel; when Hašek died, however, his friend Josef Lada chose to caricature Švejk rather than base his illustrations on Strašlipka.

SVENGALI

George du Maurier, *Trilby* (1894)

Felix Moscheles

Further reading: Daphne du Maurier, *The Du Mauriers* (1937), Felix Moscheles, *In Bohemia with George du Maurier* (1897) T.A. Armstrong, *Reminiscences of George du Maurier* (1912), L. Ormond, *George du Maurier* (1969), D.P. Whiteley, *George du Maurier – His Life and Work* (1948)

George du Maurier's artistic career was threatened, in 1857, by the loss of sight in his left eye and for the next two years he consulted experts in Holland and Belgium before accepting that a detached retina would forever deprive him of the use of the eye. During this difficult period du Maurier stayed in Malines, Belgium, and formed a close friendship with Felix Moscheles who dabbled in art and the occult with equal enthusiasm: in a drawing he did of Moscheles, du Maurier added the caption 'Moscheles, or Mephistopheles?' Moscheles was an accomplished mesmerist who used his skill to entertain and astonish du Maurier. In his book *In Bohemia With Du Maurier* (1897) Moscheles describes one of the experiments he conducted in the back parlour of a tobacconist's store: 'There I am operating on [this] stupid little Flemish boy.... All I recollect is that I gave him a key to hold, and made him believe that it was red-hot and burnt his fingers, or that it was a piece of pudding to be eaten presently, thereby making him howl and grin alternately.' Du Maurier, who sketched this incident, was greatly impressed by the power of hypnotism and later wrote to Moscheles: 'You'll see that I've used up all your Mesmerism and a trifle more in my new book.'

The new book was *Trilby* in which the attractive heroine is transformed into a great singer by the mesmeric presence of Svengali who appears as a caricature of Moscheles: 'a tall bony individual of any age between thirty and forty-five, of Jewish aspect, well featured but sinister.... He went by the name of Svengali, and spoke fluent French with a German accent, and humorous German twists and idioms, and his voice was very thin and mean and harsh, and often broke into a disagreeable falsetto.' Moscheles was delighted with the novel and proud that his hypnotic demonstrations provided du Maurier with 'the germs that were eventually to develop into Trilbyism and Svengalism.'

SWALLOWS

Arthur Ransome, *Swallows and Amazons* (1930), *Peter Duck* (1932), *Winter Holiday* (1933), *Coot Club* (1934), *Pigeon Post* (1936), *We Didn't mean to go to Sea* (1937), *Secret Water* (1939), *The Big Six* (1940), *Missee Lee* (1941), *The Picts and the Martyrs* (1943), *Great Northern?* (1947)

The Altounyan children

Further reading: Hugh Brogan, *The Life of Arthur Ransome* (1984)

Ernest Altounyan (1889-1962) was the son of a doctor who ran his own hospital in Aleppo. Around 1905 Ernest met Arthur Ransome at Lanehead, a house – on the north-eastern shore of Coniston Water (or Thurstonemere), in the Lake District – owned by the artist W.G. Collingwood, Ransome's mentor. Altounyan became friendly with Ransome, and in 1915 married Dora Collingwood, W.G.'s daughter. While Ernest pursued his medical studies, he also had literary ambitions, and approached Virginia Woolf, whose diary of 1919 refers to 'Poor, scatterbrained Altounyan' (12 July) and the 'lean fanatical figure of Altounyan' (7 September). Altounyan qualified as a doctor in 1919, and in October of that year took his wife and children to Aleppo. Every few years, however, the Altounyans returned to the Lake District to stay at Bank Ground Farm, below Lanehead. When they returned in April 1929, Ernest and Dora had by then five children: Taqui, Susie, Mavis (known as Titty), Roger and Brigit.

As his wife and family settled into the farm, Ernest Altounyan went off to buy two fourteen-foot dinghies, one of these, *Mavis*, was the family property, the other, *Swallow*, they shared with Arthur Ransome who, since 1925, had owned a home, Low Ludderburn, at Windermere.

During the summer of 1928 Ransome and the Altounyan children enjoyed themselves on the two dinghies, Ransome helping to teach them to sail. On 19 January 1929, the day after his birthday, Ransome was visited by the Altounyans at Low Ludderburn and, as Hugh Brogan says, saw 'Susie and Titty coming towards him, each holding a large and handsome red Turkish slipper and uttering cries of "Many Happy Returns" . . . He was deeply touched by this attention from the youngest members of the family that meant so much to him'. Ransome then decided he would write a sailing story, featuring *Swallow*, which the Altounyan children would enjoy back in Syria. The result was *Swallows and Amazons*, in which three of the Altounyans appear (under their own Christian names) as Susan, Titty and Roger Walker – the Swallows since they crew *Swallow*. A fourth male Walker, John, substituted for Taqui in the interests of an equal distribution of the sexes. Sending the book to Aleppo, Ransome dedicated it to 'the six for whom it was written in exchange for a pair of slippers'.

CHARLES SWANN

Marcel Proust, *Remembrance of Things Past* (1913–27)

Charles Haas (died 1902)

Further reading: George D. Painter, *Marcel Proust* (1959, 1965)

At the beginning of Proust's novel, the middle-aged narrator lies in bed remembering how, as a child, he used to despair if his mother forgot to give him a goodnight kiss. Going back to his childhood at Combray (actually Illiers, near Chartres) Marcel is upstairs in bed waiting for his mother to leave her guest, Charles Swann, and come to him. Swann, a stockbroker's son, is (in the C.K. Scott Moncrieff/Terence Kilmartin translation) 'one of the most distinguished members of the Jockey Club, a particular friend of the Comte de Paris and of the Prince of Wales, and one of the men most sought after in the aristocratic world of the Faubourg Saint-Germain'. He is also a Jew with a special interest in art. From Combray there are two walks, or ways: the Guermantes way; and Swann's way taking in the house and park of Tansonville, where Swann lives with his wife ODETTE and daughter GILBERTE. For Marcel, Swann 'seemed . . . a being so extraordinary that I found it miraculous that people of my acquaintance knew him too, and in the course of the day might run into him'. The narrator goes back in time to tell of Swann's love for Odette de Crécy for whose sake he frequented the salon of Mme de Verdurin, and later created a salon for Odette herself. Throughout the novel, the narrator expresses his immense admiration for Swann, and his regret that Odette was not worthy of Swann's love, and that Gilberte conveniently forgot, after Swann's death, the great virtues of her Jewish father. Swann is a pivotal figure in the novel: his jealous passion for Odette anticipates Marcel's attitude to Albertine; and his Jewishness introduces the Dreyfus case into the novel.

Charles Haas, who described himself (somewhat facetiously) as 'the only Jew ever to be accepted by Parisian society without being immensely rich' was the wealthy son of a stockbroker. In 1868 he was included, along with fashionable stalwarts of high society, in Tissot's painting of the balcony of the Club in the Rue Royale. As a result of his bravery in the Franco-Prussian war, he gained entrance to the exclusive Jockey Club, and in the 1880s and early 1890s he frequented the salon of Mme Strauss, who probably introduced him to Proust. Not only was Haas friendly with such aristocrats as Count Robert de Montesquiou (original of Proust's CHARLUS), but as (George D. Painter explains when identifying Haas with Swann) 'a favourite companion of Edward VII as Prince of Wales and of . . . the Comte de Paris, who lived in exile at Twickenham. Apart from social life, his chief interests were woman-chasing and Italian painting, on both of which subjects he was regarded as a connoisseur'.

T

TANNHAUSER
Richard Wagner, Tannhäuser, opera in three acts (1845)
Tanhuser, (*circa* 1230–70)

Further reading: Philip S. Barto, *Tannhäuser and the Mount of Venus* (1916)

Richard Wagner's romantic opera Tannhäuser opens with a bacchanal at the court of Queen Venus in the depths of the Venusberg. The young knight, poet and singer, Tannhäuser, sings the praises of the Queen of Love. He has given up the world and lived in the Venusberg for a long time, but in the midst of his song he expresses longing to return to the outside world. When he swears by the name of the Virgin Mary, the entire scene vanishes as if a dream, and he finds himself in the valley of the Wartburg. A young shepherd sings a song to the goddess of spring as a group of pilgrims pass. They are on the way to Rome. Tannhäuser is discovered by a group of his old associates, including Wolfram von Eschenbach and the Landgrave, father of Tannhäuser's beloved, Elisabeth. In a singing contest for Elisabeth's hand in marriage, Wolfram sings of sacred love, but Tannhäuser – in a reverie – sings in praise of Venus. He is threatened by other knights, but saved by the intervention of Elisabeth. He goes to Rome to seek atonement, which is denied him by the pope, who says: 'You may no more be pardoned than this staff in my hand could yield new branches!' Elisabeth dies of a broken heart, and Tannhäuser dies of grief on her bier. At that moment the pilgrims return from Rome, proclaiming a miracle – the staff in the Pope's hands has sprouted new leaves; Tannhäuser has been forgiven.

The real Tanhuser was a German Minnesinger (lyric poet and minstrel) who lived at the court of Frederick II in Austria. He also lived for a time at the court of Otto II, Duke of Bavaria. He wandered from court to court in various German states and kingdoms, and gathered a reputation for his compositions. He wrote mostly *Tanzlieder* and *Tanzleiche*, which are characterized by the sudden movement from a serious opening, which may be addressed to a patron, to a *ballade*, which may be satirical of the courtly love tradition, or otherwise enlivened by wit, humour and zest. Tanhuser went on a Crusade to the Holy Land. It is easy to see how the elements of the real Tanhuser become taken up and translated into the legend of Tannhaüser – his wanderings, his songs which move from serious to flippant subjects, and his pilgrimage to the Holy Land. The Venusberg has been identified with the Hörselberg, near Eisenach. Wolfram von Eschenbach, author of *Parzifal* lived *circa* 1200-20.

LUCY TANTAMOUNT
Aldous Huxley, *Point Counter Point* (1928)
Nancy Cunard (1896–1965)

Further reading: Anne Chisholm, *Nancy Cunard* (1979)

In 1920 Aldous Huxley married Maria Nys, a Belgian girl he had met at Garsington, the home of Lady Ottoline Morrell. By 1922, though, Huxley was deeply in love with Nancy Cunard who, like himself, had contributed to the Sitwells' anthology *Wheels* (1916). As Anne Chisholm says, in her biography of Nancy Cunard, Huxley 'became suddenly infatuated with Nancy; but she hardly noticed. She liked him and kept him dangling; he would wait miserably for her telephone calls or hang around her at parties or in nightclubs, which he detested. At one point she had a brief and, for her, unimportant affair with him, which left him more in love than ever; but his adoration bored her, and his jealousy irritated her.' When Nancy went abroad for the winter of 1922, Huxley considered going after her, so the following year Maria Huxley presented her husband with an ultimatum – to choose between her and Nancy. Huxley chose Maria, but his feelings for Nancy informed his fiction. Nancy appears as Myra Viveash in *Antic Hay* (1923), as Barbara in *Those Barren Leaves* (1925), and as Lucy Tantamount in *Point Counter Point*.

Lucy Tantamount, the daughter of Lord and Lady Edward Tantamount of Tantamount House, Pall Mall, London, is a woman of great sexual presence. At the beginning of the novel Walter Bidlake – whose father John had been Lady Tantamount's lover – leaves the pregnant

Marjorie Carling at home as he goes in search of Lucy. Almost in spite of himself, Walter craves Lucy's company: 'what he wanted was Lucy Tantamount. And he wanted her against reason, against all his ideals and principles, madly, against his own wishes, even against his own feelings – for he didn't like Lucy; he really hated her.' Lucy's husband Henry (her first cousin) is dead and she is able to exploit her charms. Huxley's description of her reflects Nancy Cunard, though he changes the colour of her hair from fair to dark: 'She was of middle height and slim, like her mother, with short black hair, oiled to complete blackness and brushed back from her forehead. Naturally pale, she wore no rouge. Only her thin lips were painted and there was a little blue round the eyes.' Lucy does not return Walter's love, though she sleeps with him a couple of times. He is aware of her limitations, but besotted by her.

Nancy Cunard was born at Nevill Holt, Leicestershire, the home of her father Sir Bache Cunard, and mother Lady Cunard (born Maud Alice Burke). She married Sydney Fairbairn in 1916, but quickly tired of him, separating in 1918. Thereafter her life was devoted to cultural and radical causes.

ELLIOT TEMPLETON

W. Somerset Maugham, *The Razor's Edge* (1944)

Sir Henry Channon
(1897–1958)

Further reading:
Ted Walker, *Maugham* (1980)

Elliot Templeton, the heroine's elegant uncle in Somerset Maugham's *The Razor's Edge*, is an American who does his best to live down what he regards as the vulgar connotations of his own country. Thanks to his expert knowledge of the art market and his love of social climbing he has established for himself, in Paris, impeccable social credentials. 'He was a colossal snob,' writes Maugham. 'He was a snob without shame. He would put up with any affront, he would ignore any rebuff, he would swallow any rudeness to get asked to a party he wanted to go to or make a connexion with some crusty old dowager of great name. . . . His French was fluent and correct and his accent perfect. He had taken great pains to adopt the manner of speech as it is spoken in England and you had to have a very sensitive ear to catch now and then an American intonation.'

Maugham modelled the character on Henry 'Chips' Channon as he once admitted over dinner to the original. Chips, a rich homosexual from Chicago, was always determined to identify himself with the English establishment. When prime minister Baldwin called for strike-breaking, special constables in 1926 both Maugham and Channon volunteered. In 1935 Maugham met Chips at a London lunch and was fascinated by the American's progress in English society. 'To add influence to his affluence Chips married into the aristocracy in 1933 and he and his wife, Lady Honour Guinness, made their home in Belgrave Square in a mansion next door to the Duke of Kent. 'I have put my whole life's work into my anglicization,' wrote Chips in his posthumously-published diary. His ambitions were gradually realized for he became a Conservative MP in 1936, served as private secretary to R.A.B. Butler, Under-Secretary of State for Foreign Affairs from 1938 to 1941, and was eventually knighted in 1957.

TESS

Thomas Hardy, *Tess of the d'Urbervilles* (1891)

Mary Head Hardy
(1772–1857)

Further reading:
Mrs. F.E. Hardy, *The Early Life of Thomas Hardy 1840–1891* (1928), *The Later Years of Thomas Hardy 1892–1928* (1930), C.J. Webber, *Hardy of Wessex*

Thomas Hardy's subtitle for *Tess of the d'Urbervilles* was 'A Pure Woman Faithfully Presented', a concept that caused some hostility when the book first appeared. Tragically, the tale catalogues Tess's tribulations: after being seduced by Alec d'Urberville she loses her child; after being married to Angel Clare he abruptly deserts her on hearing her confession. Eventually, in despair, Tess is driven to stab d'Urberville. There is an elemental quality to Tess as Hardy describes her: 'On these lonely hills and dales her quiescent glide was of a piece with the element she moved in. Her flexuous and stealthy figure became an integral part of the scene.'

Although Hardy's powerful conclusion to his novel is artistic invention, the basic pattern of a poor woman's suffering is taken from the life of his grandmother Mary Head Hardy. She was born in Fawley, Berkshire, and by the time she was twenty-four had moved to Reading

(1965), W.R. Rutland, *Thomas Hardy – A Study of His Writings and Their Background* (1938), Robert Gittings, *Young Thomas Hardy* (1975), *The Older Hardy* (1980)

where she gave birth to an illegitimate child in 1796. The following year she was charged with stealing a copper tea-kettle and sent to the House of Correction in Reading. At that time the penalty for larceny was hanging and Mary Head lived with this threat for three months until she was released after her accusers failed to bring evidence against her in the Quarter Sessions of 25 April. In 1799 Mary Head met Hardy's grandfather Thomas in Puddletown, Dorset, and married him when she was already three months pregnant. Hardy was devoted to his grandmother who provided him with much material that he used in his poetry and fiction. In his poem 'One We Knew' he describes her: 'With cap-framed face and long gaze into the embers – /We seated around her knees – /She would dwell on such dead themes, not as one who remembers/But rather as one who sees.'

MILLY THEALE

Henry James, *The Wings of the Dove* (1902)

Minny Temple (1846–70)

Further reading: Robert Mark, *James's Later Novels – An Interpretation* (1960), Sallie Sears, *The Negative Imagination – Forms and Perspectives in the Novels of Henry James* (1968), Leon Edel, *The Life of Henry James* (4 vols., 1953–72)

Although the innocent American victim of an English plot in Henry James's *The Wings of the Dove*, millionairess Milly Theale achieves a posthumous victory of the spirit. On learning that Milly is dying of an incurable illness Kate Croy persuades the impecunious Merton Densher to feign undying affection for the American so that he will inherit her fortune and use it as the basis of a prosperous marriage to Kate. Milly is described as a young woman whose face 'was expressive, irregular, exquisite, both for speech and for silence. When Milly smiled it was a public event.' Although she discovers Kate's deception, Milly leaves her money to Merton and so her presence dwells with the other characters. Kate observes that, like a dove, Milly 'stretched out her wings, and. . . . They cover us' and tells Merton 'Her memory's your love.'

James based the character on his cousin Minny Temple who died of tuberculosis in 1870. In a letter to his mother James writes: 'As much as a human creature may, I fancy, she will survive in the unspeakably tender memory of her friends. No attitude of the heart seems tender and generous enough not to do her some unwilling hurt – now that she has melted away into such a dimmer image of sweetness and weakness! . . . She certainly never seemed to have come into this world for her own happiness – as that of others – or as anything but as a sort of divine reminder and quickness – a transcendent protest against our acquiescence in its grossness. To have known her is certainly an immense gain. . . . There is absolute balm in the thought of poor Minny and *rest* – rest and immortal absence.' James had been delighted when he met Minny in 1860 in Newport, Rhode Island, as she had both mental agility and social grace. It is possible that he never recovered from the shock of losing her and his most beautiful heroines – including Milly and the exuberantly open Isabel Archer in *The Portrait of a Lady* (1881) – are recreations of Minny.

THERESE

George Sand, *Elle et Lui* (1859)

Armandine Aurore Lucie Dupin, 'George Sand' (1804–76)

Further reading: Curtis Cate, *George Sand – A Biography* (1975), George Sand, *Histoire de ma Vie*, in *Oeuvres autobiographiques*, edited by George Lubin (1971)

In her novel *Elle et Lui*, George Sand recounted her love affair with the poet and dramatist Alfred de Musset (see LAURENT) from her point of view. Thérèse is a young painter with a highly developed sense of duty to her art and a loving and forgiving heart. Laurent is a handsome but irresponsible young gigolo, who takes to drink and spends all the money Thérèse manages to earn selling her canvasses.

George Sand was brought up by her grandmother at Nohant. At one time intending to be a nun, she inherited her grandmother's property, married, had two children, and then left for Paris where her first novel, *Indiana*, made her famous in 1832. She had a riotous love-life. She was seduced at the age of sixteen, and never looked back. Among her lovers were Frederic Chopin, Prosper Mérimèe and Gustave Planche. She also enjoyed liaisons with lovers of her own sex, including the actress Marie Dorval.

Her relationship with Alfred de Musset was passionate and tempestuous. After one of their more serious breaks, she was in such despair that she cut off all her hair, stuffed it into a skull and had it sent to him. This was a direct imitation of an incident in her novel *Indiana*. In the version of the story written by Alfred's brother Paul, *Lui et Elle*, the hair is delivered in a parcel to Alfred, who is in company in his rooms. He begins to open the package, sees what it contains, and shoves it in a drawer. He later laments over the shorn locks. In the story as told by Alfred's later mistress, Louise Colet (see EMMA BOVARY) George Sand delivers the hair in person, sinking to the floor at the hero's feet: 'her eyes seemed dark and hollow. . . . She did not utter a word . . . but . . . touched me with her sinister offering. I brushed it aside and it rolled onto the floor at my feet. Out of it flowed a long black tress of hair.'

Aurore took her name Sand from the novelist Jules Sandeau, with whom she had developed an intimacy between 1831 and 1833. She wrote a string of novels, dealing with forbidden love and social revolt. She was an ardent feminist and enemy of bourgeois conventions. In old age she was transformed into a kind old lady.

THERSITES

William Shakespeare, *Troilus and Cressida* (1602)

Henry Cuffe (1563–1601)

Further reading: Robert Naunton, *Fragmenta Regalia* (1630)

Homer presents Thersites as a crippled and vituperative officer in the Greek army during the Trojan war, constantly railing against his commanders. Achilles strikes him to the ground with his fists and kills him. In Shakespeare's play, he becomes a blistering commentator on the folly of the war and the stupidity of the military commanders: 'Shall the elephant Ajax carry it thus? He beats me, and I rail at him. O worthy satisfaction! . . . Then there's Achilles, a rare engineer! If Troy be not taken till these two undermine it, the walls will stand till they fall themselves.' Human beings, he asserts, have only one motive: 'Lechery, lechery; still, wars and lechery; nothing else holds fashion.' In some ways he plays the role of the Fool in Shakespearean dramas, that of a detached observer who comments on the action and undercuts the illusion and pretence of the leading characters; but in Thersites this is carried to the extreme, and he is bitter, foul-mouthed, abusive and cynical.

Some have argued that *Troilus and Cressida* is an allegorical treatment of the War of the Theatres. This would make Thersites either Ben Jonson or John Marston. But a more likely identification is made by John Dover Wilson in *The Essential Shakespeare* (1932), arguing that this is a portrayal of Henry Cuffe, secretary and companion to the Earl of Essex (see ACHILLES). Cuffe was an author and politician, educated at Oxford, where he was professor of Greek 1590-96. He accompanied Essex on the Cadiz expedition as his secretary, was loyal to his master when he was in disgrace, but proved an unfortunate and reckless advisor. He probably played a considerable part in the planning of the ill-fated *coup d'état* Essex attempted, although he did not personally take part in the action. Henry Cuffe wrote several books, including *The Differences of the Ages of Man's Life* (1600) and assisted Columbanus in his edition of Longus's Pastoral of *Daphnis and Chloe*. He was arrested and imprisoned after the Essex rebellion, and later executed. Sir Robert Naunton in his *Fragmenta Regalia* (1630) describes Cuffe as: 'a vile man, and of a perverse nature', who, with others, gave Essex bad advice, so that: 'when he was in the right course of recovery, and settling to moderation, would not suffer a recess in him, but stirred up the dregs of those rude humours, which by time, and his affliction, out of his own judgement he sought to repose; or to give them all a vomit'.

SADIE THOMPSON

W. Somerset Maugham, *The Trembling of a Leaf* (1921)

Miss Thompson

In 1916, on his way to Tahiti for material for *The Moon and Sixpence*, Somerset Maugham took the steamer *Sonoma* to Pago Pago, capital of Eastern Samoa. Among his fellow passengers was a Miss Thompson, a prostitute who had lost her livelihood when the police had closed down Honolulu's red-light district. She was on her way to Western Samoa to work as a barmaid in Apia and quickly became conspicuous on board since she flaunted herself sexually and played her gramophone incessantly, to the novelist's great annoyance. Also on board were a medical missionary and his wife and they, like Maugham, found Miss Thomp-

Further reading: Ted Walker, *Maugham* (1980)

son's loud and flirtatious behaviour unacceptable. Because of a quarantine inspection all the passengers were delayed in Pago Pago and Maugham, again enduring the unavoidable presence of Miss Thompson, speculated on what might happen if the missionary and Miss Thompson competed in a contest for moral supremacy.

The result was 'Rain', included in the collection *The Trembling of a Leaf*, in which the missionary becomes Mr Davidson whose 'sincerity was obvious in the fire of his gestures and in his deep, ringing voice'. Miss Thompson was made unforgettably fictional by the addition of the first name Sadie: 'She was twenty-seven perhaps, plump, and in a coarse fashion pretty. She wore a white dress and a large white hat. Her fat calves in white cotton stockings bulged over the tops of long white boots in glacé kid.' In the story the Revd Davidson's obsessive attempts to impose his rigid notions of joykilling morality on Sadie Thompson bring him into intimate contact with her. Unable to practise what he preaches, he succumbs to Sadie's obvious charms and afterwards cuts his throat. As the story ends Sadie is once more 'dressed in all her finery, in her white dress' and aggressive in her attitudes: 'You men! You filthy, dirty pigs! You're all the same, all of you, Pigs! Pigs!'

MARY TILFORD

Lillian Hellman, *The Children's Hour* (1934)

Jane Cumming (born 1795)

From a thirty-page account of an Edinburgh trial of 1811 in William Roughhead's *Bad Companions* (1930), Lillian Hellman extracted the source of her play *The Children's Hour*. Switching the story to the USA in her own time, Hellman has an adolescent girl, Mary Tilford, convince her doting grandmother that two women teachers operating a girls' boarding school are 'in love with each other'. The two women sue the grandmother for libel, and lose their suit, after which one of them, aware of her Lesbian tendencies, shoots herself. The play was twice filmed, with scripts by Hellman, by William Wyler: as *These Three* (1936), in which extramarital sex is substituted for the Lesbianism of the play; and as *The Loudest Whisper* (1961, the US distributors retaining the title of the play).

Hellman portrays Mary Tilford as a spoilt brat who causes trouble for two decent women. Mary Tilford's original was a more complex figure. Jane Cumming was the illegitimate child of George Cumming, of the Honourable East India Company, and an Indian woman. When Jane was five, her father died, and she was sent first to a school in Calcutta, then to Scotland, where Lady Helen Cumming, George Cumming's mother, accepted her as her natural granddaughter. In 1809 two young Edinburgh teachers, Jane Pirie and Marianne Woods, set up a School for Young Ladies in Edinburgh. When Lady Helen asked them (in 1810) to accept Jane Cumming as a pupil, Pirie and Woods were at first reluctant on account of Jane's colour, but enrolled her because of Lady Helen's social position.

In the summer of 1810, Pirie and Woods vacationed in Portobello, Edinburgh's seaside resort, and took Jane Cumming with them. The two women slept in the same bed, with Jane at its foot. When they went back to the school, Pirie slept in the same bed as Jane, while Woods often came through from her adjoining bedroom at night. Jane circulated stories about the sexual impropriety of her teachers, and Pirie and Woods sued Lady Helen when she repeated these stories. In the trial, before the Court of Session in Edinburgh in 1811, Jane Cumming said 'When Miss Woods came into bed, I felt them both take up their shifts, and I felt Miss Woods move and shake the bed, and Miss Woods was breathing so high and quick. Miss Woods was lying above Miss Pirie at this time.' Pirie and Woods lost the trial, but won the appeal the following year. Lady Helen then took the case to the House of Lords, where it dragged on until 1818, when once again Pirie and Woods were vindicated. Lady Helen reluctantly settled out of court, for a sum thought to be £2,000, but the two teachers were professionally ruined as a result – so Lillian Faderman argues in *Scotch Verdict* (1985) – of the statements of an adolescent, disturbed because of her illegitimacy and colour.

TIMON'S VILLA

Alexander Pope, *Moral Essays IV: Epistle to Burlington, Of Taste* (1731)

Country house of Sir Robert Walpole (1676–1845) **at Houghton, Norfolk**.

Pope's fourth Moral Epistle takes as the subject of its satire 'the *Vanity of Expence* in people of wealth and quality'. At a time when the wealth of the nation was expanding as a result of successful colonial wars and the consequent development of overseas trade, the wealthy and fashionable vaunted their riches by conspicuous consumption on a vast scale. The ownership and extensive decoration of houses was one obvious way in which people could demonstrate their wealth, owning several properties in town and country, and adding wings and extensions to existing properties, which then could be filled with vast collections of paintings, statuary, volumes and other objects. Pope puts before us the person of the wealthy Timon who owns a huge country house: 'At Timon's villa let us pass a day,/Where all cry out, "What sums are thrown away!"/So proud, so grand: of that stupendous air,/Soft and agreeable come never there./Greatness, with Timon, dwells in such a draught/As brings all Brobdignag before your thought./To compass this, his building is a town,/His pond an ocean, his parterre a down:/Who but must laugh, the master when he sees,/A puny insect, shivering at a breeze!' Timon's house is full of books he never reads, of paintings he never regards, statues he hardly notices, his chapel given over to vanities and his banquet so lavish and punctilious that none can enjoy it.

At the time this satire was attacked as aimed at Lord Chandos's seat at Cannons. This was fabricated by Leonard Welsted (1688-1747), an enemy of Pope's, so that attention would be diverted from the real object of Pope's attack – Sir Robert Walpole's lavish expenditure on his house at Houghton, the construction of which occupied him between 1722 and 1735. His huge extravagances – he owned several properties in London, including a house in New Park, Richmond – provided his political opponents with constant ammunition in the form of claims and assertions that he appropriated public funds. It was rumoured he spent £100,000 on his collection of paintings, £14,000 on his hunting lodge at Richmond and additional thousands on his establishments at Chelsea and London. The rent-roll of his estate in Norfolk was between £5,000 and £8,000 by 1740, he made a fortune out of South Sea stock (a thousand per cent profit when he sold), and from official sources he had £9,000 a year, as well as profits made while he was Paymaster to the armed forces. He dominated British politics as leader of the Whigs until his resignation in 1742, and maintained himself in office by well-oiled political machinery which included bribery and various forms of corruption. His paintings were sold to the Empress of Russia – at a considerable profit. When he retired, with a house full of books, he said he had lost his taste for reading. (see ORGILIO and COCK-ROBIN).

Further reading:
John Barnard, *Pope – The Critical Heritage* (1973), Kathleen Mahaffrey, 'Timon's Villa—Walpole's Houghton' in *Texas Studies in Literature and Language*, IX (1967) pp. 193–222, Maynard Mack, *The Garden and the City* (1969)

TITAN

Morgan Robertson, *Futility* (1898)

White Star liner, Titanic (1912)

There is a term used in psychology for a dream or a memory of future events – *promesia*. There is an extraordinary literary example of promesia in Morgan Robertson's novel *Futility*, which was published in 1898. It narrates the story of a huge passenger liner which was perceived as a miracle of modern engineering – an unsinkable floating palace – named the *Titan*. It sinks during its maiden voyage after striking an iceberg. Almost the entire crew and passengers are drowned in the disaster, mainly because there were insufficient numbers of lifeboats. Fourteen years later, on 14 April 1912, the White Star liner *Titanic* struck an iceberg on its maiden voyage. It was at that time the largest ship afloat, and it struck the iceberg at full speed, stripping off her bilge almost from end to end. It sank within three hours. Of the 2,206 passengers only 703 were saved, picked up by the *Carpathia*, which had answered the *Titanic*'s distress signals. The commission of enquiry into the disaster concluded that the main cause of loss of life was that there were not enough lifeboats, and that boat-drill was inadequate. The *Titanic* sank on the fifth day of her trip to New York. The similarities are extraordinary. The *Titan* was 800 feet long; the *Titanic* 882.5 feet long. The *Titan's* tonnage was 75,000; and the *Titanic's* 66,000. Both vessels had three propellers. The *Titan* was travelling at the speed of twenty-five knots; the *Titanic* at twenty-three knots. There were 3,000 passengers on board the *Titan*; the *Titanic* had 2,206. The *Titan* had twenty-four lifeboats, the *Titanic* had twenty. Both ships sank in the month of April. The coincidences are striking. The *Titan* was a prescient original of the *Titanic*. The real-life disaster is meticulously detailed in Walter Lord's *A Night to Remember* (1956).

UNCLE TOM

Harriet Beecher Stowe, *Uncle Tom's Cabin* (1852)

Josiah Henson, a Maryland slave

Further reading: Edward Wagenknecht, *Harriet Beecher Stowe – The Known and Unknown* (1965), Edmund Wilson, *Patriotic Gore* (1962)

Uncle Tom's Cabin or *Life Among the Lowly*, was first serialized in the *National Era* from June 1851, an in book form became an international bestseller, translated into twenty-three languages and praised by George Sand, Turgenev, Heine and Dickens.

The political impact of this anti-slavery novel was tremendous. It pictured in colour and vividness scenes which fuelled anti-slavery sentiments. Lincoln is reputed to have said on meeting Mrs Stowe: 'So this is the little lady who made this big war!' The theme of the book is the buying and selling of slaves as if they were so much cattle, the heartless dividing of their families and the brutal treatment of the slaves by their owners. The one scene remembered by all who read the book is Uncle Tom being beaten to death by Simon Legree, deliberately portrayed as a Yankee come South to make his fortune. Mrs Stowe wrote later: 'Human nature is no worse at the South than at the North; but the law at the South distinctly provides for and protects the worst abuses to which that nature is liable.' (*Key to Uncle Tom's Cabin*, 1853.) Tom is portrayed as a true Christian martyr. He is converted at a revival meeting and subsequently acts in the manner of the primitive martyrs of the Christian church. In her view the churches of the North should defy the Fugitive Slave Law of 1850, educate escaped slaves, and help them get to Liberia and set up a true Christian republic there. The black man's ideal state was to be realized not in the USA but in Africa.

An apparently deeply religious woman, Mrs Stowe claimed that Uncle Tom was given to her in a vision during a communion service in Brunswick, Maine. Here she suddenly saw an old and ragged slave being cruelly beaten. The claim she was to make as being merely God's amanuensis must be seriously qualified by the fact that she met Josiah Henson earlier in her life. He had been abused while a slave in the South and had made his escape by the underground railway, up North to Canada, where he was instrumental in establishing an all-black Utopia in Ontario. He was something of a celebrity and was introduced to Queen Victoria in London. Mrs Stowe commented that she met him in Boston in 1850 at her brother's house and read his account of his life (seventy-six pages long) which 'furnished me many of the finest conceptions and incidents of Uncle Tom's character'.

POLLY TOODLE

Charles Dickens, *Dombey and Son* (1848)

Mrs Hayes (née Littlefair)

Further reading: Edwin Pugh, *The Charles Dickens Originals* (1912)

Polly Toodle is employed by Mr Dombey as a wet-nurse for his baby son Paul (see PAUL DOMBEY) after his wife has died in childbirth. She is a: 'Plump rosy-cheeked wholesome apple-faced young woman' and the mother of five children. She is warm-hearted and loving, and gives Paul more than mother's-milk. She provides him with love and attention far beyond the call of duty, but, for Mr Dombey, it is entirely a matter of hire and salary: 'Oh, of course', Mr Dombey says, 'I desire to make it a question of wages altogether.' He even insists that she alter her name to 'Richards', which he finds more suitable than her real name: 'Now, Richards, if you nurse my bereaved child, I wish you to remember this always. You will receive a liberal stipend in return for the discharge of certain duties, in the performance of which I desire you to see as little of your family as possible. When these duties cease to be required and rendered, and the stipend ceases to be paid, there is an end of all relations between us . . . You have children of your own . . . It is not at all in this bargain that you need become attached to my child, or that my child need become attached to you . . . When you go away from here, you will have concluded what is a mere matter of bargain and sale, hiring and letting; and you will stay away. The child will cease to remember you; and you will cease, if you please, to remember the child.' She is dismissed when she returns to see her own family, thus 'taking Paul into haunts and society which are not to be thought of without a shudder.' She lived in Staggs's Gardens, Camden Town, through which the London to Birmingham railway line was constructed. When Paul is taken ill and lies on his death-bed, he asks to see his old nurse, Polly, again.

This affectionate portrait of a loving child-nurse is drawn from the character of Mrs Hayes, who was a domestic servant to Harry Burnett, who married Charles Dickens's sister, and was the father of the little crippled child on whom the novelist based the character of Paul Dombey. When Dickens told Mrs Hayes (who came from Manchester) that she was the original of Polly Toodle, she said: 'Wot larx!'

MAX TOWN

Anthony West, *Heritage* (1955)

H.G. Wells (1866–1946)

Further reading: Anthony West, *Aspects of a Life* (1984)

At the beginning of Anthony West's novel *Heritage* the narrator, Richard Savage, lives in London with his mother Naomi, an actress. Richard is an illegitimate child, and when he goes to St Michael's school for boys he learns the identity of his father and contemplates 'the strange and unexpected discovery that my father was Max Town. He was divided from me by something harder to cross than a mere row of footlights, a barrier of print and a reputation. I had seen his photograph beside feature articles on the League of Nations and similar subjects of political aspect in the daily papers, a darkly foreboding, serious, public face, and I had seen his name on the backs of books. Such a person seemed remote and dead, as far off as Dickens and Thackeray, quite out of the world I inhabited.' Max – in the company of Lolotte, the Grafin von Essling-Sterlinghoven – visits Richard's school and impresses his son as a man of great charm. Winning the right to have access to Richard, Max welcomes his son to his apartment in Paris: 'For a week or ten days Max would give up all his time and his energy to playing with me, treating the city as if it was a fair which had been set up for our amusement.' With his warmth, and his difficult life with Lolotte (who dies during the novel), Max is a sympathetic character; a man of immense drive and incisive intellect, who is contrasted with the narrator's mother, Naomi.

As West acknowledges in the first British edition of *Heritage* (1984), Max Town and NAOMI SAVAGE were intended as portraits of his parents, H.G. Wells and Rebecca West. Wells met Rebecca West in 1912, after she had reviewed his novel *Marriage* (1912) for the *Freewoman*, a feminist weekly. The two writers were immediately attracted and West, their illegitimate child, was born on 4 August 1914. Twice married in a productive lifetime, Wells was fascinated by women, and found Rebecca West not only exciting, but intellectually his equal. 'She was,' said Wells, 'the only woman who ever made me stop and wonder when she said "Look".' Anthony West was adopted by his mother, but grew to dislike Rebecca West, and resent her hostile references to Wells, whose work he admired, and whose career he surveyed in *H.G. Wells* (1984). In an interview in the *Guardian*, prior to the British publication of *Heritage*, West said of his parents: 'she had a very large view of herself and when she realized he wasn't going to marry her, she couldn't endure the defeat as she saw it. Vexation turned to hatred and then to mania [but I] realized HG was not the comic, absurd figure she tried to make him.'

TOMMY TRADDLES

Charles Dickens, *David*

Tommy Traddles is a pupil at Salem House, and a very good friend to David Copperfield. He is best man at David's wedding. He becomes a distinguished barrister: 'Poor Traddles! In a tight sky-blue suit that

Copperfield (1850)
Sir Thomas Noon Talford (1795–1854)

Further reading: Una Pope-Hennessy, *Charles Dickens 1812–1870* (1945), Arthur L. Hayward, *The Dickens Encyclopaedia* (1924), Edwin Pugh, *The Charles Dickens Originals* (1912)

made his arms and legs like German sausages, or roly-poly puddings, he was the merriest and most miserable of all the boys. He was always being caned – I think he was caned every day that half-year, except one holiday Monday when he was only ruler'd on both hands – and was always going to write to his uncle about it, and never did. After laying his head on the desk for a little while, he would cheer up somehow, begin to laugh again, and draw skeletons all over his slate, before his eyes were dry. I used at first to wonder what comfort Traddles found in drawing skeletons; and for some time looked upon him as a sort of hermit, who reminded himself by those symbols of mortality that caning couldn't last for ever. But I believe he only did it because they were easy, and didn't want any features.' He next turns up as a law student at Mr Waterbrook's. He lodges with Micawber (see WILKINS MICAWBER), and assists in the unmasking of Uriah Heep. At the end of the novel he is happily married and about to be made a judge.

Traddles is based on Dickens's close friend Thomas Talford, who was educated at Mill Hill (a dissenting school) and at Reading School, under Richard Valpy. He studied law, and became quite a prolific essayist and poet, also writing a tragedy, *Ion*, in the Greek style. He was a friend of Charles Lamb, William Wordsworth and Samuel Coleridge. He was made a serjeant at law in 1833, and justice of common pleas in 1849. He was elected MP for Reading in 1835, 1837 and 1841. Dickens wrote of him: 'Talford delightful, and amuses me mightily. I am really quite enraptured at his success and think of his happiness with uncommon pleasure.' John Forster in his *Life of Charles Dickens* (1874) says that he adorned the bench with 'qualities that are justly the pride of that profession, and with accomplishments which have become more rare in its highest places . . . His elevation only made those virtues better known . . . he continued to be the most joyous and least affected of companions. Such small oddities or foibles as he had made him secretly only dearer to Dickens, who had no friend he was more attached to . . .' Dickens dedicated *Pickwick Papers* to Talford.

TREEBEARD

J.R.R. Tolkien, *The Lord of the Rings* (1954–55)
C.S. Lewis (1898–1963)

Further reading: Humphrey Carpenter, *J.R.R. Tolkien – A Biography* (1977), Roger Lancelyn Green and Walter Hooper, *C.S. Lewis – A Biography* (1974), Robert Giddings, *J.R.R. Tolkien – This Far Land* (1984)

Treebeard is the venerable Guardian Ent, of the most ancient race of all in Middle-earth. They were ancient as the trees they looked after, 'fathers of the fathers of trees, remembering times when they were lords'. In Treebeard's words: 'Elves began it, of course, waking trees up and teaching them to speak and learning their tree-talk.' Merry and Pippin wander away during a battle between Orcs and the Riders of Rohan, and find themselves in Fangorn Forest. They feel safe, even though they have no food and shelter, and when Pippin says that he almost felt he liked the place, a strange voice says: 'Almost felt you liked the Forest! That's good! That's uncommonly kind of you.' Very gently they are turned round by knob-knuckled hands laid on their shoulders, and they find themselves looking at Treebeard: 'a large Man-like, almost Troll-like, figure, at least fourteen-feet high, very sturdy, with a tall head, and hardly any neck . . . the arms were not wrinkled, but covered with a brown smooth skin. The large feet had seven toes each. The lower part of the face was covered with a sweeping grey beard, bushy, almost twiggy at the roots, thin and mossy at the ends . . . the eyes were now surveying them, slow and solemn, but very penetrating. They were brown, shot with a green light.' Treebeard has a remarkable voice, deep 'like a very deep woodwind instrument', and he often hummed and haahed in special Ent-like way, going 'Hrum, Hoom!'

Treebeard is the ultimate idealization of Tolkien's love for trees. He told his Oxford colleague Nevill Coghill that when he came to write this chapter, he modelled Treebeard's way of speaking 'on the booming voice of C.S. Lewis'. Lewis was a friend and colleague of Tolkien's at Oxford, and a member of that exclusive male club, The Inklings, which included Charles Williams, Hugo Dyson, Warren Hamilton Lewis (C.S. Lewis's brother) and Jim Dundas-Grant. Tolkien and Lewis were initially wary of each other; Lewis distrusted Catholics and philologists (Tolkien was both), and Tolkien sensed that as a scholar more interested in literature than in language Lewis might oppose his plans for reforms in the Oxford English syllabus. But Tolkien warmed 'to Lewis's quick mind and the generous spirit that was as huge as Lewis's shapeless flannel trousers', writes Humphrey Carpenter, in his biography of Tolkien. The friendship was very long and very close, but cooled rather when Lewis befriended Charles Williams, and later when he married Joy Davidman. Lewis was Fellow and Tutor at Magdalen College, 1925–54, and Professor of Medieval and Renaissance English at Cambridge from 1954. He wrote numerous works of scholarship as well as a series of popular religious sci-fi romances for young readers, the Narnia saga.

TRILBY

George du Maurier, *Trilby* (1894)

Carry of Malines

Further reading:
As for SVENGALI

Trilby O'Ferrall, the heroine of George du Maurier's *Trilby*, enchanted America when the novel first appeared in the pages of *Harper's Magazine* and subsequently caused a sensation in England where the book came out in three volumes. The story of the poor, tone-deaf artist's model, transformed into a celebrated singer by Svengali, produced a Trilby craze. There were Trilby hats and Trilby songs, Trilby soaps and Trilby toothpastes; and a town in Florida, USA, was named Trilby.

Du Maurier conceived the character as a result of his stay in Malines, Belgium, in the late 1850s. With his great friend Felix Moscheles, du Maurier frequented the back parlour of a local tobacco store. Octavie, the daughter of the proprietress, was nicknamed Carry (a corruption of Cigar) by Moscheles and du Maurier who both adored her. Carry's tobacco store background is alluded to in the novel when Trilby 'sat herself down cross-legged on the model throne and made herself a cigarette'. As Moscheles wrote in *In Bohemia with Du Maurier* (1897) carry 'looked upon us as superior beings, and, granting her points of comparison, not without cause; du Maurier could draw and I could paint; he could sing and I could mesmerize, and couldn't we just both talk beautifully!' Although Moscheles was unable to mesmerize Carry, du Maurier had the creative time of his life imagining what might happen to such a girl who succumbed to the hypnotic power of one she regarded as a 'superior being'. Daphne du Maurier, in *The Du Mauriers* (1937), supposes that when her grandfather came to write Trilby 'he brought [Carry of Malines] out and polished her and beautified her, and breathed a little of his own charm upon her, and Trilby, the freckled Irish giantess, was born, with her clubbed hair and fringe, her military coat, her exquisite feet thrust into a pair of men's slippers.

MRS TROTTER

John Hawkesworth, BBC/Time-Life television series, *The Duchess of Duke Street* (1976–77)

Rosa Lewis (1867-1952)

Further reading:
Daphne Fielding: *The Duchess of Jermyn Street* (1964)

The heroine of *The Duchess of Duke Street* is a cook in a rich London household. She attracts the attention of the Prince of Wales, who is a frequent house-guest. To facilitate their liaison, she goes through the process of marrying Trotter, who is also in service. Her husband takes to drink and dies, and her affair with Edward comes to an end. But she is a cook of genius and a brilliant hotel administrator. Her establishment in Duke Street becomes famous for its hospitality.

The TV series, starring Gemma Jones as Mrs Trotter, narrated the fortunes and vicissitudes of life in the hotel in Duke Street from 1909 to the end of the First World War. Notable among her staff were the porter, Star, and his dog, Fred; the melancholy butler, Merriman; and sundry maids. Mrs Trotter has a poignant affair with the young Lord Hazelmere, (Christopher Cazenove), who is killed in the war.

The series was based on Rosa Lewis, brilliant cook, and founder of the Cavendish Hotel (see LOTTIE CRUMP), who worked for the Comte de Paris and Lady Randolph Churchill. She was certainly noticed by the Prince of Wales, and it was rumoured that she was the mistress of the heir apparent and of Lord Ribblesdale. She was a very handsome young woman, tall and well-made, with silky dark brown hair and deeply set blue eyes. She married Excelsior Lewis when she was twenty-five, and he was four years older. He had been a butler to Sir Andrew Clarke, and had saved enough for them to run a boarding house in Eaton Terrace. Soon bored with this life, she took a post as a cook. Her husband now took seriously to drink. Rosa then started cooking in various distinguished households by special invitation. In Coronation year, 1902, she provided twenty-nine suppers at various balls. In the same year she bought the Cavendish Hotel in Jermyn Street, which she immortalized by her catering and hospitality. Among her staff was the famous Steffany, who was deaf and nearly blind; his face was reminiscent of gargoyle fringed with cobweb. His back was bent, he moved with ponderous dignity, and when he died he was succeeded by Moon, a grumpy, skinny old man. Her first hall-porter was named Scott, who had a fox-terrier named Freddy. She was the complete hostess, celebrated for her care of her customers' hangovers and other hazards. Evelyn Waugh recorded that when young men had been at pleasure, she would say: 'I'll get a doctor to look at your winkle.' After Rosa died the Cavendish was run by Edith Jeffrey, a friend of Rosa's. It was rebuilt in 1963.

BETSY TROTWOOD

Charles Dickens, *David Copperfield* (1850)

Miss Strong, of Broadstairs

Further reading: Edwin Pugh, *The Charles Dickens Originals* (1912)

Betsy Trotwood is David Copperfield's great aunt, who has always had a rather grim and unyielding view of David's mother. However, when Mrs Copperfield marries Mr Murdstone, and his stepfather's cruelties eventually force David to run away, he runs to Betsy in Dover. Beneath her rather austere exterior, she has a heart of gold, and a view of the world and its behaviour which is sagacious and mature. She was present when David was born, and is continuously present in the novel as David's guide, philosopher and friend. She gives him a sound education and sets him up in life. She is a very strong character, almost masculine, and has considerable resources to draw on at moments of crisis. She faces up to the Murdstones, for example, and assists in the overthrow of Uriah Heep: 'My aunt was a tall, hard-featured lady, but by no means ill-looking. There was an inflexibility in her face, in her voice, in her gait and carriage, amply sufficient to account for the effect she had made upon a gentle creature like my mother; but her features were rather handsome than otherwise, though unbending and austere. I particularly noticed that she had a very quick, bright eye.' She has an obsession with keeping donkeys away from her front door, which they frequently passed, as her house was on the coast at Dover: 'Janet had gone away to get the bath ready, when my aunt, to my great alarm, became in one moment rigid with indignation, and had hardly voice to cry out, "Janet! Donkeys!" Upon which, Janet came running up the stairs as if the house were in flames, darted out on a little piece of green in front, and warned off two saddle-donkeys, lady-ridden, that had presumed to set hoof upon it; while my aunt, rushing out of the house, seized the bridle of a third animal laden with a bestriding child, turned him, led him forth from those sacred precincts, and boxed the ears of the unlucky urchin in attendance who had dared to profane that hallowed ground. To this hour I don't know whether my aunt had any lawful right of way over that patch of green; but she had settled it in her own mind that she had, and it was all the same to her . . .'

This is a portrait of Miss Strong of Broadstairs, according to Frederick Kitton (*Charles Dickens by Pen and Pencil*, 1890): 'She occupied a double fronted cottage in the middle of . . . the sea front; and, like the admirable Betsy, she was firmly convinced of her right to stop the passage of donkeys along the road, opposite her door, deterring their proprietors by means of hostile demonstrations with a hearth broom.' Her house is now Dickens house, Victoria Parade, Broadstairs.

TOM TULLIVER

George Eliot, *The Mill on the Floss* (1860)

Central to George Eliot's novel *The Mill on the Floss* is the relationship between Maggie Tulliver and her brother Tom. Maggie is, especially in the early stages of the book, a self-portrait of Mary Ann Evans (as the author was called before adopting the pseudonym George Eliot in 1857):

Isaac Pearson Evans
(1816–90)

Further reading:
M. Blind, *George Eliot* (1883), Gerald Bullett, *George Eliot and Her Novels* (1947)

Tom, the obstinate brother, is Isaac Pearson Evans.

As Mary Ann's senior by three years Isaac was the object of her adoration, as *The Mill on the Floss* and the sonnet-sequence 'Brother and Sister' (1874) show. When Isaac turned against her, Mary Ann must have reacted like Maggie Tulliver who 'felt the hatred in his face, felt it rushing through her fibres'. In June 1840 Isaac married Sarah Rawlins and, when Mary Ann offended her father in 1842 by her refusal to go to church, he invited his sister to Griff House (her childhood home) and persuaded her to make the gesture of accompanying her father to church – which she did until his death in 1849.

A more serious crisis arose in 1854 when Mary Ann decided to live with Henry George Lewes; three years later she wrote to Isaac explaining the situation and he broke off all relations with her. A Tractarian, he did not relent and only resumed contact with her on 17 May 1880 when Lewes was dead and Mary Ann married her admirer J.W. Cross. On 29 December, that same year, Mary Ann was buried in Highgate Cemetery; among the mourners there was, said George Eliot's biographer Oscar Browning, an elderly man 'tall and slightly bent, his features recalling with a striking veracity the lineaments of the dead'. Isaac had come to pay his last respects to the sister who concluded *The Mill on the Floss* with wishful thinking: 'after the flood [the] two bodies . . . were found in close embrace . . . In their death they were not divided.'

MARY TYRONE

Eugene O'Neill, *Long Day's Journey into Night* (1956)

Ella O'Neill (1857–1922)

Further reading:
Arthur and Barbara Gelb, *O'Neill* (1962), L. Sheaffer, *Eugene O'Neill – Son and Playwright* (1968)

Eugene O'Neill's *Long Day's Journey into Night* was completed in 1941 but not performed until 1956, three years after the dramatist's death. O'Neill had decided on a posthumous production because the play is so intensely autobiographical. The Tyrone family is a group-portrait of the O'Neills with Eugene as Edmund and his alcoholic brother Jamie as Jamie Tyrone. James, O'Neill's father, is in the play (as in life) a man who has known success and celebrity as a Shakespearean actor. The truly tragic presence comes with Mary Cavan Tyrone, Edmund's mother, whose drug addiction haunts all the other characters as she drifts around the house like a ghost. During the drama Mary justifies her pitiful condition by alluding to the difficult birth of Edmund: 'I was so healthy before Edmund was born. You remember, James. There wasn't a nerve in my body. . . . But bearing Edmund was the last straw. I was so sick afterwards, and that ignorant quack of a cheap hotel doctor – All he knew was I was in pain. It was easy for him to stop the pain.'

Ella O'Neill was born Mary Ellen Quinlan in New Haven, Connecticut. At the age of fifteen she was sent to a convent and, like Mary in O'Neill's play, 'wanted to be a nun'. An accomplished pianist, she graduated in 1875 with honours in music; two years later she married James O'Neill, the handsome actor she had admired since first seeing him in her father's house in 1872. After the birth of Eugene in 1888, Ella (as James called her) was in considerable pain; accordingly a doctor friendly with James gave her morphine to comfort her. She quickly became addicted as O'Neill discovered when he came home from school one day in 1900 to find his mother in the act of injecting herself. Mary, in the play, explains the appeal of morphine for the addict: 'It kills the pain. You go back until at last you are happy beyond its reach. Only the past when you were happy is real.'

U

ARTURO UI

Bertolt Brecht, *The Resistible Rise of Arturo Ui* (1958)

Adolf Hitler (1889–1945)

Further reading: John Willett, *Brecht in Context* (1984), Ronald Hayman, *Brecht – A Biography* (1983), John Willett, *The Theatre of Bertolt Brecht* (1959)

Bertolt Brecht's *The Resistible Rise of Arturo Ui* was written in 1941, shortly before the dramatist arrived in America. He had long been fascinated by stories and films about crime in Chicago and saw in the career of a gangster like Al Capone a precedent for the ruthless rise to power of Adolf Hitler. In the play, the burning of a warehouse represents the Reichstag fire and the machine-gun massacre in a garage suggests Hitler's purge of 30 June 1934. Arturo's ambition is to achieve greatness in a criminal context and he sets out to succeed by taking over the greengrocery business in Chicago. By terrorist tactics he increases his authority over his rivals but what he seeks, above all, is an image that will impress the 'little man', the source of demagogic power. Coached by an actor, Arturo adopts pseudo-Shakespearean mannerisms as he postures as a man of honour among thieves. Addressing a group of vegetable dealers he says (in Ralph Manheim's translation) 'For such is man. He'll never put aside/His hardware of his own free will, say/For love of virtue, or to earn the praises/Of certain silver tongues at City Hall./If I don't shoot, the other fellow will.'

Hitler's actual career, up to 1935, is closely paralleled in the play. In 1933 President Hindenburg (Old Dogsborough) appointed Hitler as Chancellor on condition that the East Aid scandal, involving Hindenburg, was suppressed. Once entrusted with political office Hitler astonished his colleagues by his fierce appetite for violence. Nevertheless he also aspired to statesmanship and employed an actor to train him in the art of declamation thus increasing his already considerable gifts as an orator. After the Reichstag fire of February 1933 Hitler unleashed the deadly Night of the Long Knives as a prelude to his reign of terror. Hence, in an epilogue, Brecht warns his audience that 'The world was almost won by such an ape!'

UNA

Edmund Spenser, *The Faerie Queene* (1589, 1596)

Elizabeth I, Queen of England, (1533–1603)

Further reading: K. Williams, *Spenser's Faerie Queene – The World of Glass* (1966)

Queen Elizabeth I appears several times in the complex allegorical structure of *The Faerie Queene*. She is Gloriana, the Queen of Fairyland, whose twelve days of festivities were to be the occasion for the narration of the adventures of the twelve knights whose stories – Spenser intended – should comprise *The Faerie Queene*. She is Belphoebe, the virgin huntress, who nurses the wounded squire Timias back to health. She is also Mercila, whose kingdom is threatened by the Souldan (see GRANTORTO). Above all, she appears as Una, who is saved by the Redcrosse knight, in Book I of Spenser's epic, from the dangers variously posed by Archimago (hypocrisy), Sansfoy (faithlessness), Fidessa, who is really Duessa (see DUESSA) in disguise (falsehood), Sansloy (lawlessness), Sansjoy (joylessness), and who finally saves Redcrosse himself by preventing his suicide after he has met the spectre of Despair. Spenser portrays her radiantly: 'A lovely Ladie rode him faire beside/Upon a lowly Asse more white than snow,/Yet she much whiter; but the same did hide/Under a vele, that wimpled was full low;/And over all a blacke stole shee did throw/As one that inly mournd, so was she sad,/And heavie sate upon her palfrey slow;/Seemed in heart some hidden care she had,/And by her, in a line, a milkwhite lambe she lad.' The lamb signifies her innocence: 'So pure and innocent, as that same lambe,/She was in life and every vertuous lore;/And by descent from Royall lynage came/Of ancient Kinges and Queenes, that had of yore/Their scepters stretcht from East to Westerne shore/And all the world in their subjection held . . .' Sir Robert Naunton, writing about 1630, said of the person of Queen Elizabeth: 'She was of personage tall, of hair and complexion fair, and therewith well favoured, but high nosed, of limbs and feature neat, and which added to the lustre of those exterior Graces, of Stately and

Majestick comportment; participating in this more of her Father than Mother, who was of inferior allay, plausible, or as the French hath it, more *debonaire* and affable, vertues which might well suit with Majesty; and which descending, as Hereditary to the daughter, did render of a more sweeter temper, and endeared her more to the love and liking of the people; who gave her the name and fame of a most gracious and popular Prince; the atrocity of her Fathers nature, being rebated in hers, by the Mothers sweeter inclinations' (see PRINCE ARTHUR). Elizabeth was the daughter of Henry VIII and Anne Boleyn.

JULIAN UNDERWOOD

C.P. Snow, *In Their Wisdom* (1974)

William Gerhardie (1895–1977)

Further reading: Philip Snow, *Stranger and Brother* (1982)

C.P. Snow's novel *In Their Wisdom* concerns a legal dispute over a will that names Julian Underwood as heir to a fortune. The two women in Julian's life – his mother and Elizabeth, daughter of Lord Hillmorton – wait as he defends his iegal right to the money. Ever optimistic, Julian is convinced he will overcome any threat to his sudden financial security. Julian is a man of moods who looks, so Elizabeth thinks, 'like a wicked baby'. He is self-centred, since 'Anything which gave him pleasure, provided it didn't get in his own way, was a good idea.' Ultimately, though, he is formidable; 'It took an abnormally strong will to live as Julian had lived, doing nothing which he didn't want to do. It wasn't admirable, it could be at the same time silly and destructive, but it was there. His mother knew this. She had lost in every conflict of wills since he was a child. His women knew it, Liz most clearly of all. Maybe it gave him his power over them.'

According to the novelist's brother Philip Snow, the character of Julian Underwood was modelled on the author William Gerhardie, whose work C.P. Snow greatly admired. Born in St Petersburg, the son of a British industrialist, Gerhardie was posted, during the First World War, to the staff of the British Military Attaché at Petrograd, and in 1918 went with the British Military Mission to Siberia. After the war he was educated at Oxford, and in 1922 published his first novel *Futility*. When *The Polyglots* appeared in 1925, Gerhardie scored a great critical triumph and became, as Arnold Bennett observed, 'the pet of the intelligentsia and the darling of Mayfair'. In 1931 Gerhardie moved into Rossetti House, London, where he stayed for the rest of his life in increasing isolation. Introducing Gerhardie's posthumously published *God's Fifth Column* (1981), Michael Holroyd and Robert Skidelsky write: 'For more than forty years he travelled nowhere, but lived in increasing poverty, eventually without newspapers, radio, gramophone, television and, for much of the time, adequate heating. He was a hermit in the West End of London, his only link with the world an endless telephone line and the remembrance of things past.' The revival of interest in his work in the 1970s substantiated Snow's claim that Gerhardie was 'a comic writer of genius'.

UNREAL CITY

T.S. Eliot, *The Waste Land* (1922)

Bertrand Russell's Vision of Unreality

Further reading: Bertrand Russell, *Autobiography* (1967–9)

T.S. Eliot's *The Waste Land*, one of the masterpieces of modernism, juxtaposes several notions, including the spectacle of cultural collapse in a great city. The first section of the sequence, 'The Burial of the Dead', concludes with a passage that reads like a transcription of a nightmare: 'Unreal City,/Under the brown fog of a winter dawn,/A crowd flowed over London Bridge, so many,/I had not thought death had undone so many./Sighs, short and infrequent, were exhaled,/And each man fixed his eyes before his feet./Flowed up the hill and down King William Street,/To where Saint Mary Woolnoth kept the hours/With a dead sound on the final stroke of nine.'

One of the formative influences on Eliot was Bertrand Russell, who taught the poet symbolic logic in a Harvard postgraduate class in 1914, and, the following year, let Eliot and his first wife Vivien live with him at his flat in Russell Chambers, Bury Street, London. During the First World War, Russell was opposed to conscription, and in 1917 was sentenced to six months in prison for proclaiming his pacifist faith.

Russell was deeply disturbed by the horror of a world at war, and reacted emotionally. In his autobiography he recalled: 'After seeing troop trains departing from Waterloo, I used to have strange visions of London as a place of unreality. I used in imagination to see the bridges collapse and sink, and the whole great city vanish like a morning mist. Its inhabitants began to seem like hallucinations, and I would wonder whether the world in which I thought I had lived was a mere product of my own febrile nightmare.'

Russell spoke of his 'visions of London as a place of unreality' to Eliot, who incorporated the imagery into the *The Waste Land,* which also alludes, by means of a popular song, to the collapse of bridges: 'London Bridge is falling down, falling down, falling down' ('What the thunder said'). Writing to Russel on 15 October 1923 Eliot said; 'I was delighted to get your letter. It gives me very great pleasure to know that you like the *Waste Land* . . . I must tell you that 18 months ago, before it was published anywhere, Vivien wanted me to send you the MS. to read, because she was sure that you were one of the very few persons who might possibly see anything in it.'

PRINCESS URQUHART
D.H. Lawrence, 'The Princess' (1925)
Dorothy Brett
(1883–1977)

Further reading:
Sean Hignett, *Brett* (1984)

D.H. Lawrence's story 'The Princess' (first published in the Calendar of Modern Letters) tells of an ageing virgin's sexual encounter with a Mexican guide with whom she goes into the Rockies. Shocked by his possession of her, which extends to keeping her his prisoner, she is 'slightly crazy' by the time she is rescued by the Forest Service (one of whose men shoots the Mexican guide). Dollie Urquhart, the heroine, is known as the Princess because her father applies this pet name to her: 'People called her Princess Urquhart, as if that were her christened name.' The Princess is thirty-eight when her father dies, and unchanged in appearance: 'She was still tiny, and like a dignified, scentless flower. Her soft brownish hair, almost the colour of beaver fur, was bobbed, and fluffed softly round her apple-blossom face, that was modelled with an arched nose like a proud old Florentine portrait. In her voice, manner and bearing she was exceedingly still, like a flower that has blossomed in a shadowy place . . . She was the Princess, and sardonically she looked out on a princeless world.' Until, that is, she comes to New Mexico and meets her Mexican guide.

Princess Urquhart was modelled, according to Catherine Carswell, on the Honourable Dorothy Brett, whom Lawrence met in 1915. In 1924 Lawrence went to America in the company of his wife Frieda and 'the Brett', or 'Brett', as they called her. The daughter of Viscount Esher and sister of the Ranee of Sarawak, Brett was a painter who suffered from deafness, and became an early convert to Lawrence's projected utopian colony of Ramamin. By March 1924 Lawrence was in Taos, New Mexico, as guest of Mabel Lodge Luhan, who found 'the holy Russian idiot' Brett, complete with ear trumpet Toby, a nuisance . . . On 3 June Lawrence was writing, from the ranch he named Kiowa, 'we are alone, save for a friend, Dorothy Brett, who paints – and is a daughter of Viscount Esher . . . Everything is all right'. First Frieda, then Lawrence, lost interest in Brett, and never saw her again after 1926. In *The Priest of Love* (1974) Harry T. Moore says that 'In 1974 [Brett] revealed that the impotent Lawrence of 1926 twice tried to have sex with her. She was willing, but he failed.'

RODERICK USHER
Edgar Allan Poe, *The Fall of the House of Usher* (1839)
Edgar Allan Poe
(1809–49)

In *The Fall of the House of Usher* Roderick and his sister Madeline are twins, but are also divided personalities, two sides of the same personality. Both of them fear confinement. Madeline is entombed before she is actually dead. Roderick is sensitive almost to the point of psychosis: 'It was with difficulty that I could bring myself to admit the identity of the wan being before me with the companion of my early boyhood,' the narrator says, of his meeting with Roderick at the house of Usher: 'Yet the character of his face had been at all times remarkable. A cadaverousness of complexion; an eye large, liquid, and luminous. . .lips somewhat thin and very pallid . . . a nose of delicate Hebrew model, but with a breadth of nostril unusual in similar formations; a finely moulded chin, speaking, in its want of prominence, of want of moral energy; hair of a more than web-like softness and tenuity. . . . His action was alternatively vivacious and sullen. His voice varied rapidly from a tremulous indecision . . . to that species of energetic concision – that abrupt, weighty, unhurried and perfectly modulated gutteral utterance, which may be observed in the lost drunkard, or the irreclaimable eater of opium.'

A glance at surviving portraits, contemporary photographs or drawings by Ismael Gentz, will show that Poe is describing himself. He struck contemporaries as an oddity. His pale, delicate and intellectual face, with a curling and almost disdainful lip, his invariable black suit, his cadaverous face, strange eyes, curling hair, extensive forehead, his low voice which seemed almost cultivated – it is Roderick Usher exactly. Also Poe had the neurotic qualities he gives to Roderick – he was noticeably tense and moody, and – like his creation – he feared confinement.

Further reading:
H.P. Lovecraft, *Supernatural Horror in Literature* (1945), Thomas Woodson, *The Fall of the House of Usher* (1969), Mary E. Philips, *Edgar Allan Poe the Man* (1926)

V

PAQUITA VALDES
Honoré de Balzac, *The Girl with the Golden Eyes* (1835)
Marie Dorval (1798–1849)

Further reading: Arsène Houssaye, *Les Confessions* (1891) and Françoise Moser, *Marie Dorval* (2947)

The Girl with the Golden Eyes is set in Paris in 1815. Henri de Marsay, illegitimate son of Lord Dudley, and a member of a group of youths, 'the Thirteen', who place themselves above the law, is a mysterious and beautiful youth. He sees, and immediately falls in love with, a strikingly attractive young woman, Paquita Valdes; he is drawn to her with an almost magnetic pull: 'I came face to face with a woman, or rather with a young girl; who, if she did not throw herself at my head, stopped short, less I think, from human respect, than from one of those movements of profound surprise which affect the limbs, creep down the length of the spine, and cease only at the sole of the feet, to nail you to the ground . . .a sort of animal magnetism which becomes enormously powerful when the relations are reciprocally precise.' Her face seems to say to him: 'What, it is you, my ideal! The creation of my thoughts, of my morning and evening dreams!' What particularly strikes him are her two yellow eyes, like a tiger's: 'a golden yellow that gleams, living gold, gold which thinks, gold which loves, and is determined to take refuge in your pocket.' For Henri no other girl could surpass her: 'She is like the cat who rubs herself against your legs; a white girl with dusk coloured hair, delicate in appearance, but who must have downy threads on the third phalanx of her fingers, and all along her cheeks a white down whose line, luminous on fine days, begins at her ears and loses itself on her neck.' Paquita is well guarded, but Henri finds his way to her, and they become lovers. Though she is a virgin, he finds her an adept and fulfilling lover. This is because she is a lover of another woman, the Marquise de San-Rèal, who, unbeknown to Henri, is his half-sister. This is why Paquita falls in love with Henri: she loves both persons in different forms. Henri finds that Paquita has another lover, and with the aid of 'the Thirteen' he goes to gain his vengeance, only to find that the Marquise has already stabbed Paquita. Her dying words are: 'Too late, my beloved!' and she expires in a pool of blood.

Paquita is based on the celebrated actress Marie Dorval, who was George Sand's lover. Arsène Houssaye, who knew them well, described the caresses, fondlings and kisses he saw them indulge in: 'Both were frantic for the unforeseen and insatiable for love.' Marie was incomparable in romantic dramas; her greatest role was Kitty Bell in Alfred de Vigny's *Chatterton* (1835).

RAPHAËL DE VALENTIN
Honoré de Balzac, *The Ass's Skin* (1831)
Honoré de Balzac (1799–1850)

Further reading: Herbert J. Hunt, *Balzac's 'Comedie Humaine'* (1959)

The Ass's Skin is an oriental fable in the guise of a novel about Paris in the early 1830s. A young man, Raphaël Valentin, buys an enchanted pelt, an ass's skin, from an old and wizened antique-dealer. The skin bears the inscription in Sanskrit: 'Whosoever possesses me shall possess all things. But your life will belong to me. God has willed it so. Desire and your desires will be realized. But match your desires to your life. It is there. At every wish I will diminish like your days. Do you want me? Take me. God will hear you! So be it!' The old man in the shop explains to Raphaël that he himself has managed to live to be a hundred years old because he was very careful never to wish for anything. He says: 'In just a few words I will reveal to you the entire mystery of human life. Man expends himself in the performance of two instinctive acts. These drain away all the sources of his being. All the forms of these two agents of death may be summed up in these two words: *will* and *can*.' The message is wasted. Raphaël indulges in an orgy of feasting and womanizing. The novel is a brilliant picture of a decadent society, run for the benefit of bankers, lawyers and men about town. An elegant young man, Rastignac encourages Raphaël to climb upwards in society by marrying a beautiful rich woman, Fedora. He wastes his substance in gambling, living on credit. He desires a fortune and inherits 200,000 francs. At each wish the skin shrinks. He attempts to have the skin stretched scientifically; he attempts to retreat to the world of the natural and unspoilt life; but he dies in erotic frenzy in the company of his beloved, Pauline Gaudin.

In his wild ambitions and fantasies, and in the story of his early trials and tribulations in attempting to succeed in society, Raphaël is a portrait of Balzac himself. There is a scene early in the novel where, with his feet in the lap of a half-dressed young woman, Raphaël tells his life-story up to the moment when he bought the shagreen. It is Balzac's own early days. He was born of peasant stock and did not do well at school, though he read profusely. He studied the law and then drifted into literature. His early works were not successful and he was full of hair–brained schemes for getting rich or getting on. He intended to marry Mademoiselle Elèonore de Trumilly, daughter of a wealthy *emigré*, in order to enable him to stand for parliament. His father had always told him the secret of longevity was to economize on activities and emotions.

JEAN VALJEAN

Victor Hugo, *Les Misérables* (1862)

Pierre-François Lacenaire, 'Gaillard'

Further reading:
The Memoirs of Lacanaire, translated and edited by P.J. Stead (1952)

Les Misérables tells the story of Jean Valjean, who is wrongly convicted and sentenced to years in the galleys. He attempts to return to 'normal' life and to build up his life again, but he is hounded by a tenacious police officer who really destroys his humanity. Among the most celebrated episodes in the novel is the tale of the bishop's candlesticks which Valjean steals after being offered accommodation there for the night. When he is apprehended, the authorities find the candlesticks on Valjean's person. Out of compassion and charity, the bishop tells them that he had given Valjean the candlesticks as a present.

Victor Hugo based Jean Valjean on the real life assassin, thief and forger, known as 'Gaillard' to the French authorities. Théophile Gautier termed him: 'The Manfred of the gutters, and indeed he assumed a somewhat romantic reputation which his deeds and lifestyle hardly deserved. He was not even a brilliantly successful criminal, he spent at least three years in confinement and was executed at the age of thirty-six, but he was an articulate member of the middle classes with a flair for public relations and was able to gain a place in the public eye which brought him to the attention of Victor Hugo. Gaillard wrote poems and articles about his escapades and expressed an influential 'philosophy' of crime. Prison, he declared, was the great university of crime. In attacking the political establishment of the day – the regime of Louis Philippe – he became the darling of the radical opposition. His *Memoirs* were widely read and discussed. He became a criminal, he maintained, as a result of his parents' lack of affection for him. He always showed an enviable gift for drama and took over the prosecution in his trial as a means of making sure that his accomplices who had given him away would also go to the scaffold. Among his fellow inmates in prison he lorded it like an aristocrat. Early in his career he had public sympathy, and the people were with him when he was sentenced in 1829 for theft. When he stabbed an old bachelor and his mother for five hundred francs and was sentenced to death he no longer commanded such a public following. But he was flamboyant to the end – arrested in the provinces he was glad to be sent to Paris to be tried: 'It would have been very disagreeable to have been executed by a provincial executioner,' he said.

VANE

H.D., *Bid Me to Live* (1960)

Cecil Gray (1895–1951)

Further reading:
Barbara Guest, *Herself Defined: The Poet H.D. and her World* (1984)

H.D.'s *Bid Me to Live* begins with the autobiographical heroine, Julia Ashton, in an anxious condition at her room in Queen's Square, Bloomsbury. Her husband RAFE (based on H.D.'s husband, Richard Aldington) is having an affair with Bella Carter (Dorothy Yorke) and Julia is sustained through her epistolary relationship with the novelist RICO (D.H. Lawrence). When Rico and his wife Elsa (Frieda Lawrence) are turned out of Cornwall, Julie lets them stay in her room at Queen's Square, and she realizes that Elsa hopes she, Julia, will sleep with Rico so she, Elsa, can concentrate on the composer Vane. Julia's friendship with

Rico remains an intellectual one, and it is she, not Elsa, who turns to Vane when he arrives: 'Vane looked like a young officer on sick-leave with his stooping shoulders, his aristocratic langour . . .He said, "I want two things, I want to finish my opera and I want a beautiful relationship with a woman." He had said this before. She would go to Cornwall.' So Julia leaves London with Vane, and sees her life from a new perspective. As the novel is firmly founded on the facts of H.D.'s life in 1917–18, Vane is clearly based on the composer Cecil Gray, who was the father of H.D.'s child Perdita (born 1919).

Born in Edinburgh and educated in Edinburgh and Birmingham, Gray was living at Bosigran Castle, Cornwall, in October 1917, when he was visited by the D.H. Lawrences. It was wartime, and a light was seen from Gray's window. Gray was fined, and Lawrence was subsequently ordered out of Cornwall. Lawrence and his wife Frieda were lent H.D.'s room at 44 Mecklenburgh Square, London. At the time, H.D. (born Hilda Doolittle) was depressed by the affair between her husband Richard Aldington and Dorothy Yorke. Writing a postscript to the 1983 reprint of *Bid Me to Live*, Perdita – the child of Gray and H.D. – recalls how Gray abandoned H.D. in 1919 because the baby (Perdita herself) was 'too much for him. H.D. wrote him an impulsive note in 1936. She suggested they meet and talk about old times. He never replied.'

Cecil Gray (also the original of Cyril Scott in Lawrence's *Aaron's Rod*) was best known as a writer on music, for example his book on *Peter Warlock* (1934). He also wrote three operas to his own libretti: *Deirdre*, *Temptation of St Anthony*, and *The Trojan Women*.

DOLLY VARDEN

Charles Dickens, *Barnaby Rudge* (1841)

Maria Beadnell
(1810–86)

Further reading:
Norman and Jeanne MacKenzie, *Dickens – A Life* (1979)

Dolly Varden, one of the finest portrayals of a coquette in the works of Dickens, is the irresistible daughter of Gabriel Varden, the locksmith. She is loved by honest Joe Willet, son of the landlord of the Maypole Inn, and also by Varden's apprentice, the wily and spiteful Sim Tappertit. During the Gordon Riots she is taken by the mob, but rescued by Joe. She eventually marries him: 'A roguish face met his: a face lighted up by the loveliest pair of sparkling eyes that ever locksmith looked upon; the face of a pretty, laughing, girl; dimpled and fresh, and healthful – the very impersonation of good humour and blooming beauty.' This is how her father sees her, but her appearance is more damaging to single young men: 'When and where was there ever such a plump, roguish, comely, bright-eyed, enticing, bewitching, captivating, maddening little puss in all this world, as Dolly!'

This is Dickens's first love, Maria Beadnell, with whom he was totally infatuated when they first met in 1830, when she was eighteen. She was a born flirt, but the young Dickens found every moment spent in her company sheer heaven. Young men clustered around her. She was well aware of her charms, but Charles would have died for her, even though her parents disapproved of the match (see FLORA FINCHING). Her father sent her to Paris to complete her education, and Charles pined for her. When she returned she made her indifference to him quite plain. He sent her letters and gifts back with a message: 'Our meetings of late have been little more than so many displays of heartless indifference on the one hand; while on the other they have never failed to prove a fertile source of wretchedness and misery. . . . Believe me that nothing will ever afford me more real delight than to hear that you, the object of my first and my last love, are happy.' She sent this letter back with a note that caused him to hope, but it came to nothing. He had loved her for four years and felt that she had ruled his emotions. The young Dickens's pride had been wounded, and he thought this frustrating affair responsible for: 'a habit of suppression which now belongs to me, which I know is no part of my original nature, but which makes me chary of showing my emotions . . .' Maria appears, in the words of Christopher Hibbert (*The Making of Charles Dickens*, 1967) 'as the pretty, provocative, silly

Dolly Varden'. Dora, David's child-wife in *David Copperfield*, is also clearly based on the young Miss Beadnell.

HONORE GABRIEL VARNEY

Edward Bulwer Lytton, *Lucretia; or The Children of Night* (1846)

Thomas Griffiths Wainewright
(1794–1847)

Gabriel Varney, the son of a French father and English mother, is a characteristic and melodramatic Victorian monster and villain. He is a forger and murderer, who insures his victims for vast sums and then poisons them, claiming the insurance money which he spends lavishly. He is portrayed as a mixture of disarming – almost romantic – charm, and sinister, devilish qualities: 'It is true that he was small for his years; but his frame had a vigour in its light proportions, which came from a premature and almost adolescent symmetry of shape and muscular development. The countenance, however, had much of effeminate beauty; the long hair reached the shoulders, but did not curl; straight, fine, and glossy as a girl's and, in colour, of the pale auburn, tinged with red, which rarely alters in hue as childhood matures to man; the complexion was dazzlingly clear and fair. Nevertheless, there was something so hard in the lip, so bold, though not open, in the brow, that the girlishness of complexion, and even of outline, could not leave, on the whole, an impression of effeminacy. All the hereditary keenness and intelligence were stamped upon his face at that moment, but the expression also had a large share of. . .irony and malice.' He is eventually convicted and transported for life, which is in fact, a lingering death.

Lytton based the character and much of the narrative on Thomas Wainewright. He researched the story thoroughly, and corresponded with various officials and employees to verify Wainewright's attempts to defraud insurance firms. Wainewright was a painter, art critic and forger. He was educated at Dr Burney's Greenwich Academy and was apprenticed to the artist Thomas Philips. He was sufficiently good to exhibit at the Royal Academy 1821, 1822, 1824 and 1825. He forged powers of attorney so as to gain access to capital he had been left, when he was supposed to enjoy only the interest. He was supposed also to have poisoned victims for their insurance money, but this was never proved. (See JULIUS SLINKTON.)

Further reading:
K. Hollingsworth, *The Newgate Novel* (1963)

ABINGER VENNARD

John Buchan, *The Moon Endureth* (1912)

David Lloyd George
(1863–1945)

John Buchan's story 'A Lucid Interval' (published in *Blackwood's Magazine* in 1910, before being collected in *The Moon Endureth*) is a comic variant of Stevenson's *Dr Jekyll and Mr Hyde*. It tells of the impact on two prominent British politicians of a Hindu drug 'capable of altering a man's whole temperament until the antidote was administered. It would turn a coward into a bravo, a miser into a spendthrift, a rake into a fakir.' A wealthy Indian has been deprived of land because of the reforms of Lord Caerlaverock, former Indian Viceroy, and plans to extract revenge by having one of Caerlaverock's curries dosed with the drug. At Caerlaverock House, Alexander Cargill, the Home Secretary, and Abinger Vennard, the Secretary for India, partake of the curry, and are transformed so that both experience a 'lucid interval'. Under the influence of the drug, Cargill is transformed from a liberal apologist to a fiercely reactionary penologist; Vennard, the rising star of radical liberalism, becomes an empire-builder. Philosophically, the narrator (Lady Caerlaverock's nephew) concludes that 'the drug did not create new opinions, but elicited those which had hitherto lain dormant'. At the end of the story the antidote is administered and 'at last peace . . . descended'.

'A Lucid Interval' is a *conte a cléf*. Caerlaverock is modelled on Lord Curzon (1859-1925), Viceroy of India from 1899-1905. Alexander Cargill is based on R.B. Haldane (1856-1928), Liberal War Minister from 1905-12. Abinger Vennard is a portrait of David Lloyd George, who became President of the Board of Trade in the Liberal cabinet of 1905, and in 1908 became Chancellor of the Exchequer. Buchan, a London barrister when he wrote the story, describes Abinger Vennard's

Further reading:
David Daniell (ed.), *The Best Short Stories of John Buchan, Volume 2* (1982)

late arrival at Caerlaverock House: 'He made a fine stage entrance, walking swiftly with a lowering bow to his hostess, and then glaring fiercely round the room as if to challenge criticism . . .there could be no denying his good looks. He had a bad, loose figure, and a quantity of studiously neglected hair, but his face was the face of a young Greek.'

David Lloyd George, the Welsh wizard of political oratory, became Prime Minister of the wartime coalition in 1916. Buchan was, in 1917, Director of Information responsible to the Prime Minister; and, the following year, Director of Intelligence in the new Ministry of Information.

MR VENUS

Charles Dickens, *Our Mutual Friend* (1865)

J. Willis

Further reading: Edwin Pugh, *The Charles Dickens Originals* (1912)

Mr Venus is a taxidermist in business at Clerkenwell. He buys Silas Wegg's amputated leg, and co-operates with him in his attempts to blackmail Mr Boffin (see NICODEMUS BOFFIN). He later repents and gives Silas Wegg away, letting Boffin into the secret of what is going on. His life is considerably blighted by his unrequited love for Pleasant Riderhood, Rogue Riderhood's daughter. She objected to his trade as a taxidermist and general practitioner in bones 'human and various'. He is described as having: 'A sallow face with weak eyes, surmounted by a tangle of reddish-dusty hair. The owner of the face has no cravat on, and has opened his tumbled shirt-collar to work with the more ease. For the same reason he has no coat on; only a loose waistcoat over his yellow linen. His eyes are like the over-tried eyes of an engraver, but he is not that; his expression and stoop are like that of a shoemaker, but he is not that . . .' He expresses the blighting of his hopes by saying: 'I do not wish to regard myself, nor to be regarded in that bony light.'

It was Marcus Stone, the illustrator of *Our Mutual Friend*, who discovered the character on which Mr Venus is based, and brought him to Dickens's attention. After writing four numbers of the serial, the novelist wanted a new subject. He wrote to John Forster on 25 February 1864: 'While I was considering what it should be, Marcus (Stone), who has done an excellent cover, came to tell me of an extraordinary trade he had found out, through one of his painting requirements. I immediately went with him to St Giles's to look at the place, and found – what you will see.' What Stone had discovered was the shop of Mr J Willis, of 42 St Andrew's Street, Seven Dials. He was a preserver of animals and birds, and articulator of human bones, mainly for the medical profession. He brags to Mr Wegg: 'If you was brought here loose in a bag to be articulated, I'd name your smallest bones blindfold equally with your largest, as fast as I could pick 'em out, and I'd sort 'em all, and sort your wertebrae, in a moment that would equally surprise and charm you.' Dickens transfers the location of this extraordinary establishment to Clerkenwell. The original was discovered by Percy Fitzgerald, who was a frequent visitor to Dickens's house at Gadshill in the 1860s. Fitzgerald said to him: 'I am convinced I have found the original of Venus.' Charles Dickens agreed that he was right.

VERA

Mikhail Lermontov, *A Hero of Our Time* (1840)

Varvara Lopukhina

Further reading: Laurence Kelly, *Lermontov* (1977)

When Lermontov was a thirteen-year-old pupil at the Noble Pension, Moscow, in 1827, he met Varvara Lopukhina, daughter of friends of his family. During his university years in Moscow (1830-2), he saw Varvara as often as possible, wrote poems to her and called her 'my Madonna'. He was, he said, 'happy beyond all bounds'. In 1832 Lermontov went to the 'Junker' School in St Petersburg to train as a cavalry cornet and, though he corresponded with Varvara's sister, did little to encourage the object of his love. Then, as Laurence Kelly says, 'In May of 1835 he was thunder-struck to hear of [Varvara's] wedding to Nicholas Bakhmetiev, a rich, portly man sixteen years her senior.' Lermontov's reaction was to write a melodrama, *The Two Brothers*, in which a soldier, Yuri, hears that his former mistress Vera has married a rich Prince. It also transpires, towards the end of the play, that Yuri's brother Alexander has seduced Vera. In June 1838, in St Petersburg, Lermontov met Varvara and her husband. Recovering from the loss of a baby she was (says Kelly) 'White as a sheet, thin as a nail . . .a shadow of her former self.'

Pechorin, the cynical protagonist of Lermontov's novel *A Hero of Our Time*, comes across his former mistress Vera (another projection of Varvara) in the episode 'Princess Mary'. As Pechorin realizes, Vera is clearly ill: 'She wore a straw hat and was wrapped in a black shawl. Her head was sunk on her breast, her face hidden by her hat.' Nevertheless, the arrogant Pechorin gives Vera the benefit of a 'thrilling, passionate kiss', pities her for being tied to a rich, rheumatic husband (her second), and subsequently ponders on what she meant to him (in the 1966 translation by Paul Foote): 'I know we shall soon part again, perhaps this time for ever. We shall each take our own road to the grave, but her memory will always be sacred in my heart.' After receiving a letter from Vera, declaring her love, Pechorin panics: 'Now that I might lose her for ever Vera was dearer to me than anything else in the world – life, honour, happiness.' Soon, though, he recovers his composure and reflects on 'how futile and senseless it was to pursue lost happiness.'

After Lermontov's death, in a duel in 1841, Varvara's sister told a friend: 'Her [Varvara's] nerves are so shattered that she had to spend two weeks in bed. Her husband proposed that she should go to Moscow, she refused; or abroad, she refused and said she did not really want to be healed. Perhaps I am mistaken, but I link this to the death of Michel.'

HENRI VERDOUX

Charles Chaplin, *Monsieur Verdoux* (1947)

Henri-Désiré Landru (1869–1922)

Further reading: Charles Chaplin, *My Autobiography* (1964)

At the beginning of Charles Chaplin's film *Monsieur Verdoux* there is a shot of a tombstone inscribed 'Henri Verdoux/1880-1937'. In a voice-over, Verdoux explains that he was a bank clerk who lost his job in the depression of 1930: 'It was then I became occupied in liquidating members of the opposite sex. This I did as a strictly business enterprise to support wife and family.' The film shows Verdoux in action. His wife, Mona, is an invalid living in the country with their son Peter; at home with them Verdoux is a model husband. In order to sustain this rural idyll, Verdoux (alias Varnay, alias Bonheur, alias Floray) is a bluebeard who marries and murders women for their money. As Chaplin says in his autobiography, 'He is a paradox of virtue and vice; a man who, as he trims his rose garden, avoids stepping on a caterpillar, while at the end of the garden one of his victims is being consumed in an incinerator.' After various adventures, Verdoux is approached by a detective who has guessed the grisly truth. Verdoux poisons him, but is later arrested and put on trial for mass murder. Sentenced to death, Verdoux makes a brief speech claiming that his crimes are insignificant when compared to the murders committed by the state in time of war. The film ends as Verdoux goes to the guillotine.

Chaplin conceived *Monsieur Verdoux* after Orson Welles proposed he should star in a film based on the life of 'the celebrated French murderer, Bluebeard Landru'. Whereas Welles felt the film could be based on the records of the Landru trial, Chaplin saw the comic possibilities and developed the character as a French charmer capable of great dignity as well as marvellous comedy. The screen credits acknowledge the 'Idea suggested by Orson Welles'.

Henre-Désiré Landru, a married man with four children, made a career from exploiting the emotional weaknesses of lonely middle-aged Frenchwomen. Using aliases, he placed matrimonial advertisements in French newspapers; ten of the women who met him through these advertisements were never seen again. Though no human remains were found, Landru was charged with the murder of these women, and during his trial he revealed intelligence and wit: told that a copy of *The Great Poisoners* had been found on his premises, he answered 'You can't poison people with a book.' Before going to the guillotine Landru refused the rum and the consolations of religion; Verdoux, however, takes the rum, since he has never tasted the drink before.

MADAME VERDURIN
Marcel Proust, *Remembrance of Things Past* (1913–27)
Arman de Caillavet (1847–1910)

Further reading: George D. Painter, *Marcel Proust* (1959, 1965)

In Proust's novel Charles Swann takes several steps down the social ladder in order to keep the company of Odette de Crécy, 'a young woman of a "certain class"' who frequents the salon of Mme Verdurin. As a hostess, Mme Verdurin presides over her own cultural circle as a rich, self-centred woman who nevertheless appreciates art. Proust describes her (in the translation by C.K. Scott Moncrieff) 'sitting upon a high Swedish chair of waxed pinewood, which a violinist from that country had given her . . .she made a point of keeping on view the presents which her "faithful" were in the habit of making her from time to time, so that the donors might have the pleasure of seeing them when they came to the house. . .From this lofty perch she would take her spirited part in the conversation of the "faithful" and would revel in all their fun'. Mme Verdurin eventually has her revenge on the aristocratic 'bores' who shun her for, twice-widowed, she eventually marries the widower Prince de Guermantes, and so climbs to the top of the social ladder.

Proust frequented many salons conducted by society ladies, such as Mme Strauss (widow of Bizet, the composer), Mme Aubernon, Mme Ménard-Dorian and Madeleine Lemaire, but the chief original of Mme Verdurin was Arman de Caillavet. In the summer of 1889 Proust first visited Mme Arman's salon, at 12 Avenue Hoche, Paris, and there met Anatole France – the original of Bergotte, and Mme Arman's lover. Léontine Lippman (as Mme Arman was born) married Albert Arman in 1868, a few years before he added 'de Caillavet' to his surname, after a vine-growing chateau on his country estate. George D. Painter writes of Mme Arman: 'Like Mme Verdurin, she felt herself persecuted by *les ennuyeux*. Strangely enough, however, these bores were not people whom she despaired of luring to her salon, but those she was anxious to expel from it; just as, at the age of three, she had tried to throw her baby brother out of the window, saying: "He bores me."' Painter adds that 'Mme Arman was perhaps an intellectual snob, but she was not a social one.'

When Proust's *Les Plaisirs et les Jours* appeared in 1896 there was a rumour that the introduction, signed by Anatole France, was actually the work of Mme Arman, and she undoubtedly helped France in many ways. In 1894 Proust met Oscar Wilde at Mme Arman's, and the formidable hostess described 'Monsieur Wilde' as 'a cross between the Apollo Belvedere and Albert Wolff [the fat, foppish theatre critic of *Le Figaro*]'. When she died, Anatole France was devastated, and Proust sent a wreath of camelias, arum-lilies, lilac, roses and violets.

DIANA VERNON
Sir Walter Scott, *Rob Roy* (1817)
Jane Anne Cranstoun, Countess Purgstall (1760–1835)

Further reading: Basil Hall, *Schloss Hainfeld* (1836); Christopher Johnston, *Sir Walter's? Conge* (1931)

Diana Vernon is one of Scott's most convincing heroines; she is mature, cultivated and passionate with a rose-like purity. She makes an immediate impact on the hero, Francis: 'She extended her hand, but I clasped her to my bosom. She sighed as she extricated herself from the embrace which she permitted, escaped to the door which led to her own apartment, and I saw her no more.' They are obviously very strongly attracted to each other although her evil cousin, Rashleigh, has designs on her. There is a scene at her uncle's house where Francis and Diana are together in the library. She turns over the pages of *Orlando Furioso* when out falls a copy of some verses. As she begins to read them the hero blushes: 'It is not worthy your perusal – a scrap of translation.' She answers: 'Mine honest friend, do not, if you will be guided by my advice, bait your hook with too much humility; for, ten to one, it will not catch a single compliment. . . . There is a great deal of it.' Francis then hears the sweetest sounds which mortal ears can drink in: 'those of a youthful poet's verses . . . read by the lips which are dearest to him.' This is a portrait of Jane Anne Cranstoun, sister of a close friend of Sir Walter Scott's when he was attending classes in Civil Law in Edinburgh. At this time Scott was courting Williamina Belsches, though he saw a great deal of the enchanting Miss Cranstoun. When Bürger's famous grisly romantic ballad *Leonore* became fashionable, Scott was determined to translate it, and was encouraged to do so by Jane Anne Cranstoun. He stayed up all night finishing it, and then called to show her at six in the morning. She was full of enthusiasm for his achievement (it is still a fine translation) and it was on her advice that Scott presented Miss Belsches with a fine copy of his verse translation of Bürger's German ballad. Williamina was very pleased with the beautifully bound copy, but she gave her hand in marriage to William Forbes, Scott's rival. This is clearly the basis of the library scene in *Rob Roy*. In 1797 Jane married Count Wenzel Gottfried Purgstall, an Austrian aristocrat, and went to live at his castle in Styria. She corresponded with Scott and several of her letters are preserved at Abbotsford. They are deeply affectionate letters. When Scott married she wrote to congratulate him with warmth and affection saying that her heart burned as she read his letters to her and asserting her gratitude that those who loved her were happy and had not forgotten her: 'I have no way to express my feelings – they come in a flood and destroy me!' She met Goethe, Schiller, Kant and Mozart. She never returned to Scotland.

LILY VERNON

Christopher Isherwood, *The Memorial* (1932)

Kathleen Isherwood (1868–1959)

Christopher Isherwood's second novel *The Memorial*, subtitled 'Portrait of a Family', studies the impact of the First World War on various individuals. One of these, Lily Vernon, is an artistically-inclined war widow who clings to memories of the privileged life she led with her heroic husband Richard. Lily's nostalgia for the past is combined with a suspicion of the new generation represented by her son Eric: 'And at the thought of this new generation, so eager for new kinds of life and new excitement, with new ideas about dancing and clothes and behaviour at tea-parties, so certain to sneer or laugh at everything which girls had liked and enjoyed in nineteen hundred – at that thought Lily felt not a pang of sadness but a stab of real misery. She was living on in a new, changed world, unwanted, among enemies. She was old, finished with.' Lily is modelled on Isherwood's own mother Kathleen.

In 1903 Kathleen Machel Smith, daughter of an wine merchant, married Frank Bradshaw-Isherwood - the second son of John Bradshaw-Isherwood of Marple Hall, a big Elizabethan mansion in Cheshire. After honeymooning in Cambridge, Kathleen and Frank moved into Wyberslegh Hall and, in this house on John Bradshaw-Isherwood's estate, Kathleen gave birth to Christopher Isherwood, on 26 August 1904. As Frank was a professional soldier, the family left Wyberslegh Hall when Christopher was three, a move deeply regretted by Kathleen who loved the social graces surrounding Marple Hall. On 8 May 1915 Frank was killed at the second battle of Ypres, and Kathleen survived by switching her attention to her children Christopher and Richard (born 1911). Christopher resented his mother's snobbish, overpowering personality and – so he says in *Christopher and his Kind* (1976) – became a homosexual in an act of rebellion against Kathleen. Her high professional hopes for her son came to nothing: in 1925 Christopher deliberately failed his Cambridge examinations, and in 1928 withdrew from his course at King's College Medical School. Though she was shocked by his homosexuality, she paid £1,000, in 1936, in an unsuccessful attempt to arrange a change of nationality for Isherwood's Berlin boyfriend Heinz, and so save him from German military service. For years Kathleen lived in London, but when Isherwood inherited Marple Hall from his Uncle Henry, in 1940, she was able to return to Wyberslegh Hall for the rest of her life, Isherwood renouncing his rights in favour of his brother Richard. Over the years Isherwood's attitude to his mother mellowed, as can be seen in his book about his parents, *Kathleen and Frank* (1971), which draws on Kathleen's diaries.

ANN VERONICA

H.G. Wells, *Ann Veronica* (1909)

Amber Reeves

Further reading: V. Brome, *H.G. Wells* (1951), L. Dickson, *H.G. Wells – His Turbulent Life and Times* (1969)

The heroine of H.G. Wells's novel *Ann Veronica* is an advanced feminist whose fictional behaviour was considered deeply shocking by the Edwardian reading public. Ann Veronica Stanley rejects the domestic tyranny of her father, joins the Fabian Society, is imprisoned as a suffragette, and becomes pregnant after seducing and running off with her biology tutor. Wells describes her lovingly: 'She was slender, and sometimes she seemed tall, and walked and carried herself lightly and joyfully . . . Her lips came together with an expression between contentment and the faintest shadow of a smile, her manner was one of great reserve, and behind this mask she was wildly discontented and eager for freedom and life.'

Ann Veronica is a portrait of Amber Reeves, a girl twenty years younger than the married author she so admired. Wells got to know Amber through her parents who were well-known figures in the intellectual life of London: Hon William Pember Reeves was to become a Director of the London School of Economics and his wife was head of the Women's Section of the Fabian Society. Amber followed her mother into the Fabian Society and completed her education at Cambridge; she thus attracted Wells by her brains as well as her beauty. In 1908 the two became lovers and Amber was pregnant when she felt obliged to part from Wells. For a while she stayed in a villa, near Paris, provided for her by Wells then she returned home to tell her mother exactly what had happened. Mrs Pember Reeves was, for all her Fabian notions, shocked and disappointed in her daughter. Amber eventually decided to marry a fellow Fabian and gave birth to Wells's baby in December 1909. Nevertheless there was considerable gossip and Wells discussed the affair in letters in one of which he wrote 'I've done nothing I am ashamed of.'

THE VICAR OF BRAY

Popular song, *The Vicar of Bray* (c 1720)

Revd Simon Aleyn

(sixteenth century)

The well-known song, *The Vicar of Bray*, was put in circulation in its present form in the early eighteenth century, and celebrates the tact and skill which enables a minister of religion to survive various reigns which brought in different religious and political orthodoxicalities. His one unswerving loyalty is to the fact that whoever sits on the throne, he will continue to be the vicar of his parish: 'And this is Law, I will maintain/Until my dying day, Sir,/That whatsoever King shall reign/I will be the Vicar of Bray, Sir.' He begins his career during the reign of Charles I: 'In good King Charles's golden days/When loyalty no harm meant,/A furious High-Church Man I was/And so I gained Preferment,/ Unto my flock I daily preached/Kings are of God appointed/And damn'd are those who dare resist/Or touch the Lord's annointed.' In course of time, James II, the Roman Catholic brother of Charles II, becomes King: 'When Royal James possest the Crown/And Popery grew in fashion,/The Penal Law I hunted down/And read the Declaration;/The Church of Rome I found would fit,/Full well my Constitution;/And I had been a Jesuit,/But for the Revolution.' After the revolution of 1688-9 he accepts the succession of William and Mary, adjusting his religious practices accordingly: 'When William our Deliverer came/To heal the Nation's Grievance,/I turned the Cat in Pan again/And swore to him allegiance;/ Old Principles I did remove,/Set conscience at a distance,/Passive Obedience is a Joke,/A jest is Non-resistance.' The accession of Queen Anne requires another about-face, and he becomes an Anglican and a Tory: 'Occasional Conformists base/I damn'd and Moderation,/And thought the Church in danger was/From such prevarication.' When Anne died without producing a surviving heir, and George I became King, the vicar has to change once more, becoming a Whig, and a defender of the Protestant Church against the Old Pretender and the pope: 'The Illustrious House of Hanover/And Protestant Succession,/To these I lustily will swear,/Whilst they can keep possession;/For in my Faith and Loyalty/I never once will falter,/But George my lawful King shall be,/Except the Times should alter.'

The song is a reworking of a much earlier ballad, which celebrated the similar survival of the Revd Aleyn at Bray in Yorkshire where he was vicar between 1538 and 1565 during the reigns of Henry VIII, Edward VI, Mary I and Elizabeth I; during this time he kept his head above the varying troubled waters of successively Roman Catholic, Reformation, Anglican, Roman Catholic and Protestant crises.

VIRGIL

Ben Jonson, *The Poetaster* (1601)

William Shakespeare (1564–1616)

Ben Jonson's satirical comedy, *The Poetaster*, is supposedly set in Augustan Rome, but it really concerns contemporary persons and events in the so-called 'War of the Theatres'. (See HORACE, DEMETRIUS, CRISPINUS and CHRYSOGANUS). Horace brings before the Emperor Augustus his allegations that other poets have conspired against him. William Shakespeare appears in this charade as Virgil, and he is praised by Ben Jonson, in the role of Horace: 'I judge him of a rectified spirit,/By many revolutions of discourse,/(In his bright reason's influence,) refined/ From all the tartarous moods of common men;/Bearing the nature and similitude/Of a right heavenly body;most severe/In fashion and collection of himself; And, then, as clear and confident as Jove.' Horace is most generous about his learning and the value of his works: 'His learning savours not the school-like gloss/That most consists in echoing words and terms,/And soonest wins a man an empty name;/Nor any long or far-fetched circumstance/Wrapp'd in the curious generalities of arts;/But a direct and analytic sum/Of all the worth and first effects of arts./And for his poesy, 'tis so ramm'd with life,/That it shall gather strength of life with being,/And live hereafter more admired than now.' Virgil is then asked to deliver a sample of his current opus, his *Aeneids*, which Augustus chooses at random. Jonson here creates a rollicking parody of Shakespeare at his most bombastic: 'Meanwhile the skies 'gan thunder, and in tail/Of that, fell pouring storms of sleet and hail:/The Tyrian lords and Trojan youth, each where/With Venus' Dardane nephew, now, in fear,/Seek out for several shelter through the plain,/Whilst floods come rolling from the hills amain./Dido a cave, the Trojan prince the same/Lighted upon. There earth and heaven's great dame,/That hath the charge of marriage, first gave sign/Unto his contract; fire and air did shine,/As guilty of the match; and from the hill/The nymphs with shriekings do the region fill.' It is Virgil who announces the verdict in the trial of Crispinus and Demetrius, gives the former his emetic pills, and pardons the latter, tempering the judgements with good advice for aspiring poets.

Jonson knew Shakespeare well; he appeared in Jonson's *Every Man in his Humour* at the Globe in 1598. John Aubrey recorded: 'He was a handsome, well-shaped man: very good company, and of a very ready and pleasant smooth wit. Though, as Ben Jonson says of him, that he had little Latin and less Greek, he understood Latin pretty well: for he had been in his younger years a schoolmaster in the country. He was wont to say that he never blotted out a line in his life. Said Ben Jonson, 'I wish he had blotted out a thousand.'

Further reading: J.H. Penniman, *The War of the Theatres* (1897), R.B. Sharpe, *The Real War of the Theatres – Shakespeare's Fellows in Rivalry With The Admiral's Men 1594–1603* (1935), Alfred Harbage, *Shakespeare and the Rival Traditions* (1952)

JOHANN ULRICH VOSS

Patrick White, *Voss* (1957)

Ludwig Leichhardt (1813–48)

Ulrich Voss, the German explorer, intends to lead an expedition into the Australian hinterland. Before the party leaves they are entertained at the Sydney house of the Bonner family. Ulrich and Laura, Mrs Bonner's niece, find themselves mutually attracted. He sets off with six white companions, including Judd and Palfreyman, an ornithologist. They have two aboriginal guides. The expedition is dogged with bad luck. Their store animals are lost and the party itself is torn with tension. Judd, with half the group, sets off to return. Palfreyman is killed. Voss and the remainder go on. Voss is murdered and decapitated by Jackie, one of the guides. Judd is presumed to have died also. Towards his end, Voss has believed that Laura has been with him in spirit. Meanwhile, she is taken ill and at the height of fever – the moment of Voss's death – she cries out: 'O God! It is over!' Years later, Laura has embarked on a career as a

Further reading: B. Argyle, *Patrick White* (1968), C.D. Cotton, *Life of Ludwig Leichhardt* (1938)

teacher, when a search party returns with an old man. It is presumed that he is Judd. Although he can have no genuine knowledge of how Voss met his end, Laura accepts his account of how he closed Voss's eyes as he died.

Australia was gradually explored in the 19th century by such pioneers as Blaxland, Lawson, Wentworth, Oxley, Evans, Cunningham, Hume, Hovell, Eyre and Sturt. The mid 1840s was the period of the great inland expeditions of Ludwig Leichardt. He was born in Trebatsch, near Frankfurt-on-Oder, and went to Australia in 1841. In 1844 he set out in search of the overland route from the military station of Port Victoria, on the coast of Arnheim Land, to Moreton Bay. Initially he went along the Dawson and the Mackenzie in Queensland. From there he ascended the source of the Burdekin and he crossed the tableland to the west and reached the Gulf of Carpentaria. He skirted the shores of the Gulf as Roper and crossed Arnheim Land to reach the Alligator River. After a journey of some three thousand miles, completed within a year and three months, he reached Port Victoria. In December 1847 he attempted to cross the continent from east to west. He left the Fitzroy Downs in Queensland. His expedition was never found. His last dispatch was from the Cogoon and was dated 3 April 1848. The journals of his earlier expedition survive.

PHILIP WAKEM

George Eliot, *The Mill on the Floss* (1860)

Françoise D'Albert-Durade

Maggie Tulliver, a young woman of poetic and artisitc tastes, finds her brother Tom intellectually and spiritually undeveloped, but in Philip Wakem, a deformed son of a local lawyer, a companion who can share her interests. Philip is a shy and sensitive young man, with a humped back, but he is a very clever artist. The two find they are mutually very strongly attracted, though he fears she will not respond to him because he is deformed. He finds her very attractive not only because she is a handsome young woman but because her company is so intellectually rewarding. Maggie's father is very suspicious of Philip Wakem, and these suspicions seem confirmed when his business, Dorlcote mill, goes bankrupt in litigation in which Wakem is the other party. Maggie's brother, Tom (see TOM TULLIVER) discovers the relationship between Maggie and Philip, and they part. She has always felt the relationship tinged with guilt because it had to be kept secret, though she admits she loves him, but feels there is still something lacking in her feelings for him. In a terrible scene, Maggie's father thrashes Philip, and this action brings on Mr Tulliver's death.

Francois D'Albert-Durade was a deformed hunchback artist with whom George Eliot boarded in Geneva in the winter of 1849. She may also have used the character of another artist she met in 1845 at her half-sister's house in Baginton, who confessed his love to her, writing to say she was 'the most fascinating creature he had ever beheld'. She felt that she could not respond to his offer that they should keep in touch as he was a picture-restorer and this profession was not well-paid or very well-esteemed, but she thought him the most interesting young man she had met 'and superior to all the rest of mankind'. The friendship soon cooled.

Further reading: Mathilde Blind, *George Eliot* (1882), Mary S. Deakin, *The Early Life of George Eliot* (1913), Leslie Stephen, *George Eliot* (1882), Blanche C. Williams, *George Eliot – A Biography* (1936)

WALDEN POND

Henry David Thoreau, *Walden* (1854)

Henry David Thoreau's classic *Walden* opens on an assertion: 'When I wrote the following pages . . . I lived alone, in the woods, a mile from any neighbour, in a house which I had built myself, on the shore of Walden Pond, in Concord, Massachusetts, and earned my living by the labor of my hands only. I lived there two years and two months.'

Thoreau's beautifully written account of his idyll has been enormously influential and there are many urban dwellers who long to get away from it all and live the life Thoreau claimed to live. Readers of Walden might, however, ponder on the reality. Thoreau did not live alone; not only did he encourage hordes of visitors but he returned almost every day to his family home at Concord to see his mother. Early in his life Mrs Thoreau had taken him to see Walden Pond and it became 'the fabulous landscape of my infant dreams'; in the twenty-two months he spent commuting from Concord to Walden he never lost contact with his beloved mother who lived only a mile away from his hut.

In his book *Stuff of Sleep and Dreams* (1982) Leon Edel suggests a good reason for Thoreau's subterfuge in 1845, when he set up in the woods. He had become persona non grata in Concord on account of an act of accidental vandalism. While out fishing at Fair Haven Bay, Thoreau caught some fish and lit a fire to cook them. The result was a brush fire which spread to the woods around Concord. Before this the people of Concord considered Thoreau as an idler – now they thought of him as a menace to society. So when he retreated to Walden, Thoreau was both protecting himself from the good people and also sending out signals that he was suffering in silence. In his art, however, Thoreau transmuted the matter-of-fact into a myth which many still respond to: 'I went to the woods because I wished to live deliberately, to front only the essential facts of life.'

Further reading: Walter Harding, *The Days of Henry Thoreau* (1965), F.O. Matthiessen, *American Renaissance* (1941), J.L. Stanley, *The Making of Walden* (1957), Leon Edel, *Stuff of Sleep and Dreams* (1982)

WANDA VON DUNAJEW
Leopold von Sacher-Masoch, *Venus in Furs* (1870)
Fanny Pistor

The word masochism, signifying sexual pleasure at being cruelly treated by a member of the opposite sex, is derived from the name of Leopold von Sacher-Masoch (1836-95), an Austro-Hungarian author. Born at Lemberg, Sacher-Masoch was fascinated by dominant women from an early age. As a child, he experienced erotic excitement when chastised by his father's relative Countess Xenobia, after she discovered him spying on one of her sexual adventures. Since the Countess always wore a house-jacket trimmed with fur, Sacher-Masoch associated his submissive sexuality with a fetishistic love of fur.

As an adult, Sacher-Masoch had an affair with Fanny Pistor, a young feminist willing to act out his fantasies. Accordingly, Sacher-Masoch arranged to travel to Italy with Fanny under bizarre circumstances. Disguising himself as her servant, he signed a contract obliging him to obey Fanny unconditionally for six months, during which period she should wear furs while punishing him. To Sacher-Masoch's delight, Fanny not only carried out her part of the bargain, but increased his enjoyment by taking an Italian actor, Salvini, as her lover. Sacher-Masoch recreated his experience of self-imposed slavery in his novella *Venus in Furs*, in which he is Severin, Salvini is Alexis, and Fanny is Wanda. Here (in H.J. Stenning's translation of 1965) is Sacher-Masoch's ideal: 'Wanda swiftly approached me, her white satin dress trailed behind her in shimmering silver, like moonlight; her hair glowed like flames against the white fur of the jacket; now she stood before me, her left hand firmly on her hip, the right holding the whip . . . With savage grace she rolled back the fur-trimmed sleeve and struck me across the back.'

After the publication of *Venus in Furs* – in a three-novella collection *The Heritage of Cain* – Sacher-Masoch met Aurora Rümelin, a poor girl who admired his literary talents, and hoped he could help her make a career as a writer. They were married in 1873, and, when Aurora objected to her husband's obsession with cruel women in furs, he agreed to eliminate his fantasies from his stories if she, in turn, would satisfy him by acting out the part of Wanda. This she did, wearing furs and whipping him regularly until their marriage broke down in 1883. In 1906 Aurora published an autobiography *My Life's Confessions*, under the significant pseudonym Wanda von Sacher-Masoch. It was the erotologist Richard von Krafft-Ebbing, author of *Psychopathia Sexualis* (1886), who coined the term 'masochism'.

GLORIA WANDROUS
John O'Hara, *Butterfield 8* (1935)
Starr Faithfull (1911–31)

Further reading: E.R. Carson, *The Fiction of John O'Hara* (1961), C.C. Walcutt, *John O'Hara* (1969)

John O'Hara's *Butterfield 8* describes the squalid culmination of the career of Gloria Wandrous. Since being sexually abused as a child she has gradually disintegrated until she has lost her self-respect. At the beginning of the novel she is in despair: 'It was the kind of despair that she had known perhaps two thousand times before, there being 365 mornings in a calendar year. In general the cause of her despair was remorse, two kinds of it: remorse because she knew that whatever she was going to do next would not be any good either.' Her time is spent drinking in speakeasies and indulging in casual sex. Finally she commits suicide by jumping off an excursion steamer, her body being ripped to shreds by the side-wheel.

O'Hara came across the original story when the newspapers of 9 June 1931 reported that a young woman, Starr Faithfull, had been found washed up on shore at Long Beach, Long Island. She had been at a midnight sailing party on a liner and ignored the order telling visitors to leave the ship. In the somewhat confused circumstances there was a possibility of suicide, or even murder. Starr Faithfull had been a familiar figure in the New York speakeasies where she was known for her stunning good looks and her erratic behaviour. She had received psychiatric treatment for her alcoholism and suicidal depression, disorders possibly determined by a childhood trauma. Apparently Starr had been sexually abused in childhood by a prominent citizen who then paid twenty thousand dollars for treatment to help her over the emotional shock. It did nothing of the kind. As O'Hara noted in his novel: 'It would be easy enough to say any one of a lot of things about Gloria, and many things were said. It could be said that she was a person who in various ways – some of them peculiar – had the ability to help other people, but lacked the ability to help herself.'

GEORGE WARRINGTON

William Makepeace Thackeray, *Pendennis* (1850)

George Stovin Venables (1810–88)

Further reading: John Carey, *Thackeray – Prodigal Genius* (1977)

George Warrington is one of the more fortunate influences on the life of the unworldly and feckless Arthur Pendennis (see ARTHUR PENDENNIS). The two become friends at Oxbridge, and then, when Pendennis embarks on a literary and journalistic career, he shares chambers with Warrington, who has become a somewhat bohemian man of letters. He is attributed with: 'great natural parts and powers of pleasing . . . varied acquirements, enthusiasm, simplicity, humour, and that freshness of mind which his simple life and habits gave him . . . In Warrington's very uncouthness there was a refinement . . .' For a time Laura Bell is in love with Warrington, and George Warrington uses his influence to extricate Pendennis from the infatuation with Fanny Bolton, the porter's daughter at Shepherd's Inn. This situation is one which he is personally well qualified to understand, as he got entangled with a young woman when he was a mere eighteen, and this was a rock he struck against which – he tells Arthur – wrecked the whole of his later life: 'She was a yeoman's daughter in the neighbourhood . . . Her parents knew who my father was, and encouraged me . . . What could come of such a marriage? I found, before long, that I was married to a boor . . . Her dullness palled upon me till I grew to loathe it . . . At my father's death I paid what debts I had contracted at college, and settled every shilling which remained . . . in an annuity, upon – upon those who bore my name . . . If I had earned fame or reputation, that woman would have come to claim it . . . and I entered life at twenty . . . hopeless and ruined beyond remission . . . Beware how you marry out of your degree. I was made for a better lot than this . . .'

Some of the character details for Warrington Thackeray took from his friend George Morland Crawford, a barrister and journalist, but Warrington's tragic story is the biography of Thackeray's old school friend George Stovin Venables, who broke the novelist's nose in a boyish brawl at Charterhouse. Venables's life and career were blighted by such an imprudent marriage as Warrington's, but he was Fellow and Tutor at Jesus College, Cambridge in 1835. He was a barrister at the Inner Temple until 1882. He wrote for the *Saturday Review* and *The Times*, and was a friend of Alfred Tennyson's.

LADY CECILY WAYNFLETE

George Bernard Shaw, *Captain Brassbound's Conversion* (1900)

Dame Ellen Alice Terry (1848–1928)

Further reading: Gordon Craig and St John Ervine, *Memoirs of Dame Ellen Terry* (1932)

Captain Brassbound's Conversion is set in Morocco, where Brassbound is resolved to take revenge upon his uncle, whom he believes has misappropriated funds from the West Indian estates which should be his. Sir Howard Hallam and his sister-in-law, Lady Cecily Waynflete, have just arrived at Mogador to make an expedition up-country. It is suggested Brassbound accompany them. In the course of this adventure one of the party is wounded, and Lady Cecily persuades Brassbound to give up his bed on his boat, *Thanksgiving*, so she may nurse him. Her charm exerts great influence on Brassbound, who not only gives up his intentions of bloody revenge, but begins to fall in love with her. After they are rescued, it is her evidence at the ensuing enquiry which saves them all. Cecily is described by Shaw as being between thirty and forty, and: 'tall, very goodlooking, sympathetic, intelligent, tender and humorous, dressed with cunning simplicity . . . A woman of great vitality and humanity, who begins a casual acquaintance at the point usually attained by English people after thirty years' acquaintance when they are capable of reaching it at all . . .'

Shaw wrote this part exclusively for Ellen Terry (see CANDIDA) and said: 'Ellen's skin does not fit her body more closely than Lady Cecily fits her; for I am a first class ladies tailor, and I love Ellen and Ellen loves me.'

Ellen herself was not so happy about the play, which, she said, was 'more fitted for the closet than the stage'. Frank Harris claimed on first-hand evidence that Ellen Terry was the living original of Lady Cecily Waynflete, and he knew both parties personally. Ellen and Shaw exchanged a lengthy correspondence, which was published in 1929, revealing a relationship which was Platonic but obviously very deeply felt on both sides. Shaw wrote: 'Ellen Terry and I exchanged about two hundred and fifty letters in the 'nineties. An old fashioned governess would say that many of them were love-letters; and yet, though we were all the time within a shilling hansom-ride of one another's doors, we never saw one another in private; and the only time I ever touched her was on the first night of *Brassbound*, when I formally kissed her hand.' Her range as an actress was extraordinary. She was impressive in a wide variety of Shakespearean roles, from high tragedy to comedy. Her ability to project convincing pathos was acknowledged by the severest of reviewers. She was an outstanding Lady Teazle in *The School for Scandal*, and at the close of her career played the parts of old women.

EVERARD WEBLEY

Aldous Huxley, *Point Counter Point* (1928)

Sir Oswald Mosley (1896–1980)

Further reading: Nicholas Mosley, *Rules of the Game* (1982)

Towards the end of Aldous Huxley's *Point Counter Point*, Everard Webley is murdered by the diabolical character Spandrell. As head and founder of the fascist Brotherhood of British Freemen, Webley has many enemies, and the police are puzzled by the Webley Mystery. Eventually three of Webley's fascists murder Spandrell as a reprisal. Tall, handsome and imposing in appearance, Webley has a high regard for himself. As Lady Edward Tantamount observes, Webley 'hasn't got much sense of humour. He wants to be treated as though he were his own colossal statue, erected by an admiring and grateful nation.' Later in the novel Webley addresses a thousand British Freemen in Hyde Park: he is 'Dressed in green and wearing a sword [and speaking] from the back of his white horse, Bucephalus'.

Like Webley, Oswald Mosley – on whom Huxley's character is based – was a powerful orator with a fondness for swords. He was one of the most controversial British politicians of the 1920s, sitting in parliament as a Unionist from 1918–22, as an Independent in 1922–4, and as a Labour member in 1924 and 1926–31. Having married Lady Cynthia, daughter of Lord Curzon, in 1920 he attempted to form a Centre Party in 1921, claiming to speak for 'a confederation of reasonable men'. After joining the Labour party in 1924 he was widely regarded as 'the most brilliant man in the House of Commons', as Beatrice Webb noted in her diary, before adding 'So much perfection argues rottenness somewhere . . . some weak spot.' In 1925 Mosley expressed his economic theories – known as the Birmingham Proposals – in his pamphlet *Revolution by Reason*, advocating the creation of State Banks to establish the 'firm grip of the Socialist State over the whole remaining field of Capitalist activity'. A junior minister in the Labour Government when Huxley's novel appeared, Mosley resigned in 1930. A year later he founded the New Party, and in 1932 formed the British Union of Fascists. He married Diana Freeman-Mitford in 1936, and was interned during the Second World War until 1943, when he was released on health grounds.

ADAM WEIR

Robert Louis Stevenson, *Weir of Hermiston* (1896)

Lord Braxfield (1722–99)

Further reading: Jenni Calder, *RLS – A Life Study* (1980), Graham

Robert Louis Stevenson considered Adam Weir, the Lord Justice-Clerk of *Weir of Hermiston*, to be his most effective character. With his racy use of Scots and his 'hanging face', Weir embodies a grim view of justice and the nature of the man is suitably severe: 'He did not try to be loved, he did not care to be; it is probable the very thought of it was a stranger to his mind. He was an admired lawyer, a highly unpopular judge; and he looked down upon those who were his inferiors in either distinction.'

Stevenson based the character closely on Robert MacQueen, Lord Braxfield, Scotland's most notorious hanging judge who became Justice Clerk in 1788 and so controlled the criminal court. Braxfield was a hard-drinking, blunt Scots-speaking man who obviously enjoyed his work as he administered justice ferociously. He sentenced the revolutionary leader Thomas Muir to transportation for sedition and he told one prisoner that he would be 'nane the waur o' a hangin''. Stevenson was fascinated by Braxfield and told his friends how he intended to use him in his novel: 'Braxfield – Only his name is Hermiston – has a son who is condemned to death; plainly there is a fine, tempting fitness about this.' Stevenson died before completing the story though the description of Braxfield as Hermiston stands as a finely finished verbal portrait: 'my Lord Hermiston occupied the bench in the red robes of criminal jurisdiction, his face framed in the white wig. . . . It was plain he gloried in the exercise of his trained faculties, in the clear sight which pierced at once into the joint of fact, in the rude unvarnished gibes with which he demolished every figment of defence. He took his ease and jested, unbending in that solemn place with some of the freedom of the tavern; and the rag of man with the flannel round his neck was hunted gallowsward with jeers.'

Lord Cockburn, in his *Memorials of His Time* (1856), described Braxfield as Hermiston stands as a finely finished verbal portrait: 'my start yet. Strong-built and dark, with rough eyebrows powerful eyes, threatening lips, and a low, growling voice, he was like a formidable blacksmith.' In 1877 there was an exhibition of Sir Henry Raeburn's paintings in Edinburgh and Stevenson was struck by the portrait of Braxfield in whose face he discerned not a trace of timidity.

Balfour, *The Life of Robert Louis Stevenson* (1901), David Daiches, *Robert Louis Stevenson – A Revaluation* (1947), J. Pope-Hennessy, *Robert Louis Stevenson* (1974)

SAM WELLER

Charles Dickens, *The Posthumous Papers of the Pickwick Club* (1836)

Simon Vale, also known as Sam Vale

Sam Weller, the son of Tony Weller the coachman, was the boots at the White Hart Inn, in the Borough. He is employed by Samuel Pickwick as his valet, and, in effect – with his earthy wisdom and healthy scepticism balancing the innocent optimism of his master – he plays Sancho Panza to Pickwick's Don Quixote: 'He was habited in a coarse striped waistcoat, with black calico sleeves, and blue glass buttons; drab breeches and leggings. A bright red handkerchief was wound round his neck, and an old white hat was carelessly thrown on one side of his head.' His acceptance of the job with Pickwick is characteristically philosophical: 'I wonder whether I'm meant to be a footman, or a groom, or a gamekeeper, or a seedsman. It looks like a sort of compo of every one on'em. Never mind: there's a change of air, plenty to see, and little to do; and all this suits my complaint uncommon; so long life to the Pickvicks, say I!' Sam is the embodiment of Cockney wit and the master of an idiosyncratic epigrammatical style of utterance: 'I only assisted natur, as the doctor said to the boy's mother arter he'd bled him to death' – 'Avay with melincholly, as the little boy said ven his schoolmissis died' – 'Vich I calls addin' insult to injury, as the parrot said ven they not only took him from his native land, but made him talk the English langwidge' – 'Business first, pleasure arterwards, as King Richard the Third said when he stabbed the t'other king in the Tower, afore he smothered the babbies' – 'I hope our acquaintance may be a long 'un, as the gen'l'mun said to the fi'pun'note.'

'Dickens based Sam on the comic actor Simon Vale, who made his name as Simon Spatterdash in Samuel Beazely's farce *The Boarding House* (1822), which was full of such gags as: 'Come on! As the man said to the tight boot' – 'Let everyone take care of himself, as the jackass said when he danced among the chickens' – 'I am down upon you, as the extinguisher said to the rushlight.' This style of gagging was well established in the century before Dickens honed it to the sharpness of genius in creating such a natural philosopher as Sam Weller. There are examples in the works of Sir Walter Scott; in *Rob Roy* (1818) Andrew Fairservice says: 'Ower mony maisters – as the paddock said to the harrow when every tooth gae her a tig' [paddock = a frog or toad, tig = a sharp blow]. In *Kenilworth* (1821) Michael Lambourne says: 'I have the hope of bettering myself, to be sure, as the old woman said when she leaped over the bridge at Kingston.' But Wellerisms are more than gags – they encapsulate a world-view.

Further reading:
Edwin Pugh, *The Charles Dickens Originals* (1912)

ROGER WENDOVER

Mrs Humphry Ward, *Robert Elsmere* (1888)

Mark Pattison (1813–84)

Further reading: Gwynn Stephen, *Mrs Humphry Ward* (1917), Janet Trevelyan, *The Life of Mrs Humphry Ward* (1923)

Mary Augusta Arnold (who became Mrs Humphry Ward in 1872) was born in Hobart, Tasmania, and came to England in 1856 when her father converted to Roman Catholicism. The granddaughter of Thomas Arnold of Rugby and the niece of Matthew Arnold, Mary moved to Oxford in 1865 when her father temporarily returned to the Anglican Church. In Oxford, Mary decided to educate herself with the assistance of such scholars as Mark Pattison, who had been appointed Rector of Lincoln College, Oxford, in 1861. A man of great erudition, Pattison published his *Oxford Essays* in 1855, contributed to the *Quarterly*, and wrote various critical and biographical articles. He was bitter, on account of his long frustrating wait for the rectorship of Lincoln, and gained a reputation as a pedant who rather neglected his administrative duties. Yet he was a gifted teacher, and his advice to Mary to concentrate her mind deeply on a single subject led her to study early Spanish ecclesiastical history. This research gave her the confidence to criticize orthodox Christianity in *Robert Elsmere*, in which Pattison appears as Roger Wendover.

The novel, which enjoyed enormous success in the Victorian period, tells how Elsmere breaks with the established church and forms a humanistic Christian Brotherhood in London's East End. As a young parson, Elsmere constantly comes up against privilege and prejudice. Concerned with the poverty in cottages at Mile End, Elsmere goes to see the squire, Roger Wendover, who owns the property. Initially Wendover's attitude is one of indifference, for he does not want his studies to be disturbed: 'I am a student first and foremost, and desire to be left to my books. Mr Henslowe [Wendover's agent] is there on purpose to protect my literary freedom.' Subsequently Wendover is shocked by the conditions at Mile End, Elsmere learns to respect him as a man of letters, and the squire acknowledges that he needs more human contact: 'he suddenly realized that he had been unwholesomely solitary, and that for the scholar there is no nerve stimulus like that of an occasional interchange of ideas with some one acquainted with his *Fach*.' Squire Wendover's 'dry cynical talk' fascinates Elsmere, and stimulates him to a reassessment of his own attitude to religion.

SOPHIA WESTERN

Henry Fielding, *The History of Tom Jones* (1749)

Charlotte Cradock (died 1744)

Further reading: W.L. Cross, *The History of Henry Fielding* (1918), C.J. Rawson, *Henry Fielding* (1968)

Sophia is the beautiful daughter of the drunken and rumbustious Squire Western. Tom Jones falls in love with her, but he is rivalled by the treacherous Blifil who does all that he can to blacken Tom's name. Eventually it is discovered that Tom is really Squire Allworthy's nephew (see SQUIRE ALLWORTHY) and he marries Sophia: 'a middle sized woman; but rather inclining to tall. Her shape was not only exact, but extremely delicate: and the nice proportion of her arms promised the truest symmetry in her limbs. Her hair, which was black, was so luxuriant, that it reached her middle, before she cut it to comply with the modern fashion; and it was now curled so gracefully in her neck, that few could believe it to be her own. . . . Her eyebrows were full, even, and arched beyond the power of art to imitate. Her black eyes had a lustre in them, which all her softness could not extinguish. Here nose was exactly regular, and her mouth, in which there were two rows of ivory, exactly answered Sir John Suckling's description in those lines – "Her lips were red, and one was thin,/Compar'd to that was next her chin./Some bee had stung it newly." – Her cheeks were of the oval kind; and in her right she had a dimple, which the least smile discovered. Her chin had certainly its share in forming the beauty of her face; but it was difficult to say it was either large or small, though perhaps it was rather of the former kind. Her complexion had rather more of the lily than of the rose, but when exercise or modesty increased her natural colour, nor vermilion could equal it . . . Her neck was long and finely turned . . . Here was whiteness which no lilies, ivory, nor alabastor could match. The finest cambric might indeed be supposed from envy to cover that bosom which was much whiter than itself . . . when she smiled, the sweetness of her temper diffused that glory over her countenance which no regularity of features can give.'

This generous portrait is of Charlotte Cradock, whom Fielding loved and married in 1734. He says in *Tom Jones* 'she resembled one whose image never can depart from my breast'.

HUGH WESTON

Christopher Isherwood, *Lions and Shadows* (1938)

W.H. Auden
(1907–73)

Further reading:
Humphry Carpenter, *W.H. Auden* (1981)

Christopher Isherwood's *Lions and Shadows* is a fictionalized account of the author's life from his public schooldays to his departure for Berlin in 1929. Looking back on his days at prep school, Isherwood remembers a boy called Hugh Weston who seemed 'precociously clever, untidy, lazy and . . . insolent'. Weston re-enters Isherwood's life in the winter of 1925. Now he is a poet: 'I found him little changed. True, he had grown enormously; but his small pale yellow eyes were still screwed together in the same short-sighted scowl, and his stumpy immature fingers were still nail-bitten and stained – nicotine was now mixed with the ink.' Isherwood assumes the role of Weston's 'literary elder brother', but at the end of the book he is sufficiently impressed by Weston to go to Berlin on his recommendation. As Isherwood acknowledges in *Christopher and his Kind* (1976), Weston is a portrait of Wystan Hugh Auden.

In his last year at St Edmund's prep school, Hindhead, Isherwood met Auden, two-and-a-half years his junior. Auden was enormously impressed by Isherwood and delighted to renew the friendship seven years later when he was an undergraduate at Christ's Church, Oxford, and Isherwood was living in London. In the summer of 1926 Auden holidayed with Isherwood at Freshwater Bay, Isle of Wight. The two got together again in Berlin in 1929, since Auden had convinced Isherwood that 'Berlin meant Boys'. They frequented a homosexual bar called the Cosy Corner, and so began Isherwood's involvement in the Berlin he describes so vividly in his work. Auden's *Poems* (1930) were dedicated to Isherwood, and the two men were close enough to collaborate on three plays – *The Dog Beneath the Skin* (1935), *The Ascent of F6* (1936), *On the Frontier* (1938) – as well as on *Journey to a War* (1939), the travel-book based on the trip they made to China in 1938.

On 19 January 1939, Auden and Isherwood emigrated to the USA, thus bringing upon themselves the charge that they were deserting their native land in its hour of need. Writing in *Horizon*, Cyril Connolly called Auden and Isherwood 'far-sighted and ambitious young men with a strong instinct of self-preservation, and an eye on the main chance'. According to Isherwood, in *Christopher and his Kind*, the reason he and Auden left England was because they no longer had faith in 'the Popular Front, the party line, the anti-fascist struggle'. Auden's admiration for his friend is expressed in a poem written on 3 September 1937 for Isherwood, who is described as 'A brilliant young novelist' and 'My greatest friend'. After settling in the USA, Auden and Isherwood remained friends, though they did not collaborate on any more projects.

THE WHITE GODDESS

Robert Graves, *The White Goddess* (1948)

Laura Riding
(born 1901)

Further reading:
Martin Seymour Smith, *Robert Graves* (1982)

For Robert Graves, poetry occurs when the poet is possessed by an eternal Muse, the White Goddess. She is a Triple Goddess, the three stages of womanhood (mother of man, his mate, his mourner) and the Goddess of the heavens. The task of the poet is to evoke the religious presence of the White Goddess as embodied in a woman he loves. Expounding this theme in *The White Goddess*, Graves wrote: 'The test of a poet's vision . . .is the accuracy of his portrayal of the White Goddess and of the island over which she rules. The reason why the hairs stand on end, the eyes water, the throat is constricted, the skin crawls and a shiver runs down the spine when one writes or reads a true poem is that a true poem is necessarily an invocation of the White Goddess, or Muse . . .The White Goddess is anti-domestic; she is the perpetual "other woman".' Writing in the *Yale Review* (Winter/Spring 1956) the poet Randall Jarrell convincingly argued that Graves's conception of the White Goddess was inspired by his relationship with Laura Riding.

Born in New York, Laura Riding divorced Louis Gottschalk in 1925, and the same year went to Egypt in the company of Robert Graves, his wife Nancy Nicholson, and the four Graves children. Graves was Professor of English Literature at the University of Cairo for a year before returning to England, where he set up the Seizin Press with Laura Riding. In 1929 Laura Riding almost died after jumping from a fourth-storey window in Chiswick, and Graves and Nancy parted. Nancy took the children, and Graves took Laura Riding to Deya, a fishing and olive-producing village on the northwest coast of Majorca. Graves had finished with England, as he made clear by calling his autobiography *Goodbye to All That* (1929).

Like Nancy Nicholson, Laura Riding was a militant feminist with a powerful personality. Under her influence, Graves began to write poems asserting the feminine principle as the ultimate artistic source, an assertion elevated to a thematic theology in *The White Goddess*. In 1936, on the outbreak of the Spanish Civil War, Graves and Laura Riding left Majorca, wandered around Europe and the United States for three years, and then parted in 1939. Graves married Beryl Pritchard, after the break with Laura Riding, and continued to write poems prompted by women in whom he discerned the presence of the White Goddess.

After the publication of her collected *Poems* in 1938, Laura Riding renounced poetry. She married Schulyer Jackson in 1941. For his part, Graves continued to speak highly of Laura as a poet.

SHERIDAN WHITESIDE

George S. Kaufman and Moss Hart, *The Man Who Came to Dinner* (play, 1939)

Alexander Woolcott (1887–1943)

Further reading: Howard Teichmann, *Smart Aleck* (1976)

Influential critic, reviewer, lecturer and wit Sheridan Whiteside, falls and breaks his hip in a small town in Ohio. The Stanleys a family of means, offer to accommodate him while he recovers. Although in a wheelchair for most of the play, Whiteside dominates his world, which he turns into an idiosyncratic bedlam – sending telegrams, making telephone calls, issuing orders and ruling the Stanleys himself. He arranges for his secretary to marry the local journalist. The play is packed with sophisticated contemporary references – to H.G. Wells, Jascha Heifetz, the Lunts, Ethel Barrymore, Louella Parsons, Arturo Toscanini, Sacha Guitry, Ginger Rogers etc., as well as actually featuring caricatures of Noel Coward and Gertrude Lawrence. There is general relief when Whiteside eventually recovers. Joy turns to grief as he slips on a piece of ice and breaks his other hip. He is carried back into the Stanley house for a further period of convalescence.

Kaufman and Hart based Whiteside on the journalist and broadcaster, Alexander Woolcott, a renowned wag and egocentric, one of the most influential drama reviewers of his period. He was a make or break critic, who gave free reign to personal prejudices and predilections, but opposed sham and fully realized the possibilities of personality journalism, wielding tremendous power through his column in the *New York Times*. A member of the Algonquin set (which included Dorothy Parker) Woolcott's wit was deservedly legendary – in person, in telegrams and in the thousands of words he published in various journals including the *New Yorker*. His reviews still read well ('An unfortunate thing occurred at the Maxine Elliott Theatre last night . . .' – 'The score is by Sigmund Romberg, who knows a good tune when he hears one.') He said of himself: 'One day I shall probably talk myself to death. Those who live by the word shall perish by the word.'

VERNON WHITFORD

George Meredith, *The Egoist* (1879)

Sir Leslie Stephen (1832–1904)

To emphasize the triumph of integrity over egoism in *The Egoist* George Meredith builds his novel around two contrasting male characters. Sir Willoughby Patterne parades his wealth and enjoys the exercise of his authority; Vernon Whitford, his cousin, is devoted to his literary work with a disinterestedness that is beyond the Egoist. Throughout the novel Sir Willoughby pursues Clara Middleton because he thinks she will make a suitable Lady Willoughby of Patterne; Clara, however, succumbs to Vernon's quiet charm and chooses him rather than the Egoist. Vernon is seen, by Mrs Mountstuart, as 'a Phoebus Apollo turned fasting friar' – a description, says Meredith, that 'painted the sunken brilliancy of the lean long-walker and scholar at a stroke'.

Vernon is an affectionate portrait of Meredith's friend Sir Leslie Stephen whose critical writing established him as one of the great literary Victorians. He wrote biographies (of Johnson, Pope, Swift, George Eliot and Hobbes), helped found the *Pall Mall Gazette*, edited the *Cornhill* for eleven years with great distinction, and did outstanding editorial work on the *Dictionary of National Biography*. As befits his arrogant manner, Sir Willoughby treats Vernon as a rose in his lapel for he considers it prestigious as well as useful to have such a scholar to hand: 'Now Vernon was useful to his cousin; he was the accomplished secretary of a man who governed his estate shrewdly and diligently.... Furthermore, [Sir Willoughby] liked his cousin to date his own controversial writings, on classical subjects, from Patterne Hall. It caused his house to shine in a foreign field; proved the service of scholarship by giving it a flavour of bookish aristocracy that, though not so well worth having, and indeed in itself contemptible, is above the material and titular; one cannot quite say how . . . Sir Willoughby could create an abject silence at a county dinner-table by an allusion to Vernon "at work at home upon his Etruscans or his Dorians".'

Sir Leslie's daughter, the novelist Virginia Woolf, thought he was (as she told Vita Sackville-West) 'an adorable man, and somehow tremendous'. He was certainly a man of integrity. For example, he was ordained in 1855 but resigned his Cambridge tutorship in 1862 because he had lost his religious faith. His critical perception of the continuity of culture had an influence on F.R. Leavis and others.

Further reading:
John Gross, *The Rise and Fall of the Man of Letters* (1969), F.W. Maitland, *The Life and Works of Leslie Stephen* (1906), Noel G. Annan, *Stephen* (1951), *Leslie Stephen: The Godless Victorian* (1984)

DICK WHITTINGTON

Traditional British pantomime hero.

Richard Whittington
(died 1423)

The earliest version of the Dick Whittington story dates from a stage play and ballads licensed for the press in 1605. The stories tell of a runaway apprentice from Gloucestershire who comes to London to seek his fortune. He finds shelter in the household of the rich alderman, Fitzwarren. Fitzwarren allows his staff to invest in overseas ventures. All Dick has to send is his cat. Dick runs away because he is badly treated by the other servants. Resting at Highgate Hill he hears a voice in the sound of the bells: 'Turn again Whittington, thrice Mayor of London.' He returns to find his cat has made a fortune. It was bought by the King of Barbary, who was plagued by rats and mice. Dick marries Fitzwarren's daughter, Alice, and does in fact become Lord Mayor three times.

The real Dick Whittington was born in Pauntley, Gloucestershire. He became a mercer in London, later alderman and three times Lord Mayor – 1397-98, 1406-07 and 1419-20. He actually married Alice Fitzwarren, who was the daughter of Ivo Fitzwarren, and through this marriage acquired substantial property in the south-west counties. Richard Whittington was a substantial benefactor to the city of London, and advanced loans to Richard II, Henry IV and Henry V, subsidizing his Agincourt campaign. He left legacies towards rebuilding Newgate prison and founding almshouses. The true life history of Richard Whittington soon merged into the stuff of legend and myth – the process can be seen in John Stow's *Annals, or A General Chronicle of England* (1580) and in Richard Johnson's *Crown Garland of Roses* (1612) in which the picturesque episode of the sound of Bow Bells makes its first appearance in the narrative.

Further reading:
H.T. Riley, *Memorials of London* (1868), Samuel Lysons, *The Model Merchant of the Middle Ages* (1860), Walter Besant, *The Life of Richard Whittington* (1894), T. Keightley, *Tales and Popular Fictions* (1834)

JONATHAN WILD

Henry Fielding, *Jonathan Wild the Great* (1743)

Sir Robert Walpole
(1676–1745)

Henry Fielding uses the story of the real life English criminal, Jonathan Wild, to explore the nature of 'greatness' in society. Wild ran a gang of thieves and received stolen goods. He betrayed the members of his gang to the authorities if they would not obey him, and rewarded those who did what they were told, and kept their mouths shut. The real Wild was hanged at Tyburn in 1725. In Fielding's version of the story Wild is baptized by Titus Oates, the fabricator of the 'Popish Plot' and develops

Further reading: J.H. Plumb, *Life of Robert Walpole* (1956), Lord Chesterfield, *Characters of Eminent Personages of His Own Time* (1777)

into a consummate rogue. He learns to tread the path of crime while at school, and becomes first a pickpocket, under the leadership of Mr Snap, who keeps a sponging house. He then gradually develops a business of his own, running a large gang, contriving crimes, always taking the biggest share of the booty himself, and handing over unreliable members to the law. Snap's daughter, Letitia, becomes his wife. His main policy is to bring an old school friend of his, Heartfree, to ruin. Heartfree's jewellers business goes bankrupt and he nearly succeeds in getting Heartfree condemned for the murder of Mrs Heartfree.

This is a political satire on the Whig politician and statesman, Sir Robet Walpole, who rose to supreme power, and maintained his control of the political system by bribery, corruption and the impeachment of his enemies. He is referred to as 'Bob Booty' in John Agy's *Beggar's Opera*, but the idea of a career politician seen in terms of a master criminal gets full treatment in *Jonathan Wild*, Fielding had little cause to love Walpole; his Licensing Act of 1737 put an end to Fielding's career as a dramatist. As a young MP Walpole had been imprisoned for alleged corruption, but was in the ascendancy after the South Sea Bubble. He staved off threats to his power from Carteret, Bolingbroke, Pulteney. He resigned the premiership in 1742 and a committee investigating his affairs estimated at least £60,000 was spent in buying the press, as well as huge sums bribing MPs. He also used preferment.

THE WILDERNESSES

Malcolm Lowry, *Dark as the Grave wherein my Friend is Laid* (1969)

The Lowrys

Further reading: Douglas Day, *Malcolm Lowry* (1973)

In December 1945 Malcolm Lowry and his second wife, Margerie Bonner Lowry, flew from Vancouver to Mexico City, then took a bus to Cuernavaca, where Lowry had lived with his first wife Jan Gabrial (Ruth in the novel). On New Year's Eve, Lowry received a letter from Jonathan Cape, the publisher, demanding revisions in the text of *Under the Volcano* (1947). Depressed by this frustrating news Lowry made (according to Douglas Day's introduction to *Dark as the Grave*) 'a half-hearted and spontaneously conceived attempt to slash his wrists' on 10 January. Six days later, the Lowrys were on their way to Oaxaca, where Lowry planned a reunion with his old drinking friend Juan Marquez (Juan Fernando Martinez in the novel). Discovering that Juan Marquez had been dead for more than five years, the Lowrys left for Acapulco the next day. From the notes he and Margerie had made during their Mexican trip, Lowry shaped *Dark as the Grave wherein my Friend is Laid*, a text that rakes over the material used in *Under the Volcano*. It was not, however, published in the author's lifetime (1909-57), but prepared for publication by Margerie Bonner Lowry and Douglas Day.

In *Dark as the Grave wherein my Friend is Laid* (a title using a line from Abraham Cowley's elegy 'On the Death of Mr William Hervey') Lowry appears as Sigbjørn Wilderness who 'was, if a monumentally unsuccessful one, and of late silent, a writer'. Margerie is Primrose who 'looked young and slim and fresh in her new blue travelling suit, and her large and beautiful flowerlike eyes, with their long lashes'. Lowry met Margerie in 1939 in Hollywood, where she had formerly shone as a child star of silent movies. When Lowry moved to Vancouver, to avoid Jan Gabrial's divorce action against him, Margerie followed him to Canada. Malcolm and Margerie were married in Vancouver in 1940 and settled, among a community of squatters, in a tidal shack along the Dollarton beach, in Vancouver's upper harbour. Here they lived for fourteen years, a period in which Margerie helped Malcolm through his alcoholic binges, encouraged him to complete *Under the Volcano*, and typed *Dark as the Grave*... After Lowry's death, in Sussex, Margerie edited and championed his work. *Dark as the Grave* is a tribute to a close marriage: 'It was easy to romanticize their own kind of life. But it often seemed so much better to Sigbjørn than any other, for them, despite its disadvantages, that even to contemplate any other made him feel physically sick.'

MADGE WILDFIRE

Sir Walter Scott, *The Heart of Midlothian* (1818)

Feckless Fannie

(flourished, late 18th century)

Further reading:
The Heart of Midlothian (Border Edition 1893)

Madge Wildfire is the crazy daughter of Meg Murdockson in *The Heart of Midlothian* (see JEANIE DEANS). George Staunton, alias Robertson, the lover of Effie Deans, seduces Madge. Out of revenge for what he has done to her unwitting daughter, Meg sells Effie's child by Robertson to a vagrant woman, while her parents believe that it had died. In fact Effie had been tried for her neglect which had led to the 'death' of her baby son. In his efforts to find his son Robertson comes across a band of ruffians and in an altercation he is killed by one of them – it turns out to be his own son. Thus fate avenges his terrible treatment of Madge Wildfire. She is one of Scott's most memorable characters, a kind of Scottish Ophelia, whose inner personality is often shadowed forth in the snatches of songs and ballads that she sings: 'I glance like the wildfire through country and town;/I'm seen on the causeway – I'm seen on the down;/The lightning that flashes so bright and so free,/Is scarcely so blithe or so bonny as me.' These lines introduce her to us: 'A tall, strapping wench of eighteen or twenty, dressed fantastically in a sort of blue riding-coat with tarnished lace, her hair clubbed like that of a man; a Highland bonnet and a bunch of feathers; a riding-skirt or petticoat of scarlet camlet embroidered with tarnished flowers. Her features were coarse and masculine, yet at a little distance, by dint of very bright, wild-looking black eyes, an aquiline nose and a commanding profile (she) appeared rather handsome.' She is aware of her charms, for she sings: 'I'm Madge of the country/I'm Madge of the town,/And I'm Madge of the lad I am blithest to own –/The Lady of Beeve in diamonds may shine,/But has not a heart half so lightsome as mine./I am Queen of the Wake, and I am Lady of May,/And I lead the blithe ring round the May-pole to-day;/The wild-fire that slashes so fair and so free,/Was never so bright, or so bonny, as me.' The pathos of the scene of her death is heightened by the snatches of ballads that she sings: 'Cauld is my bed, Lord Archibald,/ And sad my sleep of sorrow;/But thine shall be as sad and cauld,/My fause true-love! to-morrow.' And finally: 'Proud Maisie is in the wood,/ Walking so early;/Sweet Robin sits on the bush,/Singing so rarely./Tell me, thou bonny bird,/When shall I marry me?/"When six braw gentlemen/Kirkward shall carry ye"./Who makes the bridal bed,/Birdie, say truly?/"The grey-headed sexton/That delves the grave duly".' Scott based Meg on Feckless Fannie, a mad wandering shepherdess of Cumnock and Moffat. She was reputedly the daughter of a northern English squire who had shot her lover. This caused her insanity, though she was quite harmless. She died in Glasgow.

WILLEMS

Joseph Conrad, *An Outcast of the Islands* (1896)

Johannes de Veer

Further reading:
Jocelyn Baines, *Joseph Conrad – A Critical Biography* (1960)

Willems is a white trader who is disowned by his fellow Europeans for dishonesty. This considerably destroys his self-respect, but he believes that paradise has been revealed to him in his love for a Malay woman, and his discovery of a secret Far Eastern trading post. But here, too, he betrays the trust of others, and he becomes an outcast among the natives. From his fellow Europeans he experiences: 'solitude and silence . . . the cruel solitude of one abandoned by men; the reproachful silence which surrounds an outcast rejected by his kind, the silence unbroken by the slightest whisper of hope; an immense and impenetrable silence that swallows up without echo the murmur of regret and the cry of revolt.' He is in a state of enslavement in his love for the Malay woman: 'With a sinking heart he thought that he really could not – somehow – live without her. It was terrible and sweet. He remembered the first days. Her appearance, her face, her smile, her eyes, her words. A savage woman! Yet he perceived that he could think of nothing else but of the three days of their separation, of the few hours since their reunion . . .' The end of his personal history finds him a spiritual vacuity: 'He would be dead. He would be stretched upon the warm moisture of the ground, feeling nothing, seeing nothing, knowing nothing; he would lie stiff, passive, rotting slowly; while over him, under him, through him – unopposed, busy, hurried – the endless and minute throngs of insects . . .

would swarm in streams, persistent, ferocious and greedy – till there would remain nothing but the white gleam of bleaching bones in the long grass... that would shoots its feathery heads between the bare and polished ribs. There would be that only left of him; nobody would miss him; no one would remember him.'

Willems was based on a Dutchman named de Veer, whom Conrad got to know when he was a merchant seaman on the *Vidar*, trading with the Malayans. He was a Dutch sailor, once a fine, well-built and upstanding man with a great sense of pride in himself, whose personality had become totally destroyed by drink, and who relied completely on Olmeijer (see KASPAR ALMAYER) and other companions in Bulungan, disowned by his fellow Europeans, and despised by the natives.

WILLIAM WILSON

Edgar Allan Poe, *William Wilson* (1839)

Edgar Allan Poe (1809–49)

Further reading: Marie Bonaparte, *The Life and Works of Edgar Allan Poe* (1949), R.P. Benton, *New Approaches to Poe* (1970)

William Wilson is one of the finest examples of the story of the Doppelgänger. Wilson is a degenerate, spendthrift and dissolute young man who drifts through school, college and into a life of gambling and irresponsibility. Wherever he goes he is accompanied by his double; he talks to him continuously, in the manner of his conscience. At the climax he kills the double, and sees in a mirror that he has killed himself: 'mine own image, but with features all pale and dabbled in blood, advanced to meet me with a feeble and tottering gait'. Poe is portraying himself. He gave Wilson the same birthday and he sets his schooling in the institution in Stoke Newington where he himself had been educated. The headmaster was the Revd John Bransby, and Poe uses the same name in *William Wilson*. He describes the school accurately: 'a large, rambling, Elizabethan house, in a misty-looking village of England'. Wilson's character and career are presented as a kind of vicious parody of Poe's: 'a cause of serious disquietude to my friends, and of a positive injury to myself... addicted to the wildest caprices... a prey to the most ungovernable passion'. This is followed by a period of 'thoughtless folly' and 'miserable profligacy' at Eton, and to a catalogue of vices at Oxford. Like Poe himself, Wilson develops into a compulsive gambler.

The account of Wilson's career at Oxford is a perverted version of Poe's at the University of Virginia, where he caroused, gambled and accumulated debts of $2,500 and left after a year in residence. Poe also talked to himself, and showed signs of derangement similar to Wilson's. Poe's literary executor, Rufus Griswold, records that 'he walked the streets, in madness or melancholy, with lips moving in indistinct curses, or with eyes upturned in passionate prayers... and at night, with drenched garments and arms wildly beating the wind and rain, he would speak as if to spirits'. The engraver, John Sartain, recorded Poe's bizarre behaviour and account of his delusions – two men in a train were plotting to murder him – he had been put in the cells where the attendants had tried to frighten him to death – his mother-in-law had been brought in and they had cut her legs off a piece at a time, 'her feet at the ankles, then her legs up to the knees, her thighs at the hips, and so on'.

PRISCILLA WIMBUSH

Aldous Huxley, *Crome Yellow* (1921)

Lady Ottoline Morrell (1873–1938)

Further reading: Sybille Bedford, *Aldous Huxley* (1973, 1974)

In 1902 Lady Ottoline Cavendish-Bentinck, sister of the Duke of Portland, married Philip Morrell, the Liberal MP for whom Bertrand Russell canvassed in 1910. The following year, in March 1911, Russell fell in love with Lady Ottoline, and decided to divorce his wife Alys. Philip Morrell bought, in March 1913, Garsington Manor, an Elizabethan house (outside Oxford) which Lady Ottoline recreated as a cultural haven for the leading intellects of the day. After she moved to Garsington in 1915 she began to lose interest in Russell, as he recalled in 'Memoirs': 'she gave me less and less while at the same time she gave more and more to others. For instance, I was never allowed to enter her bedroom but Aldous Huxley was habitually present while she undressed. (I do not think she ever had physical relations with him.) In the end I rebelled and decided that the pain and frustration were more than I could endure.'

At the beginning of Huxley's first novel *Crome Yellow*, the young writer Denis Stone goes to see Anne Wimbush at her Uncle Henry's house at Crome (modelled on Garsington). It occurs to him that his hostess, Mrs Priscilla Wimbush, might be in her boudoir in the central tower on the garden front of the house. He goes up and is invited in: 'Mrs Wimbush laughed. Her voice, her laughter, were deep and masculine. Everything about her was manly. She had a large, square, middle-aged face, with a massive projecting nose and little greenish eyes, the whole surmounted by a lofty and elaborate coiffure of a curiously improbable shade of orange . . . To-day she was wearing a purple silk dress with a high collar and a row of pearls. The costume, so richly dowagerish, so suggestive of the Royal Family, made her look more than ever like something on the Halls.'

Like D.H. Lawrence, who portrayed Lady Ottoline as Hermione Roddice in *Women in Love* (1921), Huxley saw the hostess of Garsington as a comical figure, because she took culture so seriously and collected men of letters so avidly. Her appearance was startling. Even Russell, writing about her in his *Autobiography* (1967-9) said 'Ottoline was very tall, with a long thin face something like a horse, and very beautiful hair of an unusual colour, more or less like that of marmalade, but rather darker.'

LORD PETER WIMSEY

Dorothy L. Sayers, *Whose Body?* (1923), *Clouds of Witness* (1927), *Unnatural Death* (1928), *The Unpleasantness at the Bellona Club* (1928), *Lord Peter Views the Body* (1929), *The Documents in the Case* (1930), *Strong Poison* (1930), *The Five Red Herrings* (1931), *Have his Carcase* (1932), *Murder must Advertise* (1933), *Hangman's Holiday* (1933), *The Nine Tailors* (1934), *Gaudy Night* (1934), *Busman's Honeymoon* (1937), *In the Teeth of the Evidence* (1940), *Striding Folly* (1973)

Eric Whelpton

Further reading: James Brabazon, *Dorothy L. Sayers* (1981)

Like his predecessor Sherlock Holmes, Lord Peter Wimsey combines a talent for detection with considerable cultural accomplishments. In *Whose Body?*, the first Wimsey mystery, he sends his man Bunter to a rare-book sale and tells him 'Don't lose time – I don't want to miss the Folio Dante nor the de Voragine.'

At the time that Dorothy L. Sayers created Lord Peter she was deeply in love with Eric Whelpton, a friend whose good looks and war-weariness greatly appealed to her. After the First World War, Whelpton took up a post near Paris teaching English to the French nobility; Dorothy went along as his secretary. He never returned Dorothy's passion so she consoled herself by exchanging mock-scholarly notes on popular detective fiction with her fellow enthusiast Muriel Jaeger. This correspondence led to the creation of Lord Peter Wimsey who assumed some of Whelpton's characteristics such as a flair for languages and a taste for the good life. In his book *The Making of a European* (1974) Whelpton writes 'In spite of my close association with Dorothy Sayers, I had never succeeded in finishing any of her books, though some of her friends have declared that I am the original of Lord Peter Wimsey, a suggestion that has also been made in the Sunday Press.'

Dorothy L. Sayers married, in 1926, Oswald Arthur 'Mac' Fleming and Whelpton suggested that he 'also contributed to the creation of Lord Peter'. However, the detective came complete in 1923 and hardly changed in a dozen novels though his height increased from five feet nine, in the early books, to six feet in his final full-length adventure *Busman's Honeymoon*.

WINNETOU THE WARRIOR

Karl May, *Winnetou*, three volumes (1893) Films, *Treasure of Silver Lake*, directed by Harald Reinl (1962), *Winnetou the Warrior*, directed by Harald Reinl (1964)

Cochise (died 1874)

Winnetou the Warrior is the son of an Apache chief, who becomes the blood-brother to Karl, the narrator of the Winnetou series of novels. Karl goes to St Louis, where he is appointed tutor to a German family. He is later a member of a surveying team used by the Atlantic and Pacific Railway Company. During his venture into the wilderness of the West he meets the noble Winnetou: 'His bronze-coloured force bore the imprint of a very special nobility. We seemed to be about the same age. He immediately impressed me as being endowed with an exceptional mind, and an exceptional character. We looked each other up and down. His eyes shone with a dull fire, and I thought I could detect in them the faint light of sympathy. The others told me that Winnetou has accomplished more, though still in his youth, than ten other warriors could hope to accomplish in a whole lifetime. I believed them. One day, his name

Further reading: Christopher Frayling, *Spaghetti Westerns – Cowboys and Europeans from Karl May to Sergio Leone* (1981)

would be famous through all the plains, and in all the mountains.' Karl and Winnetou admire each other, and, after Karl has been instructed in Apache lore, languages, customs and traditions, he and Winnetou become blood-brothers. Winnetou is the noblest savage of them all; he has a cultivated mind, and regularly pores over the pages of Longfellow's *Hiawatha* (see HIAWATHA). Winnetou is the last of his race, doomed to be overtaken by the white man as the frontiers extend westwards, but his nobility is memorable.' The Winnetou stories were very popular in Germany earlier this century, and made successful movies, filmed in Jugoslavia. They were among Hitler's favourite reading.

May never went to America. He was born in Hohenstein-Ernsstahl, Saxony, and read Fenimore Cooper and other travellers' tales while in prison in Zwickau. He specialized in pulp fiction located in exotic places he had never personally seen – the Wild West (*Winnetou*), the Near East (*Durch die Wüste*, 1892) and the Balkans (*Der Schut*, 1872). His stories have been translated into sixteen languages, and sold over twenty-six million copies. Christopher Frayling in *Spaghetti Westerns – Cowboys and Europeans From Karl May to Sergio Leone* (1981) argues that Winnetou is based on the historic Apache chief Cochise, who believed compromise with the white man was possible. All accounts of him stress his nobility, fine physique, gentle manners and cultivation, though he was a ferocious warrior, once provoked.

WORLDLY WISEMAN

John Bunyan, *The Pilgrim's Progress* (1678)

Paul Cobb

Further reading: Alexander Whyte, *Bunyan Characters* (ND), William York Tindall, *John Bunyan – Mechanick Preacher* (1964), Jack Lindsay, *John Bunyan – Maker of Myths* (1937), Roger Sharrock, *Bunyan* (1954)

On the restoration of Charles II in 1660 the authorities decreed that unlicensed preachers must not address their congregations. Well aware of this ruling John Bunyan, the Puritan preacher, held a meeting on 12 November 1660 and was duly arrested and held in Bedford jail. Paul Cobb, the Clerk to the Justices of Bedford, visited Bunyan and advised him to submit to the authority of the Church (of England) and State or suffer the consequences of transportation 'or else worse than that'. Bunyan was obliged to listen to Cobb's pragmatic advice: 'Well, neighbour Bunyan. . . . You may do much good if you continue still in the land: But alas, what benefit will it be to your friends, or what good can you do to them, if you should be sent away beyond the seas into Spain, or Constantinople, or some other part of the world? Pray be ruled.'

After the coronation of Charles II, Bunyan hoped to be included in the general amnesty but Cobb personally prevented Bunyan from appearing in court. In his second period of imprisonment, in 1675, Bunyan began to write *The Pilgrim's Progress* and included a portrait of Cobb as Worldly Wiseman who 'dwelt in the Town of Carnal Policy, a very great Town, and also hard by from whence Christian came'. Worldly Wiseman attempts to seduce Christian from the true path and to accept established authority instead. Evangelist explains to Christian: 'The man that met thee is one Worldly Wiseman, and rightly is he so called: partly because he savoureth only the doctrine of this world (therefore he always goes to the Town of Morality to church); and partly because he loveth that doctrine best, for it saveth him from the Cross. And because he is of this carnal temper, therefore he seeketh to prevent my ways, though right.'

WITCHFINDER GENERAL

Film, *The Witchfinder General* (American title, *The Conqueror Worm*) (1968)

Matthew Hopkins (died 1647)

The Witchfinder General, written by Michael Reeves and Tom Baker, based on the novel Ronald Bassett, and directed by Michael Reeves, became one of the cult horror movies of the late 1960s. The story is a simple one. As law and social order begins to break down during the Civil War, a cruel and dishonest lawyer, Matthew Hopkins, begins to earn a lucrative living as a travelling witchhunter. He tours the south-eastern counties with an accomplice, John Stern, who acts as his torturer and executioner. Once witches have been denounced, local magistrates are glad to pay good money to have their villages and townships cleansed. A village priest and his beautiful niece fall victims to the witchhunt. She is loved by a young soldier in Cromwell's army, and they are betrothed with the priest's blessing. Hopkins (played with sinister charm by Vincent Price, in one of his finest screen performances) offers the possibility of saving their lives, if she sleeps with him. Nevertheless, the old priest is denounced and hanged. Hopkins and Stern are pursued by her lover, and eventually cornered. He savagely kills Stern, and is in the process of sadistically beating Hopkins to death when a fellow soldier shoots the Witchfinder General out of sheer mercy, as the hero cries: 'You have taken him from me!'

This terrible story is based on the career of Matthew Hopkins, a lawyer in Ipswich and Manningtree. He gained a reputation as a witchfinder in Huntingdonshire and the eastern counties in the years 1644-7. He procured a special judicial commission from John Godbolt, judge of common pleas (died 1648), by means of which sixty women were hanged in Essex in one year alone. Hopkins hanged forty at Essex, forty were hanged at Bury, and many at Norwich and Huntingdonshire. In 1647 Hopkins published his book *The Discovery of Witches*. Hopkins was himself exposed by John Gaule, vicar of Great Staughton and author of *Select Cases of Conscience Touching Witches* (1646). Matthew Hopkins was hanged as a sorcerer in 1647, exposed by his own test – he floated bound in water – which he claimed was a sure sign of witchcraft.

Further reading:
Ronald Bassett, *Witchfinder General* (1966), Charles Mackay, *Extraordinary Delusions and the Madness of Crowds* (1841)

WOMAN IN 'A GAME OF CHESS'

T.S. Eliot, *The Waste Land* (1922)

Vivienne Eliot
(1888–1947)

Further reading:
Leon Edel, *Stuff of Sleep and Dreams* (1982)

The Waste Land first appeared in T.S. Eliot's literary quarterly, the *Criterion*, in October 1922. The same month Vivienne Eliot, the poet's first wife, wrote to Sidney Schiff explaining that the publication of *The Waste Land* had been a painful experience for her since it seemed so much a part of her, and she of it. In the second section of the poem, 'A Game of Chess', Eliot introduces a neurotic woman: 'Footsteps shuffled on the stair./Under the firelight, under the brush, her hair/Spread out in fiery points/Glowed into words, then would be savagely still./"My nerves are bad to-night. Yes, bad. Stay with me."/"Speak to me. Why do you never speak. Speak."/"What are you thinking of? What thinking? What?"/"I never know what you are thinking. Think."'

Eliot met Vivienne Haigh-Wood, an English girl six months his senior, at Oxford in 1915, and married her on 26 June 1915 in London. His parents were displeased at the match, and Vivienne's mental insecurity soon manifested itself: in a letter of November 1915 to Ottoline Morrell, Bertrand Russell described Vivienne as 'a person who lives on a knife-edge'. Eliot gradually began to break down under the strain of his life with her. While staying at Margate in 1921 – and *The Waste Land* suggests 'On Margate Sands./I can connect/Nothing with nothing' – he was so ill that Ottoline Morrell and Julian Huxley both advised him to seek help from Dr Roger Vittoz in Lausanne. Eliot responded so well to the treatment that he completed the final section of *The Waste Land* in Lausanne.

Afterwards Eliot came back to the source of most of his nervous problems – his life with Vivienne. She was receiving medical attention for her problems, he was under pressure launching the *Criterion* – named after a restaurant where Vivienne used to dine with her former lover, Charles Buckle. In his quest for stability, Eliot converted to Anglo-Catholicism in 1926, but, as Peter Ackroyd shows in his biography *T.S. Eliot* (1984), he still had Vivienne to deal with.

In 1933 Eliot had a Deed of Separation drawn up, though Vivienne did not easily relinquish her hold on him. She sought him out in the theatre and at the offices of Faber and Faber (where he was a director), and she put an advertisement in *The Times* of 17 September 1934: 'Will T.S. Eliot please return to his home 68 Clarence Gate Gardens which he abandoned Sept. 17th 1932.' She eventually met up with him at a book exhibition in 1935 but he walked away from her. She died in a mental hospital.

TOM WRENCH

Arthur Wing Pinero, *Trelawny of the 'Wells'* (1898)

Thomas Robertson (1829–71)

Further reading: *The Principal Dramatic Works of Thomas Robertson, With a Memoir by His Son* (1889), T.E. Pemberton, *The Life and Writings of Thomas Robertson* (1893), M. Savin, *Thomas Robertson* (1950)

Trelawny of the 'Wells' is without doubt among the finest plays about the theatre ever written. The theme of the play is the change in theatrical taste in mid-Victorian drama, towards a more naturalist kind of theatrical experience. This revolution in dramatic style was to a considerable extent pioneered by Thomas Robertson, who appears in Pinero's play in the character of Tom Wrench.

As the play opens Rose Trelawny, a successful actress, is preparing to leave the theatrical company as she is to marry Arthur Gower and move into society. Amid the sad farewells and general banter of various members of the company as they wish Rose all the best of happiness, Tom's theories of drama are discussed – but it seems what he wants to present is too ordinary and everyday to pass as 'theatre'. In the second act Rose's old companions call at her new address in the West End. They have been celebrating another marriage in the company, and are out on the town – Rose is tempted to give up her forthcoming marriage into the Gower family and return to tread the boards: 'I've seen enough of your life – my dear boy – to know that I'm no wife for you,' she tells Arthur. But Rose has been changed by her experience, she can no longer put on the grand manner but is subdued. In fact, the times are changing and are ready for Tom Wrench's 'new' kind of drama. Arthur Gower joins the company which, backed by capital put up in part by Gower's family, successfully mounts drama with the new style of acting. In important respects it is the case that Robertson really paved the way for Bernard Shaw.

Robertson was born into a theatrical family, and was at one time prompter at the Olympic under the management of Charles Mathews (a comic actor much admired by Dickens). He wrote successful comedies and farces, and *David Garrick*, which held the stage for many years. It was *Society* staged at the Prince of Wales in 1865 which really made his name and London flocked to see the new 'cup-and-saucer' comedy – no wit, no sparkle, no exaggeration – an attempt to portray commonplace life. *Caste* (1866), *Play* (1868), *School* (1869) and *MP* (1870) were his most famous plays.

YORICK

William Shakespeare, *Hamlet* (1601)

Richard Tarlton (died 1588)

In Act V, Scene 1 of *Hamlet*, the Prince of Denmark takes the skull cast up by the gravedigger and says: 'Let me see. Alas, poor Yorick! I knew him, Horatio: a fellow of infinite jest, of most excellent fancy; he hath borne me on his back a thousand times. . . . Here hung those lips that I have kiss'd I know not how oft. Where be your gibes now, your gambols, your songs, your flashes of merriment that were wont to set the table on a roar? Not one now to mock your own grinning.'

Tradition has it that these are references to the celebrated English comic actor and clown Richard Tarlton, who was 'discovered' by the Earl of Leicester and brought to court. He is described as having a squint and a flat nose. In 1583 he had been instituted as one of Queen Elizabeth's twelve players, and on one occasion is reputed to have pointed at Sir Walter Raleigh and said: 'See – the Knave commands the Queen!' and to have made sundry gibes at the power of the Earl of Leicester. He was renowned for his abilities as an ad-libbing comedian, improvising doggerel verses ('Tarltonising') and his skill at dancing jigs and playing the pipe and tabor.

Various biographical data appeared after his death, of varying reliability, and little is known about his early life, but many examples of his material survive, including *Tarlton's Jests*, the earliest editions of which date from circa 1600. He is supposed to have doubled the roles of the clown and the judge in *The Famous Victories of Henry V* and to have taken the part of Pedringano in Kyd's *Spanish Tragedy*. His great gift as a performer seems to have been in impromptu cut and thrust and in 'playing' an audience. This seems to be behind Hamlet's advice to the players in Act III, Scene 2: 'And let those that play your clowns speak no more than is set down for them; for there be of them that will themselves laugh, to set on some quantity of barren spectators to laugh too.' Thomas Heywood, the dramatist and actor, wrote of him in his *Apology for Actors* (1612): 'I must needs remember Tarlton, in his time gracious with the Queen his sovereign and in the people's general applause, whom succeeded Will Kemp, as well in the favour of Her Majesty as in the good thoughts of the general audience.'

Further reading: E.K. Chambers, *The Elizabethan Stage* (1923), Edmund Bohun, *A Full Account of the Character of Queen Elizabeth* (1693), Thomas Fuller, *The History of the Worthies of England* (1662)

THE YOUNG MASTER

Thomas Hughes, *Tom Brown's Schooldays* (1857)

George Edward Lynch Cotton, Bishop of Calcutta (1813–66)

Tom Brown's Schooldays is full of portraits of real people who were contemporary with Thomas Hughes's years at Rugby, 1833-42, including the school's most famous headmaster Dr Thomas Arnold (1795-1842) (see TOM BROWN, HARRY EAST, GEORGE ARTHUR). The book's most memorable character, Flashman, the immortal school bully, was apparently 'a painfully correct photograph' of a young man who could not be named when Sydney Selfe assembled his fascinating account of the school in the mid-nineteenth century, *Chapters From the History of Rugby School*. The 'young master' fresh from university, who plays such an important part in the plot, and whose class on Homer leads to the 'great fight' between Tom Brown and Slogger Williams, can be positively identified – he was George Edward Lynch Cotton, later a celebrated Bishop of Calcutta. The rather weak and pampered Arthur and Tom eventually become good friends, although their characters are strongly contrasted; Tom the rough and tumble boy who is rather slow academically, and Arthur, deeply religious and very scholarly. On one occasion their regular form master is away unwell and their construing of Homer is to be heard by the 'new master . . . quite a young man, who had only just left the University'. The boys all hope they can spin out the lesson so that the limits of their preparation will not be exceeded. They usually manage to get away with forty lines or so: 'However, notwithstanding all their efforts, the new master got on horribly quick; he

Further reading: *Memoirs of the Life of Bishop Cotton* (1871) by Mrs Cotton, his widow

seemed to have the bad taste to be really interested in the lesson, and to be trying to work them up into something like an appreciation of it, giving them good spirited English words, instead of the wretched bald stuff into which they rendered poor old Homer; and construing over each piece himself to them . . . to show them how it could be done.' Arthur's scholarship enables more of the text to be consumed than the boys had anticipated, and his being threatened as 'a little sneak' and being protected by Tom leads to the great pugilistic encounter between Slogger Williams and Tom Brown (which is also based on a celebrated fight at Rugby in Hughes's day).

George Cotton was educated at Westminster and Trinity College, Cambridge, and was a house-master at Rugby between 1837-52, then headmaster of Marlborough 1852-8. He then became Bishop of Calcutta, where he founded schools for poor Eurasian and European children. He was a tireless worker and did much to improve the position of chaplains, and exerted himself in missionary work, though he opposed the presbyterian claim to use government churches. He was drowned at Kushtea on the Ganges on 6 October 1866.

Z

ZENOBIA

Nathaniel Hawthorne, *The Blithedale Romance* (1852)

Sarah Margaret Fuller, Marchioness Ossoli
(1810–50)

Further reading:
Julia Ward Howe, *Margaret Fuller* (1883), Hyatt H. Waggoner, *Hawthorne – A Critical Study* (1955)

In 1842 Hawthorne had briefly participated in Brook Farm, the utopian community established at West Roxbury, Massachusetts, where the membership equally shared work, profit and social life. Hawthorne found the experience unlikable. He modelled the community he describes as Blithedale on his perceptions of Brook Farm. One of those taking part in this experimental way of life is Hollingsworth, said to be based on Herman Melville, who is determined to convert Blithedale into an experimental penitentiary. Zenobia, a dark and imperious young woman, falls deeply in love with the self-centred but dynamic Hollingsworth. This relationship is complicated by the arrival of another female, Priscilla, who has had a mysterious past, although she is young and innocent. She had fallen under the malevolent influence of the sinister mesmerist, Westervelt. She has come to Blithedale to escape. Hollingsworth falls in love with Priscilla. When Zenobia learns of this, she commits suicide by drowning herself. Hollingsworth is so shocked by this act, that he gives up his schemes of prison reform experiment and turns to Priscilla for support.

Zenobia is a portrait of the American bluestocking, Margaret Fuller. She was born in Cambridge, Massachusetts, and reared as a prodigy by her father. She taught languages in Boston and later at Providence, Rhode Island, published translations of Goethe, and, with the help of Ralph Waldo Emerson, founded the *Dial*, while her conversation classes for women in Boston played an important part in the womens movement. She published *Woman in the Nineteenth Century* in 1844, and her *Summer on the Lakes in 1843* (1844) was greatly admired. She moved to New York and engaged in critical reviewing. Visiting Europe in 1846, she came to England and France, settling finally in Italy, where she married the Marquis Giovanni Angelo Ossoli (ten years her junior), who was a follower of Mazzini. During the war of 1848-9 she ran a hospital in Rome. She was drowned when the ship on which she was returning to USA was wrecked on Fire Island on 16 June 1850. Margaret Fuller was called 'The High Priestess of Transcendentalism'. Horace Greeley said of her: 'All the art, the thought and nobleness in New England . . . seemed related to her, and she to it.' Nathaniel Hawthorne was less charitable: 'She was a great humbug; of course with much talent, and much moral ideality, or else she could not have been so great a humbug. But she had stuck herself full of borrowed qualities . . . which had no root in her.'

ZULEIKA

Lord Byron, *The Bride of Abydos* (1813)

Augusta Leigh
(born 1783)

Further reading:
Leslie Marchand, *Byron – A Biography* (1957), Harriet Beecher Stowe, *Lady Byron Vindicated* (1870)

The Bride of Abydos is subtitled 'A Turkish Tale' and is the story of the love between Zuleika, daughter of the Pasha Giaffir, and her cousin, Selim. Zuleika is presented as the perfection of Eastern beauty: 'So bright the tear in Beauty's eyes,/Love half regrets to kiss it dry;/So sweet the blush of Bashfulness,/Even Pity scarce can wish it less!' But it is her father's wish that she marry the rich boy of Karasman. She has never even seen him. In her distress at hearing this from her father's lips, she confesses her grief to her beloved brother, Selim. But Selim now tells her that he is not her brother, but her cousin, the son of Zuleika's uncle, who has been killed by the Pasha Giaffir. He also tells Zuleika that he is a pirate chief in disguise and asks her to run away with him. The Pasha appears and Selim is killed. Zuleika dies of grief: 'though deep – though fatal – was thy first!/Thrice happy ne'er to feel nor fear the force/Of absence, shame, pride, hate, revenge, remorse.'

The Bride of Abydos really presents the passionate and illicit love of Byron for his half-sister, Augusta. In the first draft of the poem Selim and Zuleika were actually brother and sister. Incest was a theme which had always fascinated Byron. The relationship with Augusta took place in the summer of 1813. Her husband, Colonel Leigh, was absent during the racing season and Byron and Augusta were constantly in each other's company, Byron confessed his passion in a veiled manner to Lady Melbourne. He wrote to a friend: 'I am at this moment in a far more serious, and entirely new, scrape than any of the last twelve months, and that is saying a great deal,' (letter dated 22 August 1813). He revealed the matter to Lady Melbourne. Nine months later Augusta gave birth to a daughter. He wrote to Lady Melbourne in November: 'For the last three days I have been quite shut up, my mind has been from *late* and *later* events in such a state . . . that as usual I have been obliged to empty it in rhyme, and am in the heart of another Eastern tale.' He is referring to *The Bride of Abydos*. (See also ASTARTE.)

INDEX

A

B

C

E

F

G

H

I

J

M

N

O

P

T

U